UNIVERSITY LIL ✓ **W9-COX-903**
UW-STEVENS POINT

ENVIRONMENTAL LAW HANDBOOK

Ninth Edition

J. Gordon Arbuckle, Nancy S. Bryson, David R. Case, Colburn T. Cherney,
Ridgway M. Hall, Jr., John C. Martin, Jeffrey G. Miller,
Marshall Lee Miller, William F. Pedersen, Jr., Russell V. Randle,
Richard G. Stoll, Thomas F.P. Sullivan, Timothy A. Vanderver, Jr.

Government Institutes, Inc.
Rockville, MD
1987

PUBLISHER'S NOTE

This publication is designed to provide accurate and authoritative information with regard to the subject matter covered. It is sold with the understanding that the publisher is not engaged in rendering legal, accounting or other professional service. If legal advice or other expert assistance is required, the services of a competent professional person should be sought. — From a Declaration of Principles jointly adopted by a Committee of the American Bar Association and a Committee of Publishers.

Publication of this book does not signify that the contents necessarily reflect the views and policies of Government Institutes, Inc.

All rights reserved. No part of this publication may be reproduced, stored in a retrieval system, or transmitted in any form or by any means, electronic, mechanical, photocopying, recording or otherwise, without the prior written permission of the publisher.

Ninth Edition

May 1987

Published by
Government Institutes, Inc.
966 Hungerford Drive #24
Rockville, Maryland 20850
U.S.A.

Copyright © 1987 by Government Institutes, Inc.
ISBN Number: 0-86587-706-8
Library of Congress Catalog Card Number: 76-41637

Printed and bound in the United States of America

:F
3775
E 473
1987

PREFACE

A complex body of environmental laws, regulations, and decisions is now established in the United States. Environmental law, which evolved quickly, now ranks with labor, tax, banking, communications, and several other fields as an accepted part of our legal system.

As the environmental law field has matured so have our publishing efforts. We at Government Institutes are extremely proud that our Environmental Law Handbook, the first such comprehensive text in the field and now in its ninth edition, has become a standard reference. As the environmental law field has evolved, so have our publishing activities. Although this Handbook is the "flagship" of our environmental publishing efforts, we offer over 100 books on a wide range of other environmental topics. A free catalog of all our books is available on request. In addition, suggestions for new publications and manuscripts from authors are invited because our job is to satisfy the informational needs of our clients.

I sincerely hope that our efforts help bring about a better understanding of the environmental laws, regulations and decisions. More importantly, we wish to encourage compliance with the spirit of the law, so that public health and the environment are protected, now and for future generations.

Thomas F. P. Sullivan
President
Government Institutes, Inc.

371136

CONTENTS

**Chapter 1 ENVIRONMENTAL LAW FUNDAMENTALS
AND THE COMMON LAW**

CONTENTS

CONTENTS

Chapter 2 RESOURCE CONSERVATION AND RECOVERY ACT

CONTENTS

Chapter 3 COMPREHENSIVE ENVIRONMENTAL RESPONSE, COMPENSATION AND LIABILITY ACT (CERCLA OR SUPERFUND)

CONTENTS

Chapter 4 TOXIC SUBSTANCES

CONTENTS

Chapter 5 WATER POLLUTION CONTROL

CONTENTS

Chapter 6 AIR POLLUTION CONTROL

Chapter 7 THE OCCUPATIONAL SAFETY AND HEALTH ACT

CONTENTS

Chapter 8 SAFE DRINKING WATER ACT

CONTENTS

Chapter 9 MARINE PROTECTION, RESEARCH AND SANCTUARIES ACT

Chapter 10 NATIONAL ENVIRONMENTAL POLICY ACT

CONTENTS

Chapter 11 FEDERAL REGULATION OF PESTICIDES

Chapter 12 NOISE CONTROL

CONTENTS

ABOUT THE AUTHORS

J. Gordon Arbuckle

Mr. Arbuckle is a partner of the Washington, D.C. law firm of Patton, Boggs, & Blow. His experience includes representing trade associations, industrial concerns in connection with the congressional deliberations which led to adoption of the Federal Water Pollution Control Act, the Ports and Waterways Safety Act and other legislation. He has also been involved in administrative proceedings and litigation under the Water Pollution Control Act, the National Environmental Policy Act, RCRA, TSCA, the Clean Air Act and other state and federal environmental statutes. Mr. Arbuckle holds a B.A. degree from the University of Maryland and an LL.D. degree from George Washington University.

Nancy S. Bryson

Ms. Bryson is an attorney with the Washington, D.C. law firm of Crowell & Moring where she specializes in environmental law. She is a former trial attorney and assistant chief of the Environmental Defense Section, Land and Natural Resources Division of the Department of Justice. In that capacity, she litigated many cases under all of the major environmental statutes. She has authored articles on environmental law and regulation under RCRA and Superfund. Ms. Bryson graduated summa cum laude and Phi Beta Kappa from Boston University and received her J.D. from Georgetown University Law School.

David R. Case

Mr. Case is General Counsel for the Hazardous Waste Treatment Council in Washington, D.C. He was formerly at Crowell & Moring where he specialized in environmental law. He was a Chairman of the Environmental Pollution Committee and Deputy Chairman of the Council of Natural Resources and Lands of the Federal Bar Association. He has authored articles and lectured on environmental regulation under RCRA, Superfund, the Clean Air Act, the Clean Water Act, and other federal and state environmental programs. Mr. Case has received his B.A. magna cum laude from Amherst College, his LL.B. Cantab. from Cambridge University, and his law degree from the University of Michigan Law School.

ABOUT THE AUTHORS

Colburn T. Cherney   *Ch pts 8+9*   *in Wash. D.C.*

Mr. Cherney is with the law firm of Ropes & Gray in Washington, D.C., Boston, Massachusetts, and Providence, Rhode Island. He was with the United States Environmental Protection Agency for twelve years, serving as Assistant General Counsel for Superfund and Associate General Counsel for Water. His practice includes matters arising under a wide range of state and federal environmental laws, and he is a frequent speaker at conferences on environmental issues. He is a graduate of the University of Wisconsin and the University of Wisconsin Law School.

Ridgway M. Hall, Jr.

Mr. Hall is a partner in the Washington, D.C. law firm of Crowell & Moring. Formerly Associate General Counsel of the Environmental Protection Agency, he now practices environmental law and litigation. He has authored numerous articles on environmental law and is a prominent speaker at seminars and symposia on environmental law and regulatory programs. A magna cum laude graduate of Yale University, Mr. Hall received his law degree from Harvard Law School.

John C. Martin

Mr. Martin is a member of Patton, Boggs & Blow where he specializes in environmental law and litigation. He was formerly a trial attorney with the Department of Justice's Lands and Natural Resources Division where he litigated a broad spectrum of environmental issues representing EPA. He was the recipient of a Special Achievement Award for his efforts in Superfund litigation and successfully litigated many penalty cases, including one in which the court rendered the largest judgment ever handed down in an environmental case brought by the Federal Government. He previously served as an attorney in the Solicitor's Office at the Department of the Interior.

Jeffrey G. Miller

Mr. Miller is a partner in the Washington, D.C. law firm of Verner, Liipfert, Bernhard, McPherson and Hand. He was an enforcement and permitting official in the U.S. Environmental Protection Agency for ten years and ended his government career as head of EPA's enforcement program. He practices before federal and state courts and administrative agencies on a variety of pollution control matters. Mr. Miller is the author of numerous articles and a frequent speaker on environmental issues. He is a graduate of Princeton University and Harvard Law School.

ABOUT THE AUTHORS

Marshall Lee Miller

Mr. Miller, a partner in the Washington, D.C. office of the law firm of Reid & Priest, is the former Deputy Administrator of the U.S. Occupational Safety and Health Administration, Department of Labor. His experience includes service as the Special Assistant to the first Administrator of the U.S. Environmental Protection Agency, Chief EPA Judicial Officer and Associate Deputy Attorney General in the U.S. Department of Justice. He was educated at Harvard, Oxford, Heidelberg, and Yale.

William F. Pedersen, Jr.

Mr. Pedersen is an attorney with the firm of Verner, Liipfert, Bernhard, McPherson and Hand where he practices environmental law. He formerly served as Deputy General Counsel at EPA, and as Associate General Counsel for Air and Radiation. He is an honors graduate of Harvard College and Harvard Law School, and a former clerk to the late Judge Henry J. Friendly. His articles on environmental and regulatory matters have appeared in the Yale, Stanford, Virginia, and Pennsylvania Law reviews, and in the Washington Post.

Russell V. Randle

Mr. Randle is an attorney with the Washington, D.C. law firm of Patton, Boggs & Blow, where his experience includes litigation under the Clean Water Act, Clean Air Act, CERCLA, and NEPA, as well as work under the Safe Drinking Water Act. He graduated magna cum laude from Princeton University, took his law degree from Yale Law School, where he was an editor of the Law Journal, and served as law clerk to the Honorable John H. Pratt of the United States District Court for the District of Columbia.

Richard G. Stoll

Mr. Stoll is a partner in the Washington, D.C. law firm of Freedman, Levy, Kroll & Simonds, where he specializes in environmental law--primarily in the hazardous waste area. His former positions include Deputy General Counsel of the Chemical Manufacturers Association and Assistant General Counsel of the U.S. Environmental Protection Agency. In the American Bar Association's Natural Resources Section, he is currently a member of the Council and has served as Chairman of the Solid and Hazardous Waste Committee. He is a magna cum laude graduate of Westminister College in Missouri and received his law degree from Georgetown University.

ABOUT THE AUTHORS

Thomas F. P. Sullivan

Mr. Sullivan is an attorney in Washington, D.C. who has been in the forefront of the environmental field since the 1960s. He has served as editor and author of many books in addition to being a regular contributing author for "Pollution Engineering" magazine. His lecture credits include numerous environmental engineering conferences and seminars. He also serves as president of Government Institutes, Inc. Mr. Sullivan has undergraduate degrees from Kenrick Seminary and St. Louis University, and his law degree from Catholic University.

Timothy A. Vanderver, Jr.

Mr. Vanderver is a partner in the Washington, D.C. law firm of Patton, Boggs & Blow, and specializes in environmental issues. He has practiced law with the Department of the Interior and the Department of Housing & Urban Development where he specialized in natural resources and land development law. He is a graduate of Washington & Lee University and Harvard Law School. Mr. Vanderver was awarded a Rhodes Scholarship and achieved his graduate degree in law from Oxford University in England.

Chapter 1

ENVIRONMENTAL LAW FUNDAMENTALS
AND THE COMMON LAW

Thomas F. P. Sullivan
Attorney & President
Government Institutes, Inc.
Rockville, Maryland

1.0 LAWYERS AND NON-LAWYERS

Attorneys are professionally trained to provide advice on "legal matters" but they also need a continuous supply of information on new legal developments to maintain their proficiency. Some knowledge of environmental laws and regulations is also necessary for those non-lawyers who control the operations and installations that are involved in environmental and health protection.

A basic understanding of fundamental legal principles is also beneficial to environmental managers when the need arises to work with legal counsel. Non-lawyers who have environmental responsibilities should know something about environmental law to better enable them to understand an environmental attorney's advice regarding prevention of problems. The basic information in this book can help a non-lawyer to know when to seek counsel's advice and to even evaluate counsel's performance.

This book is not intended to be another erudite tome but a useful text that will help those with responsibilities for environmental protection to comply with both the letter and the spirit of the law.

The reader should always be aware of the old axiom that a "little knowledge is dangerous." So, be careful with the knowledge you gain from reading this and other materials.

1

This chapter will present the fundamentals of environmental law. From these fundamentals can be derived many legal generalities. Generalities are difficult to sustain because the factual situation determines the actual application and, therefore, the results. It should always be remembered that exceptions are born of generalities. When generalities are applied to specific factual situations, the advice of competent counsel should be obtained. Also, the reader should be alert to the fact that this field is extremely dynamic. What is the "law" today changes with time as new laws and regulations are promulgated. In addition, the courts are regularly re-interpreting the application of the laws, regulations and legal principles in their decisions.

The majority of those who will read this book are not lawyers but have their training in the sciences or engineering. These readers should remember that scientists and lawyers deal with different kinds of laws. The laws of nature which the scientist tries to discover are inviolable. The law of gravitation, for example, or Newton's three laws of motion, cannot be disobeyed.

Human laws do not share this characteristic. The moral obligation imposed by man-made laws results precisely from the fact that it is possible to break them.

2.0 WHAT IS ENVIRONMENTAL LAW?

Environmental law encompasses all the protections for our environment that emanate from the: (1) United States Constitution, (2) state constitutions, (3) federal and state statutes and local ordinances, (4) regulations promulgated by federal, state and local regulatory agencies, (5) court decisions interpreting these laws and regulations and, (6) the common law. This chapter covers (1), (5) and (6) namely, environmental protection derived from the Constitution, the common law and court decisions. In subsequent chapters, we will cover the areas that have been pre-empted by legislation and regulation.

3.0 ENVIRONMENTAL LAW AND THE COURTS

In order to gain the proper understanding of court decisions, a basic knowledge of the United States court system is needed. As the courts interpret the environmental laws and regulations and apply them to specific factual situations, they are continually determining what the law means in actual cases.

The authority of the U.S. courts is limited to those powers (1) enumerated in Article III of the U.S. Constitution, and (2) not designated in the Constitution as responsibilities of the legislative or executive branches of the federal government.

3.1 States and United States Court Systems

Throughout the United States there are two sets of judicial systems: (1) the state and local courts, established in each state under the authority of the state government, and (2) U.S. courts, set up under the authority of the Constitution by the Congress of the United States.

The state courts have general, unlimited power to decide almost every type of case, subject only to the limitations of state law. State and local courts are located in every town and county and are the tribunals with which citizens most often have contact. The great bulk of legal business such as divorce, probate of estates, traffic accidents and all other matters except those assigned to the U.S. courts is handled by these state and local courts.

The U.S. courts, on the other hand, have the authority to hear and decide only selected types of cases which are specifically enumerated in the Constitution. The U.S. courts are located principally in the larger cities while state and local courts are found throughout the country.

3.2 Cases Which the United States Courts Can Decide

The controversies which can be decided in the U.S. courts are set forth in Section 2 of Article III of the United States Constitution.

These are first "Controversies to which the United States shall be a party." That is, cases in which the U.S. government itself or one of its officers is either suing someone else or is being sued by another party. Obviously, it would be inappropriate for the U.S. government to depend upon the state governments to provide courts in which to decide controversies to which it is a party.

Secondly, the U.S. courts have power to decide cases when state courts are inappropriate or might be suspected of partiality. Thus, federal judicial power extends "to Controversies between two or more States; between a State and Citizens of another State; between Citizens of different States; between Citizens of the same

State claiming Lands under Grants of different States . . . ." If the State of Missouri sues the State of Illinois for pollution of the Mississippi River, a U.S. court would be a more impartial forum than the courts of either Missouri or Illinois. Foreseeing the possibility of interstate rivalry, the drafters of the Constitution sought to avoid any suspicion of favoritism by vesting power to decide these controversies in the U.S. courts.

State courts are also inappropriate in "Cases affecting Ambassadors, other public Ministers and Consuls" and in cases "between a State, or the Citizens thereof, and foreign States, Citizens, or Subjects." The United States government has responsibility for diplomatic relations with other nations. Since cases involving representatives or citizens of other countries may affect our foreign relations, such cases are decided in the U.S. courts.

And, thirdly, the Constitution provides that the judicial power extends "to all Cases, in Law and Equity, arising under this Constitution, the Laws of the United States, and Treaties made, or which shall be made, under their Authority" and "to all Cases of admiralty and maritime jurisdiction." Under these provisions, the U.S. courts decide cases involving the Constitution, laws enacted by Congress, treaties, and laws relating to navigable waters. For example, in cases brought under provisions of the Clean Air Act, Clean Water Act, or other federal statutes generally the appropriate forum is the U.S. court system.

The Constitution declares what cases may be decided in the U.S. courts. The Congress can and has determined that some of these cases may also be tried in state courts and that others may only be tried in U.S. courts. Specifically, Congress has provided that, with some exceptions, cases arising under the Constitution or laws of the United States or between citizens of different states may be tried in the U.S. courts only if the amount involved exceeds $10,000 and even then may be tried in either the state or the U.S. courts. The Congress has also provided that maritime cases and suits against consuls can be tried only in the U.S. courts. When a state court decides a case involving federal law, it in a sense acts as a U.S. court, and its decision on federal law may be reviewed by the United States Supreme Court.

It should be clear from this discussion that the U.S. courts cannot decide every case which arises, but only those which the Constitution and the laws enacted by Congress allot to them.

The question of which court has jurisdiction can be a complex issue. Also, the selection of the specific court in which a case is initiated is generally a key move in the overall strategy for winning a lawsuit. The selection of the specific court as a legal strategy is called "forum shopping." When bringing a case a good lawyer will evaluate which court is more inclined toward his client's position. For example the judges of the U.S. courts in the District of Columbia are known for their pro-environmentalist record. So organizations such as the Environmental Defense Fund (EDF) and Sierra Club are inclined to initiate their lawsuits in the U.S. district courts for the District of Columbia. Industrial firms are generally more inclined to file a lawsuit in a district court in Louisiana or other such geographic area with a more conservative judicial record.

3.3 United States Court System

The structure of the U.S. court system has evolved throughout the historical development of our country. The Constitution merely provides: "The Judicial Power of the United States, shall be vested in one Supreme Court, and in such inferior Courts as the Congress may from time to time ordain and establish." Thus, the only court which is constitutionally indispensable is the Supreme Court. The authority to establish and abolish other U.S. courts is vested in and has been exercised by the Congress.

At the present time, the United States court system is pyramidal in structure. At the apex of the pyramid stands the Supreme Court of the United States, the highest court in the land. On the next level are the United States courts of appeals. On the next level down are the United States district courts including the United States district courts for the District of Columbia and Puerto Rico and the district courts in the Canal Zone, Guam, and the Virgin Islands.

A person involved in a suit in a U.S. court may proceed through three levels of decision. His case will first be heard and decided by one of the courts or agencies on the lower level. If either party is dissatisfied with the decision, he may usually have a right of review in one of the courts of appeals. Then, if he is still dissatisfied, he may petition for review in the Supreme Court of the United States. However, review is granted by the Supreme Court only in cases involving matters of great national importance.

This pyramidal organization of the courts serves two purposes. First, the Supreme Court and the courts of appeals can correct errors which have been made in the decisions of the trial courts. Secondly, the higher courts can assure uniformity of decision by reviewing cases in which two or more lower courts have reached different decisions.

State courts have a similar pyramid structure with a basic court of original jurisdiction, an appellate court and then a supreme court, but often states do not call their highest court a supreme court. So, at the state level the nomenclature can be confusing.

3.4 Courts in Practical Perspective

From a practical viewpoint, when you hear of a judicial decision of interest to you, ask which court decided the case. If the Supreme Court of the U.S. decided the case, it is a very important decision for the entire country. If a local court decided the case, it is generally of little interest nationally but of major interest to that local jurisdiction. However, any decision on a point of law is better than none at all.

Also, be aware that courts do differ in their opinions. There are many examples of two lower courts reaching conflicting opinions on a point of law. This is an extremely difficult concept for many to accept. If you are originally trained in engineering or the sciences, you are probably accustomed to dealing in data and facts. To move into the realm of "ifs" and "yes, but" seems to be like going from the "world of black and white" into a "world of gray." For those who find this troubling, remember that in almost everything, we are talking about degrees of certitude. The field of environmental law may involve a higher degree of uncertitude than most other areas because of its newness and changeability. As a result, you do your best to understand what is the meaning of the laws, regulations and court opinions, and you then take into consideration the degree of certitude involved in a particular legal issue before proceeding to a decision.

Also, keep in mind that our court system, although hailed as one of the fairest systems ever developed by mankind, is subject to human frailties. The judges, lawyers, plaintiffs, defendants and jurors all involve human interactions, another source of uncertainties.

4.0 COMMON LAW

Underlying the development of legal theory in the United States is a body of rules and principles relating to the government and security of persons and property which had its origin, development and formulation in England. Brought to the American colonies by peoples of Anglo-Saxon stock, these basic rules were formally adopted in the states in which they were in force after the American Revolution. Known as the "common law," these principles are derived from the application of natural reason, an innate sense of justice, and the dictates of conscience. The common law is not the result of legislative enactment. Rather, its authority is derived solely from usages and customs which have been recognized, affirmed and enforced by the courts through judicial decisions.

It is important to realize that the "common law" is not a fixed or absolute set of written rules in the same sense as statutory or legislatively enacted law. The unwritten principles of common law are flexible and adaptable to the changes which occur in a growing society. New institutions and public policies; modifications of usage and practice; changes in mores, trade, and commerce; inventions; and increasing knowledge, all generate new factual situations which require application and reinterpretation of the fundamental principles of common law by the courts.

As the courts examine each new set of facts in the light of past precedent, an orderly development of common laws occurs through a slow and natural process. Thus, the basic principles underlying American jurisprudence remain fundamentally constant, evolving slowly and progressively in scope as they absorb the surface ripples produced by the winds of social change.

The common law, so far as it has not been expressly abrogated, is recognized as an organic part of the jurisprudence of most of the states. The major exception is Louisiana jurisprudence, which is based on Roman law--a relic of French rule prior to the Louisiana Purchase. However, since the state court systems have functioned independently of each other, subject only to federal review in cases of national importance, the common law varies slightly from state to state.

There is also a federal common law which forms the basis for deciding cases in which a uniform standard is desirable for dealing with such claims as alleged federal rights.

The common law actions that we will discuss in subsequent sections are civil suits in which the plaintiff (the party bringing the lawsuit) seeks to remedy a violation of a private right. Civil actions are distinguished from criminal proceedings in which the state seeks to redress a breach of public or collective rights which are established in codified penal law.

Sections 6.1, 6.2 and 6.3 of this chapter review the three most frequently used types of common law actions that can be the basis of a lawsuit in the pollution control field: nuisance, trespass, and negligence. After these three actions are described, collateral matters are covered which should be of concern to industry and government officials responsible for operating facilities that have the potential of causing injury to human health or our environment.

5.0 CASE LAW

Because there is no unified codification of common law, we must look to the court records of actual judicial decisions to determine the application of common law rules and principles to a given set of facts.

To discover how the laws governing environmental controls are applied in a specific factual situation, it is necessary to analyze cases which arose from similar circumstances.

Since each case or factual situation is unique, the decisions reached in prior cases involving similar circumstances are valuable as precedents for points of law. A judicial opinion represents a synthesis of many factors such as: a careful examination of the facts, the weight of relevant precedent, the strength of the legal principles involved, the balance of equities in the case, and more.

Case law, then, is the aggregate of points of law derived from reported cases which forms the body of law established through judicial decisions. It is separate and distinct from statutory law, which is promulgated by legislative bodies.

5.1 Obiter Dicta

Obiter dicta is a Latin phrase used in the legal profession to refer to extraneous comments in a court's opinion. All that a court says is not law. A judicial opinion is, like evidence, only binding insofar as it is relevant. When a court's opinion touches upon points not at issue, the extraneous statements are not binding court opinions or precedents.

The obiter dicta in a court's opinion are not a compelling precedent. However, if the judge giving the decision is highly regarded as a legal scholar, his opinion—whether obiter dicta or not—may have some impact on succeeding cases.

6.0 TORTS

In modern legal terminology, "tort" is the word used to denote a private wrong or wrongful act for which a civil action can be brought by the injured party. Thus, a tort is clearly distinguished from a criminal act which is an offense against statutorily established public rights and is prosecuted by the state in behalf of the citizenry.

A tort arises from the existence of a generalized legal duty to avoid causing harm to others, through acts of omission, as well as of commission. By virtue of citizenship, every adult person is obliged to fulfill a duty of care for the personal and property rights of others while engaged in daily life. Carelessness in exercising this responsibility may give rise to a cause of action (a lawsuit) by means of which the injured party may seek restitution. This duty is non-contractual; that is, it does not arise from an explicit promissory agreement between the parties to the action. So a tort is also distinguished from a contract right which is dependent upon the contract itself.

Tens of thousands of tort lawsuits have been filed against the major asbestos manufacturers resulting in Johns Manville and several other large corporations filing for bankruptcy. These asbestos cases and other toxic chemical litigation have prompted some writers to allege that the 1980s will be the era of "toxic torts." It is clear that tort law will be of considerable interest to industry in the 1980s as its role expands.

Torts are divided into two general classes: (1) property torts which involve injury or damage to property and (2) personal torts which involve injuries to a person, whether to the body, reputation or feelings.

The three types of torts encountered in the environmental field are: (1) nuisance; (2) trespass, and (3) negligence.

6.1 Nuisance

The most common tort action in the field of environmental law is nuisance. Nuisance is defined as "that class of wrongs that arise from the unreasonable, unwarrantable or unlawful use by a person of his own property, either real or personal, or from his own improper, indecent, or unlawful personal conduct, working an obstruction of or injury to the right of another or of the public, and producing material annoyance, inconvenience, discomfort or hurt."[1]

The general rule is that a person may use his land or personal property in any manner he sees fit. However, this rule is subject to limitation: the owner must use his property in a reasonable manner. A nuisance arises whenever a person uses his property to cause material injury or annoyance to his neighbor.

In determining whether a given act constitutes a nuisance, the court considers the nature of the act itself, and the place and the circumstance surrounding the act. To be actionable, the injury or discomfort must amount to a material injury or annoyance. It must tangibly affect the physical comfort of ordinary people under normal circumstances or conditions.

6.1.1 Private or Public Nuisances

Nuisances may be private or public. A private nuisance may be abated by an injunction brought by the individual whose property or health is affected. A public nuisance is one which affects an indefinite number of persons in a community. A public official normally abates a public nuisance.

In the United States today, public nuisances are primarily defined by statute and ordinance. Regulation at the local level has resulted in a great variety of specific provisions; for example, local ordinances generally prohibit making loud noises in the immediate vicinity of a hospital. Nearly all states have adopted broad criminal statutes covering public nuisances without attempting to define the specific acts which are covered by them. These have come to be construed as including anything that would have been a public nuisance at common law.

The distinction between public and private nuisance rests on a determination of whether the nuisance affects the rights of the public or the rights of an individual exclusively.

It is generally held that an individual acting privately cannot initiate a legal action for a purely public nuisance, unless his damage

---

1/   Black's Law Dictionary 961 (5th ed. 1979).

is in some way distinguished from that sustained by other members of the general public. The modern trend, however, is to eliminate this distinction between private and public nuisance and to allow private individuals to initiate legal actions whether the nuisance is private or public. 2/

A public nuisance is generally a crime. It may also be a tort or private nuisance, if a plaintiff can prove that he has suffered some "special" or "particular" damage. The damage must be of a kind that is individual to the plaintiff as distinguished from that which he shares with the rest of the public.

In an Arkansas case, 3/ nine homeowners in the vicinity of a rendering plant brought suit to abate the odor nuisance created by operation of the plant. They claimed that odors from the rendering plant caused them to feel nausea and to lose sleep at night. On the witness stand, the plant manager admitted that operation of the plant violated existing law. The court found the plant to be a public nuisance, and the homeowners obtained a court order to close the plant unless conditions causing the nuisance were corrected within a time limit established by the court.

On appeal, the plant owner argued that the homeowners were not entitled to abatement of a public nuisance because they failed to show that they incurred damages beyond those sustained by the general public. The appeals court found that although the plant was found to be a public nuisance, this did not preclude it from also being a private nuisance with respect to the homeowners who brought suit. So the plant was declared a private nuisance by the appellate judge.

Some states have statutes which allow private individuals to sue in an attempt to abate a public nuisance.

6.1.2. Noise Nuisance

The most common form of environmental nuisance is noise pollution. Noise produced by human activities is a common environmental problem. In order to constitute a nuisance in the legal sense,

---

2/   Prosser, Private Action for Public Nuisance, 52 Va. L. Rev. 997 (1966).

3/   Ozark Poultry Products, Inc. v. Garman, 251 Ark. 389, 472 S.W. 2d 714(1971).

generally, noise must be of such magnitude and intensity as to cause actual or psychological discomfort to persons of ordinary sensibilities. Noise from the operation of an industrial plant constitutes an actionable nuisance if it affects injuriously the health or comfort of ordinary people in the plant's vicinity to an unreasonable extent. Neither the courts nor legislatures 4/ have been able to set an absolute standard, so this determination rests on the facts.

O'Neill v. Carolina Freight Carriers Corp. 5/ is an example of a "noise nuisance" case in which a homeowner was awarded both an injunction and damages against the operators of a nearby business. In this case, the plaintiffs showed that they were ordinary people and that the noise from trucks and loading operations at a terminal located immediately adjacent to their home was unreasonable. It caused them loss of sleep and prevented general enjoyment of their home. The court ruled that the truck terminal noises between 11:00 p.m. and 6:00 a.m. were unreasonable and that every property owner must make reasonable use of his land so as not to cause unnecessary annoyance to his neighbors.

In the O'Neill case, the facts lead readily to a conclusion of injury to health because the noise during the night could logically cause loss of sleep and resulting injury to health.

There is no fixed standard as to what degree or kind of noise constitutes a nuisance. The circumstances of each case must be considered independently, the key determination being whether or not the noise is unreasonable and causes some physical or psychological harm. This determination varies from one community to another and from one period of time to another depending on local attitudes and customs.

6.1.3 Other Nuisances

Smoke, dust, odors, other airborne pollutants, water pollutants and hazardous substances have also been held to be nuisances.

The Ozark Poultry Products case, previously cited (footnote 3), is an example of an odor being classed as a nuisance.

4/   S. D. Comp. Laws Ann. § 21-10-9; (1967) Wis. Stat. Ann. § 23.02 (West 1977); Fla. Stat. Ann. § 60.05. (West 1969).

5/   156 Conn. 613, 244 A.2d 372 (1968).

In a New York case, McCarty v. Natural Carbonic Gas Co., 6/ the plaintiffs owned a home adjacent to the defendant's manufacturing plant. The plaintiffs claimed that under specific wind conditions, black smoke settled about their home causing them discomfort, annoyance and injury. The court determined that the operation of the manufacturing plant resulted in an unreasonable use of the property, because all the damage could be avoided by the use of hard coal or by use of some modern emission control systems. Although either would involve an increase in expenses, the court held that the safety of persons, generally, is superior in right to a particular use of a single piece of property by its owner. So the court awarded the decision to the plaintiffs.

It should be noted that air pollutants only constitute a nuisance under certain circumstances. Normal air is usually considered as that common to a locality and so varies from one area to another. To be a nuisance, the air pollution must cause harm and discomfort to ordinary people to an unreasonable extent.

In the case of Chicago v. Commonwealth Edison 7/ the court refused to issue an injunction against alleged air pollution. The court found that although the public had a right to clean air, the notion of pure air has come to mean clean air consistent with the character of the locality and the attending circumstances. The court ruled that "The City has failed to answer the threshold question of whether Commonwealth Edison's Indiana facility causes substantial harm so as to constitute an actionable invasion of a public right. In order to be entitled to injunctive relief a substantial harm or injury must be clearly demonstrated." This case is a strict interpretation of the law of nuisance because it was a request for an injunction to cease operation which would have a broad impact on employment and local economics. If the action had been for damages, the court may have decided it differently by not using a strict interpretation of the law.

In Harrison v. Indiana Auto Shredders, 8/ the Seventh Circuit Court of Appeals also refused to permanently enjoin operation of an

---

6/   189 N.Y. 40, 81 N.E. 549 (1907).

7/   24 Ill. App. 624, 321 N.E.2d 412, 7 Env't. Rep. Cas. (BNA) 1974.

8/   528 F.2d 1107, 8 Env't Rep. Cas. (BNA) 1569 (7th Cir. 1975).

automobile shredding and recycling plant based on a nuisance action. The court held that under the evidence presented and in the absence of an imminent hazard to health or welfare—none of which was established—the defendant could not be prevented from continuing to engage in its operation. In addition, the court believed that the operation should be allowed a reasonable time to correct any defects not posing threats of imminent or substantial harm.

In essence, the courts were not convinced by the evidence presented in these last two cases that the harm caused by the alleged nuisance was so great as to justify forcing them to cease operation. If these facilities were shut down, many families would be injured by the forced unemployment. So the weighing of the equities by the court resulted in a determination based on all the evidence presented in favor of allowing continued operations. This is generally called "balancing the equities."

An unusual type of nuisance case of considerable notoriety and interest involved the construction of the 110-story Sears building in Chicago. 9/ In this case, the plaintiffs requested an injunction to prevent completion of the building which they claimed would constitute a nuisance by distorting television reception in surrounding areas. The court held that Sears had a legal right to use the airspace above its property, at least as much as it can occupy or use in connection with the land, subject only to legislative limitation. One can readily see the adverse consequences that such a theory could pose for solar energy.

The Earthline Corporation, a subsidiary of SCA Services, Inc., attempted to operate an industrial waste recovery, treatment, storage and disposal site on a 130-acre site in Illinois. Ninety acres are located within the Village of Wilsonville and the remaining acres adjacent to the village. The operation accepted hazardous wastes and toxic substances. The Village sued Earthline to stop the operation and also to require the removal of those hazardous wastes and toxic substances that had been deposited on the site. 10/ The court

---

9/   People ex rel Hoogasian v. Sears, Roebuck and Co., 52 Ill. 2d 301, 287 N.E. 2d 677 (1972), cert. denied, 409 U.S. 1001 (1972).

10/   Village of Wilsonville v. SCA Services, Inc., 77 Ill. App. 3d 618, 396 N.E. 2d 522 (1979), aff'd 86 Ill. 2d 1, 426 N.E. 2d 824 (1981).

ruled that the site was a public/private nuisance, issued an injunction against Earthline's further operation of the site and required them to remove all wastes and contaminated soil.

It is most important to note that this case was decided against SCA even though there was no showing that SCA had violated any government regulation. Compliance with government regulations is not a defense against a common law nuisance action. Also, the lower court decision emphasized a nuisance does not require a showing of any negligence on the part of the defendant:

> Nuisance and negligence are distinct torts and except in the cases of nuisances created by negligence, liability for nuisance does not depend upon the existence of negligence. Negligence is not an essential or material element of a cause of action for nuisance and need not be pleaded or proved especially where the thing complained of is a nuisance per se or a public nuisance or results from ultra-hazardous conduct on the part of the defendant. A nuisance is a condition and not an act or a failure to act on the part of the person responsible for the condition.

6.1.4 Some Defenses to Nuisance Actions

Nuisance actions have often come down to a question of balancing the equities (weighing the impact of the injuries to the respective parties involved in the litigation). In any balancing of the equities, the good faith efforts of the polluter, while not absolving him, would certainly be a factor if they exist. 11/

The availability of pollution control devices is, of course, a significant factor that can be considered by the court. For example, in Renkin v. Harvey Aluminum, 12/ the court noted Harvey Aluminum's failure to keep pace with the technological advances in pollution controls. In that case the court ordered adoption of such controls.

In general, the courts are moving to strict liability for environmental nuisances so that practically speaking, there are no good defenses. The solution is: do not create nuisances.

11/   McElwain v. Georgia Pacific, 245 Or. 247, 421 P. 2d 957 (1966).

12/   226 F. Supp. 169 (D. Or. 1963).

6.1.5 Coming to a Nuisance

"Coming to a nuisance" is the phrase used to describe a defense that the complainant or plaintiff affected by the nuisance moved into the area where the "complained about activity" had already been in existence.

An example of "coming to a nuisance" occurs when someone moves onto the property next to an airport or near an industrial complex and then complains of the nuisance that existed prior to his moving there. Generally, the fact that an individual purchases property with the knowledge of the existence of a nuisance or that he came to the nuisance will not defeat his right to the abatement of the nuisance or recovery of damages. 13/

However, some cases have held that if the complainant came to a nuisance, this constitutes a defense to a nuisance lawsuit. This minority view is probably a result of an old axiom of law that one who voluntarily places himself in a situation whereby he suffers an injury will not prevail. The test of liability in these cases is often the knowledge of the plaintiff regarding the consequences of his conduct.

The majority rule, however, is that the fact alone that a person moved into the vicinity of a nuisance by purchasing or leasing property in the area does not bar him from complaining in an action against the continued operation or maintenance of the nuisance.14/ The majority rule is based on the theory that pure air and the comfortable enjoyment of property are as much rights belonging to it as the right of possession and occupancy. If population where there was none before approaches a nuisance, it is the duty of those liable to put an end to it.

6.2 Trespass

In a general sense, an invasion of another's rights is a trespass. Usually, trespass is used in a more limited sense. It is to be

---

13/   Fertilizing Co. v. Hyde Park, 97 U.S. 659 (1897); Rentz v. Roach, 154 Ga. 491, 115 S.E. 94 (1922); Vann v. Bowie Sewerage Co., 127 Tex. 97, 90 S.W. 2d 561 (1936) are a few cases.

14/   A comprehensive article on this subject is found in 42 A.L.R. 3rd 344 (1972). This article includes a listing of cases by jurisdictions that recognize the majority rule.

understood as designating an injury to the person, property, or rights of another which is the immediate result of some unlawful act.

In order to constitute trespass, unlawful intent is not necessary. Intent or motive with which the act was done is immaterial except as far as it may affect the measure of damages. A person is liable even if he acted in good faith and with reasonable care.

Trespass is commonly divided into three types. These are:

(1) **Trespass to personal property** is an injury to or interference with possession, with or without the exercise of physical force. This includes destruction of personal property as well as the taking from the possession of another, or a refusal to surrender possession.

(2) **Trespass to the person** is an unlawful act committed on the person of another such as a vehicle impact or even an unauthorized operation. Mere words are not actionable trespass to the person.

(3) **Trespass to realty** is an unlawful, forcible entry on another's possession. An injury to the realty of another or an interference with his possession, above or below ground, is a trespass, regardless of the condition of the land and regardless of negligence.

Trespass to realty is the type of trespass action that is generally used in pollution control cases. In an action for trespass to realty, entry upon another's land need not be in person. It may be made by causing or permitting a thing to cross the boundary of the premises. The trespass may be committed by casting material upon another's land, by discharging water, soot or carbon, by allowing gas or oil to flow underground into someone else's land, but not by mere vibrations or light which are generally classed as nuisances.

In the case of Martin v. Reynolds Metal Co., 15/ the deposit on Martin's property of microscopic fluoride compounds, which were emitted in vapor form from the Reynolds' plant, was held to be an invasion of this property—and so a trespass.

Cases have distinguished between trespass and nuisance and held that encroachment of the space above the land is a nuisance.

15/   221 Or. 86, 342 P. 2d 790(1959), cert. denied, 362 U.S. 918 (1960).

Generally there must be physical invasion of the property to constitute a trespass.

Some courts have used trespass and private nuisance almost
interchangeably. The end result is that the distinction between trespass and nuisance is somewhat clouded.

Negligence and trespass have also been used interchangeably
as seen in the case of Stacy v. VEPCO. 16/ In this case, the court
ruled that there was "negligence and/or trespass on the part of
VEPCO" because of damage caused to Stacy's trees by the emissions
from VEPCO's Mount Storm plant. It is interesting to note that the
court in this case was convinced by the expert meteorologist's testimony that the emissions could travel the 22-mile distance from the
plant to damage the trees. The important point to remember is that
courts can and do minimize the concern with the form of the action
but endeavor to do substantive justice based on all the evidence
presented.

6.3 Negligence

Negligence is: (a) doing or omitting to do an act, (b) which a
person owes to another by virtue of a legal duty imposed upon him
by law, (c) thereby causing injury to the plaintiff or to his property.
Negligence is that part of the law of torts which deals with acts not
intended to inflict injury. If there is intent to inflict injury, then the
case becomes one of criminal law. The standard of care required by
law is that degree which would be exercised by a person of ordinary
prudence under the same circumstances. This is often defined as the
"reasonable man" rule, namely what a reasonable person would do
under all the circumstances.

In order to render the defendant liable, his act must be the
proximate cause of the injury. Proximate cause is that which in the
natural and continuous sequence, if unbroken by an efficient intervening act, produces injury and without which the result would not
have happened.

An example of a negligence action in a pollution case is Bur-
gess v. Tamano. 17/ This case involved the July 1972 spill of more

---

16/   7 Env't. Rep. Cas. (BNA) 1443 (E.D.Va. 1975).

17/   5 Env't. Rep. Cas. (BNA) 1914 (D.C. Me. 1973) and 6 Env't.
      Rep. Cas. (BNA) 1380 (D.C. Me. 1974).

than 100,000 gallons of bunker oil from the tank ship Tamano into Maine's Casco Bay. Fishermen, boat owners, and property owners allegedly damaged by the spill brought suit against the Tamano, while Maine filed suit to recover damages sustained by the state as a result of the spill. Since the federal government has a great deal of money with which to pay damages, plaintiffs contended that the proximate cause of the escape and spread of oil from the Tamano was the Coast Guard's negligent conduct of its containment and cleanup operations. The court ruled that the United States, in undertaking any task such as pollution abatement, is liable in tort for the consequences of its negligence to the same extent that a private person would be liable.

The evidence convinced the court that the Coast Guard caused injury, which could be foreseen, by its inadequate containment and cleanup operation. Since this conduct was the proximate cause of injury to the plaintiff, the court held that the Coast Guard was guilty of negligence.

Persons harmed as a result of careless and improper disposal or handling of hazardous waste can recover for their losses under a negligence cause of action. Indeed, state and federal courts have long recognized this common law theory of recovery against defendants who engage in the negligent disposal of pollutants such as hazardous waste. 18/ Where negligence can be established, it is no defense that the negligent action was in full compliance with all government regulations 19/ and permit conditions. 20/ On the other hand, noncompliance with regulations or a permit in some states may be prima facie evidence (that is, proof without any more evidence) of liability. 21/

18/ See, e.g., Knabe v. National Supply Div. of Armco Steel Corp., 592 F.2d 841 (5th Cir. 1979).

19/ Greater Westchester Homeowners Assoc. v. City of Los Angeles, 26 Cal. 3d 86, 603 P.2d 1329 (1978), 160 Cal. Rptr. 733, cert. denied, 449 U.S. 820 (1980).

20/ Brown v. Petrolane, Inc., 102 Cal. App.3d 720, 162 Cal. Rptr. 551 (1980); Belton v. Wateree Power Co., 123 S.C. 291, 115 S.E. 587 (1922).

21/ See Martin v. Herzog, 288 N.Y. 164, 126 N.E. 814, 439 N.Y.S.2d 922 (1920).

6.3.1 Res Ipsa Loquitur

As a general rule, the mere fact that an accident occurs does not give rise to a presumption of negligence. Negligence must be proved by a preponderance of the evidence. The doctrine of res ipsa loquitur does not relieve the plaintiff of proving negligence but it does rearrange the method of establishing proof. Res ipsa loquitur means that the party claiming injury has produced sufficient facts to warrant an inference of negligence.

In order to rely on res ipsa loquitur, the plaintiff must show that the instrumentality which caused the injury was, to some extent, under the exclusive control of the defendant, and the injury was such that, in the ordinary course of things, it would not have occurred, if the one having control had used proper care.

The following is a hypothetical example of res ipsa loquitur:

> A is a passenger in the airplane of B Company, a common carrier. In good flying weather, the plane disappears, and no trace of it is ever found. There is no evidence. Various explanations are possible, including mechanical failure which could not have been prevented by reasonable care, or bombs planted on the plane. In this case, however, it may be inferred by the jury that the most probable explanation for A's death is negligence on the part of B Company. 22/

In negligence cases involving pollution, it is generally difficult to link the activities of an alleged polluter with plaintiff's claimed injury from the pollution. Res ipsa loquitur helps to eliminate this difficulty. The case of California Department of Fish and Game v. SS Bournemouth 23/ presented such a case for use of res ipsa. Officers of the California Fish and Game Department took oil samples from an oil slick in a harbor and from the SS Bournemouth. The court found a scientific probability that the two samples came from the same source. The court also found, on the basis of evidence as to wind, current, and tide, that the slick could have come from the ship. There was no other ship in the general area at the

---

22/   Restatement (Second) of Torts § 328D (1966).

23/   318 F. Supp. 839 (C.D. Cal. 1970).

relevant time. Then, the court applied the doctrine of res ipsa; the oil spill probably could not have occurred unless someone was negligent; no other source of the spill was indicated; the plaintiff was not negligent; the ship was under exclusive control of the defendant; therefore, the burden of proof was shifted from the plaintiff to the defendant based on res ipsa loquitur. Damages of the cost of cleaning up the spill were awarded against the vessel by the court.

6.3.2 Violation of a Statute or Ordinance

Generally, the violation of a statute or ordinance which was passed to promote safety is negligence. But the violation of such law does not of itself give rise to civil liability. The plaintiff must show that the violation of the law was the proximate cause of the injury. The violation of a statute or ordinance, which is not designed to prevent the sort of harm about which the plaintiff is complaining, is not negligence.

An example of the application of this doctrine in an environmental lawsuit is the case of Springer v. Schlitz Brewing Company. 24/ Mr. and Mrs. Springer owned a large farm downriver from a newly constructed Winston-Salem, N.C., brewery of Schlitz. They sued Schlitz for overloading the city's sewage treatment, causing it to pollute the Yadkin river, resulting in fish kills and so interfering with their riparian rights. In North Carolina, as in many other states, a riparian landowner has a right to the agricultural, recreational and scenic use and enjoyment of the stream bordering his land. A city sewage ordinance prohibited the discharge of pollutants that interfere with the city's waste treatment process.

In this case the plaintiff did not, according to the court's opinion, prove that Schlitz was negligent in the conventional sense. Instead, the Court looked to the theory that violation of a city sewage ordinance is negligence "per se." The appeals court directed that the jury should decide if Schlitz violated the city's ordinance. If the jury decides that the ordinance was violated, it is negligence per se and if the negligence proximately causes injury, then the industry is liable irrespective of any good faith efforts on the part of the defendant.

24/   510 F.2d 468, 7 Env't. Rep. Cas. (BNA) 1516 (4th Cir. 1975).

So, violations of environmental or pollution control statutes or ordinances which are generally designed to protect the public health or safety could result in a successful negligence lawsuit by the injured party even though there is no factual showing of negligence.

6.3.3 Dangerous Substances—Strict Liability

Courts have ruled that a person who keeps a potentially dangerous substance on his land which, if permitted to escape, is certain to injure others, must make good the damage caused by the escape of the substance, regardless of negligence on the defendant's part.

This strict liability theory is very old. It was used in a 1907 case where oil escaped into the Potomac River in Washington, D.C., and resulted in injury to boats in a downstream boathouse. 25/ In this case, it was determined that a potentially dangerous substance is anything which, if permitted to escape, is certain to injure others. This description of a potentially dangerous substance is so broad as to include oil in the case under discussion plus thousands of other substances in subsequent litigation.

The reasoning for this strict liability standard is that, when persons suffer loss, no good reason can be found to charge the loss against anyone who did not contribute to it. If the defendant is engaged in an ultra-hazardous or dangerous activity for profit, he should bear the burden of compensating others who are harmed by his activities.

In making the determination of whether an activity is ultra-hazardous, courts have traditionally scrutinized six factors: (1) the existence of a high degree of risk, (2) the likelihood that the resultant harm will be great, (3) the ability to eliminate the risk by exercising reasonable care, (4) the extent to which the activity is not common in the community, (5) the appropriateness of the activity to the place where it is carried on, and (6) the activity's value to the community.

Not surprisingly, courts have applied strict liability theories in cases involving the disposal of hazardous waste and hazardous materials management.

25/   Brennan Constr. Co. v. Cumberland, 29 App. D.C. 554 (1907).

6.3.4 Defenses to an Action for Negligence

6.3.4.1 Contributory Negligence

Contributory negligence is an affirmative defense in some jurisdictions. The theory behind this concept is that a person is not entitled to benefit from his own wrong. Therefore, contributory negligence on the part of the plaintiff generally relieves the defendant of liability, unless he, the defendant, had the "last clear chance" of avoiding the accident.

The "last clear chance" doctrine 26/ presupposes a perilous situation created or existing through the negligence of both the plaintiff and the defendant. It assumes that there was a time, after such negligence had occurred, when the defendant could, and the plaintiff could not by the use of available means, avoid the accident. This doctrine is not applicable when the emergency is so sudden that there is no time to avoid it. Under the "last clear chance" doctrine, a negligent defendant is liable when he (aware of the plaintiff's peril, or unaware of it only through carelessness) had, in fact, a later opportunity than the plaintiff to avert the accident.

A comparative negligence concept (apportionment of responsibility or damages) is recognized in 12 states. 27/

6.3.4.2 Assumption of Risk

Generally any person who knows of a risk and assumes it is not permitted to recover for any injury sustained. This is based on the theory that a person should not be permitted to benefit from his own wrong. One of several exceptions to this rule is when the risk is assumed to save life.

6.3.4.3 Proving Negligence

Negligence actions in the pollution field are generally hampered by the plaintiff's difficulty in proving the defendant negligent. The plaintiff also must prove that the negligence of the defendant was the proximate cause of the plaintiff's injury. However, the increased availability to the public of plant records, monitoring, inspections and source emission data required under the

---

26/ 57 Am. Jur. 2d Negligence § 386 (1971).

27/ Id. at § 426.

various statutes and regulations will contribute to easing the evidentiary problems of proving a negligence case.

6.4 Sovereign Immunity and Torts

Theoretically, the law has granted immunity from tort liability to governments. Neither the United States nor any of the several states may be sued by a private citizen without the government's consent. The origin of this idea was the common law notion that "the King can do no wrong." But, it was not until the sixteenth century that this concept was fully established as law. When the individual sovereign was replaced by the broader concept of the modern state, the idea was carried over: that to allow a suit against a ruling government without its consent was inconsistent with the very idea of supreme executive power.

In most state jurisdictions, however, consent has been given, usually in a limited form by statutes, which provide for special procedure or create special courts of claims, or which authorize suits against the state in its own courts for particular causes of action. There is a good deal of variety to these statutes, and reference must be made to those of the particular jurisdiction.

In 1946, the United States waived its immunity, with certain exceptions, from liability in tort, and provided for litigation of tort claims against it in the federal courts by the Federal Tort Claims Act. 28/

So, for anyone contemplating bringing a pollution lawsuit based on a tort action against a government entity, the first questions are: has sovereign immunity been waived, and what are the consent restrictions?

In regard to any suit against a state brought in a federal court, the Eleventh Amendment to the U.S. Constitution states:

> The Judicial power of the United States shall not be constructed to extend to any suit in law or equity commenced or prosecuted against one of the United States by Citizens of another State or by Citizens or subjects of any Foreign State.

While the Eleventh Amendment, by its own terms, does not bar suits against a state by its own citizens, the U.S. Supreme Court

---

28/   28 U.S.C. §§ 1254 et seq. (1982).

has consistently ruled that an unconsenting state is protected from suits brought in federal courts by her own citizens as well as by citizens of another state. 29/ It is also well-settled law that even though a state is not named as a defendant, any judgment which must be paid from public funds of the state falls within the prohibitions of the Eleventh Amendment.

A successful example of the defense of sovereign immunity on the federal level is found in an environmental case entitled Byram River v. Village of Port Chester. 30/ In this case, the plaintiffs were seeking to halt the depositing of allegedly inadequately treated sewage into the Byram River. The plaintiffs named a number of defendants, including the New York State Department of Environmental Conservation.   The Court dismissed the action against New York State based on the defense of sovereign immunity as set forth in the Eleventh Amendment.

7.0 CONSTITUTIONAL LAW

7.1 Constitution and Government Authority
The federal government was created to be a government of limited authority. The powers granted to the federal government are those enumerated in the U.S. Constitution. Although the federal government's authority is theoretically limited to only those enumerated, in practice these powers have been so expanded in scope by judicial interpretation that it is hard to conceive of any environmental laws being beyond the federal authority. So this section will not review the general question of the theoretical basis of federal power but, instead, focus on the specific constitutional limits to this authority.

These limits appear to be of more pragmatic interest and concern today because they are the issues raised in lawsuits against the abuse of governmental authority.

7.2 Limits on Governmental Action

7.2.1 Search Warrants and the Fourth Amendment
The Fourth Amendment of the Constitution provides that:

29/   Hans v. Louisiana, 134 U.S. 1(1890); Edelman v. Jordan, 415 U.S. 651 (1974).

30/   7 Env't. Rep. Cas. (BNA) 1970 (S.D.N.Y. 1975).

> The right of the people to be secure in their persons, houses, papers, and effects, against unreasonable searches and seizures shall not be violated, and no Warrants shall issue, but upon probable cause, supported by oath or affirmation and particularly describing the place to be searched and the persons or things to be seized.

One of the most common abuses of governmental authority is in the collection or obtaining of evidence. Evidence is necessary for any civil or criminal enforcement program. However, federal evidence collection is limited by these Fourth Amendment prohibitions.

The courts have held that the Fourth Amendment applies to the corporate entity as well as to the private citizen. The Supreme Court has held that the requirement for a search warrant even applies to routine administrative inspections. 31/ In the Camara case, the Court held that the warrant requirement applied to a municipal health inspector's search of a private residence. A similar conclusion was reached with respect to a fire inspector's attempted search of a commercial warehouse. 32/ In these cases, the Court indicated that a lesser degree of "probable cause" would be required for an administrative search warrant than for the typical criminal search warrant. So there can be routine periodic searches of all structures in a given area based on an appraisal of conditions in the area as a whole rather than on a knowledge of conditions in a particular building. The reasonableness of such inspections is to be weighed against the invasion of rights that the search entails.

Generally warrants are only sought after entry is refused because there is no need for a search warrant when the owner or operator has given his consent.

To avoid this need for search warrants, the Congress has authorized warrantless searches in some statutes. In the famous Barlow case 33/ the constitutionality of these legislative waivers

---

31/ Camara v. Municipal Court of San Francisco, 387 U.S. 523 (1967).

32/ See v. City of Seattle, 387 U.S. 541 (1967).

33/ Marshall v. Barlow's Inc., 436 U.S. 307 (1978).

was reviewed by the Supreme Court. The Court held that Section 8 of the Occupational Safety and Health Act (OSHA) authorizing warrantless inspections violated the Fourth Amendment prohibition against warrantless searches and was unconstitutional. How does this affect you? Probably it doesn't affect you directly, but it does put some restraint on the federal government not to harass businesses with needless inspections.

The Environmental Protection Agency (EPA) has avoided the test of the constitutionality of the warrantless search authorizations given to them by Congress in the Noise Control Act and the Resource Conservation and Recovery Act by not challenging the issue. If an EPA inspector is refused admission, EPA, as standard procedure, will then obtain a search warrant and not even try to use the statutory authority. This avoids the constitutional confrontation.

It is common, in the field of environmental law, to find exceptions to the general rules. An example of an exception to the search warrant requirement is the so-called "open fields" exception described in the Supreme Court case, Air Pollution Variance Board v. Western Alfalfa. 34/ In this case, an inspector of a Division of the Colorado Department of Health entered the premises of Western Alfalfa Corporation without its knowledge or consent to make a Ringelmann reading of plumes of smoke being emitted from the company's chimneys. The Western Alfalfa Corporation claimed that the inspection violated the Fourth Amendment by entering its property to collect evidence without a search warrant. The U.S. Supreme Court ruled that the inspector was within an exception to the Fourth Amendment and had not violated the rights of the Western Alfalfa Corporation. The Court held the general rule to be that the act of conducting tests on a defendant's premises without either a warrant or the consent of defendant constitutes an unreasonable search within the Fourth Amendment. However, in this case the inspector did not enter the plant or offices. Basically he sighted what anyone in the area near the plant could see in the sky. He was on the defendant's property but there was no showing that he was on premises from which the public was excluded. The Court held that there is an "open fields" exception to the constitutional requirement for a search warrant which was applicable in this case.

34/ 416 U.S. 861, 6 Env't. Rep. Cas. (BNA) 1571 (1974).

In the vast majority of practical situations, consent is given for collection of evidence. The consent may be oral or written, with the latter being more desirable, because it simplifies subsequent problems of proof. The consent is commonly given by employees simply admitting the inspectors to the company premises or giving answers to oral or written questions by government employees.

One method of avoiding the necessity of obtaining a search warrant is to require the owner or operator of the pollution source to get a permit or license to operate. Then, a condition is included in the permit, allowing inspections without warrants. The U.S. Supreme Court has not yet ruled on the constitutionality of this method. Since permit systems are now being used more and more by federal, state and local agencies to control pollution, this method of obtaining desired evidence will be the trend of the future and provides the government with the consent needed.

7.2.2 Prohibition Against Self-Incrimination: The Fifth Amendment

The Fifth Amendment to the Constitution prohibits compulsory self-incrimination. It is limited in that it only applies to criminal cases. If the government agency collecting the evidence will use it only for civil actions, such as injunctions, the Fifth Amendment is not applicable. In addition, the Fifth Amendment applies only to persons and not to corporations or partnerships.

Most environmental statutes provide penalties for both individuals and corporations. Therefore, in a case where the evidence or samples taken might be used in a criminal action, the person in authority at the place where the evidence is to be taken should be advised of his rights to remain silent, to an attorney, and that any evidence taken may be used against him in a subsequent criminal action. If these rights are not formally observed, the evidence so collected may not be admissible in a criminal action.

7.2.3 Due Process, the Fifth and Fourteenth Amendments

The requirement that government entities not deprive anyone of due process of law is found in the Fifth and Fourteenth Amendments.

Due process is a very basic principle of our system of laws:

> The Fifth Amendment to the U.S. Constitution says: "No person shall . . . nor be deprived of life, liberty, or property, without due process of law; nor shall private property be taken for public use, without just compensation."

The Fourteenth Amendment to the U.S. Constitution states: "Section 1 . . . No State shall make or enforce any law which shall abridge the privileges or immunities of citizens of the United States; nor shall any State deprive any person of life, liberty, or property without due process of law; nor deny to any person within its jurisdiction the equal protection of the law."

The Fifth Amendment prohibition applies to the federal government and the Fourteenth applies to the states. These protections guarantee to a person the right not to be deprived of his life, liberty or property without due process of law. Simply stated due process means the law of the land, that is, according to settled usage and mode of proceeding. As long as the law preserves the fundamental rights of a person according to the law of the land, the novelty of the law does not invalidate it.

An example of the application of the legal concept of due process is found in the case, Construction Industry Ass'n. v. Petaluma. 35/ In this case the Court held that a city ordinance that limits issuance of new building permits to achieve a goal of preserving "small town" character, open spaces and low density population does not violate the due process clause of the Fourteenth Amendment. The Court's opinion explained that zoning regulations must find their justification in some aspect of the police power asserted for the public welfare to satisfy the due process mandate. The Court found that the concept of the public welfare is sufficiently broad to uphold Petaluma's desire to preserve its small town character, open spaces and low density population.

The due process argument was used against the beverage container ordinance of the City of Bowie, Maryland. 36/ The Court ruled that there was not a violation of due process because there was not a showing that the police power was exercised arbitrarily, oppressively or unreasonably. The opinion also reasoned that a law

---

35/ 522 F.2d 897, 8 Env't. Rep. Cas. (BNA) 1001 (9th Cir. 1975), cert. denied, 424 U.S. 934 (1976).

36/ Bowie Inn v. City of Bowie, 274 Md. 230, 335 A.2d 679, 7 Env't. Rep. Cas. (BNA) 2083 (1975).

should not be held void, if there are any considerations relating to the public welfare by which it can be supported.

7.2.4 Police Power and Due Process

Police power is the inherent right of a government to pass laws for the protection of the health, welfare, morals, and property of the people within its jurisdiction. In a sense, police power is but another name for the power of the government. Police power may not be bartered away by contract. It extends to all public needs. It may be put forth in the aid of what is sanctioned by usage or held by prevailing opinion to be greatly or immediately necessary for public welfare. By the exercise of reasonable police power, a government may regulate the conduct of individuals and of the use of their property and, in some instances, take property without compensation.

Although the police power of a state is very broad, it is not without limitation. It is always within the power of the court to declare a law void which, although enacted as a police regulation, is not justified as such. In other words, a law enacted as a police regulation must be reasonable. If the law is unreasonable or exercised in an arbitrary manner, it is taking life, liberty, or property without due process of law.

Two examples of the allowable exercise of police powers are given in Section 7.2.3.

Another example of the valid exercise of police power which did not violate the due process principle was in the Supreme Court case, <u>Village of Belle Terre v. Borass</u>. 37/ In this case a New York village ordinance restricted land use to one-family houses and precluded occupancy by more than two unrelated persons. The Court held this ordinance to be a valid exercise of the city's police power, stating:

> A quiet place where yards are wide, people few, and motor vehicles restricted are legitimate guidelines in a land use project addressed to family needs. The police power is not confined to elimination of filth, stench, and unhealthy places. It is ample to lay out zones where family values, youth values, and the blessings of quiet seclusion and clean air make the area a sanctuary for people.

37/   416 U.S. 1 (1974).

7.2.5 Prohibition Against Taking Property Without Compensation

The Fifth Amendment to the Constitution states that ". . . nor shall private property be taken for public use, without just compensation."

Despite numerous court opinions on this issue, the line between "takings" which require compensation and valid exercise of the "police power" which do not require compensation has never been clearly drawn. It is difficult to predict the outcome when the principles in this area are applied to factual situations.

It may be said that the state takes property by eminent domain because it is useful to the public. This taking requires compensation. When the state takes property because it is harmful, it is done under the police power and does not require compensation. What is useful to one person may be harmful to another. So, the perspective of all the conditions and circumstances is often the determining factor in choosing between useful and harmful.

The problem often comes down to one of degree. In both circumstances damages result. If the damage is suffered by many similarly situated and is in the nature of a restriction on use and ought to be borne by the individual as a member of society for the good of the public, it is a reasonable exercise of the police power not requiring compensation. However, if the damage is so great to the individual that he ought not to bear it under contemporary standards, then courts are inclined to treat it as a "taking" or unreasonable exercise of police power requiring compensation.

This "taking" issue has been in the forefront of noteworthy litigation. One important case involved the denial of operational drilling permits in the Santa Barbara Channel and was entitled Union Oil v. Morton. 38/ In this case the court reviewed the question of the degree to which the government may interfere with the enjoyment of private property by exercise of its police power without having to pay compensation and concluded that there was not a simple answer to this question. The courts under a variety of tests have recognized that regulation of private property can become so onerous that it amounts to a taking of that property. The court in this case held that a permanent unconditional suspension of permits

---

38/   512 F.2d 743, 7 Env't. Rep. Cas. (BNA) 1587 (9th Cir. 1975).

to install drilling platforms is a taking that requires compensation or violates the Fifth Amendment.

A series of cases have held that airport noise can constitute a taking of property rights. In the landmark case of United States v. Causby, 39/ the Supreme Court held that frequent low flights over the Causby's land by military aircraft landing at a nearby airport operated by the United States constituted a taking of the Causby's property without compensation in violation of the Fifth Amendment of the Constitution. The noise from the aircraft rendered it impossible to continue the use of the property as a commercial chicken farm. Although the flights did not completely destroy the enjoyment and use of the land, they were held to be so low and frequent as to constitute a direct and immediate interference with the full enjoyment of the land, limiting the utility of the land and causing a diminution in its value, and therefore constituted a taking under the Fifth Amendment.

In another major Supreme Court decision on this issue, Griggs v. Allegheny County, 40/ the Court held that Allegheny County, which owned and operated the Greater Pittsburgh Airport, was liable for a taking of property under the Fifth Amendment where the noise from taking off and landing at the airport on flight paths over the Griggs' property rendered the property undesirable and unbearable for residential use. The Court saw no difference between the county's responsibility to pay for the land on which the runways were built and its responsibility for the air easements necessary for operation of the airport. The glide path for the northwest runway is as necessary for the operation of the airport as is a surface right-of-way, wrote the Court.Several states have interpreted their own constitutions to require compensation under less strict circumstances when the noise from aircraft has diminished the market value of the homeowner's property. The interference must be substantial and sufficiently direct in the majority of jurisdictions.

7.2.6 Commerce Clause Limitations

The Constitution grants to Congress the authority ". . . to regulate Commerce with foreign Nations and among the several

---

39/   328 U.S. 256 (1946).

40/   369 U.S. 84 (1962).

States and with the Indian Tribes." So, if state statutes or regulations are found by the courts to be an impermissible burden upon interstate commerce, then they are unconstitutional and unenforceable.

It is well settled that a state regulation validly based on the police power does not impermissibly burden interstate commerce where the regulations neither discriminate against interstate commerce nor operate to disrupt its required uniformity. Where there is a reasonable basis to protect the social, as distinguished from the economic, welfare of a community, the courts will not deny this exercise of sovereign power and hold it to violate the Commerce Clause.

An example of a Commerce Clause case involved a challenge against New Jersey's Waste Control Act. 41/ This law barred disposal within the state of solid waste originating or collected outside the state's territorial borders. The U.S. Supreme Court opinion held that this statute does violate the Commerce Clause of the Constitution.

The Supreme Court held that all objects of interstate trade merit Commerce Clause protection and none is excluded from the definition of "commerce" including "valueless" out-of-state wastes. The Court ruled that the New Jersey statute was basically an economic protectionist measure, and thus virtually per se invalid, and not a law directed at legitimate local concerns that had only incidental effects on interstate commerce.

Another Commerce Clause case involved the Chicago ordinance banning the sale of detergents containing phosphates. 42/ The Seventh Circuit Court of Appeals held that the ordinance did not violate the Commerce Clause because, although it had some minor effect on interstate commerce, the benefits far outweighed these effects and the ordinance was a reasonable method to achieve a legitimate goal of improving Lake Michigan.

A similar result favorable to the legislators was reached in Oregon when the constitutionality of the Oregon "bottle-bill" which

---

41/ City of Philadelphia v. New Jersey, 437 U.S. 617 (1978).

42/ Procter and Gamble Co. v. Chicago, 509 F.2d 69, 7 Env't. Rep. Cas. (BNA) 1328 (7th Cir. 1975), cert. denied, 421 U.S. 978 (1975).

in essence banned the sale of non-returnable beverage containers was upheld. 43/

The trend is definitely one of the courts trying to uphold environmental legislation with the rationale being based on a balancing of the equities, namely weighing the benefits against the detrimental effect.

7.2.7 Equal Protection of the Laws

Section One of the Fourteenth Amendment to the Constitution prohibits the states from denying to any person the equal protection of the laws.

Does a state noise law which exempts construction equipment where there is no exemption for mining equipment deny equal protection? The Illinois Supreme Court held no in a suit entitled Illinois Coal Operators Association v. Illinois Pollution Control Board. 44/

The courts generally hold that for a classification to violate the constitutional guarantee of equal protection, there must be a showing that there is no reasonable basis for the distinction. A law is presumptively valid. Unless clear and convincing proof demonstrates that a law is arbitrary and unreasonable, the law must be upheld. The result is that few laws are ever held to violate the equal protection clause.

8.0 DEFENSES

8.1 Generally

Some of the defenses available against civil lawsuits have already been considered under the discussions of nuisance and negligence. Others not previously covered are considered in this section.

Generally, it is not a defense to an action for pollution that the defendant was not negligent; nor that he used due care; nor that his method of operation was customary.

43/ American Can Co. v. Oregon Liquor Control Comm'n, 15 Or.App. 618, 517 P.2d 691, 4 Env't. Rep. Cas. (BNA) 1584 (1973).

44/ 59 Ill.2d 305, 319 N.E.2d 782, 7 Env't. Rep. Cas. (BNA) 1315 (1974).

Some courts have taken into consideration the relative importance of the interests of the parties and have refused to abate
pollution or to grant an injunction against a plant but have relegated
the plaintiff to an action for damages. 45/ This approach is based on
the concept that closing a plant could cause more harm than good.
This is called "balancing the equities."

The question of how far individual rights must yield to the
public good is a complex issue depending on all the facts of the case
at issue. Some courts have held that an injunction will be granted to
restrain pollution without regard to the magnitude of the interest
enjoined. However, the current situation is a balancing of the
equities involved or comparing the injuries between the parties
involved in the lawsuit.

Defenses in the pollution field are few. As in other social
areas, the trend is to shift the basis of liability away from the
traditional concept of the nature of the wrong committed toward a
concern for the nature of the harm done. Under the common law,
whether one had a cause of action was a question of whether there
was a 'duty owed' by the wrong-doer to the injured party. Today, the
test of liability is the reasonable expectation of the person injured
by the act of another to be free from such injury.

Carried to their logical conclusion this trend makes futile any
hope of a defense. The situation is tantamount to strict liability.
This is helpful to aggrieved parties but makes it difficult for the
potentially resonsible parties involved.

8.2 Laches

The term "laches" generally describes the defense that is
based on the failure of the plaintiff to do something which should
have been done or to claim or enforce a right at a proper time.
Generally, there are three criteria for the equitable doctrine of
laches: (a) the defendant must show a delay in asserting a right or
claim, (b) the delay was not excusable and (c) there was undue preju-
dice to the party against whom the claim is asserted.

The defense of laches was successfully used in the Michigan
Supreme Court case Thompson v. Enz. 46/ In that case defendants

---

45/ 61A Am. Jur. 2d Pollution Control § 534 (1981).

46/ 385 Mich. 103, 188 N.W. 2nd 579, 2 Env't. Rep. Cas. (BNA)
     1842, (1971).

had obtained formal approval for a lake-front development project from all locally concerned governmental agencies, and at least tacit approval from the state. The defendants made a substantial investment in initiating the project. After all of these efforts and investments by the defendants, the plaintiff initiated a lawsuit to stop the development. The court ruled that the plaintiff would not be allowed to stop the completion of the project because of the defense of laches. The plaintiffs had allowed the defendants to proceed, and in the court's opinion, they should have filed their lawsuit in the very beginning of the project. The court indicated that it might have enjoined the project had it been promptly brought to its attention.

Laches is determined in the light of all existing circumstances and requires, generally, that the delay be unreasonable. The mere lapse of time is not sufficient.

The equitable defense of laches should see increased service to put a reasonable time limit on efforts in environmental cases.

8.3 Contractual Authorization

The right to pollute the air or a stream may be acquired by grant or license as against the grantor or licensor. A case that is an example of this defense involved oil pollution in Texas. It was ruled in this case that a release given to an oil company by a rancher for all claims arising from the operation of the oil wells on his property barred recovery of damages by the rancher for harm caused by crude oil leaking onto his property. 47/

Some contract clauses go too far in waiving rights, and are then generally ruled void, as being against public policy. This rule of voidness would probably be applicable to many pollution cases because it could be shown as against public policy to contract away environmental rights.

8.4 Public Authorization

In some jurisdictions, legislative authorization of the cause of the pollution might be a defense against liability. There is authority that a cause of action for abatement of a public nuisance does not

---

47/ Jackson v. Marathon Oil Co., 441 F.2d 511, 2 Env't. Rep. Cas. (BNA) 1533, (5th Cir. 1971).

arise, if the plant or establishment causing the pollution has legislative or administrative approval. 48/

A legislative license to create a nuisance by pollution must be given in express terms or by necessary implications. A private nuisance may arise, even though the facility has legislative sanction.

However, authority to build sewers is not authority to pollute a stream. Also, the legislature has no power to authorize the taking of property by pollution without just compensation.

8.5 Vagueness

One defense attempted against new statutory and regulatory prescriptions has been to attack them on the grounds of vagueness. However, the courts have not been responsive to this argument in pollution cases.

In Houston Compressed Steel Corp. v. Texas, 49/ the Texas Clean Air Act's broad definition of "air pollution" was upheld by the Texas Court of Civil Appeals as not to be too vague to be employed against a scrap metal company that burned railroad boxcars outdoors. The opinion stated that "since the science of air pollution control is new and inexact, and these standards are difficult to devise, if they are to be effective, they must be broad." The Texas court also felt that an air polluter should not escape the consequences of his act merely because he is able to make his contaminants difficult to measure or control.

In Air Commission v. Coated Materials, 50/ the Pennsylvania Air Pollution Control Act's definition of air pollution, as some substance "which unreasonably interferes with the comfortable enjoyment of life and property" was found to be uncertain, and was susceptible to acceptable standards of proof "since the language employed in the statute is equivalent to the definition of nuisance which is certainly established in the law."

Similarly, the Connecticut General Statutes were found not unconstitutionally vague when they required every motor vehicle to be so equipped and adjusted as to prevent excessive fumes or

---

48/   61 A Am. Jur. 2d, Pollution Control, § 571 (1981).

49/   456 S.W. 2d 768 (Tex. Civ. App. 1970).

50/   1 Env't. Rep. Cas. (BNA) 1444 (Pa. Common 1970).

exhaust smoke, since any ordinary and interested person would have no difficulty in determining whether or not a motor vehicle put out offensive or excessive exhaust fumes. 51/

Based on a review of the current case law, the argument of vagueness as a potential defense does not appear to offer a probability for success.

8.6 Unreasonableness and Impossibility of Performance

The courts do consider the reasonableness of duties imposed by statutes, regulations, standards and even court orders. An example is found in Pennsylvania v. Pennsylvania Power, 52/ where the court ruled that the regulations requiring compliance with Pennsylvania's sulfur dioxide emission standards were unreasonable because the technology adequate to meet the standards did not exist and the company acted in good faith.

The court stated:

> To impose sanctions on PPC in an attempt to force it to perform an impossible act would be both meaningless and unjust.
> It has been held that where the defendant cannot perform the duty ordered, and where that inability is not due to actions of the defendant himself that impossibility is a defense. F.T.C. v. Plaine, 308 F. Supp. 932 (N.D. Ga. 1970).

The courts have held in other cases that rules and regulations must be reasonable before the courts will enforce them.

However, the availability of the defense of economic and technological infeasibility in cases arising under the Clean Air Act resulted in contrary or partially contrary decisions in the federal circuit courts. So, the question was resolved by the Supreme Court. The question in issue was: Is technological or economic

---

51/ Connecticut v. Schuster's Express, 6 Conn. Cir. 108, 266 A.2d 902 (1970).

52/ 12 Pa. Common 212, 316 A.2d 96, 6 Env't. Rep. Cas. (BNA) 1328 (1974).

feasibility a defense against compliance with a State Implementation Plan (SIP) for air pollution control?

The U.S. Supreme Court, in a landmark decision decided on 25 June 1976, said no on this key issue but provided some additional guidance in this area of the law. In the case of Union Electric Co. v. EPA 53/ Mr. Justice Marshall writing for a unanimous Court said:

> After reviewing the relevant provision of the Clean Air Act Amendments of 1970 and their legislative history, we agree that Congress intended claims of economic and technological infeasibility to be wholly foreign to the Administrator's consideration of a state implementation plan.
>
> These requirements are of a technology-forcing character and are expressly designed to force regulated sources to develop pollution control devices that might at the time appear to be economically or technologically infeasible.
>
> This approach is apparent on the face of §110(a)(2). The provision sets out eight criteria that an implementation plan must satisfy, and provides that if these criteria are met and if the plan was adopted after reasonable notice and hearing, the Administrator 'shall approve' the proposed state plan. The mandatory 'shall' makes it quite clear that the Administrator is not to be concerned with factors other than those specified, and none of the eight factors appears to permit consideration of technological or economic infeasibility.

However, the opinion continues by setting forth that claims of infeasibility can be relevant. This infeasibility issue should be raised before the particular state agency while formulating the SIP. If the industry is not exempted in the original plan, then a variance may be submitted as a revision to the SIP. An industry denied exemption may take its claims of infeasibility to the state courts. Also, a state governor may request an extension or postponement based on infeasibility grounds. Finally, claims of technological or economic feasibility are relevant to fashioning an appropriate compliance order between EPA and the operator in controversies arising under the Clean Air Act.

53/   427 U.S. 246, 8 Env't. Rep. Cas. (BNA) 2143 (1976).

9.0 PARTIES

Parties to a lawsuit are classified as nominal, necessary and indispensable. Nominal parties are those who have some interest in the subject matter of the suit but are not affected by the judgment. Necessary parties are those who may be indirectly affected by the judgment and should be made parties (if they can be served with a subpoena to appear in court) but whose interests are separate from the others. Indispensable parties are those without whom the court cannot enter a valid judgment. Indispensable parties must be joined in the suit and must be served with process.

9.1 Standing, or Who May Sue

One of the most basic questions regarding parties that is normally asked is who may sue or in "lawyerese," the question of which parties have "standing" to file a lawsuit. This question was in the forefront of early environmental litigation.

Standing, strictly speaking, differs from who may sue. Theoretically speaking, anyone who has the fee to pay for filing a lawsuit may initiate a lawsuit. Where a party has a sufficient interest in a controversy to obtain judicial resolution of the controversy is what is traditionally referred to as the question of "standing to sue."

The general rule of law under the Administrative Procedure Act is that standing exists only when a plaintiff can satisfactorily demonstrate that (a) the agency action complained of will result in an injury in fact and that (b) the injury is to an interest "arguably within the zone of interests to be protected" by the statute in question.

The leading cases addressing the "injury in fact" question are cases involving the National Environmental Policy Act and environmental impact statements. The key case is the Supreme Court decision in <u>Sierra Club v. Morton</u>. 54/ This case involved the recreational development of the Mineral King Valley. The question in <u>Sierra v. Morton</u> was, what must be alleged by persons who claim injury of a non-economic nature to widely shared interests to give them standing. The court recognized that environmental well-being,

---

54/   405 U.S. 727 3 Env't. Rep. Cas. (BNA) 2039 (1972).

like economic well-being, is an important ingredient of our society. The fact that environmental interests are shared by the many rather than few does not make them less deserving of legal protection. But the "injury in fact" test, according to the Court, requires that the party seeking review be himself among the injured. The Sierra Club did not allege and show that it or its members would be affected in any of their activities or pastimes by the development. So, the Court ruled against them. However, this has since proven to be an easy matter to remedy, by the plaintiffs alleging that an aesthetic or other non-economic interest was injured. So, the Sierra Club established in this decision that environmental interests could be the basis for standing. This was a major development in the law.

In a subsequent Supreme Court case, SCRAP v. U.S., 55/ the Supreme Court gave some law students standing to sue the I.C.C. in a rate increase case involving recyclables. The Supreme Court ruled that standing to sue was demonstrated by the students, showing that they used the forest and streams in the Washington, D.C. area for camping and hiking and that this was disturbed by the adverse environmental impact, caused by the nonuse of recyclable goods, brought on by the I.C.C. rate increase on recyclable commodities.

The rule appears now that injury to a non-economic interest such as scenery, natural and historic objects and wildlife is a sufficient injury in fact to be a basis for a suit by a person or group who will suffer the injury directly. This covers a broad range of potential plaintiffs and cases. As a result the issue regarding standing has now shifted from the "injury in fact" question to the "zone of interests to be protected" by the statute involved in the litigation.

Citizens are given standing or access to the federal courts explicitly in the Federal Water Pollution Control Act, the Clean Air Act, the Noise Act, and many other statutes. This question of standing is only relevant when statutory authority is not available.

In summary, almost anyone who alleges an environmental concern can sue the government and most other parties.

9.2 Class Actions
Since many environmental lawsuits are brought as class actions, the basis for these is set forth in this section.

55/   412 U.S. 669 (1973).

One or more members of a class may sue or be sued as representative parties on behalf of all, only if, as a general rule:

(1) The class is so numerous that a uniting in the pleadings of all members is impractical.

(2) There are questions of law, or fact, common to the class.

(3) The claims or defenses of the representative parties are typical of the claims or defenses of the class.

(4) The representative parties will fairly and adequately protect the interests of the class.

In a true class suit, plaintiffs stand in judgment for the class. A judgment for or against the plaintiffs benefits or binds each member of the class personally under the principles of res judicata. The members of the class must, therefore, be capable of definite identification, as being either in or out of the class.

10.0. EVIDENCE

Evidence is the legal means, exclusive of arguments, for proving or disproving any <u>fact</u>, the truth of which is submitted to investigation. Since evidence is so critical to many issues in the environmental field, some key points of interest will be presented in the following sections. Evidence is an extremely complex area of the law. So, this is intended only as a brief review to give non-lawyers some basic concepts.

Please note that the law of evidence is known for its exceptions to general rules.

10.1 Burden of Proof

In the law of evidence, the phrase burden of proof is used to denote the duty of affirmatively proving the facts in dispute on an issue raised between the parties.

This burden of proof rests throughout the trial, upon the party asserting the affirmative of the issue.

The burden of proof is generally distinguished from the burden of proceeding. The duty of proceeding with a case is called the burden of proceeding, and shifts between the plaintiff and defendant during the trial.

10.2 Judicial Notice

As a general rule, a party must prove everything he alleges. The exceptions to this general rule are (1) things admitted in the pleadings, (2) things stipulated by the parties, or (3) judicial notice.

Judicial notice means that the court will take cognizance of certain facts without requiring proof. An example of judicial notice is that 12 January 1986 is a Sunday. Many facts of common indisputable knowledge need not be proven by evidence because the courts take judicial notice of this information so as not to waste time.

10.3 Presumptions

A presumption is a conclusion, which is drawn from other facts already proved. Presumptions are either (1) conclusive—which are rules of law and may not be rebutted or (2) rebuttable—presumptions which can be overcome by evidence.

10.4 Admissions

An admission is a voluntary acknowledgement of the existence of or the truth of certain facts. An admission will be recognized in court, if made by an employee against an employer within the scope of employment. As a general rule, an admission made by a party to a suit is admissible no matter when or where made. One exception to this general rule is when the admission is made in an offer to compromise. As a general rule, offers to compromise a lawsuit are not admissable. An admission made during a telephone conversation may be admissible if there is collaborating testimony or evidence.

An admission of guilt in a criminal case is a confession.

10.5 Questions Of Law and Fact

Questions arising during the course of a trial are either: questions of law or questions of fact. Generally, questions of law are decided by the court. Questions of fact are decided by a jury. One exception to that division of duties is whether a witness is an expert, which is determined by the court.

10.6 Relevant and Material

Two of the most commonly used words in the area of evidence are relevant and material. The facts or testimony presented in court must be relevant and material to the issue in question, or these irrelevant and immaterial facts or testimony are subject to exclusion. Whether the facts or testimony are relevant and material is a question of law, and so these are decided by the judge.

10.7 Res Inter Alios Acta

The Latin phrase res inter alios acta is used to denote the general rule that prior acts of a defendant or subsequent acts of precaution are not admitted in evidence, because they tend to multiply the issues or may be unfairly prejudical. There are a number of exceptions which have severely eroded this general rule.

10.8 Hearsay

Hearsay is that evidence which depends solely for its truth or falsity upon statements of a person other than the witness. Hearsay, in itself, has no evidentiary value. The witness cannot be cross-examined regarding hearsay, because the statements are those of another. Generally, hearsay is inadmissible, but there are numerous exceptions. An interesting example of inadmissible hearsay is found in the case Bebbington v. California Western States Life Ins. Co. 56/ In this case the suit was brought by the beneficiary of a life insurance policy against the insurance company (defendant). The policy provided that it was void, if the insured died in a plane crash. The insurance company in trying to prove that the decedent died in a plane crash, introduced a letter from a friend of the deceased, a telegram of condolence, and a newspaper clipping each telling of the plane accident. The court ruled that these were all written hearsay, and so inadmissible. (The insurance company should have proved the accident by an eyewitness or official records).

Usually in the case of documents, a statute provides for an official custodian or witness who will certify to their authenticity or validity to overcome the hearsay objection.

10.9 Opinion Evidence

Generally, the testimony of a witness is confined to a statement of concrete facts based upon his own observation or knowledge. Expert opinion evidence is admissible when it concerns

---

56/   30 Cal. 2d 157, 180 P.2d 673 (1947).

scientific or technical knowledge. Non-expert witnesses may be asked to express an opinion to help understand what was observed, but conjecture is not admissible. The problem with experts is that you can generally find one on either side of a case. For example the prosecutor will have his psychiatrist testify that the defendant is sane while the defendant's psychiatrist is testifying he is insane. This type of opinion evidence is common in environmental litigation.

10.10 Best Evidence Rule

The "best evidence rule" simply states that unless a sufficient reason is given, proof of the contents of a writing must be made by producing the original evidence, or at least a certified copy of the original. The best evidence possible must be submitted to the court, or the evidence is inadmissible.

10.11 Parol Evidence Rule

The general rule is that parol (oral) evidence is not admissible to vary, add to, take away from or contradict the terms of a written instrument. There are exceptions, such as explaining an ambiguity, showing a condition precedent, showing fraud and others.

10.12 Witnesses

Generally, all persons are competent to testify, but their credibility can be attacked. Leading questions (ones which suggest an answer), may generally only be asked of unwilling witnesses or adverse parties. A witness must answer all questions asked, which will provide information on the issue under investigation--unless this testimony may subject the witness to criminal prosecution. The opposing party has a right to cross-examine the witness. If the witness refuses to answer a question on cross-examination, his entire testimony may be expunged from the record. Generally, cross-examinations are limited to facts, on which a witness testified during direct examination.

10.13 Privileged Communications

Privilege is an exception to the rule that the public has the right to know every man's evidence. The reason for the exception is public policy.

At common law there was privilege only between an attorney and client, but by statutes and judicial decisions this has been extended to others such as physician and patient, clergy and laymen.

In environmental lawsuits, the concern is with the attorney-client relationship. It is the duty of a lawyer to preserve his client's confidences. This duty outlasts the lawyer's employment.

The concept of privileged communications can be used not only in lawsuits but also when providing legal advice such as during environmental audits.

Timothy A. Vanderver, Jr., a Washington, D.C. attorney who has conducted many environmental audits writes:

> By definition, the purpose of an environmental audit is to discover what may have been previously unknown violations of the law. Thus, it is highly desirable that the audit report be protected from disclosure or discovery to the maximum extent possible. For this reason, the audit should be designed and carried out so that a claim of attorney-client privilege can be successfully asserted with respect to the audit report and all pertinent information gathered in the course of the audit. Establishing an attorney-client privilege requires close involvement of legal counsel in both the design and performance phases of the audit. This is necessary in order to assure that the elements of the privilege are satisfied:
>
> o   All communications are made between the client and its attorney for the purpose of rendering legal advice on the company's compliance status.
>
> o   Communications are made for the clearly-stated purpose of seeking legal advice.
>
> o   Attorney-client communications are kept confidential during and after the audit process.
>
> o   The privilege is not inadvertently waived through disclosure.
>
> Thus, it is important that a lawyer supervise the information-gathering process during the audit, and establish procedures for controlling access to all documents generated during the audit. Of particular importance is the audit report. This should be treated as a confidential document and circulation should be limited to top-level management. 57/

57/ Environmental Audits (4th Edition, 1985), Government Institutes: Rockville, Md., p.29 et seq.

10.14 Your Own Reports as Evidence Against You

Many of the environmental laws and regulations require reports or data to be filed with the government. The laws governing occupational health, waste and air pollution all require reports. Even the reports to the Securities and Exchange Commission require disclosure of information on pollution. Most of these reports are available to the public and to competitors.

The extent to which the results of an investigation or inspection are available in private liability litigation remains uncertain. A corporation is not protected by the self-incrimination provisions of the Fifth Amendment to the U.S. Constitution. So, it may not object to the production of its books to be used as evidence against it. 58/

10.15 Samples or Physical Evidence

One of the common evidentiary problems raised in court cases is that involving physical evidence. In environmental cases the evidence is often a sample or some data. Some of the key issues normally involved with physical evidence are: (1) has the evidence or data been altered or contaminated, (2) was the equipment used in evidence collection properly calibrated, (3) were scientifically acceptable and standard methods of analysis used in evaluation and (4) who has handled the evidence (chain of custody)?

In order to lay a proper foundation for the admission of evidence, an attorney should be able to present the principals in the "chain of custody" to testify as to their involvement and appropriate expertise in the proper handling of the evidence. The courts will frequently require the parties to stipulate as to the authenticity of the evidence to avoid this tedious form of proof. In legal terminology, "to stipulate" is to agree initially on conduct or evidence for the purpose of shortening the legal proceedings.

10.16 Evidence Collection and Constitutional Rights

A problem that may arise in the collection of evidence concerns the Fourth Amendment or Constitutional rights of corporate entities and private persons.

58/   Essgee Co. v. U.S., 262 U.S. 151 (1923).

The Fourth Amendment to the U.S. Constitution prohibits all unreasonable searches and requires a search warrant for most investigations. However, no search warrant is needed in three basic situations: (1) when there is an emergency, (2) when the owner or operator gives his consent, or (3) when the samples could be taken from outside of the property (open fields exception). Search warrants are described in detail in Section 8.2.1.

In most states, search warrants are used for searches for the implements or fruits of a crime and not for mere investigation of conditions which may lead to either civil or criminal penalties. A few states authorize a special kind of search warrant, sometimes called an inspection warrant, which may be used to investigate conditions.

The Fifth Amendment prohibition against criminal self-incrimination was described earlier in Section 8.2.2. In evidence collection involving criminal charges against private parties, this Fifth Amendment right must be properly observed or the courts will not allow evidence to be introduced in the case. The Fifth Amendment protections apply only to private persons and not to corporations or partnerships.

11.0 ADMINISTRATIVE LAW

11.1 Generally

Governments are customarily divided into executive, legislative and judicial branches. The executive branches function through a system of administrative agencies. These are the governmental officials with whom environmental managers are in the most contact on a regular basis. The operations of these administrative agencies are regulated by the field of administrative law. We will briefly identify some major points in administrative law which may be of interest to environmental managers.

11.2 Powers of Governmental Agencies

Rules, regulations and general orders promulgated by an administrative agency, pursuant to its delegated powers, have the force and effect of law. They are binding on all persons subject to them without notice, and the courts take judicial notice of them. However, the power to promulgate regulations is not a power to change the law. The environmental regulations must be in conformance with the authorizing environmental law.

In order for a regulation to be the basis of a crime, it is necessary that sufficient statutory authority exists for declaring any act or omission a criminal offense.   A breach of a departmental regulation is not a crime, unless made so by the legislature. Regulations prescribed by the President of the United States and heads of departments, under authority granted by Congress, may be regulations prescribed by law. However, it does not follow that an act or omission constitutes a criminal offense when the statute does not make it so. An administrative agency may not provide for penalties or criminal liability unless specifically provided by statute.

An administrative agency has limited jurisdiction, depending entirely on that given to it by the statute.

11.3 Procedures

The procedures to be followed before an administrative agency are usually prescribed by the statute creating the agency. If the statute fails to prescribe the procedure, then the fundamental principle is that the regulations must preserve the requirements of fair play.

In general, an administrative agency is not bound by the technical or formal rules of procedure which govern trials before a court.   While the constitutional guaranty of due process of law applies to an administrative agency as well as a court, due process is not necessarily judicial process. All the formalities of a judicial proceeding are not essential to constitute due process of law in an administrative proceeding. Neither the Fifth Amendment nor the Fourteenth Amendment of the federal Constitution guarantee any particular form of procedure. In administrative proceedings due process signifies a right to be heard before a final order becomes effective.

It is not within the power of any tribunal to make a binding adjudication of the rights of any party not brought before it. Consequently, a party is entitled to notice, when a constitutional right is in question, and sufficient time to enable him to prepare a defense.

As in a judicial proceeding, notice by publication may be prescribed by statute and will sustain the jurisdiction. Consequently, it is generally held that a corporation doing business in a state, even though it has not applied for permission to do business in the state, consents to abide by the state laws, including service of notice in a proceeding before an administrative body.

Generally, the federal government announces its environmental regulations and hearing in the <u>Federal Register</u> which is published daily.

11.4 Evidence in Administrative Law

As a general rule, an administrative agency is not bound by the strict rules of evidence, which must be observed in the trial of cases in courts of law. However, unless a statute provides rules of evidence for the agency, the latter, in the exercise of its quasi-judicial powers, must provide rules of evidence which preserve fair play, such as the right of cross-examination of witnesses and the right to subpoena witnesses and documents. But the mere fact that certain evidence which would be inadmissible in a court of law is admitted at a hearing before an administrative agency does not invalidate such administrative proceedings.

Under the Administrative Procedure Act, <u>59/</u> generally hearsay evidence is admissible, but no order can issue, unless it is supported by and in accordance with reliable, probative, and substantive evidence.

11.5 Hearings

Not every administrative determination for private individuals requires notice and hearing. In order to comply with due process, notice and hearing are required only when some constitutional right is claimed to have been violated.

When the purpose of an administrative determination is to decide whether a right or privilege, which a person does not have, shall be granted or withheld in the exercise of its discretion, it is not necessary to have a notice and hearing in the absence of a statutory provision.

The constitutional guarantee of a trial by jury does not apply to an administrative hearing. Determination of facts may be left to an administrative tribunal. It is common practice to have testimony taken before an examiner, who reports the facts to the tribunal. Exceptions may be taken to the report, and argument may be had before the deciding body. The recommendation in the report is not binding on the determining body, if it is charged with the duty of making final decisions.

59/   5 U.S.C. §§ 551 <u>et</u> <u>seq</u>. (1982).

11.6 Judicial Review

What decisions an administrative agency makes depends on the statute. It is common for a federal agency to have the power to issue a cease and desist order, and in many instances an agency has the power to take affirmative action. An administrative order cannot be enforced in a court without an express provision in the statute.

Generally, before a person is able to have a court review an administrative action, he must exhaust all his administrative remedies because courts are normally reluctant to interfere with administrative action before it is completed. Once the administrative remedies have been exhausted, then the matter is considered "ripe" for judicial review.

Theoretically, the courts will not review the facts in the case but limit themselves to questions of law, or whether there has been abuse of authority and disregard of due process.

Recent cases are worthy of examination because basic concepts are being challenged in this area of administrative law as the trend develops for the courts to interject themselves more and more into examining the operation of administrative agencies.

In one case the manufacture of a mercury fungicide (use of which was ordered suspended by the secretary of agriculture, based on a single abnormal incident without a hearing), was reviewed by a federal district court. The review was undertaken by the court based on the argument that the agency order was arbitrary and capricious since there was only one incident and a hearing was not held by the Department of Agriculture. 60/

On the state level in a case before the Pennsylvania Court of Common Pleas of Dauphin County, there was a challenge of the findings of the Pennsylvania Air Pollution Commission that a coil coating plant emitted odorous gases in violation of the state Air Pollution Control Act. The court said that it could not modify the finding on the ground of credibility of evidence. 61/ The court said it only considered whether the Air Pollution Commission was arbi-

---

60/ Nor-Am Agricultural Products, Inc. v. Hardin, 435 F.2d 1133 (7th Cir. 1970), rev'd., 435 F.2d 1151 (7th Cir. 1970).

61/ Air Commission v. Coated Materials, supra, footnote 50.

trary, and left credibility of the evidence to the commission. This limited review is the usual approach taken by a court when considering an appeal from an administrative agency.

In the case of the <u>Environmental Defense Fund v. Hardin,</u> 62/ the secretary of agriculture's failure to act promptly on a conservation group's request for interim suspension of the registration of a pesticide to protect the public from an "imminent hazard" was held by the U.S. Court of Appeals for the District of Columbia to be tantamount to an order denying suspension and was, therefore, ripe for judicial review. The court held that even a temporary refusal results in irreparable injury on a massive scale, and is thus a final disposition of such rights as plaintiffs and the public may have to interim relief. In a subsequent court action on the same controversy the court's opinion was critical of the handling of the case by the Department of Agriculture. The court stated that for years courts have "treated administrative policy decisions with great deference," but they no longer will "bow to the mysteries of administrative expertise." One judge disagreed and wrote a dissenting opinion charging that "the Court is undertaking to manage the Department of Agriculture." These majority and dissenting comments show two views on review by the courts of administrative decisions.

As the general rule, if you are involved in a dispute with an administrative agency, usually you must exhaust all available administrative remedies before you can initiate court action.

Generally, in the judicial review process, the courts first determine whether or not the agency acted within the scope of its authority. If this question is answered in the affirmative, then there must be a finding whether the choice made was arbitrary, capricious or not in accordance with law. The standard of review then becomes a determination whether the decision was based on a consideration of the relevant factors and whether there has been a clear error of judgment. The courts are not empowered to substitute their judgment for that of the agency.

12.0 ATTORNEYS' FEES

One of the basic traditions of who pays the lawyers has been significantly modified in recent years. This trend is worthy of

---

62/   138 U.S.App.D.C. 391, 428 F. 2d 1093 (1970).

description in this book because the award of these fees may be a significant factor in an environmental lawsuit.

Generally, under the so-called "American Rule" the winning party in a lawsuit is awarded costs but these costs do not include attorneys' fees. The result is that each party normally is responsible for their respective attorneys' fees.

Several statutes have created exceptions to this rule by authorizing the award of attorneys' fees. These statutes include the Clean Air Act and the Resource Conservation and Recovery Act (RCRA). Successful plaintiffs were awarded attorneys' fees in several environmental lawsuits during the past few years. The matter was becoming confused with various court interpretations of the law. However, the Supreme Court has spoken on the subject of award of attorneys' fees to clarify the situation. In Alyeska v. Wilderness Society, 63/ the Supreme Court ruled that in the absence of statutory authorization or an enforceable contract, litigants must pay their own attorneys' fees.

Congress while fully recognizing this general rule has made specific and explicit provisions for the allowance of attorneys' fees in some statutes. If a statutory provision is not involved, the courts generally will not order payment of attorney fees.

13.0 CRIMINAL AND CIVIL LIABILITY OF CORPORATE EMPLOYEES

The environmental laws and regulations provide for a wide range of civil and criminal penalties for failure to comply as described in subsequent chapters.

Now, there is a quiet evolution taking place. The courts are no longer holding only a corporation liable under the statutes for a fine but are holding individuals personally liable in their corporate roles.

The U.S. Supreme Court case of U.S. v. Park 64/ is a landmark case in this area. In this case the Court held that a corporate officer could be criminally liable under the Food, Drug and Cosmetic Act if he had the corporate authority and responsibility for preventing violations of the statute but failed to do so.

63/   421 U.S. 240, 7 Env't. Rep. Cas. (BNA) 1849 (1975).

64/   421 U.S. 658 (1975).

Park, the president of Acme Markets, was convicted of violating the Federal Food, Drug, and Cosmetic Act. It states that "any person who violates a provision of [the Act] . . . shall be imprisoned for not more than one year or fined not more than $1,000, or both." Park was charged with causing interstate food shipments, being held for sale in an Acme Baltimore warehouse, to become adulterated by exposure to rat poison. Park had received notice that there was a violation in Acme's Baltimore warehouse. He had delegated responsibility for remedying the situation to some employees. The trial court was of the opinion that because he knew of a previous violation in a Philadelphia warehouse that had been ineffectively remedied and he had delegated responsibility to the same people, his delegation in the Baltimore case (which also turned out to be ineffective) was not a sufficient attempt to remedy the problem. He was convicted on five counts.

The trial court judge said that Park could be found guilty "even if he did not consciously do wrong" and even if he had not "personally participated in the situation," if it were proved beyond a reasonable doubt that he "had a responsible relationship" to the situation.

Generally, criminal violation requires some element of conscious wrong-doing or some criminal intent. In this case the Supreme Court upheld Park's conviction based on his being the responsible corporate official. This means that corporate officers can be held legally liable for their subordinates' actions or inactions in a broad range of cases.

The Supreme Court noted that a finding of guilt cannot be based solely on the officer's position in the company. There should be some measure of "blameworthiness." The test which the Supreme Court used was that a corporate officer could be held criminally responsible if such officer had, "by reason of his position in the corporation, responsibility and authority either to prevent in the first instance, or promptly to correct, the violation complained of, and that he failed to do so." 65/

Criminal liability under other environmental laws is generally not as broad as under the Food, Drug and Cosmetic Act because the other laws use a term such as "knowing" before the proposed violation to require some willfulness or intent.

65/   Id. at 672.

Governmental officials are also subject to criminal indictment. The "Watergate Cases," resulting from the Nixon re-election campaign, give a famous example of the highest government officials being convicted of crimes for their actions or inactions.

Civil penalties are a definite deterrent but criminal penalties can literally destroy individuals from both a social and economic viewpoint.

These trends toward increased severity in punishment for violation of the law should make everyone more conscious of their legal and social duties.

Chapter 2

RESOURCE CONSERVATION AND RECOVERY ACT

Ridgway M. Hall, Jr.
Nancy S. Bryson
Attorneys
Crowell & Moring
Washington, D.C.

David R. Case
General Counsel
Hazardous Waste Treatment Council
Washington, D.C.

1.0 OVERVIEW

The management of the hazardous waste which is being generated in large quantities by our modern, post-World War II economy has come to be recognized as a major environmental problem over the past ten years. On 21 October 1976, Congress enacted the Resource Conservation and Recovery Act (RCRA), the first comprehensive federal effort to deal with the problem of solid waste generally and hazardous waste specifically. 1/ RCRA is basically a regulatory statute, designed to provide cradle to grave management of hazardous waste by imposing management requirements on generators and transporters of hazardous materials and upon owners and operators of treatment, storage and disposal facilities. It does not address what has come to be recognized as the equally serious problem of abandoned and inactive sites. Legislation establishing remedies and allocating responsibilities for correcting problems at those sites is contained in the Comprehensive Environmental Response,

---

1/ 42 U.S.C 6901 et seq. (1981). Citations throughout this chapter are to sections of the act, rather than to the U.S. Code.

Compensation, and Liability Act of 1980, commonly known as Superfund, 2/ which is discussed in detail in Chapter 3.

RCRA has been amended several times since its enactment, most recently in 1984. 3/ It is currently divided into nine subtitles, A through I. The most significant of these is Subtitle C, which sets the regulatory requirements for the hazardous waste management program by governing the conduct of generators and transporters of hazardous waste and owners and operators of treatment, storage and disposal facilities.

Subtitle C, which encompasses Sections 3001-3019, establishes the following parameters for the RCRA hazardous waste management program. Section 3001 requires EPA to promulgate regulations which identify specific hazardous waste, either by listing them or identifying characteristics which render them hazardous. Persons managing such waste are required to identify themselves and their hazardous waste activities to EPA. 4/

Persons who generate or produce these wastes must comply with a set of standards authorized by RCRA Section 3002. These include preparing manifests to track the movement of the waste through ultimate disposal. Persons who transport hazardous waste are required by Section 3003 to comply with another set of regulations dealing with recordkeeping, labeling and the delivery of hazardous waste shipments to designated treatment, storage or disposal (T/S/D) facilities.

Section 3004 requires performance standards for such T/S/D facilities including statutory minimum technology requirements, groundwater monitoring, and a phased-in ban on the disposal of untreated hazardous wastes in land disposal facilities. Section 3005 requires owners and operators of T/S/D facilities to obtain permits which set forth the conditions under which they may operate. Section 3005(e) establishes the "interim status" provision for existing status T/S/D/ facilities which allows them to remain in operation

---

2/   42 U.S.C. Section 9601 et seq.

3/   PL 96-482, 94 Stat. 2334 (1980); 1984 Hazardous and Solid Waste Amendments signed by President Reagan on November 8, 1984, PL 98-616, 98 Stat. 3221.

4/   Section 3010(a).

until a site-specific permit is issued. Owners and operators of interim T/S/D/ status facilities must file a timely application for and eventually qualify for a RCRA permit under Section 3005(a). The 1984 RCRA amendments set a timetable for EPA to process and issue all such permits.

Sections 3007 and 3008 authorize site inspections and federal enforcement of RCRA and its implementing regulations. Section 3006 authorizes states to assume responsibility for the RCRA program in lieu of the federal program where the state adopts and agrees to enforce a program which is at least equivalent to the federal program.

Other provisions of Subtitle C include provisions for compiling a hazardous waste site inventory; limited monitoring and enforcement authority against previous owners of T/S/D facilities; EPA issuance of performance standards for the management of recycled oil, and an inventory of federal agency hazardous waste facilities. 5/

The 1984 amendments to RCRA, which are included in the discussion here, are extensive. They significantly expanded both the scope of coverage and the detailed requirements of RCRA. For example, they require EPA to more fully regulate an estimated 200,000 companies that produce only small quantities of hazardous waste (less than 1,000 kilograms per month). An entirely new regulatory program was created in Subtitle I ("eye") for underground storage tanks containing hazardous substances or petroleum, which will affect hundreds of thousands of facilities for the first time. 6/ The numerous constraints imposed on those who treat, store or dispose of wastes in landfills, including restrictions on the disposal of liquid wastes and other common hazardous wastes, are technically complex. For example, companies using existing unlined surface impoundments will be required to retrofit with double liners and leachate collection systems by 1988.

The amendments contain many so-called "hammer" provisions that require EPA to implement new requirements by a deadline or a congressionally formulated regulation will automatically go into

---

5/   Sections 3012, 3013, 3014, 3016.

6/   Sections 9001-9010.

effect. There are 72 major provisions in the new law, by EPA's count, and 52 required EPA action within the first two years after enactment of the 1984 amendments. This will have a substantial impact on every U.S. business that produces hazardous waste from industrial and commercial operations.

These major provisions of the Subtitle C program and the impact of the 1984 amendments are discussed in detail below, as are the requirements of other important subtitles of the act including the newly enacted Subtitle I.

2.0 POLICY GOALS AND OBJECTIVES OF RCRA, AS AMENDED

Subtitle A of RCRA declares that, as a matter of national policy, the generation of hazardous waste is to be reduced or eliminated as expeditiously as possible. In addition, all waste that is generated must be handled so as to minimize the present and future threat to human health and the environment. 7/

Subtitle A also includes a series of objectives designed to achieve these goals, including in the first instance proper management of hazardous waste, minimization of the generation and land disposal of hazardous waste, prohibition of open dumping, encouragement of state assumption of RCRA programs, encouragement of research and development activities in the waste management area and promotion of recovery and recycling as alternatives to disposal. 8/

3.0 DEFINITION OF SOLID AND HAZARDOUS WASTE

Section 1004(27) states that:

The term "solid waste" means any garbage, refuse, sludge, from a waste treatment plant, water supply treatment plant or air pollution control facility and other discarded material, including solid, liquid,

---

7/   RCRA, Section 1003(b).

8/   RCRA, Section 1003(a).

semisolid, or contained gaseous materials resulting from industrial, commercial, mining and agriculture activities and from community activities but does not include solid or dissolved material in domestic sewage, or solid or dissolved materials in irrigation return flows or industrial discharges which are point sources subject to permits under section 402 of the Federal Water Pollution Control Act, as amended (86 Stat. 880), or source, special nuclear, or byproduct material as defined by the Atomic Energy Act of 1954, as amended (68 Stat. 923). (Emphasis supplied.)

The statute therefore applies to potentially any waste regardless of its physical form.

The Subtitle C regulatory program of RCRA covers the management of those solid wastes categorized as hazardous. As defined in Section 1004(5), the term "hazardous waste" means a solid waste, or combination of solid wastes, which because of its quantity, concentration, or physical, chemical, or infectious characteristics may—

"(A) cause, or significantly contribute to an increase in mortality or an increase in serious irreversible, or incapacitating reversible illness; or

"(B) pose a substantial present or potential hazard to human health or the environment when improperly treated, stored, transported, or disposed of, or otherwise managed."

These general statutory definitions have been greatly amplified and explained by EPA regulations implementing RCRA, the first set of which was issued on 19 May 1980. 9/ These regulations are discussed in the following section which describes the Title C program in detail.

9/   45 FR 33066.

4.0 SUBTITLE C: The HAZARDOUS WASTE MANAGEMENT PROGRAM

4.1 Identification of Hazardous Wastes Under the Implementing Regulations 10/

New regulations adopted by EPA on 4 January 1985 define solid waste to include any discarded material that is not otherwise subject to a regulatory exclusion or a specific variance granted by EPA or an authorized state. 11/ "Discarded material" is in turn defined as any material that is abandoned, recycled or "inherently waste-like." 12/ A material is abandoned if it is disposed of, burned or incinerated, or accumulated, stored or treated prior to or in lieu of abandonment. A material can be a solid waste if it is recycled in a manner constituting disposal, by burning for energy recovery, by reclamation, or by speculative accumulation. Materials that are not solid wastes when recycled are materials that are directly used or reused as ingredients or feedstocks in product processes, or as effective substitutes for commercial products, or that are recycled in a closed-loop production process. A material is inherently waste-like if EPA so defines it by regulation. 13/

These interlocking definitions result in EPA regulating a universe of materials that may not commonly be understood to be "wastes" for a particular industry or company.

Once a material is found to be a solid waste, the next question is: is it a "hazardous waste"? EPA's regulations automatically exempt certain solid wastes from being considered hazardous wastes. Generally these regulatory exemptions include:

10/ For a more comprehensive description of the regulatory provisions of RCRA, the reader is referred to Hall, Watson, Davidson, Case and Bryson, RCRA/Hazardous Wastes Handbook (Government Institutes, 7th ed. 1987).

11/ 40 CFR 261.2(a), 50 FR 664 (4 January 1985). The list of regulatory exemptions appears at 261.4(a) and is very limited. See pp. 6-7 infra.

12/ 40 CFR 261(a)(2), 50 FR 614 (4 January 1985).

13/ 40 CFR 261.2, 50 FR 614 (4 January 1985).

(1) household waste;

(2) agricultural wastes which are returned to the ground as fertilizer;

(3) mining overburden returned to the mine site;

(4) utility wastes from coal combustion;

(5) oil and natural gas exploration drilling waste;

(6) wastes from the extraction, benefaction, and processing of ores and minerals, including coal;

(7) cement kiln dust wastes;

(8) arsenical-treated wood wastes generated by end users of such wood;

(9) certain chromium-bearing wastes. 14/

EPA has also provided some limited regulatory exemptions under particularly defined circumstances such as for hazardous waste that is generated in a product or raw material storage tank, transport vehicle, pipeline or manufacturing process unit. EPA has also exempted waste samples and other samples collected for monitoring and testing, which are subject to limited regulation.

If a solid waste does not qualify for one of the many exemptions, it will be deemed a hazardous waste if it is listed by EPA in 40 CFR Part 261, Subpart D, if it exhibits any of the four hazardous waste characteristics identified in 40 CFR Part 261, Subpart C, or if it is a mixture of a listed waste and a solid waste. 15/

4.1.1 Hazardous Waste Lists

EPA has established three hazardous wastes lists: (1) hazardous wastes from nonspecific sources (e.g., spent nonhalogenated solvents, toluene, methyl ethyl ketone. . .); 16/ (2) hazardous wastes from specific sources (e.g., bottom sediment sludge from the

---

14/ 40 CFR 261.4(b), 45 FR 33120, 45 FR 72037 (30 October 1980), 45 FR 76620 (19 November 1980), 45 FR 78531 (25 November 1980).

15/ 40 CFR 261.3(a).

16/ 40 CFR 261.31.

treatment of wastewaters from wood preserving); 17/ and (3) discarded commercial chemical products, and all off-specification species, containers, and spill residues thereof. 18/

The first two hazardous waste lists are largely self-explanatory. A company need only compare its solid waste stream to those lists to determine if it manages a hazardous waste.

The third list sets forth commercial chemicals which, when discarded, must be treated as hazardous wastes. This hazardous waste list actually consists of two distinct lists. One list sets forth chemicals deemed toxic and, therefore, hazardous if discarded (40 CFR 261.33(f)). These are regulated like the other listed hazardous wastes. A second list contains wastes which EPA identifies as acutely hazardous (40 CFR 261.33(e)) for which more rigorous management requirements apply.

Hazardous waste regulation under the commercial chemical list can be triggered when a company decides to reduce inventory and discards a listed commercial chemical product in its pure form. Another situation that will also trigger the commercial chemical list is an accidental spill. 19/ If a listed commercial chemical is spilled, the spilled chemical and any contaminated material, i.e., dirt and other residue, is likely to be discarded and thus becomes a hazardous waste. Therefore, even companies that generally do not discard or intend to discard any of the commercial chemical products on the list must be prepared to comply with the RCRA hazardous waste regulations in the event of an accidental spill. 20/ This will involve, as discussed below, obtaining an EPA identification number and complying, at a minimum, with applicable generator standards.

17/ 40 CFR 261.32.

18/ 40 CFR 261.33, 45 FR 33122-27, 45 FR 47833-36 (16 July 1980); 45 FR 72039 (30 October 1980); 45 FR 74890 (12 November 1980); 45 FR 78541-44 (25 November 1980); 46 FR 27476-77 (20 May 1981).

19/ 40 CFR 261.33(d), 45 FR 78541 (25 November 1980), 46 FR 27477 (20 May 1981).

20/ See 45 FR 76629 (19 November 1980).

Since the RCRA program became effective in 1980, many companies have filed "delisting petitions" with EPA to remove wastes generated at their facilities from the RCRA hazardous waste lists at 40 CFR Part 261. The granting of a delisting petition exempts the waste generated at a particular facility from the RCRA hazardous waste program requirements, provided the waste is not hazardous by characteristic. In the past, EPA could grant these companies "temporary exclusions" from the hazardous waste list based on a substantial likelihood that their delisting petitions would be granted, pending the public notice and comment required for a final decision on the petitions. The 1984 amendments now require EPA to act on a delisting petition within two years of receiving a complete petition, thus restricting the agency's discretion to grant lengthy temporary exclusions.

Prior to the 1984 RCRA amendments, a company seeking a delisting had to demonstrate that the particular waste generated at its facility did not contain the hazardous constituents for which EPA listed the waste. Congress has now directed EPA to restrict delisting petitions by requiring companies to demonstrate that their wastes do not contain any constituents that could cause the waste to be hazardous, not just the constituents EPA considered in listing the waste.

For example, a company seeking to delist a waste which would otherwise be included under F006 (wastewater treatment sludge from electroplating operations) must show not only that the concentrations of chromium, nickel, and cyanide for which the waste was listed are below levels of regulatory concern, but also that no other heavy metals or other constituents are present that may cause the waste to be hazardous. This is expected to substantially increase the cost and the EPA processing time for delisting petitions. As a practical matter, in anticipation of the new law EPA had already begun implementing this requirement.

4.1.2 Hazardous Waste Characteristics

Non-listed wastes are covered by RCRA if they possess one of four hazardous waste characteristics: ignitability, corrosivity, reactivity, or toxicity. 21/

21/ 40 CFR 261.3, 40 CFR 261.20.

The hazardous waste characteristic of ignitability was established to identify solid wastes capable during routine handling of causing a fire or exacerbating a fire once started. 22/ A solid waste is deemed to exhibit the characteristic of ignitability if it meets with one of the following four descriptions. First, if it is a liquid, other than an aqueous solution containing less than 24 percent alcohol by volume, with a flash point of less than 60 degrees centigrade (140°F). Second, if it is a nonliquid which under normal conditions can cause fire through friction, absorption of moisture or spontaneous chemical changes and burns so vigorously when ignited that it creates a hazard. Third, if it is an ignitable compressed gas as defined by the DOT regulations set forth at 49 CFR 173.300. Finally, a waste exhibits ignitability if it is an oxidizer as defined by the DOT regulations set forth at 49 CFR 173.151.

The hazardous waste characteristic of corrosivity was established because EPA believed that wastes capable of corroding metal could escape their containers and liberate other wastes. 23/ In addition, wastes with a pH at either the high or low end of the scale can harm human tissue and aquatic life and may react dangerously with other wastes. Therefore, EPA determined that any solid waste is deemed to exhibit the characteristic of corrosivity if it is (1) aqueous and has a pH of less than or equal to 2.0 or greater than or equal to 12.5, or (2) a liquid and corrodes steel at a rate greater than 6.35 millimeters (.250 inches) per year under specified testing procedures.

EPA established the hazardous waste characteristic of reactivity to regulate wastes that are extremely unstable and have a tendency to react violently or explode during stages of its management. 24/ The regulation lists several situations where this may happen which warrant specific consideration (e.g., the behavior of the substance when mixed with water, when heated, etc.). Instead of developing a precise scientific description of this characteristic, EPA has promulgated a descriptive, prose definition of reactivity

---

22/ 40 CFR 261.21.

23/ 41 CFR 261.22.

24/ 41 CFR 261.23.

since suitable test protocols for measuring reactivity are unavailable.

The toxicity characteristic is designed to identify wastes which are likely to leach hazardous concentrations of specific toxic constituents into groundwater under improper management conditions, one of the more significant dangers posed by mismanagement of hazardous waste. 25/ This characteristic is determined based on a mandatory testing procedure which extracts the toxic constituents for a solid waste in a manner which EPA believes will stimulate the leaching action which occurs in landfills. 26/ If the extract obtained by use of the toxicity testing protocol exhibits concentrations of a toxic constituent at levels of regulatory concern, then that waste will be deemed to exhibit the characteristic of toxicity.

4.1.3 Mixtures of Hazardous Wastes and Solid Wastes

A mixture including a listed hazardous waste and a solid waste is treated as a hazardous waste unless such a mixture qualifies for the following exemption: (1) the listed hazardous waste in the mixture was listed solely because it exhibits a hazardous characteristic and the mixture does not exhibit that characteristic; or (2) the mixture consists of certain specified hazardous wastes and wastewater the discharge of which is subject to regulation under the Clean Water Act. To qualify for the second exemption, the concentrations must not exceed certain specified concentrations. 27/ On the other hand, a mixture including a characteristic hazardous waste and a solid waste will be deemed hazardous only if the entire mixture continues to exhibit a hazardous characteristic. 28/

4.1.4 Used, Reused, Recycled or Reclaimed Hazardous Wastes

On 4 January 1985, EPA issued final regulations redefining the term "solid waste" to extend coverage to many recycling activities which were previously exempted. 29/ This redefinition is

---

25/ 40 CFR 261.24.

26/ 40 CFR Part 261, Appendix H.

27/ See 40 CFR 261.3(a)(2), 46 FR 56588-89 (17 November 1981).

28/ See 45 FR 33095 (19 May 1980).

29/ 50 FR 614.

complex. Conceptually, the analysis required to apply the definition requires knowledge of two things—the secondary material being recycled and the manner in which it is being recycled.

Secondary materials that are solid wastes when recycled include spent materials, listed and characteristic sludges, listed and characteristic by-products, commercial chemical products and scrap metals. These are all solid wastes when recycled with two exceptions. Characteristic sludges and by-products are not solid wastes when they are reclaimed. Commercial chemical products are not solid wastes when they are either reclaimed or speculatively accumulated.

The recycling activities that are regulated are (1) use in a manner constituting disposal (e.g. land application), (2) burning for energy recovery, (3) reclamation, and (4) speculative accumulation. 30/ Two types of activities are excluded. 31/ The first involves direct use or reuse of secondary materials as either ingredients or feedstocks in product processes or as effective substitutes for commercial products. The second is "closed-loop production processes" which return secondary materials to the original primary production process in which they were generated without first reclaiming them.

Generally speaking, hazardous wastes waiting to be recycled are subject to the Part 262 and 263 regulations for generators and transporters and to the storage facility requirements in Part 264 and 265 until the recycling activity is completed. 32/

Case-by-case variances from classification as solid waste are available in three cases from either the appropriate EPA regional administrator or an authorized state. Materials eligible for these variances are those which are (1) accumulated without sufficient amounts being recycled; (2) reclaimed and then reused within the original primary production process in which they were generated; or (3) reclaimed but must be reclaimed further before material recovery is completed.

30/ 40 CFR 261.2(c).

31/ 40 CFR 261.2(e).

32/ 40 CFR 261.6(b)(1).

EPA has adopted a broad definition to provide regulatory authority over many types of activities. The various permutations and combinations of these regulations bear close scrutiny.

4.1.5 1984 Amendments Relevant to Fuel Containing Hazardous Waste and Used Oil

In the 1984 RCRA amendments Congress directed EPA to impose technical standards that are protective of human health and the environment on companies that produce, transport, distribute, market or burn fuel containing hazardous wastes. 33/ EPA had previously exempted such wastes from RCRA regulation.

The new law required companies that produce, distribute, market or burn hazardous waste fuels to file a notification with EPA by 8 February 1986, which gives the location, type of facility, and the hazardous waste that is used as fuel. This provision applies to listed and characteristic hazardous wastes (including commercial chemical products used as fuel), mixtures of such hazardous wastes and other materials, and used oil. The new law makes it unlawful for any person who is required to file a notification to distribute or market any hazardous waste-derived fuel without the following legend on the invoice or bill of sale:

WARNING: THIS FUEL CONTAINS HAZARDOUS WASTE
(followed by a list of the hazardous wastes).

This legend must appear in conspicuous type which is clearly distinguishable from other printed matter on the invoice or bill of sale.

EPA has also promulgated the first set of standards for utility and industrial boilers and furnaces that burn hazardous waste fuels. 34/ Such fuels may no longer be burned in residential, commercial, and institutional boilers and furnaces. Generators and transporters of hazardous waste fuels are now subject to full RCRA regulation. Marketers of hazardous waste fuels may only sell to persons who will burn such fuels only in qualified boilers and furnaces. Both marketers and burners are subject to certain storage

---

33/ RCRA, Sections 3004(q), (r) and (s).

34/ 40 CFR Part 266, Subpart D; 50 FR 49164 (29 November 1985).

standards for containers and tanks in 40 CFR Parts 264 and 265. The actual burning of hazardous waste fuels continues to be exempt from RCRA regulation.

In the 1984 amendments, Congress also directed EPA to make a final determination by November 1986 on whether to identify used automobile and truck crankcase oil as hazardous waste. EPA missed that deadline as it continues to study the regulatory options available under both TSCA and RCRA for regulating used oil destined for disposal. If EPA finally decides that used oil that is disposed of should be a hazardous waste, companies that generate, transport, store, treat or dispose of such used oil will likely become subject to the RCRA hazardous waste regulations, as modified by any regulations EPA may promulgate especially for used oil. 35/

Congress also directed EPA to establish a special regulatory scheme for companies that generate and transport used oil which is recycled. These used oil recycling standards may not include a manifest requirement or any recordkeeping and reporting (except records of agreements for delivery of used oil) for generators that send used oil to qualified recycling facilities. EPA is to promulgate special standards for recycling facilities, which are then deemed to have a RCRA permit if they comply with such standards.

4.2 Notification of Hazardous Waste Management Activities

RCRA Section 3010(a) requires that any person who manages a hazardous waste (i.e., generators, transporters, and owners or operators of T/S/D facilities) must file a notification with EPA within 90 days after regulations are promulgated identifying the waste as hazardous. EPA has published Form 8700-12 as the Section 3010(a) notification form. 36/ The reporting company must identify itself, its location and the EPA identification numbers for the listed and non-listed hazardous wastes it manages. It is important to remember that notifications are required to be filed for each site (e.g., plant) at which hazardous waste is managed.

Persons managing hazardous wastes under EPA's initial RCRA regulatory program in 1980 37/ should have filed the Section 3010(a)

35/ See 1984 amendments, Section 241.

36/ 45 FR 12746 (26 February 1980).

37/ 45 FR 33066 (19 May 1980).

notification form not later than 18 August 1980. Failure to file makes the transport, treatment, storage or disposal of hazardous wastes unlawful. 38/ Companies that failed to file due to excusable oversight may request the EPA exercise its enforcement discretion and permit continued operation if it is in the public interest. 39/

4.3 Generators of Hazardous Waste

Generators play a crucial role in the overall RCRA hazardous waste regulatory scheme. The failure of a generator to properly identify and initiate the management of a hazardous waste may mean that the waste never enters the "cradle to grave" hazardous waste program. Thus the requirements imposed on generators under RCRA Section 3002 and EPA's implementing regulations at 40 CFR Part 262 are of key concern.

EPA's regulations define the term "generator" as "any person, by site, whose act or process produces hazardous waste identified or listed in Part 261 of this chapter or whose act first causes hazardous waste to become subject to regulation." 40/ This definition refers explicitly to the particular site of generation. A corporation with several plants must evaluate and comply with the generator requirements individually for the site of each facility.

A generator is initially required to determine whether any of its solid waste is a "hazardous waste" under the criteria described above. 41/ If it is, the generator must obtain an EPA Identification Number before the waste can be transported, treated, stored or disposed of by persons who also have obtained their EPA Identification Numbers. 42/

The generator also has the responsibility of preparing the Uniform Hazardous Waste Manifest, 43/ a control and transport

---

38/ 45 FR 76632 (19 November 1980).

39/ Id.

40/ 40 CFR 260.10(a)(26).

41/ 40 CFR 262.11.

42/ 40 CFR 262.12(c).

43/ See the current Uniform Manifest at 51 FR 35193 (1 October 1986).

document that accompanies the hazardous waste at all times. 44/ The generator must specify the name and EPA Identification Numbers of each authorized transporter and the permitted T/S/D facility or other designated facility which will accept the waste, describe the waste as required by DOT regulations, certify that it is properly packaged and labeled, and sign the manifest certification by hand.

In the new era of RCRA, companies must develop new management strategies and new technologies to reduce the volume, quantity, and toxicity of hazardous wastes. As an action-forcing mechanism, Congress has now required all generators to certify on manifests that:

> the generator of the hazardous waste has a program in place to reduce the volume and toxicity of such waste to the degree determined by the generator to be economically practicable and that the proposed method of treatment, storage or disposal is that practicable method currently available to the generator which minimizes the present and future threat to human health and the environment.

A sufficient number of copies of the manifest must be prepared so that all parties listed on the manifest as handling the hazardous waste will be provided with a copy, and a final copy can also be returned to the generator from the T/S/D facility. A copy of the final signed manifest must be kept for a period of three years from the date of acceptance of the waste by the initial transporter. 45/

A generator, in addition, must properly prepare the waste for transportation off-site. EPA has adopted the DOT regulations issued under the Hazardous Materials Transportation Act, 49 USC 1802 et seq., with respect to the packaging, labeling, marking, and placarding of hazardous waste shipments. 46/ In addition to the DOT

44/ 40 CFR 262.20 - 262.23. Small quantity generators must make a modified certification of waste minimization. See 51 FR 35190 (1 October 1986).

45/ 40 CFR 262.40.

46/ 40 CFR 262.31.

regulations, EPA requires that any container of 110 gallons or less must be specifically marked with the generator's name, address, manifest document number, and the words:

> HAZARDOUS WASTE — Federal law prohibits improper disposal. If found contact the nearest police or public safety authority or the United States Environmental Protection Agency. 47/

A generator is allowed to accumulate up to 55 gallons of hazardous wastes at or near the point of generation in "satellite accumulation areas." 48/ The containers must be properly marked, the containers must be in good condition, and the waste must be moved into storage once the container is full. A generator is also allowed to store hazardous waste on-site prior to shipment for a period of up to 90 days in tanks or containers without having to obtain a permit for a storage facility. The generator must comply, however, with the Part 265 standards for containers and tanks (e.g., secondary containment structures) and the requirements for personnel training, contingency planning, and emergency preparedness and response.

A generator must file biennial reports with EPA or an authorized state. The biennial report is filed on March 1 of even numbered years and must include (1) the name, address and EPA identification number of the generator, (2) the EPA identification number for each transporter used during the preceding year, (3) name, address and identification number of each T/S/D facility to which wastes were sent, and (4) waste identification information including the DOT hazard class, EPA hazardous waste identification number, and the quantity of the wastes. 49/ Many states require annual reports. The 1984 amendments require that the reports now also include information on the "waste minimization" efforts undertaken to reduce the volume and toxicity of the hazardous wastes, and the results actually achieved in comparison with previous years.

47/ 40 CFR 262.32.

48/ 40 CFR 262.34.

49/ 40 CFR 262.41.

Generators must also submit an exception report in the event that a manifest is not received back in a timely or properly executed manner. The regulations specifically provide that a generator must contact the transporter and/or the T/S/D facility to determine what happened to the manifest and the hazardous waste. If, after the 45th day, the generator has not received a manifest with the proper signature from the T/S/D facility, the generator must submit an exception report to the EPA regional administrator including (1) a copy of the manifest for which the generator does not have confirmation of delivery; and (2) a cover letter which describes the efforts taken to locate the waste and the manifest and the result of those efforts. 50/

Both the biennial reports and the exception reports, like the manifests, are required to be kept for a three-year period. In addition, the records of any test results, waste analyses, or determinations that a waste is hazardous must be kept for three years from the date the waste was last sent to a T/S/D facility. As a practical matter, in view of the liability imposed by Superfund, discussed in Chapter 3, generators should seriously consider maintaining RCRA reports for substantially longer than the minimum three-year period.

4.3.1 Small Generators

As directed by the 1984 RCRA amendments, EPA has promulgated special regulations for small quantity generators that produce hazardous wastes in a total monthly quantity of less than 1,000 kilograms (2,200 pounds), as well as for transporters and T/S/D facilities that handle such wastes. 51/ The regulations vary somewhat from the standards that currently apply to hazardous wastes of larger quantity generators. For example, small quantity generators may still store up to 1,000 kilograms of hazardous waste on site for 180 days without a permit. If the waste must be shipped over 200 miles, the limit is increased to 6,000 kilograms (13,200 pounds) for up to 270 days. Besides using the Uniform Manifest, small quantity generators must have their waste treated, stored (except short-term storage on site) and disposed of at an interim status or permitted T/S/D facility, and no longer at a state or municipally licensed

---

50/ 40 CFR 262.42.

51/ 40 CFR 261.5, 262.20; 51 FR 10146 (24 March 1986).

landfill. Small quantity generators of less than 100 kilograms per month are still conditionally exempt from RCRA, but they are subject to certain minimum standards.

4.4 Transporters of Hazardous Wastes

A transporter is any person engaged in the off-site transportation of hazardous waste by air, rail, highway or water. 52/ Off-site transportation includes both interstate and intrastate commerce. 53/ Thus, the reach of RCRA includes not only shippers and common carriers of hazardous wastes, but also the private company that occasionally transports hazardous wastes on its own trucks solely within its home state.

Anyone who moves a hazardous waste that is required to be manifested off the site where it is generated, or the site where it is being treated, stored and disposed of, will be subject to the transporter standards. The only persons not covered are generators or operators of T/S/D facilities who engage in on-site transportation of their hazardous waste. Once a generator or a T/S/D facility operator moves its hazardous waste off-site—which can be just a few hundred feet down a public road—he is then considered a transporter and must comply with the regulations.

EPA has promulgated standards for all transporters of hazardous wastes at 40 CFR Part 263. These standards are closely coordinated with the standards issued by the Department of Transportation under the Hazardous Materials Transportation Act for the transportation of hazardous materials. 54/ For the most part, EPA's regulations incorporate and require compliance with the DOT provisions on labeling, marking, placarding, using proper containers, and reporting discharges. In addition, all transporters must obtain an EPA Identification Number prior to transporting any hazardous waste and may only accept hazardous waste which is accompanied by a manifest signed by the generator. 55/ The transporter himself must sign and date the manifest acknowledging acceptance of the

---

52/ 40 CFR 260.10(a).

53/ Section 3003.

54/ 49 U.S.C. §1801, et seq., 49 CFR 171-179.

55/ 40 CFR 263.11, 263.20.

waste and return one copy to the generator before leaving the generator's property.

At all times the transporter must keep the manifest with the hazardous waste. When the transporter delivers the waste to another transporter or to the designated T/S/D facility, he must (1) date the manifest and obtain the signature of the next transporter or the T/S/D facility operator, (2) retain one copy of the manifest for his own records, and (3) give the remaining copies to the person receiving the waste. 56/ If the transporter is unable to deliver the waste in accordance with the manifest, he must contact the generator for further instructions and revise the manifest accordingly. 57/ The transporter must keep the executed copy of the manifest for a period of three years. 58/

Finally, the transporter may hold a hazardous waste for up to ten days at a transfer facility without being required to obtain a RCRA storage permit. 59/ A transfer facility generally includes a loading dock, storage area, and similar areas where shipments of hazardous wastes are held during the normal course of transportation.

Transporters of hazardous wastes may become subject to the Part 262 requirements for generators if, for example, the transporter mixes hazardous wastes of different DOT descriptions by placing them into a single container. 60/ Also, a hazardous waste which accumulates in a transport vehicle or vessel or a product or raw material pipeline will trigger the generator standards when the waste is removed.

If an accidental or intentional discharge of a hazardous waste occurs during transportation, the transporter is responsible for its

---

56/ 40 CFR 263.20. Special requirements apply to rail or water transporters of hazardous waste, and those who transport hazardous waste outside of the United States. 40 CFR 263.20(e), (f) and (g), 263.22(b), (c) and (d).

57 40 CFR 263.21(b).

58/ 40 CFR 263.22.

59/ 40 CFR 263.22.

60/ 40 CFR 263.10(c).

clean up and must take immediate action to protect human health and the environment. Such action includes treatment or containment of the spill and notification of local police and fire departments. 61/ DOT's discharge reporting requirements are incorporated into the RCRA regulations. 62/ They identify the situations in which telephone reporting of the discharge to the National Response Center and the filing of a written report are required. That telephone number is 800/424-8802 or 202/426-2675.

Transporters are subject to both DOT and EPA enforcement. Under a memorandum of understanding executed by the two agencies, DOT conducts an ongoing program of inspections of transporters to monitor their compliance. 63/ DOT will immediately advise EPA of "any possible" violations of the RCRA transporter regulations so that EPA can take enforcement action.

The 1984 RCRA amendments will not result in any material change in the standards applicable to transporters of hazardous waste, although transporters are affected by several of the amendments. For example, EPA is required to establish requirements for the transportation of hazardous waste–derived fuels (as discussed above). In addition, transporters who haul used oil for recycling will be subject to the special standards required by the 1984 amendments for handlers of used oil and will be obligated to deliver the used oil to a permitted recycling facility. The new law also shields railroads from the RCRA "citizen suit" and "imminent hazard" enforcement provisions (discussed below) if the railroad merely transports the hazardous waste under a sole contractual agreement and exercises due care.

4.5 Statutory and Regulatory Requirements for Treatment, Storage, and Disposal (T/S/D) Facilities

The term "T/S/D" is commonly used to refer to the three different hazardous waste management activities that are regulated under RCRA Section 3004, and which thus require a permit under

---

61/ 40 CFR 263.30(b).

62/ See 49 CFR 171.15 and 171.16 (1979).

63/ 45 FR 51645 (4 August 1980).

RCRA Section 3005. These activities are treatment, storage and disposal. Section 3004, prior to the 1984 amendments, directed EPA to establish a comprehensive set of regulations governing the management of all aspects of operation of T/S/D facilities. The regulations adopted include both requirements of general applicability to all T/S/D facilities and specific requirements for particular types of facilities. They apply to any T/S/D facility that was active after the effective date of the Subtitle C regulations, 19 November 1980. 64/

In 1984, Congress added a number of important provisions to Section 3004. These establish, among other things, a ban on the disposal of liquids in landfills, and minimum technological requirements for existing and new surface impoundments and landfills. In addition, Congress directed EPA to make a number of regulatory decisions in short order. The most significant provision sets a rigid timetable under which EPA must decide whether to ban land disposal of all untreated hazardous wastes. Failure by EPA to meet the deadlines in the new law will result in a self-enacting statutory ban. The requirements of the current standards and the impact of the new amendments are discussed below.

A facility will be regulated as a "treatment" facility if the operator handles hazardous waste by utilizing any method, technique, or process designed to change the physical, chemical, or biological character or composition of any hazardous waste so as to neutralize such waste, to recover energy or material resources from the waste, to render the waste nonhazardous or less hazardous, safer to transport, store or dispose of, or amenable for recovery, amenable for storage, or reduced in volume. 65/ A "storage" facility is defined as one which engages in the holding of hazardous waste for a temporary period, at the end of which the hazardous waste is treated, disposed of, or stored elsewhere. 66/

A "disposal facility" is one at which hazardous waste is intentionally placed into or on any land or water, and at which waste will

---

64/ See 45 FR 33170.

65/ 40 CFR 260.10(a).

66/ Id.

remain after closure. 67/ The term "facility" is separately defined to include "all contiguous land, and structures, other appurtenances, and improvements on the land." 68/ Clarification of the application of the foregoing definitions can be sought during the permitting process.

A number of different types of T/S/D facilities and hazardous waste activities are currently exempted from regulation all together. This list may change as a result of the 1984 amendments and continued regulatory activity. However, the list presently contains the following exclusions:

(1)   Facilities that dispose of hazardous waste by means of ocean disposal pursuant to a permit issued under the Marine Protection, Research, and Sanctuaries Act (except as provided in a RCRA permit-by-rule).

(2)   The disposal of hazardous waste by underground injection pursuant to a permit issued under the Safe Drinking Water Act (except as provided in a RCRA permit-by-rule).

(3)   A Publicly Owned Treatment Works (POTW) that treats or stores hazardous wastes which are delivered to the POTW by a transport vehicle or vessel or through a pipe.

(4)   T/S/D facilities that operate under a state hazardous waste program authorized pursuant to RCRA Section 3006.

(5)   Facilities authorized by a state to manage industrial or municipal solid waste, if the only hazardous waste handled by such a facility is otherwise excluded from regulation pursuant to the special requirements for less than 100 kilograms for small quantity generators.

67/   Id.

68/   Id.

(6)   A facility that treats or stores hazardous wastes which are subject to the special requirement for recyclable materials, except as provided in Part 266.

(7)   Temporary on-site accumulation of hazardous waste by generators.

(8)   Farmers who dispose of waste pesticides from their own use in compliance with 40 CFR 262.51.

(9)   Owners or operators of a "totally enclosed treatment facility."

(10)   Owners and operators of elementary neutralization units and wastewater treatment units.

(11)   Persons taking immediate action to treat and contain spills.

(12)   Transporters storing manifested wastes approved in containers at a transfer facility for 10 days or less.

(13)   The act of adding absorbent material to hazardous waste in a container, to reduce the amount of free liquids in the container, if the materials are added when wastes are first placed in the container.

4.5.1 Standards of General Applicability

As discussed more fully in the permits discussion below, two categories of T/S/D facilities currently exist—interim status facilities and permitted facilities. Interim status facilities are those which are currently operating without final RCRA permits based upon a legislative decision recognizing that issuance of permits would be a time consuming process. These facilities had to meet a three-part statutory test of:

(1)   being in existence on 19 November 1980, or the effective date of statutory or regulatory changes that rendered the facility subject to the need for a RCRA permit,

(2)   notifying EPA pursuant to RCRA Section 3010(a) of its hazardous waste management activities, and

(3)   filing a preliminary permit application. 69/

A facility's interim status will end when the facility receives a permit. This in turn is based upon technical standards issued by EPA, or a State with an approved program, which are incorporated into the permit. As discussed in the next section on permits, the 1984 amendments specify timetables for issuance of all such permits. All other T/S/D facilities, including new facilities that were not "in existence" on 19 November 1980 and facilities that have otherwise failed to qualify for interim status, must obtain an individual RCRA permit and may not operate until they do.

Separate standards have been issued for interim status facilities 70/ and permitted facilities. 71/ Both the interim and permanent status regulations for T/S/D facilities include standards of general applicability (e.g., personnel training, security, financial responsibility), as well as specific design and operating standards for each different type of T/S/D facility (e.g., storage tanks, landfills, incinerators). The standards of general applicability are discussed first below.

An operator of a T/S/D facility is required to obtain an EPA identification number. 72/ The operator must also obtain or conduct a detailed chemical and physical analysis of a representative sample of a hazardous waste before the waste is treated, stored, or disposed of at the facility. 73/ This is to ensure that the operator has

---

69/ Section 3005(e); 40 CFR 265.1. As discussed below, a permit application consists of Part A (two forms) and Part B (detailed information on the facility filed at a later date). Part A must be filed to obtain interim status.

70/ 40 CFR Part 265.

71/ 40 CFR Part 264.

72/ 40 CFR 265.11, 264.11.

73/ 40 CFR 265.13, 264.13.

sufficient knowledge of the particular waste being handled to be able to properly manage it. Operators must install a security system to prevent unknowing entry, and to minimize the potential for unauthorized entry, of people or livestock to the active portion of a T/S/D facility. 74/ This may be either a 24-hour surveillance system or a barrier around the facility and a means to control entry, and posted "Danger" signs. Operators are required to prepare and implement an inspection plan specifically tailored to the circumstances at their facility. 75/ Permitted facilities to be sited in areas prone to seismic activity or floodplains are subject to location standards designed to reduce the additional risks. 76/

T/S/D facility personnel also are required to have expertise in the areas to which they are assigned, thus reducing the chances that a mistake due to lack of training might lead to an environmental accident. The training may be by formal classroom instruction or on-the-job training. The program must be directed by a person trained in hazardous waste management procedures. 77/

Special precautions must be taken to prevent accidental ignition or reaction of ignitable or reactive wastes. While many of the requirements for handling ignitable, reactive, and incompatible wastes are largely common sense practices, specific requirements regarding the mixing of such wastes also are included in the regulations. Compliance with the regulations concerning management of ignitable, reactive or incompatible wastes must be documented. 78/

Regulations for preparedness and prevention have been promulgated to minimize the possibility or effect of an explosion, spill, or fire at a T/S/D facility. 79/ Facilities must have, unless unnecessary due to the nature of the wastes handled, the following equipment:

74/ 40 CFR 265.14, 264.14.

75/ 40 CFR 265.15, 264.15.

76/ 40 CFR 265.18(b), 264.17(c), 264.18(a).

77/ 40 CFR 265.16, 264.16.

78/ 40 CFR 265.17, 264.17.

79/ See generally 40 CFR 265.30-.49, 264.30-.49.

(1)   an internal alarm or communications system,

(2)   a device capable of summoning emergency assistance from local agencies,

(3)   fire and spill control equipment, and

(4)   decontamination equipment.

Operators are required to have a contingency plan for the facility designed to minimize hazards to human health and the environment in the event of an actual explosion, fire, or unplanned release of hazardous wastes. 80/ They are also required to obtain liability insurance or other instruments to provide coverage during the operating life of a facility for claims arising out of injuries to persons or property which result from hazardous waste management operations. 81/

Numerous recordkeeping requirements apply to T/S/D facilities. 82/ Upon receipt of a manifested shipment of hazardous waste, the operator of a T/S/D facility must immediately sign, date, and give to the transporter a copy of the manifest prepared by the generator. Within 30 days, the operator must return another copy of the manifest to the generator and retain a copy of each manifest at the facility for at least three years from the date of delivery. All T/S/D facilities also must maintain a complete operating record until closure. 83/ Required information includes, among other things, a description and the quantity of each hazardous waste received and the method and date of its treatment, storage and disposal, the location of each waste within the facility, records and results of waste analysis and trial tests and inspections.

There are also basic reports which the T/S/D facility operator is obligated to file with the EPA regional administrator or an authorized state. These include a biennial report of waste management

---

80/ See generally 40 CFR 265.50-.56, 264.50-.56.

81/ 40 CFR 265.143(e), 264.143(f).

82/ See generally 40 CFR 265.71-.72, 264.71-.72.

83/ 40 CFR 265.73, 264.73.

activities for the previous calendar year, 84/ an "unmanifested waste" report which the operator must file within 15 days of accepting any hazardous waste that is not accompanied by the required manifest, 85/ and certain specialized reports, e.g an incident report, in the event of a hazardous waste release, fire, or explosion.

There are general closure requirements applicable to all T/S/D facilities, and additional requirements for each specific type of facility. 86/ "Closure" is the period after which hazardous wastes are no longer accepted by a T/S/D facility and during which the operator completes treatment, storage or disposal operations. "Post-closure" is the 30-year period after closure when operators of disposal facilities only must perform certain monitoring and maintenance activities. Generally, an owner or operator must have a detailed written closure plan and schedule therefore. It must be approved by EPA or the state and amended when any changes in waste management operations affect its terms. Post-closure care must continue for 30 years after the date of completing closure and include groundwater monitoring and maintenance of monitoring and waste containment systems. Post-closure care is required where hazardous waste will remain at the site after closure.

Financial responsibility requirements have been established to ensure that funds for closure and post-closure care are adequate and available. 87/

4.5.2 Standards for Specific Types of T/S/D Facilities

The standards discussed above are generally applicable to all T/S/D facilities, from the simple container storage area to the most complex commercial landfill. EPA has also promulgated specific design, construction, and operating standards for each of ten different types of T/S/D facilities that constitute the universe of facilities regulated under RCRA. These are: (1) containers, (2) tanks, (3) surface impoundments, (4) waste piles, (5) land treatment units,

---

84/ 40 CFR 265.75, 264.75.

85/ See 40 CFR 261.5.

86 See generally 40 CFR 265.110-.120, 264.110-.120.

87/ See generally 40 CFR 265.140-.151, 264.140-.151.

(6) landfills, (7) incinerators, (8) thermal treatment units, (9) chemical, physical, and biological treatment units, and (10) underground injection wells. 88/ In the years ahead, additional classes of facilities may also be addressed by distinct sets of standards such as these.

Discussion of the detailed regulatory requirements for all of these types of facilities, including groundwater monitoring requirements for land disposal facilities, 89/ is beyond the scope of this chapter. 90/ Moreover, the regulations applicable to four of these types of facilities—surface impoundments, waste piles, land treatment units and landfills—are undergoing extensive change as a result of the 1984 RCRA amendments. The clear thrust of the amendments is that Congress viewed EPA's regulatory activities in this area to date as too little and too late. The major amendments affecting land disposal facilities are discussed below.

4.5.3 Impact of the 1984 Amendments

4.5.3.1 Prohibitions on Land Disposal of Certain Wastes

Perhaps the most significant provision of the new law calls for EPA to determine whether to ban or restrict, in whole or in part, the disposal of all RCRA hazardous wastes that are not pretreated in landfills and other land disposal facilities. Congress has set forth a phased program for EPA to implement the restrictions. First, the land disposal of hazardous wastes containing dioxin or solvents is banned after November 1986, unless the wastes are pretreated as discussed below. 91/ EPA may lift the ban only for those methods of

----

88/ 40 CFR 265, Subparts J-R, 264, Subparts J-O.

89/ See generally 40 CFR 265.90-.94, 264.90-.101.

90/ These requirements are discussed in detail in chapter 7 of the RCRA/Hazardous Waste Handbook (Government Institutes, 7th ed. 1987).

91/ The dioxin containing wastes are those chlorinated dioxins, -dibenzofurans, and -phenols proposed by EPA for listing as acutely hazardous wastes. 48 FR 14514 (4 April 1983). The solvents are those listed as F001, F002, F003, F004 and F005 at 40 CFR §261.31. See generally Section 201 of the 1984 Amendments, PL 98-616, 98 Stat. 3221 (8 November 1984).

land disposal of particular hazardous wastes which EPA determines will be protective of human health and the environment, based on a reasonable degree of certainty that there will be no migration of hazardous constituents from the land disposal facility, and taking into account the persistence, toxicity, mobility, and propensity to bioaccumulate the hazardous waste and the long-term uncertainties associated with land disposal.

Second, the land disposal of certain hazardous wastes which California has already banned will become subject to a national ban under RCRA after July 1987, unless again EPA lifts the ban for particular wastes. The "California list" includes: (1) liquid hazardous wastes, including free liquids associated with any sludge, containing free cyanides greater than 100 mg/l; (2) specified concentrations of heavy metals (arsenic, cadmium, chromium, lead, mercury, nickel, selenium and thallium); (3) acids below a pH of 2; (4) PCBs; and (5) halogenated organic compounds. 92/

Third, EPA has published a ranking of all listed hazardous wastes based on their intrinsic hazard and volume, with a schedule for determining whether to ban the land disposal of such wastes. By August 1988, EPA must decide whether to ban from certain kinds of land disposal some or all of the first one-third of the highest priority hazardous wastes on the ranking list. By June 1990, EPA must decide whether to ban the middle of the ranked hazardous wastes. Then by May 1991, EPA must determine whether to ban all RCRA listed hazardous wastes. At each phase of the schedule, EPA can decide not to impose the ban on a particular method of land disposal for a particular hazardous waste if EPA determines that human health and the environment will be protected, taking into account the relevant factors discussed above.

Congress wanted to promote treatment of hazardous wastes in lieu of or prior to any land disposal. Therefore at the same time EPA promulgates these land disposal restrictions, it must also promulgate regulations specifying the methods of treatment, if any,

---

92/ Disposal by deep well injection is subject to special provisions and a different schedule for implementing the ban. EPA has until August 1988 to decide the extent of the ban on deep well injection of dioxin-containing and solvent hazardous wastes and the California list.

that substantially diminish the toxicity or reduce the likelihood of migration of the waste from land disposal facilities. A company that treats its hazardous waste in accordance with these pretreatment standards will not have the treated waste or residue subject to the land disposal ban.

EPA has limited authority to extend the ban deadlines for specific hazardous wastes to the earliest date on which adequate alternative treatment, recovery, or disposal capacity will be available. EPA can also grant a one-year extension, renewable only once, to a company that demonstrates on a case-by-case basis that a binding contractual commitment has been made to construct or otherwise provide alternative treatment, recovery, or disposal capacity, but due to circumstances beyond its control the alternative capacity cannot reasonably be made available by the ban deadline.

Again Congress has used a "hammer" to compel EPA action by the statutory deadlines. If EPA fails to decide whether to ban the land disposal of the hazardous wastes in accordance with the priority ranking and schedule, the ban will automatically go into effect. The only exception is for generators that certify that the only practicable alternative currently available to them is the disposal of their hazardous waste at a landfill or surface impoundment meeting the "minimum technological requirements" of the 1984 law (discussed below).

4.5.3.2 Liquids in Landfills

EPA has by regulation already placed substantial restrictions on the disposal of liquid hazardous wastes in landfills. Congress has now gone further and banned the disposal in landfills of bulk or non-containerized liquid hazardous wastes, and hazardous wastes containing free liquids. EPA has also promulgated regulations that minimize disposal of containerized liquid hazardous wastes in landfills. In order to discourage the use of absorbent materials (e.g., "kitty litter") to reduce free liquids in containerized wastes, EPA's regulations also prohibit the landfilling of liquids that have been absorbed in materials that biodegrade or that release liquids when depressed during routine landfill operations.

In addition, Congress has banned the disposal in RCRA landfills of any liquids that are not hazardous wastes, unless the owner can demonstrate that disposal in its landfill will not present a risk of contamination of any underground source of drinking water, and the only reasonably available alternative is disposal at another landfill or unlined surface impoundment which contains hazardous wastes.

4.5.3.3 Existing Surface Impoundments and Minimum Technological Requirements

During congressional consideration of the 1984 RCRA amendments, one of the most controversial questions was whether companies that are currently using unlined surface impoundments should be required to retrofit by installing liners to prevent groundwater contamination. According to EPA, there are an estimated 200,000 unlined pits, ponds, and lagoons used for the storage, treatment, and disposal of hazardous waste across the nation. EPA believes these impoundments are a major source of groundwater contamination, but the cost of retrofitting or closing all these impoundments is estimated to be very high.

In the end, Congress decided to require companies to retrofit all interim status surface impoundments with double liners, leachate collection systems, and groundwater monitoring systems by November 1988. EPA can modify these requirements only if the operator can demonstrate that the impoundment is located, designed, and operated so as to ensure that there will be no migration of any hazardous constituents to the groundwater or surface water at any future time. 93/ The retrofit requirements are expected to result in the closing of many surface impoundments.

Congress created two carefully limited exemptions. First, a surface impoundment that has at least one liner, is located more than one-quarter mile from an underground source of drinking water, and is in compliance with groundwater monitoring requirements is exempt. EPA expects, however, that very few surface impoundments are, in fact, located more than one-quarter mile from an underground drinking water source. Second, a surface impoundment which is part of a wastewater treatment facility regulated under the Clean Water Act, and which is used to contain treated wastewater during the secondary or subsequent phases of an "aggressive biological treatment" system, may be exempt. 94/ In order to obtain these

---

93/ See 1984 amendments, Sections 215, 202 and 203.

94/ The initial impoundment must have a maximum five-day hydraulic retention time, or maximum 30-day retention time if the sludge in the impoundment is not EP Toxic, or activated sludge treatment must be used in the first portion of the secondary treatment.

exemptions, however, companies that operate such surface impoundments must apply to EPA, or an authorized state, by not later than 8
November 1986. After that time, the exemptions are deemed to be
waived.

4.5.3.4 Expansion During Interim Status

Under EPA's 1980 regulations, the existing portion of a
surface impoundment, landfill or waste pile that qualified for
interim status was not subject to any liner requirements. This
allowed operators to replace or expand these existing land disposal
units without complying with the more stringent requirements for
new facilities.

Congress has changed that. Now, every new unit, replacement of an existing unit, or lateral expansion of an existing unit at
an interim status surface impoundment or landfill must have two or
more liners and a leachate collection system above (for a landfill)
and between the liners. Waste piles must have single liners. Groundwater monitoring is also required. 95/ To expedite permitting of
interim status surface impoundments and landfills, the operator
must submit a Part B permit application within six months of receiving hazardous wastes in a new, replacement, or expansion unit. If a
liner and leachate collection system are installed in good faith under
the new requirements, no different liner or leachate collection system may be required as a condition of the first RCRA permit issued
to the facility, unless EPA has reason to believe that a liner is
leaking.

4.5.3.5 Corrective Action Beyond Facility Boundary

When EPA began implementing the interim status and permit
programs, it stated that RCRA did not provide authority to require
cleanup of pollution beyond the property boundary of a T/S/D facility which may have occurred before RCRA was enacted. Congress
has now given EPA that authority. As a condition to receiving a
RCRA permit, the T/S/D facility standards now require that the
operator take corrective action beyond the facility boundary where
necessary to protect human health and the environment. 96/ As

---

95/ See 1984 amendments, Section 243.

96/ See 1984 amendments, Section 207.

discussed in Section 4.6 below, a companion provision requires corrective action of releases at any T/S/D facility holding or seeking a permit. 97/

This type of authority for cleanup is analogous to that which exists under the Comprehensive Environmental Response, Compensation and Liability Act of 1980 ("CERCLA" or "Superfund"), and will have a very substantial impact on some facilities.

4.5.3.6 Minimum Technological Requirement for New Landfills and Surface Impoundments

In significant new provisions, Congress has directed that any RCRA permit issued by EPA for a new landfill or surface impoundment must require the installation of two or more liners, a leak detection system, and a leachate collection system above (for a landfill) and between the liners. 98/ Groundwater monitoring will also be required as a permit condition. Land disposal facilities operating under interim status were required to certify in November 1985 that they were in compliance with all applicable groundwater monitoring requirements, or interim status was lost. 99/ EPA has amended its regulations to implement these "minimum technological requirements."

A company can use alternative design and operating practices in lieu of liners if it can demonstrate that such practices, together with the location characteristics of its facility, will prevent the migration of any hazardous constituents into groundwater or surface water as effectively as liners and leachate collection systems. The double-liner requirement may also be waived for monofills containing certain types of waste.

Location standards specifying criteria for the acceptable location of new and existing T/S/D facilities have also been established by EPA, along with guidance criteria identifying areas of vulnerable hydrogeology.

97/   See 1984 amendments, Section 206.

98/   See 1984 amendments, Section 202.

99/   See 1984 amendments, Section 203.

4.6 Permits

RCRA requires every owner or operator of a T/S/D facility to obtain a permit. 100/ Different permit application procedures apply to interim status facilities and to new facilities or existing facilities that failed to qualify for interim status. A T/S/D facility which was in existence on 19 November 1980 or the date of the statutory or regulatory change that made the facility subject to RCRA, notified EPA of its hazardous waste management activities, and filed a Part A application, was authorized to continue operations without having been issued a site-specific permit. 101/ A new facility or an existing facility that failed to qualify for interim status must obtain a permit before commencing operations.

A Part A application is a form application containing certain basic information about the facility, such as name, location, nature of business, regulated activities, and a topographic map of the facility site, 102/ and must be filed as soon as an existing T/S/D facility becomes subject to the hazardous waste regulatory program. For most existing facilities, this was 19 November 1980. For other existing facilities which subsequently become subject to RCRA because of changes in regulations, the deadline for filing the Part A application will be specified by EPA in the preamble. A T/S/D facility that qualifies because it loses its special status—such as a small generator—must file a Part A application within 30 days of the loss of its exemption. 103/

A Part B application requiring substantially more detailed information must be filed after the effective date of the applicable technical standards for T/S/D facilities, and following request for it by EPA or the state. 104/

100/ Section 3005.

101/ See the interim status standards for T/S/D facilities in 40 CFR Part 265.

102/ 40 CFR 270.13.

103/ See 46 FR 60446 (10 December 1981).

104/ See generally 40 CFR 270.13-270.21.

The final permit will govern the application of these standards to the particular facility. New facilities must submit Part A and B applications simultaneously. A permit is required to be issued before operation. 105/

Permit applications will be requested and final permits will be issued by states authorized under RCRA to administer their own programs, and by the EPA regional administrator in all other states. Permit issuance must be based on a determination that the T/S/D facility will comply with all requirements of RCRA.

After a complete RCRA permit application is filed, the rules in 40 CFR Part 124 establish the procedures for processing the application and issuing the permit. These include preparation of draft permits, public comment and hearing, and the issuance of final decisions.

In the 1984 amendments, Congress has taken steps to accelerate the permitting of existing interim status T/S/D facilities. Congress has provided that interim status for any existing land disposal facility must terminate on 8 November 1985, unless the owner or operator has submitted a Part B application for a final permit and a certification that the facility is in compliance with groundwater monitoring and financial responsibility requirements. 106/   EPA, or an authorized state, must then process all permit applications for land disposal facilities within four years, all incinerator permit applications within five years, and applications for all other facilities within eight years.

The new law also provides that permits for land disposal facilities, storage facilities, incinerators and other treatment facilities can be issued for a ten-year fixed term. While permits may be reviewed and modified at any time during their terms, permits for land disposal facilities must be reviewed five years after issuance. At such time, the terms of a permit may be modified to ensure that the permit continues to incorporate the standards then applicable to land disposal facilities. 107/

105/ See 1984 amendments, Section 211. An exception is provided for facilities constructed under the Toxic Substances Control Act for the incineration of PCBs.

106/ See 1984 amendments, Section 213.

107/ See 1984 amendments, Section 212.

In addition, newly issued permits also must require the owner or operator of a T/S/D facility to take corrective action for all releases of hazardous waste and constituents from solid waste management units at the facility regardless of when the waste was placed in the unit, or whether the unit is currently active. 108/

4.7 State Hazardous Waste Programs

States are authorized by RCRA to develop and carry out their own hazardous waste programs in lieu of the federal program administered by EPA. 109/ Congress anticipated that states would gain authorization for their programs in two stages. States with legislative authority for hazardous waste programs first obtained "interim authorization" from EPA to carry out their programs upon a showing that the state program was "substantially equivalent" to the federal program.

Regardless of whether a state received interim authorization, any state may apply for "final authorization" to administer the RCRA hazardous waste program. The conditions for approval are intended to ensure uniformity among the states. To support a grant of final authorization, the state program must meet three standards. It must be "equivalent" to the federal program, it must be "consistent" with federal and authorized state programs, and must provide adequate enforcement of compliance with the requirements of RCRA Subtitle C. 110/ The deadline for receiving final authorization was extended by the 1984 amendments to 31 January 1985. 111/

EPA regulations that implement the 1984 amendments take effect in states having final authorization on the same day that they take effect under the federal program. A state may submit evidence to EPA that its existing state program contains a requirement substantially similar to the EPA regulation, and may request interim

---

108/ See 1984 amendments, Section 206.

109/ Section 3006; see generally 40 CFR Part 271.

110/ Cooperative agreements are a third type of arrangement whereby states which do not qualify for interim authorization may nonetheless administer portions of their programs. 45 FR 33784-86 (20 May 1980).

111/ See 1984 amendments, Section 227.

authorization to administer the requirement under the state program in lieu of direct administration by EPA. 112/ The state can then apply for final authorization for the new requirement after promulgating an equivalent regulation.

4.8 Inspection and Enforcement

RCRA provides that any officer, employee or representative of EPA or of a state with an authorized hazardous waste program may inspect the premises and records of any person who generates, stores, treats, transports, disposes of, or otherwise handles hazardous waste. 113/ EPA's inspection authority extends to persons or sites which have handled hazardous wastes in the past but no longer do so. The owner/operator must provide government officials access to records and property relating to the wastes for inspection purposes. Copying and sampling are authorized.

In the 1984 amendments, Congress has directed EPA and authorized states to improve and regularize RCRA inspections. EPA and authorized states must now conduct inspections of all privately-operated T/S/D facilities at least once every two years. Federally-operated T/S/D facilities must be inspected on an annual basis by EPA or an authorized state. Similarly, EPA must conduct annual inspections of T/S/D facilities which are operated by a state or local government to ensure compliance with the requirements of the act. 114/

All organizations should have an established policy and procedure for handling RCRA inspections, including consideration of whether or not a warrant should be required.

112/ See 1984 amendments, Section 228.

113/ Section 3007. EPA's inspection activities under RCRA Section 3007 are subject to the Fourth Amendment's protection against unreasonable searches or seizures, which the Supreme Court has applied in holding that a warrant is generally required for an inspection by an administrative agency. Marshall v. Barlow's, Inc., 436 U.S. 307 (1978) involving the inspection provisions of the Occupational Safety and Health Act.

114/ See 1984 amendments, Sections 229, 230 and 231.

EPA can bring several types of enforcement actions under RCRA. These include administrative orders and civil and criminal penalties. Whenever EPA determines that any person is violating Subtitle C of RCRA (including any regulation or permit issued thereunder), it may at its option either issue an order requiring compliance immediately or within a specified time period, or seek injunctive relief against the violator through a civil action filed in a U.S. District Court. Any person who violates any requirement of Subtitle C is liable for a civil penalty of up to $25,000 for each day of violation, regardless of whether the person had been served with a compliance order. A person subject to RCRA can not rely on EPA to tell him when he is in violation, then take the required corrective action, and thus avoid a penalty. Failure to comply with an administrative order may also result in suspension or revocation of a permit.

RCRA also imposes criminal liability of up to $50,000, two years imprisonment, or both for persons who "knowingly" commit certain violations. The 1984 amendments significantly expand the list of these criminal violations. Fines and imprisonment can be imposed on generators who knowingly allow hazardous waste to be transported to an unpermitted facility, knowing violations of federal interim status standards, or counterpart state requirements, material omissions or the failure to file reports required under RCRA by generators, transporters, and T/S/D facility operators which are committed knowingly, and knowing transport of hazardous waste without a manifest. 115/

The statute also creates a crime of "knowing endangerment." The purpose of this sanction is to provide more substantial felony penalties for any person who commits the acts described above and "who knows at that time that he thereby places another person in imminent danger of death or serious bodily injury." Upon conviction, an individual faces a fine of up to $250,000 and/or up to fifteen years' imprisonment. An organizational defendant is subject to a maximum fine of $1 million. All of this is part of the message from Congress to EPA and the Justice Department that more rigorous enforcement of the nation's hazardous wastes laws is the federal policy.

115/ See 1984 amendments, Section 232.

5.0 REGULATION OF UNDERGROUND STORAGE TANKS

A last-minute Senate amendment to the 1984 RCRA amendments established under a new Subtitle I ("eye") in RCRA a comprehensive regulatory program for underground tanks containing "regulated substances." "Regulated substances" are all "hazardous substances" as defined under Superfund (except RCRA hazardous waste, which would be regulated under Subtitle C) and liquid petroleum substances. 116/ Every owner of an underground storage tank containing a regulated substance was required to notify the state of the existence of the tank. No notification was required, however, for underground storage tanks taken out of the ground, or for tanks that were taken out of operation before 1 January 1974. A company that now begins using an underground storage tank must notify the state within thirty days.

The installation of an underground storage tank for regulated substances is now prohibited unless certain statutory design and construction standards are met. EPA is directed to promulgate additional standards applicable to all new underground storage tanks by November 1987. The regulations must require a monitoring system to detect leaks, the maintenance of records on the leak detection system, the reporting of releases, corrective action in response to a release, performance standards for new tanks, and regulations on tank closure which will prevent releases of regulated substances into the environment.

The new law allows states to take over the regulatory program for underground storage tanks by submitting "release detection, prevention, and correction programs" for review and approval by EPA. The state program must include the components of the federal program, provide for adequate enforcement of compliance, and have performance standards for new tanks that are no less stringent than federal standards.

116/ See 1984 amendments, Section 601. In a separate Section 207(w), Congress also directed EPA to promulgate permit rules for underground tanks that contain hazardous wastes as defined under Subtitle C.

6.0 STATE OR REGIONAL SOLID WASTE PLANS

Regulation of non-hazardous waste is the responsibility of the states pursuant to Subtitle D of RCRA. The federal involvement is limited to establishing minimum criteria that would prescribe the best practicable controls and monitoring requirements on solid waste disposal facilities.

In the 1984 amendments, Congress directed EPA to conduct a study to answer whether current guidelines and criteria provide sufficient groundwater protection and to submit that study to Congress by 1987. In addition, Congress ordered EPA to revise the criteria for facilities receiving hazardous waste from households or from small generators to enable detection of groundwater contamination, provide for corrective action as necessary, and facility siting. 117/ Compliance with the minimum requirements determines whether a facility is classified as an "open dump" or not. Disposal of solid waste in "open dumps", (i.e., those facilities not meeting the criteria) is prohibited. Existing dumps were allowed to make modifications that will permit them to meet the requirements, and it is the state's responsibility to ensure that such upgrading occurs or the open dumps are closed.

EPA was not given any enforcement authority, however, for the ban on open dumps. EPA's enforcement authority under RCRA only covers hazardous wastes. EPA cannot take action against a person disposing of non-hazardous wastes in an open dump or against the state for failing to close open dumping, other than terminating certain grant funds available to the state under RCRA. Recognizing this problem, Congress has asked EPA, as part of its study, to make recommendations on the need for additional enforcement authorities. 118/

RCRA also envisions that the state, with the help of federal grant funds, will develop regional solid waste management plans. The program is patterned on Section 208 of the Clean Water Act and relies upon a comprehensive regional planning approach to solving solid waste problems. The state is responsible for identifying

---

117/ See 1984 amendments, Section 302(a)(1).

118/ Id.

appropriate management areas, developing regional plans through the use of local and regional authorities, inventorying and closing or upgrading existing open dumps, and generally assessing the need for additional solid waste disposal capacity in the area.

Of particular significance is a requirement that states not have any bans on the importation of waste for storage, treatment or disposal, or have requirements that are substantially dissimilar from other disposal practices that would discourage the free movement of wastes across state lines. Although enforcement of this requirement may be difficult, in light of the limited enforcement authority available to EPA, it does evidence a congressional policy for a national approach to solid waste disposal and prevents localities from shielding themselves from disposal to the detriment of other jurisdictions.

7.0 ROLE OF THE DEPARTMENT OF COMMERCE

Subtitle E of RCRA gives the Department of Commerce (DOC) responsibility for developing standards for substituting secondary materials for virgin materials, developing markets for recovered materials, and for the promotion of resource recovery technology generally.

The authorities given to DOC are similar to those assigned to EPA in other sections of the act, specifically Subtitle H on Research, Development, Demonstrations and Information. Nevertheless, DOC has not received sufficient funding to support a major role.

8.0 FEDERAL RESPONSIBILITIES

Subtitle F requires that all federal agencies and instrumentalities comply with all federal, state, interstate, and local requirements stemming from RCRA unless exempted by the President. It also requires the federal government to institute a procurement policy which encourages the purchase of recoverable materials when available at reasonable prices and which, because of their performance, can be substituted for virgin materials.

9.0   ADDITIONAL ENFORCEMENT PROVISIONS: CITIZEN SUITS AND IMMINENT HAZARD ACTIONS

In addition to the enforcement provisions specifically included in Subtitle C and discussed above, Subtitle G authorizes, among other things, citizens' suits and suits by the federal government to remedy imminent hazards.

Citizen suits are envisioned by Congress and many others as a key enforcement tool for environmental protection. As originally enacted, the RCRA citizen suit provision provided that any person may bring a civil action against any alleged violator of the act's requirements or against the EPA administrator for a failure to perform a nondiscretionary duty. Further, any person may petition the EPA administrator for promulgation, amendment or repeal of any regulation. Courts were authorized to award costs including attorneys' fees to any party. 119/

The 1984 amendments substantially enhance the role accorded to these suits. The citizen suit provision has been expanded to authorize suits in cases where past or present management or disposal of hazardous wastes has contributed to a situation that may present an imminent or substantial endangerment. However, citizen suits are prohibited (1) with respect to the siting and permitting of hazardous waste facilities; (2) where EPA is prosecuting an action under RCRA or Superfund; (3) while EPA or the state is engaged in a removal action under Superfund or has incurred costs to engage in a remedial action; or (4) where the responsible party is conducting a removal or remedial action pursuant to an order obtained from EPA. Affected parties may be allowed to intervene in ongoing suits. Plaintiffs must notify EPA, the state, and affected parties ninety days prior to commencement of a citizen suit. Attorneys' fees may be awarded to the prevailing or substantially prevailing party. 120/

In addition, EPA is authorized in Section 7003 to bring suits to restrain an imminent and substantial endangerment to health or the environment. 121/ EPA has construed "imminent and substantial

---

119/ Section 7002.

120/ See 1984 amendments, Section 401.

121/ Section 7003.

endangerment" to mean posing a "risk of harm" or "potential harm" but not requiring proof of actual harm. 122/ This interpretation was upheld in United States v. Vertac Chemical Corp., 123/ the first published decision interpreting RCRA Section 7003. In issuing a preliminary injunction to contain the migration of dioxin from land-fills and a treatment basin into a creek, the court held that under the endangerment provisions of both RCRA and the Clean Water Act harm need only be threatened rather than actually occurring.

In response to conflicting federal court decisions, Congress reworded the "imminent hazard" provision in 1984 to clarify that actions which took place prior to the enactment of RCRA are covered by this provision. Thus a non-negligent generator whose wastes are no longer being deposited at a particular site may still be ordered to abate the hazard resulting from the leaking of previously deposited wastes. 124/

The 1984 amendments also require EPA to provide for public notice and comment, and the opportunity for a public meeting in the affected area, prior to entering into a settlement or covenant not to sue in any imminent hazard actions. 125/ This expands on existing Department of Justice practice with respect to consent decrees.

10.0 RESEARCH, DEVELOPMENT, DEMONSTRATION, AND INFORMATION

In cooperation with federal, state, and interstate authorities, private agencies and institutions and individuals, EPA is directed to conduct, encourage and promote the coordination of research, inves-tigations, experiments, training, demonstrations, surveys, public education programs and studies. These R & D efforts can relate to

---

122/ Memorandum, 25 January 1980, from Douglas MacMillan, Acting Director of EPA's Hazardous Waste Enforcement Task Force, to Regional Enforcement Division Directors and others.

123/ 489 F. Supp. 870 (E.D. Ark. 1980).

124/ See 1984 amendments, Section 402.

125/ See 1984 amendments, Section 404.

the protection of health; planning, financing and operation of waste management systems including resource recovery; improvements in methodology of waste disposal and resource recovery; reduction of the amount of waste generated, and methods for remedying damages by earlier or existing landfills; and methods for rendering landfills safe for purposes of construction and other uses.

EPA was also directed to carry out a number of special studies including the following subjects: small-scale and low technology approaches to resource recovery; front-end separation for materials recovery; mining waste; sludge; and airport landfills.

11.0 NATIONAL GROUNDWATER COMMISSION

The 1984 RCRA amendments also established a National Groundwater Commission to study and assess, among other things, the groundwater resource, the extent of its contamination, methods of abatement and improved future management of groundwater. The Commission has reported its findings and recommendations to Congress and the President. 126/

12.0 CONCLUSION

As the foregoing discussion amply demonstrates the RCRA program is complex. The 1984 amendments have added many new requirements which represent a challenge to the will and imagination of the regulated community. Industry has been challenged to find new ways to treat and dispose of hazardous waste. This may include methods of destruction or detoxification using technologies many of which are only recently developed or not yet even on the drawing boards. Never has the incentive been greater to reuse, recycle, or reclaim wastes, or to search out new products, processes, and raw materials which do not result in the generation of hazardous waste in the first place.

126/ See 1984 amendments, Section 704.

Chapter 3

COMPREHENSIVE ENVIRONMENTAL RESPONSE,
COMPENSATION, AND LIABILITY ACT
(CERCLA OR SUPERFUND)

Richard G. Stoll, Esq.
Freedman, Levy, Kroll & Simonds
Washington, D.C.

1.0 INTRODUCTION

1.1 CERCLA's Basic Purposes

In 1980, Congress enacted the Comprehensive Environmental, Response, Compensation, and Liability Act, usually referred to as "CERCLA" or "Superfund." 1/ CERCLA's most basic purposes are to provide funding and enforcement authority for responding to hazardous substance spills and for cleaning up the thousands of hazardous "waste sites" that have been created in the U.S. over the past decades.

With respect to hazardous waste disposal, CERCLA joins with the Resource Conservation and Recovery Act (RCRA) to provide "wrap-around" coverage. While RCRA establishes a cradle-to-grave regulatory program for present hazardous waste activities, CERCLA establishes a comprehensive response program for past hazardous waste activities.

It should be noted that many CERCLA provisions, which will be discussed below, go beyond the old waste-site cleanup program.

1/   42 U.S.C. §§9601 et seq.

Thousands of business establishments, for instance, are subject to reporting requirements for spills and other kinds of environmental "releases." The overwhelming emphasis of CERCLA has been and will continue to be, however, on old waste sites. The organization of this chapter reflects that emphasis.

1.2 CERCLA: Center of Controversies

Certainly no environmental statute in the 1980s has consumed more of EPA's and Congress' time and energy than CERCLA. Bitter disputes over CERCLA policies were at the heart of the "great purges" of 1982 when the EPA administrator and nearly all of her top assistants were forced out of office.

Unfortunately for the American public, over the last three years Congress has been preoccupied with raking EPA over the coals and attempting to amend CERCLA in a manner that would drastically curtail EPA's discretion. This preoccupation and the resulting delays in reauthorizing CERCLA have significantly disrupted the waste site cleanup program.

1.3 1986 Amendments to CERCLA

In the very last days of the 99th Congress, Congress finally passed (and the president signed on October 17, 1986) massive new amendments to CERCLA. 2/ These amendments (176 pages) are exactly four times longer than the 1980 law (44 pages) they amend. Overall, these amendments greatly curtail EPA's discretion and/or create additional confusion with lengthy, complex, and detailed language. The amendments also require EPA to perform many more tasks and demand that activities start at many more sites on tight schedules.

Unfortunately, the level of complexity in the new statutory language is almost certain to create additional delays as EPA, interested parties, and the courts fight over a multitude of interpretative issues. In addition, new provisions which will drastically increase the costs of cleaning up each site are likely to make cleanup "settlements" much more difficult to obtain. And because EPA's cleanup program has been slowed down so much because of congressional reauthorization delays, it will take a long time for

---

2/ Public Law No. 99-499.

EPA to regain the momentum it had been building. While Congress has certainly raised great expectations with its grandiose 1986 amendments, it has also probably made it impossible for EPA to live up to these expectations.

1.4 Interpreting the 1986 Amendments

Before turning to an analysis of the statute, there is one major caveat. The 1986 amendments alter CERCLA in so many fundamental ways that one can analyze most key issues only by analyzing the amendments. Yet as this is being written (October 1986), the ink on the amendments is barely dry. EPA and court interpretations of these numerous complex statutory provisions are obviously months and in some cases years away.

Moreover, the 1986 legislative history is unhelpful on many key issues. Provisions in the final House bill were generally very different from the final Senate bill, and the House-Senate conferees had a most difficult time crafting compromise legislative language. Once compromises were reached, they were extremely delicate, and staffers writing the Conference Report 3/ were generally unable to add the kind of expansive "gloss" to which they are accustomed. In large part, then—at least on the most controversial issues—the Conference Report offers nothing more than a cold and unilluminating summary of the legislative language.

On the other hand, there were many individual interpretative statements entered into the Congressional Record to "explain" the final bill. These statements were not subject to any such restraints, and many of them offer wild views of what the Act "really" means. 4/ Moreover, these statements are often blatantly contradicted by other members' statements.

As Mr. Dingell, chairman of the House Conferees, aptly remarked: "Such statements are nothing more than opinions of individual members about what the legislation might have said or what they wish it said." 5/

3/ H.R. Report 99-962, October 3, 1986, is referred to throughout this paper as the "Conference Report."

4/ See Congressional Records of October 3, 1986, S. 14895-14943, and October 8, 1986, H. 9561-9634.

Thus, in the absence of legislative history which is both informative and reliable, and with the current absence of administrative or judicial interpretations, the 1986 amendments can only be analyzed by reference to the statutory language. At least some of this language is sufficiently plain, and much of it builds upon language and concepts in prior legislative and/or administrative policies, so worthwhile analyses can still be performed at this time.

2.0 CERCLA OVERVIEW

In analyzing CERCLA, it is first important to understand a few key concepts and definitions. These will be explored in Section 3.0.

As indicated above, CERCLA's most fundamental purposes are to provide for inactive waste site cleanups and for spill (and other "release") reports and responses. The waste site cleanup program will be described in Section 4.0 and the release reporting and emergency response program will be discussed in Section 5.0.

In the 1986 CERCLA amendments, Congress added a totally new title for "Emergency Planning and Community Right-to-Know." This new title was added in reaction to disasters or near-disasters in India and West Virgina, and will be discussed in Section 6.0.

In both 1980 and 1986, Congress rejected hard-fought proposals to extend CERCLA into a full-blown damage assessment and collection program for alleged personal injury or private property damages. This has generally been referred to as the "Victims Compensation" issue. Nevertheless, the 1986 amendments contain elements which are designed to facilitate and promote private "toxic tort" suits, and they will be discussed in section 7.0.

Unlike most federal environmental programs which are funded out of general revenues, CERCLA activities are funded out of a special "Superfund" trust fund. Congress enacted special industry taxes in 1980 to provide most of this funding, and enacted new types of industry taxes in 1986. In 1980, Congress established a $1.6 billion funding level. EPA has now spent (or obligated) this amount, and in 1986, Congress established a $9 billion funding level to be raised over the next five years. The taxes enacted to raise these Superfund dollars will briefly be described in section 8.0.

Finally, there are several miscellaneous provisions which

5/   Congressional Record, October 8 1986, H. 9563, col. 1.

should be noted. These provisions will be briefly discussed in section 9.0.

3.0 KEY CONCEPTS AND DEFINITIONS

Certain basic concepts and definitions help tie together the various parts of CERCLA. Above all, it is important to understand that the overall scope of CERCLA is far broader than any of the other federal environmental statutes. The word "Comprehensive" in the statute's title is certainly accurate.

While the Clean Air Act deals with air and the Clean Water Act deals with water, CERCLA covers all environmental media: air, surface water, groundwater, and soil. Moreover, unlike the specific media statutes, CERCLA can apply directly to any type of industrial, commercial, or even non-commercial facility regardless of whether there are specific regulations affecting that type of facility and regardless of how that facility might impact on the environment (i.e., through stacks, pipes, impoundments, etc.)

Events that may trigger CERCLA response or liability would be the release or "threat of" release into the environment of a hazardous substance or pollutant or contaminant. Each of these terms is defined quite broadly in CERCLA.

3.1 CERCLA "Hazardous Substance" Defined

Under CERCLA §101(14) a "hazardous substance" is any substance EPA has designated for special consideration under the Clean Air Act (CAA), Clean Water Act (CWA), or TSCA (Toxic Substances Control Act), and any "hazardous waste" under RCRA. Moreover, EPA must designate additional substances as hazardous which "may" present substantial danger to health and the environment. 6/ EPA maintains and updates a list of all such "hazardous substances" in 40 CFR part 302. As of this writing, there are a total of 717 substances on the list. 7/

Congress has excluded only two basic types of substances from the definition of "hazardous substances": (1) petroleum and (2) natural gas (and synthetic gas usable for fuel). 8/ As will be seen

---

6/   §102(a).

7/   See section 5.2 of this chapter.

8/   §101(14), last sentence.

below, petroleum might be regulated in certain ways under
CERCLA, but not as a "hazardous substance."

3.2 CERCLA "Pollutant or Contaminant" Defined

Under CERCLA §101(33) a "pollutant or contaminant" can be
any other substance not on the list of hazardous substances which
"will or may reasonably be anticipated to cause" any type of adverse
effects in organisms and/or their offspring.   Again, petroleum and
natural gas are excluded. 9/

By the time one reads together the definitions of "hazardous
substance" and "pollutant or contaminant," one can safely conclude
that any substance EPA might ever want to cover is covered by
CERCLA authority.   One might in fact wonder why Congress even
bothered to distinguish between "hazardous substances" and "pollutants or contaminants."

There are at least two fundamental consequences of this distinction.   First, while EPA can respond to either type of substance,
private parties may be liable for cleanup costs and natural resources
damages only to the extent "hazardous substances" are involved.
Second, private parties are liable for reporting certain "releases"
only to the extent "hazardous substances" are involved. With respect
to most other major provisions of CERCLA, however, the distinction
has no real consequence.

3.3 CERCLA "Release" Defined

A "release" is defined extremely broadly so that any way a substance can enter the environment is covered ("spilling, leaking,
pumping," etc.). 10/ Congress has for policy or political reasons
excluded four types of activities from the definition, however:
(1) workplace exposures (covered by OSHA); (2) vehicular engine
exhausts; (3) certain radioactive contamination covered by other
statutes; and (4) the "normal" application of fertilizer. 11/

There is also a "federally permitted release" concept, keyed
to eleven types of releases specifically allowed under other environ-

---

9/   §101(33), last sentence.

10/ §101(22).

11/ §101(22).

mental statutes (CAA, CWA, etc.). 12/ For instance, any release in compliance with an NPDES permit under the CWA is a "federally permitted release." 13/

The "federally permitted release" versus other kinds of "releases" distinction is analogous to the "hazardous substance" versus "pollutant or contaminant" distinction discussed above. That is, EPA has full response and cleanup authority with respect to federally permitted releases; but private parties neither have liability for such releases, nor are they obligated to report them. 14/

3.4 CERCLA "Environment" Defined

Finally, "environment" is defined almost as broadly as possible. 15/ It includes all navigable and other surface waters, groundwaters, drinking water supplies, land surface or subsurface strata, and ambient air within the U.S. jurisdiction. Perhaps the only limitation of note would be that "indoor" air is not included, as EPA's Clean Air Act regulations have always defined "ambient" air to exclude indoor air. 16/

4.0 INACTIVE WASTE-SITE CLEANUP (OR "REMEDIAL") PROGRAM

The program for providing long-term remedial action at inactive waste sites is CERCLA's primary focus.

4.1 Distinctions between "Removal" and "Remedial" Actions and Selection of National Priorities List (NPL) Sites for Remedial Action

Under Section 104(a)(1), whenever there is a "release" or "substantial threat" of a release into the "environment" of any (1) hazardous substance or (2) pollutant or contaminant under cir-

---

12/ §101(10)(A).

13/ §101(10)(A).

14/ §§107(j); 103(b)(2).

15/ §101(8).

16/ 40 CFR §50.1(e).

cumstances where the pollutant or contaminant "may" present an imminent and substantial danger, EPA is authorized to undertake "removal" and/or "remedial" action. Both these terms are defined in CERCLA §101.

4.1.1. Removal or Remedial Action

In general terms a "removal" is a short-term, limited response to a more manageable problem while a "remedy" is a longer term, more permanent and expensive solution for a more complex problem. For instance, EPA may respond to a tank truck spill by siphoning all spilled materials and digging up and hauling away a few inches of contaminated soil so that there is no contamination left at the site. This would be a "removal." Or EPA may enter a site where a few dozen drums of old waste are stored and haul them away. Again, this would be a "removal." On the other hand, an old landfill covering 60 acres with waste 100 feet deep may require a 4-year construction program and a 30-year groundwater pumping and treating program. This would be a "remedy."

Of course, at some sites, both a "removal" and a "remedy" might be appropriate. For instance as a preliminary stage toward a final "remedy" at an old landfill, it may be necessary to step in and "remove" a bunch of old drums quickly to avoid fires or explosions, or prevent extra leaking that would only make the final remedy more difficult.

The remainder of this section 4.0 will focus on the "remedial" program under CERCLA (again, with the understanding that "removal" actions might often be part of a "remedy.") "Removal" actions will be discussed in section 5.0.

4.1.2 State Contract or Cooperative Agreement

There are two basic prerequisites to undertaking a remedial action which should be understood at the outset. First, CERCLA precludes EPA from taking any remedial action at a site unless EPA has first entered into a "contract or cooperative agreement" with the state in which the site is located. This agreement must obligate the state to undertake several measures, 17/ the most important of which is that the state agrees to to finance 10 percent of the

---

17/ See §104(c)(3).

remedy (or 50 percent in the case of a state-operated site).

4.1.3 National Priorities List

Second, under EPA regulations, only those sites listed on the "National Priorities List" (NPL) will be eligible for remedial action. 18/ It is thus important to understand what the NPL is and how sites may be placed on it.

Since the 1980 CERCLA, §105(8) has required EPA to develop "criteria" for determining priorities among sites for purposes of taking remedial actions and to develop and maintain a "list" of such "national priorities" when such sites have been examined in accordance with these criteria.

As part of its National Contingency Plan (NCP) regulations, discussed in greater detail in section 4.4 below, EPA has set forth a structured program for evaluating sites and placing some of them on the NPL. Generally, from among the over 20,000 sites reported to EPA which might need remedial action, EPA has established a "winnowing down" process. Any site which comes to EPA's attention will receive a "preliminary assessment" (often an "armchair" review of data) to determine if further attention is currently needed.

Sites not "discarded" at this stage will next receive a physical "site inspection." After such an inspection many sites will become candidates for a more thorough evaluation and "scoring" under the "hazard ranking system" (HRS). 19/ Under the HRS (also known as the "MITRE model") pertinent data about a site are evaluated and "scored." A site may be given various scores for waste volume, waste toxicity, distance to population, distance to underground drinking water, etc. Under current EPA policy, any site that receives a score of 28.50 or above will be included on the NPL. As of October 1986, EPA has placed 703 sites on the NPL and has proposed to add an additional 185 sites. 20/

4.2 Steps in the Remedial Process for NPL Sites

18/ 40 CFR §300.66(c)(2).

19/ 40 CFR 300.66(b).

20/ 51 FR 21054, June 10, 1986.

As will be described more fully below, providing a "remedy" for an NPL site can be a massive and complex legal/scientific/engineering/construction undertaking. For each site there must be a distinct "pipeline" of activities, and it would be impossible to initiate work at all sites at once. The following generally describes EPA's approach to sites once they are on the NPL. 21/

4.2.1 Superfund Comprehensive Accomplishments Plan (SCAP)

EPA does not have the resources to process cleanup activities for all NPL sites at once. It accordingly develops a plan for each fiscal year—the "Superfund Comprehensive Accomplishments Plan" or "SCAP." The SCAP shows for each fiscal quarter which stage of the cleanup process (if any) is scheduled for each NPL site. The SCAP, which can be obtained under the Freedom of Information Act, may provide useful planning intelligence to parties who suspect they may be involved with a particular site.

4.2.2 Studies and Remedy Selection

Under the relevant statutory and regulatory provisions discussed in section 4.4 below, EPA may select a cleanup remedy at a site from a great variety of options, and the costs of these options may vary widely. This is the process in which EPA determines "how clean is clean" and "how expensive is expensive."

For this crucial process, there are basically two stages: (1) the performance of a "Remedial Investigation/Feasibility Study" (RI/FS), following the preparation of a "Work Plan" for the RI/FS; and (2) EPA's selection of the remedy with a "Record of Decision" (ROD).

4.2.3 Remedial Investigation/Feasibility Study (RI/FS)

The "Remedial Investigation" and "Feasibility Study" are two studies which are almost always performed together. The RI will attempt to characterize with precision the conditions at a site. The

---

21/ The description of the remedial process in section 4.2 is largely derived from a chapter by David B. Graham and Richard G. Stoll to be included in a forthcoming ALI-ABA book entitled "Practical Guide to Environmental Law." This chapter has also been published in ALI-ABA's Practical Real Estate Lawyer, Vol. 2, No. 5, September 1986, at p.41.

RI will identify the source and extent of contamination, the pathways of possible migration or releases to the environment, and the extent of potential human or other environmental exposure to contamination. The RI will present data on these matters in sufficient detail to develop and evaluate remedial alternatives.

Based upon the RI information, the FS will present a series of specific engineering or construction alternatives for cleaning up a site. For each major alternative presented, there will be a detailed analysis of the costs, effects, engineering feasibility, and environmental impact.

The RI/FS study process is a major effort which often takes more than a year. EPA's guidance documents for performing the RI and the FS total 340 pages. EPA has estimated the average cost of an RI/FS to be $800,000, and many have cost substantially more.

One recent EPA practice, now that RI/FSs have become such a major project, is to require a "work plan" to precede an RI/FS. The work plan—which may itself cost $30 to $50 thousand—sets forth in detail such things as the proposed type of groundwater and soil sampling (number and parameters to be tested), the location and depths of monitoring wells, the timing for accomplishing certain tasks, and generally the degree to which the site will be studied and how alternatives will be developed.

The degree to which various study requirements are written into or excluded from the work plan will largely determine the cost of the RI/FS. The work plan will also directly affect the scope of the RI/FS, and may accordingly affect the scope of remedial options presented.

4.2.4 Record of Decision (ROD)

Once the RI/FS has presented EPA with the detailed cost/effectiveness estimates of several cleanup options, EPA must select the appropriate option in light of the requirements of new CERCLA §121 (discussed in section 4.4 below.) In some RI/FSs, as many as ten to fifteen alternatives may be presented, ranging from a "no action" alternative (costing perhaps nothing) to a "total exhumation and incineration" alternative costing a billion dollars. Under the 1980 CERCLA, the more likely candidates were somewhere in between; under the 1986 CERCLA the more likely candidates will almost certainly be on the high side.

4.2.5 Public Participation in Records of Decision
EPA prepares and publishes a proposed "Record of Decision" (ROD) in which it announces and explains its tentative selection from among the RI/FS options. EPA will then provide an opportunity for written comments and the opportunity for an informal hearing.

Under the 1986 amendments, this process will be much more formal and elaborate than in the past. Under new CERCLA §117, EPA must abide by detailed "public participation" requirements at each site. Moreover, to assure that the "public" will "participate" (even if they had otherwise not been so inclined) EPA can at each site now give "Supergrants" of $50,000 and even more to anyone to "facilitate" public participation. 22/

As if federally-funded citizens' "participation" were not enough, new CERCLA §121(f) requires EPA to go to extraordinary lengths to assure "State involvement" in the ROD process. When all is said and done, EPA's final ROD selection is certain to have been accomplished only after jumping extensive and arduous procedural hurdles.

Finally, EPA will issue a ROD document in which is responds to the public comments and further explains the basis for its final decision.

4.2.6 Design and Construction
At the ROD stage, the remedial alternative which EPA selects will be presented in fairly basic and conceptual terms and the costs will be only estimates. It is at the "design" stage that the detailed engineering plans are developed, site specifications are calculated, and all site-specific factors are incorporated into the general remedial concept. These detailed plans and specifications usually take 9-12 months to prepare and can cost in the low millions.

Finally, once design is complete, a construction contract or contracts may be awarded for the actual remedial work. These "constructions" are often complex, multi-phase projects involving many discrete tasks and different types of subcontractors over time.

In addition to the capital costs of the initial construction, there is often a long-term (20-30 years) "operation and maintenance" ("O&M") phase which is an integral part of the project. For instance,

---

22/ §117(e)(2).

after some waste has been removed, the site has been capped, and
slurry walls have been erected during "construction," there may be a
30-year program of groundwater pumping and treating in the "O&M"
phase. The costs of this phase can be considerable.

4.3 Liability of Responsible Parties and Financing Options for Remedial Actions

It is obvious that the site planning, investigation, study,
remedy selection, design, construction, and operation and
maintenance processes all cost money—sometimes very significant
sums. Where does this money come from?

CERCLA authorizes EPA to draw upon two basic types of
resources to pay for waste site remedies: (1) from the "Superfund"—
the federal trust fund discussed in section 8.0 below; and (2) under
the liability scheme of CERCLA, from the pockets of "responsible
parties" with certain types of relationships to the site. Responsible
parties' liabilities cover not only the actual construction costs, but
also the investigation, RI/FS, and design costs. The types of parties
who may be liable for site remedial costs are specified in CERCLA
§107(a) as follows:

(1)   present and past "owners or operators" of the site;

(2)   parties who transported wastes to the site ("trans-
        porters"); and

(3)   parties (usually referred to as "generators") who arranged
        for wastes to be disposed or treated at the site, either
        directly with an owner/operator or indirectly with a
        transporter.

To illustrate, assume that a commercial landfill accepted
hazardous wastes for disposal from 1960 to 1970, during which time
the landfill was owned and operated by company A. In 1975, five
years after the landfill was totally closed, company B bought the
property on which the landfill is located.

Assume further that during the landfill's operation, companies
C, D, E and F were in the hauling business and transported hazardous
wastes from manufacturing plants to the landfill for disposal.
Assume finally that during these years, companies G through Z were
in various manufacturing businesses (aircraft, auto, chemical,
computers, oil, steel, etc.), produced ("generated") hazardous waste

as a byproduct of their manufacturing, and had individually arranged with transporter C, D, E and/or F to have their waste disposed.

Now, in 1986, the landfill is a NPL site and EPA has determined through the RI/FS and ROD process that a $150 million cleanup is necessary. Under CERCLA, as interpreted by numerous court decisions, any of parties A through Z may be liable or some or all of the $150 million. This liability has the following characteristics:

(1)   it is retroactive, because parties are liable for acts or omissions occurring well before the date of CERCLA's enactment (1980); 23/

(2)   it is strict, because it is irrelevant that a generator selected a licensed hauler to take waste to a licensed landfill, that all legal requirements at the time were fully met, and/or that a party used all due care; 24/

(3)   it may in appropriate cases be joint and several, because one party out of many may be held liable for more than his/her "share" under any fair allocation, and may in fact be held liable for the entire site cleanup. 25/

The 1986 CERCLA amendments make few significant changes to the basic liability scheme. They exempt from the definition of "owner or operator," however, a unit of state or local government which acquired ownership involuntarily (through tax delinquencies, abandonments, etc.). 26/

And the 1986 amendments contain a limited defense for owners of facilities who acquire them after all disposal has taken place 27/.

23/ Caldwell v. Gurley Refining Company, 755 F.2d 645 (8th Cir. 1985) U.S. v. South Carolina Recycling and Disposal, Inc., 21 Env't. Rep. Cas. 1577 (D.S.C. 1984).

24/ State of New York v. Shore Realty Corp., 759 F.2d 1032 (2d Cir. 1985).

25/ U.S. v. Chem-Dyne Corp., 572 F. Supp. 802 (S.D. Ohio 1983); U.S. v. A&F Materials Company, 578 F. Supp. 1249 (S.D. Ill. 1984).

26/ § 101(20)(D).

27/ § 101(35).

Essentially, a "subsequent" owner seeking to avail himself of such a defense must show that after all reasonable efforts consistent with "good commercial practice in an effort to minimize liability," he still did not know "and had no reason to know" that disposal took place on the property. 28/

4.4 Determining the Appropriate Extent of the Remedy at a Site ("How Clean is Clean" or "How Expensive is Expensive")

4.4.1 Overview and Introduction

CERCLA's "how clean is clean" policy has developed in four basic stages, from:

(1)   the 1980 statute which gave EPA almost total discretion to make rational decisions on a site-by-site basis; to

(2)   1982 EPA regulations which preserved most of this discretion; to

(3)   1985 EPA regulations with many new ambiguous provisions but with an overall thrust towards more expensive cleanups; to

(4)   the 1986 CERCLA amendments which greatly curtail EPA's discretion and point inexorably toward even more expensive cleanups—in almost total disregard of whether there will be any further health/environmental benefits at a site.

As will be seen, under the 1986 amendments, this entire issue might be better described as "how expensive is expensive." In fact, senior EPA officials have already projected the costly impacts. Gene A. Lucero, EPA's Director of Waste Programs Enforcement, recently predicted that average cleanup costs could go from $9 million per site under prior law to between $30-$50 million under the 1986 statute. Lucero added that when the new statute's groundwater cleanup requirements are considered, just one site's cleanup under the new statute could cost between $300-600 million. 29/

28/ Id.

29/ 1 BNA Toxics Law Reporter, No. 16, p.451, September 24, 1986.

4.4.2   Background and History

One of the most chronically difficult CERCLA issues has been how to determine the "appropriate extent of the remedy" at a particular site. Among CERCLA cognoscenti, this is known as the "how clean is clean" issue.

For instance, should all waste and contaminated soil at an old landfill be completely excavated for offsite disposal or incineration? Or should the waste and contaminated soil be "contained" in place to prevent further migration? If so, by which of many alternative containment methods? Or should the nearby groundwater that now has X parts per billion (ppb) of a hazardous substance be treated down to Y ppb or even zero ppb?

The answers to these questions could, up to a point, present different results in the degree of health and environmental protection at any site and will present extremely different results in terms of cleanup costs. One remedial option may cost $20 million and provide X level of protection; another may cost $40 million and provide 3X level of protection; while another may cost $400 million and still provide 3X level of protection.

4.4.2.1 1980 CERCLA: Flexibility

The 1980 CERCLA did not answer these questions. Instead, it gave EPA discretion to deal with sites on a case-by-case basis. The statute simply directed EPA to ensure that cleanup measures "protect the public health and welfare and the environment." 30/ While the statute required cost analyses of alternatives and "cost-effective" cleanup options, 31/ it did not elaborate any further. Rather, it directed EPA to publish "National Contingency Plan" (NCP) regulations which would set forth "methods and criteria for determining" the appropriate extent of the cleanup remedies. 32/

30/ §104(a)(1).

31/ § 105(2) and (7).

32/ §105(3).

4.4.2.2 1982 NCP and the Emerging Dispute Over "Standards"
EPA published in 1982 an NCP which detailed requirements for analyzing the nature of the problem and arraying the costs and effectiveness of several types of cleanup alternatives at each site. This NCP did not, however, specify any "cleanup standards." It simply directed that each remedy represent the lowest cost alternative that effectively protects public health, welfare, or the environment. 33/

In adopting this flexible approach, EPA rejected environmental groups' arguments that CERCLA cleanups should meet uniform, nationally applicable standards developed under other environmental laws. For instance, EPA has promulgated innumerable standards under the Resource Conservation and Recovery Act (RCRA) that apply to new and currently operating hazardous waste facilities. 34/

EPA has also issued numerical concentration standards under the Safe Drinking Water Act that public water systems must ensure are not exceeded in their customers' household water. It has also approved many state water quality standards under the Clean Water Act that generally are designed to protect a "fishable-swimmable" water quality in surface waters. Because none of these standards were developed with the old waste site problem in mind, EPA stated in 1982 that a "rigid requirement" to apply such standards at old waste sites would "impose the use of potentially inappropriate levels of cleanup." 35/

As will be seen below, this 1982 dispute over using standards from other environmental laws has been at the center of the "how clean is clean" controversy. As will also be seen, EPA's 1982 position has been turned around about 179 degrees.

4.4.2.3 1985 NCP: First Resolution of Standards Issue
The Environmental Defense Fund and the State of New Jersey petitioned for judicial review of the 1982 NCP, and they raised the "lack of specified cleanup standards" as their primary issue. To

---

33/ 47 FR 31180, et seq., July 16, 1982.

34/ Facilities closed by 1980 are generally not subject to RCRA regulations for hazardous wastes.

35/ 47 FR at 10978.

resolve this litigation, EPA entered into a settlement agreement in early 1984 under which EPA agreed to propose NCP amendments requiring that "relevant" standards and criteria from other federal environmental programs "be used," with the opportunity for "adjustment" in determining the appropriate extent of remedy. 36/

EPA issued its NCP revisions on November 20, 1985. 37/ In this regulation, EPA took a giant and unfortunate leap forward from its judicial obligation to "use" standards with the opportunity for "adjustment." Instead, it obligated itself to meet certain standards in certain (albeit vague) situation.

Among the most basic requirements of EPA's 1985 NCP were:

(1)   Any remedy at any site must protect health and the environment;

(2)   Each remedy (except as noted below) must meet "applicable or relevant and appropriate Federal public health and environmental requirements that have been identified for the specific site";

(3)   Other federal criteria, guidance, and state standards must be considered and may be used, with "adjustments for site-specific circumstances"; and

(4)   The foregoing requirements could be waived in five circumstances:

   (i)   where the cleanup in question is only a stage toward a more comprehensive cleanup;

   (ii)   where Superfund dollars are to be used, and for "fund-balancing" concerns, there is a need to conserve fund dollars for use at other sites;

   (iii)   where a selected remedy would be technically impracticable from an engineering perspective;

36/   EDF v. EPA, D.C. Cir. No. 82-2234, Settlement Agreement entered February 1, 1984.

37/   50 FR 47912 et seq.

(iv) where the remedy would have unacceptable environmental impacts; or

(v) where the remedy is to be achieved through litigation against liable parties and the litigation would "probably not result" in the desired remedy. 38/

EPA's NCP regulations did not define just what "applicable/ relevant/appropriate" meant at a particular site. 39/ From EPA's practice in applying ARA, however, it is certainly clear that most RCRA standards will be applied at CERCLA land disposal sites. Thus under EPA's interpretations, if an old pre-RCRA landfill is being closed, a RCRA "cap" would be required and the RCRA "ground-water protection standard" would have to be met.

4.4.3 1986 CERCLA Amendments; New Cleanup Standards

Section 121(a) of the 1986 amendments adds a new Section 121 to CERCLA. This lengthy new section is entitled "Cleanup Standards" and is organized into six subsections.

4.4.3.1 Selection of Remedial Action—§121(a)

This subsection states the basic rule that all CERCLA response actions—whether fund financed under §104 or privately performed under §106—must assure compliance with the new cleanup standards. This subsection also provides, as the original CERCLA stated, that remedial actions are to be "cost effective."

Those who might infer from that phrase that costs play a meaningful role will—as explained below—have their hopes dashed by the remaining provisions of Section 121. Moreover, §121(a) makes clear that in evaluating cost-effectiveness, EPA must consider the "total short and long-term costs" for the entire period during which such activities will be required.

38/ 40 CFR 300.68(i), 50 FR 47975, November 20, 1985.

39/ Because Congress adopted this phrase in the 1986 CERCLA amendments and it is a pivotal concept which will be mentioned often below, it is hereby dubbed "ARA."

Thus, in the past EPA may have found it was more "cost effective" to spend $20 million now on site stabilization and then $2 million a year for 40 years on groundwater pumping and treatment, as compared to spending $80 million now to remove all hazardous substances from the soil and water. Under the new law, §121(a) would strongly lead toward the latter result and, as seen below, other subsections would even more strongly favor more "permanent" solutions.

4.4.3.2 General Rules—§121(b)

This subsection states two basic principles that are to govern the selection of remedies at all sites:

(1) "Treatment" is strongly preferred over "disposal" or "leaving in place" options. Treatment which "permanently and significantly reduces" the hazardous substances involved is to be "preferred" over other remedies and EPA must select remedies that utilize "permanent solutions" and alternative treatment technologies "to the maximum extent practicable."

Moreover, this subsection directs EPA in assessing alternatives to take into account factors which logically push for a strong bias in favor of destruction, treatment, and "permanent" remedies as opposed to less expensive "containment" or disposal options.

(2) Offsite disposal is clearly disfavored. Offsite transport and disposal of untreated waste is the "least favored" alternative where "practicable" treatment technologies are available. To further bias the matter, §121(b) essentially provides in paragraph (2) that a technology may be "available" even if it has never been used before.

In deciding whether to require such an unproven technology, EPA may take into account the technology's "degree of support" by parties "interested in the site." Presumably, EPA can therefore allow the "good vibrations" of citizens' groups or other interests to override the judgment of engineers and scientists as to a technology's availability.

It is interesting to note that there are no biases against offsite transport for treatment, even if the transportation would be coast-to-coast. As explained below, §121(d)(3) further skews the bias against offsite disposal.

4.4.3.3. Review—§121(c)

To further emphasize the bias toward total and permanent treatment/destruction, this subsection requires the following whenever the remedy will result in "any hazardous substances, pollutants, or contaminants remaining at the site" (emphasis added):

(1)   EPA must review the site at least each five years to assure that health and the environment are still being protected;

(2)   EPA must take additional action at such sites any time in the future when warranted; and

(3)   EPA must report to Congress on all such sites and the results of all reviews and/or actions.

4.4.3.4 Degree of Cleanup—§121(d)

This is the most lengthy and complex subsection and gets to the heart of the "standards" issue.   It is organized into four paragraphs.

4.4.3.4.1 General Cleanup Principles

Paragraph §121(d)(1) repeats the basic principle that all remedies must assure protection of health and the environment. It also states—echoing EPA's last NCP and foreshadowing the details of paragraph (d)(2)—that remedial actions are to be "relevant and appropriate" to the circumstances.

4.4.3.4.2 Applicable/Relevant/Appropriate Concepts

Paragraph §121(d)(2), which contains probably the most important provisions in Section 121, builds upon and expands many of EPA's "applicable/relevant/appropriate" (ARA) concepts from the last NCP. It is important to note that it applies when "any" hazardous substance, pollutant or contaminant will remain onsite. 40/ Thus, in light of the five-year review procedures of §121(c) discussed above, even sites that meet all the requirements of paragraph (d) must still be reviewed each five years (unless by operation of paragraph (d) all hazardous substances, pollutants, and contaminants are removed). Moreover, EPA is strongly encouraged to select a remedy

---

40/ §121(d)(2)(A), first sentence.

that <u>totally</u> removes <u>all</u> hazardous substances from a site so EPA will not have to fool around with all the incredibly complex words and phrases of §121(d).

4.4.3.4.2.1 General "ARA" Requirements

Paragraph §121(d)(2) first provides that if certain types of federal <u>or state</u> requirements are "legally applicable" to the substance or pollutant or contaminant "concerned," or are "relevant and appropriate" under the circumstances, then the remedial action shall require that each substance of concern "at least attain" such requirement. The types of federal/state requirements subject to this ARA standard are specified in §121(d)(2)(A) as follows:

(i)   Any standard, requirement, criteria, or limitation under any Federal environmental law, including, but not limited to, the Toxic Substances Control Act, the Safe Drinking Water Act, the Clean Air Act, the Clean Water Act, the Marine Protection, Research and Sanctuaries Act, or the Solid Waste Disposal Act [RCRA];

(ii)   Any promulgated standard, requirement, criteria, or limitation under a State environmental or facility siting law that is more stringent than any Federal standard, requirement, criteria, or limitation, including each such State standard, requirement, criteria, or limitation contained in a program approved, authorized or delegated by the Administrator under a statute cited in subparagraph (A), and that has identified to the President by the State in a timely manner.

With respect to federal requirements, the paragraph does not nail down precisely which are "applicable" or "relevant or appropriate" in which circumstances, so there will still be much for EPA and the courts to interpret. It is safe to assume from prior EPA practice with these words, however, that at landfill cleanups, virtually all substantive RCRA standards will be applied. It is important to note that the statute here significantly expands upon EPA's NCP by requiring adherence to <u>state</u> requirements and to federal <u>criteria</u> (not just standards).

The only additional guidance provided in §121(d) is that remedial actions must "at least attain" maximum contaminant level "goals" under the Safe Drinking Water Act and water quality criteria under the Clean Water Act where such goals or criteria are relevant and appropriate under the circumstances. 41/ Moreover, with respect to determining whether water quality criteria are relevant or appropriate, EPA is to consider several factors, such as the "designated or potential use of the surface or groundwater" and the purposes for which such criteria were developed. 42/

4.4.3.4.2.2 Severe Restrictions on Alternative Concentration Limits ("ACLs")

As noted earlier, RCRA standards would probably be the most widely applied set of ARA requirements for most Superfund waste sites. Under EPA's RCRA regulations for land disposal, EPA has established a "groundwater protection standard." 43/ That standard can be met at each RCRA site either (1) by showing compliance with a number of concentration limits which have been established under the Safe Drinking Water Act, or (2) respecting constituents of concern at a site for which such concentration limits have not been set, by showing no excess above "background" for such constitutents. 44/

In issuing its RCRA regulations, EPA realized that rigid adherence to such stringent levels (background in many cases) in all locations could produce great overkill. Because of the distance of some monitoring points from any source of drinking water and/or other hydrogeologic factors, some points in the groundwater can not rationally be assumed related to drinking water. To require stringent and extremely expensive controls at such points would provide no health benefits—such expenditures would benefit only the construction contractor or treatment facility carrying out the remedy.

EPA accordingly provided within its RCRA groundwater protection standard the opportunity—on a site by site basis—for the site owner to demonstrate that some alternative level of control at a particular point in the groundwater would be fully protective of public health and the environment. If the owner could carry this

---

41/ §121(d)(2)(A), last sentence.

42/ §121(d)(2)(B)(ii).

43/ 40 CFR §264.92

44/ 40 CFR §264.94

burden, he would then have to meet an "alternative concentration limit" (ACL) that would still have to be sufficiently stringent to protect health and the environment at that site. 45/

In one of the most controversial and hotly debated provisions in §121, Congress included major new restrictions on how EPA—in applying RCRA groundwater protection standards—can utilize these health-protective ACLs. By virtue of §121(d)(2)(B)(ii), an ACL cannot be used for any point which assumes human exposure beyond the facility boundary except in extremely limited conditions. These conditions would basically assure that ACLs could be used only where the waste site is near a river except in cases of very large "facilities." (Presumably where a river is nearby, the concentrations of concern would be diluted into undetectable levels through the flow and volume of the river.) Even in this situation, any conceivable human exposure to the groundwater (from the facility to the river) must be "precluded" through "enforceable measures."

In essence, the new CERCLA ACL policy assumes that all groundwater beyond the facility boundary—no matter where it is located and what its real or designated uses are—must be cleaned to meet the most stringent possible limits under the assumption that it will be used for drinking. The fact that some particular portion of groundwater will not or could not be used for drinking is—except possibly if it is near a river—irrelevant.

4.4.3.4.2.3 Safe Drinking Water Act Standards Status

By way of postscript to this section, it should be obvious that EPA's activities in setting standards under the Safe Drinking Water Act are taking on crucial importance to the level of control that may be required under CERCLA. As of October 1986, EPA has issued national primary drinking water regulations establishing maximum contaminant levels (MCLs) for 23 contaminants and published recommended MCLs (RMCLs) for nine contaminants under the Safe Drinking Water Act. 46/ In accordance with the SDWA Amendments of 1986, EPA is required to issue new national primary

---

45/ 40 CFR §264.94(b)

46/ See 40 CFR Part 141, Subpart B and G (MCLs) and Subpart F (RMCLs).

drinking water regulations which establish MCLs and publish "MCL goals" for 83 contaminants (which include the 23 already covered by existing MCLs) in accordance with a schedule set out in §101(b) of the Act. "MCL goals" under the new SDWA amendments are the equivalent of what was termed an "RMCL" prior to enactment of the amendments.

4.4.3.4.3 Offsite Disposal

Paragraph §121(d)(3) gives real life to the general statement in §121(b)(1) that offsite transport and disposal is the "least favored alternative." It provides that any offsite disposal facility, to be qualified to accept waste from a CERCLA site, must meet two extremely hard-to-meet requirements:

(1)   The waste management "unit" which will accept such waste is not releasing any hazardous waste into the groundwater, surface water, or soil; and

(2)   All other units at the facility are "being controlled" by an approved RCRA "corrective action" program.

4.4.3.4.4 Exceptions to the ARA Requirements

Paragraph §121(d)(4) provides six exceptions to the basic ARA requirements of §121(d)(2). It is important to note that §121(d)(4) does not provide any exception to the basic requirement that all remedies be sufficient to protect health and the environment. These six exceptions, which are largely adopted from EPA's most recent NCP (see discussion above), are as follows:

(A)   The selected action is only part of a total remedial action that will comply with the ARA requirements when completed;

(B)   Compliance with the ARA requirements would present greater health/environmental risks than alternative options;

(C)   Compliance with the ARA requirements is "technically impracticable from an engineering perspective";

(D)   The selected remedy will attain a "standard of performance" which is "equivalent" to an ARA-required standard
through use of another "method or approach";

(E)   With respect to a state requirement, the state has not
demonstrated consistent application of the requirement
in similar circumstances; and

(F)   Where the remedy is to be Fund-financed, meeting the
ARA standard would not provide "balance" between the
need for cleanup at the site in question considering the
amount of Fund resources that must be utilized at other
sites in need of cleanup. 47/

It remains to be seen how EPA and the courts will interpret
these exceptions, but (C), (E), and (F) may have some potential for
producing more reasonable remedies than would otherwise be required through rigid adherence to the ARA doctrine.

4.4.3.5 Permits and Enforcement
    The first paragraph 48/ of this subsection resolves a long-
standing controversy in EPA's favor. It provides that no "Federal,
State, or local permit" shall be required for any portion of a
CERCLA remedial action that is conducted on the site of the
facility being cleaned up.
    The second paragraph 49/ involves enforcement and is not
related to the extent of remedy issue. It generally gives the states
standing to enforce any federal or state requirement which must
apply at a site by virtue of §121 and provides that all consent
decrees arising from such state enforcement must include stipulated
penalties for decree violations in amounts not to exceed $25,000 per
day.

47/ §121(d)(4).

48/ §121(e).

49/ §121(e)(2).

4.4.3.6 State Involvement
This subsection 50/ contains detailed requirements for assuring "substantial and meaningful involvement" by each state in all phases of the selection of the remedy at all sites within the state. Working in tandem with the general "public participation" provisions of new §119 (which even include the authority for federal "technical assistance" grants of $50,000 or more to citizens groups at each site), EPA's determination of remedy process for each site is virtually guaranteed to be protracted and arduous.
This subsection also gives states standing in federal court to challenge EPA's selection of a remedy with which the state disagrees in certain situations.

4.4.4 Transition and "Grandfathering"
Finally, section 121(b) of the amendments (which does not actually amend CERCLA), specifies when the new rules of §121 would take effect at a particular site. It essentially provides as follows:

(1)   New §121 applies to any remedial action for which EPA has not formally entered a "record of decision" (ROD) prior to October 17, 1986; unless

(2)   the ROD is formally entered by November 16, 1986, and EPA certifies that the remedy selected complies "to the maximum extent practicable" with new §121; provided, that

(3)   Any existing ROD which is "reopened" after October 17, 1986 to "modify" or "supplement" the selection of remedy shall be subject to new §121.

Thus, under this "grandfather" provision, it is very possible that expensive work which has been ongoing at many sites for years could be rendered partially, largely, or totally superfluous and EPA or responsible parties might have to go back to "square one." For instance, parties may have spent $1 million over the last two years at a site performing an RI/FS that was designed to select a remedy under EPA's old NCP. But because a ROD has not been issued by

---

50/ §121(f).

October 17, 1986, new §121 now applies at the site. EPA (or interested citizens groups) might argue successfully at some sites that the emerging RI/FS is largely useless to determine the extent of remedy under new §121 and force a new RI/FS.

4.5 Procedures and Policies for Obtaining "Settlements" with Responsible Parties

4.5.1 Background

In accomplishing a cleanup (or any phase of a cleanup) EPA has a combination of options it may utilize. EPA may perform remedial work with Superfund dollars, and then sue responsible parties for reimbursement under the "cost recovery" authority of CERCLA §107, or EPA may issue an administrative order (or initiate litigation) seeking to compel responsible parties to perform remedial work with their own funds under the "abatement" authority of CERCLA §106.

Or EPA may seek through negotiations to persuade responsible parties to perform and/or pay for any or all stages of the remedial action at a site. This performance and/or payment would be in discharge of some or all of the parties' potential liabilities under §§106 and/or 107 of CERCLA.

EPA's policy has generally been to attempt to seek such "private party settlements" at any site where it appears there are parties willing and able to undertake such a cleanup. This "settlement" policy is grounded in large part on the fact that there are limitations on EPA's resources to perform cleanups and yet there are a tremendous number of current and future NPL sites. Accordingly, the national cleanup program can be greatly expedited if private parties can clean up some sites with their own management and resources at the same time EPA leads the cleanup at other sites (presumably where there are no financially sound responsible parties or where the parties involved are unable to agree to a cleanup).

At any particular site, different phases of a remedy might be handled by EPA or by the parties. For instance, at one site, EPA may fund and perform the entire remedy from RI/FS work plan through construction, then seem reimbursement through cost recovery. At another site, EPA may perform the RI/FS but the responsible parties may agree to fund an carry out the design and construction. At another, the parties may agree to perform the RI/FS but not the design and construction. At another, the parties may fund and perform the entire remedy.

In analyzing "settlement" policies for waste sites, it is important to understand that at many sites, hundreds of parties may have contributed to the site problem over a period of years. And sites vary in the degree to which solvent responsible parties can be found. Today's problem sites were generally caused by activities carried on years or even decades ago; records (if they ever existed) can get lost, witnesses can lose their memories or die, and companies can out out of business or go bankrupt. Moreover, at many sites, even among dozens or hundreds of "solvent" parties who are identified, they may be willing to consider settlements in many different degrees, ranging from "peace at any price" types to "over my dead body" types.

4.5.2 Key Settlement Issues and EPA's 1985 Policy

In EPA's implementation of CERCLA before the 1986 amendments, many issues developed regarding the degree to which EPA would enter into "settlements" with parties for site cleanups. EPA's positions on several key issues evolved in three basic stages: (1) in reaction to vicious congressional criticism about the alleged "sell out" nature of some early settlements, an extremely rigid "all or nothing" approach in late 1982 and early 1983 which made multiple party settlements virtually impossible; (2) a "draft memo" dated December 12, 1983 which took a slightly more flexible approach on certain issues; (3) a formally issued "Settlement Policy" in the Federal Register on February 5, 1985 51/ which took an even more flexible approach.

EPA's "evolution" on the most basic of these issues will first be described. 52/ Then Congress' response in the 1986 amendments will be explained.

4.5.2.1 No More 80 Percent Threshold

As a prime manifestation of the "all or nothing" approach, EPA officials had stated they would entertain settlements only for 100

51/ 50 FR 5034.

52/ This description of EPA's settlement policy evolution is largely derived from Stoll and Graham, Need for Changes in EPA's Settlement Policy, Natural Resources & Environment (ABA), Fall 1985, at 3 and 7.

percent of a site's cleanup costs. To illustrate, assume the following: at a site with 100 solvent parties, 5 of them contributed 50 percent of the waste. These five offer to "settle" their liabilities by paying 75 percent of the cleanup costs and leaving it up to EPA to collect the extra 25 percent from the remaining 95 parties. Under the early EPA policy, this offer would be automatically rejected.

By late 1983, EPA modified this policy by stating in a memo that it would at least "consider" settlement offers for less than 100 percent—but in no event would it entertain offers which accounted for less than 80 percent of a site's cleanup costs.

The 1985 Settlement Policy contained no such arbitrary threshold. Rather, it directed the regional offices to negotiate whenever there is an offer for a substantial proportion of the cleanup costs.

4.5.2.2 Use of Superfund Dollars for the "Orphan" Share

At many sites, numerous parties may have contributed wastes over the years. The facts may often reveal that some significant portion of the wastes is attributable to parties who are now insolvent, unknown, dead, or otherwise judgment-proof. This portion is known as the "orphan share" of waste at the site.

A long-standing issue has been whether the government would use Superfund dollars to pay for the orphan share when reaching settlements with solvent parties willing to pay their own shares. In 1983, EPA unequivocally stated that it would not allow Superfund dollars to be used in this fashion. The 1985 Settlement Policy stated that Superfund dollars may be used to cover the orphan share.

4.5.2.3 Information Sharing

If private parties are expected to work together to allocate costs and develop cleanup proposals, it is essential that they have relevant data and facts showing their respective roles and other parties' roles at the site (volume and nature of waste are among the most critical factors). EPA has in the past been inconsistent in its policies for releasing such information.

In the 1985 Settlement Policy, EPA stated that it would release such types of site information to the parties to facilitate discussions for settlement. The policy also provided that the regional offices could release such information to the negotiating parties even before all of the parties have responded to EPA's information requests.

4.5.2.4 Willingness to Accept "De Minimis" Contributors' Cash-Outs

At many multiple-party sites, some parties may account for extremely small portions of the total waste contributed. In the past, such parties have often wanted to settle by making an early cash payment to EPA and thereby avoid extensive and costly negotiations and litigation with EPA or many other parties.

EPA has in the past refused to recognize such types of de minimis cash-outs. The 1985 Settlement Policy acknowledged this procedure as an option.

4.5.2.5 Settlements in Phases; Responsible Party Performance of RI/FS

As another manifestation of an "all or nothing" approach, EPA had taken the position that it would not enter into a settlement for any particular phase of site cleanup (RI/FS, design, removal, remedy) unless the settling parties agreed to perform all phases of the cleanup. The 1985 Settlement Policy reversed this position, and EPA in fact began encouraging parties to at least enter into RI/FS settlements.

4.4.2.6 "Releases" from Liability

The degree to which EPA will enter into releases from liability, or "covenants not to sue," with respect to potential future liabilities has been an extremely controversial and difficult issue. On the one hand, EPA recognizes that a more complete release produces a stronger inducement for responsible parties to settle. This is because generally, when a party seeks to settle a matter, it is willing to trade the uncertainties of litigation for payment of a sum certain. Under a system in which a party can consider its "settlement" check only as a down payment to precede unspecified future installments, there will naturally be a great reluctance to settle.

On the other hand, EPA may be uncertain whether a particular long-term remedy for a site will perform as predicted. If contrary to expectations, the site is still in need of further cleanup after a remedy is performed, EPA has expressed a wish to keep responsible parties "on the hook" for these costs.

After a great deal of vacillation, EPA finally provided some guidance on this difficult issue in the 1985 Settlement Policy. The most basic position could be summarized as follows: "The better the remedy, the better the release." As the Settlement Policy articulated this general "sliding-scale" approach, "The [EPA] regions will have the flexibility to negotiate releases that are relatively expansive or relatively stringent, depending upon the degree of confidence that the Agency has in the remedy."53/

The Settlement Policy presented two examples of how EPA might have "confidence." First, with respect to remediation of groundwater contamination, it would regard an agreement to meet a "health based performance standard" as preferable to an agreement simply to install and apply a particular treatment technology. Second, a remedy that involved treatment of waste (such as burning in an industrial furnace) would be preferable to a remedy that involved land disposal. 54/

4.5.2.6.1 Reopeners

Regardless of how "expansive" the regions may wish to be in using this sliding-scale approach, the Settlement Policy imposed several significant limitations. For instance, it prescribed that "at a minimum" all settlement agreements must include a "re-opener" clause that allows the government to "modify" the agreement whenever the site conditions may in the future present an "imminent and substantial endangerment" because: (1) previously unknown conditions are discovered, or (2) additional scientific information becomes available about the conditions known at the time of the agreement. 55/

4.5.2.6.2 Releases for "Second Site" Disposal

In some remedies, EPA may decide to remove waste from the CERCLA site and dispose of it in a RCRA site (the "second site"). Many parties have long urged EPA in such situations to grant releases to the generators involved in the first site from any potential liability respecting the "second site." In its 1985 Settlement Policy, EPA refused to recognize this type of release.

53/ 50 FR at 5039.

54/ Id.

55/ 50 FR at 5040.

4.5.3 Settlements: The 1986 Amendments

The 1986 amendments add a new section 122 to CERCLA, entitled "Settlements." This section contains rather lengthy and detailed provisions which address many of the same issues EPA had been grappling with in its administrative settlement policies.

In general, this entire section gives EPA a great deal of discretion to enter into settlements under certain circumstances and with certain conditions, but it does not <u>require</u> EPA to enter into any type of settlement at any site. In fact, section 122 specifies that EPA's decision <u>not</u> to undertake settlement negotiations at a site is "not subject to judicial review." <u>56/</u>

With respect to the "80 percent threshold" issue, there is no requirement in §122 for <u>any</u> particular threshold. Presumably, EPA has the authority to enter into agreements with parties representing any portion of the total site cleanup costs. In fact, there is a paragraph entitled "mixed funding" which specifically authorizes EPA to agree to cover "certain [unspecified percentages] costs" of remedial actions responsible parties have agreed to perform. <u>57/</u>

Similarly, with respect to the "orphan share" issue, nothing in §122 (or any other section of CERCLA) precludes EPA from deciding that a certain portion of the site cleanup costs should be covered by Superfund dollars to account for "orphans." In the "mixed funding" paragraph mention above, <u>58/</u> there is a general exhortation for EPA to make "all reasonable efforts" to recover dollars it has used in mixed funding situations from non-settlors. The Conference Report stresses that the "burden of mixed funding should be shifted to non-settlors." <u>59/</u> This does not say, however, that EPA cannot recognize an "orphan" share where there are no "non-settlors." Moreover, the Conference Report does not demand that EPA recover against non-settlors in all cases, for it recognizes that there may be cases in which "it would be unreasonable to undertake such efforts." <u>60/</u>

<u>56/</u> §122(a), last sentence.

<u>57/</u> §122(a)(1).

<u>58/</u> §122(b)(1).

<u>59/</u> Conference Report, p. 252.

<u>60/</u> <u>Id.</u>

With respect to the "settlement in phases" issue, the 1986 amendments confirm EPA's 1985 position. The amendments provide that a settlement can cover "any response action" so long as EPA "determines that such action will be done properly." 61/

The 1986 amendments contain a new restriction on responsible party performance of RI/FS work, however. By way of background, EPA's policy of encouraging private party RI/FS work greatly distressed environmental groups and the State of New Jersey. They argued that this would be akin to a "fox guarding the chicken coop," because—apparently in their view—the parties would assure that a cheap and ineffective remedy would be selected and EPA would be powerless to do anything about it.

In reaction to this criticism, one close-to-final version of the House Bill actually prohibited EPA from allowing responsible parties to perform the RI/FS at a site. The 1986 amendments reflect a compromise on the issue.

Under the compromise, EPA can agree to allow responsible parties to perform an RI/FS, but only where:

(1)   EPA determines that the parties are "qualified" to do so;

(2)   EPA contracts with a "qualified person" to "oversee" and "review" the conduct of the RI/FS; and

(3)   The responsible parties agree to reimburse EPA for the costs of this extra oversight. 62/

With respect to the "release" issue, the 1986 amendments specifically authorize EPA to enter into "covenants not to sue" when settling with parties. In one passage, Congress has directed EPA to "be guided by the principle that a more complete covenant not to sue shall be provided for a more permanent remedy." 63/ This is very much like the EPA Settlement Policy's "sliding scale" approach. In addition, Congress has specified "factors" that EPA must consider in deciding whether and to what extent to grant a covenant not to

---

61/ §122(a).

62/ §104(a)(1).

63/ §122(c)(1).

sue. 64/ In general, these factors point strongly towards the idea that a more permanent remedy will result in a more complete remedy.

Similar to EPA's most recent policy statements, Congress has specified that covenants not to sue must generally be subject to "reopeners" for conditions unknown at the time of the agreement. 65/ There are four exceptions to this "reopener" requirement, however:

(1)   In the case of "de minimis" settlements covered by §122(g) (discussed below);

(2)   In the case of any other settlement, when warranted by "extraordinary circumstances" after considering numerous factors including "strength of evidence," "ability to pay," "litigative risks," "inequities," and when there are "all reasonable assurances" that health and the environment will be protected in the future; 66/

(3)   Where (1) EPA has rejected a remedial alternative that does not contemplate offsite disposal, and (2) EPA requires offsite disposal, and (3) the offsite disposal facility meets numerous specified requirements of RCRA 67/; or

(4)   Where there is a treatment/destruction remedy which is so complete that there are no longer any "current or currently foreseeable future" risks from the substances treated or the byproducts of such treatment. 68/

Thus, at least in the four limited circumstances specified above, CERCLA now specifically recognizes the concept of a "complete release." Moreover, CERCLA does not explicitly prohibit EPA from granting complete releases in any other situations.

64/   §122(f)(4).

65/   §122(f)(6).

66/   §122(f).

67/   §122(f)(2)(A). This is Congress' response to the "secondary site" release issue discussed above.

68/   §122(f)(2)(B).

As to "information sharing," there is a "special notice procedure" in new §122(e) which EPA may (but is under no obligation to) use. If EPA decides to "trigger" this procedure, it is directed to provide all identified parties, "in advance," with the following information, "to the extent it is available":

(1)   the names and addresses of potentially responsible parties;

(2)   the volume and nature of substances contributed by each potentially responsible party; and

(3)   a "ranking by volume" of the substances at the facility. 69/

This new subsection also allows but does not require EPA to prepare a "nonbinding preliminary allocation of responsibility" (NPAR) for the responsible parties' use in trying to allocate cleanup costs among themselves. This NPAR may be based upon any weighing of any factors which EPA may consider relevant, including volume, toxicity, mobility, strength of evidence, ability to pay, litigative risks, and "inequities." 70/

An NPAR at a site (if one is ever done) is really nothing more than an "initial cut" that the parties can accept, use as a "starting point," or totally reject. Congress has made clear that NPARs cannot be admissible in evidence and are non-reviewable in court. 71/ Moreover, they shall "not constitute an apportionment or other statement on the divisibility of harm or causation." 72/

The statute makes clear that EPA can in its discretion reject any offer based upon an NPAR, even if "substantial," and such rejection shall not be judicially reviewable. 73/ Perhaps the only thing that is real about an NPAR is that whenever EPA performs one, it will charge the responsible parties for the costs. 74/

69/ §122(e).

70/ §122(e) (3)(A).

71/ §122(e)(3)(C).

72/ Id.

73/ §122(e)(3)(E).

74/ §122(e)(3)(D).

Finally, with respect to the de minimis issue, §122(g) provides explicit authority for EPA to allow "buy outs" in certain circumstances. This new subsection says that EPA "shall as promptly as possible reach a final settlement" with a responsible party under certain conditions as follows:

(1)   where "practicable and in the public interest, as determined by EPA;"

(2)   for non-owners of the facility, where both the volume and the toxicity contributed by the party are "minimal in comparison to other hazardous substances at the facility;"

(3)   for site owners, where the owner did not "conduct or permit" the generation or placement of any hazardous substance at the facility and did not "contribute" to the release or threat of release "through any act or omission." 75/

4.6 Judicial Issues

4.6.1 Judicial Review of Remedies
One long-standing issue has been the appropriate time a court may "judicially review" the selection of a remedy. for instance, EPA may have gone through the RI/FS-ROD process described above and, from options A through E, selected option C (which will cost $100 million).

A group of responsible parties (who will in all likelihood have to pay for the cleanup through EPA's "cost recovery" authority) may feel strongly that EPA should have selected option B which would cost $50 million. An environmental group may feel strongly that EPA should have selected option E which would cost $200 million.

Either group may therefore wish to challenge EPA's remedy in court. And of course, they would want to do so before EPA took all the time and spent all the money to complete the remedy, for after that has been done, the practical chances for obtaining meaningful judicial relief would probably evaporate.

EPA has always maintained, however, that courts should not be allowed to review EPA's remedial decisions in separate litigation, but only in connection with cases initiated by EPA to force parties

---

75/ §122(g).

to perform a remedy (under CERCLA §106) or to recover costs for the amounts it has expended (under CERCLA §107). The 1980 CERCLA was silent on this issue, but the courts have rather unanimously agreed with EPA's position. 76/

The 1986 amendments now address this issue explicitly, and basically adopt EPA's long-standing position. New Section 113(h) provides that EPA's removal or remedial decisions may be judicially reviewed only at the following times:

(1)   in a §107 cost recovery or contribution action;

(2)   in an action to enforce (or recover penalties under) a §106 order;

(3)   in an action for "reimbursement" under §106(b)(2);

(4)   in a "citizens suit" (under new section 310) alleging that a removal or remedy taken was in "violation of the Act," but such an action may not be brought with regard to a removal "where a remedial action is to be undertaken at a site;" and

(5)   a lawsuit in which EPA seeks to compel cleanup under §106.

Situations (3) and (4) deserve further discussion. The "reimbursement" referred to in situation (3) relates to new §106(b)(2), which was added to address constitutional concerns raised by the Court in Aminoil v. EPA and other cases. 77/

The concern was based upon the following type of scenario. EPA could issue a §106 order to a party (or group of parties) demanding that they perform a certain cleanup. Suppose this cleanup was going to cost $100 million and the parties felt that a $50 million cleanup was entirely adequate to comply with CERCLA.

_____

76/ See, e.g., Wheaton Industries v. EPA, 781 F.2d 354 (3rd Cir. 1986); Lone Pine Steering Committee v. EPA, 777 F.2d 882 (3rd Cir. 1985); J.V. Peters & Co. v. EPA, 767 F.2d 263 (6th Cir. 1985).

77/ 599 F. Supp. 69 (D.C. Cal. 1984).

Under EPA's theories, however, a party could not seek judicial review of the remedy simply because EPA had issued the order; rather, judicial review would be appropriate only if and when EPA initiated litigation to enforce the order, seek penalties, and/or to recover its costs (if EPA went ahead and performed the remedy itself).

EPA is, however, under no obligation to go to court at any particular time. EPA could simply issue an order, and if the parties did not comply, go ahead and clean up the site on its own time and seek cost recovery in court at some later date.

Nevertheless, §107(c)(3) allows EPA to seek treble damages against those who fail to comply with §106 order "without sufficient cause." This left the parties who had received the order with quite a dilemma. They could refuse to obey in hopes that ultimately a reviewing court would agree with their position that the remedy was over-extensive and that they had "sufficient cause" to reuse to comply. This may be an extremely cheeky strategy, however, since if you guess wrong you can be out $300,000,000.

On the other hand, they could go ahead and comply by spending the $100,000,000 (which was twice what they honestly felt was required). But if they did, they would forever lose their right to judicial review because EPA would then never need to bring an enforcement or cost recovery action.

Because the Aminoil decision referenced above raised troubling questions about the constitutionality of this scenario, Congress came up with an alleged remedy in §106(b)(2). The main thrust of the remedy is that a party's compliance with an order need not shut-off judicial review rights.

Rather, if a party complies with an order (that is, in the example above, spends the $100,000,000), that person may "petition" EPA for reimbursement from the Superfund under the "claims" procedures of §112. If EPA fails to grant a petitioner its requested relief, the petitioner may then seek judicial review under §113.

If a petitioner convinces EPA (or the reviewing court) that the remedy was excessive under the law (under an "arbitrary/capricious" standard), it may be entitled to reimbursement to the extent of the excess. 78/ If a petitioner convinces EPA (or the reviewing court) that it is "not liable for response costs," it may be completely

---

78/ §106(b)(2)(D).

reimbursed. 79/ This latter opportunity is of very little practical comfort at CERCLA sites, where the threshold for establishing liability is so low.

Situation (4) refers to a new "citizens suit" provision (§310) in CERCLA, which, like similar provisions in other environmental statutes, gives citizens standing to sue EPA in certain circumstances. The plain words of the statute are that such a suit cannot be brought until after a remedy is complete: "An action . . . alleging that the . . . [EPA] action taken . . . was in violation . . . . Such an action may not be brought with regard to a removal where a remedial action is to be undertaken at the site." 80/

Despite the last sentence quoted above, the Conference Report says "an action under Section 310 would lie following completion of each distinct and separate phase of the clean-up." 81/ Apparently, the intent is to allow "distinct" phases of the remedy (but not removal) to be separately reviewed. It remains clear, however, that judicial review must always await "completion" of the activities being reviewed.

4.6.2 Contribution Rights of Liable Parties; Protection for Settlers

As noted earlier, many courts have held that there is "joint and several" liability under CERCLA. Fewer courts have addressed the corollary issue of whether a party held jointly and severally liable may turn around and sue another party (or group of parties) for "contribution." The few courts to address it have generally held that contribution rights exist, 82/ and Congress ratified this point in the 1986 amendments. 83/

79/ Id.

80/ §113(h)(4).

81/ Conference Report, p. 224.

82/ E.g., Colorado v. Asarco, Inc., 608 F. Supp. 1484 (D. Colo. 1985).

83/ §113(f).

Congress also addressed and resolved an important dispute over the timing of contribution actions and the effect of settlements on potential future contribution actions. Before explaining the new statutory provisions, it may be useful to set forth examples to illustrate the import of these issues in a waste site setting.

Assume EPA spends $100 million to clean up a site, and has identified 100 responsible parties at the site. In seeking cost recovery, it decides to sue only five parties with the largest relative volume at the site.

Assuming that these five parties may be "jointly and severally" liable for the $100 million, can they nevertheless seek "contribution" from some or all of the other 95 parties? If so, when?

EPA maintained through much of the CERCLA legislative debates that while contribution rights should exist, parties sued by EPA should be precluded from joining other parties to the litigation until after EPA had concluded its litigation against the few parties it selected for suit. Others maintained that sued parties should have the right to bring in other parties at any time.

Congress resolved this issue in the 1986 amendments by providing that a party may seek contribution from any other party during or following EPA's litigation. Congress also made clear that this does not preclude a contribution suit where no EPA suit has been filed. 84/

Alternatively, assume that at the site in question EPA reached a settlement with 90 of the parties to pay $60 million, with the understanding that EPA would press litigation against the other 10 parties for the remaining $40 million. What if the 10 sued parties (non-settlors) believe that the 90 settlors got "too good a deal," and under any fair scheme, the 10 non-settlors believe they should be liable for no more than $10 million (not $40 million). Could those non-settlors bring the 90 settlors back in to the litigation by way of "contribution" claims or any other theories?

Congress resolved this issue in the 1986 amendments by providing that a party who has "resolved its liability" to EPA or a State in "an administrative or judicially approved settlement" shall not be liable for contribution claims by others for matters addressed

---

84/ §113(f)(1).

in the settlement. 85/ This principle is repeated twice (in different contexts) in the "settlement" section of CERCLA. 86/

4.6.3 CERCLA Statute of Limitations

By apparent oversight, the 1980 CERCLA specified no statute of limitations with respect to EPA cost recovery actions. This could cause (and was in fact causing) great consternation in the business community. For instance, what if EPA spent $20 million to clean up a site and a company believes that EPA might seek to recover part or all of those costs against the company. The company has honest and valid reasons for wanting to know how long it must wait to find out for sure whether EPA is going to sue. When 2, 3, or 6 years go by, can the company finally commit funds to capital expansion that it was otherwise reserving for the potential litigation? Or can it finally stop noting the potential liability in its SEC statements? Or can the company's officers cut back on their Maalox dosage?

The 1986 amendments provide answers, although with respect to remedial actions, companies may have a long wait. The new amendments basically provide that EPA must bring a cost recovery suit for removal actions within 3 years after "completion of the removal."

For remedial actions, it should be recalled that EPA may incur costs over a period of several years. In an effort to compromise the interests of (1) providing certainty to parties as to whether suit will ever be brought and (2) making the whole process more manageable, Congress provided as follows:

(1) EPA must bring "an initial action" within 6 years after initiation of physical on-site construction;

(2) During this "initial action" courts are to enter declaratory judgments respecting parties' liability for response costs that will be binding on "subsequent" cost recovery claims at the site; and

---

85/ §113(f)(2).

86/ See §122(g)(5) relating to de minimis settlements; §122(h)(4) relating to cost recovery settlements.

(3)   A "subsequent" action or actions for "further" response costs may be brought "at any time during the response action, but must be commenced no later than 3 years after the date of completion of all response action." 87/

The new amendments also provide a general 3 year limitation period for "contribution" claims under specified circumstances. 88/

5.0 RELEASE REPORTING AND EMERGENCY RESPONSE

5.1 Reporting of Releases

To have a workable system for tracking "releases" so that any necessary responses can be timely, CERCLA has established an elaborate system for reporting. The basic statutory scheme is that under CERCLA §102, EPA is to establish "reportable quantities" for all hazardous substances. 89/

Under CERCLA §103, any person in charge of any facility, as soon as he has knowledge of any release (except a "federally permitted" release) of a hazardous substance in excess of the "reportable quantities" established under §102, must immediately notify the National Response Center of the release. There are civil and criminal penalties for failure to comply. 90/

EPA's regulations for this release reporting program are contained in 40 CFR part 302. This part contains the lengthy list of hazardous substances in alphabetical order. For each substance, a table indicates the Chemical Abstracts Service Registry Number (CASRN), any common "regulatory synonyms," and the designated "quantity." If a particular substance also happens to be a RCRA

87/ §113(g)(2).

88/ See §113(g)(3).

89/ As noted in Section 3.0, CERCLA §101(14) broadly defines "hazardous substance" to include hundreds of substances already designated under the CAA, CWA, RCRA, etc. CERCLA §102(a) also authorizes EPA to designate additional substances as hazardous.

90/ CERCLA §103(b).

listed waste, the table sets forth the appropriate RCRA waste number. 91/

For instance, if a plant was handling bromine cyanide, the appropriate plant personnel could consult the table in part 302 and obtain the following information. For purposes of ascertaining the correctness of the terminology, they would see that the CASRN is 506683 and that the common regulatory synonym is "cyanogen bromide." If they have a RCRA waste stream with this substance, they can see by cross-referencing that the RCRA waste number is U246.

Most importantly, they can see that the "reportable quantity" for this substance is 1,000 pounds, or 454 kilograms. Thus, if and when 1,000 pounds of this substance are "released" to the "environment" (see part 3.0 above for a discussion of the breadth of these terms), the plant's reporting requirements may be triggered.

The basic notification requirement is set forth in §302.6. Whenever a release exceeds the relevant reportable quantity in any 24-hour period, the person in charge of the facility shall immediately notify the National Response Center in Washington, DC at (800) 424-8802 (in D.C., call 426-2675).

What if in a 24-hour period, a plant released 1,500 pounds of a mixture, 900 pounds of which were bromine cyanide and 600 pounds of which were a substance which is not on the hazardous substance list? Because the release did not involve bromine cyanide in its "reportable quantity" of 1,000 pounds, the release need not be reported. EPA's regulations specify that releases of "mixtures and solutions" trigger the requirement to notify only where "a component hazardous substance of the mixture or solution is released in a quantity equal to or greater than its reportable quantity." 92/

What if certain solids are released in an amount exceeding the reportable quantity, but the particle sizes are large enough to be unlikely to present risks? EPA's regulations address this issue by exempting releases of solid particles of the following metals so long as the "mean diameter" of the particles released is larger than 100 micrometers (0.004 inches): antimony, arsenic, beryllium, cadmium, chromium, copper, lead, nickel, selenium, silver, thallium, and zinc. 93/

91/ See 40 CFR §302.4.

92/ 40 CFR § 302.6(b).

93/ 40 CFR §302.6(c).

As noted in Section 3.0 above, there is no obligation to report "federally permitted" releases. One additional important exemption is provided in the regulations. CERCLA reporting requirements do not apply to the application of a pesticide product registered under FIFRA or to the handling and storage of such a product by an agricultural producer. 94/

In several rulemaking phases over the last few years, EPA has published reportable quantities. Its most recent final rule appeared in the Federal Register of September 29, 1986. 95/

There are currently 717 hazardous substances under CERCLA. With its September 29, 1986 final rule, EPA has now established reportable quantities for 442 substances, and still needs to establish levels for 275. Warning: this does not mean there are no reporting requirements for these 275 substances. By operation of CERCLA §102(b), there is a statutorily-imposed reportable quantity of one pound until EPA takes regulatory action on a particular substance.

One important statutory provision is designed to insure that certain "continuous" releases do not have to be continuously reported. So long as a release is "continuous, stable in quantity and rate," it does not have to be reported every day or hour. Generally, a one-time-only notice will suffice. 96/

Strangely enough, EPA has never defined the term "continuous release" in its regulations. While EPA has raised this issue for comment in numerous regulatory proposals over the years, it has continuously avoided resolving it. There are many different bona fide ways to interpret the statutory language, and EPA's silence is producing great confusion among EPA regions, the states, and the regulated industry. Nevertheless, EPA announced once again on September 29, 1986 (approximately six years after the phrase became law) that it is still in "the process" of trying to clarify this issue. 97/

94/ 40 CFR §302.7(c).

95/ 51 FR 34534 et seq.

96/ § 103(f)(2).

97/ 51 FR 34536, col. 1.

5.2 Emergency Reponse

There may be many old sites which will never make it to the NPL and for which, if any response is necessary, a (relatively) inexpensive "removal" will suffice to protect health and the environment. Moreover, there may be many current "releases" from existing facilities which may warrant a "removal." There is actually very little in CERCLA to restrain EPA's discretion in dealing with these non-NPL removal situations. Compared to the complex detail of new §121 explained above, EPA is simply directed to take such actions as may be "necessary to protect the public health or welfare or the environment." 98/

One significant restriction in the 1980 CERCLA to these "non-remedial" responses, however, was that EPA could not spend more than $1,000,000 or continue a response for more than six months unless there was a true "emergency" situation. The 1986 amendments have raised these numbers to $2,000,000 and 12 months, respectively. 99/

6.0 EMERGENCY PLANNING AND "RIGHT-TO-KNOW"

After the Bhopal, India disaster and several incidents in West Virginia soon thereafter, there was widespread criticism of EPA's alleged weaknesses in dealing with emergency situations under CERCLA. The result of all this criticism is a totally new federal/state program under a new Act entitled the "Emergency Planning and Community Right-to-Know Act of 1986." For acronym aficionados, we now have the virtually impossible "EPCRTKA."

This new act was part of the 1986 CERCLA Amendments (Title III), but it will be "free standing" as a separate act and not codified as part of CERCLA. It is quite comprehensive, taking up 32 printed pages of the 1986 amendments.

Nothing in this new act supersedes or amends the CERCLA 102/103 reporting program; rather it appears designed to build upon this program and provide a tremendous new federal/state infrastructure to assure that reported releases may be better responded to and that would-be disasters can be better headed off.

98/   §104(a)(1).

99/   §104(e) of the amendments, amending CERCLA §104(c)(1).

One important element of the new act is the establishment of an entirely new list of "extremely hazardous substances" (EHSs). The basic idea behind the concept is that for such substances, many legal safeguards must be employed beyond CERCLA release reporting to assure (1) that the potential for release be minimized and (2) that adequate and timely responses will be made to protect surrounding populations.

Section 302 of the act requires EPA, no later than November 17, 1986, to publish a list of EHSs. Congress specified that this initial list was to be the same list that EPA had previously published in a 1985 guidance document, but that EPA could add or delete substances through rulemaking. 100/

For each EHS, EPA is to establish a "threshold planning quantity" (TPQ). As described below, for any facility in the U.S. at which an EHS "is present" in TPQ amounts, numerous requirements under the new act will be triggered.

On November 17, 1986, in accordance with the act's deadline, EPA published the EHS list and established TPQs for each EHS. 101/ EPA designated 402 substances as EHSs, listed them alphabetically and by CAS number, and set TPQs for each. The TPQs ranged from 2 pounds (i.e., chloromethyl ketone, chromic chloride) to 10,000 pounds (i.e. thiometon, isobutyronitrile). 102/

Before explaining the requirements these EHSs and TPQs may trigger at a facility, it is first necessary to explain other provisions of the new act. Section 301 requires the establishment of a totally new state and local infrastructure for emergency planning and response. It requires the governor of each state, no later than April 17, 1987, to appoint a state "emergency response commission." 103/ By July 17, 1987, each state commission must designate local "emergency planning districts," 104/ and by August 17, 1987, each state

---

100/ § 302(a)(2), (4).

101/ 51 FR 41570 et seq.

102/ See Appendix D, 51 FR at 41582.

103/ §301(a).

104/ §301(b).

commission must appoint a "local emergency planning committee" for each local district. 105/

The purpose behind all this infrastructure is to create and implement "comprehensive emergency response plans" under Section 303. By October 17, 1988, each local committee is to complete such a plan and assure that resources are available to carry it out. The plan is to be prepared under federal guidelines 106/ and be reviewed by the state commission. 107/ Each plan must include at least the following elements: 108/

(1) Identification of (a) covered facilities within the emergency planning district, (b) routes likely to be used for the transport of EHSs, and (c) additional facilities contributing or subjected to additional risk due to their proximity to covered facilities, such as hospitals or natural gas facilities;

(2) Methods and procedures to respond to releases of EHSs;

(3) Designation of a community emergency coordinator and facility emergency coordinators;

(4) Procedures assuring timely notification of releases by facility emergency coordinators and the community emergency coordinator to persons designated in the emergency plan, and to the public;

(5) Methods for determining the occurrence of a release, and the area or population likely to be affected by such release;

(6) A description of emergency equipment and facilities in the community and at each covered facility, and an identification of the persons responsible for such equipment and facilities;

105/ §301(c).

106/ §303(f).

107/ §303(e).

108/ §303(c).

(7) Evacuation plans, including provisions for a precaution-
ary evacuation and alternative traffic routes;

(8) Training programs, including schedules for training of
local emergency response and medical personnel; and

(9) Methods and schedules for exercising the emergency
plan.

As EPA stressed in its preamble to the November 17 rules,
the emergency planning requirements are applicable to all facilities
which "store, manufacture, process, use, or otherwise handle at any
time" an EHS in TPQ amounts. 109/ A "facility" includes all of a
plant with its various buildings at the same site and even contiguous
sites. 110/ Thus, assume that at any given time, a plant uses 200
pounds of substance X in one building, stores 300 pounds of substance X in another building, and stores 500 pounds of substance X in
a storage shed. If substance X is an EHS and the TPQ for X is 1,000
pounds, the plant will be subject to the emergency planning requirements.

For facilities subject to these requirements, numerous duties
are triggered. First, the facility must notify the state commission
by May 17, 1987 that the facility is subject to the new act. Any time
in the future that a facility first becomes subject to the act, it must
notify the State commission of this fact within 60 days. 111/

Second, by September 17, 1987, each covered facility must
select a "facility emergency coordinator" to participate in the local
emergency planning process and inform the local emergency planning committee of the selection. 112/ Thereafter, whenever
requested by the committee, the facility must "promptly provide"
information necessary for developing and implementing the emergency plan.

Section 304 establishes additional notification requirements
for covered facilities. Generally, whenever there is a "release" (as

---

109/ 51 FR 41573.

110/ §329(4).

111/ §302(c).

112/ §303(d).

defined in CERCLA) of an EHS, the facility must notify the appropriate local committee(s) and the appropriate state commission(s)
"for any area likely to be affected by the release." 113/ The
notification must contain numerous items of information, including:
the name of the substance; estimates of quantities, time, and duration of the release; the medium or media into which the release
occurred; known "or anticipated" risks, and "advice" regarding
medical attention; advice as to public precautions; and a name and
phone number for further information. 114/

With respect to the community "right to know" elements of
the new act, any facility which is required to prepare or maintain a
"material safety data sheet" (MSDS) for any chemical under OSHA
must submit such sheets for each chemical to the local committee,
the state commission, and the fire department with jurisdiction over
the facility. 115/ The local committee is required to make these
MSDSs available to any member of the public on request. 116/

In addition to the MSDS for each chemical, each facility must
also prepare a new "inventory form" which shows the amounts and
locations of each MSDS chemical. This must also be submitted to
the appropriate local committee, state commission, and fire department. 117/

Finally, under Section 313, some facility owners will be
requested to complete and submit toxic chemical release forms (or
"emissions inventories") on an annual basis. EPA must maintain all
such data and make it available to the public. 118/

113/ §304(b).

114/ §304(b)(2).

115/ §311(a).

116/ §311(c)(2).

117/ §312(a).

118/ §313(j).

7.0 FACILITATION OF TOXIC TORT SUITS

Each time Congress has addressed CERCLA authorization or reauthorization, there have been massive proposals put forward for "Victims Compensation" schemes. These proposals have taken the form of administrative claims mechanisms and/or a new federal "cause of action" in tort. The main thrust behind these proposals has been to make it easier for people who claim they have been made sick (or will become sick), or have otherwise allegedly been adversely affected by hazardous substances, to recover damages. The main assumption behind these proposals is that the current state tort law system is inadequate to provide this recovery.

In the 1980 CERCLA, all victims compensation proposals were defeated. CERCLA has, however, indirectly assisted in the development of toxic tort suits.

For every NPL site, as described in section 4.0 above, EPA develops a tremendous amount of information through the RI/FS-ROD process and through identification of responsible parties. This is usually public information or may easily become public through judicial discovery and/or the Freedom of Information Act.

This information can be extremely helpful to plaintiffs' attorneys in finding out who put what waste at a site in what volumes and what the site conditions are. From this information, which might otherwise have taken years to develop, they can simply file their complaints. Many toxic tort suits being filed today are really "tag-ons" to the work EPA is doing at CERCLA sites.

In the 1986 amendments, virtually all "victims compensation" proposals were again defeated. This time, however, there is one new "statute of limitations" provision which is certain to promote more toxic tort suits in a direct manner; and there are major new data-gathering provisions which appear designed to promote more toxic tort suits in an indirect manner.

One common complaint about the tort system is that some states have "date of exposure" rules in their statutes of limitations. For instance, if the law said that all tort claims must be filed no later than three years form the date of exposure, practically all claims for cancer and genetic defects could be barred because such adverse effects may not even manifest themselves for 15 to 20 years after exposure. (Actually very few states still have such restrictive statutes.)

Congress took care of this problem with a bang in the 1986 amendments, and enacted (if constitutional) a new nationally-applicable statute of limitations for toxic torts which goes well beyond even what most "modern" state laws provide.

Section 203 of the amendments adds a new §309 to CERCLA. This new §309 applies to all personal injury or property damage tort suits related to alleged exposure to hazardous substances (or even "pollutants or contaminants").

It requires that a state statute of limitations for such actions can not begin to run until "the date the plaintiff knew (or reasonably should have known)" that the injury/damages "were caused or contributed to" by certain hazardous substances or pollutants or contaminants. This new statute of limitations could extend the period for filing suits for a particular alleged injury indefinitely, as science and environmental politics may always develop over the years to provide new theories on which to base allegations.

Moreover, the 1986 CERCLA amendments provide a continuous mother-lode of free data and information for plaintiffs' attorneys. Section 110 of the amendments add dozens of new requirements to existing CERCLA §104(i) (which was originally designed to find out what sort of links could be made between waste sites and disease but which was never aggressively implemented).

This new information includes not only detailed generic data about many substances commonly found at waste sites, including each substance's potential health effects, but also site-specific "health assessments" at each facility on the NPL. Thus, while the current CERCLA materially assists plaintiffs in developing their case as to which parties to name and what type of exposure might be created, the new CERCLA will materially assist plaintiffs in building the toxicological/scientific portions of their cases.

8.0 FUNDING

The 1980 CERCLA was designed to derive 1.6 billion over five years from special industry taxes (87.5 percent) and general revenues (12.5 percent). The special industry taxes were largely on the petrochemical industry, with a combination of a tax on crude oil and on certain organic and inorganic chemical "feedstocks."

The 1986 amendments are designed to raise $9 billion over five years from the following sources:

Source	Billions $
Domestic crude oil	1.250
Imported crude oil	1.500
Chemical "feedstocks"	1.400
"Environmental tax"	2.500
General revenues	1.250
Interest and cost recovery	.600
Fuel tax (for UST program)	.500
	9.000

The "environmental tax" listed above (§516) represents a major victory for the petrochemical industry, which has campaigned for years to "spread the base" of Superfund taxes. The argument has been that at most CERCLA waste sites, all basic manufacturing is well-represented on the list of responsible parties (auto, aircraft, electronics, etc.). This tax, while too complicated to explain here, applies to a broad segment of large American manufacturing corporations.

9.0 MISCELLANEOUS ISSUES

9.1 Natural Resource Damages

Since 1980, CERCLA has provided for liability not only for response (cleanup) costs, but also "natural resource damages." 119/ "Natural resources" as defined in CERCLA must be governmentally owned or controlled; private property is not covered. 120/

While there have been some claims and some litigation, this area of CERCLA has not been particularly active yet (relative to the issues respecting cleanup). This may in large part be due to delays (by the Department of Interior) in issuing regulations for assessing natural resource damages under §301(c) of CERCLA.

The 1986 amendments contain a new requirement that Interior issue these regulations by April 17, 1987. The 1986 amendments

_____

119/ See §107(a)(4)(C).

120/ §101(16).

also made numerous miscellaneous changes respecting natural resource damages.

9.2 Contractors' Liability

Because CERCLA liability has been extended so broadly to any party who had anything to do with a waste site, cleanup contractors have become very concerned about their liabilities for (1) future cleanup costs and (2) toxic torts, even if they performed a remedy totally in accordance with all EPA specifications. Because environmental liability insurance is unavailable, this fear of liabilities has kept many of the larger ("deep pocket") construction firms—who actually have the expertise and ability to perform cleanup work most effectively—from participating in site cleanup work.

These contractors sought various protections in the 1986 amendments so they could safely enter the waste site cleanup business and new CERCLA §119 is the result of their efforts. They got some protection, but not as much as they sought.

For instance, they had sought (and the House bill had included) a federally-imposed "negligence standard" that would preempt application of strict liability in all federal/state cleanup/tort actions. The 1986 amendments insulate cleanup contractors from strict liability under CERCLA, but do not touch the issue of federal or state tort law. The 1986 amendments also provide EPA with the discretion to <u>indemnify</u> contractors (with Superfund dollars) with respect to the potential CERCLA/tort liabilities.

9.3 Underground Storage Tanks (UST)

"Petroleum" has long been totally excluded from CERCLA coverage. <u>121</u>/ Petroleum product storage had also long been excluded from RCRA because a product is not a "waste." In 1984, however, Congress amended RCRA to impose a new program for underground petroleum (and hazardous substance) storage tanks. These RCRA amendments provided EPA with massive regulatory and enforcement authority, but did not provide funding for EPA to take corrective actions when necessary (in the case of unwilling or insolvent tank owners).

Section 205 of the 1986 amendments amends RCRA to beef up certain enforcement and regulatory authority under the existing

---

<u>121</u>/ §§101(14); 104(a)(2).

UST program. The 1986 amendments also provide $500 million (from a tax on fuel use) for federal response authority where necessary.

9.4 Schedules

Section 116 of the amendments adds a new §116 to CERCLA which is designed to speed-up EPA's allegedly slow "pace" of cleaning up NPL sites. Section 116 has both "goals," which EPA must "explain" if it misses, and "mandatory schedules," for which EPA can be sued if it misses.

The "goals" are as follows:

(1)   Complete preliminary assessments of all known sites (over 22,000) by January 1, 1988;

(2)   Complete all site inspections as necessary by January 1, 1989; and

(3)   Perform "hazard ranking" evaluation for NPL listings for all sites as necessary by October 17, 1990.

The "mandatory schedules" are:

(1)   Commence new RI/FSs at 275 NPL facilities by October 17, 1989. But if this schedule is not met, EPA must commence RI/FSs at an additional 175 sites by October 17, 1990, an additional 200 sites by October 17, 1991, for a total of 650 sites by October 17, 1991; and

(2)   Commence "substantial and continuous" new physical construction at 175 NPL sites by October 17, 1989 and at an additional 200 NPL sites by October 17, 1991.

Chapter 4

TOXIC SUBSTANCES

Marshall Lee Miller
Reid & Priest
Washington, D.C.

1.0 INTRODUCTION

The problem of toxic chemicals, including pesticides and especially hazardous wastes, is acquiring increasing importance with the public realization that thousands of carcinogenic (cancer-causing), teratogenic (birth defect-causing) and mutagenic (genetic-damaging) substances are present in our environment. Both the World Health Organization and the National Cancer Institute have estimated that between 60 and 90 percent of cancers are environmentally induced. 1/ The Toxic Substances Control Act (TSCA) of 1976 provides EPA with authority to require testing of chemical substances, both new and old, entering the environment and to regulate them where necessary. This authority supplements sections of existing toxic substances laws, such as Section 112 of the Clean Air Act, 2/ Section 307 of the Water Act, 3/ and Section 6 of the

---

1/ See for example, "WHO Reports on Cancer," cited in In Re Shell, 6 ERC 2047, 2051. The term "environment," of course, encompasses a wide range of possible exposures from industrial chemicals to food and cosmic radiation.

2/ Clean Air Act, 42 U.S.C. § 1857 et seq., PL 91-604 (1970).

3/ Federal Water Pollution Control Act, 33 U.S.C. § 1251 et seq., PL 92-500 (1972).

156

Occupational Safety and Health Act, 4/ which already provide regulatory control over toxic substances. It may also be used to regulate the development of biotechnology and genetic engineering.

2.0 PROBLEM OF UNREGULATED CHEMICALS

Prior to the passage of the Toxic Substances Control Act of 1976, there was no general federal requirement that the thousands of new chemicals developed each year be tested for their potential environmental or health effects before they were introduced into commerce. An estimated two million chemical compounds have been recognized, with thousands of additional substances being developed each year. 5/ While most such chemicals never reach the market, EPA calculates that approximately a thousand of these new chemicals are produced annually in commercial quantities. Of these, only a fraction are subject to mandatory testing requirements under the Pesticide Act (FIFRA) or the Food, Drug and Cosmetic Act (FDCA). 6/

Recent tragic experiences illustrate the consequences of this lack of testing. In the late 1960s, there arose national concern over the widespread contamination of food, water, and soil by certain highly toxic compounds of organic mercury. By 1972 the government had authority under the Clean Air Act and the Federal Water Pollution Control Act to control direct emissions of mercury into the environment, but there was no federal authority to require testing of the effects of various mercuric compounds or to regulate the multiple uses of mercury in industrial, commercial, and consumer products.

4/ 29 U.S.C. § 651 et seq., PL 91-596, 84 Stat. 1950 (1970).

5/ New York Times, 8 July 1975, estimated as high as 250,000.

6/ Only three federal statutes give the government authority to require chemical manufacturers to test their products. They are the Federal Insecticide, Fungicide and Rodenticide Act, as amended (7 U.S.C. § 135 et seq.), dealing with pesticides; the Federal Food, Drug and Cosmetic Act, (21 U.S.C. § 321 et seq.) requiring testing of drugs and food additives; and Section 211 of the Clean Air Act (42 U.S.C. § 1857 et seq.), providing authority to require testing of fuel additives.

Another episode in the early 1970s involved polycholorinated biphenyls (PCBs), used in such diverse applications as printing inks and dielectric fluids. PCBs are similar to DDT, Aldrin-Dieldrin, and other chlorinated hydrocarbons in their pervasiveness and persistence in the environment and in their suspected carcinogenicity.

A host of other chemicals have also received recent public attention. A partial list includes asbestos, lead (including tetraethyl lead), arsenic, fluorocarbons (freon), nitrosamines, methyl butyl ketone, cadmium, and fluorides.

Vinyl chloride was involved in one of the most publicized episodes. In January 1975, a link was confirmed between worker exposure to vinyl chloride monomer (VCM) and a rare form of cancer, angiosarcoma of the liver. Except for the extreme rarity of this disease and the unusual number of workers in whom it was found, the carcinogenic properties of VCM might have remained undetected. Medical experts now fear that it may also result in damage to the brain and other key organs. An OSHA standard in 1975 set a permissible limit at one part per million (1 ppm) but not before three decades of workers had been exposed to levels as high as several hundred parts per million. 7/

The incident which contributed directly to the passage of TSCA was the discovery in mid-1975 that workers in a small Virginia manufacturing plant had sustained severe neurological and reproductive damage from exposure to the chemical Kepone. Federal and state health agencies were widely criticized for failure to prevent this tragedy. The head of one agency responded, "We could accomplish a great deal if we were able to keep track of what toxic chemicals are entering our environment. Toxic substances legislation . . . is therefore an important need." 8/ While Kepone may not actually

---

7/ OSHA "Vinyl Chloride Standard," 29 CFR 1910, 1017. This was upheld unanimously by the Court of Appeals in Society of Plastics Industry v. U.S. Dept. of Labor, 509 F.2d 131 (2nd Cir. 1975); the Supreme Court denied certiorari, sub. nom. Firestone Plastics Co. v. U.S. Dept. of Labor, 95 S.Ct. 1998 (1975).

8/ Testimony of the Assistant Secretary of Labor for OSHA before a Subcommittee of the Senate Committee on Agriculture and Forestry (2 February 1976).

be a good example of this need (as a pesticide, it had long been screened and registered with EPA), the national attention engendered by such tragedies finally prodded Congress to enact the Toxic Substances Control Act.

3.0 THE NEED FOR A TOXIC SUBSTANCES CONTROL ACT

Prior to the passage of the Toxic Substances Act, significant gaps existed in the federal government's authority to test and regulate problem chemicals. The Clean Air Act, the Federal Water Pollution Control Act, and other laws dealt with chemical substances only when they entered the environment as wastes (emissions to the air or discharges into the water). In many cases controls could not be easily fashioned or required without severe economic consequences. Toxic substances legislation, which theoretically would require testing before a chemical reached the production phase, overcame this difficulty.

Other statutes, such as the Occupational Safety and Health Act and the Consumer Product Safety Act, deal only with one phase of the chemical's existence (worker exposure or direct consumer exposure) and contain no authority to address environmental hazards. While both of these statutes are clearly needed, the life cycle of a chemical, from production to ultimate disposal, provides many opportunities for its escape into the environment and human exposure, and federal authority to deal with the overall cycle is fragmented. The Toxic Substances Control Act was designed to fill these gaps, both in regulatory powers and in authority to require that tests be conducted before the human or environmental exposure occurs.

4.0 LEGISLATIVE BACKGROUND

In 1970 the President's Council on Environmental Quality (CEQ) recommended that the administrator of EPA be empowered "to restrict the use or distribution of any substance which he finds is hazardous to human health or to the environment." 9/ This was incorporated in the President's Message to Congress on the Environment in February 1971. 10/ Both the House and Senate passed toxic

---

9/ See CEQ, Environmental Quality, August 1971, p. 306.

10/ Ibid., Appendix F.

substances bills during the 92nd Congress, but the House acted too late in the session to permit a resolution of the differences between the two bills. In the 93rd Congress, both houses approved toxic substances legislation, but were unable to reach a compromise in conference.

The fundamental disagreement was whether the proposed law would require new chemicals to be <u>registered</u>, as with pesticides or drugs, or simply that EPA be <u>notified</u> of plans to manufacture. Senator William Spong (D-Va.) favored the former view, but more senators were influenced by EPA's desultory pesticide registration record to avoid this time-consuming approach.

The 94th Congress, beginning January 1975, considered a variety of toxic substances legislative proposals. A bill similar to that passed by the Senate in the previous Congress was introduced as S.776 by Senators John V. Tunney (D-Cal.), Philip Hart (D-Mich.), and Warren Magnuson (D-Wash.). After considerable debate, the Senate passed a redrafted but substantively similar bill S.3149, on 26 March 1975, by a vote of 60-13, with only three significant amendments.

Three separate bills were introduced in the House. One, H.R.7229, sponsored by Congressman Robert Eckhardt (D-Tex.), was reported with amendments from the Subcommittee on Commerce and Finance to the full House Commerce Committee. The Ford administration, however, actively supported a more limited bill (H.R.12336) sponsored by Representative John McCollister (R-Neb.) and most of the chemical industry. A third bill, introduced by Rep. William Broadhead (D-Mich.), was supported by organizations such as Ralph Nader's Health Research Group. The bill that emerged, H.R. 14032, was a compromise that the House passed on 23 August 1976. <u>11</u>/

On 28 September 1976, a House and Senate conference committee agreed on a final version of the Toxic Substances Control Bill, which was enacted on 11 October 1976 and signed into law by the President. It became effective, with one exception, on 1 Janu-

---

<u>11</u>/ See H.R.   94-1341,   accompanying   H.R.14032,   and   the Conference Report at 94-1679; S.R. 94-698 and the Senate Conference Report, 94-1302.

TOXIC SUBSTANCES 161

ary 1977. 12/ On 22 October 1986, a new law was passed amending the Toxic Substances Control Act by adding a Title II to the act. This amendment establishes asbestos abatement programs in schools. 13/ (See Section 17.0.)

5.0 TOXIC SUBSTANCES CONTROL ACT OF 1976

The Toxic Substances Control Act (TSCA) has two main regulatory features:

First, acquisition of sufficient information by EPA to identify and evaluate potential hazards from chemical substances;

Second, regulation of the production, use, distribution, and disposal of such substances where necessary. The principal provisions of the act are described in the following sections.

6.0 PREMANUFACTURE NOTIFICATION—STATUTORY PROVISIONS

The heart of TSCA is the requirement for premanufacture notification (PMN). Under Section 5(a), a manufacturer must notify EPA ninety days before producing a new chemical substance, defined as any chemical not listed on a specially compiled inventory list (discussed later). Notification is also necessary even for older chemicals, already on that list, if the administrator concludes that there is a significant new use which increases human or environmental exposure. 14/ In either case, EPA may extend the notifi-

---

12/ The exception is Section 4(f), which only took effect two years later. Actually, without implementing regulations, none of the sections had immediate force on 1 January 1977, except for Section 8(e) requiring the reporting of significant adverse effects.

13/ The Asbestos Hazard Emergency Response Act of 1986, PL 99-519.

14/ TSCA § 5(a). The criteria the administrator must consider for a new use determination (Significant New Use Regulation—SNUR) include the expected production volume, increased quantity or duration of human and environmental exposure, and hazards of manufacturing and distribution.

cation processing period for one additional ninety days, but the reasons for requiring longer consideration may be challenged in court. 15/

Many companies may wish to notify EPA well before the ninety day period in order to forestall last-minute delays in marketing. There are disadvantages to this, however: competitors will thereby be tipped off to the company's marketing plans, and EPA has warned that PMN data submitted too far in advance may be rejected as lacking sufficient certainty of the ultimate intention to manufacture.

Within five days of receiving the notice, EPA must publish in the Federal Register an item identifying the chemical substance, listing its intended uses, and a description of the toxicological tests required to demonstrate that there will be no "unreasonable risk of injury to health or the environment."

If the administrator decides that the data submitted is "insufficient to permit a reasoned evaluation" and that the chemical may pose a risk to man or the environment, he may restrict or even prohibit any aspect of the chemical's production or distribution. Such an order, however, must be issued no later than forty-five days before the expiration of the notification period, meaning that the agency must respond very quickly. The manufacturer then has thirty days to submit specific objections to the order. 16/

Finally, for those chemicals on the priority list for which special testing is required, the administrator is required to publish in the Federal Register his reason for not taking action to limit production and use, before the end of notification period. 17/

By statute, Section 5 was to take effect thirty days after the publication of the inventory list, which was due in November 1977. Since this did not occur until the summer of 1979, implementation of the manufacturing notification requirements was delayed for almost three years after passage of the act.

15/ TSCA § 5(c). Such a challenge is subject to the confidentiality restrictions of Section 14.

16/ TSCA § 5(e)(1). This description, although complex, is nevertheless an oversimplication.

17/ TSCA § 5(g). This publication, however, is not a prerequisite for the production or marketing of the product.

6.1 PMN Regulations Proposed and Reproposed

In January 1979, EPA proposed voluminous PMN regulations, 18/ which required not only the submission of data specified by Congress in Section 5(d) but also extensive reporting and record-keeping derived presumably from Section 8. The proposed requirements would include complete flow charts of the production process, a risk assessment of production and distribution, certification that processors and consumers have been notified regarding the chemical's properties, detailed information on hourly emissions and effluents, and approximately 110 pages of forms with other requirements. 19/

The EPA-commissioned Arthur D. Little, Inc. study on the economic burden of complying with the proposed PMN regulations estimated that the paperwork alone would cost from $2500 to $41,000, depending on the assumptions. Preparation would also require hundreds of hours, exclusive of the still unknown testing costs. The report concluded that at $10,000 per chemical for PMN, half of the new chemicals normally introduced each year would not be released. At $40,000, 90 percent would not be introduced. 20/ The effects on small companies, which are responsible for a disproportionate amount of chemical innovation, 21/ would be disastrous if they were not granted some relief. 22/ The irony is that the original EPA estimates on PMN costs, made before passage of the act, were

---

18/ 44 FR 2242, 10 January 1979.

19/ See also EPA, "Explanatory Appendix: Premanufacture Notice Forms," January 1979; "Support Document: Premanufacture Notification Requirements and Review Procedures," January 1979; and "TSCA: Questions and Answers on the Proposed PMN Regulations," February 1979.

20/ EPA, "Impact of TSCA Proposed PMN Requirements," December 1978, p. 13.

21/ Ibid, p. III-18.

22/ Statement of Ervin Colton, CERAC Inc. of Milwaukee, at EPA PMN hearing 13 February 1979, p.5. The definition of small business in the proposal was annual sales of one million dollars, compared with five million under Section 8. Also, the one thousand pound presumption for exempt R & D was dropped entirely under the proposed Section 5 regulations.

negligible. They assumed that companies would be required to submit information which most would have developed anyway. 23/

In October 1979, EPA responded to public criticism of its voluminous notification regulations by issuing a new PMN proposal. 24/ This eliminated or made optional many previous agency demands for "a considerable amount of information that is not related to EPA's decision-making." EPA claimed this revised rule would reduce mandatory PMN compliance costs to a $1200 - $8900 range per chemical, provided neither health questions nor confidentiality was raised. Despite requests, the October reproposal again did not provide special treatment for low-volume substances of, say, less than one metric ton a year, but EPA did specifically request additional comments on this issue. An exemption from supplementary reporting was provided for small business, defined as companies with annual sales below one million dollars, 25/ and they were promised extra latitude in answering many of the PMN information forms with "not available."

6.2 Interim PMN Policy and Final Regulations

In November 1980, just after the presidential election, the outgoing Carter administration published a revised interim policy to be followed until final rules were promulgated. 26/ With the advent of the Reagan administration, a much-simplified PMN procedure was promised that would minimize the burden on the reporting industries, but this shorter version did not prove any easier to prepare. Thus, after almost seven years, no final regulation had yet appeared. Meanwhile companies were complying with Section 5 as best they could, given EPA's shifting attitudes. That meant submitting a

---

23/ Letter from Gary H. Baise, Director of EPA's Office of Legislation, to Senator John V. Tunney (D-Calif.), no date but approximately June 1973, reprinted in Senate Commerce Committee Report No. 93-254 on S.426, pp. 50-51.

24/ 44 FR 59764, October 1979.

25/ The figure under Section 8(b) was five times higher, while under 8(a) a proposal set the level as thirty million.

26/ 45 FR 74378, 7 November 1980.

notification and hoping the agency would not find it inadequate in whole or in part.

The PMN regulations were finally issued in May 1983. 27/

6.3 Proposed Testing Guidelines Under Section 5

In March 1979, EPA issued proposed guidelines for testing under Section 5. 28/ Although TSCA's testing rules are to be issued under Section 4, EPA took this additional step because of widespread industry concern that Section 5(e) might be used to delay production indefinitely. Under that section, the administrator is empowered to seek an injunction to prevent the manufacture or distribution of a substance for which data is insufficient and from which there might be an unreasonable risk. Producers therefore wished to know what data EPA would regard as sufficient. Their concern was heightened by a provision in the proposed PMN regulation that the 90-day clock would stop on a notice found to be deficient in some respect. 29/ Despite agency denials, many companies feared that this was an imaginative loophole created to extend the statutory 90/180-day notice period and thereby to convert the process into a certification program akin to FIFRA or FDA.

6.4 PMN Exemption: Section 5(h)(4)

The statute provides that the administrator can exempt a manufacturer of a new substance from all or part of PMN if he decides that its production, distribution, use, and disposal "will not present an unreasonable risk of injury to health or the environment." 30/

In 1980, Polaroid requested EPA for a blanket exemption on minor changes made from time to time in the formulation of instant photographic film. 31/ After similar requests from other companies, prolonged debate, and an initial rejection of the exemption by the

---

27/ 48 FR 21742, 13 May 1983; codified at 40 CFR § 720.

28/ 44 FR 16240, 16 March 1979.

29/ 44 FR 2242 at 2272, proposing 40 CFR § 720.34.

30/ TSCA § 5(h)(4).

31/ See BNA, Chemical Reporter, 17 October 1980, p. 913.

White House's Office of Management and Budget (OMB) as (ironically) too restrictive, 32/ the agency finally approved the first Section 5(h)(4) exemption in a rule published in June 1982. 33/

In July 1982, in response to industry petitions, EPA proposed other rules under Section 5(h)(4) which would exempt about half of all new chemicals produced in the U.S. 34/ They would provide that manufacture of certain polymers, chemicals used solely at the plant site, and low volume chemicals (defined generally by the companies as 25 thousand pounds annually). 35/ For chemicals produced in volumes under one thousand kilos a year, only a brief notice was to be submitted to EPA under the polymer exemption proposal: namely, manufacturer's name, location, chemical identity, and the polymer's molecular weight. Another category of polymers, those produced in quantities of between one thousand and ten thousand kilograms annually, would have to be submitted with somewhat more information under an abbreviated 14-day PMN. Environmentalists, such as the NRDC, predictably reacted with alarm to the proposals. 36/ In April 1985 EPA published a rule expediting PMN review for low volume chemicals (described as 1,000 kilograms or less a year). A chemical eligible for this exemption undergoes a 21-day review, rather than a 90-day, and has fewer information requirements. 37/

32/ Ibid., 23 October 1981, p. 803; 30 October 1981, p. 819.

33/ 47 FR 24308, 4 June 1982.

34/ 47 FR 32609, 28 July 1982.

35/ Section 26 provides that action taken for a single chemical may also be taken for a group; so, to grant a broad Section 5(h)(4) exemption, EPA must follow the rulemaking procedures of TSCA § 6(c)(2) and (3). Within five days of receipt EPA under Section 5(d)(2) must publish in the Federal Register, subject to Section 14 provisions on confidentiality, information on the new substance and its uses. Section 5(c) allows a 90-day extension period, if necessary for good cause, subject to section 5(e) and (f) regulatory triggers.

36/ BNA, Chemical Reporter, 30 July 1982, p. 555.

37/ 50 FR 16477, 26 April 1985.

6.5 Significant New Use Regulations (SNURs)

Although commonly forgotten, Section 5's PMN requirements apply not only to new chemicals but to significant new uses of existing chemicals or even an appreciable increase in their utilization for an existing purpose. According to Section 5(a)(2), relevant factors include:

(A)   the projected volume of manufacturing and processing of a chemical substance,

(B)   the extent to which a use changes the type or form of exposure of human beings or the environment to a chemical substance,

(C)   the extent to which a use increases the magnitude and duration of exposure of human beings or the environment to a chemical substance, and

(D)   the reasonably anticipated manner and methods of manufacturing, processing, distribution in commerce, and disposal of a chemical substance.

Determining when a use is a new one, especially for a chemical already having scores of applications, can be difficult. EPA found that drafting rules concerning a multitude of such situations was even harder than anticipated. After several unsuccessful attempts, the agency decided to issue SNURs on an ad hoc basis. Then, after a pattern perhaps developed, regulations could be prepared.

EPA therefore examined approximately thirty separate chemicals with purported new uses, and on 19 November 1980 proposed its first SNUR on N-methanesulfonyl-p-toluenesulfonamide. Despite evidence of some adverse effects, exposure was considered minimal because annual production for this use was only four hundred pounds a year. The manufacturer was required to give the agency 90-days notice if it should increase production over one thousand pounds (450 kg) a year or change the use. 38/

The significance of its first SNUR was muted, however, by the accompanying explanation from senior EPA officials, such as Deputy Assistant Administrator Warren Muir, that it was not a good example of what they expected in future SNURs. This uniqueness was reinforced when the incoming Reagan administration indicated

---

38/ BNA, Chemical Reporter, 28 November 1980, p. 1105.

its own misgivings about the program. Referring to the candidates for SNUR classification, Muir's successor, Don Clay, expressed doubt that most of the hundred then suggested were actually sufficiently hazardous enough to warrant special treatment; perhaps Section 8(a) reporting requirements (discussed below) might be more appropriate. 39/ The Chemical Manufacturers Association (CMA) favored this latter approach. 40/

The first final SNUR, on two potassium phosphate chemicals, was issued only in September 1984. The manufacturer was required to notify EPA if the concentration of these substances in consumer products exceeded 5 percent to avoid eye irritation. 41/ In another case, at the same time, the agency decided to use the monitoring authority of Section 8(a), rather than issue a SNUR on a chlorinated napthalene. 42/

For whatever reason, EPA still has done little to implement Section 5(a), either by general rule or on a substance-by-substance basis.

6.6 Rejection of PMNs

In December 1979, EPA rejected its first PMN because of inadequate information concerning production volume, disposal methods, and other essentials. The company, which EPA declined to identify, responded that it had assumed only the facts set forth in Section 5(d)(2) were needed. 43/ The reply was unconvincing because Section 5(d)(1), specifying the required data, referred directly to the information listed in Section 8(a)(2).

EPA officials lamented the scarcity of information provided in the early PMNs but, as already discussed, were obliged to deal with the problem on ad hoc basis. 44/ For example, EPA would review the submitted toxicological data and, after critical remarks, would induce the affected company to withdraw its notification, either permanently or pending further submissions or tests. 45/

39/ E.g., ibid., 18 September 1981, p. 555.

40/ Ibid., 8 January 1982, p. 1045; 26 February 1982, p. 1223.

41/ 49 FR 35011, 5 September 1984.

42/ 49 FR 33649, 24 August 1984.

43/ BNA, Chemical Reporter, 4 January 1980, p. 1557.

44/ Ibid, 25 January 1980, p. 1636.

45/ See, for example, ibid., 14 November 1980, p. 1057.

A more formalistic procedure is provided in the lengthy Sections 5(e) and (f) of the act. If the administrator determines that there could be environmental risk and that the information provided is inadequate to make a "reasoned evaluation," he may prohibit chemical production. 46/ If the agency decides that there is an actual indication of hazard, rather than simply insufficient evidence to rebut, Section 5(f) provides that it may prohibit, limit, or otherwise restrict production or use, as set forth in various portions of Section 6. 47/

The first Section 5(e) notice, announced in April 1980, proposed delaying the manufacture of six new but questionable chemicals. The firm dropped its manufacturing plans shortly thereafter. 48/ In September 1980, EPA issued another order to block production of a new chemical pending development of additional information on its human health rules. 49/ That has been the pattern, and to date no manufacturer, either foreign 50/ or domestic, has contested the determinations in federal district court, as permitted in Section 5(f). 51/

It is still not clear under the law what happens next, for the statute is ambiguous; there are as yet no court decisions, and the legislative history offers two inconsistent views. Senator Warren Magnuson (D-Wash.) explained that the House-Senate compromise language here was based on procedure in the FDA law, 52/ whereby the agency could determine if the objections had merit: "If the Administrator determines that valid objections have been filed, then he is required either to seek an injunction or to dismiss the order. If he decides that the objections are not reasonable, then the proposed order becomes effective upon the expiration of the premarket

---

46/ TSCA, § 5(e).

47/ TSCA, § 5(f), esp. (f)(2) referring to TSCA §§ 6(a) and 6(d)(2)(B).

48/ BNA, Chemical Reporter, 25 April 1980, p. 91.

49/ BNA, Chemical Reporter, 5 September 1980, p. 753.

50/ BNA, Chemical Reporter, 16 October 1981, p. 787.

51/ TSCA, § 5(f)(3)(B).

52/ Food, Drug, and Cosmetic Act § 701(e); see also Pfizer v. Richardson, 434 F.2d 536 (2nd Cir. 1970).

notification." 53/ Rep. James T. Broyhill (R-N.C.), on the other hand, informed the House that a company objection, no matter how frivolous, blocks the effect of the administrator's order and forces him to resort to a federal district court for injunctive relief. 54/

When EPA concludes that there is sufficient information to classify a chemical as an unreasonable risk, it may issue a proposed order restricting manufacture, processing, or distribution. It may also directly seek an injunction which, like the above procedure for insufficient data, is also necessary if a company challenges the prospective order. 55/

7.0 INVENTORY LIST: SECTION 8(b)

Because the notification rules apply primarily to new chemical substances, there obviously needs to be a list available of pre-existing chemicals. Under Section 8(b), EPA was therefore required to compile an inventory of chemicals manufactured or processed in the United States. This was not to cover every chemical ever produced but was statutorily limited to those substances produced within the three-year period preceding the promulgation of applicable regulations, namely since 1 January 1975. 56/

The statute required that this list be prepared and published "not later than 315 days after the effective date of this act." This 11 November 1977 deadline proved far too optimistic, for the inventory reporting regulations were not even published until late December 1977, six weeks afterward. 57/ This gave chemical

---

53/ 122 Congressional Record 16803. 28 September 1976: see TSCA § 5(e)(2). The Senate interpretation seems more consistent with the actual language of the act and is probably the approach which EPA will adopt.

54/ Ibid., H-11344.

55/ TSCA, § 5(f). See also the section in this chapter on Enforcement, Part 11.0.

56/ TSCA, § 8(b). The regulations according to Section 8(a) were supposed to have appeared 180 days after the effective date or 1 July 1977. However, they were signed on 12 December 1977 effective 1 July 1978.

57/ 42 FR 64572, 23 December 1977. Regulations were first proposed on 9 March 1977 (42 FR 13130) and after modification were reproposed on 2 August 1977 (42 FR 39182).

companies until 1 May 1978 to submit their products for inclusion in
the inventory, which was finally scheduled for publication in June
1979. 58/ Processors and importers had an additional 210 days to
report any other chemicals, and only after that was a final revised
inventory list published. 59/ This process thus turned into a rather
lengthy one, which consequently considerably delayed the implementation of other parts of the act, particularly premarket notification. 60/

58/ Some manufacturers complained that EPA itself should have
compiled the basic inventory list and then asked chemical companies only to fill in any gaps. This proposal was rejected as
infeasible. See, e.g. Appendix A, Comment 2, 42 FR 64580.

59/ 42 FR 64572, 23 December 1977.

60/ EPA published inventory reporting regulations on 23 December
1977 (42 FR 64572) and supplemented them on 6 March 1978 (43
FR 9254) and on 17 April 1978 (43 FR 16178). In October 1978
(43 FR 49688), a policy for revised inventory reporting was
published. Then, in May 1979, distribution of the initial inventory list, containing over 44,000 chemical substances, began.
Supplement I was published on 9 November 1979 (44 FR 65180).

A second inventory reporting period lasting 210 days began on 1 June 1979. During this period, a person who processed
or used a chemical substance for a commercial purpose or
imported a chemical substance as part of a mixture or article
could report a chemical substance that was not included on the
published Initial Inventory, if the substance was manufactured,
processed, or imported for a commercial purpose since 1 January 1975. The notice of availability of a cumulative supplement
and revised inventory was published in the Federal Register on
29 July 1980 (45 FR 5544).

EPA has also engaged in considerable debate, again cen-
tered on synfuels, whether the particular production process
should affect the definition of a substance on the inventory list.
Initially, the agency said it did. In the case of one substance,
EPA ruled that since the chemical on the 8(b) list was produced
by a method using other raw materials, an identical chemical
with identical properties produced by another method was not
on the inventory list and hence was not "grandfathered." In
early 1984, however, the agency reconsidered the logic of this
position and reversed this stance. In November 1984, EPA made
a similar decision regarding (surprisingly) the very definition of
petroleum.

Any substance not reported for the Inventory by 30 August 1980, or subsequently added under the PMN process, must undergo premanufacture review before it may be manufactured or imported for a commercial purpose. This applies even if a producer can demonstrate that a substance was, in fact, produced before then. The converse, however, does not hold true: EPA has removed from the list certain substances, notably ones involved in synthetic fuels, which it claims were improperly registered as commercial products, and hence "grandfathered," when in fact they were only in research and development at the time. 61/

The obligation to report did not extend to all companies dealing with chemical substances. By regulation, EPA limited this to manufacturers and others with (a) over thirty percent (by weight) of their products classified under SIC code categories 28 or 2911; 62/ or (b) the total chemical production or importation exceeding one million pounds; or (c) special reporting for any substances produced in quantities over a hundred thousand pounds at one site in 1977. 63/

Small manufacturers, defined in the regulations under Section 8 as those with total sales less than five million dollars, were given a limited exemption from some of the reporting requirements. 64/ They were required to submit a list of substances produced but did not need to give production volumes, except for chemicals produced in excess of a hundred thousand pounds, nor separate volume figures for each plant site. This rather trivial exemption is not available to small companies owned or controlled by a larger, non-eligible company. 65/

61/ BNA, Chemical Reporter, 7 August 1981, p.428; 18 June 1982, p. 390.

62/ 40 CFR § 710.3(a). SIC is the abbreviation for "Standard Industrial Classification."

63/ As elsewhere in the act, production includes manufacturing, processing, or importing.

64/ For Section 5 purposes, however, EPA initially proposed defining small business by total sales of less than one million dollars, 44 FR 2242, 10 January 1979.

65/ 40 CFR § 710.2(x). The original Section 8 proposal defined small business as a company having total sales under a hundred thousand dollars. 42 FR 39191 (2 August 1977), EPA officials later confided that this unreasonably low figure was never really serious.

All these "exemptions" were illusory. It was not a benefit for, say, a small company not to report on chemicals it was using; if they were put on the Section 8(b) inventory list, they were "grandfathered" and therefore not subject to burdensome PMN requirements.

Another exemption is for chemical substances produced in "small quantities for purposes of scientific experimentation or analysis or chemical research." The regulation declares a legal presumption that any chemical produced in a quantity of under a thousand pounds annually is for research and development and may therefore not be reported on the inventory, unless the producer can demonstrate otherwise. 66/ A subsequent EPA regulation attempted to clarify this question by suggesting that a manufacturer request his customers to certify that a chemical is not used for purposes other than R & D. 67/

A third exclusion is for "mixtures" which are not considered to be "chemical substances" under Section 8(b). A mixture is defined as any combination of substances which is not the result of chemical reaction and which does not occur in nature. 68/ Remember, however, that mixtures are only excluded from some of the requirements of TSCA; they may still be subject, for example, to the provisions of Sections 4 and 5. 69/

Also exempt from inventory requirements are naturally occurring substances, tobacco, food and food additives, and other chemicals such as drugs and pesticides which are regulated under other federal environmental acts. 70/

66/ 40 CFR § 710.2(y). Section 8(b) of the statute says, "The Administrator shall not include in such list any chemical substance which is manufactured only in small quantities (as defined by the Administrator by rule) solely for purposes of scientific experimentation or analysis of, such substance or other substance, including such research or analysis for the development of a product."

67/ 43 FR 9254, 9255, 6 March 1978.

68/ TSCA, §§ 3 and 8(b). See also 122 Congressional Record H-11020, 23 September 1976.

69/ TSCA, §§ 4(a) and 5(a).

70/ The general exemptions from the definition of "chemical substance" under the Act are set forth in § 3(2)(B). EPA has issued several further clarifications on inventory coverage, such as for natural gas streams (43 FR 16178, 17 April 1978) and natural latex (43 FR 9254, 6 March 1978).

The essential point is, however, that exclusion from the inventory reporting requirements was a mixed blessing. Since placing a substance on the list "grandfathered" it from future PMN requirements, except for significant new uses, it was obviously a benefit for a producer or processor to have everything possible in the inventory.

EPA intends periodically to update the inventory list to include products for which notification forms have been submitted. The most recent compilation was released in the summer of 1985. Future manufacturers can therefore consult the revised list and know that no futher notification to EPA is required, unless special testing under Section 4 is necessary.

8.0 REPORTING REQUIREMENTS

8.1 Section 8(a)

Under Section 8(a) of TSCA, the administrator must promulgate rules under which each person who "manufactures or processes or proposes to manufacture or process a chemical substance" must keep records and make reports to the administrator as is deemed necessary for the effective enforcement of the act. The administrator may require such information as molecular structure, categories of use, amounts produced, description of by-products, disposal methods, and all existing data concerning the environment and health effects of each substance. Manufacturers and processors are persons who manufacture or process chemicals for "commercial purposes."

Section 8 generally exempts small manufacturers or processors from the provisions, although they may be subject under certain circumstances. 71/ In the case of manufacturers or processors of mixtures or of small quantities of research and development chemicals, reports and records may be required to the extent "necessary for the enforcement of this Act."

8.2 Proposed 8(a) Regulation, 1980

Rules governing Section 8(a) were to be promulgated no later than 180 days after TSCA went into effect. However, the proposed rules were not published until 29 February 1980, 72/ more than 2 1/2 years after the deadline for final rules.

71/ Section 8(a)(3)(A)(ii).

72/ 45 FR 13646.

The proposal required chemical manufacturers, including miners and importers, and some processors to report production and exposure-related data on approximately 2300 chemicals, chosen because of toxicity or exposure levels. EPA intended to use this data for preliminary risk assessment and for ranking chemicals.

The proposed rules contained two phases of reporting. First, manufacturers and importers of the chemicals listed had to answer several questions including questions on customer use. Second, if they were unable to report customer use, EPA could require customers to submit information.

Under the Section 8(a) proposal, small manufacturers were defined as having:

(1) total sales for all products at all sites together of less than $30 million for the reportable year, and

(2) production volume at each site for the chemical reported less than 100,000 pounds (45,400 kilograms) for the reportable year.

In October 1980, EPA proposed a generic small business reporting exemption under Section 8(a). This eliminated all record-keeping requirements for qualifying companies, unless they planned to manufacture or process (a) a substance subject to a Section 4 testing rule, (discussed below), (b) a substance categorized as an unreasonable risk under Section 5(b)(4), (c) a restricted substance under Section 6, or (d) one subject to a Section 5(e) rule for additional testing information. 73/

In a planned subsequent rulemaking, the agency wanted to propose Section 8(a) reporting rules for the follow-up of selected new chemicals after they had passed through the PMN process.

8.3 Section 8(a) Final Regulations

The final Section 8(a) regulation, when issued in June 1982 74/, cut the reporting list down drastically from almost 2,300 to only 245 chemicals. Manufacturers must report production, release and

---

73/ 45 FR 66180, 6 October 1980.

74/ 47 FR 26992, 22 June 1982.

exposure data, which will then be used to determine which chemicals deserve further testing. 75/

EPA also published concurrently a 3-part proposed rule under Section 8(a), requiring processors to report on the listed 250 chemicals whenever the manufacturers' reports fail to account for use of 80 percent of the substance. The proposal added another fifty chemicals for consideration for inclusion in the final list. 76/

Subsequently, EPA has indicated an intention to use Section 8(a) to monitor suspect chemicals that are not deemed to merit regulation under Sections 4(f), 5(e), 6, or other sections. There are also plans to follow up all PMN chemicals for several years using this procedure. 77/

On 12 June 1986, EPA issued a final inventory update 78/ under Section 8(a) requiring manufacturers and importers of certain chemical substances in the TSCA Chemical Substances Inventory to report current data on the production, volume, plant site, and site-limited status of the substances. Four categories of substances are generally exempt: polymers, inorganic substances, micro-organisms, and naturally occurring substances. Small manufacturers and firms making less than 10,000 pounds of a subject chemical per year are also exempt. After the initial reporting, recurring reporting will be required every 4 years for as long as the rule is in effect.

In October 1986, EPA proposed a comprehensive assessment information rule (CAIR) under Section 8(a) which would be used by the agency to gather information for use in risk assessments and in developing regulatory strategies for 47 substances. 79/

— 100-page standardized report

— would allow EPA to add chemicals to the CAIR list in a shorter period of time than the current procedures allow

---

75/ See, e.g., 49 FR 25856, June 1984.

76/ 47 FR 26992, 22 June 1982; BNA Chemical Reporter 25 June 1982, pp. 412 and 423ff; 2 April 1982, p. 3.

77/ See, e.g., ibid., 9 March 1984, p. 1707.

78/ 51 FR 21438.

79/ 51 FR 35762.

— would centralize data collection in the Office of Toxic Substances.

8.4 Reporting of Health and Safety Studies: Section 8(d)

Section 8(d) requires the administrator to promulgate rules requiring any person who manufactures, processes, or distributes in commerce any chemical substance or mixture to submit to the administrator:

(1) lists of health and safety studies (A) conducted or initiated by or for such person with respect to such substance or mixture at any time, (B) known to such person, or (C) reasonably ascertainable by such person, except that the administrator may exclude certain types or categories of studies from the requirements of this subsection if the administration finds that submission of lists of such studies are unnecessary to carry out the purposes of this act; and

(2) copies of any study contained on a list submitted pursuant to paragraph (1) or otherwise known by such person. 80/

In July 1978 EPA promulgated rules governing this subsection of TSCA, 81/ requiring manufacturers, processors, or persons distributing in commerce the chemicals on the first Interagency Testing Committee priority list to submit lists and copies of health and safety studies on those chemicals. 82/

The Manufacturing Chemists Association filed a petition requesting EPA to amend or repeal the rule in September 1978. EPA rejected the petition, with minor exceptions. 83/

On 15 September 1978, the Dow Chemical Company filed a petition for review of the rule in the U.S. Court of Appeals for the

---

80/ TSCA, § 8(d)(1) and 8(d)(2).

81/ 43 FR 30984, 18 July 1978.

82/ Two minor corrections were made to the rule shortly thereafter (43 FR 36249, 16 August 1978 and 43 FR 41205, 15 September 1978).

83/ 43 FR 56724, 4 December 1978.

Third Circuit, questioning EPA's authority to obtain studies on chemicals manufactured or processed for research and development purposes, since it was claimed such chemicals are not manufactured or processed for "commercial purposes," or on chemicals from companies that do not manufacture, process or distribute those chemicals. In addition, Dow asserted that EPA had not provided adequate notice and fair opportunity to comment on some of the provisions of the rule.

Although the Court denied Dow's challenge of EPA's authority on 24 August 1979 84/, and EPA itself had no doubt that the provisions of the rule were within the agency's statutory authority, EPA decided that Dow had raised substantial questions on whether adequate notice and comment were provided with respect to some provisions of the rule. Therefore the rule was revoked on 31 January 1979. 85/

A new proposed rule was published in the Federal Register on 31 December 1979 86/ requiring reporting of lists and copies of studies on all chemicals included in the 18 July rule, as well as additional chemicals recommended by the ITC and other chemicals separately selected by EPA. The agency specifically requested comment on whether it should exercise authority to obtain copies of studies on substances from persons in possession of such studies whether or not they manufacture, process, or distribute the substances. The proposal also established an obligation to list on-going studies for five years after a chemical appears on the Section 8(d) list.

The final rule, which appeared in September 1982, 87/ after extensive public comment, somewhat reduced the reporting requirements set forth in the earlier rule.

First, the sweeping definitions of "known to" or in the "possession of" were replaced with a procedural definition that would better indicate when an extensive search could be considered final, for purposes of the act. Companies, henceforth, need only search

---

84/   Dow Chemical Co. v. EPA, 605 F. 2d 673 (3rd Cir. 1979).

85/   44 FR 6099, 31 January 1979.

86/   44 FR 77470, 31 December 1979.

87/   47 FR 38780, 2 September 1982, 40 CFR Part 716.

"the company files in which they ordinarily keep studies and records kept by employees whose assigned duty is to advise the company on health and environmental effects of chemicals." 88/ This search may be limited to records developed after 31 December 1979, when the revised rule 8(d) was proposed.

However, companies which manufactured a chemical within the past ten years, even if they are not currently doing so, are obliged to submit copies of studies but need not provide lists of other known studies. This could be helpful where, say, a company's research uncovered that one of its chemicals was potentially harmful and therefore discontinued it, although other manufacturers continued production unaware.

Distributors are exempted from Section 8(d) reporting by this revised regulation. They do not normally conduct studies anyway, and a review of all submissions under the provisions of the Section 8(d) rule indicated none were from distributors.

Also exempted were seven types of studies that the agency had not found useful in assessing risks but which were burdensome to compile. These exceptions include studies of impurities (which, however, would presumably exempt reports on, say, hazardous dioxin impurities), published studies, and studies submitted previously to EPA or on non-confidential basis to another federal agency.

EPA declined, however, to retreat from its previous position that research and development studies are nevertheless "for commercial purposes" and therefore reportable. Because the agency's contention had already been judicially approved, a subsequent change would have been difficult. The final rule nevertheless relied on a different argument, namely that the purpose of Section 8(d) "is to give the agency access to information from which it can assess the nature and significance of chemical hazards and risks. TSCA is intended to address these hazards and risks to health or the environment whether or not the chemicals are desired commercial products." 89/

8.5 Reports of Health and Safety Studies

Companies routinely test their chemical products for efficiency and safety. Section 8(d) directs that EPA issue rules

---

88/   Ibid.

89/   Ibid., p. 38781.

requiring any person manufacturing, etc., a chemical to provide the agency with copies of such health and safety studies. 90/ But the rule is broader than just that. If the company has copies of, knows of, or reasonably could ascertain that other experimental reports or studies exist regardless of who performed or conducted them, it must also provide copies or lists of those reports. 91/

The administrator is given the statutory authority to exclude certain categories of studies, however, if he determines they are "unnecessary to carry out the purposes of this Act." 92/

This seemingly straightforward section has been the source of considerable controversy. One issue involved a query from a major industry-supported but independent testing lab which had important studies; since it was not a manufacturer, however, it contended it had no obligation under Section 8(d) to report them to EPA. (The information was, of course, provided to EPA in due course.)

A chemical company challenged an obligation to report studies conducted for research and development on substances produced in small quantities and not offered for sale. The company contended that the statutory definition of "manufacture" under Section 8 meant "manufacture or process for commercial purposes" and that this excluded R & D. 93/ The Court of Appeals held, however, that Section 8(d) included just such limited manufacture and, therefore, EPA was authorized to seek the data. 94/

In September 1982 EPA issued a final rule requiring companies to provide the agency with unpublished studies. 95/ The specifically requested information on forty chemicals and chemical categories—thirty-nine recommended for Section 4(e) testing by the eight-agency Federal Interagency Testing Committee (ITC) through

---

90/ TSCA, § 8(d)(1)(A).

91/ TSCA, § 8(d)(1)(B), (C), and 8(d)(2).

92/ TSCA, § 8(d)(1)(C).

93/ TSCA, § 8(f).

94/ Dow Chemical Co. v. EPA, 605 F. 2d 673 (3rd Cir. 1979).

95/ 47 FR 38780, 2 September 1982.

June 1981 (actually about 175 substances), plus asbestos added by EPA. 96/

At the same time, the agency proposed adding another sixty-five chemicals more recently recommended by the ITC. 97/

9.0 HAZARD REPORTING REQUIREMENTS

9.1 Substantial Risk Notification: Section 8(e)

The sweeping general notification requirements of TSCA have swamped EPA with data that, however inadequate, is still more than it could properly analyze and absorb. For the next few years, until comprehensive screening criteria are established, this could mean that information on potentially hazardous substances could languish unanalyzed in EPA files while some chemical tragedy occurs. Indeed, even if analyzed, there is no assurance that the EPA reviewers could differentiate the hazardous from the non-hazardous chemicals. The field of chemical structure analogies is much shakier than the drafters of TSCA assumed. This suggests that notification—the key feature of the entire statute—may require a scientific sophistication that may not be developed for many years.

If health effects cannot be confidently predicted in advance, then EPA must learn of them as soon as they are discovered. Section 8(e) places upon chemical manufacturers, etc., the responsibility for reporting any indication of adverse effect. In the words of the act, any person:

> who obtains information which reasonably supports the conclusion that such substance or mixture presents a substantial risk of injury to health or the environment shall immediately inform the Administrator of such information unless such person has actual knowledge that the Administrator has been adequately informed of such information. 98/

Such a reporting requirement is not unprecedented. Section 6 of FIFRA has a similar provision for "factual information regarding

---

96/ See this Chapter, Paragraph 10.3.

97/ 47 FR 38800, 2 September 1982. This process of adding to, and removing, chemicals from the list continues apace.

98/ TSCA, § 8(e).

unreasonable, adverse effects on the environment. 99/ However, FIFRA's use of the word "unreasonable" assumes, perhaps naively, that the manufacturer himself will make an adverse risk-benefit analysis and then report it. TSCA insists that any evidence of "substantial risk" must be reported. Hard and unmistakable evidence is not required; instead any "information which reasonably supports the conclusion" of possible substantial risk must be reported. Failure to report may subject any individual or company to civil penalties and even criminal prosecution. 100/

EPA issued regulations implementing Section 8(e) in March 1978. 101/ This placed upon corporation presidents and other top officials the responsibility for ensuring that adverse information is reported. 102/ The regulations state, however, that:

> An employing organization may relieve its individual officers and employees of any responsibility for reporting substantial-risk information directly to EPA by establishing, internally publicizing, and affirmatively implementing procedures for employee submission and corporate processing of pertinent information. 103/

99/ FIFRA, § 6(a)(2). A more formal system of five-year post-market surveillance is suggested in the proposed FDA law revisions submitted to Congress in March 1978. FDA Proposal § 108(g).

100/ TSCA, §§ 15(3), 16, and 17. It is interesting to note that in the first major criminal case against a company (Velsicol) for failure to disclose adverse data on the pesticides chlordane and heptachlor, the Justice Department chose to use the general federal criminal laws rather than FIFRA, § 6(a)(2).

101/ 43 FR 11110, 16 March 1978.

102/ This is not an empty threat. The Supreme Court held that a chief executive officer was personally and criminally liable under federal health laws for not preventing rodent contamination of food in one of his warehouses, even though he had delegated responsibility to a corporate vice president. U.S. v. Park, 421 US 658 (1975). This was based on a much older case, U.S. v. Dotterweich, 320 US 277 (1943).

103/ 43 FR 11110, supra, Section II.

In defining substantial risk, the regulation excludes from consideration the "economic or social benefits of use, or cost of restricting use." Moreover the regulation takes a strongly health protectionist view by directing that the extent of exposure is to be given little weight in assessing human health risks, since "the mere fact the implicated chemical is in commerce constitutes sufficient evidence of exposure." 104/

9.2 Significant Adverse Reactions: Section 8(c)

A subsection surprisingly similar to Section 8(e) is Section 8(c). Why are both provisions necessary?

Under Section 8(c) of TSCA, any person who manufactures, etc., any chemical substance or mixture shall maintain records of "significant adverse reactions" alleged to have been caused by the chemical. Those records relating to possible health reactions of employees must be kept for thirty years, during which time they may be inspected by or submitted to anyone he designates. All other recorded allegations need be preserved for only five years.

A comparison of Section 8(c) indicates that both the standard of proof and the required response is appreciably lower than for Section 8(e).

	TSCA § 8(c)	TSCA § 8(e)
Trigger	"Significant adverse reactions"	"Substantial risk of injury"
Evidence	"Alleged"	"Information which reasonably supports the conclusion"
Response	Record and retain for 5 or 30 years	Notify EPA immediately
Regulation	Final 1982	Final 1978

The proposal, published by EPA in July 1980 105/ defined "significant adverse reactions" as "reactions which may indicate a tendency

---

104/ Ibid., at 11111, Section V.

105/ 45 FR 47008, 11 July 1980.

of a chemical substance or mixture to cause long-lasting irreversible damage to health or the environment." Second, all manufacturers, processors and chemical distributors—except retailers—were included in the rule (an estimated 580,000 firms). And third, oral as well as written allegations were required to be recorded.

The final version in September 1982 106/ reflected the Reagan administration's desire for less burdensome regulations. First, the definition was changed to place more emphasis on the word "significant":

> Significant adverse reactions are reactions that may indicate a tendency of a chemical substance or mixture to cause long-lasting or irreversible damage to health or the environment.

Moreover, only previously "unknown" effects need be recorded. This borrows a concept from Section 8(e) that may be appropriate there, where the goal is to inform EPA of new hazards, but is not fitting in a section that essentially provides for a log of health problems and complaints.

Second, the requirement to record oral allegations is dropped, although realistically that is the form in which most worker complaints would be made. Third, only processors in certain SIC code industries (namely, SIC categories 28 and 2911) are covered, while manufacturers of "naturally-occurring" substances are exempted entirely. This reduces the number of affected firms by over 98 percent, to only 10,000. And fourth, while the statute gave EPA an alternative of record inspection or submission, the final regulation opted for the former, with no automatic reporting requirement.

10.0 TESTING REQUIREMENTS

10.1 General Testing Requirements: Section 4(a)

Section 4(a) of TSCA permits EPA to require the testing of any chemicals, both old and new, if an unreasonable risk to health or the environment is suspected. 107/ Testing may also be required if a

---

106/ 47 FR 38780, 2 September 1982; see also EPA Concept Paper on Section 8(c), 8 July 1982.

107/ TSCA, § 4(a)(1)(A).

chemical will be produced in such quantities that significant human or environmental exposure could result. 108/

Mixtures are also subject to the above rules, but only when the effects cannot be determined or predicted by testing the individual chemical substances which comprise the mixture. 109/ This should reduce the testing burden, particularly for small producers and formulators.

Note that not all questionable chemicals need be tested—only those for which EPA makes a specific determination that additional data is necessary and issues a formal testing rule. This standard may prescribe the biochemical effects to be investigated, the tests to be conducted, and even the experimental protocols to be followed. 110/ The statute itself, in Section 4(b), details many of the studies that may be required, including carcinogenicity, mutagenicity, teratogenicity, behavioral modification, synergism, and various degrees of toxicity. Moreover, EPA must review each testing standard at least once a year and revise them where warranted. 111/

In setting these testing standards, the EPA administrator is to consider the relative costs and availability of facilities and personnel, and the period within which they can reasonably be per formed. 112/ This little-noticed provision could have considerable future significance, if and when the agency ever gets serious about issuing testing rules, for the present animal testing capability in this country could be saturated by a sudden increase in demand.

108/ TSCA, § 4(a)(1)(B).

109/ TSCA, § 4(a)(2).

110/ This rulemaking is subject to the Administrative Procedure Act, 5 U.S.C. § 551, including requirements for a transcript.

111/ TSCA, § 4(b)(2). An earlier bill required EPA to propose test protocols within one year of enactment but this was not in the final version. See Senate Committee on Commerce, "Toxic Substance Control Act of 1973, Report on S.426," (D.C: G.P.O., 1973), p. 7.

112/ TSCA § 4(b)(1).

EPA's effort to develop test standards under Section 27 is presently encountering serious technical difficulties. Consequently, publication of these important protocols could be delayed. 113/

A company intending to run tests on a chemical for which EPA has issued no standard under Section 4(a) but may do so in the future, can formally request from EPA testing rules for that product. 114/ This could help avoid later charges that the tests were inadequate or otherwise not in conformity with EPA requirements. It would also help a company in litigation with OSHA or other parties, even if no Section 4(a) rule is ever issued.

In 1981, for example, EPA took 14 test rule actions and decided not to regulate testing on three other chemicals. 115/ This was overshadowed, however, by the Reagan administration's penchant for voluntary testing over required rules, despite charges from environmental groups that it undermines TSCA. 116/ In August 1984, a federal district court agreed with the environmentalists and held that the voluntary system subverted the mandatory system set forth in the statute.

10.2 Testing Reimbursement

Because toxicological testing is so expansive, TSCA borrowed from the pesticide act a provision for sharing of testing costs. 117/ The reimbursement period is generally five years from date of submission but may be modified by the administrator to conform to the time that was necessary to develop such data. 118/ If the manufac-

---

113/ TSCA, § 27.

114/ TSCA, § 4(g). EPA has sixty days to grant or deny the petition. Then, if granted, it has only seventy-five days to issue test standards; if denied, the Agency must publish reasons for the denial in the Federal Register.

115/ BNA, Chemical Reporter, 26 March 1982, p. 1323.

116/ Ibid., 9 July 1982, p. 468.

117/ FIFRA, § 3(c)(1)(D), 7 U.S.C. § 136a(C)(1)(D). This issue is discussed later, in the chapter on Pesticides.

118/ TSCA, § 4(c)(3)(B).

turers cannot decide among themselves a proper allocation of costs, the administrator—as formerly in FIFRA—is required to adjudicate the dispute after consultation with the Attorney General and the Federal Trade Commission. 119/ Sharing such data exempts subsequent producers from having to conduct or submit duplicative test results.

The agency has proposed a reimbursement rule under Section 4 which will share the cost of testing between producers in proportion to their production volume. The proposal also suggests a mechanism for adjudicating disputes on cost claims. 120/

The equivalent section in the pesticide act has been the source of more controversy, uncertainty, and administrative inconvenience than any other issue. Except that the testing burden for notification is less than for registration of pesticides, this section of TSCA is unlikely to be a greater success under TSCA than FIFRA.

10.3 Priority List for Chemical Testing

There are tens of thousands of potentially toxic substances. Congress recognized that if EPA tried simultaneously to regulate all of them with its limited resources, it might actually accomplish nothing. 121/ This was important, for an earlier agency attempt to keep short the first list of regulated toxic substances under Section 307 of the Clean Water Act had failed when challenged by environmentalists in court. 122/

Section 4(e) of the act therefore provided for a priority list of chemicals for testing and directed that it "may not, at any time, exceed 50." 123/ The "list of 50" may contain groups of chemicals

---

119/ TSCA, § 4(c).

120/ BNA, Chemical Reporter, 11 June 1982, p. 349.

121/ Congressional authorization for the first year of TSCA implementation was originally only ten million dollars, a fraction of the sum allocated for other EPA programs at their inception. This has since been substantially increased. See TSCA, § 29.

122/ N.R.D.C. v. Train, 8 ERC 2120 (D.D.C. 1976).

123/ TSCA, § 4(e)(1)(A).

as well as individual substances. This permits considerable expansion of the list's scope, if the administrator so desires. The final list will leave a number of vacancies that can be filled if important new chemical hazards are discovered.

The procedure for preparing this list is spelled out in excruciating detail: a committee of eight members, each from a designated government agency, 124/ was given until the end of September 1977 to submit a candidate slate, based on toxicity and exposure, to EPA administrator for public comment and his final decision. 125/ Within twelve months he must either initiate a rulemaking under Section 4(a) or publish the reasons why not. 126/

The preparation of the inventory priority list began with an initial list of approximately 3650 chemicals compiled from nineteen scientific sources. Next, substances under the jurisdiction of other federal laws, such as pesticides and drugs, were deleted. These and other deletions led to a Master File of 1700, which was then screened for production volume and population exposure to produce a Preliminary List of 330 chemicals which was published in July 1977. This list was in turn reduced to a candidate list of eighty.

In October 1977 the Interagency Testing Committee (ITC) nominated the first group of ten substances (six categories of chemicals and four individual substances) to the administrator. 127/ A

124/ These include EPA, OSHA, CEQ, NIOSH, NIEHS, NCI, NSF, and the Department of Commerce. Several other agencies overlooked by the statute, such as FDA, have unofficially become a part of the committee. Others include the Consumer Product Safety Commission (CPSC), and the Department of Defense and Interior. Members serve four years, may not have any financial interest, or accept employment for one year from anyone subject to TSCA.

125/ TSCA, § 4(e)(2). The priority list is supposed to be updated every six months.

126/ TSCA, § 4(e)(1)(B). One observer, who believed the nine month period was too long, had earlier described the process as confirmation of Parkinson's law that work expands to fit the time. He was overly optimistic.

127/ 42 FR 55026, 12 October 1977. This group included alkyl epoxides and phthalates, chlorinated benzenes and paraffins, chloromethane, cresols, hexachlorobutadiene, nitrobenzene, toluene, and xylenes.

second set of eight recommendations (four categories and four individual substances) was submitted in April 1978. 128/

The third report of the ITC recommended the addition of three substances (two categories of chemicals and one individual substance) in October 1978. 129/ Twelve new substances (one category of chemicals and eleven individual substances) were added in April 1979. 130/

In October 1978, twelve months after the publication of the initial priority list, EPA decided it was not yet prepared to issue rules by the statutory deadline, so it withdrew that first group and declared that it would postpone testing rule-making until appropriate standards were developed. 131/ This action was widely criticized as both illegal and unimaginative. On 8 May 1979, the National Resources Defense Council (NRDC) instituted an eventually successful suit against EPA for failure to develop testing rules on the initial ITC recommendations. 132/

The chairman of the ITC under the Reagan administration, Elizabeth Weinburger, announced in March 1982 that the committee would no longer examine broad categories of chemicals, but half of the first group listed were categories rather than individual substances. 133/ This group of highest priority testing candidates was as follows:

128/ 43 FR 16684, 19 April 1978. This listed acylamide, aryl phospates, chlorinated naphthalenes, dichloromethane, halogenated alkyl epoxides, polychlorinated terphenyls, pyridine, and 1,1,1-trichloroethane.

129/ 43 FR 50630, 30 October 1978. This group listed dichloropropane, glycidol and its derivatives, and chlorinated benzenes—tri, tetra, and penta.

130/ 3 BNA, Chemical Regulation Reporter, 4 May 1979, p. 110. This list includes acetonitrile, aniline and chloro-, bromo-, and nitroanilines; antimony; antimony sulfide; antimony trioxide; cyclohexanone; hexachlorocyclopentadiene; isophorone; mesityl oxide; 4,4-methylenedianiline; methyl ethyl ketone; and methyl isobutyl ketone.

131/ 43 FR 50134, 26 October 1978.

132/ N.R.D.C. v. Costle, 14 ERC 1858 (S.D. N.Y. 1980).

133/ BNA, Chemical Regulation Reporter, 26 March 1982, p. 1323.

The Original TSCA Section 4(e) Priority List

Entry	Date of Designation
1. Acetonitrile	April 1979
2. Acrylamide (environmental effects)	April 1978
3. Alkyl epoxides	October 1979
4. Aniline and bromo-, chloro-, and/or nitroanilines	April 1978
5. Antimony (metal)	April 1979
6. Antimony (sulfide)	April 1979
7. Antimony trioxide	April 1979
8. Aryl phosphates	April 1978
9. Biphenyl	April 1982
10. Bis(2-ethylhexyl) terephthalate	October 1982
11. Chlorinated benzenes, mono- and, di- (environmental effects)	October 1977
12. Chlorinated benzenes, tri-, tetra-, and penta-(environmental effects)	October 1978
13. Cresols	October 1977
14. Cyclohexanone	April 1979
15. Dibutyltin bis(isooctyl maleate)	October 1982
16. Dibutyltin bis(isooctyl mercaptoacetate)	October 1982
17. Dibutyltin bis(lauryl mercaptide)	October 1982
18. Dibutyltin dilaurate	October 1979
19. 1,2-Dichloropropane	October 1978
20. Dimethyltin bis(isooctyl mercaptoacetate)	October 1982
21. 1,3-Dioxolane	October 1982
22. Ethyltoluene	April 1982
23. Formamide	April 1982
24. Glycidol and its derivatives	October 1978
25. Halogenated alkyl epoxides	April 1978
26. Hexachloro- 1,3-butadiene	October 1977
27. Hexachlorocyclopentadiene	April 1979
28. Hydroquinone	November 1979
29. Isophorone	April 1979
30. Mesityl oxide	April 1979
31. 4,4'-Methylenedianiline	April 1979
32. Methyl ethyl ketone	April 1979
33. Methyl isobutyl ketone	April 1979
34. Monobutyltin tris(isooctyl mercaptoacetate)	October 1982
35. Monomethyltin tris(isooctyl mercaptoacetate)	October 1982

36.	Pyridine	April 1978
37.	Quinone	November 1979
38.	4-(1,1,3,3,-Tetramethylbutyl) phenol	October 1982
39.	Toluene	October 1977
40.	1,2,4-Trimethylbenzene	April 1982
41.	Tris(2-ethylhexyl) trimellitate	October 1982
42.	Xylenes	October 1977

This list, it should be noted, is not a permanent one. A chemical is placed on it until designated for testing or determined to be inappropriate. There has thus been a parade of substances on and off the 4(e) list. So far there have been almost a hundred substances on and off this list.

11.0 EPA'S REGULATORY ROLE

EPA is given broad authority to take whatever regulatory measures are deemed necessary to restrict chemicals suspected of posing harm to man or the environment. The procedures are modeled basically on the pesticide act, although there are several important differences. Like FIFRA, there is a regulatory distinction between substances presenting unreasonable risks (Section 6) and those more severe cases which constitute an imminent hazard (Section 7). 134/

11.1 Section 6
TSCA borrows its definition of hazard for invoking "cancellation" directly from FIFRA: "unreasonable risk of injury to health or the environment." 135/ There is, however, one small change—the phrase is preceded by the words "presents or will present." This was added to avoid the contention that "risk" meant a certainty of harm,

---

134/ Compare FIFRA, §§ 6(b) and 6(c) with TSCA, §§ 6 and 7. Note that while TSCA does not use the terms "cancellation" or "suspension," since there is no registration to cancel or suspend as under FIFRA, these are nevertheless convenient terms to use for the process in Section 6 and 7.

135/ TSCA, § 6(a).

as had been proposed by an appellate court panel (later reversed) in a case under Section 211 of the Clean Air Act. 136/

Section 6 authority is not restricted to removing a chemical from the market. It may also include limiting the amount that can be produced, prohibiting or limiting specific uses considered most hazardous, requiring labels and warnings, mandating extensive manufacturing and monitoring records, controlling disposal, "or otherwise regulating any manner or method of commercial use of such substance or mixture." Restrictions may even be applied in some geographical areas and not in others. Quality controls in manufacturing or processing may be required if there is a potential problem of highly toxic impurities, such as TCDD in the herbicide 2,4,5-T. The manufacturer or processor may be required to replace or repurchase products held to constitute a hazard. 137/

The regulations for implementing Section 6 rulemakings were issued in final in December 1977. 138/ These emphasized flexible procedures, rather than strict adherence to the Administrative Procedure Act, although a limited right of cross examination is provided. Subpoena authority is also available, although to be used sparingly.

11.2 PCB, CFC and Asbestos

One of the most controversial chemicals EPA has had to deal with is polychlorinated biphenyls (PCBs). Congress sought to insure that EPA would confront the problem by specifically mandating action and a regulatory timetable in Section 6(e). This unusual step prodded EPA into banning some uses of PCBs in 1977 and most production and use in April 1979. 139/ EPA estimates that the new

---

136/ Ethyl Corp. v. EPA, 7 ERC 1353 (CADC 1975): reversed en banc by 541 F. 2d 1, 8 ERC 1785 (CADC 1976); cert. denied 426 U.S. 941, 8 ERC 220 (1976). Section 112 of the Clean Air Act authorizes regulation of potentially harmful fuel additives, especially lead.

137/ TSCA, § 6(a) and (b).

138/ 40 CFR Part 750, 2 December 1977.

139/ 3 BNA Chemical Regulation Reporter, 20 April 1979, p.49. See also Preamble to EPA Final Rules for PCBs Manuf., 17 April 1979.

more stringent standard will bring nearly a million additional pounds of PCBs under control. 140/ PCB regulation and enforcement has become so important under TSCA that the next main heading in this Chapter, 12.0, is devoted exclusively to it.

Another widely publicized chemical group is the chlorofluoro-carbon. On 17 March 1978, EPA promulgated final regulations prohibiting almost all of the manufacturing, processing, and distribution of chlorofluorocarbons for those aerosol propellent uses subject to TSCA. 141/ These regulations became effective 15 October 1978. More recently, EPA has proposed to ban five uses of asbestos under Section 6 and to force users to find alternatives to asbestos over a 10-year period. 142/

11.3 Imminent Hazards: Section 7

Although "imminent hazard" determinations have been invoked repeatedly under FIFRA (i.e., suspension), and the agency has been criticized for not using it more, the equivalent provision under TSCA, Section 7, has not once been used. It has rarely even been seriously considered as a regulatory option.

The standard for "suspension" actions under Section 7 of TSCA is, as with pesticides, an "imminent hazard." This is defined more stringently than in FIFRA, however, as "a chemical substance or mixture which presents an imminent and unreasonable risk of serious or widespread injury to health or the environment." 143/

EPA may also take action during premarket notification where there is insufficient information to evaluate health or environmental effects. EPA must go to court in order to halt the manufacture or prohibit a specific use of a substance, if the manufacturer objects to the proposed EPA ban, or where there is adequate evidence that the substance presents an unreasonable risk. 144/

Unlike FIFRA, enforcement orders under TSCA cannot be issued solely on the agency's own authority, challengeable only

---

140/ BNA, Chemical Regulation Reporter, 6 April 1979, p. 3.

141/ 43 FR 55241, 27 November 1978.

142/ 51 FR 3738, 23 January 1986.

143/ TSCA, § 7(f).

144/ TSCA, § 5(f).

before the court of appeals. Instead, if a proposed restrictive rule is contested, EPA must seek an injunction from a federal district court, which will itself determine whether there is sufficient basis for legal action. EPA may also initiate a civil suit in district court seize an imminently hazardous chemical. 145/ Judicial review of final EPA orders is limited to the circuit of courts of appeals, which must determine whether the agency action is supported by substantial evidence on the record as a whole. 146/

The rulemaking procedures assure manufacturers of a full range of due process safeguards, including reasonable hearing procedures, the right of cross-examination during rulemaking, and the right of appeal. EPA's authority to propose an immediately effective rule to ban or limit manufacture of an existing chemical is limited by the requirement that it first obtain a court injunction based on the same legal criteria as applied in cases of imminent hazard. Therefore, a substantial degree of proof is required, procedural safeguards afforded, and assurance provided that EPA cannot act without good cause.

While the agency has used its Section 6 authority sparingly apart from the specific instance of Section 6(e) PCB regulation, it has not used Section 7 at all yet.

12.0 PCB REGULATION

The regulation of polychlorinated biphenyls (PCBs) is an anomaly. Nowhere else in the environmental laws is a substance banned by name, although there have been occasional requirements that EPA examine specific substances—such as asbestos, mercury, beryllium and cadmium under Clean Air Act Section 112—for possible eventual regulation. Because of perennial dissatisfaction with various agency actions, Congress has discussed utilizing this device further, either to restrict additional chemicals or, especially with FDA on saccharin, to prevent regulators from restricting a chemical. Thus, the PCB issue is interesting not only because of the broad public attention it has received but also as a possible regulatory precedent for future actions.

145/ TSCA, § 7(a), (b); see also § 6(c),(d).

146/ TSCA, § 19.

PCBs have been used as transformer fluids and dielectics, but their darker side was not revealed until a tragic episode in Japan in 1969. Cooking oil somehow became contaminated with PCB leaking from a transformer. Whether from the PCBs themselves or from furans and other contaminants, this resulted in deaths, central nervous system damage, serious stomach and liver disorders, and possibly cancer. Immediate steps were taken in Japan to prevent this problem from recurring. No action was taken in the United States, however, until several more years and several serious incidents later.

PCBs are ubiquitous in the environment. They are stable even at high temperatures, and may not break down into non-toxic compounds for many years. PCBs sealed in a transformer may last 15, 20, or perhaps 25 years before needing replacement because of eventual leaks.

Following a number of episodes in Michigan and elsewhere (actually due largely to the unrelated polybrominated biphenyls) Congressman John Dingell (D-Mich.) and other representatives inserted Section 6(e) into the final version of TSCA. It provided for a schedule which would first stop PCB manufacture and then gradually curtail its use. EPA, as usual, missed most of the deadlines but did finally issue a series of regulations implementing the statute.

Section 6(e) directed EPA to phase-out PCB manufacture and use according to a statutorily-mandated timetable. After one year from the passage of the act (that is, by October 1977) no one was allowed to manufacture, process, distribute, or use any PCB except in "a totally enclosed manner." 147/ Unless the administrator finds no unreasonable risk, 148/ no one may manufacture PCBs at all after two years, nor distribute it after 2 1/2 years. 149/ If needed, the administrator may utilize any other provision of TSCA or of any other federal law to regulate PCBs. 150/

At the time of enactment, these provisions seemed to pose no problem. There was only one remaining PCB manufacturer in the

---

147/ Defined in TSCA, § 6(e)(2)(C).

148/ See TSCA, § 6(e)(3)(B).

149/ TSCA, § 6(e)(3).

150/ TSCA, § 6(e)(5).

United States and it intended to abandon the business. Utilities and other owners of PCB-filled electric transformers and capacitors were permitted to maintain their equipment for its working life, provided it did not leak or require major servicing. Congressmen could therefore vote for tough regulation of unpopular PCBs a month before national elections, without any appreciable political risk.

EPA's initial regulations addressed four categories: PCB transformers (those having over 500 parts per million of PCB in the transformer fluid); PCB-contaminated transformers (having between 50 and 500 parts per million); and a category not specifically defined except by exclusion, which would be non-PCB transformers, defined as those less than 50 parts per million. The fourth category, not discussed here, was railroad transformers.

Such transformers were required to be appropriately labeled, standards were set for transport of PCB, and disposal of techniques were outlined including incineration.

The statute exempted transformers and other uses that were "totally enclosed." If a transformer were not "totally enclosed," it must be banned. But how would EPA know; and did a tiny, well-contained leak of a thimblefull a year constitute a non-enclosed use requiring tens of thousands of dollars for equipment replacement? First of all, there is a problem called "sweating"—a fancy word EPA likes for small leaks, and in March 1980 it requested comments on the extent "weeping" or "sweating" was a problem for PCB transformers. The answers the agency received were quite varied, ranging from estimates of 80-90 percent sweating to a fraction of that. EPA decided not to issue regulations, hoping the issue would just fade away.

An environmental group, the Environmental Defense Fund (EDF), brought suit against EPA's 1978 and 1979 implementing regulations 151/ and persuaded the court of appeals to strike them down as "unsupported by the record." 152/ Because of the broad nature of the suit, this meant that EDF won not only on the issue that prompted the suit, namely a desire for stringent inspection and maintenance of electrical equipment, but on most other issues as

---

151/ 43 FR 7150, 17 February 1978; 44 FR 31542, 31 May 1979.

152/ Environmental Defense Fund v. EPA, 636 F. 2d 1267, 15 ERC 1081 (CADC, 1980).

well. This included the 50 ppm cut off level for regulation, which was admittedly arbitrary but reflected the consensus of authorities. And that led to problem number two.

Many chemical processes involving aromatics and chlorine were found to produce small but measureable traces of PCBs as unintended by products. This could affect up to a quarter of all American chemical operations, most of whom did not (and probably still do not) realize they were vulnerable to EPA enforcement or citizens' suits for "manufacturing" PCBs in violation of the law.

After a series of chemical and electrical industry surveys, EPA proposals, 153/ and public hearings, EPA decided to issue three sets of regulations. 154/ Rule One, published in August 1982, 155/ applied to electric transformers and capacitors. It prohibited PCB-filled equipment near food and feed after October 1985 (the proposed rule allowed indefinite use, subject to weekly self-inspections), authorized most other electrical equipment for the remainder of its useful life, subject to (for large transformers) a quarterly self-inspection, allowed storage for disposal of non-leaking equipment outside of qualified storage facilities, and provided for retaining three years of maintenance records.

Rule Two, issued in October 1982, 156/ exempted byproduct manufacture which took place entirely within closed systems or separated as designated waste for disposal by EPA-approved methods. Although originally requested by the companies, the lengthy final version was opposed because it promised an "exemption" for which few if any companies could honestly qualify. None did.

153/ See 47 FR 24976, 8 June 1982.

154/ Ironically, despite the Reagan administration's expressed preference for agreements instead of edicts, the agency rebuffed a negotiated settlement proposed in late 1982 by an unusual coalition of chemical industry and environmentalist groups. The final regulation two years later was insubstantially different.

155/ 47 FR 37342, 25 August 1982.

156/ 47 FR 46980, 21 October 1982.

Rule Three, applying generally to the incidental by-product problem in the chemical industry, is currently in preparation. A related question involved in protracted litigation is whether monochlorinated biphenyls are polychlorinated biphenyls. Despite linguistic and persistence arguments, EPA decided they were and brought a major enforcement action against a leading chemical company. The company's challenge to the regulations was dismissed for lack of jurisdiction, 157/ then pursued through a protracted series of hearings and appeals within EPA. The agency judicial officer, Ron McCallum, ruled in July 1982 that the company had indeed violated the PCB rules and that the courts of appeals, not an enforcement proceeding, was the proper forum for a challenge to the definition of PCB. 158/

Meanwhile, the debate continues. The definition of "totally enclosed" had to be modified, with comments obtained in September 1984. For "inadvertent generation" of PCB by-products, EPA prepared new rules in 1984 which showed an annual average of 25 ppm and a maximum concentration of 50 ppm. PCBs vented into the outside air cannot exceed 10 ppm. 159/

The transformer rule issued in 1982 exempted approximately 140,000 potentially dioxin-containing electrical transformers. But the concern has grown that this did not do enough to prevent transformer fires in heavily populated areas that could emit large quantities of dangerous fumes. Therefore, EPA prepared proposed regulations in 1984 to isolate transformers from ventilation ducts and require the removal of combustibles stored near transformers. 160/ A final rule restricting the use of certain PCB transformers in commercial buildings was issued 17 July 1985. 161/ The rule is a more stringent version of the electrical transformers rule published by EPA in October 1984.

157/ Dow Chemical Co. v. Costle, 484 F.Supp. 101 (D. Del., 1980).

158/ BNA, Chemical Reporter, 20 August 1982, p. 645; see also 30 July 1982, p. 558.

159/ Ibid., 7 September 1984, p. 590; Washington Post, 2 July 1984.

160/ Washington Post, 2 April 1984, 17 October 1984.

161/ 50 FR 29170.

The once-simple PCB issue remains a troublesome one, because of this lawsuit and its consequences, because the agency was long unwilling to make decisions on incineration and on other disposal techniques, and because the problem is technically and legally more complex than anyone imagined. Meanwhile, Congress has grown impatient with the delays. As it pointed out rather bitterly to EPA on the eve of the current litigation, even four years after decisive action was ordered, 99 percent of the PCBs in the United States are still in existence.

13.0 CONFIDENTIALITY

Since a principal function of TSCA is the collection of voluminous information on chemical substances, concern for the protection of genuine trade secrets continues to be a hotly debated topic.

Section 14 provides that EPA may not release any information which is not exempt from mandatory disclosure under the Freedom of Information Act (FOIA). 162/ This excludes "trade secrets and commercial or financial information obtained from a person and privileged or confidential." 163/ TSCA does not prohibit the disclosure of health and safety studies nor, of course, the release of information to federal officials in the performance of their duties. Data may also be disclosed to protect "against an unreasonable risk of injury to health or the environment" in a legal proceeding. There is interestingly no allowance for release of information to state health authorities, despite the lessons of the Kepone tragedy, although perhaps they could qualify by being made "contractors with the United States." 164/

EPA's general regulations for dealing with FOIA requests under its various statutes were issued in September 1976. 165/ Although they tend strongly to favor disclosure, EPA had relatively few business secrets in its files, so industry has had few objections

---

162/ TSCA, § 14(a).

163/ Administrative Procedure Act § 2, 5 U.S.C. § 552(b)(4).

164/ TSCA § 14(b) and (a); see also 40 CFR § 2.301(h), 43 FR 2637, 18 January 1978.

165/ 41 FR 36902, 1 September 1976.

so far to these procedures. The exception is pesticides regulation, which for several years has been entangled by litigation over release of data. 166/

Some chemical industry representatives have complained that existing laws are not sufficiently protective of confidential business information. The president of the Manufacturing Chemists Association, for example, has expressed concern that as long as the trade secret exemption under the FOIA remains permissive, "there is no assurance that privately developed information submitted to the government in confidence will not be disclosed." 167/

EPA modified some portions of the original March 1977 inventory reporting proposal 168/ to assuage certain industry fears, such as by deleting the requirement that a toxicological bibliography be submitted. 169/ The agency has also established a task force to establish computer security precautions to protect information submitted or stored on magnetic tape. 170/

Polaroid Corporation challenged the adequacy of protection provided for chemical trade secrets which the company was required to furnish EPA under the reporting regulations. In June 1978, a U.S. district judge denied the request that Polaroid be excused from reporting the information, but also issued an injunction ordering EPA not to disclose the information outside the agency. 171/

166/ Mobay Chemical Corp v. Train, F. Supp., 8 ERC 1227 (D.C. W. Mich. 1975); dismissed per curiam U.S., 8 January 1979.

167/ Letter from former MCA President William J. Driver to Sen. James Abzourek (D-S.D.), Chairman of the Administrative Practice and Procedure Subcommittee of the Senate Judiciary Committee, 18 January 1978, quoted in BNA Environment Reporter, 1978, p. 1468.

168/ 42 FR 13130, 9 March 1977.

169/ 42 FR 39182, 39188, 2 August 1977, reproposing 40 CFR 710.7(e).

170/ See, e.g., 42 FR 53804, 53805, 3 October 1977; 43 FR 1836, 12 January 1978.

171/ Polaroid Corp. v. Costle, No. 78-11335 (D. Mass. 1978).

Then on 8 September 1978, EPA issued amendments to its confidential business information regulations 172/ providing substantial protection for TSCA confidential information and providing for notice to affected businesses before confidential information is disclosed outside EPA. 173/ Polaroid withdrew its suit and the Court order was vacated. The problem of confidentiality nevertheless will continue to be a sensitive issue for the foreseeable future.

EPA has consistently insisted that requests for confidentality be accompanied by an explanation to why it is needed. Merely calling something a trade secret does not make it so. Although the first policy issued by the Reagan administration on Section 5 provided that under PMN a manufacturer could withhold data as confidential without providing a rationale, 174/ Congress is monitoring this area very closely and has threatened to pass legislation restricting the scope of confidentiality if companies abuse the privilege. 175/

14.0 TSCA ENFORCEMENT

EPA has recently announced a stricter enforcement policy through stiffer penalties. For example, in the summer of 1985, six chemical manufacturers were fined a total of $6.9 million for allegedly failing to notify the agency prior to making new chemicals.

At around the same time, Chemical Waste Management Inc. was required to pay a $2.5 million fine for violations of TSCA Section 6 regulations governing processing, storage, distribution, recordkeeping, marking, and disposal requirements for PCBs. EPA initially sought $6.8 million. Yet, the $2.5 million fine is still the largest in the history of EPA.

172/ 40 CFR Part 2, 43 FR 3997, 8 September 1978.

173/ This provision for notification to the company was already set forth in Section 14(c) of the statute.

174/ BNA, Chemical Reporter, 7 February 1982, p. 443.

175/ See, e.g., reports in ibid., 3 August 1984, p. 483. The head of EPA's toxics office, John Moore, requested that companies claim less data as confidential, to ease the evaluation by his staff. Ibid., 6 April 1984, p. 3.

On 1 March 1985, EPA proposed to fine Union Carbide Corporation $3.9 million for its alleged delay of Section 8(e) reporting safety data on diethyl sulfate, the second largest fine ever proposed by EPA. Four months later Diamond Shamrock Corporation agreed to pay $800,000 in penalties after it was charged with illegally disposing of wastes contaminated with PCBs.

The first enforcement cases under Section 13 chemical import certification requirements and Section 4 chemical testing requirements were announced by EPA on 3 October 1985.

15.0 CITIZEN ENFORCEMENT AND LEGAL FEES

Private citizens are allowed, even encouraged, to participate in TSCA administrative and judicial proceedings. 176/ Section 21 provides that any person may petition the administrator to take action on rules under Sections 4-8, excepting imminent hazard determinations under Section 7; the administrator then has 90 days either to grant or deny the petition. If he denies the petition, a citizen may initiate civil action in a federal district court. 177/

The section has been used by the Service Employees International Union requesting asbestos standards for schools (granted), a company wishing to leave PCB-contaminated soil in a mine shaft (denied), and an association wishing to delete the inventory designation of inorganic glass as mixtures (denied). 178/ Despite its name, it has been little used by ordinary citizens.

Citizens may also file suit under Section 20 to compel the administrator to perform any non-discretionary duty, or against anyone including the government alleged to be in violation of any rules issued under Sections 4-6. The plaintiff, however, must give

---

176/ The citizen participation sections were missing in whole or part from earlier versions of TSCA. For example, H.R. 5356 of 1973 had neither section, while the Senate bill (S.426) had a citizens suit provision (§ 19) but only an oblique reference to citizen petitions (§ 24a). See House Report 93-360 (1973) and Senate Report 93-254 (1973).

177/ TSCA, § 21.

178/ EPA Office of Toxic Substances, Bulletin, March 1984; ibid., May 1984; 49 FR 36844, 20 September 1984.

EPA the traditional 60 days notice before he may commence his litigation. 179/
    The exclusion of Section 7 from both the citizens petition and citizens suit sections of TSCA is particularly striking, considering that under FIFRA the imminent hazard area has been a prime focus of activity by environmental groups.
    Attorney and witness fees may be awarded by the courts to persons litigating under TSCA. There is no requirement that the person's legal position has prevailed, or that such an award be limited to so-called public interest groups, although that is surely its main concern. The statutory test is simply that costs and reasonable fees may be granted "if the court determines that such an award is appropriate." 180/

16.0 BIOTECHNOLOGY: TOXIC REGULATION

    The field of biotechnology promises great advances in human well being, such as the creation of industrial enzymes which would be capable of, among other things, purifying water and degrading toxic chemical wastes. However, because genetic engineering is so new, still being developed, and little understood, it has been surrounded by controversy over both its safeness and who should regulate it.
    On 18 June 1986, President Reagan signed a Coordinated Framework for Regulation of Biotechnology, which sets out specific agency roles and statutory authority and ensures the industry's environmental safety and economic viability. Legislation has also been proposed recently in Congress to set up a regulatory structure for reviewing the safety of genetically engineered products under TSCA. However, the Biotechnology Science Coordination Act (HR 4452) was criticized by industry for defining genetically engineered organisms too narrowly. The bill was also criticized for not giving EPA enough discretion to regulate genetically engineered products on a case-by-case basis. EPA's ability to regulate biotechnology under TSCA has also been questioned.

179/ TSCA, § 20.

180/ TSCA, § 19(d).

Despite the efforts to regulate biotechnology, there are some who are dissatisfied that the efforts have not regulated the biotechnology industry enough. Jeremy Rifkin, who heads the environmental group called Foundation for Economic Trends, is one of the most determined opponents. In fact, he believes that biotechnology should be banned altogether. Although most of his attention has been focused on biotechnology developments and efforts in the pesticides field (see Chapter 11 on pesticides), he has also fought the biotechnology industry in all other areas, including toxics.

For example, on 2 September 1986, Rifkin filed suit in the U.S. District Court for the District of Columbia against the Department of Defense (DOD) to enjoin the U.S. military from testing, developing and producing toxic biological warfare materials until the military prepares environmental impact statements. The foundation first sued DOD in November 1984 to prohibit the military from building a proposed biological warfare testing facility in Utah. An injunction was granted in May 1985 and is still in effect.

A landmark case decided in 1980, which Rifkin lost and which should be mentioned here, is Diamond v. Chakrobatry 181/ in which the Supreme Court ruled in June 1980 that genetically altered organisms may be patented. Now when individuals and firms put time and money into biotechnology research they can be assured of earning economic rewards. Rifkin's foundation had filed a "friend of the court" brief supporting the U.S. Attorney General's office in its contention that the federal patent laws should not cover such organisms.

17.0 ASBESTOS AMENDMENT

On 22 October 1986 President Reagan signed into law a measure, PL 99-519, amending the Toxic Substances Control Act to require school systems to identify and abate asbestos hazards in school buildings. Previously, school districts were required to inspect facilities for asbestos and inform teachers and parents of the inspection results, but were not required to take any abatement action.

This new law amends the Toxic Substances Control Act by adding a new Title II, the Asbestos Hazard Emergency Response Act of 1986. At this time the abatement provisions affect only schools; however, there has been considerable support to include commercial buildings in the future.

181/ 100 S.Ct. 2204, 447 U.S. 303.

Under this law, EPA is required to issue regulations defining what response actions must be taken in school buildings containing friable (i.e., crumbling) asbestos. Furthermore, before April 1987 EPA must propose regulations prescribing proper asbestos inspection procedures, standards for asbestos abatement, procedures for periodic re-inspection of buildings with encapsulated or remaining asbestos, and the establishment of a model contractor accreditation program for the states. Final rules are due by October 1987.

Under the current asbestos law, the Asbestos School Hazard Abatement Act, EPA distributes loan and grant money to financially needy schools to help pay for abatement costs. This amendment to the Toxic Substance Control Act establishes an Asbestos Trust Fund where funds received from schools that receive loans are to be deposited. Under the previous law, funds were simply returned to the U.S. Treasury.

In cases where the asbestos is not crumbling or threatening to disperse into the environment, many experts believe that the asbestos is best left in place but monitored closely with a self-inspection system, since attempted removal could pose more risk (as well as being enormously expensive) than leaving the material in place.

18.0 RELATIONSHIP OF TSCA TO OTHER FEDERAL LAWS

TSCA was enacted to fill gaps left by other laws, but Congress was also concerned that it not lead to jurisdictional conflicts with other agenices or even between different divisions of EPA. There was no wish to see a repetition of the bitter OSHA-EPA dispute of 1973 over pesticide re-entry standards. 182/ Consequently, Section 9 sets forth in some detail the coordination procedures to be followed when two health regulatory laws overlap.

Under Section 9, the EPA administrator may ask another agency to undertake regulation of a substance that presents an "unreasonable risk" which may be prevented by the other agency. The receiving agency must then take whatever regulatory measures it deems necessary, or reply in the Federal Register with a "detailed

---

182/ Under pressure of lawsuit by a migrant farmworkers' group, OSHA sought in spring 1973 to assert jurisdiction over conditions of fieldworker exposure to pesticides. This account is related in the chapter on Pesticides, Section 9.5.

statement" why no action is warranted. There the matter rests, whether EPA is in accord with the decision or not. (A citizen suit against the second agency is nevertheless possible.) EPA cannot thereafter bring an enforcement action of its own under Sections 6 or 7 concerning that hazard. 183/

EPA issued its first referral on 26 June 1985 when it referred regulatory control over 4,4'-methylene-dianiline to OSHA because of its exclusively workplace-related risks. Earlier, in the same year, EPA referred the regulation of asbestos to OSHA, but rescinded that decision after much controversy, especially criticism from Congress that reflected a low opinion of OSHA's capabilities.

For other laws administered under EPA, the administrator is given the flexibility to apply them where they would be most useful or to rely on the provisions of TSCA. He is not relieved of the procedural or substantive requirements in those other laws, however, if he chooses to rely on them. 184/

Finally, Congress added a special provision concerning OSHA, stating the Environmental Protection Agency's exercise of authority under TSCA did not constitute a preemption of OSHA jurisdiction under OSH Act Section 4. 185/

In the past several years, congressional frustration with OSHA has exceeded even that with EPA. This has led to proposals that TSCA be used to regulate some occupational exposure to hazardous substances. Despite the clear intrusion in OSHA's jurisdiction, this now has been endorsed by the Senate Environment and Public Works Committee. According to the bipartisan leadership, Sen. Robert Stafford (R.-Vt.) and Jennings Randolph (D.-W.Va.), the fact that Section 5 is directed at pre-manufacture notification, rather than just pre-market, shows that workers too were to be

---

183/ TSCA, § 9(a). EPA could try to circumvent this bar by first initiating an enforcement action and then sending the notification to the other agency, although this Section 9(a)(3) "loophole" is rather narrow for such a statutory departure.

184/ TSCA, § 9(b). At least theoretically, the application of the doctrine to all laws "administered in whole or in part by the Administration" also includes the Food, Drug, and Cosmetic Act. See the chapter on Pesticides, Section 9.1.

185/ TSCA, § 9(c); OSH Act, § 4(b)(1).

protected. Section 9 is interpreted as merely for coordination. 186/
This view is exceedingly imaginative but of questionable public
policy. If Congress wants OSHA to perform its functions better or
differently, it should address that problem, rather than expect
another agency with probably similar appointments and philosophy to
do the job.

18.1 Existing Toxic Substances Laws

The term "toxic substance" has become so identified with this
new act that one often forgets there is considerable legislation dealing with chemical substances already on the books. In one sense,
almost all of the recent environmental laws have in fact been
directed at toxic substances.

One generally excludes from the term "toxic substance" the
six original air pollutants regulated by EPA under Sections 108-110
of the Clear Air Act; carbon monoxide, hydrocarbons, photochemical
oxidant, sulfur dioxide, nitrogen oxides, and particulate matter. In
sufficient concentrations most of these substances can be immediately deadly and all have serious long-term effects on health. They
tend, however, to be the ubiquitous products of combustion, the
waste products of an industrial society, and their control necessitates a general national policy that cuts across many diverse industries. Similarly, a number of the substances controlled under the
water pollution laws are usually excluded from the definition,
including suspended soil particles and decaying organic products
which adversely affect the biological oxygen demand (BOD) of the
water.

18.2 Clean Air Act

Section 112 of the Clean Air Act, entitled "National Emission
Standards for Hazardous Air Pollutants," is specifically directed
toward toxic substances. Although this provision has so far been
used only for asbestos, mercury, beryllium, and vinyl chloride, it
could develop into one of the most important parts of the act.
Arsenic and benzene are currently under consideration for regulation
under this section. One reason for its infrequent use is its deliberate
omission of economic or technical feasibility in standard setting; the
only relevant factor for the administrator is "the level which in his

---

186/ BNA, Chemical Reporter, 1 June 1984, p. 276.

judgment provides an ample margin of safety to protect the public health from such hazardous air pollutants." 187/　EPA tacitly ignored this unusual provision in the vinyl chloride deliberations 188/ and this, if deemed successful, could lead to greater use of this sec tion in the future. 189/

Congress has been irritated that Section 112 has been so little used over the past decade and a half. For the last couple of years, therefore, legislation has been debated which would mandate the addition of over three dozen substances to the regulatory list.

18.3 Water Pollution Act

Another key law is Section 307 of the Federal Water Pollution Control Act entitled "Toxic and Pre-treatment Effluent Standards." 190/ This provides specifically for the listing and setting of standards with an "ample margin of safety" for hazardous chemicals discharged into the nation's waterways. In September 1973, EPA listed nine chemicals, mostly pesticides, on this list, including DDT, Aldrin-Dieldrin, PCBs, Toxaphene, and cadmium and mercury compounds. 191/ Effluent standards for these substances do not apply to all industries but only to about two dozen broad categories such as non-ferrous metal smelters, textile manufacturers, and agricultural fertilizer manufacturing. 192/ By the consent decree between EPA

187/　Clear Air Act, § 112(b)(1)(B).

188/　EPA, "Proposed Standard for Vinyl Chloride," 16 December 1975.

189/　The original Clean Air bill considered by Congress had two toxic substances sections—the present one for extreme hazards and a milder version allowing economic considerations for the less serious toxic pollutants. The House-Senate Conference Committee in 1970 dropped the latter section from the final bill without giving any reason.

190/　Federal Water Pollution Control Act, § 307, 33 U.S.C. § 1317.

191/　38 FR 24342, 7 September 1975. The rules of practice under § 307 were amended by 41 FR 1765, 12 January 1976.

192/　For more detailed information, see Chapter 5 on Water Pollution Control.

and the Natural Resources Defense Council in June 1976, a total of sixty-five substances comprising several hundred individual chemicals was added to the Section 307 list. 193/ This decree was subsequently written into the 1977 amendments to the Clean Water Act. 194/

Under Section 311 entitled "Oil and Hazardous Substance Liability," EPA is to regulate "spills" of hazardous substances into the nation's waterways and coastal zones. The administrator is required to list those elements and compounds which should be designated "hazardous substances." Within 180 days of this designation he is to establish a unit of measurement and a monetary penalty for the discharge of a unit into the water. EPA finally proposed such a list in December 1975. It announced that although the act authorizes the imposition of fines up to five million dollars, the agency would voluntarily limit penalties to $5000 unless gross negligence by the polluter is demonstrated. 195/

The administrator also has emergency authority under Section 504 of the Clean Water Act to seek to enjoin any person from discharging any pollutants which are "presenting an imminent and substantial endangerment to health or welfare." 196/ This section has rarely been invoked by EPA, despite numerous situations for which it would be appropriate.

18.4 Occupational Safety and Health Administration

The Occupational Safety and Health Act, although not usually regarded as a toxic substance act, is potentially the most important

---

193/ N.R.D.C. v. Train, 8 ERC 2120 (D.D.C. 1976); see also N.R.D.C. v. Train, 510 F.2d 692 (D.C. Cir. 1974).

194/ PL 95-217. There has been some dispute about the degree to which Congress incorporated the consent decree into the amendments. Rep. Ray Roberts (D-Tex.) insisted that it didn't, or at least modified it considerably; Sen. Edmund Muskie (D-Me.) said that it did. The latter view is preferred.

195/ EPA, Notice of Proposed Rulemaking, Designation of Hazardous Substances, 40 FR 59960-60017 (30 December 1975). 40 CFR Parts 116-19.

196/ Federal Water Pollution Control Act § 504, 33 U.S.C. § 1364.

statute in the field. 197/ Although limited to occupational situations, the act covers over 80 million workers, many of whom have much greater exposure to highly toxic chemicals than they are ever likely to encounter in the general environment. Section 6 of the act 198/ requires OSHA to set strict health standards at a level "which most adequately assures, to the extent feasible, on the basis of the best available evidence, that no employee will suffer material impairment of health or functional capacity even if such employee has regular exposure to the hazard dealt with by such standard for the period of his working life. 199/ This act, if fully implemented, could have a tremendous effect.

In the decade and a half since the passage of this act, however, OSHA has put out only seven final health standards—asbestos, vinyl chloride, coke oven, arsenic, benzene, lead, and a group of carcinogens. In late 1975, after a change in OSHA's top management, standards were proposed for a dozen other substances, including ammonia, beryllium, and trichloroethylene, but these still are pending. In addition, OSHA has a list of approximately 400 substances with threshold limits adopted from the recommended lists of private industrial hygiene organizations. 200/

18.5 Consumer Product Safety Commission

The Consumer Product Safety Act and related statutes such as the Hazardous Substances Act administered by the Consumer Product Safety Commission (CPSC) also confer jurisdiction over certain forms of toxic substances. One should note, however, that "hazardous substances" as used in this act includes devices and equipment, and thus is much broader than the term toxic substances. Furthermore, the CPSC may address only human safety questions derived from the use of consumer products, and thus it has no authority over environmental problems.

197/ 29 U.S.C. § 651 et seq., PL 91-596, 84 Stat. 1590.

198/ OSH Act § 6, 29 U.S.C. § 655.

199/ OSH Act, § 6(b)(5).

200/ These have been reviewed as part of the Standards Completion Process to convert the bare threshold numbers into a full standard with monitoring, medical, and other requirements.

In the past, the CPSC has exhibited little activity in the chemical area, except for limited involvement in cases concerning two spray can propellants, vinyl chloride and freon, and a fumbled effort on asbestos hair dryers. It issued a detailed cancer policy document modeled closely on that proposed by OSHA but was forced to withdraw it in April 1979 because of procedural deficiencies.

Because of budget and staff cuts, this disfavored agency is unlikely to be a more important factor in the next few years.

19.0 THE PROPOSED FEDERAL CANCER POLICY

The proposed Federal Cancer Policy, initiated by OSHA in October 1977, considered by all four health regulatory agencies— OSHA, EPA, FDA, and CPSC—and currently on hold by the Reagan administration—could potentially have more effect on toxic chemical control than the better-known Toxic Substances Control Act. This cancer policy, if effectively applied, could directly impact hundreds or thousands of chemical substances throughout American industry. It is currently undergoing "revision," after the OSHA administrator who suspended it decided such a policy could be useful after all. But he has since left the government and the present staff has neither the will nor the ability, at present, to repropose a more coherent policy. Some modification will be needed, in any case, to ensure that the policy is in accord with the Supreme Court's subsequent decision in the Benzene case. 201/

19.1 Goals of the Federal Cancer Policy

The three goals hoped to be reached through OSHA's Federal Cancer Policy are (1) to avoid repetitious scientific debate at OSHA hearings and ad hoc decisions on health standards involving carcinogens, (2) to streamline OSHA's ponderous standard setting process by "prefabricating" the essential elements of several alternative versions, and (3) ultimately to harmonize the policies of the four health regulatory agencies. The regulatory requirements, derived from the cancer principles, spell out monitoring and medical tests in rigorous detail and set a goal of reducing levels of "confirmed" carcinogens to near zero.

201/ Industrial Union v. American Petroleum Institute v. Donovan, 100 S. Ct. 2478 (1981).

19.2 Background of the Policy

Efforts to develop a cancer policy at both OSHA and EPA date from the Aldrin-Dieldrin pesticide suspension decision at EPA in October 1974. This set forth tentative principles of carcinogenicity which the agency could apply to future regulatory cases. 202/ EPA subsequently established a task force to analyze this fledgling policy and recommended a final version. The focus shifted to OSHA in 1975 with the transfer of several former EPA officials to that agency. In January 1976, a lengthy OSHA draft proposal was widely circulated, but the change of administrations forestalled its issuance. Finally, the proposal, different in only a few details from the version prepared nine months earlier, was signed by the head of OSHA on 28 September 1977 and subsequently appeared in the Federal Register on 4 October 1977, entitled "Identification, Classification and Regulation of Toxic Substances Posing a Potential Occupational Carcinogenic Risk." 203/ The policy in final form was issued in January 1980. 204/

19.3 Scientific Principles of the Cancer Policy

The policy takes a hardline regulatory approach to carcinogens, namely that exposure should be reduced to zero, or as close to zero as feasible. If safer alternative chemicals are available, they should be substituted.

The leading scientific policy conclusions in the proposal are as follows:

(1) A carcinogen is defined as a substance or condition which increases the incidence of generally irreversible benign or malignant tumors, reduces the latency period, or produces unusual tumors in animals or man.

(2) The results of cancer tests on animals, particularly rodents and other animals, are relevant to human exposure. ("Any substance which is shown to cause tumors in animals should be considered carcinogenic and, therefore, a potential cancer hazard for man.")

202/ In re Shell, 6 ERC 2047 (1974).

203/ 42 FR 54148, 4 October 1977.

204/ 45 FR 5002, 22 January 1980.

(3)   A threshold or "no effect" level may theoretically exist
        for carcinogens but this has not been conclusively
        demonstrated; and, even so, it would have to be deter-
        mined separately for each substance. Therefore, the
        only safe level is zero.

(4)   Most carcinogens are neither species-specific nor organ-
        specific.

(5)   A substance may be termed a confirmed carcinogen
        after replicated tests in only one species. ("If carcino-
        gens are not species-specific, it logically follows that
        the demonstration of carcinogenic effect in more than
        one species is not absolutely necessary for finding of
        carcinogenicity.") Note that EPA has recently com-
        mented that under some circumstances even replication
        should be waived as unnecessary.

(6)   In evaluating test data, no distinction will be made be-
        tween benign and malignant tumors. ("The Agency pro-
        poses to place as much weight on an experiment in
        which only benign tumors are observed, as upon experi-
        ments in which both malignant and benign tumors are
        induced.")

(7)   Positive test results (i.e., indicators that a substance is
        carcinogenic) outweigh negative findings.

(8)   Chemical structural similarity of a suspect chemical to
        a known carcinogen may be a guide for testing priority
        but is itself insufficient to classify the former as a
        carcinogen.

(9)   Induced tumors appearing in animals at the point of
        application, or due to physical rather than chemical
        effect, may be disregarded.

(10)   The administration of high doses is a methodological
        device necessary for finding gross effects in small test
        samples. "Consequently, a substance that will induce
        cancer in experimental animals at any dose level, no
        matter how high or low, should be treated with great
        caution."

(11)   The Ames test or other in vitro experiments using non-
        mammalian species are not an appropriate basis for
        regulatory action, but positive results plus carcino-
        genicity in one mammalian species may be.

(12)   Human epidemiological studies are generally an insensi-
        tive indicator of carcinogenicity, unless the study is
        exhaustively controlled or the particular cancer is quite
        unusual (e.g., angiosarcoma from vinyl chloride).

19.4 Implementation Regulations of the Cancer Policy

The implementation regulations and model standards (Part II) are an attempt to convert the scientific principles discussed above into full OSHA standards through a modular format. There are five such formats:

(1)   Category I—Emergency Temporary Standard for Confirmed Carcinogen

- Lowest levels feasible within the six-month period of the ETS.

- Most of the medical surveillance, waste disposal, recordkeeping, and other precautions that are required under a permanent standard, allowing for the short compliance period.

(2)   Category I—Permanent Standard for Confirmed Carcinogen

- Level set at zero exposure or as low as feasible.

- Feasibility is not really defined in the entire document, nor is it clear whether it is limited to technological feasibility, as OSHA insists, or can also include economic risk-benefit calculations.

- A full battery of monitoring, medical and protective equipment requirements designed to safeguard employees from exposure to carcinogens in the workplace.

- This category can be triggered by a finding of carcinogenicity in tests with two animal species, one species if replicated, one species unreplicated if accompanied by a positive in vitro test, or other evidence determined sufficient by the Secretary of Labor.

- These regulations are unusually specific, dealing in detail with everything from the laundering of work clothes to the application of cosmetics by employees in the workplace.

(3)   Category II—Suspected Carcinogens

- This category can be applied to all the toxics substances for which the data is "suggestive" of carcinogenicity but for which the tests for Category I are either not met or partially rebutted.

- The standard level will be set sufficient to prevent acute or chronic non-carcinogenic effects.

- Most of the medical, monitoring, and other requirements applicable to Category I are required.

(4) Category III—Acquitted Chemicals
(or "Guilt Unproved")

- This class encompasses substances which have either been cleared of suspicion of carcinogenicity, or which still deserve some additional research.

(5) Category IV—Foreign Toxic Substances

- This provision was merely an attempt to close the loophole by which a toxic substance for which no federal standard exists could be imported to the U.S. from abroad.

- As in Category III, no special regulations other than publication are provided for this group.

- This section was determined to be superfluous in the final versions.

In July 1980, as the final step in the implementation of the policy, OSHA brought out a long, tentative list of cancer candidates for regulation. 205/ In its final version, the candidate list of the substances numbered 204; half were borrowed from an EPA compilation by its Carcinogen Assessment Group (CAG), while the remaining half were submitted by an outside consulting firm on contract to OSHA. 206/ The plan was to select up to twenty for the development of full health standards, ten for Category I and ten for Category II.

The Reagan administration, under considerable business pressure, put a hold on the cancer policy within days of its coming to office. In December 1981, OSHA announced that it was subjecting the entire issue to extensive review, 207/ and in July 1983 the

---

205/ OSHA Press Release, 14 July 1978.

206/ 45 FR 53672, 12 August 1980.

207/ OSHA Press Release, 31 December 1981; 47 FR 187, 5 January 1982.

agency published a notice suspending the candidate project pending further review by OSHA and, though not mentioned, the development of a government-wide policy 208/ currently under consideration by a committee headed by White House Science Advisor, George Keyworth. The principal reason for this stay was concern that the process could constitute a blacklist of chemicals and cause undue alarm.

20.0 CONCLUSION

The Toxic Substances Control Act got off to a slow start, due in part to the delay in filling top EPA positions. 209/ The ponderous pace did not accelerate thereafter, however, so the Act may require an entire decade to implement fully. We should recognize the considerable administrative burden this cumbersome statute places on EPA; the Agency needs not only technical expertise but also extensive managerial and legal resources.

For the immediate future TSCA will be essentially an information-gathering act, although the Administrator has promised soon to initiate legal proceedings under Section 6 against a number of particularly hazardous substances. The concurrent slowdowns at OSHA, FDA, and the CPSC have created a back pressure which could create an impetus for change in the next few years. Even if this occurs, however, past experience is not comforting that the new administration will be any more proficient than its predecessors.

Nevertheless, in the long run, the importance of TSCA is likely to expand gradually, much as the requirements of FIFRA and the FDA Act increased substantially long after their enactment.

208/ 48 FR 241, 4 January 1983. See also Administrative Conference of U.S., Recommendation 82-5, "Federal Regulation of Cancer-Causing Chemicals", 18 June 1982.

209/ See, for example, the story entitled, "Search for Toxic Chemicals in Environment Gets A Slow Start, Is Proving Difficult and Expensive," Wall Street Journal, 9 May 1978, p. 48. Similar criticism, almost a year later, arose from congressional oversight hearings before the House Subcommittee on Consumer Protection on 8 March 1979.

Chapter 5

WATER POLLUTION CONTROL

J. Gordon Arbuckle, Timothy A. Vanderver, Jr.,
and Russell V. Randle
Attorneys
Patton, Boggs & Blow
Washington, D.C.

1.0 INTRODUCTION—THE HISTORICAL PERSPECTIVE

In 1972, Congress put the basic framework for federal water pollution control regulation in place by enacting the Federal Water Pollution Control Act, which was significantly modified in 1977 to deal with toxic water pollutants, and renamed the Clean Water Act.

This act has been amended several times including the most recent and extensive amendments, entitled the Water Quality Act of 1987.

The act has five main elements: a permit program, a system of minimum national effluent standards for each industry, water quality standards, provisions for special problems such as toxic chemicals and oil spills, and a construction grant program for publicly-owned treatment works (POTWs).

Some history makes these program elements more understandable, and puts a detailed discussion of pollution control programs into perspective. Prior to 1970, standards were generally set by the states for pollutant parameters for various water bodies. Although this approach was theoretically attractive, it worked badly in most states. Major problems included:

— Inability to determine precisely when a discharge violated applicable standards;

— Inapplicability of federal-state water quality standards to intrastate waters;

217

— Lack of state initiative in making load allocations required to set enforceable discharge standards; and

— Cumbersome enforcement mechanisms and the requirement of state consent for federal enforcement.

Although a few states made the water quality approach work, it was clear by 1970 that an effective nationwide approach would require implementation of a permit program based on federal minimum "end-of-pipe" effluent criteria enforceable directly against the discharger.

When legislation proposed in 1969 to provide this mechanism failed to pass, and when courts and citizens groups "discovered" that the Refuse Act penalized discharges of pollutants which had not been approved by the Army Corps of Engineers and provided a "bounty" to citizens who provided information for the government to bring actions to enforce those penalties, the Nixon administration initiated the Refuse Act permit program in late 1970. 1/

The Refuse Act is an archaic 1899 statute designed to protect navigation. It does, however, prohibit almost all discharges into navigable waters or tributaries thereof unless a permit is obtained from the Corps of Engineers prior to commencing the discharge. 2/ By using this authority to require all industrial dischargers to apply for and obtain permits, the granting or denial of which would be based on environmental factors, the administration was able, for the first time, to pose a credible threat of prosecution. Hundreds of cases were initiated under the Refuse Act.

The Refuse Act was not drafted as a comprehensive water pollution control statute. Consequently, the permit program encountered severe problems:

— The act provided no standards for the grant or denial of permits, nor were any regulations promulgated to provide such standards;

_____

1/   33 U.S.C. § 407; Ex. Ord. No. 11574, 35 F.R. 19627 (Dec. 23, 1970).

2/   The only exception recognized by the statute is for "refuse matter . . . flowing from streets and sewers and passing therefrom in a liquid state." Thus, the regulation of stormwater discharges, which has proven controversial under the Clean Water Act, see § 5.2 below, could not have been accomplished under the Refuse Act.

— As a result of a court decision, Kalur v. Resor, 3/ environmental impact statements had to be prepared for every permit decision, further taxing the inadequate staff in charge of processing the applications;

— Penalties under the act were thought by many to be inadequate;

— The relationship of the act to other federal and state water pollution control efforts was unclear, and created considerable confusion.

By late 1971, it was evident that comprehensive water pollution control legislation was a prerequisite for a workable control program.

In late 1972, Congress finally passed, over President Nixon's veto, a comprehensive recodification and revision of federal water pollution control law. The 1972 act, Public Law 92-500, 4/ made the Environmental Protection Agency (EPA) responsible for setting effluent standards on an industry-by-industry basis and required such standards to be based on the capabilities and costs of pollution control technologies. EPA had to meet a stringent timetable for setting these standards.

The act continued requirements for water quality standards so that more stringent discharge standards could be imposed where effluent standards were insufficient to assure that the quality of receiving waters did not deteriorate to, or remain at, unacceptable levels. States could take over the administration of the permit program when state control programs met rigorous federal standards.

The basic framework of the 1972 act—the permit program, national effluent limitations, water quality standards, special provisions for oil spills and toxic substances, and a POTW construction grant program—proved reasonably sound and remains so today. Congress significantly amended the act in 1977 in an effort to deal more effectively with toxic pollutants, and to resolve numerous definitional and policy issues raised by court and EPA decisions. The act was revised again in 1978 to deal with spills of hazardous substances and in 1980 and 1981 to change certain aspects of the construction grant program for POTWs. Over President Reagan's veto, Congress passed significant amendments in 1987.

3/   335 F. Supp. 1 (D.D.C. 1971).

4/   33 U.S.C. § 1251 et seq.

2.0   FEDERAL-STATE WATER POLLUTION CONTROL PROGRAM —OVERVIEW

The regulatory program established under the Clean Water Act, as amended, has two basic elements—a statement of goals and objectives and a system of regulatory mechanisms calculated to achieve those goals and objectives.

2.1 Goals and Objectives

The act's stated objective (Section 101) is to "restore and maintain the chemical, physical and biological integrity of the nation's waters." To achieve that objective, the act establishes as "national goals":

—   Achieving a level of water quality which "provides for the protection and propagation of fish, shellfish, and wildlife" and "for recreation in and on the water" by 1 July 1983; and

—   Eliminating the discharge of pollutants into United States waters by 1985.

The "no-discharge" goal was written into early drafts of the 1972 act in order to encourage the adoption of sewage treatment systems relying on land application of effluent. The "no-discharge" language remained after the legislative emphasis shifted away from land application, in part to encourage the reuse and recycling of industrial process water and chemicals. Even though they are unattainable in the short run, these national goals significantly affect the stringency of limitations imposed.

2.2 Mechanisms for Achieving These Goals and Objectives

The principal means to achieve the act's goals is a system to impose effluent limitations on, or otherwise to prevent, discharges of "pollutants" into any "waters of the United States" from any "point source." This system includes five basic elements:

(1) A permit program (the National Pollutant Discharge Elimination System—NPDES) requiring dischargers to disclose the volume and nature of their discharges, authorizing EPA to specify the limitations to be imposed on such discharges, imposing on dischargers an obligation to monitor and report as to their compliance or non-compliance with the limitations so imposed,

and authorizing EPA and citizen enforcement in the event of non-compliance. Citizen enforcement actions have become an important factor in recent years.

(2) A two-stage system of technology-based effluent limits establishing base-level or minimum treatment required to be achieved by direct industrial dischargers (existing and new sources) and Publicly Owned Treatment Works (POTWs) and a complementary system of pretreatment requirements applicable to dischargers to POTWs. EPA has now set almost all of these standards and the compliance dates for most of them have passed.

(3) A program for imposing more stringent limits in permits where such limits are necessary to achieve water quality standards or objectives.

(4) A set of specific provisions applicable to certain toxic and other pollutant discharges of particular concern or special character (e.g., oil spills, discharges of toxic chemicals, and non-process discharges such as contaminated plant site runoff).

(5) A grant program to help fund POTW attainment of the applicable requirements. This grant program has been significantly scaled back as pressures on the federal budget have increased, and may be phased out and/or replaced with a loan program.

The act is, of course, far more complex than this five-part framework indicates. In order to grasp how the act applies in concrete situations, it is essential to understand the definitional and policy decisions which translated these broad legislative directives into reality.

3.0 PERMITTING UNDER THE NATIONAL POLLUTANT DISCHARGE ELIMINATION SYSTEM

The act's primary mechanism for imposing limitations on pollutant discharges is a nationwide permit program established under Section 402 and referred to as the National Pollutant Discharge Elimination System (NPDES). EPA's present regulations are found at 40 CFR Parts 121-125. This section will consider three basic permit program issues—the program's scope and applicability, the procedures followed in permit issuance, and the nature of the conditions normally included in permits.

3.1 Program Scope and Applicability

Under the NPDES program, any person responsible for the discharge of a pollutant or pollutants into any waters of the United States from any point source must apply for and obtain a permit.

Although the definition of "pollutant" in Section 502(6) of the act includes only the materials specifically listed in that section 5/ the definition is nevertheless quite broad and has been broadly interpreted to include virtually all waste material, whether or not that material has value at the time it is discharged. 6/

The term "discharge of a pollutant or pollutants" under the act is defined in Section 502(12) to mean the addition of any pollutant to waters of the United States from any point source. The act's requirement that there must be an addition of a pollutant in order for a discharge to be regulated has been successfully used in some situations to preclude the imposition of limitations on the discharge of materials in a waste stream which are present only by reason of presence in intake waters, if the intake water is drawn from the same body of water into which the discharge is made and if the pollutants present in the intake water are not removed by the discharger as part of his usual operations. 7/ The term does not include discharges of water from dams, even if a dam's operations adversely affect the temperature and dissolved oxygen content of the water. 8/

The point source element of the discharge definition has been one of the most difficult aspects of the permit program to implement. Section 502(14) of the act defines the term "point source"

5/ Dredged spoil, solid waste, incinerator residue, sewage, garbage, sewage sludge, munitions, chemical wastes, biological materials, radioactive materials, heat, wrecked or discarded equipment, rock, sand, cellar dirt and industrial, municipal, and agricultural waste discharged into water.

6/ See Weinberger v. Romero-Barcelo, 456 U.S. 305 (1982) (bombs dropped on naval target range held to be pollutants); United States v. Standard Oil Co., 384 U.S. 224 (1966) (accidental discharge of gasoline held to be pollutant discharge under Refuse Act).

7/ See NPDES regulations, § 122.45(h).

8/ National Wildlife Federation v. Gorsuch, 693 F.2d 156 (D.C. Cir. 1982).

to include "any discernible, confined and discrete conveyance, . . . from which pollutants are or may be discharged." The "may be" language is important because it means that permits are required for facilities such as surface waste impoundments from which discharges are not normally anticipated except under unusual but foreseeable conditions such as excessive rainfall. The "discrete conveyance" language of the definition is so comprehensive as to cover a number of types of discharges, such as storm sewers, irrigation flows and the like, which are not efficiently regulated through the issuance of permits. For this reason, a number of statutory and administrative exemptions from the point source definition or the scope of the permit program have been adopted. These include irrigation return flows, the discharge of sewage from vessels regulated under Section 312 of the act, effluent from properly functioning marine engines, certain agricultural and silvicultural discharges, and certain discharges of dredged or fill material regulated under Section 404 of the act. Regulations of the Environmental Protection Agency also exclude from the definition of "point source" stormwater discharges which occur outside urbanized areas, provided that the runoff is not from lands or facilities used for industrial or commercial activities. The 1987 amendments amend Section 502(14) in order to codify the exclusion of agricultural stormwater discharges from the definition of point source.

The term "waters of the United States" is defined by EPA regulations 9/ to include (1) navigable waters; (2) tributaries of navigable waters; (3) interstate waters; and (4) intrastate lakes, rivers and streams (a) used by interstate travelers for recreation and other purposes, or (b) which are a source of fish or shellfish sold in interstate commerce, or (c) which are utilized for industrial purposes by industries engaged in interstate commerce. The intent of this definition is to cover all waters over which the broadest constitutional interpretation would allow the federal government to exercise jurisdiction. 10/ The definition clearly covers wetlands, and the Supreme Court has upheld an expansive definition of wetlands under regulations governing dredge-fill activities under section 404 of the

---

9/ 40 CFR § 122.2.

10/ NRDC v. Callaway, 392 F. Supp. 685 (D.D.C. 1975).

act. 11/ Few exclusions to the definition have been recognized and those which have been accepted to date seem to be limited to situations where the waterway in question is wholly confined on the property of the discharger, does not result in any flow beyond the property line, and is not available for significant public use.

One remaining major issue is the extent to which discharges to publicly or privately owned sewage systems constitute discharges to waters of the United States so as to be subject to the NPDES permit requirement. It is fairly well accepted that a discharge to a sewage system which is not connected to an operable treatment works is a discharge subject to the NPDES program, but that a discharge to a publicly owned treatment works which is capable of meeting its effluent limits is excluded from the NPDES permit requirement. 12/ All industrial dischargers to POTWs are required to comply with general pretreatment standards 13/ and many must also comply with industry-by-industry ("categorical") standards, promulgated together with effluent limitations for each industry. These pretreatment standards, as discussed more fully below, are intended to prevent pollutants produced by industrial dischargers from interfering with POTWs or passing through untreated. There are flexible permit requirements for discharges to privately owned treatment works which give the Environmental Protection Agency substantial discretion to consolidate or issue separate permits as needed to meet effluent standards.

To summarize, though there are important exclusions, the scope of the NPDES permit program is exceedingly broad. The basic intent is to regulate all pollutants discharged from all facilities into virtually all waters in the United States.

3.2 Permitting Procedures

Under Section 402 of the Clean Water Act, the Environmental Protection Agency is the issuing authority for all NPDES permits in a state until such time as the state elects to take over program

---

11/ United States v. Riverside Bayview Homes, Inc., __ U.S. __, 106 S.Ct. 455 (1985).

12/ 40 CFR § 122.3(c).

13/ 40 CFR Part 403.

administration and obtains EPA approval of its program. About three-fourths of the states have approved NPDES programs and function as the issuing authorities for permits in their jurisdictions. Where the state is the issuing authority, permitting procedures are generally comparable to the EPA procedures discussed below, with certain exceptions. For example, the states, unlike EPA, are not required to provide for an evidentiary hearing, though many do. Where the state is the issuing authority, procedures for judicial review of permit issuance are those provided under the state's administrative procedure act rather than under the Clean Water Act and the federal Administrative Procedure Act. State permit issuance is not a federal action subject to the requirements of the National Environmental Policy Act. 14/

Permits issued by states are subject to review by EPA and a state permit may not be issued if the EPA Administrator objects within ninety days after the state's proposed issuance. The administrator must state the reasons supporting the objections and must provide a statement of the limitations and conditions which would be included in the permit if it were to be issued by EPA. States are entitled to a public hearing regarding the administrator's objections and if the objections are not resolved, at the hearing or otherwise, the administrator can issue the permit. EPA has the authority to withdraw its approval of a state program and take over the entire program administration if it finds that the state is not carrying out the program in accordance with the act's requirements.

Procedures for permit issuance are generally as follows: A permit application, on the appropriate form, must be submitted to the EPA regional administrator (or the state, if it is the issuing authority) at least 180 days in advance of the date on which a proposed discharge is to commence or the expiration of the present permit, as the case may be. Where EPA is the issuing authority, it will require, for new dischargers, submission of a new source questionnaire before it will process the permit application. This questionnaire serves as the basis for an EPA determination as to whether the facility is a "new source." If the facility is determined to be a new source, the applicant will be required to prepare an environmental assessment for

---

14/ See Chesapeake Bay Foundation, Inc. v. Virginia State Water Control Bd., 453 F. Supp. 122 (E.D.Va. 1978).

EPA's use in determining whether an environmental impact statement is required by the National Environmental Policy Act. 15/
After the application is filed, the district engineer of the Corps of Engineers must be given an opportunity to review the application to evaluate the impact of permit issuance upon anchorage and navigation. Other federal agencies, and specifically the Fish and Wildlife Service of the Department of the Interior and the National Marine Fisheries Service of the Department of Commerce, are provided a similar opportunity to comment on the application.
Where EPA is the issuing authority, the state in which the discharge will occur must be provided with an opportunity to review the application. Based on that review, the state is asked to certify, pursuant to Section 401 of the act, that the permitted discharge will comply with applicable provisions of Sections 301, 302, 303, 306, and 307 of the act. Since provisions in Sections 301 and 303 deal with the question of compliance with state water quality standards, the state, in effect, is asked to certify that the discharge in question will comply with all limitations necessary to meet water quality standards, treatment standards, or schedules of compliance established pursuant to any state law or regulations.
Although the applicable regulations would appear to require the applicant for an NPDES permit to provide EPA with the required certification, in practice EPA forwards applications received without a certification to the appropriate state and keeps the state advised throughout the permit proceedings. If a state does not either certify or deny certification within a reasonable time after the receipt of the permit application, it will be deemed to have waived the certification requirement. Because this time period starts to run on the state's receipt of an application, it is advisable for the applicant to send a copy of the application to the state rather than waiting for EPA to do so. EPA is barred from issuing any NPDES permit unless the state has either certified the permit or waived its right to certify.
In processing the application, the issuing authority makes tentative determinations as to whether a permit should be issued, and, if so, as to the required effluent limitations, schedules of compliance, monitoring requirements and so forth. These tentative determinations are organized into a draft permit and the discharger is normally given an opportunity to review and comment on this draft. The public is

---

15/ Clean Water Act, § 511(c).

given notice of the permit application proceeding and the issuing authority's preliminary determinations with respect thereto. 16/

The regulations provide for a period of not less than thirty days during which the public may submit written comments and/or request that a public hearing be held. The issuing authority is required to hold a public hearing if there is a significant degree of public interest in a proposed permit or group of permits. The public must be notified of such hearings and interested persons must be given at least thirty days in which to prepare for the hearings. Following the public hearing, the issuing authority issues a final determination regarding permit issuance after taking into account the comments received. Where the final determination is substantially unchanged from the tentative determination outlined in the original public notice, the issuing authority must forward a copy of the determination to any person who submitted written comments regarding the permit. Where the issuing authority's decision substantially changes the tentative determinations and draft permit, public notice must be given.

Within thirty days following the date of the notice of final determination, any interested person may request an evidentiary hearing or a legal review to reconsider the determination.

The granting of an evidentiary hearing or legal review stays the effective date of all contested provisions of the permit. 17/ The hearing is an on-the-record quasi-judicial proceeding presided over by an administrative law judge. 18/

The decision reached on the basis of the evidentiary hearing may be appealed to the EPA administrator. 19/ Where EPA is the issuing authority, the entire permit issuance proceeding, of course, is subject to judicial review under the federal Administrative Procedure Act. Where the state is the issuing authority, the state administrative procedure act probably governs.

16/ If a variance request or other effort to secure relaxation of generally applicable effluent limits is indicated, it is appropriate to submit the request at this point in the proceedings. If this is done, a stay of further action on the permit, pending disposition of the request, would be appropriate.

17/ 40 CFR § 124.16(a).

18/ Id., § 124.81.

19/ Id., § 124.91.

Contested provisions of the permit become effective, and a final permit is issued, upon completion of these review proceedings. The issuance of a permit under the Clean Water Act will be deemed to fulfill the permit requirements of the Refuse Act of 1899, as well as those under the act itself except for requirements under Section 307(a) covering discharge of toxic pollutants presenting human health risks. It should be noted, however, that issuance of a permit does not mean that no further action will be required during the permit term. As the permit makes clear, additional applications must be filed and processed whenever modifications to the facility or method of operation will result in changes to the discharge. Thus, keeping permits up-to-date will often be a continuous endeavor.

3.3 Permit Conditions

An NPDES permit performs two basic functions in the Clean Water Act regulatory process. It establishes specific levels of performance the discharger must maintain and it requires the discharger to report failures to meet those levels to the appropriate regulatory agency.

Many conditions typically included in industrial permits are either negotiable or susceptible to legal attack. Accordingly, proposed permit conditions should be carefully analyzed and, if inappropriate, modified and if need be, contested. The more significant permit conditions are discussed below.

Monitoring and Reporting—The monitoring requirements in an NPDES permit are critically important. The effectiveness of the permit program in assuring compliance with applicable effluent limitations, water quality standards, pretreatment standards and other requirements established pursuant to the act will depend, in major part, on the effectiveness of monitoring and data maintenance requirements included in permits pursuant to Section 308. 20/ Under that section, EPA is authorized to require the owner or operator of any point source to establish and maintain specified records, make specified reports, install, use and maintain monitoring equipment and methods, take specified samples, and provide other information which EPA may reasonably require. As with the permit program in general,

---

20/ POTWs subject to the act's permit requirements must also require industrial dischargers to monitor their discharges to the POTWs.

the states have the opportunity to administer their own monitoring programs and, upon obtaining EPA's approval of an appropriate monitoring program, the state becomes the monitoring authority for all point sources within its jurisdiction.

The enforcing authority will have the right to enter the premises of the discharger at any reasonable time, inspect the records required to be maintained, take test samples and so forth. All data obtained under Section 308 is required to be open to the public except to the extent non-disclosure is necessary to protect trade secrets. This public disclosure requirement is an essential underpinning of the act's provision for citizen enforcement actions against non-complying dischargers.

The NPDES regulations specify the manner in which effluent limitations are to be included in permits and thus imposed on permittees. 21/ The monitoring requirements in various sections of Part 122 are intended to assure compliance with the limits included in permits. Under these provisions, limits are to be imposed and monitoring is to take place at the point of discharge except in limited situations where monitoring at point of discharge is infeasible. The regulations do provide the permit issuer with authority to require monitoring of internal waste streams in certain situations such as where the final discharge point is inaccessible, where wastes at the point of discharge are so diluted as to make monitoring impracticable, or where interference among pollutants at the point of discharge would prevent detection or analysis. A permittee is required to monitor, as specified in his permit, to determine (1) compliance with the limitations on amounts, concentrations or other pollutant measures specified in the permit, (2) the total volume of effluent discharged from each discharge point and (3) otherwise as required by the permit. 22/

The permit must include requirements for maintenance and proper installation of the monitoring equipment, must specify monitoring methods and frequencies adequate to provide reliable data regarding the volume of flow and quantity of pollutants discharged, and must specify the test methodology to be utilized in analyzing the samples taken. The regulations put the burden on the applicant, if he believes that the monitoring requirements specified in a draft permit

---

21/ 40 CFR §§ 122.44, 122.45.

22/ 40 CFR § 122.44(i).

are inadequate to yield accurate data, to request additional monitoring requirements which are sufficient to achieve an acceptable degree of accuracy. Compliance with the effluent limits set in the permit will be assessed through application of the monitoring methods which the permit provides. Thus, unless inadequate monitoring requirements are contested during the permit issuance procedures, it may be difficult to use alleged inadequacy as a defense in any later enforcement action.

Monitoring records, including charts from continuous monitoring devices and calibration and maintenance records, must be maintained for a minimum period of three years, and that period may be extended by request of the permit issuing authority at any time. 23/ As the statute of limitations applicable to permit violations is the five-year limitation in 28 U.S.C. § 2462 (1982), 24/ it would be wise to maintain the records for that longer five-year period.

The results of monitoring must be reported periodically to the permit issuing authority on forms provided by the authority. Frequency of reporting is governed by the terms of each individual permit and must be at least annual. In addition to the periodic reporting requirement, certain toxic discharges must be reported within twenty-four hours. 25/ Failure to properly monitor and report is a violation of the permit and any person who knowingly makes any false statement in monitoring records, monitoring reports, or compliance or non-compliance notifications is subject upon conviction to substantial fines and criminal penalties, both under the Clean Water Act and under the applicable provisions of the federal criminal code, including 18 U.S.C. Section 1001.

It is evident from the foregoing that the monitoring requirements may occupy a considerable amount of employee time, require

---

23/ 40 CFR § 122.41(j).

24/ E.g. Chesapeake Bay Foundation v. Bethlehem Steel Corp., 608 F.Supp 440, 446-50 (D.Md. 1985); Connecticut Fund for the Environment v. Job Plating Co., 623 F.Supp 207, 211-13 (D.Conn. 1985); Atlantic States Legal Foundation v. Al-Tech Specialty, 635 F.Supp 284, 287 (N.D. N.Y. 1986).

25/ Id., §§ 122.41(k)(6), 122.42(a). The non-compliance reporting requirements are specific and detailed and should be carefully reviewed by all permittees.

the installation of sophisticated sampling devices, extensive analysis and testing, and detailed recordkeeping and reporting. Many companies may find it appropriate to develop additional in-house technical capability in order to meet the Section 308 requirements as imposed in the permit.

Schedules of Compliance—Although the act itself establishes firm deadlines for the achievement of the required levels of treatment, the issuing authority has considerable latitude to require compliance or interim steps towards compliance at earlier dates. The act also provides mechanisms to extend compliance deadlines in limited situations, as where compliance is dependent on connection to a yet-to-be constructed public treatment works or where use of innovative technology is involved. Most of the statutory bases for extensions, however, have now expired.

Effluent Limitations—Where a permit issues prior to the publication of effluent limitations for a particular pollutant or applicable industrial category or subcategory, the determination of the precise effluent limitations to be included in the permit are to be based on "engineering judgment," which is obviously more flexible than published rules. This situation is now most likely to arise as EPA works to promulgate limitations for toxic pollutants, or for facilities for which no specific set of limitations is wholly applicable.

Even after promulgation of limitations, the applicant may in certain cases seek modification of limits in the permit, and there is also considerable opportunity for the permitting authority to impose discharge limitations more stringent than the "base-level" effluent guidelines, where necessary to meet water quality standards, water quality related effluent limitations, the requirements of state planning processes, or other applicable limitations. Thus, there is considerable room for discussion regarding limits to be imposed in permits and a careful engineering analysis of proposed permit limits is a prerequisite to intelligent evaluation and negotiation of permit requirements. By the same token, once a permit has been issued on the basis of "Best Engineering Judgment" and it proves more stringent than the promulgated regulations require, the 1987 amendments include an "anti-backsliding" provision which makes it quite difficult to relax stringent permit conditions a discharger is actually meeting. 26/

26/ Water Quality Act of 1987, PL 100-4, § 404, Stat.__(1987).

Additional Effluent Limitations—Until recently, NPDES permits normally specified four or five pollutants as being subject to effluent limitations; a far greater number are now included in permits as a result of EPA's toxics strategy, which is discussed below. EPA's NPDES permit application and related regulations (Section 122.21) require extensive waste stream analysis in order to file permit applications, extensive cataloging in the application of virtually all chemicals in the waste stream, and imposition of controls on the discharge of those chemicals. Implementation of these requirements complicates the permit process and requires more extensive monitoring than was true in the past.

Duration and Revocation—Permits may be valid for terms of up to five years, and may be subject to revocation or modification based on a very minimal showing of "cause." A company's interest in connection with the permit process will generally be best served by obtaining a permit with the maximum duration and with as much specificity as is obtainable in regard to the possible grounds of revocation or modification. On the permit's expiration, the permittee, in order to obtain reissuance, must demonstrate compliance with any more stringent criteria which have been promulgated during the term of the original permit. The application for reissuance should be filed well in advance of the existing permit's expiration date.

Other—Depending on the precise nature of the applicant's operation, consideration might be given to bypass and upset provisions, start-up exclusions and so forth. Those who will be responsible for complying with the permits are well advised to make every reasonable effort to predict potential compliance problems and discuss them fully during the permit issuance process rather than in later enforcement proceedings.

4.0 ESTABLISHING THE LIMITATIONS FOR INCLUSION IN THE PERMIT—TECHNOLOGY AND WATER QUALITY-BASED LIMITS

The most difficult questions which EPA has faced in the development of the Clean Water Act program have involved the establishment of limits to be imposed in the permits issued under the NPDES mechanism. As previously noted, the act contemplates a two-part approach: (1) nationwide base-level treatment to be established through an assessment of what is technologically achievable and (2) more stringent treatment requirements for specific plants where necessary to achieve water quality objectives for the particular body of water into which that plant discharges. According to some commentators, Congress intended EPA to implement this combination of standards in a way which would force control technology innovation. 27/

While these concepts seem simple, their execution requires EPA and the courts to answer questions which have proved exceedingly complex:

— What specific pollutants should be addressed in establishing the limitations?

— How can technology-based effluent limits adequately take into account all factors relevant to the question of what is achievable and how can plant-to-plant variability be accommodated?

— What are the mechanics for deciding when more stringent limitations are required to meet water quality objectives and how are the necessary analyses to be performed prior to making permit issuance decisions?

These questions and the process by which they have been answered furnish the subject matter for this section.

4.1 Pollutants to be Addressed

Although the act broadly defined pollutants subject to regulation and permitting, it furnished little guidance before 1977 with regard to toxic pollutants. For that reason, and because the 1972 act imposed unrealistic deadlines on EPA's limited staff, EPA focused almost entirely on gross or "conventional" pollutants such as Biochemical Oxygen Demand (BOD), Suspended Solids (SS) and acidity and alkalinity (pH) when it developed the effluent limitations required by the act. As long as this approach was followed, EPA's basic system of effluent limits and permit requirements failed to address the dangers posed by more toxic pollutants such as chlorinated organic chemicals,

---

27/ See, e.g. Chemical Manufacturers Association v. Natural Resources Defense Council, 105 S.Ct. 1102, 1123 (1985) (Marshall, J., dissenting) (and sources cited therein).

heavy metals, pesticides and so forth, and at the same time may have overemphasized removal of solids and oxygen demanding materials contained in conventional wastes. 28/ Regulation of "toxic" pollutants was thought to be the exclusive province of Section 307 (a) of the act, which authorized EPA to identify and regulate, on a chemical-by-chemical rather than industry-to-industry basis, substances which it could prove to have toxic effects on identified organisms in affected waters.

Because of the stringent burden of proof and extensive procedures which the pre-1977 Section 307 required, EPA failed to establish a workable program to control the discharge of toxic pollutants. Only a limited number of substances were identified as toxic substances; long delays were encountered before final effluent limits were adopted for any of them.

EPA's failure to develop an effective toxics strategy under the 1972 act led the Natural Resources Defense Council (NRDC), an environmental organization, to sue the Environmental Protection Agency. That litigation was settled, and in the process of settlement, EPA and NRDC developed a policy which focused all of the regulatory mechanisms provided by the 1972 act upon the effective regulation of toxic or priority pollutant discharges. In developing this policy, the parties identified (1) the pollutants which would be the primary subject of regulation; (2) the industries which would be the primary concern in applying the regulations; and (3) the methods of regulating toxic discharges with the act's existing legal mechanisms. The agreements reached in these negotiations were embodied in a settlement decree, 29/ and that decree as modified 30/ has become the blueprint for toxics control strategy under the Clean Water Act.

The decree mandates full use of all the available regulatory tools under the act with a specific focus on the identified "priority pollutants." Pursuant to the decree, EPA must develop a program to regulate the discharge of 65 categories of "priority pollutants" (including at least 129 specific chemical substances—see Annex A, at

---

28/ It should be noted, however, that conventional treatment frequently, if unintentionally, removes substantial amounts of the more toxic wastes.

29/ NRDC v. Train, 8 E.R.C. 2120 (D.D.C. 1976).

30/ 12 E.R.C. 1833 (D.D.C. 1979).

the end of this chapter) by 34 industry categories which include over 700 subcategories. More than 70 percent of the nation's industry are affected by the decree. The 34 industry categories are listed in Annex B.

The consent decree required adoption of best available technology effluent limitations for each priority pollutant in each industrial category by 30 June 1983. These limitations had to be applicable to at least 95 percent of the point sources in each identified industry category or subcategory. Similar technology-oriented requirements had to be adopted for new sources and sources discharging into publicly owned treatment works. The basis for excluding a category of point sources from the toxic-focused system of technology-based effluent limitations is quite limited.

In addition to these stringent industry-by-industry toxic effluent limits, the consent decree made specific provision for full implementation of the waterway segment-by-segment approach.

The NRDC consent decree provided a judicial mandate for full use of the Clean Water Act's enforcement mechanisms in a carefully tailored effort to reduce discharges of toxic pollutants.

The 1977 amendments adopted this mandate and enacted it into federal statutory law. The amendments:

— Adopted the consent decree list of priority pollutants as the list of toxic substances to be given primary emphasis in the implementation of the Clean Water Act (This list of toxic substances is reproduced as Annex A.);

— Required adoption of best available technology effluent limitations for each listed substance by 1 July 1980, a deadline EPA failed by a substantial margin to meet;

— Required compliance with these BAT effluent limitations by 1 July 1984 (instead of 1 July 1983, as required by the consent decree);

— Permit EPA to add to or remove from the list of "toxic" substances (Although the act provides no specific criterion for making such additions or deletions, the Conference Committee Report states that a decision by the administrator to add or remove a substance from the list is final unless it is based on arbitrary and capricious action);

— Require compliance with BAT effluent limitations for toxic pollutants subsequently added to the list within three years of the establishment of the limitations;

— Provide a new system for upgrading and enforcing pretreatment regulations based on both the effluent limitations on the discharge from publicly owned treatment works and the intended use of the sludge from the facilities;

— Authorize EPA to adopt regulations establishing best management practices to control the discharge of the listed pollutants in the form of runoff or other uncontrolled discharges from industrial plant sites, parking lots and so forth;

— Require effluent limitations based on best available technology for other non-conventional pollutants by 1 July 1987; and

— Require the administrator to publish information related to the factors necessary to maintain fish, shellfish and wildlife in waterway segments.

In short, the 1977 amendments confirm and institutionalize the consent decree with some modifications.

The 1977 amendments did not, however, fully replace the consent decree. Instead, that decree has been the primary mechanism by which the toxics control program has been modified. The consent decree was amended in 1979 to reflect the changes made by the 1977 amendments and to respond to the operational problems perceived by EPA since the decree was originally issued in 1976. 31/ The modification also extended the deadlines for the development of technology-based effluent limitations for the thirty-four industrial categories and expanded the permissible bases upon which EPA may exclude substances from regulation pursuant to the consent decree. These deadlines were extended somewhat in May 1982, but the District Court rejected a bid by EPA and various industry groups for extensions of up to thirty months. Pursuant to the deadlines set in the decree, EPA has promulgated final effluent limitations for all but two of the thirty-four industry categories. The 1987 amendments require final regulations for the two remaining industries—organic

––––––––––––––––––––

31/ 12 E.R.C. 1833 (D.D.C. 1979).

chemicals and pesticides—to be promulgated by the end of 1986, a deadline EPA has missed. 32/ Challenges to the consent decree have twice been rejected by the courts. 33/

Under the revised consent decree, the Environmental Protection Agency can exclude industry categories from regulation of certain substances where only "trace amounts" of the substance are found. The administrator is also authorized to exclude pollutants from coverage under the direct discharge effluent limitations if the amount and toxicity of such pollutants within a category or subcategory does not, in his judgment, justify the development of regulations having nationwide applicability.

The basis for excluding pollutants from the applicability of pretreatment standards was similarly expanded. EPA is authorized to make such exclusions when it finds that the amount and toxicity of all incompatible pollutants discharged by a category or subcategory taken together is so small that regulations of nationwide applicability governing pretreatment of those pollutants is not justified.

In the water quality standards area, the modified consent decree makes more specific the program required for identifying bodies of water which the technology-based effluent limitations are inadequate to protect toxic-related water quality objectives. To date, this portion of the toxics program has had little effect because of EPA's long delays in identifying the affected wastes and developing a control program. The 1987 amendments impose a two-year deadline for the states to identify water bodies which fail to meet water quality standards because of toxic discharges by particular point sources, and require the imposition of additional effluent limitations on such responsible point sources, and compliance with them, three years after that.

The consent decree as confirmed by the 1977 and 1987 amendments and modified by the court has transformed the entire Clean Water Act program and focused EPA and industry attention on the most dangerous pollutants. The industry-by-industry technology-

---

32/ PL 100-4, § 301(f), 101 Stat.___(1987).

33/ Environmental Defense Fund v. Costle, 636 F.2d 1229 (D.C. Cir. 1980); Citizens for a Better Environment v. Gorsuch, 718 F.2d 1117 (D.C. Cir. 1983), cert. denied, 104 S. Ct. 2668 (1984).

based effluent limitations have been transformed from limited requirements focused on three or four conventional pollutants to a very specific system of limitations potentially applicable to 129 or more different pollutants for each industry category. Water quality standards will become far more important to industry, although EPA's lengthy delays in this regard have greatly limited the effect of such standards to date.

4.2 Required Level of Treatment—Technology-Based Limits for "Existing" Direct Discharges

Section 301(b) of the 1972 act provided for the establishment of nationally applicable technology-based effluent limitations on an industry-by-industry basis. These effluent limitations were to establish a nationwide base-level of treatment for existing direct discharge sources in every significant industrial category. This level of treatment was to be achieved in two phases. For "existing" 34/ industrial discharges, Section 301 directs the achievement:

> by July 1, 1977, of effluent limitations which will require application of the best practicable control technology currently available, and by July 1, 1983, of effluent limitations which will require application of the best available technology economically achievable.

As the time for achievement of Best Practicable Technology (BPT) is long past, its primary relevance now is as a basis for setting subsequent standards. EPA defined BPT as the "average of the best existing performance by well-operated plants within each industrial category or subcategory." The word "control" in Section 301 emphasized Congress' expectation that, in establishing the 1977 effluent guidelines, EPA would emphasize end-of-pipe treatment rather than in-plant control measures. EPA did so. However, Section 304(b)(1) of the act makes it clear that the alternative of in-plant process changes may be considered, at least for the purpose of determining whether a proposed effluent limitation is "practicable." Under the statute, the

---

34/ The act's "existing discharge" provisions will in fact apply to some newly constructed facilities since they cover any source for which a new source performance standard (see Part 4.3) has not been proposed.

word "practicable," was to be read together with the provisions of Section 304(b)(1)(B), and so required that effluent limitations be justifiable in terms of the "total cost of (industry-wide) application of (the required) technology in relation to the effluent reduction benefits to be achieved." This determination was to take into account a number of specific factors such as the age of the equipment and facilities involved, the process employed, and non-water quality environmental impacts. Thus, in developing the BPT limitations, the Environmental Protection Agency was required to make what amounted to a cost-benefit balancing test that took into account a broad range of specific engineering factors relating to the ability of plants within a category or subcategory to achieve the limits. The BPT definition was essentially unchanged by the 1977 amendments.

EPA defined Best Available Technology (BAT) as the "very best control and treatment measures that have been or are capable of being achieved." The agency can consider in-plant process changes in addition to end-of-pipe treatment measures in establishing these limitations, which had a 1983 compliance deadline under the 1972 act. Although EPA is required to consider the cost of achieving the required effluent reduction in determining whether a BAT limitation is economically achievable, it is not required to balance cost against effluent reduction benefit as it is in the case of the BPT standards. The engineering factors required to be considered—age of equipment and facility, process employed, process changes, non-water quality environmental impacts and so forth—are the same for BAT as for BPT.

The BAT definition was essentially unchanged by the 1977 amendments but its scope of applicability was radically altered and its date for attainment was extended until 1984. The BAT effluent limitations now focus primarily on the priority pollutants listed in the NRDC consent decree and on additional toxic pollutants identified pursuant to Section 307(a) of the act. These priority and toxic pollutant-oriented best available technology effluent limitations were to be adopted in accordance with a detailed time schedule established by the consent decree as modified and were required to be complied with by 1 July 1984 for the pollutants identified in the consent decree. That date has slipped past 1986 for several industry categories for which EPA was late in promulgating standards. The 1987 amendments nonetheless require EPA to have promulgated final standards for all such industries by the end of 1986. 35/ For pollutants not listed in the consent decree but identified as toxic pollutants under Section 307(a)(1) of the act, compliance with BAT effluent limits is required no later than three years after the date on which the limitations are established.

The "conventional" pollutant measures, which were the primary focus of EPA's pre-1977 BAT effluent limitations are specifically excluded from the scope of coverage of the BAT limits provided by the 1977 amendments. Those pollutants are subject to an entirely new treatment standard established for the first time in the 1977 amendments—Best Conventional Pollutant Control Technology.

The Best Conventional Technology (BCT) effluent limitations were, like the BPT and BAT limitations, to be adopted on an industry-by-industry basis but were to apply for each affected industry only to pollutants which were identified as "conventional." The compliance deadline for the BCT limitations was 1 July 1984. The 1977 amendments specifically included within the definition of "conventional pollutants" Biological Oxygen Demand (BOD), Suspended Solids (SS), fecal coliform bacteria, and pH. EPA is authorized to include additional pollutants within the conventional pollutants definition, but to date has added only oil and grease to the statutory list of conventional pollutants. The act specifically excludes heat from the conventional pollutant definition as there are special statutory provisions for thermal discharges. 36/ The BCT limitations were to be adopted by EPA based on a consideration of the reasonableness of the relationship between the cost of attaining a reduction in effluents and the effluent reduction benefits which will result. The cost of providing treatment to comply with these limits was expected by the Congress to be generally comparable to the cost of achieving the secondary treatment limitation for publicly owned treatment works. As with BPT and BAT limits, EPA was required, in adopting Best Conventional Technology effluent limits, to take into consideration factors such as the age of the equipment and facilities involved, the process employed, engineering aspects, process changes and non-water quality environmental impacts (including energy requirements).

35/ PL 100-4, § 301(f), 101 Stat. ___ (1987).

36/ Clean Water Act, § 316.

The Congress anticipated that EPA, in developing the Best Conventional Technology limits, would conduct a review of the old BAT limits for conventional pollutants and reduce the stringency of such limits to the extent indicated by the economic justification and cost comparability with secondary treatment requirements of the Best Conventional Technology definition in the 1977 amendments.

EPA's first effort at developing BCT regulations was reversed because the agency failed to consider adequately cost-effectiveness in the development of these rules. 37/ EPA then promulgated revised regulations and methodology, which are far less costly than the original rules. In many and perhaps most industry categories, EPA's new methodology resulted in BCT limitations no more stringent than those established for BPT.

The last of the three categories of technology-based effluent limits for existing industry direct discharges which the 1977 amendments provide is the system of effluent limitations to be adopted for "nonconventional nontoxic" pollutants. This is essentially an "everything else" category which applies to all pollutants other than those identified as priority pollutants, toxic pollutants or conventional pollutants under the preceding sections of Section 301. To date, only about ten substances have been so regulated; most could probably be regulated just as well either as toxic or conventional pollutants. The 1977 amendments require compliance with best available technology effluent limits to be adopted for these pollutants by 1 July 1984 or three years after the date the limitations are established by EPA regulations, whichever is later, but in no case later than 1 July 1987.

The 1987 amendments extend compliance deadlines for toxic pollutant limitations, BCT limitations, and BAT limitations until three years after the date of promulgation or March 31, 1989, whichever is sooner. 38/

4.3 Required Level of Treatment—Technology-Based Limits for "New Source" Direct Discharges

The establishment of effluent limitations for "new sources" (defined as any facility the construction of which is commenced "after the publication of proposed regulations" prescribing an

---

37/ American Paper Institute v. EPA, 660 F.2d 954 (4th Cir. 1981).

38/ PL 100-4, § 301, 101 Stat.___(1987).

applicable standard of performance) is separately dealt with in Section 306 of the act. Although the general approach for establishment of new source performance standards under Section 306 is similar to the approach for the establishment of Section 301 effluent limitations (discussed in the previous section) there are significant differences both as to the level of treatment required and the manner of applying the limitations established. These differences remain important because of EPA's delay in promulgating many BPT and BAT limitations, and because the new source standards will govern replacement of certain equipment at an existing discharger. 39/

Section 306(a)(1) of the act defines the term "standard of performance" as "a standard for the control of the discharge of pollutants which reflects the greatest degree of effluent reduction . . . achievable through application of the best available demonstrated control technology, processes, operating methods, and other alternatives, including, where practicable, standards permitting no discharge of pollutants" (emphasis added). The primary difference between this criteria and the Section 301 criteria is the requirement in Section 306 that EPA consider not only pollution control techniques, but also various alternative production processes, operating methods, in-plant control procedures and so forth. Accordingly, in the establishment of Section 306 New Source Performance Standards (NSPS), alternatives or supplements to end-of-pipe treatment will be emphasized. Production process alternatives, which, though less economic, may have a significantly reduced pollution potential may, as a practical matter, be required.

A second major difference regarding criteria for development of new source performance standards is the absence of the kind of requirements for detailed consideration of economic and technological factors which are established by Section 304 for existing source effluent limitations procedures. The absence of such required considerations reflects a presumption that if a source is yet to be constructed, there is greater flexibility to alter total facility design so as to achieve stringent effluent limitations. Thus EPA has greater discretion in the promulgation of new source performance standards than it does with respect to existing sources.

A third, and major, factor to be taken into account when considering the applicability of new source performance standards is

---

39/ 40 CFR § 122.29(b).

that the act provides almost no flexibility for moderating the impact of those standards when applied to specific facilities. The fundamental factors variance and other modification authorities provided by the act are not applicable in the new source situation and, accordingly, strict conformity with the new source performance standards, where applicable, is essential.

Finally, where EPA is the issuing authority, the issuance of a permit for a new source discharge is a federal action subject to the review requirements of the National Environmental Policy Act. 40/ Thus, where the issuance of a new source discharge permit is found to be a major action with a significant effect on the environment, an environmental impact statement will be required. The result will be both substantial delay in the issuance of the new source permit and the potential inclusion of stringent requirements in permits which are issued, requirements which may address a host of other environmental issues besides water pollution discharges and the quality of receiving waters.

Because a determination that a facility is a new source significantly affects both the stringency of applicable treatment standards and the length of time required in order to obtain a permit, the question of when a facility "commences construction" for purposes of applying new source performance standards has proven controversial. This issue is addressed in considerable detail by Section 122.29 of EPA's NPDES regulations, court decisions, and opinions of EPA's General Counsel. The question remains difficult because it depends so heavily on the facts of each case. Companies planning new facilities or major modifications of older ones should carefully review these factual and legal issues with counsel early in the planning process.

Section 306 does offer both to new sources and to new dischargers which are not new sources one important protection which is not available to existing sources under Section 301. Section 306 specifically provides that any new facility constructed to meet all applicable new source standards of performance in effect as of the time it is constructed, may not be subjected to any more stringent standards for ten years from the date construction is completed or for the period of depreciation under the Internal Revenue Code, whichever is shorter. This protection from more stringent standards of

---

40/ Clean Water Act, § 511(c).

performance, as EPA construes the act, is inapplicable to any more stringent permit conditions which are not technology-based, i.e. limitations based on water quality standards, toxic pollutant prohibitions, or to any new permit conditions which govern pollutants not controlled by the applicable new source performance standards with which the facility complied at the time of construction. It should be noted that, on the expiration of the ten-year protection period, immediate compliance with the standards in effect at the time of such expiration will be required. No implementation period for compliance with those standards will be allowed.

4.4 Required Level of Treatment—Technology-Based Limits for Indirect Dischargers (Pre-Treatment)

Industrial facilities that discharge into Publicly Owned Treatment Works (POTWs) are regulated not by the requirements governing direct discharges, but rather by comparable treatment requirements—pretreatment standards—adopted pursuant to Section 307(b) of the act. Pretreatment standards are calculated to achieve two basic objectives: (1) to protect the operation of POTWs and (2) to prevent the discharge of pollutants which pass through publicly owned treatment works without receiving adequate treatment. The dual objectives of the pretreatment program result in a two-part system of controls under the applicable EPA regulations. General requirements are imposed under 40 CFR Part 403 and requirements specific to particular industries, so-called categorical standards, are developed and imposed together with other effluent limitations governing each such industry.

The first part of the general pretreatment regulation focuses primarily on preventing the discharge into POTWs of pollutants which will interfere with the proper operation of the receiving treatment works. This "protection" standard 41/ prohibits the introduction into any publicly owned treatment works of:

(i)   Pollutants which create a fire or explosion hazard in the POTW;

(ii)   Discharges with a pH lower than 5.0 unless the works is specifically designed to accommodate such discharges;

41/ 40 CFR § 403.5.

(iii)   Solid or viscous pollutants in amounts which obstruct the flow in a sewer system;

(iv)   Discharges, including discharges of conventional pollutants, of such volume and concentration that they upset the treatment process and cause a permit violation (e.g., usually high concentrations of oxygen demanding pollutants such as BOD); and

(v)   Heat in amounts which will inhibit biological activity in the POTW resulting in interference, but in no case heat in such quantities that the temperature influent at the treatment works exceeds 40° C (104° F) unless the works are designed to accommodate such heat.

The second major objective of the pretreatment regulations-- preventing the discharge in the publicly owned treatment works of pollutants which pass through those treatment works without receiving adequate treatment--is to be achieved by "categorical" pretreatment regulations. These categorical regulations are applicable only to "incompatible" pollutants—e.g., pollutants other than biochemical oxygen demand, suspended solids, pH and fecal coliform bacteria, and which are not adequately treated in the POTW treatment process. 42/ These categorical pretreatment regulations, like the BAT regulations and new source performance standards, focus primarily on the thirty-four industries and sixty-five toxic pollutant categories specified in the NRDC consent decree. For each discharger into a POTW, these categorical standards are intended to result in the same level of treatment prior to discharge from the POTW as that which would have been required had the industrial facility discharged those pollutants directly to the receiving waters. The stringency of these categorical standards can be reduced through the mechanism of removal credits, which takes into account the removal of these pollutants consistently achieved by the POTW in question.

Accordingly, the industrial facility discharging into a POTW will be required to achieve, in meeting the applicable pretreatment

---

42/ Additional pollutants may be identified as "compatible" for a particular treatment works if it can be shown that the facility in question adequately treats those pollutants.

limits, a level of treatment performance equivalent to the applicable BAT effluent limitations or new source performance standards unless the receiving POTW has an approved pretreatment program and requests removal credits against the applicable pretreatment limit. This removal credit is to be based on the POTW's demonstrated capability to consistently remove that pollutant in its treatment process. In order to qualify for a revision, the POTW must provide consistent removal of each pollutant for which a discharge limit revision is sought, and its sludge use or disposal practices must, at the time of the application and thereafter, remain in compliance with all applicable criteria, guidelines and regulations for sludge use and disposal. EPA modified its regulations in an effort to account for process variations by POTWs, 43/ but that effort was reversed by the court of appeals. 44/

Pretreatment requirements are directly enforceable by EPA and states with NPDES permit issuance authority, but the EPA regulations contemplate eventual delegation of primary enforcement responsibility to individual POTWs with EPA and the states receding to a backup role.

Under the regulations, any POTW (or combination of POTWs operated by the same authority) having a total design flow greater than five million gallons per day must have developed and implemented a pretreatment program by 1 July 1983, if it receives incompatible industrial waste. A POTW must have an approved pretreatment program in order to grant removal credits although it may grant conditional removal credits while EPA is considering approval of the POTW's pretreatment program. POTW programs must meet funding, personnel, legal, and procedural criteria sufficient to ensure that the POTW's enforcement responsibilities can be carried out. Once the program is developed and approved, the POTW will be responsible for enforcement of the national pretreatment standards. A POTW may exercise enforcement authority through a number of methods including contracts, joint powers agreements, ordinances, or otherwise.

43/ 40 CFR § 403.7, 49 FR 31221, 3 August 1984.

44/ Natural Resources Defense Council v. EPA, 24 E.R.C. 1313, petition for cert. filed, 55 U.S.L.W. 3128 (U.S. Aug. 26, 1986) (No. 86-239).

Finally, pretreatment regulations establish extensive reporting requirements for both industrial users and POTWs in order to monitor and demonstrate compliance with categorical pretreatment standards.

The pretreatment regulations significantly affect industries subject to categorical pretreatment standards, as well as other industrial users of POTWs which will have to comply with general pretreatment requirements.

4.5 Technology-Based Treatment Standards for Industrial Dischargers Dealing with Process Variability

As the technology-based effluent limits address increased numbers of pollutants, setting proper limitations becomes much more difficult. As standards become more complex, valid application of technology-based effluent limits will, in many cases, demand some mechanism by which plant-to-plant variations can be taken into account.

The statutory mechanisms to permit plant-to-plant flexibility are exceedingly limited. Section 301(c) grants the administrator authority to modify the 1984 BAT requirements or the related pretreatment requirements if it can be shown that the economic capability of the discharger necessitates less stringent limitations. A further prerequisite to such a modification is a showing that it will result in further progress toward elimination of the discharge of pollutants. Though this basis for granting a variance is reasonably broad, the circumstances in which it can be granted are strictly limited. The Section 301(c) variance does not apply to the "Best Conventional Technology" effluent limitations, and Section 301(l) of the act precludes the modification of any effluent limitation regulating a toxic or priority pollutant. Accordingly, the Section 301(c) variance authority applies only to the "nonconventional nontoxic" pollutants so its utility is minimal.

Section 301(g) is also applicable only to the few nonconventional nontoxic pollutants (excluding heat). The 1987 amendments have substantially revised section 301(g), and reopened the application period.

The final statutory basis for modification of BAT and BCT effluent limits and pretreatment standards is set forth in Section 301(k). That subsection as amended in 1987 authorizes the administrator or state issuing authority to issue a permit providing for a compliance date extension of two years if a source seeks to achieve the applicable limits through the use of innovative technology which has the potential for industry-wide application and has a substantial likelihood of achieving greater effluent reduction than the effluent limitations or will result in significantly lower costs. It is unclear whether this innovative technology variance may be granted for toxic pollutant limits in view of the prohibition against modification of toxic pollutant effluent limitations set forth in Section 301(l).

With respect to the 1977 BPT effluent limits, the act provided only one now-obsolete basis for extending the time for compliance.

Although the statutory variance authority was of limited utility, EPA provided by administrative interpretation, and the courts approved, a more helpful variance mechanism, now codified and tightened by the 1987 amendments. 45/ This variance—the "fundamentally different factors" variance—was initially applied to the 1977 BPT effluent limitations through the inclusion in each set of effluent limitations regulations of a variance clause. This clause allowed a discharger to demonstrate that the limitations should not apply to its facility because of the existence of factors which were fundamentally different from those considered by EPA in the process of developing the effluent limitations.

The scope of the required variance clause was expanded in the case of Appalachian Power Company v. Train, 46/ and EPA's recognition of the necessity of some sort of variance mechanism for "fundamentally different factors" was applauded by the Supreme Court in the Dupont case. 47/ The need for a fundamental factors variance arises from the process EPA uses to develop industry-wide effluent limitations under the Clean Water Act. It is impossible to consider all of the factors required to be considered by Section 304 in a full and timely fashion for every type of plant in every industrial category. Consequently, there must be some way to weigh factors not fully considered in the regulatory development process when the time comes to apply effluent limitations to a particular facility in the form of an NPDES permit.

45/ PL 100-4, § 306, 101 Stat.___(1987), adds § 301(n) to the Clean Water Act, setting forth the "fundamentally different factors" variance.

46/ 545 F.2d 1351 (4th Cir. 1976).

47/ 430 U.S. 112 (1977).

Thus, in both the pretreatment regulations and NPDES permit program regulations discussed above, EPA allows dischargers to obtain the fundamental factors variance. The variance is available with respect to the categorical pretreatment regulations, as well as for all of the technology-based effluent limits for existing sources. It is unavailable for new source performance standards (because a facility yet to be constructed has greater design flexibility) or for water quality-related effluent limitations. The Supreme Court has ruled that the fundamental factors variance is available with respect to toxic pollutants under the Clean Water Act. 48/ The 1987 amendments have codified the fundamental factors variance and made it more difficult to obtain. 49/

In order to obtain a fundamental factors variance, the discharger must show that factors applicable to this facility are fundamentally different from those considered in the development of the effluent limitations guidelines. Factors which Section 125.31 of the regulations allowed to be considered as fundamentally different were:

(1) The nature or quality of the pollutants contained in the raw waste load of the applicant's process waste water;

(2) The volume of the discharger's process waste water and effluent discharged;

(3) Non-water quality environmental impacts of control and treatment of the discharger's raw waste load (are these impacts fundamentally more adverse than those considered during the development of national limits?);

(4) Energy requirements of the application of control and treatment technology (are they fundamentally greater than those assessed in developing national limits?);

(5) Age, size, land availability and configuration as they relate to the discharger's equipment or facilities, processes employed; engineering aspects of the application of control technology; and

---

48/ Chemical Manufacturers Association v. Natural Resources Defense Council, _ U.S. _ 105 S.Ct. 1102 (1985).

49/ PL 100-4, § 306, 101 Stat._(1987).

(6)   Cost of compliance with required control technology (is it "wholly out of proportion" to the
removal costs considered in developing national
limits?).

If it finds that a fundamentally different factor exists, the
Environmental Protection Agency may adopt alternative effluent
limitations for the facility in question. It should be noted that those
limits may be either more or less stringent than the effluent limitations with respect to which the variance is granted.

The fundamental factors variance is not available simply
because the cost of compliance with BPT limitations would force
plant closure. 50/ Instead, the costs of BPT compliance are relevant
in deciding if fundamentally different factors exist at a plant and, if
so, whether the alternate effluent limitations are as cost-effective as
those imposed on the industry in general. 51/ (The language of the
1987 amendments make it unclear whether cost can be considered at
all.)

Finally, it should be noted that although the fundamental
factors variance is an important mechanism and will become increasingly so as effluent limitations become more detailed and address
more pollutants, its potential availability increases the necessity for
careful monitoring of the development process for applicable effluent
limitations to assure that the factors which are considered during that
process are properly assessed and applied. Under the 1987 amendments, an applicant must show that it raised the fundamentally
different factors during the development of the regulation or show
why it did not have a reasonable opportunity to raise the factors in
such process. 52/ Arguably, the only meaningful relief available for
improper application of factors actually considered during the
development process is an appeal to the courts. Unless this appeal is
taken within ninety days after the applicable effluent limits are
published in final form, the right to raise these issues may be waived.

50/   EPA v. National Crushed Stone Association, 449 U.S. 64 (1980).

51/   Weyerhauser Co. v. Costle, 590 F.2d 1011, 1036 (D.C. Cir.
1978).

52/   PL 100-4, § 306, 101 Stat.___(1987).

4.6   Technology-Based Treatment Standards—Publicly Owned Treatment Works

For discharges from publicly owned treatment works (POTWs), Section 301 directs that by 1 July 1977, they achieve effluent limitations based on secondary treatment, as defined by EPA, and any more stringent limitations necessary to comply with water quality standards or treatment standards imposed by state law. The 1977 and 1981 amendments provide for extension of the 1977 secondary treatment and other deadlines where, because of lack of federal funding or otherwise, planned facilities have not been completed. The extension shall be to the earliest date on which funding can be provided and construction completed but no later than July 1988. Industrial dischargers whose permits require discharge to a treatment works and who had enforceable contracts for such discharge or who were included in a treatment works facility plan filed with a grant application may be granted an extension on much the same basis as the treatment works itself.

EPA defined "secondary treatment" for purposes of Section 301 in 1973 and modified that definition late in 1984. 53/ The effluent levels prescribed by these regulations are as follows:

	% Removal 30 day average	Concentration (mg/1) Monthly Average	Weekly Average
BOD (5 day)	85	30	45
Suspended Solids (SS)	85	30	45
Coliform		200/100 ml.	400/100 ml.
pH		6.0 to 9.0	

The regulations make special provision for upwards revision of the "secondary treatment" effluent limits (1) where necessary to take into account storm water infiltration into combined sewers during wet weather periods; and (2) where necessary to take into account the fact that the Section 301 and Section 306 effluent limitations applicable to major industrial dischargers into the treatment works (those exceeding 10 percent of the design flow) would permit an industrial

_____

53/ See 40 CFR Part 133.

user to directly discharge greater concentrations than those set forth
in the table. In the latter case, the permitted discharge from the
POTW which is attributable to the industrial waste received for treatment may be increased to equal, but not exceed, that which would be
permitted, under the applicable effluent limitations, if the industrial
facility were discharging directly into a waterway.

In the 1981 amendments, Congress revised the definition of
secondary treatment so that such biological treatment facilities as
oxidation ponds, lagoons, and ditches and trickling filters are deemed
to be the equivalent of secondary treatment. 54/ These modes of
treatment are considerably cheaper than other treatment modes,
especially for small communities. The changes made pursuant to this
standard allow trickling filters and stabilization ponds to meet
secondary treatment requirements if the discharge meets the following parameters 55/:

	% Removal	Concentration (mg/1) 30-Day Average	Concentration (mg/1) 7-Day Average
BOD (5 day)	65	45	65
Suspended Solids	65	45	65
pH		6.0 to 9.0	

The relative stringency of the POTW effluent limitations and
the fact that, under the 1972 act, POTWs were, for the first time,
subjected to effective and directly enforceable federal effluent
limitations and permit requirements, gave municipal authorities a
strong mandate to rigorously enforce flow and concentration
limitations on industrial users of their systems. In some cases, the
"pretreatment requirements" imposed by municipal authorities
pursuant to this mandate have been more stringent than the federal
pretreatment standards discussed above. In addition, as noted below,
the increasing need for high levels of performance by POTWs result in
new or upgraded facilities which can drastically increase the cost to
industry of waste treatment services.

**4.7 More Stringent Treatment Required to Meet Water Quality-
Related Effluent Limitations**

As has been noted, the technology-based effluent limitations
discussed above function as nationwide minimum or base level treatment standards. The act provides two separate mechanisms for the

---

54/ Clean Water Act, § 304(d)(4).

55/ 40 CFR § 133.105.

imposition of more stringent requirements where dictated by the need to protect or maintain water quality in specific bodies of water.

Section 301(b)(1)(C) of the act requires both industrial dischargers and POTWs to achieve, no later than 1 July 1977, any effluent limitations more stringent than the minimum technology-based standards which may be necessary to meet applicable federal-state water quality standards. This requirement is incorporated into permits issued by EPA through the state certification requirement under Section 401 of the act. (See Part 3.2 above.)

Section 302 of the act authorizes EPA directly to establish effluent criteria more stringent than the applicable BAT limits where necessary for the attainment or maintenance in a specific body of water quality which "shall assure protection of public water supplies, agriculture and industrial uses, and the protection and propagation of a balanced population of shellfish, fish and wildlife, and allow recreational activities in and on the water. . ." EPA has interpreted this Section 302 authority as providing a selective tool for the agency to impose more stringent requirements where necessary to protect important water resources. Although this section has received little use to date, it does have great potential impact in that it authorizes EPA to adopt its own effluent limitations for any body of water as to which a state fails or refuses to adopt water quality standards sufficient to maintain fishing and swimming uses.

The water quality standards and water quality-related effluent limitations imposed by these two mechanisms may well require levels of treatment considerably higher than those required by the technology-related effluent limits particularly for water bodies with heavy concentrations of discharges, or exceptionally poor water quality and correspondingly stringent water quality standards, or water bodies with limited assimilative capacity because of hydrologic factors. The potential stringency of these limitations is increased by the absence of any variance provision applicable to Section 301 water quality standards. (Section 302 does contain a limited variance mechanism for standards imposed under its mandate, including a potential five-year variance from certain toxic pollutant standards. 56/) The requirement for compliance with water quality standards is inflexible and mandatory, thus increasing the importance of carefully following the development of such standards as they apply to particular water bodies and dischargers to them.

56/ PL 100-4, §308, 101 Stat.__(1987).

The procedures for setting water quality standards are quite complex. States, acting pursuant to the procedures set out in 40 CFR Section 131.20, are to hold public hearings every three years for the purpose of reviewing and revising state water quality standards. EPA does not set specific minimums for state standards; instead the rules require that such standards specify and protect appropriate water uses (e.g., water supply, fish, wildlife), 57/ and set specific criteria to attain these ends. 58/ The state standards must attain the Clean Water Act's goal of fishable, swimmable waters wherever attainable, and must, at a minimum, maintain the uses designated in the standards and current uses, 59/ unless the state can demonstrate that the designated use is unattainable or infeasible for one of a short list of reasons, primarily concerning other physical or biological aspects of the water body. 60/ In addition, no degradation of "outstanding national resource" waters, such as those in national and state parks, is to be permitted. 61/

The pollutants required to be addressed by state water quality standards were addressed by criteria for a number of pollutants of specific concern, published in "Quality Criteria for Water," July 1976, the so-called Red Book. These criteria were replaced in large part when EPA adopted criteria for the priority pollutants listed in the NRDC consent decree, 62/ in addition to those earlier criteria, the 1976 Red Book. The 1976 Red Book criteria have been rescinded.

Adoption of water quality criteria and standards for priority pollutants will have no effect until these standards are translated into end-of-pipe effluent limitations to be imposed on dischargers. Section 303(e) of the act requires states to inventory all waters within their jurisdictions to identify those waters as to which BAT and other technology-based effluent limits are inadequate to promote and maintain

---

57/ §§ 131.6, 131.10.

58/ § 131.11.

59/ § 131.10(h).

60/ § 131.10(g).

61/ § 131.12(a)(3).

62/ 45 FR 79318 (28 November 1980).

compliance with water quality standards (water quality-limited segments), to establish maximum loadings for water quality limited segments, and to provide a system for allocating those maximum loadings among all dischargers to the affected waters. This requirement has not been fully implemented because of the extreme technical difficulty in performing the necessary mathematical modeling and other studies.

The 1981 amendments required states to review, and if appropriate, to revise water quality standards every three years. 63/ These standards were also to be reviewed by EPA for consistency with the act. The 1987 amendments require an additional state review of standards for water bodies failing to meet water quality standards for toxic pollutants, and require the imposition of additional controls on such toxic discharges. Under the act, even before the 1981 amendments, EPA has the authority to set its water quality standards for particular water bodies where state standards are inadequate. EPA has done so in several instances.

Because of the slow pace of the Section 303 planning process, water quality-related effluent limitations have often not been included in permits when they should have been, a situation which has been changing as EPA implements the NRDC consent decree and review mandated by the 1981 amendments. That decree requires these water quality related effluent limits to be incorporated into discharge permits. 64/ (The 1987 amendments largely codified the water quality requirements of the consent decree. 65/) For discharges to water-quality limited segments, the issuing authority cannot issue a permit unless it finds that the facility will not cause or contribute to the violation of water quality standards applicable to the water into which the discharge is made. These requirements result in a system similar to that now applicable to the location of new facilities in non-attainment areas under the Clean Air Act, where pressure for new industrial growth results in the imposition of increasingly stringent requirements on existing sources in order to permit new facilities to operate without violation of applicable standards.

63/ 33 U.S.C. § 1313a.

64/ 40 CFR § 122.43(d).

65/ PL 100-4, § 308, 101 Stat.___(1987).

EPA has borrowed another concept from the Clean Air Act —the "bubble"—for use in the water pollution context. Under the "bubble" concept, EPA would permit facilities to cumulate the discharges from different outfalls of the plant and meet a single effluent limitation, rather than outfall-by-outfall limitations. So far, the bubble is limited to steel plants. 66/ This approach may lead to appreciable cost savings depending on whether it can be used in water-quality limited areas and whether it applies to toxic pollutants. Two subcategories in the steel industry—cokemaking and cold forming—were not permitted to use the bubble, in part because of toxic pollutant concerns. 67/

In summary, it seems clear that, both as to industrial direct discharge and pretreatment requirements, water quality standards on certain bodies of water can be expected, during the next five to ten years, to increase the stringency of treatment requirements imposed on industrial and other dischargers. The toxics orientation of the water quality standards, together with the policy changes and enforcement mechanisms discussed above, merit careful consideration by potentially affected companies. Those companies would be well advised to participate actively in state proceedings related to the review and revision of existing water quality standards and the carrying out of the Section 303 planning process.

5.0   CONTROLLING NON-PROCESS-RELATED WASTE DISCHARGES

Although the system of effluent limits imposed through the NPDES permit program is an effective means of regulating waste discharges which result from normal industrial or municipal processes and which are amenable to treatment prior to discharge, this system is an inappropriate means of regulating and controlling accidental and unanticipated discharges or discharges which, by their nature, are not subject to confinement and treatment (e.g., area-wide or plant site runoff). For this latter class of discharges, the focus of regulation must be on preventing the discharge (in the case of the accidental spill) or on minimizing the volume of pollutants carried (in the case of

---

66/ 40 CFR § 420.03.

67/ 47 FR 23265-66, 23271-74 (21 May 1982), 40 CFR § 420.03(b)(3).

area-wide and plant site runoff). Since accidental spills and "non-point source" discharges are responsible for a large percentage of the total pollutants introduced into the nation's waterways, the act provides a number of mechanisms, supplemental to the NPDES permit program, to control discharges which are unrelated to industrial process wastes. This system of supplemental regulatory controls is the subject of this section and the next one.

5.1 Controlling Area-Wide Non-Point Source Pollution— Section 208 Planning

The primary mechanism contemplated by the 1972 act for controlling area-wide non-point source pollution was the planning and regulatory program created by Section 208. This section required each state to identify areas of the state which, due to urban industrial concentrations or other factors, have substantial water quality control problems. For each of these designated "waste treatment management areas," a representative of state and local officials would be identified and charged with the responsibility of developing a comprehensive area-wide plan for solving the area's water quality control problems.

After several years, however, Congress stopped funding the development and implementation of 208 plans. As a consequence, little progress has been made under Section 208 since fiscal year 1980. There has been little done since then to address the problem of non-point sources although several EPA task forces have recently begun to consider different regulatory and legislative options.

5.2 Stormwater Discharges and Best Management Practices

The regulation of municipal and industrial stormwater discharges has proven controversial since enactment of the 1972 amendments. That controversy persisted in large part because Congress failed to devise a regulatory program tailored to stormwater discharges, leaving EPA the unpleasant choice of regulating all stormwater discharges from point sources in the same fashion as process waste water from major industries or to leave all such discharges unregulated. The first choice is unworkable because of the potentially vast number of such discharges and the high cost of treating all of them; the second choice would have left a number of major discharges of toxic and other pollutants completely unregulated, and so cause significant harm to the environment.

EPA arrived at a middle course, regulating discharges from industrial areas and municipalities above a certain size. The 1987 amendments adopt but substantially modify this approach. 68/ The amended act now requires that five categories of municipal or industrial stormwater discharges be regulated as NPDES discharges:

(1) discharges which have NPDES permits issued as of February, 1987;

(2) discharges "associated with industrial activity";

(3) discharges "from a municipal separate storm sewer system serving a population of 250,000 or more";

(4) discharges "from a municipal separate storm sewer system serving a population of 100,000 or more but less than 250,000";

(5) other discharges designated by the EPA administrator or the state if such discharge "contributes to a violation of a water quality standard or is a significant contributor of pollutants to waters of the United States." 69/

For discharges associated with the industrial activities, NPDES permits must meet the applicable effluent limitations imposed upon the industry in question. Many industrial dischargers, of course, already have NPDES permits governing the discharge of stormwater from plant yards and other ancillary areas. These continue to be regulated under existing permits.

Stormwater discharges "associated with industrial activity" which do not currently have permits are subject to different procedures. By February 1989 (two years after enactment), the EPA must establish permit application requirements for such discharges. By February 1990 (three years after enactment), permit applications must be filed, and by February 1991, EPA (or the state) must issue or deny such permit. The permittee must comply with the permit "as expeditiously as practicable, but in no event later than 3 years after the date of issuance of such permit," or February 1994 if the earlier steps are completed in a timely fashion.

Large municipal discharges, i.e., from stormwater sewer systems serving more than 250,000 people, must meet the same schedule for permit application regulations, application filing, and

---

68/ PL 100-4, §405, 101 Stat.___(1987), adds a new subsection (p) to
    section 402 of the act.

69/ Clean Water Act § 402(p)(2).

deadlines for permit issuance and compliance. Thus, EPA's application regulations must be issued by February 1989, permit applications
must be filed by February 1990, EPA (or states) must decide and issue
permits by February 1991, and permittees must comply with them by
February 1994.

The 1987 amendments allow the EPA administrator flexibility
to issue permits for discharges from municipal storm sewers on either
a system or jurisdiction-wide basis. The permit must "include a
requirement to effectively prohibit non-stormwater discharges into
storm sewers." The amendments impose substantive requirements on
the permitted discharges. Such permits

> shall require controls to the maximum extent practic-
> able, including management practices, control tech-
> niques and systems, design and engineering methods,
> and such other provisions as the Administrator or the
> State determines appropriate for the control of such
> pollutants. 70/

Although smaller municipal storm sewer systems (i.e., serving
100,000 to 250,000 people) are subject to these same substantive
permit requirements, the timetable for applications, permit decisions,
and compliance is longer than for large municipal systems. Thus, EPA
must issue permit regulations for these smaller dischargers by
February 1991, permit applications must be filed by February 1992,
permits must be granted or denied by February 1993, and compliance
is required within three years of such issuance, or February 1996, if
the timetable is met.

This permit system is the primary mechanism for regulating
plant site runoff where toxic and hazardous pollutants are not
involved. In addition, Section 304(e), which was added by the 1977
amendments, authorizes EPA to require permittees to adopt "Best
Management Practices" to control toxic pollutants resulting from
ancillary industrial activities. EPA also is authorized to prescribe
regulations to control plant site runoff, spillage or leaks, and sludge
or waste disposal. The legislative history of this provision indicates
that Congress anticipated that EPA's regulations would specify treatment requirements, operating procedures, and other management
practices by classes and categories of point source discharges.

70/ Clean Water Act, § 402(p)(3)(B)(iii).

EPA proposed sweeping regulations to implement the best management practices provisions of Section 304(e), 71/ but issued final regulations of more modest scope. 72/ Both the proposed and final regulations, however, attempt to apply the BMP requirements on an across-the-board basis, instead of by categories, an administrative short-cut which may cause difficulties when applying BMP requirements to particular operations.

The final regulations emphasize BMPs of a procedural nature (especially preventive maintenance and housekeeping) and BMPs requiring only minor construction. EPA stated that these regulations are the first of two or more steps; Spill Prevention, Control and Countermeasure (SPCC) plans for hazardous substances (which have been proposed but never promulgated) and possibly additional BMP provisions are scheduled as regulatory requirements in the future.

The existing BMP requirements are applicable to all dischargers who use, manufacture, store, handle or discharge any pollutant listed as toxic under Section 307 or as hazardous under Section 311 for all ancillary manufacturing operations which may result in significant amounts of toxic or hazardous pollutants reaching waters of the U.S. Any BMPs required by a Section 304(e) effluent limitations guideline must be expressly incorporated into an NPDES permit and BMPs may be so incorporated if EPA or the State agency determines this to be "necessary to carry out the provisions of the Act . . . ." These requirements appear to have been specifically contemplated by Congress when it added the BMP provisions in 1977.

In addition, the regulations require the permittee to develop a "Best Management Practices program," which must be submitted as part of the permit application and which will be subject to all permit issuance procedures. This program must be written, must establish toxic and hazardous substances control objectives, and must establish specific BMPs to meet these objectives. The program must also address a number of points concerning ancillary activities such as materials inventory and compatibility, employee training, visual inspections, preventive maintenance, housekeeping, and security. It is clear that these requirements will impose considerable administrative burdens on affected permittees.

71/ 43 FR 39282 (1 September 1978).

72/ 40 CFR Part 125, Subpart K.

6.0 OIL AND HAZARDOUS SUBSTANCES

Section 311 of the act extensively regulates accidental or intentional discharges of oil and hazardous substances. This elaborate provision was first enacted as part of the Water Quality Improvement Act of 1970, 73/ which the 1972 amendments revised and incorporated into the Federal Water Pollution Act of 1972 as section 311. The 1977 amendments modified Section 311 in several ways, principally with respect to the limits on the liability of a discharger of oil or of hazardous substances. Congress further amended Section 311 in 1978, primarily in order to make the section's provisions with respect to hazardous substances more workable. In 1980, Congress enacted the Comprehensive Environmental Response, Compensation and Liability Act (CERCLA), which has significantly expanded EPA's authority and resources to clean up hazardous substances. Spills of petroleum products continue to be regulated solely under Section 311 of the Clean Water Act.

Although oil and hazardous substances are covered by the same Clean Water Act provisions, they have traditionally been treated separately by EPA. The following discussion analyzes each in turn.

6.1 Oil

The act prohibits the discharge of "harmful quantities" of oil into navigable waters. EPA regulations 74/ have defined the term "harmful quantities" to cover all discharges which "violate applicable water quality standards or cause a film or sheen upon the surface of the water. . ." Thus virtually all discharges of oil are prohibited. 75/

Industry's responsibility under this section has several facets. Owners and operators of large oil (including mineral or vegetable oil) storage facilities (1,320 gallons above ground or 42,000 gallons below

---

73/ § 102, PL 91-224, 84 Stat. 91-99 (April 3, 1970).

74/ 40 CFR § 110.3.

75/ It is arguable that the oils and greases contained in an NPDES permitted discharge are not covered by the Section 311 limitations and reporting requirements. However, many NPDES permits contain a condition making it clear that the permit does not in any way excuse Section 311 compliance.

ground) must comply with EPA regulations 76/ which seek to minimize the risk that an oil spill will occur by requiring the development,
implementation and maintenance of Spill Prevention, Control and
Countermeasure (SPCC) Plans. Plan implementation is often costly
because the installation of containment structures, the conduct of
regular inspections, and other preventive measures are often necessary plan elements. Failure to prepare and maintain a plan in accordance with the regulations subjects the violator to civil penalties of up
to $5,000 for each day of violation. 77/ Coast Guard regulations apply
similar, but more stringent, planning and accident avoidance requirements to vessels and associated oil transfer operations. 78/

In addition, vessels must demonstrate financial responsibility
to meet potential liability under Section 311(p)(1) of the act. Owners
and operators of inland oil barges must demonstrate financial responsibility in the sum of $125 per gross ton or $125,000, whichever is
greater. Owners and operators of vessels carrying oil and hazardous
substances as cargo must demonstrate financial responsibility in the
sum of $250,000 or $150 per gross ton, whichever is greater. Other
vessels must establish responsibility in the sum of $150 per gross
ton. Financial responsibility may be established by insurance, surety
bonds or qualification as a self-insurer.

If, despite compliance with applicable spill avoidance requirements, a spill does occur, additional obligations arise. The owner or
operator of the source from which the discharge originates must immediately report the discharge to the Coast Guard and/or EPA. 79/
Failure to comply with this requirement results, upon conviction, in a
fine of up to $10,000 and/or imprisonment for not more than one
year. 80/ It should be kept in mind that this reporting requirement is
broadly construed and may apply to oil spills which originate several
miles inland (e.g., if the spill goes into a storm sewer which outlets to
navigable waters).

76/ 40 CFR Part 112.

77/ 40 CFR § 112.6.

78/ 33 CFR Parts 154-157.

79/ 33 CFR § 153.203; 40 CFR § 110.9.

80/ Clean Water Act, Section 311(b)(5).

In addition to giving notice, the discharger must either contain and clean up the spill or pay the cost of clean up efforts by responsible government agencies. 81/ Section 311(f) limits the discharger's liability for the government's actual removal costs to $50 million unless there is willful negligence or willful misconduct in which case there is no limit on liability. Removal costs include so-called natural resources damages, defined as "any costs or expenses incurred by the federal government or any state government in the restoration or replacement of natural resources damaged or destroyed as a result of a discharge of oil or a hazardous substance in violation of [§ 311(b)]." 82/ EPA is authorized to establish lower limits of liability for facilities having small storage capacity (1000 barrels or less). 83/ Generally, effective private clean up measures are less costly than similar efforts by the government and, in addition, those efforts are of considerable practical importance in mitigating the civil penalties discussed below.

The discharger must also pay a civil penalty of not more than $5,000 for each spill. 84/ Although the Coast Guard (which is the agency administering the penalties section) must assess a penalty, it has considerable discretion to reduce the amount of the penalty based on the size of the business of the discharger, the effect of the penalty on his ability to continue in business, and the gravity of the violation. The act provides the right to notice and a hearing in connection with civil penalty assessments.

Alternatively, the government may bring a civil penalty action in district court against the discharger, for a civil penalty of up to $50,000, and in cases of "willful negligence or willful misconduct," up to $250,000. 85/

6.2 Hazardous Substances

Although Section 311 also governs the discharge of hazardous substances, EPA was slow to implement the hazardous substances

---

81/ Sections 311(c), 311(f).

82/ Section 311(f)(4).

83/ 40 CFR Part 113.

84/ Section 311(b)(6)(A).

85/ Section 311(b)(6)(B).

provision, and shortly after regulations were promulgated in March 1978 suffered an embarrassing court defeat, in which the court enjoined significant parts of the regulations before they became effective. Congress responded to the court's action by amending Section 311 to simplify and clarify its provisions along the lines agreed to in a compromise between EPA and the industry plaintiffs in that case. 86/ The 1978 amendments were directed toward the two most significant problems identified by the court: the elements necessary to establish what was to be considered a harmful quantity and the relationship of Section 311 to the NPDES program.

Pursuant to these amendments, EPA has designated approximately 300 substances as hazardous and thus subject to the Section 311 program. 87/ In addition, the agency has designated quantities of these substances that may be harmful (called a "reportable quantity"). 88/ Hazardous substances are placed in one of five categories: X, A, B, C, D. A harmful quantity of a category X substance is one pound, of a category A substance is 10 pounds, of a category B substance is 100 pounds, of a category C substance is 1000 pounds, and of a category D substance is 5000 pounds. 89/

The second principal feature of EPA's hazardous substance regulations is the exclusion of discharges made in compliance with an NPDES permit. Since a primary purpose of the amendments was to limit Section 311 to "classic" hazardous substance spills, the regulations specify that they are not applicable to chronic discharges of designated substances if the discharge complies with an NPDES permit. 90/ Such discharges, of course, remain subject to regulation under the NPDES program.

Further, if an NPDES facility has intermittent, anticipated spills of hazardous substances (i.e., into plant drainage ditches), it should determine whether these discharges ought to be brought within the terms of its NPDES permit. The regulations give the facility the

---

86/ PL 95-576, 92 Stat. 2467 (1978).

87/ 40 CFR Part 116.

88/ 40 CFR Part 117.

89/ 40 CFR § 117.3.

90/ 40 CFR § 117.12.

option of having such discharges regulated through the NPDES program or pursuant to Section 311.

Discharges of hazardous substances may also reach navigable waters through municipal sewers and publicly owned treatment works. Discharges from industrial facilities to a POTW are not covered by the regulations at present. The regulations do apply to all discharges of reportable quantities of hazardous substances to POTWs by a mobile source such as trucks unless the discharger has met certain requirements. 91/

A facility owner or operator who spills a harmful quantity of a hazardous substance must report the spill; failure to do so will subject him to criminal penalties. If there is a spill, the violator is also subject to a fine of up to $5000. In lieu of this fine, EPA can seek a penalty through a civil action in federal courts; this penalty can range up to $50,000 or up to $250,000 if the discharge was the result of willful negligence or willful misconduct within the privity and knowledge of the owner/operator.

Finally, it should be noted that the reporting requirements for spills of hazardous substances (as well as other defined wastes) have been substantially supplemented by the Comprehensive Environmental, Response, Compensation and Liability Act (also known as CERCLA or Superfund). For a fuller description of these requirements, see Chapter 3.

The nature of these regulations and the potential penalties thereunder place a premium on developing compliance procedures before a spill occurs. A facility should first be evaluated to determine whether it discharges, or might discharge, a reportable quantity of any hazardous substance to the waters of the United States. If there is a risk of such a discharge, the exemptions established by the regulations should be considered in order to determine if they will be applicable to the potential discharge. If no exemption is available, it may be advisable to develop a program to prevent such discharges. Further it is essential to implement a contingency plan capable of assuring a prompt and appropriate response in the event of a nonexempt reportable discharge.

91/ 40 CFR § 117.13.

7.0 ENFORCEMENT

The Clean Water Act provides many enforcement options to EPA and the states, as well as a citizen suit provision. These enforcement options have been substantively increased by the 1987 amendments and applicable penalties for certain violations stiffened. Enforcement has taken on increasing importance as EPA finishes developing most standards and has them incorporated into federal and state discharge permits. This understandable shift in focus by the regulatory agencies has been accompanied by a vigorous and largely successful citizen enforcement effort by many environmental groups.

7.1 Federal and State Enforcement

In order to assure compliance with the regulatory program, Congress wrote elaborate enforcement provisions into the act. Dischargers who fail to obtain permits under the act or who violate the act's effluent limitations, pretreatment requirements, or monitoring provisions, or any permit conditions required to implement these may be proceeded against under the Refuse Act of 1899, under the Clean Water Act (although there is at least some question as to whether the Section 309 sanctions apply to a failure to obtain a permit), and under the state laws providing for implementation of the NPDES program. All of the foregoing sanctions may be pursued concurrently, although it is likely that EPA will defer to state enforcement action if such actions are expeditiously commenced. As the emphasis of the regulatory program moves from the establishment of standards and the issuance of permits to concerns about compliance with the terms of standards and permits, provisions for dealing with violations will become more and more important.

EPA has a number of enforcement options under the Clean Water Act: (1) issuance of a compliance order; (2) obtaining injunctive relief under Section 309; (3) seeking civil penalties; and (4) initiating criminal prosecution. In addition, Sierra Club v. Train 92/, held that EPA can elect to take no formal enforcement action at all. Should EPA decide not to take any formal action, it can either ignore a violation as being de minimis or attempt to resolve the violation by informal procedures. EPA's decision not to pursue enforcement action does not insulate a discharger from citizen suits to enforce discharge limitations.

92/ 557 F. 2d 485 (5th Cir. 1977).

Compliance orders are administrative orders by which EPA directs the violator to come into compliance with the applicable statutory, regulatory, or permit term. These orders are subject to judicial review. Violation of such orders after they become final will subject the discharger to significant penalties.

EPA's second option, obtaining injunctive relief pursuant to Section 504, is applicable to discharges which present an imminent and substantial endangerment to the health, welfare or livelihood of persons. In such circumstances, EPA is empowered to bring suit in a United States district court to immediately stop the discharge of pollutants causing such a situation.

EPA can also seek injunctive relief under Section 309(b). The U.S. district court hearing such an action has jurisdiction to restrain the violation of any condition or limitation which implements Sections 301, 302, 306, 307, 308, 318, and 405 and to require compliance with the condition or limitation.

Violations of these same sections or of permit conditions implementing these sections can be punished by sizable civil penalties. Finally, any person who "wilfully or negligently" violates such provisions or permit conditions (and any person who violates a properly issued administrative order will certainly meet the test) is subject to substantial fines for each day of violation or imprisonment or both. "Responsible corporate officers" are subject to the same fines and criminal sanctions (including imprisonment) as are their companies. Fines are doubled for second time offenders. The act also provides fines and imprisonment for willful false statements or incorrect entries in any information required to be filed or maintained under the act.

The 1987 amendments have substantially strengthened applicable penalties, and empowered EPA itself to impose monetary penalties up to $125,000 in administrative proceedings. The applicable civil penalties in court proceedings have increased to $25,000 per day of violation. Criminal offenses have been broken into three categories: negligent, knowing, and knowing endangerment. The applicable penalties for negligent criminal violations remain $2,500 to $25,000 per day of violation and a year's imprisonment. The penalties for a knowing violation have been raised to $5,000 to $50,000 and three years' imprisonment per day of violation. The penalties for knowing endangerment are now up to $250,000 and 15 years' imprisonment for an individual, and up to a $1,000,000 fine for a corporation.

In addition to these EPA weapons, those states which have assumed NPDES permit responsibility are also responsible for enforcement. These states have their own enforcement laws, policies and personnel, all of which may be quite different from those of EPA. The situation is further complicated because EPA does not always agree with, and is not bound by, state enforcement decisions. If EPA disagrees, Section 309(a)(1) permits it to intervene to assure that "appropriate" enforcement action is taken.

From the foregoing, it is evident that where a violation occurs there will be considerable uncertainty about whether and who will bring enforcement action, and if so, in what form. Much of this uncertainty springs from EPA's and states' significant discretionary authority concerning enforcement. A discharger who is or may be faced with a potential enforcement action for a violation of the act or of a permit issued thereunder (and this category includes almost every discharger) must be aware of this discretion and of EPA's efforts to set enforcement guidelines or priorities.

EPA has issued several sets of guidelines concerning the assessment and settlement of penalties under the Clean Water Act and other statutes, efforts which have sought to promote uniformity in enforcement and effective deterrence of violations. These guidelines are very complicated, and unrealistically mechanical in the evaluation of subjective factors affecting successful criminal prosecution or a successful civil penalty action, prosecutions controlled not by EPA but by the Department of Justice. Despite these shortcomings, and changes in emphasis over time, these guidelines are good indications of EPA's enforcement priorities and settlement policy objectives. EPA plainly intends to remove any economic benefit that a violation has conferred on a discharger, both in terms of deferring capital investment in control equipment and in avoiding operation and maintenance costs. EPA has developed considerable sophistication in estimating what these avoided costs are, a sophistication based on expertise developed in setting standards and in refining its noncompliance penalties under Section 120 of the Clean Air Act. It is also clear that EPA will treat violations which cause (or threaten) greater harm to the environment or people's health more seriously than those which do not. (This emphasis is also reflected in the 1987 amendments.) Under the penalty policy, self-reporting of violations beyond what is required by law can be a significant mitigating factor. By the same token, actions which threaten the integrity of the self-reporting system, such as tampering with monitors or falsifying data, are viewed as extremely serious violations, appropriate for criminal prosecution under both the Clean Water Act and the applicable provisions of the federal criminal code such as 18 U.S.C. § 1001.

This penalty policy may change substantially in the future, as it is presently focused on dischargers who have not yet installed the appropriate control technology, and not on those dischargers who occasionally violate requirements after installation of appropriate controls.

A second effort to guide EPA's enforcement discretion is a 1982 EPA memorandum concerning criminal enforcement priorities. This memorandum identifies factors to be considered in deciding whether to bring criminal proceedings, including the intent of the alleged violator, the threat to human health caused by the violation, the effect on EPA's regulatory programs (e.g., falsification of monitoring data), deterrence, and the compliance history of the alleged violator. The memo lists highly specific violations under the Clean Water Act and other statutes in the order of their importance. 93/ EPA has added a significant criminal enforcement staff for the first time although the agency's criminal enforcement resources seem to be focused more on RCRA and other hazardous waste violations than on Clean Water Act violations.

In addition, these enforcement priorities are not binding on the Department of Justice, the federal agency responsible for these prosecutions. Nonetheless, it may be appropriate to focus compliance efforts on avoiding violations with a higher probability of criminal prosecution.

The broad enforcement discretion enjoyed by EPA and the states, coupled with the requirement of publicly filing monitoring reports, including those showing violations, requires potential violators to take the initiative in dealing with compliance problems. In the event of a possible violation, a discharger must be prepared to spend substantial time and effort with all relevant agencies. When several parts of EPA and several different state agencies are involved, there is no assurance that they are pursuing a coherent strategy or, indeed, are even talking to each other. Thus the discharger must be prepared to keep all federal and state agencies fully

---

93/ See the reproduction of this memorandum in the 22 October 1982 "Current Developments" section of the BNA Environment Reporter.

informed, preferably in a way that will ensure the most favorable processing of any potential violations. In doing this, the discharger should attempt to accomplish the following three goals:

— Convince the relevant enforcement agencies of its good faith. The EPA civil penalty policy makes it clear that "recalcitrance" is an aggravating factor and cooperation a mitigating one. Since the enforcement agencies will not, for the forsecable future, be able to move against every violation, a discharger's good faith or bad faith will be an important factor in deciding who to move against, and, if so, how severely.

— The discharger must attempt to deal with any major health or environmental problems caused by a potential violation in a manner that is as serious as the manner EPA or the state enforcement agency would adopt. Discharges which may create public health problems, or create unique environmental impacts, or which are likely to be the subject of adverse publicity are recognized as aggravating factors in the EPA's civil penalty policy. To the degree possible, special efforts should be made to avoid discharges of such substances and to quickly control and clean up any spill.

— The discharger must realistically appraise not only its chances of ultimately prevailing in any enforcement litigation, but the bureaucratic constraints such as the civil penalty policy on EPA and the Department of Justice in settlement negotiation. In any settlement calculus, a discharger must understand that even a successfully defended enforcement action will likely result in substantial adverse publicity, negative exposure which is not fully overcome by a favorable verdict.

Although these guidelines are not a panacea to the problems involved in dealing with potential enforcement actions, they can reduce the uncertainty surrounding the present enforcement system.

7.2 Citizen Suits

Section 505 of the act provides an additional impetus to vigorous enforcement of the act's provisions. It authorizes any person "having an interest which is or may be adversely affected" to commence civil actions either against a discharger, for violation of any effluent standard or limitation under the act, or against EPA for failure to proceed expeditiously to enforce the act's provisions. Experience under the Clean Water Act indicates that citizen suit provisions are highly effective in increasing the number of enforcement actions brought. While the Clean Water Act, unlike the Refuse Act, does not make provision for the payment of a "bounty" to a citizen providing information leading to successful enforcement, it does make specific provision for the payment of attorney and expert witness fees. More importantly, the Clean Water Act plainly authorizes citizen actions, while the Refuse Act, which provides only criminal penalties, was construed by the courts not to permit citizen suits.

Between January 1983 and July 1984, more than 120 notices of intent to bring citizen suits against dischargers were filed with EPA. The pace of such notices since then has remained brisk. Giving such notice is the first step in bringing a citizens' enforcement action, and is frequently the start of settlement negotiations between the discharger and the citizens' group. Normally in citizens' enforcement actions which are litigated, the plaintiffs use a discharger's required Daily Monitoring Reports (DMRs) to establish the discharger's liability. As some courts have held that dischargers are strictly liable for permit violations, intent is not a good defense. Most of the recent citizen suits have been settled on the basis of some combination of:

(1) payment of civil penalties;

(2) adoption of a compliance schedule;

(3) stipulated penalties for failure to meet the schedule; and

(4) attorney's fees and costs to plaintiffs.

Although EPA's minimal enforcement efforts in the early years of the Reagan administration were a primary cause of the recent flurry of citizens' enforcement actions, EPA's view of the enforcement action can be an important factor in settlement negotiations. In several cases, EPA has refused to agree to settlement conditions worked out by environmentalist plaintiffs and dischargers, on the ground that the conditions were too generous to the discharger. EPA's leverage in these negotiations derives from its statutory right to intervene in any citizen's enforcement action. The 1987 amendments have formalized EPA's role in reviewing consent decrees in citizen suit cases, and allow EPA 45 days to object in court. 94/

The bulk of recent reported citizen enforcement cases have been litigated in Connecticut, New York, New Jersey, the Chesapeake Bay area, Louisiana and California. A number of new cases is contemplated in the Pacific Northwest, and in the Midwest. Frequently, national environmental groups such as the Sierra Club or Natural Resources Defense Council will work with local environmental groups such as the Connecticut Fund for the Environment or the Chesapeake Bay Foundation.

Courts ruling on motions to dismiss these citizens' suits have generally held that the members of these groups have standing—the right to file the action—and have sometimes extended standing to the groups themselves. In addition, the courts have resolved a number of other potential procedural obstacles to the citizen suits favorable to the environmentalists, holding that:

1. the five-year federal statute of limitations for civil penalties, 28 U.S.C. §2462, governs these proceedings, and not shorter state limitations periods;

2. defects in the required 60-day notice to the violator, EPA and the state are seldom held to be fatal to citizens' suits;

3. the pendency of state or federal administrative enforcement proceedings, filed either before or after the citizens' suit begins, does not bar or stay the citizens' suit in federal court (the pendency of a federal or state enforcement case which is being "diligently prosecuted" does bar the filing of a separate action by citizens, but they may intervene in the enforcement action as a matter of right);

4. the citizens' suits can be used to recover civil penalties assessed by the court and payable to the federal government, as well as to obtain injunctive relief against the violator.

_____

94/ PL 100-4, § 504, 101 Stat.___(1987).

The primary limitation placed on citizen's suits by the courts has been the Fifth Circuit's (Texas, Louisiana, Mississippi) insistence that violations must be ongoing in order to file a citizens' suit against a violator. 95/ That view is in the minority of reported cases, and is now before the Supreme Court so that a split between the Fifth, Fourth, and First Circuit's approaches can be resolved. 96/

Substantial fines have been assessed against some violators as a result of these cases. In an action filed by the Chesapeake Bay Foundation and NRDC against one discharger, almost 1.3 million dollars in civil penalties were assessed. 97/ Fines of over a million dollars were recently imposed in another Chesapeake Bay case, which involved several years of reporting violations. 98/ It is evident from this record that citizens' suits can be a potent enforcement tool.

8.0. PROVISIONS HAVING SPECIAL APPLICABILITY

8.1 Discharges to Ground Waters

One byproduct of the Clean Air Act and the Clean Water Act has been increased pressure to dispose of waste materials on or below land and the consequential increased threat of groundwater contamination. However, aquifers are a class of water bodies which the act's definition of "waters of the United States" does not clearly include. Thus, although the act, in Section 402(b)(1)(D), requires states, as a precondition to approval of their NPDES programs, to "control the discharge of pollutants into wells," it gives EPA no direct authority to regulate disposal of pollutants by subsurface injection.

Although EPA initially sought to regulate underground discharges pursuant to the Clean Water Act, it met with mixed results.

95/ Hamker v. Diamond Shamrock Chemical Co., 756 F. 2d 392 (5th Cir. 1985).

96/ Id. The Supreme Court granted certiorari on January 12, 1987, No. 86-473, 55 U.S.L.W. 3463.

97/ Chesapeake Bay Foundation v. Gwaltney of Smithfield, 611 F. Supp. 1542 (E.D. Va 1985) which the Court of Appeals has reviewed and affirmed. 791 F.2d 304 (4th Cir. 1986).

98/ Sierra Club, v. Simkins Industries, Inc., 617 F. Supp. 1120 (D. Md. 1985).

The courts disagreed as to whether EPA had authority to regulate disposal into wells under that statute. 99/ EPA is now relying on the authority of the Safe Drinking Water Act (SDWA), 100/ to regulate such discharges and is encouraging the states to develop underground injection control programs pursuant to 40 CFR Part 146.

Part C of the SDWA applies to injection wells. However, well injection is broadly defined as the:

> subsurface implacement of fluids through a bored, drilled or driven well; or through a dug well, where the depth is greater than the largest surface dimension.

Thus, the state underground injection programs will have broad applicability.

Pending adoption by the state of underground injection control programs, EPA is regulating the injection of hazardous wastes under the Resource Conservation and Recovery Act. Waste lagoons and ponds will continue to be regulated by EPA and the states pursuant to the hazardous waste program.

Thus, many companies which may be exempt from wastewater discharge regulation under the Clean Water Act because they did not discharge to navigable waters are subject to requirements governing wastewater discharges pursuant to the Safe Drinking Water Act and the Resource Conservation and Recovery Act.

8.2 Dredged or Fill Material

Section 404 of the Clean Water Act substantially affects development in areas adjacent to navigable waters. The section stringently controls dredging activity and the disposal of dredged or fill material into navigable water by granting the Corps of Engineers the authority to designate disposal areas and issue permits to discharge dredged and fill material therein rather than making such discharges subject to the general permit program provided by Sections 301, 304, 402 of the act. The stringency of these requirements has been reinforced by three factors:

99/ See United States Steel v. Train, 556 F.2d 822 (7th Cir. 1977), and Exxon Corp. v. Train, 554 F.2d 1310 (5th Cir. 1977).

100/   42 U.S.C. § 300 et seq.

— Section 404 has been construed to extend to all waters of the United States, 101/ including wetlands which are themselves very broadly defined in a definition upheld by the Supreme Court. 102/ Accordingly, the Corps permit program under Section 404 is applicable to many dredge and fill projects which would not have required permits under prior law;

— The Corps has construed Section 404 broadly, so as to cover not only disposal of dredged or fill material, as the section would seem to contemplate, but also the emplacement of dredge or fill material for development purposes and the construction of structures; 103/ and

— Section 511(c) of the act covers only permits issued by the EPA administrator, so that Section 404 permits, unlike most other permits under the act, are subject to NEPA and possibly to the EIS requirements.

Congress extensively revised Section 404 in the 1977 amendments. The principal change was to authorize the states to establish permit programs for dredge and fill activities in nonnavigable waters. 104/ In order to establish such a program, a state must comply with extensive requirements prescribed by the act and must obtain EPA's approval of the program. There are also requirements for the state's operation of its program, including a requirement that a copy of each permit application and each proposed permit be sent to EPA. EPA, the Corps of Engineers, and the United States

---

101/   N.R.D.C. v. Callaway, 392 F. Supp. 685 (D.D.C. 1975).

102/   United States v. Riverside Bayview Homes, Inc., 105 S. Ct. 455 (1985).

103/   33 CFR § 323.2 (1).

104/   It is generally thought that, if a state does establish its own program, it will not be subject to NEPA constraints in its permit issuing activities.

Fish and Wildlife Service have the right to comment on applications and proposed permits, and provision is made for the situation in which EPA objects to issuance of a permit. (Section 208 was also revised to assure that dredge and fill activities are considered in the water pollution control planning process.)

A second change authorized the Corps of Engineers (or a state having an approved program) to issue "general" permits for specified categories of activities involving the discharge of dredge and fill materials. To issue such a permit, there must be a finding that the activities in the category are similar in nature and will have minimal adverse effects. Any activity covered by a general permit can be conducted without obtaining an individual Section 404 permit so long as the requirements and standards set forth in the general permit are complied with. The Corps expanded the scope of its general permit program to reduce the regulatory burden on a number of activities which involve incidental dredge or fill work. 105/ As part of a settlement agreement with environmental groups which had challenged these regulations, the Corps changed these rules to assure that they are only applied in practice to activities which have a minimal environmental impact. 106/

Finally, Section 404(f) exempts certain dredge and fill discharges from regulation under Section 404 if specified effects on navigable waters are avoided. The activities thus excluded from the scope of Section 404 include maintenance operations, the construction of temporary sedimentation basins, temporary farm, forest and mining roads, and several types of agricultural activities.

The Corps of Engineers, through the United States attorney for the district in which a violation occurs, has the power to bring enforcement action in the name of the United States not only to collect fines but to compel restoration of areas which have been dredged or filled without obtaining a necessary permit, or in violation of permit conditions. The Supreme Court recently heard a case involving such restoration work and penalties. 107/ That case raises

---

105/　　33 CFR Parts 320-330.

106/　　49 FR 37482 (5 October 1984).

107/　　United States v. Tull, 769 F.2d 152 (4th Cir.), No. 85-1239, 55 U.S.L.W. 3487 (U.S. argued January 21, 1987).

the issue of whether a defendant in a civil penalty action has the right to a jury trial, an issue which, if decided in the petitioner's favor, may substantially affect many federal regulatory programs, including those beyond the environmental area.

8.3 Ocean Discharge Criteria

Section 403(c) of the act directed EPA to promulgate guidelines for determining the effects of pollution discharges on ocean water quality and other aesthetic, recreational, and economic values of the oceans. No permit for an ocean discharge may be issued unless the permit issuing authority determines that the discharge will not cause unreasonable degradation of the environment, and permit conditions may be imposed to insure that such degradation will not occur. 108/ An ocean discharge applicant may be required to submit substantial additional information about receiving waters.

The 1981 amendments to the Clean Water Act extended the time for municipalities to apply for waivers of secondary treatment requirements for ocean discharges. 109/ In some circumstances, primary treatment may also be waived. The 1987 amendments have tightened the requirements to assure that waivers of primary treatment were granted only in unusual circumstances. 110/ EPA has announced that it will process municipal waiver applications in groups from the same geographic areas.

8.4 Thermal Discharges

Although heat is defined as a pollutant by the Clean Water Act and thereby is subject to technology-based effluent limitations imposed on industrial dischargers and POTWs, Congress included special provisions for the regulation of thermal discharges, in order to avoid unnecessary control costs. If the discharger can show that the technology based effluent limitations under Section 301 or under a new source performance standard are more stringent than necessary to assure protection and propagation of a balanced, indigenous population of shellfish, fish and wildlife in and on the body of water where

---

108/ 40 CFR Part 125, Subpart M.

109/ PL 97-117, 95 Stat. 1632.

110/ PL 100-4, § 303, 101 Stat.___(1987).

the discharge is to occur, the administrator or state may adjust the effluent limitation to a less stringent level, which will still assure such protection and propagation.

This provision—Section 316—is particularly important to power plants because heat is such a significant part of their discharge and because EPA established a "no-discharge" BAT requirement for heat. Even though this effluent limitation was overturned by the courts, 111/ permit issuers most often initially propose no-discharge of heat as an effluent limitation under Section 402(a).

Section 316 proceedings are quite complex; EPA requires substantial amounts of scientific data. There are difficult questions regarding what is the "indigenous" population; when a population is "balanced"; and how heat will in fact affect the aquatic organisms. Nonetheless, this provision does excuse thermal dischargers from control requirements to the extent such requirements are unnecessary to protect the environment.

9.0 THE EPA CONSTRUCTION GRANTS PROGRAM

The stringent treatment requirements imposed on POTWs by the 1972 act made a major federal assistance program a necessity if most municipalities were to be able to construct the facilities necessary to comply with the new effluent limitations. The construction grant program which the 1972 act established in response to this need is one of the largest public works programs now being funded by the federal government. The 1987 amendments will convert the grant program into a revolving loan program beginning in 1970, with moneys disbursed after that time taking the form of loans, the repayment of which will fund additional construction. The future of the grant program through 1990 remains uncertain because of federal deficit problems: the 1987 amendments <u>authorize</u> appropriations, but the appropriations themselves must be made in separate appropriations acts.

Under the grant program enacted by the 1972 act, the federal share of the cost of approved treatment works was originally 75 percent, but that percentage was decreased to 55 percent in 1981, where it will remain until replaced by the revolving loan program in 1990. This federal grant is supplemented in many

---

111/ <u>Appalachian Power Co. v. Train</u>, 545 F.2d 1351 (4th Cir. 1976).

instances by a 15 percent state grant so that, at present, the grantee local government may pay only 30 percent of the eligible costs of the total facility. The act and EPA's implementing regulations 112/ impose substantial conditions governing factors such as the share of operating costs which industrial users must pay, the eligibility of different parts of the plant and related sewer systems and so forth. The objective is to assure that grants will fund the construction of plants which will meet applicable treatment limits in a cost-effective manner. These conditions can substantially affect the costs of POTW treatment to industrial users.

9.1 The Cost Recovery Program and User Charges

When the 1972 act was enacted, Congress feared that the substantial grant assistance available to municipalities could function as an indirect subsidy to industrial users of the funded treatment works and that this subsidy would give users of POTWs an unfair competitive advantage over direct dischargers. Consequently, the act required that municipalities provide for repayment of that portion of the construction grant allocable to industrial users.

From the industrial user's viewpoint, the Industrial Cost Recovery (ICR) requirement converted the construction "grant" to the equivalent of a long-term, no-interest loan. However, ICR proved quite difficult to administer and was repealed in 1980 after a legislative moratorium on such projects had expired.

Some local communities continue to assess ICR payments even though they are no longer required by federal law. Such local ICR requirements are often of questionable legality under state law.

As the cost recovery regulations defined industrial users' proportionate share of the capital cost of new, grant funded treatment facilities, the user charge regulations establish requirements to be met by a municipal system for industrial sharing of the annual operating and maintenance charges of such facilities. Section 204 of the act requires, as a condition of federal construction grant assistance, a finding that the applicant has adopted or will adopt:

a system of charges to assure that each recipient of waste treatment services within the applicant's jurisdiction . . . will pay its proportional share . . . of the costs of operation

---

112/ 40 CFR Part 35, Subpart E.

and maintenance (including replacement) 113/ of any waste treatment services provided by the applicant.

The EPA regulations 114/ elaborate on the statutory requirement for proportionate distribution 115/ of O&M costs as follows:

> A grantee's user charge system based on actual use (or estimated use) of waste water treatment services may be approved if each user (or user class) pays its proportionate share of operation and maintenance (including replacement) costs of treatment works within the grantee's service area, based on the user's proportionate contribution to the total waste water loading from all users (or user classes).

> To insure proportional distribution of operation and maintenance costs to each user (or user class), the user's contribution shall be based on factors such as strength, volume, and delivery flow rate characteristics.

113/ The term "replacement" has been defined by EPA to mean "expenditures for . . . equipment . . . which are necessary to maintain . . . capacity and performance during the service life of the treatment works . . . ."

114/ 40 CFR § 35-929-1.

115/ The 1977 amendments included a provision authorizing applicants which, prior to enactment of the amendments, used a system of dedicated ad valorem taxes as a basis for funding costs of operation and maintenance of their facilities, to continue such system as the user charge system for their facility, with respect to small residential users as defined by EPA. EPA has defined a small residential user to include industrial users which introduce no more than the equivalent of 25,000 gallons per day of domestic sanitary waste to the treatment works. All industrial users whose flows exceed the 25,000 gallon per day domestic equivalent limit and all users of systems not having in effect an acceptable ad valorem system on the effective date of the 1977 amendments are required to pay user charges based on actual use. The authorization to use ad valorem tax systems for user charge collection applies only where the system results in a proportionate distribution of costs.

Quantity discounts to large volume users are not acceptable. EPA's philosophy is that savings resulting from economies of scale should be apportioned to all users or user classes. This policy would not, however, appear to preclude recognition of the other efficiencies that some large volume users are able to provide to the treatment facility to which they discharge. These efficiencies may include flow equalization or other measures to control delivery flow rate. User charges may be established based on a percentage of the charge for water usage only in cases where the water charges are based on a constant cost per unit of consumption and thus may be reasonably reflective of the amount of wastewater discharged. The regulations also specifically provide that an industrial user which discharges, to a treatment works, wastewater containing toxic pollutants that cause an increase in the cost of managing the effluent or sludge from the treatment works, must pay for those increased costs. Finally, it should be noted that user charges, unlike cost recovery payments, are to be based on actual use of the facility and not on reserved shares, as is sometimes erroneously asserted by some municipalities.

Appendix B to EPA's regulations sets forth in more detail the guidelines for user charge computations and provides sample formulae for use in that connection. The guidelines are necessarily complex and technical. There is considerable potential for misapplication, particularly by small municipalities. A company which is a sub-stantial contributor to a treatment works should thus pay close attention to the municipality's adoption of a user charge system.

As indicated above, the treatment works operator is obligated to develop a user charge mechanism, which will require each user to pay its proportionate share of the cost of waste treatment. This obligation is not fulfilled if, due to the selection of an inappropriate or defective formula or improper application of the formula selected, industrial users are required to subsidize waste treatment services performed for other users of the system. EPA approval of any planned federal construction grant application could, if necessary, be contested on that basis.

The basic approach in discussions with the POTW operating entity should be to make certain that the formula adopted (1) gives recognition to economies, other than economies of scale, which may be inherent in the nature of the company's discharge (e.g., the dis-charge may occur at non-peak periods, it may be low in suspended solids as compared to domestic sewage) and (2) does not give exces-sive weight to characteristics of the company's discharge, such as

BOD content, which do not result in additional treatment costs. For example, if the treatment works is primarily flow dependent, a high surcharge based on strength of effluent may well be inappropriate. Numerous other technical questions such as the following may arise and should be addressed:

— If the industrial user pretreats its effluent so that its strength is less than that of domestic waste, shouldn't it be entitled to a cheaper rate?

— Shouldn't an industrial user's charge be reduced if it holds its effluent for discharge at non-peak flow periods, thereby contributing to the efficiency of the treatment works?

— If the particular type of industrial effluent makes the treatment works operate more efficiently, shouldn't that factor be recognized? (For example, iron in industrial discharges is used by some municipalities to help remove phosphorous from waste water.)

— If an industrial user's wastes are phosphorous and nitrogen-deficient, isn't it inappropriate to require that user to pay the portion of plant operation and maintenance expense allocable to removal of those pollutants?

— If a substantial portion of the plant capacity is for treatment of water flowing into the system during periods of rainfall due to infiltration and inflow, shouldn't costs allocable to the treatment of this wastewater be primarily allocated to residential connections which are the primary cause of this circumstance?

These and many other similar questions are commonly answered by local authorities when they develop the user charge system which will be proposed for EPA acceptance. As user charges are an increasingly important cost component of waste treatment services provided by POTWs, affected users must be alert to the proposal of ordinances establishing new user charge systems and must ask questions such as these when such proposals are made.

9.2 Cost Effectiveness and Eligibility

Both POTW officials and industrial dischargers which use POTWs have an immediate and substantial interest in minimizing the costs of constructing and operating such works. The POTW owner-grantee, however, may be unsophisticated in the waste treatment area (or underfunded) and need technical and other assistance to assure that their waste treatment program is cost-effective. The statute requires that grant-eligible facilities be demonstrated to be the most cost-efficient alternative for compliance with applicable effluent limits over the facility's useful life 116/, but there unfortunately have been numerous cases where plants have been designed to achieve levels of treatment beyond that required by the applicable permit limits, or with capacities in excess of that necessary to serve foreseeable needs. The procedures mandated for the development of Section 201 facilities plans, the preparation of related environmental assessments, and the conduct of value engineering studies provide both industry and concerned citizens with considerable opportunities to help municipalities avoid these wasteful practices.

The final issue which should be considered in any effort to minimize the cost of industrial participation in a grant-funded POTW program is the question of whether all or only some of the elements of the POTW are eligible for federal grant funding. Treatment works costs which are found to be ineligible must be fully funded by the grantee, through a bond issue or otherwise, and industrial users are generally called upon to pay their proportionate share of the cost of amortizing the required bonds. Thus, where a portion of the facilities is found to be ineligible, industrial users will be called upon to pay, not only the costs of the treatment works over its useful life, but also their share of the bond interest on that facility.

As federal budget deficit problems mount, it seems likely that EPA will subject grant applications to increasingly rigorous scrutiny. Consistent with the general objective of minimizing expenditure of federal grant funds, EPA has narrowly interpreted the act's eligibility provisions as they apply to treatment facilities designed to handle industrial wastes. Thus though the act's definition of treatment works would appear to apply to facilities which handle industrial wastes, EPA's regulations specify that allowable projects do not include "(1) costs of interceptor or collector lines constructed exclusively or almost exclusively to serve industrial users or (2) costs allocable to the treatment for control or removal of pollutants in wastewater

---

116/ Section 212(2)(B).

introduced into the treatment works by industrial users, unless the applicant is required to remove such pollutants introduced from non-industrial sources." The scope of this exclusion in individual circumstances is subject to considerable interpretation and there are also considerable legal questions regarding the statutory authorization for this provision. Its application does merit careful attention in a number of situations. 117/

9.3 Construction Grants—Summary
The factors referenced above make it clear that users of POTWs are no longer insulated from the substantial costs of complying with Clean Water Act requirements. In many circumstances, POTWs can be an expensive way for an industrial discharger to meet the act's requirements. The economics of alternative on-site treatment and direct discharge should be carefully examined before making or continuing commitments to rely on a POTW as a method of compliance.

10.0 POLLUTION CONTROL PLANNING IN THE CURRENT REGULATORY CLIMATE

Compliance with the Clean Water Act requirements outlined above would be difficult and costly under the best of circumstances. These difficulties are compounded by inconsistencies in EPA (and state) enforcement policies, EPA's tardiness in developing standards, and the periodic congressional rewriting of statutory requirements for the construction grant program. Consequently, the questions of how the law will be interpreted and enforced are often not amenable to predictable answers. Participation in the development of standards and continuing contact with officials responsible for permitting and enforcement is necessary if industrial dischargers wish to operate in a more consistent and predictable regulatory environment.

117/ The 1977 amendments do make provision for funding of privately-owned treatment works serving commercial users where it can be demonstrated that such a facility is the most cost-effective way of providing waste treatment services and governmental entities have certified that the facility will be operated and maintained consistent with the requirements of the act (Section 202(h)).

10.1   EPA Standards Development Programs

The suitability and practicability of the standards and regulations which EPA promulgates under the act are dependent on EPA's thorough understanding of the processes and products to be regulated, the availability of detailed and reliable data on the applicability and limits of available treatment technology, and careful consideration of the economic and environmental impacts involved. Except for industry inputs, most standards (whether done by EPA staff or through outside contractors) tend to be based principally on technical data readily obtainable through review of existing literature. In some cases, these data are outdated, unreliable or inadequate. Thus, absent effective and technically documented participation by industry spokesmen, the standards which EPA promulgates are likely to have unanticipated effects when applied to real world conditions. Particular process or design factors may not have been considered and may be inequitable when applied to a specific plant or product.

Thus, early and active participation in the standards development process, either directly or through appropriate industry organizations, is advisable. Although EPA has completed the development of most standards, the toxics strategy and development of toxics water quality standards and discharge limitations based on them will continue to require such participation, as will any updating and revision of existing standards. Such participation could properly involve the following steps:

1.   Assess the probability that standards (or revisions) applicable to your company's operations will be promulgated.

2.   Determine the procedure which will be followed in developing the standard, the contemplated time schedule, and the areas under consideration where data available to EPA may be deficient.

3.   Assess the standards development procedure to determine whether it provides for taking into account any unusual aspects of your plant process or product design. Make comments to EPA and any private contractor involved as to how the procedure could be improved.

4. Consider providing EPA and/or the appropriate private contractor any relevant technical data possessed by companies in the industry which is unpublished or otherwise not generally accessible.

5. If the time schedule permits, consider the desirability of industry sponsored research or analytical projects to fill gaps in existing data on available technology or environmental and economic impact. In this connection, consideration should be given to consulting with EPA on the structuring of the project and exploring the possibility of EPA involvement in the conduct of the project.

6. After a proposed standard is published in the Federal Register, the company or its spokesmen should participate in the usual comment procedure and consider the possibility of obtaining judicial review if the standard, as finally promulgated, is still unreasonable. In this connection, it should be kept in mind that if objections to standards are not timely asserted in judicial review proceedings, then they are waived. Further, it is generally wiser to litigate a standard at a time when your company does not stand accused of a violation.

10.2 Negotiation of Permit Conditions

Whether a company's authorization to discharge is in the form of an NPDES permit for direct discharge into a waterway or a contract with a municipality for use of its treatment facilities, the terms and conditions of that permit or contract may be every bit as important, in terms of impact on profits, as a major corporate contract. Like such a contract, they can be the subject of negotiations. Accordingly, pollution control managers should determine the areas in which the act and regulations leave room for negotiation and, based on a careful assessment of the company's long-term interests, should negotiate actively in an effort to obtain favorable permit terms and conditions. These negotiations will be more important and much more complicated if toxic pollutants are involved.

10.3 Discussions With Regional Office and State Officials

No matter how good the standards are or how carefully permits are drawn, there will inevitably be situations where companies are forced to make major investment decisions which are affected by significant uncertainties in determining the applicable environmental control requirements. In these circumstances, serious consideration should be given to obtaining advance guidance from the appropriate EPA regional office and/or state enforcement personnel —whether or not the applicable statute makes provision for obtaining such guidance. A written indication that the cognizant authority has reviewed your proposal and found it acceptable, while perhaps not legally binding, can be of great future benefit. If the proposal is not acceptable to EPA or the state, it may be better to find that out before money has been spent. The chances of acceptance are generally far greater when the company goes to the regulator, rather than the other way around.

10.4 State and Local Planning Activities

Industry would also be well advised to pay considerable attention to the substantial planning requirements which are imposed by the act on state and local governments. The state and regional water quality implementation plans, continuing planning processes and areawide waste treatment management plans may well be as important as federal rules and regulations in determining a company's future abatement costs. If properly carried out, these planning processes can be of immeasurable aid to business planners in predicting and planning for the future.

11.0 CONCLUSION

The implementation of and compliance with the Clean Water Act has been and remains complex, difficult, and expensive for all concerned. The increasing focus on toxic pollutants, while environmentally sound, increases the complexity of regulations, the costs of compliance, and the difficulty of monitoring.

Under these circumstances, it is obvious that the development and implementation of a workable and effective program will require the best efforts of regulators, environmentalists, and the regulated community. EPA, for its own part, must establish priorities and allow both industry and its own enforcement personnel to concentrate their attention on resolving the problems which are most significant in terms of impact on human health and the environment. It does little for the environment to spend time, money and effort identifying and monitoring pollutants which are present in inconsequential amounts and to which significant portions of the population are not exposed.

Environmentalists, for their part, must focus their attention on problems which make the most difference in protecting human health and the environment. The NRDC consent decree is a good example of this focus. Environmental progress is better measured by improvements in the quality of life rather than costs inflicted on industry. Industry, for its part, must participate fully in the development of EPA standards, if it is to avoid wasteful and frequently unsuccessful litigation to resolve EPA mistakes and omissions.

Pollution abatement costs can constitute a substantial portion of the total cost of many companies' final product. Consequently, the effectiveness with which a company plans its pollution control program may determine the extent to which the company remains competitive in its industry.

With this kind of cooperative effort there is at least some hope for achieving a regulatory environment in which a company can intelligently plan for compliance with water pollution control requirements—when the requirements established are (1) predictable and understandable; (2) equally applicable to and equitably enforced against all companies; (3) technologically and economically feasible; (4) announced sufficiently in advance of effectiveness to permit lead time for compliance; and (5) constant for a reasonable period of time after final adoption.

Achievement and maintenance of a regulatory climate which facilitates cooperative and intelligent planning is the best, and perhaps the only way of achieving the pollution control objectives announced by Congress when it passed the 1972 act and repeatedly ratified by Congress since. These goals will best be met where all parties avoid unnecessary confrontations, focus on the real regulatory issues, and develop a program which reasonably and cost-effectively achieves essential water quality objectives without major economic or social dislocation.

ANNEX A — SECTION 307 — TOXIC POLLUTANTS

Acenaphthene
Acrolein
Acrylonitrile
Aldrin/Dieldrin
Antimony and compounds*
Arsenic and compounds
Asbestos
Benzene
Benzidine
Beryllium and compounds
Cadmium and compounds
Carbon tetrachloride
Chlordane (technical mixture and metabolites)
Chlorinated benzenes (other than dichlorobenzenes)
Chlorinated ethanes (including 1,2-dichloroethane, 1,1,1-ethane and
        hexachloroethane)
Chlorinated naphthalene
Chlorinated phenols (other than those listed elsewhere; includes
        trichlorophenols and chlorinated cresols)
Chloroalkyl ethers (chloromethyl, chloroethyl, and mixed ethers)
Chloroform
2-chlorophenol
Chromium and compounds
Copper and compounds
Cyanides
DDT and metabolites
Dichlorobenzenes (1,2-, 1,3-, and 1,4-dichlorobenzenes)
Dichlorobenzinine
Dichloroethylenes (1,1-and 1,2-dichloroethylene)
2,4-dichlorophenol
Dichloropropane and dichloropropene
2,4-dimethylphenol
Dinitrotoluene
Diphenylhydrazine
Endosulfan and metabolites
Endrin and metabolites
Ethylbenzene

---

*   The term "compounds" shall include organic and inorganic
     compounds.

ANNEX A (continued)

Fluoranthene
Haloethers (other than those listed elsewhere; includes chlorophenyl-
    phenyl ethers, bromophenylphenyl ether, bis (dischloroiso-
    propyl) ether, bis-(chloroethoxy) methane and polychlorinated
    diphenyl ethers)
Halomethanes (other than those listed elsewhere; includes methylene
    chloride methylchloride, methylbromide, bromoform,
    dichlorobromomethane, trichlorofluoromethane, dichlorodi-
    fluoromethane)
Heptachlor and metabolites
Hexachlorobutadiene
Hexachlorocyclohexane (all isomers)
Hexachlorocyclopentadiene
Isophorone
Lead and compounds
Mercury and compounds
Naphthalene
Nickel and compounds
Nitrobenzene
Nitrophenols (including 2,4-dinitrophenol, dinitrocresol)
Nitrosamines
Pentachlorophenol
Phenol
Phthalate esters
Polychlorinated biphenyls (PCBs)
Polynuclear aromatic hydrocarbons (including benzanthracenes,
    benzo-pyrenes, benzofluoranthene, chrysenes, dibenzanthra-
    cenes, and indenopyrenes)
Selenium and compounds
Silver and compounds
2,3,7,8-Tetrachlorodibenzo-p-dioxin (TCDD)
Tetrachloroethylene
Thallium and compounds
Toluene
Toxaphene
Trichloroethylene
Vinyl chloride
Zinc and compounds

ANNEX B — INDUSTRY CATEGORIES

1. Adhesives and Sealants
2. Aluminum Forming
3. Asbestos Manufacturing
4. Auto and Other Laundries
5. Battery Manufacturing
6. Coal Mining
7. Coil Coating
8. Copper Forming
9. Electric and Electronic Components
10. Electroplating
11. Explosives Manufacturing
12. Ferroalloys
13. Foundries
14. Gum and Wood Chemicals
15. Inorganic Chemicals Manufacturing
16. Iron and Steel Manufacturing
17. Leather Tanning and Finishing
18. Mechanical Products Manufacturing
19. Nonferrous Metals Manufacturing
20. Ore Mining
21. Organic Chemicals Manufacturing
22. Pesticides
23. Petroleum Refining
24. Pharmaceutical Preparations
25. Photographic Equipment and Supplies
26. Plastic and Synthetic Materials Manufacturing
27. Plastic Processing
28. Porcelain Enamelling
29. Printing and Publishing
30. Pulp and Paperboard Mills
31. Soap and Detergent Manufacturing
32. Steam Electric Power Plants
33. Textile Mills
34. Timber Products Processing

Chapter 6

AIR POLLUTION CONTROL

William F. Pedersen, Jr. 1/
Attorney
Verner, Liipfert, Bernhard, McPherson & Hand
Washington, D.C.

1.0 INTRODUCTION

Although generally described as environmental legislation, the Federal Clean Air Act, 2/ was enacted primarily because of growing concern, on the part of Congress and the general public, about the potential adverse public health effects of air pollution.

After almost two decades of tight health-based control at the federal level, however, that perception may be changing. The next round of Clean Air Act amendments is likely to give a higher priority than past revisions to welfare issues such as visibility and acid rain.

As with most "police power" functions, air pollution control was initially left to the states and local governments. However, the political and economic obstacles to controlling sources of air pollution proved too difficult for these governments to overcome and the need for federal control efforts became apparent, particularly since air pollution does not always honor political boundaries.

1/ Former Deputy Counsel and Associate General Counsel, U.S. Environmental Protection Agency. This chapter is a revision and update of versions written for previous editions of the Environmental Law Handbook by G. William Frick, Lydia N. Wegman, Robert L. Baum, Esq. and Michael A. James, Esq. to whom credit should be given for their contribution.

2/ 42 U.S.C. Section 7401 et seq.

The Clean Air Act of 1970 3/ was the result. It created a wide ranging, coordinated federal/state scheme of regulation that now pervades our social order and national economy, and affects virtually every corporate or individual citizen in the country.

2.0 HISTORY

The first regulatory "Clean Air Act" was passed in 1963. 4/ It provided for grants to air pollution control agencies and established a pollution abatement conference procedure, to be used in very limited circumstances, and useful in fact in fewer still.

In 1965, Congress amended the act to add Title II, The Motor Vehicle Air Pollution Control Act 5/, which authorized federal emission standards for new vehicles. In 1967, in PL 90-148, 80 Stat. 485, Congress considerably broadened the act with respect to stationary source control. The 1967 amendments gave the federal government authority to adopt emission control regulations in designated areas with air pollution problems. It also provided a system of limited federal enforcement.

In late 1970, after extensive hearings and debate, the Congress, in the Clean Air Act Amendments of 1970, adopted a radically new and completely restructured approach to the problem. While continuing to look to state and local governments as the primary focus of regulatory efforts, Congress provided the newly created United States Environmental Protection Agency (EPA) with authority to establish, in accordance with specific congressional directives, the minimum air quality and regulatory goals for the state and local authorities to achieve. Congress also took the step—unusual at that time—of establishing very stringent, and in many cases unrealistic, deadlines for action by the states and the federal government. Where states failed to meet those deadlines Congress often directed EPA to act for them instead. The 1970 act also provided a more vigorous new motor vehicle control program with congressionally

---

3/ PL 91-604, amended extensively in 1977, (P.L. 95-95).

4/ In 1955, the "Air Pollution Control—Research and Technical Assistance Act," PL 84-159, 69 Stat. 322, had been enacted, but it contained no regulatory authority.

5/ PL 89-272, 79 Stat. 991.

adopted emission limitations, and conferred authority for certain national emission standards that would be applicable regardless of air quality in the area where the source was located.

In 1977, Congress added new provisions to prevent significant deterioration of air quality, impose a new and tighter set of planning requirements in areas that had failed to attain national standards, restrict the use of dispersion techniques, and strengthen enforcement of the statutory provisions.

3.0 ESTABLISHMENT OF AIR QUALITY STANDARDS

3.1 Air Quality Criteria

Section 108 of the act requires that the EPA administrator publish and periodically revise a list of pollutants which he determines "may reasonably be anticipated to endanger" public health or welfare, and which are emitted from numerous or diverse stationary or mobile sources. Such "listing" of a pollutant sets in motion the process for establishing ambient air quality standards for it. 6/ The administrator must compile and publish a criteria document for each pollutant before setting an air quality standard for it. The criteria are scientific compendia of all available studies documenting the health effects of that pollutant at various concentrations in the ambient air.

3.2 National Ambient Air Quality Standards

Section 109 of the act requires the administrator to establish National Ambient Air Quality Standards (NAAQS) for each pollutant covered by a criteria document under Section 108. The administrator must establish a primary and secondary NAAQS for each criteria pollutant. The "primary" NAAQS for a pollutant must specify the level of air quality that, based on the criteria "and allowing an adequate margin of safety," will protect the public health. 7/ The

---

6/ EPA considers the initial decision to list a pollutant to be discretionary. However, flexibility was diminished by the court decision in NRDC v. Train, 411 F. Supp. 864, (S.D.N.Y.), aff'd 545 F.2d 320 (2d Cir. 1976) which required the administrator to list lead as a pollutant once he had conceded that it met the two substantive tests quoted above.

7/ CAA § 109(b)(1).

secondary NAAQS must specify the level of air quality that protects the public welfare from any known or anticipated adverse effects associated with the presence of that pollutant in the ambient air. 8/

Two points concerning the primary standards are important. First, the language and history of the act make it clear that the standards are to be set at levels which protect not only the normal healthy majority of the population, but even especially sensitive persons with pre-existing illnesses or conditions that pollution might exacerbate, although not cause, as long as these people belong to an identifiable subgroup of the population (such as infants or heart disease patients). The second, and perhaps more significant point, is that the primary NAAQS are to be established using health protection as the sole test. Cost, technical feasibility or any factor other than public health cannot be considered in setting the standards. Such factors cannot be the basis for a legal challenge to the standard. The act appears to establish a similar basis for the secondary (welfare-based) standards, but the question has never been definitively resolved.

The act expansively defines the components of public welfare that must be considered in setting the secondary standard. Section 302(h) requires such standards to protect against harm to "soil, water, crops, vegetation, man-made materials, animals, wildlife, weather, visibility, and climate, damage to and deterioration of property, and hazards to transportation, as well as effects on economic values and on personal comfort and well-being." In short, secondary standards must protect against any type of adverse effect, even if it could not be scientifically shown to affect man's physiological well-being in any medical sense.

The Environmental Protection Agency promulgated ambient standards for six pollutants on 30 April 1971. 9/ The six were sulfur dioxide (SO_2), particulate matter, carbon monoxide (CO), hydrocarbons (HC), nitrogen dioxide (NO_2), and photochemical oxidants. The secondary standards for the last four NAAQS listed were the same as the primary. However, for SO_2 and particulate matter, secondary standards were set at more stringent levels than the primary to protect against effects on vegetation and materials.

8/   CAA § 109(b)(2).

9/   40 CFR Part 50.

EPA originally included hydrocarbons in the NAAQS because they contribute to the formation of ozone. As a class, hydrocarbons alone do not cause direct health or welfare effects at ambient levels. The hydrocarbon NAAQS was only to be used as a guide for determining achievement of the ozone NAAQS. EPA revoked the hydrocarbon NAAQS on 5 January 1983. 10/ Hydrocarbon emissions, however, will still be controlled as part of the ozone NAAQS control strategy.

On 8 February 1979, EPA redesignated the oxidants NAAQS to an ozone standard and increased the acceptable pollution level by 50 percent. 11/ Pursuant to court order, EPA established NAAQS for lead on 5 October 1978. 12/

Despite the importance of the NAAQS to the entire structure of the act, only one portion of one of the original six NAAQS was challenged in the courts. 13/ The suit caused EPA to withdraw a portion of the secondary standards for sulfur dioxide, but no extensive opinion was written. Instead, the relevant judicial precedents were set by the D.C. Circuit (which has exclusive jurisdiction over challenges to NAAQS) in reviewing challenges to EPA's lead standard, 14/ and its revision of the ozone standard. 15/

In the 1977 amendments, Congress directed the agency to completely review all the criteria documents and NAAQS and to make appropriate revisions to the NAAQS by the end of 1980. However, as of the date of this chapter (October, 1986) EPA has yet to issue any final decisions as a result of this review.

The NAAQS establish ceilings for individual pollutant concentrations that should not be exceeded anywhere in the United States. They, therefore, determine the degree of control that will be

---

10/ 48 FR 628.

11/ 44 FR 8202 et seq.

12/ 43 FR 46258.

13/ Kennecott Copper Corp. v. EPA, 462 F.2d 846 (D.C. Cir. 1972).

14/ Lead Industries Ass'n v. EPA, 647 F. 2d. 1130 (D.C. Cir. 1980).

15/ American Petroleum Insitute, v. Costle, 609 F. 2d. (D.C. Cir. 1979).

imposed on existing sources and the restrictions on location of new sources, depending on whether air quality is better or worse than the NAAQS in the particular area where the source is or will be located.

Despite their critical importance to the scheme of the Clean Air Act, NAAQS are not directly enforceable. They are the controlling force behind the development and implementation of emission limitations and other controls pursuant to other sections of the statute. It is those requirements that are actually enforced against polluters, rather than the NAAQS itself.

3.3 Air Quality Control Regions

Prior to the 1970 Clean Air Act, Congress had recognized the difficulties states and their political subdivisions had in coordinating efforts to control air pollution. Consequently, the 1967 act directed the Secretary of Health, Education and Welfare (who administered federal air pollution control before EPA was formed) to designate "Air Quality Control Regions" (AQCRs). These are interstate or intrastate areas which, because of common meteorological, industrial and socioeconomic factors, should be treated as a single unit for the purpose of air pollution control. The 1970 amendments preserved the concept of ignoring jurisdictional boundaries in order to treat regional air pollution problems. Indeed, they required the entire country to be divided into AQCRs. 16/

The 1977 amendments in section 107(d) reduced the significance of the AQCRs by requiring the states to identify, and EPA to designate formally, areas of the country which meet NAAQS, do not meet NAAQS, or for which there are insufficient data.17/ It did not require this effort to be geared to the AQCRs, and county boundaries have now become the accustomed accounting unit instead.

Classification of an area very largely determines what actions the state and EPA must take to regulate air pollution from existing and new emission sources.

16/ The 247 AQCRs designated by HEW and EPA are identified in the Code of Federal Regulations (hereafter CFR) in Title 40, Part 81.

17/ 43 FR 8962, 3 March 1978.

4.0 STATE IMPLEMENTATION PLANS (SIPs)

4.1 Content of SIPs

The key regulatory section of the act is Section 110. It provides a structure under which states are expected to establish the regulatory framework necessary to achieve the NAAQS. It also directs the Environmental Protection Agency to impose the necessary regulations if state governments do not.

The structure of Section 110 is as follows. Within nine months of the promulgation of an NAAQS, each state, after public hearings, is to submit to the administrator of EPA for his approval a statewide plan for attaining it. 18/ (Under the timetable in the 1970 act, the first set of State Implementation Plans (SIPs) were due on 30 January 1972.) The law then gives the administrator of EPA four months to approve or disapprove the SIP. If a state fails to submit a plan or submits a plan which the administrator deems inadequate, the administrator must promulgate federal regulations to substitute for or supplement that portion of the state's plan. 19/ Approval of a state plan makes its provisions enforceable by the federal government as well as the state. 20/

A SIP must include a description of the air quality in each AQCR, an emissions inventory of sources that emit the pollutant in question, emission limitations and compliance schedules to reduce pollutant emissions to a level low enough to achieve the NAAQS, a permit program for review of new source construction to insure new emissions will not cause a violation of NAAQS, monitoring and reporting requirements, and enforcement procedures.

The 1970 version of the Clean Air Act gave states substantial flexibility to choose which sources to regulate, and to vary the degree of control among sources. Because air quality varied greatly throughout the country, the emission limitations also varied substantially. Some areas already had air quality better than the NAAQS,

---

18/ EPA's minimum requirements for approvable state plans are set forth in 40 CFR Part 51.

19/ Section 110(c).

20/ See 40 CFR Part 52.

while others have such serious problems that they still have not achieved the standards. Indeed, it is questionable whether certain areas will ever achieve certain standards.

The act originally required that the SIP attain the primary standards "as expeditiously as practicable," but in no event later than three years from the date of plan approval, with the possibility of a single two year extension under § 110(e).

The Clean Air Act, then as now, requires SIPs to provide for attainment of the secondary standard within a "reasonable time." The term "reasonable time" is not defined in the act and states can consider technological and economic problems in deciding on an appropriate date for achievement. 21/

Although the provisions of Section 110 in the 1970 act were relatively simple and straightforward, the development and adoption of effective emission controls involved complex technical, economic and political decisions, and many states failed to submit SIPs that could be approved in their entirety. Beyond that, a large number of plans failed to achieve the. NAAQS for one or more pollutants in some regions of the state. Consequently, Congress, in its 1977 amendments, imposed more demanding provisions in Section 110 to reinvigorate the SIP program.

As noted above, the 1977 amendments required EPA to identify the areas that had not attained the NAAQs on schedule. They then required additional rounds of SIP submissions from these areas. Revised SIPs had to be submitted by January 1, 1979, and had to be in effect by July 1, 1979. If an area could make a special showing of inability to achieve the standard for ozone or carbon monoxide, the deadline for establishing some new SIP requirements was moved to December 31, 1982.

Section 172 required SIPs for all these areas to require existing sources to install, at a minimum, "reasonably available control technology." To obtain an extension to 1987 of the deadline for achieving the NAAQs for ozone and CO, which are primarily related

---

21/ EPA by regulation indicated that, where controls were reasonably available, a "reasonable time" for achievement of the secondary standards for sulfur oxides and particulates would be three years, unless the state could show that good cause exists for choosing a later date. 40 CFR 51.13(b)(1) and (2).

to automobiles, states had to adopt a vehicle inspection and maintenance program and adopt other vehicle control measures. In all nonattainment areas, states must also show "reasonable further progress" toward achievement of the NAAQS, which is defined in Section 171 as the accomplishment of "annual incremental reductions in emissions." As an "incentive" to states to adopt these more stringent provisions, Congress provided that if the required new SIP provisions for an area were not adopted and approved by EPA by 30 June 1979, there was to be no construction of new or modified sources of the air pollutants for which NAAQS were exceeded in that area. 22/

EPA stated that this "construction ban" became applicable as a matter of law to all nonattainment areas that did not have the required new SIP provisions in place on July 1, 1979. 23/ The ban imposed at this time, which originally applied to all nonattainment areas, has gradually been removed as the missing SIP provisions were supplied so that it is now in effect only in a handful of areas.

Since then, EPA has done what it can to make the imposition of further construction bans a discretionary act. It has stated, for examle, that a construction ban is not required just because a state did not submit the required 1982 SIP revisions on time, or even because it did not achieve the standards at all. 24/

In addition to the prohibition on new facilities, if states do not adopt adequate revisions to SIPs to implement the nonattainment requirements, there are other sanctions built into the nonattainment program under the 1977 amendments. States can lose federal highway funds if transportation control measures would be necessary for attainment and they are not making "reasonable efforts" to impose them. 25/ A state's failure to implement its SIP will subject it to cutoff of EPA Clean Air Act grants. 26/ Finally, the entire federal government is directed by Section 176(c) not to

---

22/ Section 110(a)(2)(I).

23/ 44 FR 38471 (July 1, 1979).

24/ 48 FR 50686 (Nov. 2, 1983).

25/ Section 176(a).

26/ Section 176(b).

fund, approve, license or permit any activity that is inconsistent
with an applicable SIP. However, EPA has once again successfully
maintained that the decision whether or not to impose these
"sanctions" falls within its discretion.

The Congress did address one deadline problem in the Steel
Industry Compliance Extension Act 27/ which amended Section
113(e) to provide that steel production facilities may have their
compliance date extended to as late as 31 December 1985. In return
the company had to show that the funds thus released from being
spent immediately for compliance with environmental requirements
would be used for investment in production facilities to improve
efficiency and productivity.

4.1.1 Role of Technology and Economics

Industry challenges to the first SIPs raised the question
whether EPA, in determining whether to approve a state SIP, must
consider the technological and economic feasibility of the measures
in the plan. EPA took the position that this choice had been left to
the states by Congress and that EPA's only job was to determine
whether the states had provided an adequate measure of air pollution control. Moreover, the statutory requirement that primary
NAAQS be achieved within three years overrode any considerations
based on cost or availability of technology; sources could always be
shut down. Section 116 gave a state the right to adopt any requirements it wanted even if it had more stringent requirements than
necessary to achieve the NAAQS. Consequently, if the plan when
properly enforced would result in achievement of the NAAQS, EPA
would approve it regardless of any misgivings it might have regarding the technological or economic feasibility of the particular
approach chosen by the state. EPA, however, conceded the possibility of a limited review of such issues in federal enforcement actions.

The Supreme Court ultimately upheld EPA. 28/ The Court
read the act to necessitate a review of each state-submitted SIP
only to determine whether it meet the requirements explicit in
Section 110, i.e., that it include specific measures and ensure the
attainment and maintenance of the NAAQS. The opinion noted that

---

27/   PL 97-23, 17 July 1981.

28/   Union Electric Company v. EPA, 427 U.S. 246 (1976).

challenges concerning technological and economic feasibility could be made at the state level through administrative and judicial channels, and suggested that a source might obtain some review on its particular feasibility problems should the SIP be enforced against it in federal district court. The Court chose specifically not to decide what consideration EPA must give to technological or economic feasibility when it itself promulgates SIP measures.

EPA has encouraged states to choose the most cost effective means to meet emission requirements by the use of "emissions trading." 29/ This policy, also called the "bubble" policy, allows a source which is subject to several SIP emission limits at the same facility to achieve different reductions at various emission points (higher than required in some cases and lower than required in others) as long as the total emissions from the plant are no higher than they would have been if the facility met all of the requirements originally imposed. In other words, the entire plant is treated as if encased in a "bubble," with only the total emissions from the "bubble" as a whole considered important.

As discussed below, EPA has encouraged analogous approaches to implementing the "new source review" provisions of the 1977 Clean Air Act amendments.

4.1.2 Use of Dispersion Techniques

One of the major debates under the 1970 act concerned whether SIPs might rely on techniques other than continuous emission reduction to demonstrate attainment of the NAAQS. To some extent, any air quality management program relies upon the natural dispersion capacities of the meteorology and topography of the area being managed. However, many sources, particularly isolated facilities, proposed to go beyond that inevitable reliance by monitoring meteorological conditions and curtailing operations and emissions intermittently, as needed to meet the NAAQS without relying on technology or other means of achieving continuous emission control. A related approach was to rely upon tall stacks to disperse emissions.

In three major lawsuits brought by industry and by environmental groups, the courts uniformly held that dispersion dependent techniques such as intermittent control and tall stacks are

---

29/   51 FR 43814 (Dec. 4, 1986).

permisible to attain NAAQS under Section 110 of the act only if all available constant emission controls are first applied. 30/

In Section 123 of the 1977 act, Congress forbade intermittent controls except for nonferrous smelters and fuel-burning sources ordered to burn coal in strictly limited cases. Section 123 also allows SIPs to give credit in their control strategies to stack heights representing Good Engineering Practice (GEP), but not for the height of the stack above GEP. EPA published regulations defining "good engineering practice" on 8 February 1982. 31/ The regulations generally provided that a source will be given credit for emissions from a stack 2-1/2 times the height of nearby structures. Those regulations were overturned in part and remanded to EPA by the U.S. Court of Appeals for the District of Columbia Circuit in 1983. 32/ EPA has promulgated new regulations in response to the remand. The litigation on this issue has been renewed and is now well into its second decade.

4.1.3 Transportation Control Plans

It was clear to Congress in 1970 that the standards for automobile related pollutants (HC, CO, oxidants, and NO_2) could not be met everywhere on schedule by the use of conventional control approaches. It therefore required SIPs to include such "transportation controls" as were needed to achieve the standards on schedule.

The courts eventually required EPA to implement these provisions, and the agency began promulgating Transportation Control Plans (TCPs) in late 1973. TCPs included the following types of measures: exclusive bus and bicycle lanes; bridge tolls; area-wide computer systems to identify and bring together potential car poolers; surcharges on parking spaces in urban areas to force people for economic reasons to look to alternative means of transportation; state inspection and maintenance systems; requirements that older

---

30/ NRDC v. Train, 489 F.2d 390 (5th Cir. 1974); Big Rivers Electric Cooperative v. Train, 523 F.2d 16 (6th Cir. 1975); Kennecott Copper Corp. v. Train, 526 F.2d 1149 (9th Cir. 1975).

31/ 47 FR 5864 et seq.

32/ Sierra Club v. EPA 719 F.2d 436 (D.C. Cir.).

cars be retrofitted with devices to reduce emissions; requirements for improvements of mass transit systems; and finally, where achievement of the standards could not be reliably predicted, gas rationing to whatever extent necessary to reduce vehicle miles traveled in the problem areas. 33/

The TCPs created enormous controversy, and it soon became clear that the states and the general public were not ready to support such pervasive measures. Congress reacted to the public mood and, in connection with energy legislation, 34/ adopted provisions of law that deferred any EPA regulations regarding parking management. It also revoked EPA's authority to impose parking surcharges. Since that time, EPA has not stressed any air pollution control measures that would affect the free use of automobiles.

4.1.4 Variances

Historically, the grant of a variance was the chief regulatory means by which states postponed the requirement that a source comply with applicable requirements.

EPA took the position that such a variance could be approved as a simple revision to the implementation plan as long as it would not interfere with timely attainment of the NAAQS. If interference with the standards was shown, the source had to proceed under Section 110(f) of the act, which involved a lengthy formal hearing process.

The Natural Resources Defense Council challenged this approach, claiming that all variances to regulations included in a SIP required approval under Section 110(f). After seven United States courts of appeals arrived at three different views on the legality of EPA's interpretation, the Supreme Court heard the case and decided for EPA. 35/

33/ A good example of a comprehensive TCP is the one first proposed for Boston, 38 FR 30960, 8 November 1973. This plan contains virtually every measure which EPA believed feasible to reduce car use. Other TCPs contained these types of measures plus gas rationing.

34/ The "Energy Supply and Environmental Coordination Act of 1974," PL 93-319, 22 June 1974.

35/ Train v. NRDC, 421 U.S. 60 (1975).

Major noncomplying sources that cannot meet this test for a SIP revision and cannot meet the standards are handled through enforcement actions, either federally under Section 113 of the act, or by the States. The 1977 amendments placed significant new restraints on EPA's administrative handling of non-complying sources, but allowed issuance of delayed compliance orders to sources if several requirements were met. EPA's preferred approach to the problem, however, is to seek a federal court order, either litigated or on consent, which provides the source with the time it actually needs for compliance but exacts penalties—often substantial penalties—for the noncompliance.

4.2 New Source Review in Nonattainment Areas

Section 110(a)(2)(D) as enacted in 1970 required SIPs to include a program for preconstruction review of new or modified stationary sources to ensure that such sources would not interfere with attainment or maintenance of NAAQS. After the date for achievement of the ambient standards under the original 1970 statute passed, it became difficult to justify allowing construction of any new facilities in light of this mandate; any new facility emitting a pollutant for which NAAQS were violated would obviously "interfere" with attainment. To prevent a "no growth" situation in such areas, EPA issued its "offset ruling" on 21 December 1976, interpreting this section to allow growth under certain conditions. 36/ The primary condition imposed on the construction of a new source was that a reduction in emissions (an offset) be obtained from existing sources, whether owned by the applicant or not, which would not otherwise have occurred and which would provide a more than one-for-one counterbalance to the emissions from the new or modified facility.

The offset policy also required the source to install the Best Available Control Technology (BACT), and to certify that other sources of air pollution under common ownership in the same state also met applicable legal requirements.

The 1977 amendments adopted the EPA offset policy (with some changes) as a starting point 37/, until states adopted revised

---

36/   41 FR 55524-30.

37/   The current version of the offset policy is set out in 44 FR 3274, et seq.

SIP provisions incorporating a preconstruction review program as set forth in Section 172.

The program required by Section 172 for areas not achieving NAAQS must provide for a permit program for all new or modified "sources" with the potential (design capacity) to emit one hundred tons or more per year of the nonattainment pollutant. A source was "modified" if its emissions increased by more than a specified de minimis amount.

EPA initially defined a "source" subject to this requirement as any piece of equipment with the capacity to emit more than the permitting threshold, even if it was only one of a number of pieces of equipment at a plant site. 38/ The effect of this definition was to require review whenever any change at a piece of equipment at a plant increased emissions by more than the applicable review threshold, even if other emissions at the plant had simultaneously declined by an equal or greater amount. At the same time that it issued this definition EPA also defined "source" for purposes of the PSD program for clean air areas to include the entire plant, not just individual pieces of equipment. In order to allow more flexibility to sources in nonattainment areas to utilize the bubble approach to compliance, EPA, on 14 October 1981, revised the nonattainment requirements to employ the same definition of "source" as in PSD areas. 39/ That decision, after protracted litigation, was upheld by the Supreme Court in the case of Chevron v. NRDC. 40/

A source or modification classified as "major" for new source review purposes must undergo procedural review designed to determine its compatibility with NAAQS attainment. These sources must also be controlled to a level reflecting the Lowest Achievable Emission Rate (LAER), which is a defined term meaning the most stringent emission standard in any SIP (unless it is shown to be unachievable) or the lowest emissions any source in the same category has achieved in practice. Moreover, a new source cannot receive a permit unless other sources owned or operated by the applicant in the state are meeting all applicable emission limits or

---

30/   45 FR 52746, 7 August 1980.

39/   47 FR 50766.

40/   467 U.S. 1984.

at least meeting all compliance schedule steps. Finally, the new source must either provide "offsets" to its emissions or show that the SIP includes provisions that curtail other sources so that allowances for growth have been built into the control strategy.

4.3 Prevention of Significant Deterioration (PSD)

The 1970 Clean Air Act contained no special measures to protect air quality that was <u>cleaner</u> than the national standards required, and EPA originally took the position that it had no authority to require such measures. The Sierra Club had challenged that determination, arguing that the statement of purpose in section 101(b) indicated the act was to "protect and enhance" the quality of the nation's air resources, a statement that required measures to protect the air in pristine areas. In litigation which reached the Supreme Court, Sierra Club won its case when the Court divided 4 to 4. 41/ This had the effect of affirming the lower court decisions, holding not only that EPA had such authority but also was required to issue implementing regulations.

EPA's final regulations issued in response on December 5, 1974, 42/ were immediately the subject of litigation, both by environmental groups, which considered the regulations inadequate, and by other interests, which considered the regulations more stringent than necessary. These regulations allowed state and local governments to determine what degradation would be "significant" in terms of local conditions. They provided for three types of areas with certain "increments" of additional pollution allowed in each. Class I areas had increments of permissible deterioration so low as to effectively preclude any substantial growth. The increments for Class II areas were designed to allow moderate, controlled growth. (All areas in the country were initially classified as Class II.) The Class III areas allowed additional pollution up to the secondary

---

41/ In <u>Sierra Club v. Ruckelshaus</u>, 344 F. Supp. 253 (D.D.C. 1972), affirmed sub nom. <u>Fri v. Sierra Club</u>, 412 U.S. 541 (1973), the District Court enjoined EPA from approving portions of state implementation plans that did not provide for prevention of any significant deterioration of air quality in those regions that have air cleaner than the secondary ambient air quality standards.

42/ 30 FR 42510.

standard. The only pollutants covered by the regulations were SO_2 and particulate matter.

On 2 August 1976, the United States Court of Appeals for the District of Columbia Circuit upheld the regulations in their entirety. 43/ The Supreme Court agreed to review the case but, before briefs were filed, Congress adopted the 1977 amendments, which included a specific national policy to prevent significant deterioration and detailed how that policy is to be implemented.

Congress in 1977 built on the approach taken in EPA's initial regulations. It classified certain national parks and other similar areas as Class I and the rest of the country as Class II. The limited amounts of additional pollution allowed in each area are set forth in Section 163, and are more restrictive than EPA's regulations. Although the statute establishes increments for SO_2 and particulates only, it directed EPA to develop increments for other pollutants within two years from the date of enactment of the 1977 amendments, something that has not yet been done.

States and Indian governing bodies are permitted to reclassify most Class II areas to Class I or III if they follow detailed procedural requirements which emphasize public involvement, consideration of competing interests, and the approval of local governing bodies, and which are essentially impossible to complete. Certain federal lands may not be reclassified to Class III.

EPA promulgated regulations implementing the new statutory PSD requirements on 19 June 1978. 44/ EPA's regulations were challenged by environmental groups and various industries. They were upheld in part but remanded in part by the United States Court of Appeals for the District of Columbia Circuit. 45/ EPA then substantially changed its regulations and published a new round of final regulations on 7 August 1980. 46/ These regulations were also

---

43/ Sierra Club, et al. v. EPA, 540 F.2d 1114 (D.C. Cir. 1976).

44/ 43 FR 26380, et seq.

45/ Alabama Power Company v. Costle, 636 F.2d. 323 (D.C. Cir. 1979); see also, Citizens to Save Spencer County v. EPA, 600 F.2d. 844 (D.C. Cir. 1979).

46/ 45 FR 52676, et seq.

AIR POLLUTION CONTROL 309

challenged by various parties and a settlement agreement is in the doubtful process of being implemented. 47/

The PSD program is administered primarily through review of new sources and modifications to existing sources. Each state implementation plan must have provisions that require review of such sources. Where they do not, EPA administers a permit system, established in 40 CFR Section 52.21. A source must undergo new source review if it falls in one of 28 specifically designated industrial categories and has the "potential to emit" more than 100 tons of any pollutant regulated by the Clean Air Act, not just SO_2 or particulates. (The amount is 250 tons for sources outside the twenty-eight specific categories.) "Potential to emit" means the maximum design capacity of the source after application of pollution controls. For a modification to undergo review, it must be a modification of an existing major stationary source which creates a "significant net increase," as defined by EPA, in emissions of a pollutant regulated under the Clean Air Act.

In determining the "source" to which the regulations apply, EPA will examine the largest grouping of pollutant-emitting activities located on contiguous or adjacent properties which are under the control of the same person and within the same SIC code major group. 48/ The definition of source is important because new source review applies only to a net increase in emissions from the source. If emissions can be reduced at other locations within the source to levels below 100 tons, new source review may be avoided. Thus, the larger the number of emitting activities which constitute the source, the greater the possibilities for avoiding review.

A source subject to new source review must make several demonstrations before it will be allowed to construct. First, it must show that it will not cause a violation of NAAQS. Second, it must show that any emission of particulates or SO_2 will not cause a violation of the statutory PSD increments. Third, it must show that it will employ Best Available Control Technology (BACT) for each pollutant regulated under the CAA that it emits. This is defined in Section 165(a)(4) of the act as a case-by-case determination of the

─────────────────────────────

47/ See e.g., proposed revisions at 48 FR 38745, 25 August 1983.

48/ 40 CFR Section 52.21(b)(6).

maximum emission reduction that facility can achieve, taking into consideration cost, energy, non-air environmental impacts, and other factors. BACT cannot be less stringent than NSPS.

Public hearings are required on applications for permits. An applicant must make a technical showing on the effect of the proposed source's emissions on visibility and vegetation and describe any general growth in the area which may result from the source's existence.

The comprehensive preconstruction review programs developed for nonattainment areas and PSD areas between them apply nationwide. Because air quality will be either better or worse than NAAQS in all areas, any major new stationary source or major modification to an existing source will be subject to one or the other of these reviews for every pollutant for which there is an NAAQS, and may be subject to both.

4.4 Visibility Protection

Congress in 1977 also set in motion, under section 169A, a program designed for "the prevention of any future, and the remedying of any existing, impairment of visibility" in Class I areas from man-made air pollution. The inclusion of the section in the Clean Air Act is somewhat anomalous, for if the secondary air quality standards and the PSD program really did the job they are theoretically supposed to do, there would be no need for such a provision. In addition, only very limited regulatory steps are required under this provision. EPA is now in the process of taking at least some of those limited steps in response to a court order.

5.0 NATIONAL STATIONARY SOURCE EMISSION STAMDARDS

The Clean Air Act provides authority for nationally applicable emission standards that are imposed regardless of the quality of ambient air in the particular location where the source is located. New Source Performance Standards (NSPS) under Section 111 are technology-based while National Emission Standards for Hazardous Air Pollutants (NESHAP) under Section 112 are based on health protection.

5.1 New Source Performance Standards (NSPS)

Section 111 authorizes the administrator to identify those sources which ". . . contribute significantly to air pollution which causes or contributes to the endangerment of the public health or welfare." He is then to set emission standards applicable to new sources of the types identified, as well as to modifications of existing sources of that type. The standards must reflect the "degree of emission reduction achievable" through the best technology the administrator determines has been "adequately demonstrated," considering costs and a number of other factors.

The NSPS apply to any new facility or modification of an existing facility that commences construction after the date of proposal of the NSPS. As originally conceived, the NSPS provision had two purposes. First, it reflected the congressional view that new plants should bear a special control burden because they had the greatest flexibility to incorporate the latest, most effective pollution control technology. Second, it expressed a policy of requiring the same degree of control on all technically similar new sources, regardless of where they were located, thereby preventing some states from adopting more lenient air pollution requirements than other states and creating "pollution havens" as a means of attracting industry. The NSPS were also said to conserve air resources for future growth.

With the development of the programs to prevent significant deterioration and for nonattainment areas, the purposes of NSPS have changed substantially. In many cases, NSPS may be only a point of departure for determining BACT or LAER for a new source —although NSPS will always apply as a ceiling on emissions in those determinations.

Nevertheless, the 1977 act underlined the importance that Congress continues to attach to NSPS by requiring that, within one year after enactment, EPA list all major stationary source categories for which NSPS had not been established and then set NSPS for those categories over the following four years.

The most controversial amendment to Section 111 in the 1977 amendments required EPA to set NSPS for fossil-fuel burning sources, such as electric utility plants, that would require the standard to include a percentage reduction requirement as well as an absolute emission level. This provision requires flue gas desulfurization (scrubbers) or other technology to be installed in all cases, and forbids compliance simply by the use of low sulfur fuels as in the past. The requirement is intended to discourage sources from switching to low-sulfur Western coals from high-sulfur Eastern and Midwestern coals and make use of the high-sulfur coal desirable.

EPA revised its NSPS for power plants to meet these standards on 11 June 1979, 49/ was promptly challenged by both industry and environmental groups, and prevailed in court on all the issues presented. 50/
     In response to repeated requests from EPA, Congress included in Section 111 authority for EPA to set NSPS as design, equipment, work practice or operational standards where numerical emission limitations would be infeasible. EPA must allow alternative control methods if they are equally effective, and must revise the NSPS to numerical limits if it becomes feasible to do so.
     A little-noticed but potentially important part of Section 111 is subsection (d), which requires the states to regulate emissions from existing sources in any source category for which EPA sets an NSPS for new and modified sources. This requirement applies only to pollutants not covered by NAAQS, such as sulfuric acid mist and fluorides. States are now in the process of developing standards for those pollutants under control technology guidelines established by EPA. EPA must approve each state's standards or establish its own substitute standards—an approach patterned on the SIPs.

5.2 National Emission Standards for Hazardous Air Pollutants (NESHAP)

     Particularly dangerous air pollutants that may not be emitted by enough sources to justify an NAAQS are dealt with by national emission standards for hazardous pollutants (NESHAPs) pursuant to Section 112. The pollutants to be covered by Section 112 are those which ". . . may reasonably be anticipated to result in an increase in mortality, or an increase in serious irreversible, or incapaciting reversible illness." Asbestos, beryllium and mercury section 112 standards were promulgated on 6 April 1973. 51/ On 21 October 1976, EPA set standards for vinyl chloride emissions from plastics industry plants. EPA has also more recently set NESHAPs for benzene, radionuclides and arsenic.

49/   44 FR 33580.

50/   See, Sierra Club v. Costle, 657 F.2d. 298 (D.C. Cir. 1981).

51/   40 CFR Part 61.

The statute requires NESHAPs to be set at a level adequate to protect the public health with an ample margin of safety; it does not on its face authorize the administrator to consider costs or availability of control technology.

In reality, EPA does review the costs involved and the availability of technology to control emissions to the desired level. EPA gives less consideration to those factors than in other regulatory decisions under the act, but absent an overwhelming health hazard, EPA will be reluctant to shut down an industry by requiring zero emissions. Two questions central to decision making under section 112 were recently decided by the D.C. Circuit Court of Appeals: whether EPA can decline to regulate a hazardous air pollutant on the ground that the risk it poses, though greater than zero, is "not significant," and whether, in cases that fall above this risk level, EPA can consider costs in deciding how tightly to regulate. The court upheld EPA on both counts. 52/

NESHAPs apply to existing as well as new sources. The latter must comply at the time of commencement of operations. Existing sources, however, may delay compliance for a period of up to two years.

The 1977 amendments revised Section 112 to authorize the EPA to set design, equipment, work practice or operational standards where numerical emission limits would not be practicable. Because EPA has promulgated such a limited number of NESHAPs, EPA has received substantial criticism from the environmental community and Congress. EPA, in tacit cooperation with Congressman Dingell has attempted with considerable success to defuse that criticism by agreeing to issue "regulatory decisions" (which are not necessarily the same as regulations) on twenty-five chemicals that are candidates for section 112 regulation. EPA is now engaged in this task.

6.0 INFORMATION GATHERING AUTHORITY

Any agency responsible for carrying out or overseeing important regulatory programs must be able to obtain the information relevant to those programs. In Section 114 of the 1970 act, Congress

---

52/ NRDC v. EPA; 25 ERC 1105 (D.C. Cir 1986).

gave EPA broad powers to obtain information necessary for the programs under Title I of the act, especially Sections 110 through 113 and 120. This authority includes an EPA ability to require a source owner to test the source's emissions, to enter the premises of the source to test emissions itself, or to inspect aspects of the source's operations relevant to its emissions. EPA may also require source owners to maintain records and submit reports regarding their emissions and controls.

The Supreme Court's decision overturning the Occupational Safety and Health Administration's warrantless searches in Marshall v. Barlow's, Inc., 53/ arguably could also apply to this Clean Air Act authority. However, the agency as a general policy has already adopted the practice of obtaining search warrants where voluntary inspection is refused, thus in effect conforming its conduct to this decision.

7.0 ENFORCEMENT AUTHORITY

The act sets forth a relatively simple procedure for federal enforcement of applicable implementation plans and other specified requirements of the act. 54/ Where EPA finds a violation, it issues a "Notice of Violation" through the appropriate EPA regional office. The notice describes the specific violation and is sent to the alleged violator, as well as to any appropriate state or local control agency. If the violation continues for more than thirty days after the notice issues, EPA may either commence a civil action or issue an administrative order to the source.

At the request of EPA, Congress included in the 1977 amendments authority to seek from a court civil penalties up to $25,000 per day of violation. Civil penalties were attractive to the agency because a court can consider them outside the complexities of a criminal trial.

Notices of violation are not required where EPA finds violations of NSPS, hazardous emission standards, or certain reporting requirements. In these cases, the administrator may immediately issue an administrative order or bring an appropriate civil action. The absence of a notice of violation requirement here makes it

---

53/   436 U.S. 307 (1978).

54/   Section 113(a).

relatively clear that notice in the SIP context is designed not to assist the violator but to give the state an opportunity to begin the action instead of EPA.

Section 113 also provides that where the administrator finds that violations in a state are so widespread that it appears the state generally is failing to enforce its plan, he may initiate a period of federally assumed enforcement, which continues until the administrator determines that the state has resumed the needed enforcement activities. EPA has never invoked this authority.

Paragraph (c) of Section 113 authorizes criminal penalties for "knowing" violations of the law. For "knowing" offenses, the law authorizes a fine of not more than $25,000 per day and/or imprisonment for up to one year. For subsequent convictions, the sanctions are doubled. In Section 113(c)(2), a $10,000 fine and/or imprisonment for up to six months is authorized for the making of false statements or tampering with monitoring devices required by the act.

7.1 Compliance Orders and Noncompliance Penalties

The 1977 amendments made two major changes in enforcement practices of EPA. Expressing dissatisfaction with EPA's pre-1977 practice of avoiding the strict deadlines of the act through administrative enforcement orders that prescribed later compliance dates, Congress provided that the administrator cannot authorize noncompliance through such orders except pursuant to the elaborate Delayed Compliance Order (DCO) procedures of Section 113(d). 55/ Such DCOs may be issued only until 1 July 1979, or three years from the date the SIP requires compliance, whichever is later. In addition, the orders must meet several other requirements, including containing a schedule and time table for compliance. This restriction on EPA's authority to issue enforcement orders, coupled with the directive in Section 113(b) requiring the administrator to bring civil actions against major stationary source violators, has helped lead to increased emphasis on litigation (including consent decrees) to enforce the Clean Air Act.

The second major change in enforcement strategy under the act was the adoption of Section 120, which provides for fines to be

---

55/   Section 110(i).

paid by noncomplying sources, in amounts calculated to eliminate the economic advantage of noncompliance. The section's fundamental policy is to recover as a penalty any economic costs a source owner or operator may be avoiding by not making the capital outlays or operation and maintenance expenditures that would be necessary to comply with an SIP or Section 111 or Section 112 standards.

Although the noncompliance penalty program was heralded as being an effective alternative to traditional enforcement systems—indeed, the first significant such alternative to be adopted by Congress—interest in the program has slackened considerably. Congress declined to include a similar provision in the Clean Water Act Amendments of 1977. EPA's regulations 56/ became effective on 27 October 1980. They calculate the fine based upon a complex computer analysis incorporated in the regulations, that requires information from the company on approximately fifteen different variables. The complexity of the process, however, has proved to be a deterrent and EPA has considered using it in only a very limited number of situations. Future use of the procedure will also probably be limited.

8.0 EMERGENCY AUTHORITY

Like all the other major environmental statutes, the Clean Air Act provides specific authority to act in emergencies outside the usual regulatory framework. For this purpose, the act's Section 303 authorizes the adminstrator to seek a federal court order directing any type of air pollution source to stop emitting, or to take other appropriate action, when he finds that air pollution is "presenting an imminent and substantial endangerment to the health of persons." The 1977 amendments added authority to issue a short-term administrative order to begin abatement actions while a lawsuit is being prepared.

This authority has been invoked only once, in Birmingham, Alabama in 1973. However, EPA personnel have been ready in several other cities when episodes have occurred to take necessary legal action if the state or local agency response proved inadequate.

56/   40 CFR Part 66.

9.0 OZONE PROTECTION

In 1975, scientists began to announce the results of studies on depletion of the ozone layer in the stratosphere. Ozone, which at ground level is part of the photochemical oxidants complex and injurious to human health when breathed, is essential twenty miles and more up in the stratosphere to screen out harmful ultraviolet radiation that can cause skin cancers and reduced crop yields at excessive exposures.

The chemical agents implicated in ozone depletion are the halogenated compounds known as "halocarbons." Though stable in the lower atmosphere, scientists believe they become unstable in sunlight at higher levels and react with ozone, forming new compounds, thereby depleting the ozone available for screening. These halocarbons are in widespread use, as aerosol propellants, refrigerants, and foaming agents, and are released in the atmosphere when aerosol-packaged products are used and through leakage or destruction of refrigeration equipment.

Congress reacted to these concerns in its 1976 enactment of the Toxic Substances Control Act (TSCA), which included regulatory authority broad enough to allow EPA to deal with halocarbons. The 1977 amendments to the Clean Air Act essentially replaced that authority with a new regulatory scheme designed specifically for the regulation of halocarbons, and required numerous federal agencies to participate in a study of the problems, culminating in a report to Congress two years after the enactment of the amendments.

The regulatory approach prescribed in the new Sections 150-159 is relatively simple, compared to the complex scientific questions involved. The administrator may issue regulations controlling halocarbons or "any substance, practice, process, or activity" that affects the stratosphere, if the effect "may reasonably be anticipated to endanger public health or welfare." Since ozone depletion would be a world-wide problem caused by world-wide activities, EPA's efforts in this field likewise have a heavy international emphasis.

10.0 MOTOR VEHICLE EMISSION CONTROL

10.1 Introduction

Since 1965, the federal government has had authority to set emission standards applicable to new motor vehicles and engines.

Standards are to be set for pollutants which the administrator determines ". . . cause, or contribute to, air pollution which may reasonably be anticipated to endanger public health and welfare." Limitations on emissions of hydrocarbons and carbon monoxide were applied to 1968 model year vehicles and all subsequent model years. An emission standard for oxides of nitrogen went into effect beginning with 1973.

10.2 Statutory Standards and Suspension

In the belief that motor vehicle pollutants constituted the single most difficult air pollution problem facing the nation, and noting the limited progress in abating it, Congress in 1970 took the unusual step of actually prescribing the numerical level of auto emission standards. The law 57/ required a 90 percent reduction of hydrocarbons and carbon monoxide from 1970 levels, and a 90 percent reduction in nitrogen oxides emissions from levels attained in 1971 model year vehicles. The 90 percent reductions in HC and CO were to be achieved in 1975, and the NO_x reductions in 1976. In each case, the administrator was permitted to suspend for one additional year the 90 percent reduction requirements if he found, after public hearing, that the needed technology was not available, and that the manufacturer applying for the suspension had made good faith efforts to meet the standards.

Manufacturers applied for the suspension of the 1975 standards at the first opportunity, viz., January 1972. After evaluating the written and oral information submitted, EPA determined that the manufacturers had failed to prove that technology was not available, and accordingly denied the one-year suspension. The manufacturers took their case to the United States Court of Appeals for the District of Columbia Circuit. The Court, speaking through Judge Leventhal, assessed in detail the technical and policy aspects of the problem, 58/ and found that EPA had not adequately supported its conclusion that the standards could be met. Specifically, EPA had not adequately considered whether the available technology,

---

57/ Section 202(a)(1) and (2).

58/ International Harvester v. Ruckelshaus, 478 F.2d 615 (D.C. Cir. 1973).

catalytic mufflers, would be available for a sufficient variety of model lines or in sufficient quantities to meet market demands.

Subsequent to the decision, EPA held new hearings and granted a suspension. Then, in accordance with the statutory mandate, EPA set interim standards which (although not equal to the 90 percent reduction desired by Congress) were quite stringent. Renewed suspensions were granted in 1975 after an amendment to the law had made them available.

In the 1977 amendments Congress, after often heated discussions, enacted what amounted to another postponement of what were once the 1975 statutory standards. The hydrocarbon standard was set back to model year 1980; the carbon monoxide level deferred to 1981 with the potential of an administrative suspension for two more years. For oxides of nitrogen Congress went further and significantly loosened the stringent number originally set for the 1976 models. Section 202 now prescribes a 1.0 grams per vehicle mile standard beginning in model year 1981. Each of the standards postponed or loosened by the 1977 amendments has now been achieved on production vehicles.

In the 1977 amendments, Congress for the first time took charge of standard setting for heavy duty vehicles, i.e., larger trucks, a field previously left to EPA's discretion. EPA was left with the authority to substitute standards reflecting what the best available technology can achieve, if the statutory standards prove infeasible.

Section 206(g) of the CAA, added in 1977, took the innovative step of providing for a "nonconformance penalty." This would allow trucks to be certified and sold if they did not exceed the standard by more than a margin set by EPA, if the manufacturer paid a penalty set so as to remove any competitive advantage that trucks not meeting the standards might have. Such a penalty must increase from that baseline "periodically."

10.3 Certification

Under the Clean Air Act, no manufacturer may introduce vehicles subject to emission standards into commerce, unless they have been certified by EPA to conform to the standards. 59/ The certification procedure consists of a lengthy test on prototype

---

59/ Clean Air Act § 203(a)(1).

vehicles. Most of these tests are conducted by a manufacturer at its own facility, but a few vehicles are sent to EPA's laboratory at Ann Arbor, Michigan for confirmatory testing. A limited number of cars are run to 50,000 miles and their emissions tested periodically to determine the durability of the vehicles' emission controls. A "deterioration factor" is determined by observation of the increase in emissions from the 4,000 mile test to the 50,000 mile test. This factor is then applied to a single test on a somewhat larger group of the same "family" of cars. This procedure indicates whether or not a prototype vehicle has been designed to meet the standards for the useful life of the vehicle. 60/

If the tests are successful, a certificate of conformity covering that type of engine/vehicle combination is issued. The manufacturer is then free to begin producing cars of the same design as the certified prototypes.

10.4 Compliance by Production Vehicles

Certification verifies the capability of a prototype design to comply with the applicable emission standards, but provides little assurance that production vehicles will comply either at the time of their manufacture or thereafter, when operated and maintained by their owners. At the time Congress was considering the 1970 act, it was presented with data showing significant failures of compliance by vehicles in use, and decided to adopt measures to enable EPA and the vehicle owners to ensure vehicles' compliance throughout their useful life.

The provisions adopted authorized EPA to test production vehicles on the assembly line and to revoke the certificate of conformity for any noncomplying vehicle. They also required compliance by vehicles through a "useful life" of five years or 50,000 miles, required manufacturers to warrant compliance for the useful life period, and authorized EPA to require manufacturers to recall vehicles found not to comply for the specified period.

10.4.1 Assembly Line Testing

Section 207(b) authorizes the administrator to conduct assembly line testing of new vehicles. If, based on such tests, he determines that certain vehicles do not conform to the regulations, he

---

60/   Section 206, 40 CFR Part 86.

can suspend or revoke the certificate of conformity covering the class of vehicles, until such time as the manufacturer has corrected the deficiency. The manufacturer is entitled to a formal trial-type hearing on the determination by the administrator, and may appeal to the United States Court of Appeals if the final administrative decision goes against it.

The agency has developed an assembly line testing program called Selective Enforcement Audit (SEA), 61/ which uses a statistical approach to overcome the impossibility of conducting the lengthy federal test procedure on all production vehicles.

Very briefly, SEA functions as follows: EPA orders a manufacturer to conduct tests on a relatively small number of cars chosen at random on the assembly line. If those tests indicate that the cars are meeting standards, the program with respect to that line of vehicles terminates. If, however, the tests indicate that there is a question about compliance, the size of the sample is increased and testing continues. A sufficient number of vehicles will be tested to support a valid judgment as to the status of the entire class of cars. If the judgment is that the class is not meeting the standards, the certificate of conformity is revoked, and no vehicles covered by that certificate may be marketed.

10.4.2 Warranties

The act's imposition of statutory warranties was perhaps a "first" in the history of regulatory legislation. It represents an attempt to make the regulated industry directly responsible to the people who purchase its products.

Section 207(a) requires the manufacturer to warrant to the owner that the vehicle is designed, built, and equipped to conform at the time of sale with applicable standards, and that it is free from defects in materials and workmanship which would cause noncompliance. Both of these warranties carry with them rather substantial problems of proof for the owner, and have not proved to be effective remedies.

Section 207(b) provides a potentially more important check on emissions. It requires a manufacturer to warrant that the vehicle "if properly maintained and used" will perform in compliance with the

---

61/ The Selective Enforcement Audit Program was promulgated on 28 July 1976, 41 FR 31472.

applicable standards for its useful life. As vehicle inspection and maintenance programs become more widespread, warranty claims under this provision from owners whose cars prove unable to meet the standards of that program are also likely to increase in number.

10.4.3 Recall

Section 207(c) gives the administrator authority to order manufacturers to recall and repair or modify groups of vehicles which exceed the emission standards when in actual use. The manufacturer has the right to a hearing to contest EPA's finding that its vehicles do not meet standards. These are formal hearings before an administrative law judge.

EPA has required several manufacturers to recall thousands of automobiles for failure to meet the standards to which they were certified. Generally, the needed repair or replacement was readily identifiable. One recall order has been contested through the hearing appeal route. 62/

10.4.4 Vehicle Inspection

The 1977 amendments mandate vehicle inspection and maintenance programs for areas that cannot meet NAAQS for motor vehicle-related pollutants by the end of 1982. These programs provide for periodic emissions tests of all registered automobiles with a "short test" that correlates (often rather roughly) with the full-scale federal emissions test procedure. The highest emitting cars must then undergo maintenance to reduce their pollution levels. The emissions "short-test" to implement these requirements was upheld in Motor Vehicle Manufacturers Association v. Ruckelshaus. 63/ Failure to adopt or implement an I + M program in an area subject to these nonattainment requirements can result in a cutoff of certain federal funds, including highway monies.

10.5 Enforcement

Enforcement of the motor vehicle regulatory program is exclusively through the courts. The act provides for injunctive relief to stop violations (Section 204) and for civil penalties of up to $10,000 per violation per vehicle (Section 205). A few large civil penalties have been imposed on manufacturers in violation.

62/   Chrysler Corp. v. EPA, 631 F.2d. 865 (D.C. Cir. 1980).

63/   719 F.2d. 1159 (D.C. Cir. 1983).

11.0 FUEL AND FUEL ADDITIVE PROVISIONS

11.1 Registration

The Congress expressed its concern about the possible harmful effects of the byproducts of fuel additives, which are so widely used in gasoline, by including in the 1967 act a requirement that fuel additives be registered with the government for purposes of gathering information about their composition and combinations. This program was broadened considerably in Section 211 of the 1970 act. In addition to adding the regulatory authority discussed below, this provision extended the registration requirement to fuels as well as additives, and authorized EPA to require information on the products and byproducts of the combustion of fuels and additives, as well as on their effects on health, welfare, and motor vehicle emission control systems.

Regulations implementing the revised registration program were issued in November 1975. 64/

11.2 Regulatory Authority

The law establishes two grounds for the control or prohibition of automobile fuels and fuel additives.

Under Section 211(c) (1)(B), the administrator is authorized to regulate the manufacture or sale of motor vehicle fuels or additives, if he finds that products of the additives will impair, to a significant degree, the performance of an existing or proposed emission control device.

EPA determined that in order to attempt to meet the stringent 1975 emission standards, automobile manufacturers primarily intended to rely on the catalytic converter—a device which is "poisoned," i.e., rendered ineffective, by lead. As a result of this finding, the agency promulgated regulations, 65/ which require one grade of unleaded gasoline to be generally available throughout the country at the larger gasoline stations. 66/

64/   40 CFR Part 79, 40 FR 52009.

65/   40 CFR Part 80.

66/   In addition to various labeling requirements, the Part 80 regulations require that the unleaded gasoline be dispensed from a special nozzle, and that cars with catalytic converters have gasoline inlets designed to mate with the special nozzles.

In paragraph (A) of Section 211(c)(1), the administrator is also given authority to control the use of fuel additives, if he finds they will "endanger the public health or welfare." EPA determined that lead emitted from automobiles as a result of the use of leaded gasoline posed an endangerment to public health, particularly among urban children. On 6 December 1973, 67/ EPA adopted regulations that required the gradual phasing down of the amount of lead used in leaded gasoline. The schedule called for a maximum of 1.7 grams per gallon on 1 January 1975, and then reduced annually the allowable amount to 0.5 grams per gallon by 1979.

The regulations were challenged in the United States Court of Appeals for the District of Columbia, set aside by a panel, and then upheld by the court en banc. The Supreme Court declined to review the case. 68/

Small refineries (50,000 barrels per day of gasoline or less) owned by small refiners (total capacity of 137,500 barrel per day of gasoline or less) were provided additional time to meet the 0.5 grams per gallon standard. In Section 211(g) of the act, Congress determined that these smaller firms might have greater difficulty in raising capital or making other necessary capital investments and should be given until 1982, a three-year extension, to meet the standards. Those facilities were required to meet interim levels based upon a statutory scale depending on their size. EPA regulations implementing Section 211(g) were promulgated 7 August 1979. 69/

After initially proposing to weaken the lead phase-down effort early in the Reagan administration, EPA reversed course and tightened the rules instead, eliminating in the process the special treatment for small refiners.

Final regulations were promulgated on 29 October 1982,70/ and were substantially upheld by the D.C. Circuit in 1983, Small Refiner Lead Phase-Down Task Force v. Gorsuch. 71/ Since then

---

67/   40 CFR 80.20.

68/   Ethyl Corp. v. EPA, 541 F. 2d 1 (D.C. Cir. 1976), cert. denied, 426 U.S. 941.

69/   44 FR 53146, 40 CFR Section 80.20(b).

70/   47 FR 49322, et seq.

71/   705 F.2d. 506 (D.C. Cir. 1983).

EPA has once more tightened the lead in gasoline regulations, this time without provoking any legal challenge. 72/

12.0 AIRCRAFT EMISSION CONTROL

Section 231 empowers the administrator to establish emission standards for aircraft and aircraft engines, following the regulatory pattern set forth in Section 202(a) for motor vehicles. EPA has established emission standards for most classes of new aircraft and aircraft engines and for the most significant emitters among existing aircraft and engines. 73/

These standards, which can be issued only if the Secretary of Transportation agrees that they do not create safety problems, are required by the act to be enforced by the Department of Transportation, which has issued regulations for that purpose.

13.0 CITIZENS SUITS

Congress, in 1970, offered the public opportunity to assist in the process of enforcing the act against both industry and the administrator by opening a door to direct judicial action. Section 304 of the act authorizes two types of suits by citizens: one to enforce control requirements against sources, and one to enforce duties against EPA.

Under Section 304(a)(1), a person may sue any other person, including the United States government or other political jurisdictions, alleged to be in violation of emission standards or limitations, or enforcement orders issued by the administrator or a state. In short, Section 304 is designed to make the act enforceable in federal district courts by anyone with the interest and resources to do so.

Information concerning violations should be readily available to interested citizens. Section 110(a)(2)(f) requires that sources periodically report emission data to the state, and that such reports must be available to the public. Section 114, which authorizes the administrator to inspect sources and require reports, specifically

---

72/   50 FR 9386 (March 7, 1985).

73/   40 CFR Part 87.

exempts "emission data" 74/ from information which might be withheld from the public on the grounds that it constitutes a trade secret. Again, in Section 208, emission data on motor vehicles is excluded from restrictions which might otherwise allow it to be withheld from public disclosure.

The 1977 act expanded the jurisdiction of the federal district courts to hear citizens suits. Citizens can now sue to enforce most of the major requirements imposed under the act, as opposed to just emission standards and limitations. The act does not specifically authorize citizens to seek penalties or damages.

While citizen suits against polluters, at least under the Clean Air Act, have never attained the importance some had expected of them, suits against the administrator have had an enormous impact. Under § 304(a)(2), citizens are authorized to bring actions against the administrator of EPA, ". . . where there is alleged a failure. . . to perform any act or duty under this Act which is not discretionary . . ." In those few words, Congress established a mechanism by which the judicial branch of the government would, if asked, oversee a portion of EPA's implementation of the law.

It was a citizen suit in California 75/ which forced EPA to propose a transportation control plan for the South Coast Basin which included a provision requiring in excess of 80 percent gas rationing. It was under the citizen suit provision that the Sierra Club successfully litigated the issue of prevention of significant deterioration. A citizen suit forced EPA to set an ambient air quality standard for lead. There are other examples where suits under this section have forced the agency to act at a time, and sometimes in a manner, it would not have chosen of its own accord.

Citizens are required to give sixty days notice, before bringing a Section 304 suit, to the administrator of EPA, the state and the violator. If EPA or the state is diligently prosecuting an enforcement action against the violator, the citizen may not sue himself, but may intervene in that litigation.

74/ Section 114(c).

75/ City of Riverside v. Ruckelshaus, 4 ERC 1728 (C.D. Cal. 1972).

14.0 JUDICIAL REVIEW

Because of the potential importance and the controversial nature of EPA regulatory decisions implementing the Clean Air Act, many decisions are challenged in court by environmentalists, by industry or both. To expedite the judicial review of EPA's regulations, in view of the short statutory deadlines, Congress provided for direct review of all "final" regulations in the United States courts of appeals and required that challenges be brought within certain time limits.

The 1970 act required persons who wished to challenge an agency action to file a petition for review in the appropriate court of appeals within thirty days after the action was taken. The courts have upheld this time limit on judicial review by dismissing late petitions. In the 1977 amendments, Congress lengthened the deadline to sixty days. Congress also barred attacks on a regulation as a defense in an enforcement action, if the issue could have been raised in a court of appeals challenge. The 1977 act also followed the courts in providing that, in order to get judicial review after the deadline, a person must petition the agency and demonstrate that information is available which was not available when the EPA action was being developed.

Courts reviewing decisions under the Clean Air Act apply the familiar three-part test established by the Administrative Procedure Act. A rule will be reversed if it was (a) established through improper procedures, (b) outside the agency's legal authority, or (c) "arbitrary, capricious, [or] an abuse of discretion." Though courts do generally defer both to EPA policy choices and to EPA views of the law, they have often insisted on a substantial explanation by EPA of the legal and policy considerations that led to the agency's decision. 76/

The 1977 Clean Air Act amendments added a number of new provisions to the judicial review section. First, they codified and expanded prior case law by establishing detailed rulemaking provisions for EPA to follow designed to generate a suitable "record" for agency decision and judicial review. 77/ Second, they established a

---

76/ Portland Cement Ass'n v. Ruckelshaus, 486 F.2d. 375 (D.C. Cir. 1973) (Leventhal, J.).

77/ § 307(d).

rule of "harmless error" under which procedural errors could not be grounds for reversing EPA rulemaking decisions unless they were significant to the ultimate policy choice. 78/ Finally, they expanded the number of Clean Air Act actions that could only be reviewed in the United States Court of Appeals for the District of Columbia Circuit. 79/

15.0 ACID RAIN

One of the most controversial issues not dealt with directly by the Clean Air Act is the question of acid deposition or "acid rain." For some time there has been growing evidence that lakes and streams, primarily in the northeast portion of the United States and in Canada have become more acidic than they originally were, causing a reduction, or in some cases total elimination, of fish and other life in those bodies of water. Acid deposition is also suspected of reducing forest productivity. Many people believe that the acidity is due to long-range atmospheric transport of sulfur emissions, principally from power plants in the Midwest. The sulfur eventually precipitates as sulfates in the rain where it causes adverse effects to the land and water. There is, however, intense scientific and political debate over the causes of acid rain, the contribution of power plants, and the appropriate methods for addressing the problem, (e.g., reduction in sulfur emissions or treatment of lakes and land to neutralize the acid). A ten-year study of acid rain was authorized by the Congress under the auspices of the National Academy of Science.

Although the 1977 amendments to the Clean Air Act do provide for some redress for air pollution caused by out-of-state sources, the statute was not drafted with a pollution problem such as acid rain in mind. Rather, the act is premised on state-by-state control strategies for individual sources and the identification of specific sources which contribute to a particular pollution problem that results in a violation of a NAAQS, a PSD increment or visibility requirements. EPA has generally held that it lacks authority under the act to address the acid rain problem directly.

78/ § 307(d)(8).

79/ § 307 (b)(1).

The National Commission on Air Quality recommended increased authority for EPA to regulate long-range transport and recommended that there be a significant reduction by 1990 in sulfur dioxide emissions. Canada has also pressed vigorously for control of power plant emissions by the federal government. A number of proposals have been considered by the Congress to address acid rain. These range from stepped-up research to major regulatory programs. One of the most comprehensive statutory proposals would require specific reductions, (e.g., ten million tons of sulfur dioxide) from sources, primarily power plants, within thirty-one eastern states. The exact form of increased authority for EPA to address the problem of acid rain has been and will continue to be hotly contested. Due to the strong political and public pressure for action on this issue, it is quite likely that the next substantive amendments to the Clean Air Act will contain some provision on acid rain.

Chapter 7

OCCUPATIONAL SAFETY AND HEALTH ACT 1/

Marshall Lee Miller
Reid & Priest
Washington, D.C.

1.0 INTRODUCTION

The U.S. Occupational Safety and Health Administration (OSHA) has been called the most unpopular agency in the federal government. It has justifiably been criticized for its confusing regulations, chronic mismanagement, and picayune enforcement. With somewhat less accuracy, some business groups have likened it to an American gestapo, while labor unions have denounced it as unresponsive and bureaucratic.

It is not often recognized, however, that OSHA is also perhaps the most important environmental health agency in the government. Even the Environmental Protection Agency (EPA), with far greater resources and public attention, deals with a smaller range of much less hazardous exposures than does OSHA. After all, individuals are more likely to be exposed to high concentrations of dangerous chemicals in their workplaces than in their backyards.

2.0 COMPARISON OF OSHA AND EPA

There are several distinct differences between OSHA and EPA, besides the obvious occupational jurisdiction. First, OSHA has

---

1/ A section-by-section outline of the key provisions of the statute can be found at the end of this chapter as Appendix A.

major responsibility over workplace safety as well as health. Second, OSHA is essentially an enforcement organization, with a majority of its employees as inspectors, performing fifty thousand or more inspections a year. This "highway patrol" function, inspecting and penalizing thousands of businesses large and small, is the major reason for OSHA's substantial unpopularity. At EPA, on the other hand, inspections and enforcement are a relatively minor part of the operation.

Third, whereas EPA is an independent regulatory agency, albeit headed by presidential appointees, OSHA is a division of the Department of Labor. This organizational arrangement provides not only less prestige and, in theory, less independence for OSHA, but poses an internal conflict whether OSHA should be primarily a health or a labor-oriented agency. Nevertheless, OSHA and EPA regulate different aspects of so many health issues—asbestos, vinyl chloride, carcinogens, hazard labeling, and others—that it is reasonable to regard them both as overlapping environmental organizations.

3.0 LEGISLATIVE FRAMEWORK

OSHA was created in December 1970—the same month as EPA—with the enactment of the Occupational Safety and Health Act (OSH Act), 2/ and officially began operation in April 1971. When compared with other environmental acts, the OSH Act is very simple and well drafted. This does not mean that one necessarily agrees with the provisions of every section, but it is clearly and concisely written so that details can be worked out in implementing regulations. And unlike the other environmental laws which have been amended several times, the OSH Act has not been amended or modified since its original passage. 3/

3.1 Purpose of the Act

The act sets an admirable but impossible goal: to assure that "no employee will suffer material impairment of health or functional

---

2/ Occupational Safety and Health Act of 1970, PL 91-596, 84 Stat. 1590.

3/ Its annual appropriations legislation, however, has been modified several times to restrict OSHA authority over small businesses, farming, hunting, and other subjects.

capacity" from a lifetime of occupational exposure. 4/ It does not require a balancing test nor a risk-benefit determination. The supplementary phrase in the OSH Act, "to the extent feasible," was not meant to alter this. This absolutist position, comparable only to one provision in the Clean Air Act, 5/ reflects Congress' displeasure at previous, flexible state standards which traditionally seemed always to be resolved against workers' health. In fact, the concession to "feasibility" was added almost as an afterthought. 6/

Business groups did obtain two provisions in the law as their price for support. First, industry insisted that states should be encouraged to assume primary responsibility, thereby minimizing the role of the federal OSHA. Second, because of their distrust for the allegedly pro-union bias of the Department of Labor, responsibility for first-level adjudication of violations would be vested in an independent, three-member panel of judges in a separate Occupational Health and Safety Review Commission. Both of these provisions may be mistakes, and (as discussed below) the first has openly been acknowledged as such by many industry leaders.

Congress did reject, however, an industry effort to separate the standard setting authority from the enforcement powers of the new organization. A special role for the National Institute for Occupational Safety and Health (NIOSH) was intended to assure it a primary position in the standard-setting process. Thus, the three main roles of OSHA are (1) setting of safety and health standards, (2) their enforcement through federal and state inspectors, and (3) public education and consultation.

3.2 Coverage of the Act

In general, coverage of the act extends to all employers and their employees in the fifty states and all territories under federal

---

4/ OSH Act § 6(b)(5), emphasis added.

5/ Clean Air Act § 112, 42 U.S.C. § 1857. There is considerable controversy whether this section, the National Emission Standards for Hazardous Air Pollutants (NESHAPS), was really intended by Congress to have this effect.

6/ The Supreme Court's consideration of this issue will be discussed in a later section.

government jurisdiction. 7/ An employer is defined as any "person engaged in a business affecting commerce who has employees but does not include the United States or any State or political subdivision of a State." 8/ Coverage of the act was clarified by regulations published in the Federal Register on 21 January 1972. 9/ These regulations interpret the coverage as follows:

(1) The term "employer" excludes the United States and states and political subdivisions.

(2) Any employer employing one or more employees is under its jurisdiction, including professionals, such as physicians and lawyers; agricultural employers; and nonprofit and charitable organizations.

(3) Self-employed persons are not covered.

(4) Family members operating a farm are not regarded as employees.

(5) To the extent that religious groups employ workers for secular purposes, they are included in the coverage.

(6) Domestic household employment activities for private residences are not subject to the requirements of the Act.

(7) Workplaces already protected by other federal agencies under other federal statutes (discussed later) are also excluded.

4.0 FEDERAL AND STATE EMPLOYEES

The exclusion of federal and state employees 10/ has been the topic of much discussion and debate. Although Section 19 of the act designates the responsibility for providing safe and healthful working

---

7/ OSH Act § 4(a)–4(b)(2).

8/ OSH Act § 3(5). The appropriations language, as mentioned, has excluded several "peripheral" categories of employers in the past few years.

9/ Ibid.

10/ Ibid, 37 FR 929, 21 January 1972, 29 CFR § 1975.

conditions to the head of each agency and implementing regulations have been published according to various Executive Orders, many commentators feel the individual agencies' programs are inadequate and inconsistent.

In 1980, a new Presidential Executive Order 11/ was issued, which broadened the responsibility of federal agencies for protecting their workers, expanded employee participation in health and safety programs, and designated circumstances under which OSHA will inspect federal facilities. In the operation of their internal OSHA programs, agency heads will have to meet requirements of basic program elements issued by the Department of Labor and will have to comply with OSHA standards for the private sector unless they can justify alternatives.

5.0 HEALTH STANDARDS

Health issues, notably environmental contaminants in the workplace, have increasingly become OSHA'S primary concern over the past few years. Health hazards are much more complex, more difficult to define, and because of the delay in detection, perhaps more dangerous to a larger number of employees. Unlike safety hazards, the effects of health hazards may be slow, cumulative, irreversible, and complicated by non-occupational factors.

If a machine is unequipped with safety devices and maims a worker, the danger is clearly and easily identified and the solution usually obvious. However, if workers are exposed for several years to a chemical that is later found to be carcinogenic, there may be little help for those exposed.

In the nation's workplaces there are tens of thousands of toxic chemicals, many of which are significant enough to warrant regulation. Yet OSHA only has a list of 400 substances with simple threshold limits adopted from the recommended lists of private industrial hygiene organizations.

The promulgation of health standards involves many complex concepts. To be complete, each standard needs medical surveillance requirements, recordkeeping, monitoring, and multiple physical reviews, just to mention a few. At the present rate, promulgation of

---

11/ Executive Order 12196, signed 26 February 1980, 45 FR 12769, superseding E.O. 11807 of 28 September 1974.

standards on every existing toxic substance could take centuries. OSHA has explored various generic or categorical approaches to standard setting, but so far these have been poorly organized.

6.0 SLOW PACE OF STANDARDS DEVELOPMENT: THE NOISE EXAMPLE

Many of the criticisms lodged against OSHA stem from the slow standard setting process, and those complaints are generally valid. A good example of footdragging by the agency is its attempt to issue a noise standard. The Labor Department began regulating noise as far back as 1968 under the Walsh-Healy Public Contracts Act of 1936. 12/ With the creation of OSHA, responsibility for noise regulation was transferred to that agency, and in 1972 NOISH submitted a criteria document, which led to an OSHA proposed standard for 85 dB(A) (decibels). 13/ Issuance of the final revised OSHA noise standard has been promised for so long that predictions are no longer taken seriously. For instance, in October 1976, an OSHA official stated that a standard for noise regulation would be published within three months. 14/

In the meantime, labor leaders were complaining about the delay, hinting that political motives were responsible. 15/ In January 1977, a new administration assumed office that was considered to be more friendly to organized labor; but three years later, they still had not released the long-awaited, or long-dreaded, noise standard. The administrator of OSHA indicated in July 1977 that a task force was being established and that the standard would be ready by "early 1978." 16/ It was not, however, and OSHA did not even reopen the rulemaking record to introduce new information and up-

---

12/ 41 U.S.C. §§ 35-45.

13/ NOISH, "Criteria Document on Noise," 18 October 1972.

14/ BNA, Noise Regulations Reporter, no. 64, 25 October 1976, pp. A34-35.

15/ Ibid., no. 63, 11 October 1976, pp. AA-1 et seq.

16/ Ibid., no. 83, 18 July 1977, p. A-25.

dated cost data until April 1980. 17/ On 16 January 1981, a hearing conservation program was developed, 18/ but the main noise standard is now not expected in this decade and even the present standard is being reviewed for modifications.

7.0 STANDARD SETTING

To meet the objectives defined in the act, three different standard setting procedures were established. These three standard setting procedures are:

(1)   Consensus Standards, Section 6(a).
(2)   Permanent Standards, Section 6(b).
(3)   Emergency Temporary Standards, Section 6(c).

We can all recognize the amount of time that could be expended in this process. There are thousands of chemical substances, electrical problems, fire hazards, and many other dangerous situations prevalent in the workplace for which standards needed to be developed.

7.1 Consensus Standards: Section 6(a)

Congress realized that OSHA would need standards to enforce while it was developing its own. Section 6(a) allowed the agency, for a two-year period which ended on 25 April 1973, to adopt standards developed by other federal agencies or to adopt consensus standards of various industry or private associations. This wholesale adoption pleased industry and removed some of the burden from OSHA, at least temporarily. When the agency found a conflict between any existing national consensus standard and an established federal standard, it was to promulgate the standard affording the greater protection to affected employees. This hurried initial standards package was published for the most part in June 1974. 19/ This has resulted in a list of several hundred common toxic chemicals, such

---

17/ 45 FR 26366, 18 April 1980.

18/ 46 FR 4161, 16 January 1981, amending 29 CFR § 1910.95.

19/ 39 FR 23502, 27 June 1974.

as hydrogen cyanide, with maximum permitted air concentrations specified in parts per million (PPM) and in milligrams per cubic meter (mg/M^3).

There are several problems inherent in these standards. First, these threshold values are the only elements to the standard. There are no required warning labels, monitoring, medical recordkeeping, nor do they distinguish between 8-hour, 15-minute, peak, annual average, and other periods of exposure. Second, being thresholds, they are based on the implicit assumption that there are universal no-effect levels, below which a worker is safe. This is a controversial subject. There may conceivably be a no-effect level for each individual, with a broad average for a large population, but the scientific data is not able to determine what it might be. Moreover, with carcinogens, the prevailing view is that there may be no threshold: the dose-response curve continues down to zero.

Third, most of the standards were originally established not on the basis of firm scientific evidence but, as the name implies, on the basis of consensus among various industry and governmental hygienists. These various lists had been around for years, with no urgency to keep them current. By the time they were adopted by OSHA, many were out of date. They are now frozen in time, probably for decades, until OSHA goes through the full Section 6(b) process, described below.

Whatever the disadvantages, Congress was undoubtedly correct in requiring the compilation of such a list. Otherwise, there would have been no OSHA health standards at the beginning; there are virtually no others even now.

7.1.1 Standards Completion Process

The agency has attempted to deal with one of the above objections to the Standards Completion Process for the 6(a) standards. Over a number of years, OSHA has taken a half-dozen or more threshold standards and added various medical, monitoring, and other requirements. The numbers themselves cannot be updated, for legal reasons, 20/ but at least a broader range of protection is offered to exposed workers.

20/ Since the 6(a) process ended in April 1972, the standards promulgated thereunder can be revoked, reproposed, or otherwise dealt with afresh, but they cannot be modified or revised without going through the notice and comment administrative procedures under Section 6(b).

7.2 Permanent Standards: Section 6(b)

Permanent standards must now be developed pursuant to Section 6(b). This is the present standard setting process. Permanent standards may be initiated by a well-publicized tragedy, court action, new scientific studies, or (usually) the receipt of a criteria document from the National Institute of Occupation Safety and Health (NIOSH), an organization described in Section 13.0 of this Chapter. The criteria document is a compilation of all the scientific reports on a particular chemical, including epidemiological and animal studies, along with a recommendation to OSHA for a standard. The recommendation, based supposedly only on scientific health considerations, includes suggested exposure limits (8-hour average, peaks, etc.) and appropriate medical monitoring, labeling, and other prescriptions.

Congress apparently assumed that NIOSH would be the standard-setting arm of OSHA although the two are in different government departments (HHS and Labor, respectively). Theoretically, OSHA would take the recommendations from NIOSH, factor in engineering and technical feasibility, and then promulgate as similar a standard as possible. However, the system has never worked this way. Instead, OSHA's own standards office has regarded NIOSH's contribution as just one step in the process—and not one entitled to a great deal of deference. Criteria documents vary considerably in quality, depending in part on to whom they were subcontracted, but another problem is that too often they are insufficiently discriminating in evaluating questionable studies. That is, one study is regarded as good as any other study, without regard to the quality of the data or the validity of the protocols. Of course, another factor in OSHA's attitude just might be the "not invented here" syndrome.

Following receipt of the criteria document, or some other initiating action, OSHA will study the evidence and, in theory, publish a proposed standard. Most candidate standards never get this far: the hundreds of NIOSH documents, labor union petitions, and other serious recommendations have resulted in (depending on the count) only slightly over a dozen health standards since 1970. 21/

The proposed standard is then subjected to public comment for a sixty or ninety day period, after which the reactions are

---

21/ This meager number does not reflect OSHA's scientific judgment that the other candidates are unworthy or that the agency has sharply different priorities, although these may be partial factors. More important reasons are: poor leadership, technical inexperience, and a bit of politics.

analyzed and (usually) informal public hearings are scheduled. In a few controversial instances, there may be more than one series of hearings and comments. Then come the post-hearing comments, which are perhaps the most important presentations by the parties. After considerable further study, a final standard is eventually promulgated. The entire process could be accomplished in under a year, but in practice it takes a minimum of several years and possibly even decades.

Even when issued in "final," the process may not be completed. Some standards are obviously defective. The present asbestos standard for example, does not even acknowledge that the substance is a human carcinogen. The standard was reproposed as such in late 1975, then issued as an emergency standard eight years later, only to be promptly overturned by a court as a dubious emergency. 22/

On 10 April 1984 OSHA issued a proposed rule to revise the 1974 standard 23/ but no other regulatory action was taken until a year later when, on 19 March 1985, OSHA announced its plans to issue two separate asbestos exposure standards, one covering just the construction industry and the other covering general industry and maritime establishments.

Final asbestos standards for general industry and construction were finally published on 20 June 1986. 24/ The rule is identical to the emergency temporary standard struck down by the Fifth Circuit earlier. Although most provisions of the standard took effect 21 July 1986, some provisions have been stayed.

EPA, meanwhile, has proposed to ban five uses of asbestos and to force users to find alternatives to asbestos in other products over a 10-year period 25/

Under the Reagan administration, another form of revision has developed. Standards which have become final and survived legal challenge all the way up to the Supreme Court, such as cotton dust and lead standards, have nevertheless been called into

---

22/ Asbestos Information Association/North America v. OSHA), 727 F. 2d 415, (5th Cir., 1984).

23/ 49 FR 14116.

24/ 51 FR 22612.

25/ 51 FR 3738.

question. 26/ With this revision caveat, the following is a list of the final health standards which OSHA has promulgated to date:

(1)   Asbestos 27/
(2)   "14 carcinogens" 28/
        -4-nitrobiphynyl 29/
        -alpha-nephthylamine 30/
        -methyl chloromethyl ether 31/
        -3,3'-dichlorolenzidine 32/
        -bis-chloromethyl ether 33/
        -beta-naphthylamine 34/
        -benzidine 35/
        -4-aminodiphenyl 36/
        -ethyleneimine 37/
        -beta-propiolactone 38/
        -2-acetylaminofluorene 39/
        -4-dimethylaminoazobenzene 40/

26/   47 FR 5906, 9 February 1982 - "While the agency has deter-
        mined that the application of cost-benefit analysis to this
        standard is precluded by the Supreme Court's decision, the
        agency has concluded that it is totally appropriate to re-
        examine new health data and alternative compliance ap-
        proaches, as well as matters relevant to the implementation
        and enforcement of the cotton dust standard." 47 FR 26557, 18
        June 1982—"OSHA is currently undertaking a thorough recon-
        sideration of the lead standard . . . ."

27/   29 CFR § 1910.100.
28/   29 CFR § 1910.100.
29/   § 1310.1003.
30/   § 1310.1004.
31/   § 1910.1006.
32/   § 1910.1007.
33/   § 1910.1008.
34/   § 1910.1009.
35/   § 1910.1010.
36/   § 1910.1011.
37/   § 1910.1012.
38/   § 1910.1013.
39/   § 1910.1014.
40/   § 1910.1015.

-N-nitrosodimethylamine <u>41</u>/
-(MOCA—stayed by court action)

(3)   vinyl chloride <u>42</u>/
(4)   inorganic arsenic <u>43</u>/
(5)   lead <u>44</u>/
(6)   coke oven emissions <u>45</u>/
(7)   cotton dust <u>46</u>/
(8)   1,,2-dibromo-3-chloropropane <u>47</u>/
(9)   acrylonitrile <u>48</u>/
(10) ethylene oxide <u>49</u>/
(11) cotton dust <u>50</u>/

7.3 Emergency Temporary Standards

The statute also provides for a third standard-setting approach, specified for emergency circumstances where the normal, ponderous rulemaking procedure would be too slow. Section 6(c) gives the agency authority to issue an emergency temporary standard (ETS) if necessary to protect workers from exposure to "grave danger" posed by substances "determined to be toxic or physically harmful or from new hazards." <u>51</u>/ Such standards are effective immediately upon publication in the <u>Federal Register</u>. An ETS is only valid, however,

---

<u>41</u>/ § 1910.1016.
<u>42</u>/ § 1910.1017.
<u>43</u>/ § 1910.1018.
<u>44</u>/ § 1910.1025.
<u>45</u>/ § 1910.1029.
<u>46</u>/ § 1910.104.
<u>47</u>/ § 1910.1044.
<u>48</u>/ § 1910.1045.

<u>49</u>/ § 1910.1047. This is the only OSHA health standard for a specific substance issued in the first four years of the Reagan administration. 49 CFR 25796, 22 June 1984. A revised asbestos standard was issued in an emergency form, as mentioned, but was overturned by the courts.

<u>50</u>/ OSHA published a final rule on cotton dust on 13 December 1985 (50 FR 51120) amending the final cotton dust rule of 23 June 1978 (43 FR 27350).

<u>51</u>/ OSHA Act § 6(c)(1).

for six months. OSHA is thus under considerable pressure to conduct an expedited rulemaking for a permanent standard before the ETS lapses. For this reason, a quest for an emergency standard is the preferred route for labor unions or other groups seeking a new OSHA standard. In fact, most of the existing 6(b) standards began as emergency standards under Section 6(c).

8.0 SAFETY STANDARDS

This chapter emphasizes the health aspects of OSHA. Most press attention and the agency's own emphasis since the mid-1970s has been on health standards. Nevertheless, OSHA is also an occupational safety organization. The two parts of the organization are quite distinct: there are separate inspectors and standards offices for each, and the two groups are different in terms of background, education, and age. There are also far more safety than health inspectors.

Safety hazards are those aspects of the work environment which, in general, cause harm of an immediate and sometimes violent nature, such as burns, electrical shock, cuts, broken bones, loss of limbs or eyesight, and even death. The distinction from health hazards is usually obvious, with mechanical and electrical considered as safety problems, while chemicals are considered health problems. Only noise is difficult to categorize; it is classified as a health problem.

The Section 6(a) adoption of national consensus and other federal standards, created chaos in the safety area. It was one thing for companies to follow guidelines that, in many cases, had not been modified in years; it was another thing for those guidelines actually to be written down as law. The act provided two years for OSHA to produce standards derived from these existing standards. The agency should have gone through these standards, simplified them, deleted the ridiculous and unnecessary ones, and promulgated final regulations that actually identified and eliminated hazards to workers. But it did not happen that way.

Almost all of these so-called "Mickey Mouse" standards were safety regulations, such as the requirement that fire extinguishers had to be attached to the wall exactly so many inches above the floor. Undertrained OSHA inspectors often failed to recognize major hazards while citing industries for minor violations "which were highly visible, but not necessarily related to serious hazards to workers' safety and health." 52/

At a conference on Occupational Safety and Health Regulations in 1978, then Deputy Director of the Safety Standards Program at OSHA, John Proctor, stated:

> New standards will be needed to fill major gaps and respond to priority needs disclosed by work injury data or safety research into the causes of injury as well as the means of control or elimination of hazards and risks. The ability to anticipate the potential hazards of new technology or to advance the state of the art for engineering controls and means of safeguarding of exposed employees will be a major goal for OSHA's safety standards staff. 53/

Section 6(g) of the OSH Act directs OSHA to establish priorities based on the needs of specific "industries, trades, crafts, occupations, businesses, workplaces, or work environments." The Senate report accompanying the OSH Act stated that the agency's emphasis initially should be put on industries where the need was determined to be most compelling. 54/ "OSHA's early attempts to target inspections, however, were sporadic and, for the most part, unsuccessful." 55/ The situation has improved somewhat in recent years, for both health and safety, in part because of the recent requirement that some priority scheme be used that could justify search warrants, but that has brought its own problems. 56/

52/ Statement of Basil Whiting, Deputy Assistant Secretary of Labor for OSHA, before the Committee on Labor on Human Resources, U.S. Senate, 21 March 1980, pp. 5-6.

53/ Proceedings of the Occupational Health and Safety Regulations Seminar, (Washington, D.C.: Government Institutes, 10-11 April 1978) p. 15.

54/ For the legislative history of the act, see especially the Conference Report 91-1765 of 16 December 1970, as well as H.R. 91-1291 and S. Rpt. 91-1282.

55/ Basil Whiting Statement, op.cit., p. 4.

56/ See Marshall v. Barlow's Inc., 436 U.S. 307 (1978), which will be discussed later in this chapter.

9.0 Areas Covered by the Standards

To give the reader an idea of the areas covered by the standards, the following is a subpart listing from the Code of Federal Regulations, Part 1910, Occupational Safety and Health Standards. The health standards are contained in Subpart Z; the others are safety related, except for Subparts A, B and C which cover both.

Subpart   A -   General (purpose and scope, definitions, applicability of standards, etc.)

Subpart   B -   Adoption and Extension of Established Federal Standards (construction work, ship repairing, longshoring, etc.)

Subpart   C -   General Safety and Health Provisions (preservation of records)

Subpart   D -   Walking-Working Surfaces (guarding floor and wall openings, portable ladders, requirements for scaffolding, etc.)

Subpart   E -   Means of Egress (definitions, specific means by occupancy, sources of standards, etc.)

Subpart   F -   Powered Platforms, Manlifts, and Vehicle-Mounted Work Platforms (elevating and rotating work platforms, standards organizations, etc.)

Subpart   G -   Occupational Health and Environmental Control (ventilation, noise exposure, radiation, etc.)

Subpart   H -   Hazardous Materials (compressed gases, flammables, storage of petroleum gases, effective dates, etc.)

Subpart   I -   Personal Protective Equipment (eye and face, respiratory, electrical devices, etc.)

Subpart   J -   General Environmental Controls (sanitation, labor camps, safety color code for hazards, etc.)

Subpart   K -   Medical and First Aid (medical services, sources of standards)

Subpart   L -   Fire Protection (fire supression equipment, hose and sprinkler systems, fire brigades, etc.)

Subpart   M -   Compressed Gas and Compressed Air Equipment (inspection of gas cylinders, safety relief devices, etc.)

Subpart N - Materials Handling and Storage (powered industrial trucks, cranes, helicopters, etc.)

Subpart O - Machinery and Machine Guarding (requirements for all machines, woodworking machinery, wheels, mills, etc.)

Subpart P - Hand and Portable Powered Tools and Other Hand-Held Equipment (guarding of portable power tools, sources of standards, etc.)

Subpart Q - Welding, Cutting and Brazing (definitions, sources of standards, etc.)

Subpart R - Special Industries (pulp, paper and paperboard mills, textiles, laundry machinery, telecommunications, etc.)

Subpart S- Electrical (application, National Electrical Code)

Subpart T - Commercial Diving Operations (qualification of team, pre- and post-dive procedures, equipment, etc.)

Subpart U-Y- [Reserved]

Subpart Z - Toxic and Hazardous Substances (air contaminants, asbestos, vinyl chloride, lead, benzene, etc.)

10.0 VARIANCES

10.1 Temporary Variances

Section 6(b)(6)(A) of the OSH Act establishes a procedure by which any employer may apply for a "temporary order granting a variance from a standard or any provision thereof." According to the act, the variance will be approved when OSHA determines that the requirements have been met and establishes that (1) the employer is unable to meet the standard "because of unavailability of professional or technical personnel or of materials and equipment," or because alterations of facilities cannot be completed in time; (2) that he is "taking all available steps to safeguard" his workers against the hazard covered by the standard for which he is applying for a variance; and (3) he has an "effective program for coming into compliance with the standard as quickly as practicable." 57/

57/ OSH Act § 7(b)(6)(A).

This temporary order may be granted only after employees have been notified and, if requested, there has been sufficient opportunity for a hearing. The variance may not remain in effect for more than one year with the possibility of only two six-month renewals. 58/ The overriding factor an employer must demonstrate for a temporary variance is good faith. 59/

10.2 Permanent Variances

Permanent variances can be issued under Sec. 6(d) of the OSH Act. A permanent variance may be granted to an employer who has demonstrated "by a preponderance" of evidence that the "conditions, practices, means, methods, operations or processes used or proposed to be used" will provide a safe and healthful workplace as effectively as would compliance with the standard.

11.0 COMPLIANCE AND INSPECTIONS

11.1 Field Structure

The Department of Labor (DOL) has divided the territory subject to the OSH Act into ten federal regions (EPA also uses the same boundaries), each containing from four to nine area offices. When an area office is not warranted because of a lack of industrial activity, district offices or field stations are established. Each region is headed by a regional administrator; each area by an area director. In the field, compliance officers represent area offices and inspect industrial sites in their vicinity.

11.2 Role of Inspections

The only way to determine compliance by employers is inspections, but inspecting all the workplaces covered by the OSH Act would require decades. Each year there are over fifty-thousand federal inspections, and twice as many state inspections, but there are several million workplaces. Obviously, a priority system for high-hazard occupations is necessary, along with random inspections just to keep everyone "on his toes."

58/ Ibid.

59/ E. Klein, Variances, in Proceedings of the Occupational Health and Safety Regulations Seminar, (Washington D.C.: Government Institutes, 1978) p. 74.

11.3 Training and Competency of Inspectors

There has been a major problem with OSHA inspectors in the past—the training program has not adequately prepared them. In the early days there was tremendous pressure from the unions to get an inspection force on the job as soon as possible, so training was minimal. Inspectors would walk into a plant where kepone dust was so thick workers could not see across the room, and, because there was no standard as such, would not think there was a problem. Yet had there been a fire extinguisher in the wrong place, and had the inspector been able to see it through the haze, he would have cited the plant for safety violation.

> Competency among staff has markedly improved since the early days of the program. Both in-house training efforts by OSHA and increased numbers of professional training programs conducted by colleges and universities have contributed to these improvements. There is also a greater sensitivity towards workers and their representatives. 60/

11.4 Citations

If the inspector discovers a hazard in the workplace, a citation is in order. Citations can be serious, nonserious, willful, or repeated. A serious violation is found if there is "substantial probability that death or serious physical harm could result from a condition which exists, or from one or more practices, means, methods, operations, or processes which have been adopted by or are in use, in such place of employment unless the employer did not, and could not with the exercise of reasonable diligence, know of the presence of the violation." 61/ A penalty is mandatory for a serious violation; a nonserious violation is discretionary. Even several nonserious violations considered together do not make up a serious violation unless the combination somehow would be likely to lead to death or serious physical harm to an employee.

60/ Statement of Lane Kirkland, President, AFL-CIO, before the Senate Committee on Labor and Human Resources on Oversight of the Occupational Safety and Health Act, 1 April 1980.

61/ OSH Act § 17(k).

11.5 Willful Violations

The administration has a powerful weapon with which to threaten those employers who are careless of, or indifferent to, their obligations under the act. Any employer who is aware of a hazardous condition in his plant, yet makes no effort to rectify it, may be held to be a willful violator and penalized as such. A "willful" violation is "properly defined as an act or omission which occurs consciously, intentionally, deliberately or voluntarily as distinguished from accidentally." 62/

> The critical element of proof necessary is that of knowledge . . . . OSHA would have to establish that the employer was aware that a hazardous condition existed and then took no reasonable steps to eliminate the condition. 63/

Penalties for willful violations considerably exceed those for serious or nonserious violations; a penalty of $10,000 may be assessed for each violation.

11.6 Repeat Violations

The same penalty may be applied for repeated violations, with each day being in theory a separate violation. A citation for a repeated violation cannot be issued unless the employer has been cited for a violation, has abated the violation, and has thereafter again violated the same standard or permitted the same hazard to exist in his plant. In the case of a company having multiple sites or plants, in different states or OSHA regions, the issue of repeatedness is more complex. OSHA has changed its definitions several times, and the policy is not yet firm.

When enough time has been allowed for the correction of a violation, OSHA may reinspect the plant to verify compliance with the issued citation. If the employer has failed to abate, a penalty of up to $1000 per day will be assessed "for each day during which such failure or violation continues." 64/

62/ Guidebook to Occupational Safety and Health (Chicago: CCH, 1974) p. 149.

63/ OSH Act § 17(d).

64/ Ibid.

11.7 Enforcement

OSHA appears recently to be getting tough on enforcement. On 1 April 1986, OSHA cited the Union Carbide Corporation in Institute, West Virginia for 221 alleged safety and health violations, including a failure to report injuries and forcing workers to use their "sense of smell" to detect chemical leaks. The $1.38 million penalty is the largest in the history of OSHA.

More recently, OSHA announced that it is seeking $910,000 in fines against the Chrysler Corporation for a "willful" failure to keep accurate records about employee injuries at its plant in Belvidere, Illinois. However, these enforcement measures may be temporary and a reaction to heavy pressure put on it after the Bhopal incident.

11.8 Criminal Prosecutions

OSHA penalties are not the only sanction an errant employer must fear. Private tort actions and other lawsuits are always a threat, depending on state law. But the most feared of all is criminal liability. In the leading case, on 1 July 1985, three executives of a company called Film Recovery Systems, Inc. were sentenced in Illinois state court to 25 years in prison and each fined $10,000 for the murder of an employee from cyanide explosion. The court declared that the defendants were aware of the deadly hazard of their silver recovery system, but did not take adequate precautions and did not warn their employees—most of whom were of foreign origin and unable to read English—that they were handling dangerous chemicals.

12.0 STATE OSHA PROGRAMS

The federal OSHA program was intended by many legislators and businessmen to only fill the gap where state programs were lacking. The latter were to be the primary regulatory control. It has not happened that way, of course, but approximately two dozen state programs, albeit often limping, are still important.

12.1 The Concept

The OSH Act requires OSHA to encourage the states to develop and operate their own job safety and health programs, which must be "at least as effective as" the federal program. 65/ Until effective state programs are approved, federal enforcement of

---

65/ OSH Act §§ 2(b)(11) and 18 (c)(2).

standards promulgated by OSHA preempt state enforcement. 66/ State laws remain in effect when no federal standard exists.

Before approving a submitted state plan, OSHA must make certain that the state can meet criteria established in the act. 67/ Once a plan is in effect, the secretary may exercise "authority... until he determines, on the basis of actual operations under the State plan, that the criteria set forth are being applied." 68/ But he cannot make such a determination for three years after the plan's approval. OSHA may continue to evaluate the state's performance in carrying out the program even after a state plan has been approved. If a state fails to comply, the approval can be withdrawn, but only after the agency has given due notice and opportunity for a hearing.

12.2 Critiques

The program has not worked as anticipated, although almost half the states have their own system. Industry has cooled to the local concept, which requires multi-state companies to contend with a variety of state laws and regulations instead of a uniform federal plan. Moreover, state OSHAs are often considerably larger than the local federal force, so there can be more inspections. Organized labor has never liked the state concept, because of its poor experience with the previous local organizations and a realization that its strength could more easily be exercised in one location—Washington, D.C.—than in all fifty states and territorial capitals. This has meant, ironically, that some of the better state programs, in areas where unions had the most influence, were among the first rejected by state legislators under strong union pressure.

Organized labor and industry are not alone in their criticism of the state programs. Health research organizations, OSHA's own national advisory committee (NACOSH), and some of the states themselves have also voiced disapproval of the state program policy. Ineffective operations at the state level, disparity in federal

---

66/ OSH Act § 18(a).

67/ OSH Act § 18(c)(1) - (c)(8).

68/ OSH Act § 18(c).

funding, and lack of the necessary research capability are just a few of the criticisms lodged. 69/

OSHA had not developed articulate, coherent programs for achieving fully effective enforcement. State plans, in other words, are likely to be defective because they have been formed around defective criteria. OSHA must now go back and redo, to a certain extent, those criteria and reevaluate the state plans. 70/

There is some defense of state control, however. "To the extent that local control increases the responsiveness of programs to the specific needs of people in that area, this [a state plan] is a potentially good policy." 71/ But reevaluation and revision will be necessary in the next several years if OSHA's policy for state programs is to be accepted by all the factions involved.

13.0 CONSULTATION

Employers subject to OSHA regulation, particularly small employers, need on-site consultation to determine what must be done to bring their workplaces into compliance with the requirements of the OSH Act. These consultations should be free from citations or penalties. As in so many other areas of OSHA regulation, there has been a great deal of controversy surrounding the consultation process. Union leaders have always feared that OSHA could become merely an educational institution rather than one with effective enforcement. But Section 21(c) of the act does mandate consultation with employers and employees "as to effective means of preventing occupational injuries and illnesses." 72/

69/ Robert Hayden, "Federal and State Roles" in Proceedings of the Occupational Health and Safety Regulation Seminar, (Washington, D.C.: Government Institutes, 1978) pp. 9-10.

70/ Ibid., p. 11.

71/ Nicholas A. Ashford, Crisis in the Workplace: Occupational Disease and Inquiry, (Boston: MIT Press, 1976) p. 231.

72/ OSH Act § 21(c)(2).

Along with the consultation provisions, the statute provides for "programs for the education and training of employers and employees in the recognition, avoidance, and prevention of unsafe or unhealthful working conditions in employments covered" by the act. 73/ OSHA produces brochures and films to educate employees about possible hazards in their workplaces. But, there are problems at every stage of the information process, from generation to utilization. It can be an overwhelming task to generate all the information needed for a particular hazard. But even when useful and pertinent information is gathered and disseminated, decision-makers may be slow in using it.

In 1979, OSHA instituted a New Directions Training and Education Program, which made available up to $2.7 million in grants to support the development and strengthening of occupational safety and health competence in business, employee, and educational organizations. This program supported a broad range of activities, such as training in hazard identification and control; workplace risk assessment; medical screening and recordkeeping; and liaison work with OSHA, the National Institute for Occupational Safety and Health, and other agencies. "The goal of the program was to allow unions and other groups to become financially self-sufficient in supporting comprehensive health and safety programs." 74/ This program, criticized by some as a payoff to constituent groups, especially labor unions, has been a natural target of Reagan administration budget cutters, but the concept of increased consultation has been given even greater emphasis.

There is also a provision that state plans may include on-site consultation with employers and employees to encourage voluntary compliance. 75/ The personnel engaged in these activities must be separate from the inspection personnel and their existence must not detract from the federal enforcement effort. These consultants not only point out violations, but also give abatement advice.

73/ OSH Act § 21(c)(1).

74/ U.S. Department of Labor, "OSHA News," 12 April 1978.

75/ 29 CFR § 1902.4 (c)(2)(xiii).

14.0 OVERLAPPING JURISDICTION

There are other agencies involved with statutory responsibilities that affect occupational safety and health. These agencies indirectly regulate safety and health matters in their attempt to protect public safety.

One example of an overlapping agency is the Department of Transportation and its constituent agencies, such as the Federal Railroad Administration and the Federal Aviation Administration. These agencies promulgate rules concerned with the safety of transportation crews and maintenance personnel, as well as the traveling public, and consequently overlap similar responsibilities of OSHA.

Section 4(b)(1) of the OSH Act states that when other federal agencies "exercise statutory authority to prescribe or enforce standards or regulations affecting occupational safety or health," the OSH Act will not apply to the working conditions addressed by those standards. Memorandums of understanding (MOUs) between these agencies and OSHA have eliminated much of the earlier conflict.

The Environmental Protection Agency is the organization that overlaps most frequently with OSHA. When a toxic substance regulation is passed by EPA, OSHA is affected if that substance is one that appears in the workplace. For instance, both agencies are concerned with pesticides, EPA with the general environmental issues surrounding the pesticides and OSHA with some aspects of the agricultural workers who use them. During the first half of 1973, there was a heated interagency conflict over field reentry standards for pesticides (see Chapter 10 on Pesticides), a struggle which spilled over into the courts and eventually had to be settled by the White House in EPA's favor. 76/

Thus, although the health regulatory agencies generally function in a well-defined area, overlap does occur. As another example, there are toxic regulations under Section 307 of the Federal Water Pollution Control Act, Section 112 of the Clean Air Act, and under statutes of the FDA and CPSC. These regulatory agencies realized

---

76/ *Florida Peach Growers Assn. v. Dept. of Labor*, 489 F.2d 120 (5th Cir. 1974). To avoid this type of confrontation, in 1976 Congress provided in Section 9 of the Toxic Substances Control Act the detailed coordination procedures to be followed when jurisdictional overlap occurs.

the need for coordination, particularly when dealing with something as pervasive as toxic substances, and under the Carter administration combined their efforts into an interagency working group called the Interagency Regulatory Liaison group (IRLG). Although the IRLG was abolished at the beginning of the Reagan administration, the concept of interagency working groups is a good one. The federal agencies involved in regulation should rid themselves of the antagonism and rivalry of the past and cooperate with one another to meet the needs of the public.

15.0 OCCUPATIONAL SAFETY AND HEALTH REVIEW COMMISSION

The OSH Act established the Occupational Safety and Health Review Commission (OSHRC) as "an independent quasi-judicial review board" 77/ consisting of three members appointed by the President to six year terms. Any enforcement actions of OSHA that are challenged must be reviewed and ruled upon by the Commission. 78/

Any failure to challenge a citation within fifteen days of issuance automatically results in an action of the Review Commission to uphold the citation. This decision by default is not subject to review by any court or agency. When an employer challenges a citation, the abatement period, or the penalty proposed, the Commission then designates a hearing examiner who hears the case; makes a determination to affirm, modify or vacate the citation or penalty; and reports his finding to the Commission. 79/

> The report of the hearing examiner shall become the final order of the Commission within thirty days after such report by the hearing examiner, unless within such period any Commission member has directed that such report shall be reviewed by the Commission. 80/

77/ Ashford, Crisis, p. 145.

78/ OSH Act § 12(a)-(b).

79/ OSH Act § 12(j).

80/ Ibid.

The employer or agency may then seek a review of the decision in a federal appeals court.

One of the major problems with the Review Commission is the question of its jurisdiction. "The question has arisen of the extent to which the Commission should conduct itself as though it were a court rather than a more traditional administrative agency."81/ The Commission cannot look to other independent agencies in the government for a resolution of this problem "because its duties and its legislative history have little in common with the others." 82/ It cannot conduct investigations, initiate suits, or prosecute; therefore, it is best understood as an administrative agency with the limited duty of "adjudicating those cases brought before it by employers and employees who seek review of the enforcement actions taken by OSHA and the Secretary of Labor."83/

Another problem inherent in the organization of the Commission is the separation from the President's administration. There has been a question of where the authority of the administration ends and the authority of the Commission begins. Because of the autonomous nature of the Review Commission, it cannot always count on the support of the Executive agencies. In fact, OSHA has generally ignored Review Commission decisions, and few inspectors are even aware of the Commission interpretations on various regulations.

16.0 NATIONAL INSTITUTE OF OCCUPATIONAL SAFETY AND HEALTH

Under the act, the Bureau of Safety and Health Services in the Health Services and Mental Health Administration was restructured to become the National Institute for Occupational Safety and Health (NIOSH), so as to carry out HEW's responsibilities under the act. 84/ (HEW—The Department of Health, Education, and Welfare —has since become the Department of Health and Human Services.) Since mid-1971, NIOSH has claimed the training and research

---

81/ Ashford, Crisis, p. 145.

82/ Ibid. pp. 281-82.

83/ Ibid.

84/ OSH Act § 22(a).

functions of the act, along with its primary function of recommending standards.

For this latter task, NIOSH provides recommended standards to OSHA in the form of criteria documents for particular hazards. These are compilations and evaluations of all available relevant information from scientific, medical, and (occasionally) engineering research.

> The order of hazards selected for criteria development is determined several years in advance by a NIOSH priority system based on severity of response, population at risk, existence of a current standard, and advice from federal agencies (including OSHA) as well as involved professional groups. 85/

The criteria documents may actually have some value apart from their role in standards-making. Even though they do not have the force of law, they are widely distributed to industry, organized labor, universities, and private research groups as a basis to control hazards. The criteria documents also serve as a "basis for setting international permissible limits for occupational exposures." 86/

To the extent that certain criteria documents may be deficient, as discussed earlier, this expansive role for them among laymen poses a real problem. This problem may unfortunately become worse, if NIOSH declines in both funds and morale. Nevertheless, there is some benefit in having the two organizations separate. OSHA has been able to take action on some matters, such as clarifying that carbon black is not a carcinogen, which NIOSH was bureaucratically unable to resolve. 87/ And NIOSH has not hesitated to criticize OSHA for regulatory decisions, such as issuing no standard on formaldehyde, which the former believed was scientifically untenable. 88/

85/ John F. Finklea, "The Role of NIOSH in the Standards Process," in Proceedings of the Occupational Health and Safety Regulation Seminar, p. 38.

86/ Ibid, p. 39.

87/ Letter from John Miles, Enforcement Chief, to author, November 1982.

88/ See G. Fishbein, op. cit., 8 June 1982.

17.0 REPRISALS AGAINST WORKER COMPLAINTS: SECTION 11(c)

Congress assumed that the workers in a given workplace would be best aquainted with the hazards there. It therefore statutorily encouraged prompt OSHA response to worker complaints of violations. 89/ And since this system could be undermined if employers penalized complaining employees, the act in Section 11(c) provides sanctions against such retaliation or discrimination:

> No person shall discharge or in any manner discriminate against any employee because such employee has filed any complaint or instituted or caused to be instituted any proceeding under or related to this Act or has testified or is about to testify in any such proceeding or because of the exercise by such employee on behalf of himself or others of any right afforded by this Act. 90/

If discrimination occurs, particularly if an employee is fired, a special OSHA team intervenes to obtain reinstatement, back wages, or—if return to the company is undesirable—a cash settlement for the worker. If agreement cannot be reached, the agency resorts to litigation.

This entire system has not worked as expected. First, the worker complaints have suprisingly not been a very fruitful source of health and safety information. Far too many of the complaints came in bunches, coinciding with labor disputes in a particular plant. OSHA has therefore finally abandoned its policy of trying to investigate every complaint.

Second, the 11(c) process has worked slowly and uncertainly, so even though an employee may receive vindication, the months (or even years) of delay and anguish are a strong disincentive for workers to report hazards. Third, it is often difficult to determine whether a malcontented worker was fired for informing OSHA or for a number of other issues which might cloud the employer-employee relationship. Does the complaint have to be the sole cause of dismissal or discrimination, or can some (fairly arbitrary) allocation be made.

89/ OSH Act § 8(f)(1).

90/ OSH Act § 11(c)(1).

Fourth, there is continuing controversy over whether 11(c) should protect workers complaining of hazards to other than OSHA, even if the direct or indirect result is an OSHA inspection. In the Kepone case of 1975, an employee complained of hazardous chemicals to his supervisor, was fired, and only then went to OSHA. Not only was he declared unprotected by the act, but his complaint, no longer being a worker complaint, was not even investigated at the time. 91/

A related current issue is whether an employee who reports a hazard to the press, whose ensuing publicity triggers an OSHA investigation, was protected by 11(c). In one notable instance, OSHA regional officials decided in favor of the worker and won the subsequent litigation in federal district court. The Solicitor of Labor, however, disagreed and attempted in late 1982 to withdraw the agency from a winning position. 92/

For all these reasons, therefore, a worker must still complain at his peril.

18.0 CONSTITUTIONAL CHALLENGES: THE BARLOW CASE

Litigants have challenged OSHA's constitutionality on virtually every conceivable grounds from the First Amendment to the Fourteenth. 93/

The one case that has succeeded has led to the requirement of a search warrant, if demanded, for OSHA inspectors. For diverse reasons, however, this decision has limited impact.

In sustaining the challenge by a businessman from Pocatello, Idaho, the Supreme Court in Marshall v. Barlow's Inc. 94/ decided that the Fourth Amendment to the Constitution, providing for

---

91/ See Marshall Lee Miller "Report on OSHA," submitted to Assistant Secretary Bingham, 20 January 1976, pp. 4-5.

92/ Washington Post, "About Face Considered in OSHA Suit," 20 October 1982.

93/ A good, if dated summary of these challenges is found in Volume I of Walter B. Connolly & Donald R. Crowell, II, A Practical Guide to the Occupational Safety and Health Act, (New York: New York Law Journal Press, 1977).

94/ 436 U.S. 307 (1978).

search warrants, was applicable to OSHA. Section 8(a) of the act, in which Congress had authorized warrantless searches was held unconstitutional.   There are circumstances in which warrants are not required, such as federal inspection of liquor dealers, 95/ gun dealers, 96/ automobiles near international borders, 97/ and in other matters with a long history of federal involvement. And despite the political furor over OSHA, even the John Birch Society has not objected to elevator and food inspectors. Since governmental regulation of working conditions arguably has a firmer historical basis than those other areas, which also have definitive constitutional limits, 98/ requiring a search warrant for inspecting working conditions was not an inevitable result for the court to react.

    While the court held OSHA inspectors are required to obtain search warrants if denied entry to inspect, it added that OSHA need meet only a very minimal "probable cause" requirement under the Fourth Amendment in order to obtain them. As Justice White explained,

> Probable cause in the criminal sense is not required. For purposes of an administrative search such as this, probable cause justifying the issuance of a warrant may be based not only on specific evidence of an existing violation but also on a showing that "reasonable legislative or administrative standards for conducting an . . . inspection are satisfied with respect to a particular [establishment]. 99/

    Moreover, if too many companies demanded warrants, so that the inspection program was seriously impaired, the Court indicated it might reconsider its ruling. This ironically would make enjoyment of a Constitutional right partly contingent on few attempting to exercise it. It is therefore not surprising that commentators, both

---

95/ Colonnade Catering Corp. v. U.S., 397 U.S. 72 (1970).

96/ U.S. v. Biswell, 406 U.S. 311 (1972).

97/ U.S. v. Ramsey, 431 U.S. 606 (1977).

94/ U.S. Constitution, Amendments II and XXI.

99/ Marshall v. Barlow's Inc., supra, quoting Camara v. Municipal Court, 387 U.S. 523 at 538 (1967).

liberals and conservatives, were critical of the decision. Conservative columnist James J. Kilpatrick declared flatly,

> If the Supreme Court's decision in the Barlow case was a "great victory," as Congressman George Hansen proclaims it, let us ask heaven to protect us from another such victory anytime soon. 100/

19.0 HAZARD COMMUNICATIONS REGULATION

OSHA's output of health standards has never been an impressive volume. In recent years, it has tried two new approaches to get around this bottleneck. The first was the cancer policy designed to create a template for dealing in an expedited fashion with a number of hazardous chemicals. This is described at the end of the chapter on toxic chemicals.

The other, characterized by one OSHA official as the agency's most important rulemaking ever, is the hazard communication regulation issued in November 1984. 101/

19.1 Reason for the Regulation

This standard, sometimes known as the "worker right to know" rule, provides that hazardous chemicals must be labeled, material safety data sheets on hazards be prepared, and workers and customers should be informed of potential chemical risks.

How could a rule with such far-reaching consequences be issued from an administration that has stressed deregulation and has deliberately avoided issuing other protective regulations? The answer lies in an almost unprecedented grassroots movement at the state and municipal level to enact their own "worker right to know" laws which, many businessmen feel, could be a considerable burden on interstate commerce.

They therefore lent their support to OSHA in its confrontation with the Office of Management and Budget (OMB) at the White House. A federal regulation on this subject would arguably preempt the multiplicity of local laws.

100/ Washington Star, 2 June 1978.

101/ 49 FR 52380, 25 November 1983.

19.2 Scope and Components

Published on 25 November 1983, OSHA's Hazard Communication or "Right-to-Know" Standard 102/ went into effect in November 1985 for chemical manufacturers, distributors, and importers and last May for manufacturers that use chemicals. It requires that employees be provided with information concerning hazardous chemicals through labels, material safety data sheets, training and education, and lists of hazardous chemicals in each work area.

Every chemical manufacturer, importer and distributor must assess the toxicity of chemicals it makes based on guidelines set forth in the rule. Then it must provide this material downstream to those who purchase the chemicals through material safety data sheets (MSDS). The employers are then required to assemble a list of the hazardous materials in the workplace, label all chemicals, provide employees with access to the material safety data sheets, and provide training and education. While all chemicals must be evaluated, the "communication" provisions apply only to those chemicals known to be present in the workplace in such a way as to potentially expose employees to physical or health hazards.

Special provisions apply to the listing of mixtures which constitute health hazards. Each component which is itself hazardous to health and which comprises 1 percent or more of a mixture must be listed. Carcinogens must be listed if present in quantities of 0.1 percent or greater.

The Hazard Communication Standard is a performance-oriented rule. While it states the objectives to be achieved, the specific methods to achieve those objectives are at the discretion of the employer. Thus, employers have considerable flexibility to design programs suitable for their own workplaces. However, this may mean the employers will have questions on how to comply with the standard.

Limited to only the manufacturing sector, 103/ public employees, the general public, and the construction and agricultural sectors are not covered under the standard. The standard applies only to chemicals known to be present in the workplace and totally exempts those chemicals not expected to be hazardous. Also exempt are wood or wood products, chemicals brought into the workplace

---

102/ 48 FR 53280; 29 CFR 1200.

103/ SIC Codes 20-39.

for the personal consumption of the employees (e.g., tobacco), chemicals specifically regulated by other federal agencies, and in some cases, laboratories.

The purpose of labeling is to give employees an immediate warning of hazardous chemicals and a reminder that more detailed information is available. Containers must be labeled with identity, appropriate hazard warnings, and the name and address of the manufacturer. The hazard warnings must be specific. For example, if inhalation of a chemical causes lung cancer, the label must specify that and cannot simply say "harmful if inhaled." Pipes and piping systems are exempt from labeling, as are those substances required to be labeled by another federal agency.

Material safety data sheets (MSDS), used in combination with labels, are the primary tools for transmitting detailed information on hazardous chemicals. A MSDS is a technical document which contains all known information about a chemical. Chemical manufacturers and importers must develop a MSDS for each hazardous chemical produced or imported and pass it onto the purchaser at the time of the first shipment. The employer must keep these sheets where employees will have access to them at all times.

The purpose of employee information and training programs is to inform employees of the labels and MSDS and to make them aware of the actions required to avoid or minimize exposure to hazardous chemicals. The format of these programs is left to the discretion of the individual employer. Training programs must be provided at the time of initial assignment and whenever a new hazard is introduced into the workplace.

19.3 Hazard Evaluation

Chemical manufacturers are required to evaluate all chemicals they sell for potential health and physical hazards to exposed workers. Purchasers of these chemicals may rely on the supplier's determination or may perform their own evaluations.

There are really no specific procedures to follow in determining a hazard. Testing of chemicals is not required, and the extent of the evaluation is left to the manufacturers and importers of hazardous chemicals. However, all available scientific evidence must be identified and considered. A chemical is considered hazardous if it is found so by even a single valid study.

Chemicals found on the following "master" lists are automatically deemed hazardous under the standard:

*   the International Agency for Research on Cancer (IARC) monograph;

*   the Annual Report on Carcinogens published by the National Toxicology Program (NTP)'

*   OSHA's "Subpart Z" list, found in Title 29 of the Code of Federal Regulations, Part 1910; or

*   Threshold Limit Values for Chemical Substances and Physical Agents in the Work Environment, published by the American Conference of Governmental Industrial Hygienists

If a substance meets any of the health definitions in Appendix A, it is also to be considered hazardous. The definitions given are for a carcinogen, a corrosive, a chemical which is highly toxic, an irritant, a sensitizer, a chemical which is toxic, and target organ effects.

Appendix B gives the principal criteria to be applied in complying with the hazard determination requirement. First, animal as well as human data must be evaluated. Second, if a scientific study finds a chemical to be hazardous, the effects must be reported whether or not the manufacturers or importers agree with the findings.

Appendix C of the standard gives a lengthy list of sources which may assist in the evaluation process. The list includes company data from testing and reports on hazards, supplier data, MSDS or product safety bulletins, scholarly text books, and government health publications.

19.4 Trade Secrets

Although there is agreement that there must be a delicate balance between the employee's right to be free of exposure to unknown chemicals and the employer's right to maintain reasonable trade secrets, the exact method of protection has been under considerable dispute.

Under the standard, a trade secret is considered to be defined as in the Restatement of Torts; i.e., something that is not known or used by a competitor. However, OSHA had to revise its definition to conform with a court ruling which said that a trade secret may not include information that is readily discoverable through reverse engineering.

Although the trade secret identity may be omitted from the MSDS, the manufacturer must still disclose the health effects and other properties about the chemical. A chemical's identity must immediately be disclosed to a treating physician or nurse who determines that a medical emergency exists.

In nonemergency situations, any employee can request disclosure of the chemical's identity if he demonstrates through a written statement a "need to know" the precise chemical name and signs a confidentiality agreement. The standard specifies all purposes which OSHA considers demonstrate a need to know a specific chemical identity.

The standard initially limited this access to health professionals, but on 24 May 1985, the U.S. Court of Appeals for the Third Circuit in Philadelphia ruled that trade secrets protections must be narrowed greatly, allowing not only health professionals, but also workers and their designated representatives the same access as long as they follow the required procedures. 104/ In response to this order, EPA issued on 27 November 1985 an interim final rule expanding and assuring employee access to information on hazardous chemicals. 105/ The ruling also says that the Hazard Communication may not exclude non-manufacturing workers unless the Labor Department can prove their inclusion infeasible. In response to this ruling, OSHA issued a final rule on trade secrets on 30 September 1986. 106/ The final rule narrows the definition of "trade secret" not giving protection to chemical identity information that is readily discoverable through reverse engineering. It also permits employees, their collective bargaining representatives, and occupational nurses access to trade secret information. A final rule on expanding the scope of the industries covered has not yet been issued.

Upon request, the employer must either disclose the information or provide written denial to the requestor within 30 days. If the request is denied, the matter may be referred to OSHA, whereupon evidence to support the claim of trade secret, and alternative information that will satisfy the claimed need.

104/ United Steelworkers of America, AFL-CIO-CLC, et al. v. Auchter, et al., 12 OSHC 1337; 763 F.2d 728.

105/ 50 FR 48750.

106/ 51 FR 34590.

19.5 State Preemption

Several states and labor groups have filed suits challenging the Hazard Communication on the grounds that it preempts many state laws which are more protective. New Jersey, for example, has enacted the toughest labeling law in the nation, requiring industry to label all its chemical substances, whether they are hazardous or not, and supply the information to community groups and health officials, as well as to workers. These groups area also concerned that, because the final standard only covers the manufacturing sector, more than 50 percent of the workers (such as those workers in the agricultural and construction fields) will be unprotected. Moreover, they argue that OSHA will be incapable of enforcing worker protection because of the staff cuts made by the Reagan administration.

The chemical industry, on the other hand, has favored a uniform federal regulation because they believe it will be less costly and easier to comply with one federal rule as opposed to several state and local rules. Industries argue that a number of diverse labeling rules burden interstate business operations and impede worker protection because the laws often conflict or are confusing.

On 10 October 1985, the U.S. Court of Appeals for the Third Circuit ruled that the federal hazard communication standard does not preempt all sections of New Jersey's right-to-know laws designed to protect workers and the public from chemical exposure —only those which apply to the manufacturing sector. In so doing, the court overturned a lower court ruling. 107/ Thus, while some parts of a state law may be preempted, the broader provisions are probably not.

On 12 September 1986 the U.S. Appeals Court for the Third Circuit also found that the federal hazard communication standard does not entirely preempt requirements under the Pennsylvania right-to-know act pertaining to worker protection in the manufacturing industry. However, on 17 September 1986, the U.S. Court of Appeals for the Sixth Circuit ruled that a right-to-know ordinance enacted by the city of Akron, Ohio, is preempted by the federal standard in manufacturing sector workplaces.

107/ New Jersey State Chamber of Commerce, et al. v. Robert E. Hughey, et al., 12 OSHCX 1489.

APPENDIX A

OUTLINE OF KEY PROVISIONS
OCCUPATIONAL SAFETY AND HEALTH ACT OF 1970

PL 91-596, 84 Stat. 1590, 29 U.S.C.
(29 December 1970)

§ 1 Title: Occupational Safety and Health Act of 1970

§ 2 Findings and Purpose
    (a)   States findings—injuries are "a substantial burden upon...interstate commerce" because of lost wages, medical expenses, and compensation
    (b)   States purpose—"to assure so far as possible every working man or woman in the Nation safe and healthful working conditions"
        (b)   (3)   Authorizes Secretary of Labor to set mandatory standards—(also § 2 (b) (9))
        (b)   (7)   "By providing medical criteria which will assure insofar as practicable that no employee will suffer diminished health, functional capacity, or life expectancy as a result of his work experience"
        (b)   (9)   "By providing for the development and promulgation of occupational safety and health standards"
        (b)   (10)   Establishes enforcement program and prohibits advance notice of any inspection
        (b)   (11)   Authorizes state programs, provides grants, encourages improvements in ministration and experimental projects

§ 3 Definitions
    (1)   (5)   "Employer"—anyone, excluding U.S. or local governments, who has employees
    (8)   O.S.&H. "standard"—practices, methods, etc., "reasonably necessary or appropriate" for safe and healthful employment
    (9)   "National consensus standard"—(1) adopted by a "nationally recognized standards-producing organization" under circumstances (2) giving interested persons chance to comment and (3) designated as such by Secretary of Labor

(10)   "Established Federal standard"—any U.S. agency standard or law, as of enactment date

§ 4 Applicability
    (b)   (1)   Excludes AEC authority (42 U.S.C. 2021 under AEC Act § 274)
    (b)   (2)   Supersedes Walsh-Healy Act (41 U.S.C. 35 et seq.), Service Contract Act of 1965, etc., but those standards deemed to be issued under this Act
    (b)   (4)   "Nothing in this Act shall be construed to supersede or in any manner affect any workmen's compensation law or to enlarge or diminish or affect any manner the common law or statutory rights, duties, or liabilities of employers and employees under any law...."

§ 5 Duties
    (a)   (1)   General Duty Clause: "Each employer shall furnish to each of his employees employment...which are free of recognized hazards that are causing or are likely to cause death or serious physical harm to his employees"
    (a)   (2)   Employer shall comply with standards issued under the Act
    (b)   Employees shall comply with standards applicable to him

§ 6 Standards
    (a)   Secretary to promulgate national consensus and established federal standards on occupational safety and health within 2 years of effective date of Act [21 April 1973 cutoff], without regard for APA procedures; if conflict of standards select most protective rule
    (b)   Rules may be modified or promulgated as follows—
    (b)   (1)   NIOSH recommendation, possible advisory committee recommendation for standard to be published within 90-days (limit extendable to 270 days)
    (b)   (2)   Proposal and comment to be published within 30 days, advisory committee 60 days after report
    (b)   (3)   Hearing set 30 days after end of comment period, if requested

(b)   (4)   Rule to be issued within 60 days of hearing completion, with effective date not more than 90 days later

(b)   (5)   Secretary shall set standard "which most adequately assures, to the extent feasible, on the basis of the best available evidence, that no employee will suffer material impairment of health or functional capacity even if such employee has regular exposure to the hazard...for the period of his working life." The primary consideration is the "attainment of the highest degree of health and safety protection for the employee" but other factors include the "feasibility" of the standard. Performance (rather than design) standards preferred, if possible.

(b)   (6)   Applications for variances from standards (temporary)

(b)   (7)   Labels, protective equipment, medical examinations and other items to be in standard

(b)   (8)   Explanation required when standard differs substantially from consensus standard

(c)   Emergency standards for "grave danger" available within 6 months after publication of emergency standards but effective until superseded

(d)   Applications for variances from standards (permanent)

(f)   Provides for legal challenge to a standard to be filed within 60 days. Filing of petition not to operate as a stay of standard unless court so orders. Test for judicial review: "The determination of the Secretary shall be conclusive if supported by substantial evidence in the record considered as a whole." (See also § 11 "Judicial Review" for non-standards.)

§ 7 Advisory Committees

(a)   Establishes National Advisory Committee on Occupational Safety and Health (NACOSH)

(b)   Appoints special advosry committees of up to 15 members to be chosen for standard-setting

§ 8 Inspections and Recordkeeping
  (a)   Authorizes Secretary to inspect working places upon presentation of credentials and at reasonable times
  (b)   Provides for witnesses and evidence in inspections and investigations
  (c)   Empowers Secretary of Labor or of HEW [now HHS, Health and Human Services] to require records and posting of notices, reports of injuries, exposure to toxic substances, and warnings to employees
  (d)   Directs authorities to minimize the burden to small businesses
  (e)   Allows employer and employee representatives to accompany inspector
  (f)   Allows employees to request inspection of violation or imminent hazard
  (g)   Authorizes Secretary to respond to § 8 (f) if he believes such danger exists

§ 9 Citations
  (a)   Details procedure for OSHA issuing citations for violations and setting abatement procedures; de minimis violations need not be cited
  (b)   Requires posting of citation
  (c)   Sets limit of 6 months on citations after violation (§ 9 (c))

§ 10 Enforcement Procedures
  (a)   Notifies employer he has 15 days to contest citation, otherwise a final order is not reviewable
  (b)   Sets procedure if employer fails to correct violation
  (c)   Sets procedure for contesting citations with Review Commission (5 U.S.C. 554, excl. (a) (3))

§ 11 Judicial Review
  (a)   Allows review of court of appeals within 60 days but no automatic stay (§ 11 (b) gives appeal rights to Secretary of Labor)
  (c)   Prohibits discharge or discrimination against complaining worker
  (2)   Allows 30 days after violation to file complaint
  (3)   Allows DOL response within 90 days

§ 12 Review Commission
  (a)   Establishes 3 member commission named by President
  (b)   Sets terms to run 6 years
  (f)   Sets quorum of 2
  (h)   Compels witnesses to appear, testify and produce evidence
  (j)   Appoints hearing examiners who are to produce report which will be final within 30 days

§ 13 Counteraction of Imminent Dangers
  (a)   Gives jurisdiction to district courts to restrain conditions where a danger could "reasonably be expected to cause death or serious physical harm immediately"
  (d)   Gives right of a citizen suit against Secretary of Labor for mandamus

§ 14 Representation in Litigation
       Allows Solicitor of Labor to represent Secretary in civil litigation (cf. 28 U.S.C. 518 (a) exception)

§ 15 Confidentiality of Trade Secrets
       Protects trade secrets (18 U.S.C. § 1905) but allows disclosure to officials and in regulatory proceedings

§ 16 Variances for National Defense
       Provides variances, tolerances, and exemptions "to avoid serious impairment of the national defense" after due process
       Limits effect to 6 months unless notice and hearing opportunity given to affected employees

§ 17 Penalties
  (a)   Willful or repeat violations—civil penalty up to $10,000 for each violation
  (b)   Serious violation—civil penalty up to $1,000 per violation
  (c)   Non-serious—civil penalty up to $1,000
  (d)   Failure to correct violation after citation—civil penalty up to $1,000 a day
  (e)   Willful violation resulting in death—$10,000 fine and up to 6 months prison; on subsequent convictions, $20,000 and one year, or both
  (f)   Tip off of inspectors coming—fine of $1,000 and/or 6 months in prison

(g) False statements—$10,000 and 6 months prison

(h) Violation of 18 U.S.C. 1111 or 1114 resulting in death of official—liable for imprisonment up to life

(i) Violation of posting requirements—$1,000 per violation

(j) Commission's authority to assess all civil penalties, considering size of business; gravity of violation, good faith of employer; previous violations

(k) Definition of "serious" violation: "serious probability" of death or serious injury and that employer knew or should have known of the violation

(l) Specifies civil penalties are to be paid to U.S. Treasury

§ 18 State Plans

(a) State not preempted where no federal § 6 standard exists

(b) Gives state authority to develop own OSHA programs

(c) Provides for procedures and requirements for approving a state plan

(d) Gives opportunity for state to have notice and hearing if plan rejected

(e) Allows three-year probation period after state plan approved

(f) Affirms federal supervision of state's effectiveness and authority to withdraw plan approval

(g) Gives court of appeals review of OSHA approval or rejection decisions

(h) Allows federal-state agreements on partial enforcement pending § 18 (b) decision

§ 19 Federal Safety Programs

(a) Establishes responsibility of federal agencies to maintain effective safety programs

(b) OSHA report to be submitted annually to President and Congress

(c) Amendment of 5 U.S.C. § 7902 (c) (1)

(d) Gives OSHA access to records of federal agencies unless to be kept secret for national interest

§ 20 Research
  (a) (1) Directs Secretary of HEW, [HHS] after con-
      sultation with OSHA, to provide grants,
      research, and other activities
  (a) (6) Authorizes HEW [HHS] to develop and
      update a list of toxic substances
  (a) (7) Directs Secretary to conduct and publish
      studies of chronic or low-level exposures
  (b) Authorizes HEW [HHS] to make § 8 inspections
  (e) Delegates functions of Secretary to NIOSH

§ 21 Training and Education
  (a) Directs Secretary to provide educational pro-
    grams, grants, and contracts by qualified personnel
  (c) Provides for education and consultation programs
    with employees and employers

§ 22 NIOSH
  (a) Establishes National Institute of Occupational
    Safety and Health at HEW [HHS]
  (b) Specifies a 6-year term for Director

§ 23 State Grants
  (a) Authorizes funding for § 18 state programs
    development
  (d) Designates appropriate state agency by governor
  (f) Establishes federal share may not exceed 90 per-
    cent of application for approval
  (g) Provides for continuing grants to states approved
    under § 18 limited to 50 percent

§ 24 Statistics
  (a) Establishes responsibility of Labor Department and
    HEW [HHS] to develop occupational safety
    statistics
  (b) authorizes federal grants and contracts

Chapter 8

SAFE DRINKING WATER ACT

Colburn T. Cherney 1/
Attorney
Ropes & Gray
Washington, D.C.

Jeffrey G. Miller 2/
Attorney
Verner, Liipfert, Bernhard, McPherson & Hand
Washington, D.C.

1.0 OVERVIEW AND BACKGROUND

The Safe Drinking Water Act (SDWA) 3/ was originally
enacted in 1974 as an amendment to the Public Health Service Act.
The act is intended to assure safe drinking water supplies, protect
especially valuable aquifers, and protect drinking water sources
from contamination from underground injection of contaminants.
Implementation of the SDWA was far down on the list of the Environmental Protection Agency's (EPA) priorities—very few regulatory
standards were developed and enforcement was at best lax. In 1986,

---

1/   Mr. Cherney was with the Office of General Counsel, U.S.
Environmental Protection Agency, for twelve years, where he
served as Assistant General Counsel for Superfund and
Associate General Counsel for Water.

2/   Mr. Miller was an Environmental Protection Agency enforcement official for ten years, ending his government career in
charge of EPA's entire enforcement program.

3/   42 U.S.C. § 300(f) et seq.

Congress passed amendments to the SDWA 4/ in an atmosphere of growing concern over contamination of public drinking water supplies and dissatisfaction over EPA's implementation and enforcement of the act. These amendments reduce EPA's discretion in developing regulations and standards, provide stronger enforcement authority, expand protection of sole source aquifers, and create a new program for wellhead protection.

2.0 PUBLIC WATER SUPPLIES

2.1 Drinking Water Standards

The 1986 amendments greatly simplify the regulatory process EPA must follow in establishing drinking water standards. The new process also limits EPA's discretion in deciding which contaminants to regulate and provides an ambitious schedule for regulation.

The 1986 amendments require EPA to regulate 83 contaminants listed in 1982 and 1983 Advance Notices of Proposed Rulemaking. 5/ Maximum Contaminant Level Goals (MCLGs) and National Primary Drinking Water Regulations (NPDWRs) must be promulgated by June 1987 for nine of the listed contaminants, by June 1988 for an additional forty, and the remaining contaminants by June 1989. EPA may deviate somewhat from the list; if the administrator identifies a contaminant which if regulated would be more likely to be protective of public health, he may regulate that contaminant in lieu of a listed contaminant. Only seven such substitutions are permitted, and the schedule for regulation must still be met. 6/ Substitution may occur only after public comment, 7/ but EPA's decision to substitute is not subject to judicial review. 8/

In addition to this ambitious regulatory agenda, EPA must publish MCLGs and NPDWRs for any other contaminant which in the judgment of the administrator, may have any adverse effect on the

---

4/   PL 99-339, June 19, 1986.

5/   47 FR 9352; 48 FR 45502. See SDWA § 1412(b)(1).

6/   § 1412(b)(2)(A).

7/   § 1412(b)(2)(B).

8/   § 1412(b)(2)(D).

health of persons and which is known or anticipated to occur in public water systems. EPA must publish a list of contaminants which
may require regulation under this standard by January 1, 1988, and
update it every three years. 9/ Within two years of publishing this
list, EPA must propose regulations for at least 25 of the listed contaminants; 10/ final regulations are required one year thereafter. 11/

An MCLG must be set at a level at which no known or anticipated adverse effects on the health of persons occur and which
allows an adequate margin of safety. 12/ As its name suggests, the
MCLG is a goal, not an enforceable standard. 13/ NPDWRs are
enforceable, however, and may be promulgated in either of two
forms. An NPDWR may establish a Maximum Contaminant Level
(MCL), which is set as close to the MCLG as "feasible," which is in
turn defined as feasible with the use of the best technology (BAT),
treatment techniques, and other means which EPA identifies. 14/

9/   § 1412(b)(3)(A). Any contaminant that is eliminated from
      earlier regulation by substitution automatically is listed on this
      priority list. § 1412(b)(2)(C).

10/ § 1412(b)(3)(B).

11/ § 1412(b)(3)(D).

12/ § 1412(b)(4).

13/ An MCLG is, however, "enforceable" under the Comprehensive
      Environmental Response, Compensation, and Liability Act
      (CERCLA) because, in selecting remedial actions, EPA "shall
      require a level or standard of control which at least attains
      Maximum Contaminant Level Goals established under the Safe
      Drinking Water Act . . . where such goals . . . are relevant and
      appropriate under the circumstances of the release or
      threatened release." See Section 121(d)(2)(A) of the Superfund
      Amendments and Reauthorization Act of 1986, PL No. 99-499.

14/ § 1412(b)(5). Granulated Activated Carbon (GAC) is explicitly
      defined by statute as feasible for treatment of synthetic
      organic chemicals. Thus, BAT must be at least as effective as
      GAC in controlling synthetic organic chemicals. § 1412(b)(3).

If it is not economically or technologically feasible to ascertain the level of a contaminant, EPA may promulgate an NPDWR which requires use of a treatment technique, in lieu of establishing an MCL. 15/ EPA is also to promulgate National Secondary Drinking Water regulations for aesthetic values such as odor or appearance. 16/ Secondary regulations are not federally enforceable and may or may not be adopted by the states. 17/ (EPA is only authorized to enforce NPDWRs, 18/ and states need only adopt NPDWRs to obtain primary enforcement authority. 19/)

Finally, the amendments establish new provisions concerning filtration and disinfection of drinking water. By December of 1987, EPA is to promulgate NPDWRs specifying criteria under which filtration of water supplies would be required. 20/ States are then to make case-by-case decisions on which systems are required to filter. 21/ Not later than June 1989, EPA must establish regulations requiring disinfection of water supplies, with specific allowances for variances under certain circumstances. 22/

Regardless of one's opinion of these new amendments, it is easy to understand Congress' displeasure with EPA's progress under the act. In the twelve years EPA has had to implement the SDWA, it has established primary regulations for only 23 contaminants or groups of contaminants. 23/ Although Congress adopted the new deadlines from EPA's projected deadlines for regulating the

---

15/ § 1412(b)(7).

16/ § 1412(c).

17/ Id.

18/ § 1414(a) and (b).

19/ § 1413(a).

20/ § 1412(b)(7)(C).

21/ Id.

22/ § 1412(b)(8).

23/ 40 CFR §§ 141.11-141.16.

contaminants, it remains to be seen whether the ambitious program and schedule mandated by Congress can be fully carried out by EPA.

2.2 The Regulated Public

Once promulgated, standards apply to "public water systems," systems which regularly supply water to fifteen or more connections or to twenty-five or more individuals at least sixty days a year. 24/ This definition applies to most industrial and commercial establishments which supply water to employees and/or customers, although only residential systems are required to meet all the NPDWRs. Systems are excluded from all coverage, however, if they: only store and distribute water; obtain water from a regulated public water supply; sell no water; and are not a carrier of persons in interstate commerce. 25/ EPA proposed in 1985 to require certain non-residential systems (e.g., factories, schools) to meet NPDWRs. 26/

2.3 Variances and Exemptions

The SDWA provides variances and exemptions for public water supply systems which cannot meet the primary drinking water standards. If a system cannot meet an MCL despite application of the best treatment technology, it may receive a variance. Cost considerations and the nature of raw water supplies are taken into account for issuing such variances. Variances also require eventual compliance and cannot be granted if it would result in an unreasonable risk to public health. 27/ Eventual compliance may be illusory because EPA may specify "an indefinite time period for compliance" awaiting the development of new treatment technology. 28/ A variance may also be granted to a system from a treatment technology specified by a primary standard, if the nature of the system's raw water supply makes such treatment unnecessary to protect public

---

24/   § 1401(4), 40 CFR § 141.11(e).

25/   § 1411, 40 CFR § 141.3.

26/   50 FR 46918.

27/   SDWA § 1415, 40 CFR §§ 142.40-.46.

28/   40 CFR § 142.43(e).

health. Such a variance need not require eventual compliance with the standard.

If a system cannot meet an MCL for reasons other than the nature of its raw water supply or cannot install a treatment technology specified by a primary standards, it may receive an exemption. Exemptions, however, require compliance within three years and cannot be granted if they could result in an unreasonable risk to public health. Exemptions cannot be granted to new systems unless there is no reasonably available alternative source of drinking water. Special flexibility is allowed for systems that elect to comply by entering into enforceable agreements to become part of a regional public water system. 29/   Small systems may receive renewable exemption. 30/

2.4 State Role

SDWA provides for state implementation, upon application, if a state has drinking water standards "no less stringent" than the federal standards, "adequate" enforcement procedures, and variance and exemption conditions "no less stringent" than the federal conditions. 31/   These relatively lax entry requirements and the fact that virtually all states already operated a drinking water program have led all but two states to assume SDWA primacy. States with primary enforcement authority must notify EPA upon granting a variance or exemption and must submit an annual status report on all public water supply systems within the state. 32/

EPA is to review state-granted variances and exemptions. If it finds that in a substantial number of cases a state failed to include a schedule of compliance or abused its discretion in granting variances or exemptions, EPA may, after notice and hearing, rescind the variances or exemptions or correct their deficiencies. 33/ This is

---

29/   SDWA § 1416, 40 CFR §§ 142.50-142.55.

30/   § 1416(b)(2)(C).

31/   § 1412, 40 CFR §§ 142.10-142.15.

32/   40 CFR § 142.15.

33/   §§ 1415(d), 1416(d).

a particularly ineffective review mechanism, allowing the correction of deficiencies only if a substantial number of deficiencies exist and allowing corrective action only if an abuse of discretion is shown. Abuse of discretion is a tough legal standard and for EPA to find that a state has abused its discretion presents a very difficult political hurdle. This may explain why EPA has only taken one action to revoke variances. 34/

2.5 Enforcement

The 1986 amendments strengthen and streamline enforcement authorities for violations of drinking water regulations. Maximum civil penalties are raised from $5,000 per day of violation to $25,000, and the requirement that violations be knowingly committed was eliminated. 35/ The amendments also authorize for the first time EPA administrative orders requiring compliance with regulations or other requirements. 36/ Failure to comply with such orders may result in civil penalties of up to $25,000 per day, 37/ or administrative penalties assessed by EPA of up to $5,000, after opportunity for hearing in accordance with Section 554 of the Administrative Procedure Act. 38/

Federal enforcement shall be commenced in states with primary enforcement authority, if, 30 days after EPA's notice to the state, the state has not commenced "appropriate enforcement action." 39/

These strengthened enforcement provisions were enacted in large part in response to Congress' extreme dissatisfaction with EPA's enforcement record. 40/ In order to encourage EPA to use

---

34/   51 FR 23468 (June 27, 1986).

35/   § 1414(b).

36/   § 1414(g).

37/   § 1414(g)(3)(A).

38/   § 1414(g)(3)(B).

39/   § 1414(a)(1)(B).

40/   H.R. Rep. No. 99-168, 99th Cong., 1st Sess. at 260 (1985) and S.Rep. No. 99-56, 99th Cong., 1st Sess. at 9 (1985).

these new tools, Congress strongly implied that EPA enforcement was mandatory whenever a violation is detected. 41/ While this may well lead to an increase in enforcement actions, it will not necessarily focus EPA's limited enforcement resources on the most serious violations, and, in fact, could lead to pro forma orders for all violations, both serious and minor.

The amendments also create a new section of the act which makes tampering with a public water supply a criminal offense, subject to imprisonment of up to five years and a fine of $50,000. 42/ Threats or attempts to tamper can lead to imprisonment of up to three years and a fine of up to $20,000. 43/

The SDWA may be enforced by private citizens in federal court. However, they must give sixty days prior notice to EPA, the state, and the alleged violator. 44/

An unusual enforcement feature of SDWA is the requirement that public water supply systems notify customers of violations of MCLs, failure to install required treatment technology, failure to conduct required monitoring, the procurement of a variance and exemption, and any violations of the compliance schedule in a variance or exemption. Notice must be given both in the news media and in customer bills. Failure to give notice is subject to the same penalties as an NPDWR violation. 45/ EPA's regulations attempt to restrict this requirement somewhat. Among other things they allow a state to waive notice if no longer appropriate. 46/ In order to

---

41/ Id.

42/ § 1432(a).

43/ § 1432(b).

44/ SDWA § 1449. For a discussion of citizen enforcement, see J. Miller, "Private Enforcement of Federal Environmental Laws," Part I, 13 Environmental Law Reporter 10309 (October 1983); Part II, 14 Environmental Law Reporter 10063 (February 1984); and Part III, 14 Environmental Law Reporter 10407 (November 1984).

45/ § 1414(c).

46/ 40 CFR § 141.32(b)(3).

qualify for primary enforcement responsibility, a state must have authority to require public notification. 47/

3.0 UNDERGROUND INJECTION CONTROL

The SDWA's most direct effect on industry is through regulation of underground injection to protect usable aquifers from contamination. Underground injection is the subsurface emplacement of fluid through a well or dug-hole whose depth is greater than its width. It can include emplacement through a septic tank or cesspool. 48/ The regulation most directly affects hazardous waste disposal, the reinjection of brine from oil and gas production, and certain mining processes.

3.1 The Regulatory Scheme
SDWA requires EPA to publish both a list of states where underground injection control (UIC) programs would be necessary to prevent endangerment of drinking water and to propose regulations governing the approval of state UIC programs. 49/ EPA listed all states as requiring UIC programs and states were supposed to submit their applications by the end of January 1981. 50/ To be approved, state programs must: prevent underground injection unless authorized by permit or rule; authorize underground injection only where the applicant demonstrates it will not endanger drinking water sources; and maintain records, reports, inspection programs, and other such provisions. 51/ EPA may allow temporary permits, either to authorize existing injection until state permitting can catch up, or to authorize temporary injection when no other means of disposal is technologically or economically feasible. Approved programs must protect aquifers that are or may reasonably be expected to be sources of drinking water supply. These programs must be designed

---

47/   40 CFR §§ 142.10(b)(6)(V) and 142.16.

48/   40 CFR §§ 144.1(g) and .3.

49/   §§ 1421(a) and 1422.

50/   40 CFR § 144.1(e).

51/   § 1421(b).

to protect such aquifers from contamination that violates an MCL or otherwise adversely affects human health. 52/

Congress imposed several constraints upon EPA'as regulations, reflecting deference to state programs and a desire not to disrupt oil and gas production. EPA's regulations are supposed to reflect geological and historical differences between the states.53/ Unless absolutely necessary to protect public health, EPA may not issue regulations that would interfere with existing UIC regulation in a substantial number of states. 54/ EPA is also prevented from issuing regulations that interfere with the reinjection of brine from oil and gas production or gas storage requirements or with secondary or tertiary oil or gas recovery, unless essential to protect public health. 55/

If EPA disapproves a state's application for approval of a UIC program or a state does not seek approval of a UIC program, EPA must promulgate a UIC program for the state within ninety days. 56/ As of November 1986, EPA has approved full UIC programs for 23 states and partial programs for 6 states and has promulgated full programs for 18 additional states and partial programs for 6 states that did not submit approvable programs. 57/

3.2 UIC Permits

Once a UIC permit is in existence, no underground injection may take place except as authorized by permit or rule. 58/ EPA has authorized most existing injections by rule. 59/ In the meantime, injection must comply with substantive and reporting requirements

---

52/　§ 1421(d).

53/　§ 1421(b)(3)(A).

54/　§ 1421(b)(3)(B).

55/　§ 1421(b)(2).

56/　§ 1422(c).

57/　40 CFR Part 147.

58/　40 CFR § 144.11.

59/　40 CFR § 144.21.

that are abbreviated versions of ultimate permit requirements. 60/ Permit application, issuance, and appeal procedures and permit conditions are based on those of the more familiar NPDES permitting program under the Clean Water Act. 61/ There are some noteworthy differences. Substantive permit requirements may be less stringent than established by EPA's regulations if the injection does not result in an increased risk of fluid movement into an underground source of drinking water, 62/ and states may, subject to EPA review, classify aquifers as not being underground sources of drinking water if they meet specific criteria. 63/ Permits may be issued on an area basis as well as on an individual well basis, except for hazardous waste injection. 64/ Short term temporary permits may be issued in emergencies, which include the loss or delay in production of oil and gas, and may be continued until a final permit is issued. 65/

3.3 UIC Regulatory Enforcement

Enforcement is one of the few areas in the UIC program to undergo major modifications in the 1986 amendments. Civil penalty liability was raised to a maximum of $25,000 per day. 66/ In addition, EPA was given authority to issue administrative orders and assess administrative penalties of up to $10,000 per day, up to a maximum total penalty of $125,000. 67/ A hearing is required before assessment of an administrative penalty, but it need not afford the full process of the Administrative Procedure Act. 68/

60/   40 CFR §§144.26 to 144.28.

61/   40 CFR §§ 144.31 to 144.61 and Part 124.

62/   40 CFR § 144.16.

63/   40 CFR § 144.7.

64/   40 CFR § 144.33.

65/   40 CFR § 144.34.

66/   § 1423(b).

67/   § 1423(c).

68/   § 1423(c)(3)(A).

3.4 UIC Permit Substantive Requirements

A UIC permit's substantive requirements depend on the type of injection taking place. The most stringent conditions are for wells injecting wastes classified as hazardous under RCRA. These are called Class I wells.

3.4.1 Class I Wells

Class I wells may not be located where another known well penetrates the injection zone within the area of the zone expected to be influenced by the Class I well, if the other well could act as a conduit for wastes to escape from the injection zone. 69/ Class I wells must inject below the lowest underground source of drinking water, must be cased and cemented, and must have a packer or approved fluid seal set between the injection tubing and the casing, immediately above the injection zone. 70/ The mechanical integrity of the well must be determined from both construction logs and mechanical integrity testing. Also, mechanical integrity demonstrations must be repeated at least once every five years. 71/ The injected wastes must be sampled and analyzed periodically, presumably to determine compatibility with the injection equipment and the injection formation. 72/

The injection rate of the injection fluid and the pressures maintained on both the injection fluid in the injection tubing and the annular fluid between the injection tubing and the well casing must be continuously recorded. 73/ Monitoring wells must be located in underground sources of drinking water to detect fluid movement or pressure from the injection. 74/ A maximum operating pressure for

---

69/ 40 CFR §§ 144.55, 146.6 and 144.7.

70/ 40 CFR § 146.13.

71/ 40 CFR §§ 146.13(b)(3) and .8.

72/ 40 CFR § 146.13(b)(1).

73/ 40 CFR § 146.13(b)(2).

74/ 40 CFR §§ 146.6 and .13(b)(4).

the injection tubing is to be established to prevent fractures of the injection zone or the confirming zone above it. 75/ However, stimulation, e.g., controlled fracturing of the injection zone to increase its injection capacity, is allowed. 76/ Pressure on the annular fluid between the injection tubing and the casing in also to be regulated. 77/ Diesel fuel is often used as an annular fluid, which should be innocuous. Pressure on the annular fluid should be maintained at a higher rate than on the injection fluid so that a leak in the injection tubing will result in a flow of innocuous annular fluid into the tubing rather than possibly hazardous injection fluid leaking out. Injection at a constant rate with constant pressures on both injection and annular fluids is indicative of a properly functioning well. Changes in any one of them may indicate a malfunction and should be investigated. Loss of annular fluid, other than the minimum amount routinely lost through the packer or seal assembly, indicates a leak in the tubing or casing. With good equipment, potential leaks of a few gallons a day can be detected, enabling prompt detection and repair of problems with the integrity of injection well. All of this is not clearly required in the regulations, but should be.

Class I wells must be plugged and abandoned at the end of their useful lives by specified methods to prevent migration of wastes from the injection zone. 78/

Class I wells into which hazardous wastes are injected are hazardous waste disposal facilities and therefore subject to RCRA permitting requirements. For the moment, however, the RCRA program has deferred to the UIC program and exempts UIC permitted Class I wells from RCRA permitting requirements and from interim status regulations. 79/ However, UIC wells may be subject to some of the RCRA interim status and permit requirements. 80/ Any

---

75/   40 CFR § 146.13(a)(1).

76/   40 CFR § 146.13(a)(1).

77/   40 CFR § 146.13(a)(2).

78/   40 CFR § 146.10.

79/   40 CFR §§ 264.1(d), 265.1(c)(2), and 265.430.

80/   40 CFR §§ 265.1(c)(2) and 265.430.

related surface facilities for storage, treatment or disposal of hazardous waste, however, require RCRA permits and are subject to RCRA interim status or permit regulations. 81/ Moreover, the UIC regulations subject owners and operators of Class I wells to some RCRA regulations. 82/ Through a regulation patterned on the RCRA financial responsibility requirements, owners of Class I wells must establish their financial ability to properly plug and abandon the wells at the end of their useful lives. 83/

The 1984 RCRA amendments contain a number of provisions directly applicable to Class I wells. They were prompted by congressional dissatisfaction with the protection afforded by the existing UIC program. The most important of these are the so called "hammer" provisions. 84/ Under these provisions EPA must serially review all RCRA listed hazardous wastes to determine whether injection of other land disposal of those wastes may continue. If it fails to make the determination by the statutorily mandated schedule, injection is automatically prohibited, with no possibility of an administrative reprieve. The schedule for EPA action on injection of those wastes is somewhat different than the schedule for its action on other means of land disposal of the wastes. The schedule for EPA determination is:

(1)   August 8, 1988, wastes containing free cyanides or certain heavy metals in significant concentration, PCBs in concentrations greater than 50 ppm, halogenated organic compounds in excess of 1,000 ppm, specified dioxin containing waste streams, or specified solvents, or with a pH of less than 2.0 and one-third of RCRA listed wastes;

(2)   June 8, 1989, another third of RCRA listed wastes; and

(3)   May 8, 1990, the final third of RCRA listed wastes. 85/

81/   See comments to 40 CFR §§ 264.1(d) and 265.1(c)(2).

82/   40 CFR § 144.14.

83/   40 CFR §§ 144.60 to .70.

84/   RCRA §§ 3004(f)-(g), 42 USC §§ 6924(f)-(g).

85/   With regard to when a particular RCRA listed waste is to be reviewed, see 51 FR 19300, May 28, 1986.

EPA is considering a regulatory scheme which would enable well operators to petition for a determination that their well is not affected by the prohibitions because injected wastes will not escape the injection zone and will not migrate in the injection zone sufficiently to cause damage to public health or the environment. Such a determination may be viable for RCRA listed hazardous wastes because the prohibition applies "except for methods of land disposal which the administrator determines will be protective of public health and the environment for as long as the waste remains hazardous." It is more difficult for the other wastes, injection of which EPA must prohibit "if it may reasonably be determined that such disposal may not be protective of human health or the environment for as long as the waste remains hazardous." Pretreatment of wastes may avoid the prohibition if it substantially reduces their toxicity or mobility, 86/ but this is not likely to be of appreciable benefit for Class I wells.

Other provisions of the 1984 RCRA amendments applicable to Class I wells include prohibitions against injection into salt domes, mines and caves. 87/ These prohibitions can be overcome if EPA: (1) promulgates standards for such injection; (2) finds that the particular injection is protective of public health and the environment; and (3) issues a RCRA permit for the particular injection.

3.4.2 Class II and III Wells

EPA's regulations establish similar requirements for the injection of fluids associated with oil and gas production or oil and gas storage (Class II wells) and for Frasch mining of sulfur, in situ production of uranium and other metals or solution mining of salts or potash (Class III wells). Regulations for Class II and III wells are tailored to the industries to which they apply. 88/

3.4.3 Class IV and V Wells

Wells which inject radioactive wastes or wastes classified as hazardous under RCRA into or above underground sources of

---

86/   RCRA § 3004(n), 42 U.S.C. § 6924(n).

87/   RCRA § 3004(b), 42 U.S.C. § 6924(b).

88/   40 CFR §§ 146.21-146.25 and 146.31-146.35.

ENVIRONMENTAL LAW HANDBOOK

drinking water or those which inject such wastes and are not Class I wells (Class IV wells) are now banned. 89/

Only reporting and notification requirements are in effect for Class V wells at this time. 90/ Because a well injecting a harmful substance, not yet classified as hazardous under RCRA, directly into a public water supply would be a Class V well, this lack of regulation perturbs some. If injection into a Class V well causes a violation of a MCL, EPA or a UIC state may require the owner or operator to obtain a permit or take other corrective action. 91/

4.0 AQUIFER AND WELLHEAD PROTECTION

The new amendments greatly expand the former aquifer protection program and call for states to establish programs for wellhead protection areas. Section 1427 establishes procedures for development of demonstration programs designed to protect "critical aquifer protection areas." Any state or state subdivision may apply to EPA for the selection of an area for a demonstration program. In order to be eligible, the area must be within an area designated as a sole or principal source aquifer. 92/ In addition, the area must either be subject to an areawide plan approved under the Clean Water Act or meet criteria that EPA is to develop related to vulnerability of the aquifer, number of persons using the aquifer as a drinking water source, and the benefits of maintaining groundwater of high quality. The application must contain a very comprehensive plan for managing the aquifer area. 93/ If approved, states may receive matching federal grants of up to 50 percent (not to exceed $4,000,000) for implementing the program.

89/   RCRA Section 7010, 42 USC § 6979(a).

90/   40 CFR §§ 144.26 and 146.52.

91/   40 CFR § 144.12(d).

92/   An aquifer may be designated as a sole or principal source aquifer where the aquifer, if contaminated "would create a significant hazard to public health." § 1424(e).

93/   § 1427(f).

In addition, states must adopt and submit to EPA by June 1989 a program to protect "wellhead" areas within the state from contaminants which may have any adverse effects on the health of persons. 94/ "Wellhead Protection Area" is defined as "the surface and subsurface area surrounding a water well or wellfield, supplying a public water system, through which contaminants are reasonably likely to move toward and reach such well or wellfield." 95/

Both these new programs represent an unprecedented federal role in groundwater protection, traditionally an area of state concern. In addition, their full implementation would seem to involve issues of land use planning, another area of historically local concern. Finally, federal agencies would be required to bring any facilities within a wellhead protection area into compliance with the applicable state plan, unless the President determines it is not in the "paramount" interest of the United States. 96/

5.0 PROHIBITION ON USE OF LEAD PIPES

The 1986 amendments prohibit the use of lead solder, pipes, or flux in drinking water systems (including those in homes and buildings) by requiring "lead-free" materials. 97/ "Lead free" is defined as not more than 0.2 percent lead in solders and flux and not more than 8 percent lead in pipes. 98/ The ban takes effect in all states in June 1988. 99/ Public water systems must identify and provide notice to customers that may be affected by lead contamination of their drinking water, regardless of whether they meet the MCL for lead. 100/ This notification and prohibition on future use

---

94/   § 1428(a).

95/   § 1428(e).

96/   § 1428(h).

97/   § 1417(a)(1).

98/   § 1417(d).

99/   § 1417(b).

100/   § 1417(a)(2).

of lead appears to have arrived none too soon. The media began reporting in November 1986 that draft EPA studies suggest that lead contaminated drinking water may be a significant problem in many areas of the country.

6.0 SDWA IN PERSPECTIVE AND IN RELATION TO OTHER ENVIRONMENTAL LAWS

The ambitious and groundbreaking 1986 amendments have focused new attention on this long-neglected statute. Although EPA's implementation has just begun, it is obvious that the SDWA will be of higher priority and prominence in EPA's planning.

As environmental legislation and regulation further develop, the lines between the "media-specific" statutes become more blurry. Regulation of groundwater contamination under the SDWA is intertwined with regulations under RCRA, both scientifically and legally. MCLGs and MCLs are required by law to be considered in developing remedial actions under CERCLA. 101/ Establishment of an MCLG (particularly if set at zero) has ramifications under other environmental statutes. In short, the SDWA may be on the verge of joining the mainstream of environmental regulation.

101/ Superfund Amendments and Reauthorization Act of 1986, PL No. 99-499, § 121(d)(2)(A).

Chapter 9

MARINE PROTECTION, RESEARCH AND SANCTUARIES ACT

Colburn T. Cherney 1/
Attorney
Ropes & Gray
Washington, D.C.

Jeffrey G. Miller 2/
Attorney
Verner, Liipfert, Bernhard, McPherson & Hand
Washington, D.C.

1.0 BACKGROUND AND PERSPECTIVE

The Marine, Protection, Research and Sanctuaries Act, 3/
(MPRSA), often called the Ocean Dumping Act, was enacted in 1972
to regulate the dumping of materials at sea, preventing or strictly
limiting the dumping of materials "which would adversely affect the
human health, welfare, amenities, or the marine environment ecological systems, or economic potentialities." 4/ The MPRSA is very
different from other environmental laws in a number of important

---

1/ Mr. Cherney was with the Office of General Counsel, U.S.
Environmental Protection Agency, for twelve years, where he
served as Assistant General Counsel for Superfund and
Associate General Counsel for Water.

2/ Mr. Miller was an Environmental Protection Agency enforcement official for ten years, ending his government career in
charge of EPA's entire enforcement program.

3/ 33 U.S.C. §§ 1401 et seq.

4/ § 1401(b).

respects, resulting in a regulatory program which does not neatly fit in an overall waste management scheme. First, Congress did not clearly articulate a fundamental tenet of the law: whether its intention was to end all ocean dumping or to allow it only where it is the best disposal alternative and will not unduly affect the marine environment. This ambiguity has created a continuing tension in the act's administration and interpretation. This tension is highlighted by the comparative inexpensiveness of ocean dumping when compared to other waste disposal methods. It is further highlighted by the desire of land-poor metropolitan areas on the East Coast to dispose of sludge from new and expanded sewage treatment plants built to comply with the Clean Water Act (CWA) and the desire of communities relying on ocean shore tourism to be free of even the threat of possible ocean pollution.

Second, an ocean dumping permit application must document the "need" for the proposed dumping, in contrast with other laws where a permit applicant need only meet technical and/or health and environmental standards without any judgment on whether the permit is "necessary." Moreover, the extent of the "need" to be demonstrated is not spelled out: must there be no other alternative, no other more environmentally preferable alternative, no less expensive alternative, or some combination? This issue has been debated at length within the Executive Branch without creation of a clear and consistent policy.

Third, activities under the MPRSA are also governed by an international treaty, the "Convention on the Prevention of Marine Pollution by Dumping of Wastes and Other Matter," commonly referred to as the London Dumping Convention. Thus, in addition to being subject to the domestic political pressures common to all environmental laws, ocean dumping is also affected by international law-making and politics.

Fourth, there is a fundamental policy anomaly inherent in MPRSA and its administration. The act imposes different, and in most cases more stringent, limitations on discharging materials into the open ocean than other statutes impose on discharging materials into surface waters, which ultimately or directly drain into marine estuaries. These non-ocean discharges have a far greater potential adverse human impact than ocean discharges. Moreover, because marine estuaries are hosts to a very large part of the marine ecosystem at critical junctures, such non-ocean discharges also have a greater adverse impact on the marine ecosystem. Even in the enforcement sections, Congress provided penalties of $50,000 a day

for violation of MPRSA, 5/ while establishing only a $10,000 penalty for violating the CWA. 6/
  Finally, federal court decisions rendered in 1980 and 1981 remanded key portions of EPA's regulations governing ocean dumping. EPA has yet to revise the regulations, creating further uncertainty as to how the program will be administered.

2.0 REGULATORY SCHEME

2.1 Dumping Permit Program
  A permit under MPRSA 7/ is required for:

(1) transportation from the United States for the purpose of dumping in the ocean; 8/

(2) transportation from any location by any employee or agency of the United States or any vessel or aircraft registered in the United States for the purpose of dumping in the ocean; and

(3) transportation from outside of the United States for the purpose of dumping into the territorial sea 9/ or waters contiguous 10/ to the territorial sea.

5/ MPRSA § 105(a), 33 U.S.C. § 1415(a).

6/ CWA § 309(b) and (c), 33 U.S.C. § 1319(b) and (c).

7/ For transportation by an employee or agency of the United States or by a vessel or aircraft registered in the United States, from a country signatory of the London Dumping Convention, a permit from that signatory will suffice. MPRSA § 112(e), 33 U.S.C. 1412(e), § 1411.

8/ "Ocean" is defined as waters beyond the baseline from which the territorial sea is measured. MPRSA § 3(b), 33 U.S.C. § 1402(b).

9/ "Territorial sea" is not defined in MPRSA or regulations promulgated under it, but see the definition in CWA § 502(8), 33 U.S.C. § 1362(8).

10/ The "contiguous zone" is not defined in MPRSA or regulations promulgated under it, but see the definition in CWA § 502(9), 33 U.S.C. § 1362(8).

A permit may not be issued for the dumping of radiological, chemi-cal, and biological warfare agents and high-level radioactive waste. 11/ CWA completes this regulatory picture by controlling discharges to the territorial sea of materials, whether or not they are transported from outside the United States. Fish wastes are generally exempt from regulation under MPRSA, 12/ although dis-charge of fish wastes into the territorial sea or waters contiguous to it is regulated by the Clean Water Act. 13/

Congress charged EPA with the responsibility of establishing criteria for reviewing applications for ocean dumping permits issued by EPA and the Army Corps of Engineers (COE). The criteria must consider, among other things:

(1)　the need for dumping, including alternative recycling and disposal methods and their impact;

(2)　the effect of the dumping on human health and welfare, including economic, aesthetic, and recreational values; and

(3)　the impact of the dumping on the marine ecosystem, including the persistence and permanence of such effects. 14/

In establishing the criteria for review of permit applications EPA is required to apply the standards and criteria binding upon the U.S. under the London Dumping Convention, but only to the extent that in so doing the requirements of the MPRSA are not relaxed. 15/

11/　§ 1412.

12/　MPRSA permits are necessary when fish wastes are transported for dumping into harbors, protected or enclosed coastal waters, or other waters where EPA finds that an endangerment to health or the environment may occur. MPRSA § 102(d), 33 U.S.C. § 1412(d).

13/　For an effluent guideline applicable to fish wastes under the CWA, see 40 CFR Part 408.

14/　MPRSA § 102(a), 33 U.S.C. § 1412(a).

15/　Id.

No permit may be granted which will violate applicable water quality standards. 16/

2.2 EPA and Ocean Dumping Permits

EPA is authorized to issue permits for transportation of materials (other than dredged materials) for ocean disposal and for disposal of such materials in the territorial sea or water contiguous to the territorial sea. 17/

In 1977, Congress amended the MPRSA to require EPA to "end the dumping of sewage sludge and industrial wastes into ocean waters." 18/ It allowed short-term research permits for industrial wastes, 19/ but left no such open door for sewage sludge. 20/ Despite this seeming drastic move, however, Congress changed nothing, for it defined sewage sludge and industrial wastes as materials which unreasonably degrade or endanger human health or the environment, thus returning decisions back to the original criteria Congress charged EPA with developing.

EPA's regulations setting forth ocean dumping criteria are found at 40 CFR Part 227. Subpart B establishes Environmental Impact Criteria, Subpart C addresses the need for ocean dumping, and Subparts D and E relate to other impact on the ocean. Although major provisions of these regulations were held to be invalid, 21/ they remain in the Code of Federal Regulations, unrevised.

If the materials proposed for dumping do not satisfy the Environmental Impact criteria of Subpart B, the permit must be denied without examination of "need" or other factors. 22/ If the material

---

16/   Id.

17/   MPRSA § 102, 33 U.S.C. § 1412.

18/   MPRSA § 112a, 33 U.S.C. § 1412a.

19/   MPRSA § 112a(b), 33 U.S.C. § 1412a(b).

20/   MPRSA § 112(a), 33 U.S.C. § 1412(a).

21/   City of New York v. EPA, 543 F.Supp. 1084 (S.D. N.Y. 1981), discussed below.

22/   40 CFR § 227.3.

passes Subpart B, a permit may be granted unless there is no need for the dumping and alternative means of disposal are available or if there are other unacceptable adverse effects. 23/

The "conclusive presumption" against dumping contained in § 227.3 was held to be arbitrary and capricious and inconsistent with the statute in New York v. EPA, infra. The court held that the statutory term "unreasonably degrade" requires an "informed balancing process," and thus demonstration of need cannot be ignored (at 1099). 24/

In an Amendment to Final Judgment, the court allowed EPA to continue to review permit applications in accordance with applicable law and regulations "except insofar as they establish a conclusive presumption of unreasonable degradation" based solely on the environmental impact criteria. 25/ The City of New York and eight other nearby municipalities continue to dump pursuant to Consent Decrees pending promulgation of revised regulations. 26/

2.3 Dredged Materials Permits

The Secretary of the Army, through the Corps of Engineers (COE), is authorized to issue permits for transporting dredged materials for ocean disposal. 27/ The COE has promulgated regulations applicable to such activity, 28/ which is also subject to EPA's substantive review criteria, 29/ unless EPA waives the criteria. 30/

23/   40 CFR § 227.2.

24/   The opinion was also strongly critical of EPA's generally inconsistent administration of the MPRSA, noting that EPA was unreasonably lenient in some cases and unreasonably rigid in others.

25/   80 Civ. 1677 (ADS) (S.D. N.Y.).

26/   Id.

27/   MPRSA § 103, 33 U.S.C. § 1413.

28/   33 CFR Part 324.

29/   MPRSA § 103(b) and (c), 33 U.S.C. § 1413(b) and (c).

30/   MPRSA § 103(d), 33 U.S.C. § 1413(d), 40 CFR Part 225.

The Court of Appeals has upheld EPA's discretion in promulgating somewhat different criteria for evaluation of applications for permits to dump dredged and non-dredged materials, 31/ but remanded the regulations for failure to explain a rationale for the disparate treatment. 32/ EPA has not yet provided the rationale.

2.4 Dump Sites

EPA is also to establish criteria for designating dump sites and then designate sites for dumping and sites where dumping will not be allowed. 33/ When EPA first promulgated its comprehensive ocean dumping regulations, it had not yet done baseline and other studies necessary to determine whether its criteria could be met. Accordingly, EPA designated sites already in use on an interim basis. Environmental groups strongly objected to continued use of sites which had not undergone the requisite studies and review. Following litigation, a consent decree was entered which imposed schedules for EPA to conduct the studies and decide whether to designate 22 interim dredged spoil sites. 34/ COE may use disposal sites for dredged spoils at locations other than designated by EPA for disposal of other materials. 35/ EPA assumed additional obligations by voluntarily adopting a policy of preparing Environmental Impact Statements (EIS) for all site designations. 36/ This policy has proved to be a substantial hurdle in final site designations.

More than 140 interim dredge material sites and about 15 sites for other materials have been designated, although not all are

---

31/ See 40 CFR § 227.2.

32/ National Wildlife Federation v. Costle. 629 F.2d 118 (D.C. Cir. 1980).

33/ MPRSA § 102(a)(g), 33 U.S.C. § 1412(a)(g), 40 CFR § 228.4.

34/ National Wildlife Federation v. Costle, Civ. No. 80-0405 (D.C. D.C., October 1980).

35/ 40 CFR § 228.4(e)(2).

36/ 39 FR 16186 (May 7, 1974), 39 FR 37419 (October 21, 1974), 40 CFR § 228.6(b).

currently in use. 37/   EPA is currently planning to delegate to its
regional offices the authority for designating dump sites.

Perhaps the most controversial dump site designation involved "dedesignating" a site in the New York Apex, only 12 miles
from New York, and requiring the dumping to take place 106 miles
from the city. Nine municipalities are currently phasing out their
dumping activities at the Bight Site pursuant to Consent Decrees.

2.5 Ocean Incineration

Ocean incineration is considered a type of ocean dumping and
therefore requires a permit under MPRSA. Only research permits
have been granted to date, and extremely strong opposition has led
to the denial of the most recent application for a research
permit. 38/ The great controversy and emotion surrounding ocean
incineration probably means that little activity will take place in the
near future.

2.6 Marine Sanctuaries

In a complementary part of the act, the Secretary of Commerce, acting through the National Oceanic and Atmospheric
Administration (NOAA), is given authority to designate marine sanctuaries and to regulate activities within them to assure their protection. 39/

2.7 Permit Applications

Permit applications must contain general information, as well
as information sufficient to demonstrate that the criteria for permit
issuance have been met and that no additional factors would require
denial of a permit. 40/ This information must include data to support
designating the proposed disposal site for ocean dumping, if EPA has

---

37/   40 CFR § 228.12.

38/   51 FR 20344 (June 4, 1986).

39/   MPRSA § 301, 16 U.S.C. § 1431 et seq., see 15 CFR Parts 935
      through 938.

40/   40 CFR Part 221.

not already so designated it. 41/ EPA has established such criteria and has designated a number of interim disposal sites. 42/ Permit application fees may be specified 43/ and there is sentiment at EPA to amend MPRSA to mandate that fees be calculated to recoup the cost of evaluating and processing the application. In the case of controversial permits, this cost would be enormous.

Within thirty days after receiving a permit application, EPA must make a finding on the completeness of the application, although a completeness finding will not preclude EPA from requiring further information. 44/ Thirty days after receipt of a completed application, EPA must make 45/ and give public notice of a tentative determination on the application, although the notice requirements may be ignored in bona fide emergency situations. 46/ EPA must consider public comments and hold an informal public hearing if a request for a hearing raises genuine material issues. 47/ Permits are to be issued on the basis of the record before EPA, including, if an informal hearing is held, the recommendations of the hearing officer. 48/

2.8 Permit Appeals

Permitting decisions may be appealed in a formal adjudicatory hearing, 49/ with final decisions based on the record of the

---

41/ 40 CFR § 221.1(f).

42/ 40 CFR Part 228.

43/ MPRSA § 104(a), 33 U.S.C. § 1414(a). They are currently $1,000 or $3,000, depending on various factors. 40 CFR § 221.5.

44/ 40 CFR § 222.2(a).

45/ 40 CFR § 222.2(b).

46/ 40 CFR § 222.3.

47/ 40 CFR §222.4 through 222.7.

48/ 40 CFR § 222.9.

49/ 40 CFR §§ 222.9 and 222.10.

hearing, including the hearing officer's findings of fact, conclusions of law, and recommendations. 50/ If such decision is made by the regional administrator, it may be appealed to the administrator. 51/ The final determination of the administrator may be appealed to the applicable district courts of the United States under the Administrative Procedures Act, no other appeal jurisdiction having been established. 52/

2.9 General, Special, and Research Permits

General permits may be issued upon application, or by regulation without application, for material having minimal environmental impact which is disposed of in small quantities. 53/ EPA has promulgated regulations generally authorizing ocean dumping for the purposes of burial at sea, the sinking of Navy target vessels, and disposal of vessels (subject to specified limitations). 54/ Permits for ocean disposal of materials meeting EPA's discharge criteria are called "special permits" and may be issued for three-year terms. 55/ Research permits can be issued for some materials with a term of eighteen months. 56/

3.0 ENFORCEMENT

Surveillance to determine or detect violations of the act is to be conducted by the Coast Guard and other appropriate federal

---

50/   40 CFR § 222.11.

51/   40 CFR § 222.12.

52/   National Wildlife Federation v. Benn, 491 F.Supp. 1234 (S.D. N.Y. 1980); Save Our Sound Fisheries Ass'n v. Callaway, 387 F.Supp. 292 (D.R.J. 1974).

53/   40 CFR § 220.3(a).

54/   40 CFR § 220.3(a).

55/   40 CFR § 220.3(b).

56/   40 CFR § 220.3(e).

agencies. 57/ Violations of the act or of permits issued under it are subject to:

(1) an administratively assessed penalty of up to $50,000 per day of violation;

(2) injunctive relief in court;

(3) criminal penalties of up to $50,000 and/or imprisonment of up to one year;

(4) seizure of the offending vessel; and

(5) citizen enforcement for injunctive relief in court. 58/

4.0 OCEAN DISPOSAL REALITIES

Common sense and congressional mandates are eliminating many of yesterday's waste disposal options. Even with increased waste minimization and recycling, there remains a great need for more waste management capacity. Ocean disposal, including ocean incineration, must at the least be given greater and more open-minded consideration as a possible component to a comprehensive national waste management program.

57/ MPRSA § 107, 33 U.S.C. § 1417.

58/ MPRSA § 105, 33 U.S.C. § 1415. For a discussion of citizen enforcement, see Miller, "Private Enforcement of Federal Pollution Control Laws," Parts I, II and III, 13 Environmental Law Reporter 14-10063 (February 1984), and 14 Environmental Law Reporter.

Chapter 10

NATIONAL ENVIRONMENTAL POLICY ACT

Timothy A. Vanderver, Jr.,
and John C. Martin
Attorneys
Patton, Boggs & Blow
Washington, D.C.

1.0 INTRODUCTION

The National Environmental Policy Act of 1969 1/ commonly referred to as "NEPA," was signed into law by President Nixon on New Year's Day, 1970. NEPA is a short, general statute: it declares a national environmental policy and promotes consideration of environmental concerns by federal agencies. Despite its relative brevity and generality, however, NEPA is one of only a few statutes that have had a pervasive effect on the federal decisionmaking process.

In great measure, NEPA's disproportionate impact has resulted from the vast amount of litigation it precipitated. Consequently, a large body of NEPA case law has been developed, fleshing out and giving specific force to NEPA's general provisions. In response, even recalcitrant federal agencies have incorporated NEPA requirements into their routine procedures, and the early flurry of NEPA litigation has abated.

1/ PL 91-190, 42 U.S.C. §§ 4321-4347, as amended by PL 95-52 (3 July 1975) (appropriations) and PL 94-83 (9 August 1975) (delegation to States to prepare environmental impact statements in certain limited cases).

2.0 OVERVIEW

NEPA is divided into two titles. Title I declares a national environmental policy and goals, provides a method for accomplishing those goals and includes some guidance on the fundamental question of how NEPA relates to other federal law. Title II creates the Council on Environmental Quality (CEQ) and defines its responsibilities. In turn, CEQ has promulgated regulations which guide the NEPA process. 2/

2.1 Policy and Goals

The national environmental policy declared in Title I of NEPA is the first ever enacted by Congress. It announces a general commitment to "use all practicable means" to conduct federal activities in a way that will promote "the general welfare" and be in "harmony" with the environment. NEPA's six related goals are set with an eye toward assuring "safe, healthful, productive and esthetically and culturally pleasing surroundings" for all generations of Americans.

2.1.1 Enforceability of Title I Policy and Goals

An important practical question about the policy and goals embodied in NEPA is whether they create any enforceable "substantive rights." That is, does NEPA require that a federal agency make a particular decision in certain circumstances or does the statute only require that the agency consider specified environmental factors in its decisionmaking process. Although there was once a split of opinion in the United States Courts of Appeals on this question, the Supreme Court has resolved that conflict.

In Vermont Yankee Nuclear Power Corp. v. NRDC, 3/ the Court found that although "NEPA does set forth significant substantive goals for the Nation, . . . its mandate to the agencies is essentially procedural." And in Strycker's Bay Neighborhood Council v. Karlen, 4/ the Court reversed a Second Circuit decision that looked

---

2/   40 CFR § 1500 et seq.

3/   435 U.S. 519 (1978).

4/   444 U.S. 223 (1980).

to the provisions of NEPA for the substantive standards necessary to review the merits of agency decisions. In so doing, the Court ruled that:

> Once an agency has made a decision subject to NEPA's procedural requirements, the only role for a court is to insure that the agency has considered the environmental consequences; it cannot "interject itself within the area of discretion of the executive as to the choice of action to be taken." 5/

Thus, the Supreme Court has held that the policy and goals set forth in Title I of NEPA create no judicially enforceable substantive rights, but impose only a procedural duty on federal agencies to consider NEPA's aims when making decisions. So, although federal agencies are bound to exercise their decisionmaking discretion in ways that are consistent with NEPA's ends, NEPA does not require agencies to make decisions promoting the preservation or protection of the environment.

Because NEPA creates no new substantive rights, NEPA's importance stems almost entirely from procedural provisions designed to insure that agencies do in fact consider the environmental consequences of federal actions before they are taken.

2.2 Council on Environmental Quality (CEQ)

CEQ, established under Title II of NEPA, is charged with monitoring progress toward achieving our national environmental goals as set forth in Section 101 of NEPA. The specific statutory duties of CEQ are set out in Section 204 of NEPA. CEQ is to "assist and advise the president in the preparation of the Environmental Quality Report." Issues as broad as its title implies are addressed in this annual report, and an analysis of the need for any further legislation is specifically required to be included in it by Section 201. It is also the duty of CEQ to gather environmental information and to conduct studies on the conditions and trends in environmental

---

5/   444 U.S. at 227 (citations and footnote omitted). The Court also added that "the reviewing Court may not elevate environmental concerns over other legitimate considerations in its decision-making process." Id. at 228 n.2. See also, Baltimore Gas & Electric Co. v. NRDC, 426 U.S. 87, 101 (1983).

quality. Moreover, CEQ is charged with developing and recommending to the president national policies and legislation to protect the environment.

There has been a wide range of opinion concerning CEQ's performance. It has been lauded for its efforts, derided for being ineffective, chastised for failing to achieve its potential, and praised or criticized for intervening in decisionmaking processes when significant environmental impacts were involved. Although these views are certainly colored by various perspectives, there is no doubt that CEQ has performed unevenly in its advisory role. It is nevertheless true that CEQ studies of particular environmental problems have sometimes been the forerunners to major changes or developments in policy and legislation. Good examples are its reports on offshore drilling, toxic substances, and marine pollution.

In addition to its role as advisor to the president on environmental issues, CEQ has also been afforded the duty of providing guidance to other federal agencies on compliance with NEPA. In discharging this obligation, CEQ has promulgated regulations governing the NEPA process for all federal agencies.

2.3 CEQ's Procedural Regulations

The regulations promulgated by CEQ set out procedures which may be broken down into six general stages of NEPA implementation: (i) agency guidance and categorical exclusions; (ii) the environmental assessments; (iii) the scoping process; (iv) the draft environmental impact statement; (v) the final environmental impact statement; and (vi) the agency decision and its accompanying record of decision. Any project within the purview of NEPA will proceed through these steps as required by the regulations.

The CEQ regulations require that federal agencies simplify the NEPA process by providing broad guidance concerning the degree to which projects are subject to NEPA. Agencies are to establish specific criteria for classes of action: (i) which usually require environmental impact statements; (ii) which require neither an environmental impact statement nor an environmental assessment (the "categorical exclusion"); and (iii) which normally require an environmental assessment (EA) but do not necessarily require an environmental impact statement. 6/ The categorical exclusion

---

6/ 40 CFR § 1507.3(b)(2).

generally provides the first clearly defined exemption for a federal action. If the agency has determined by way of a regulation that the subject is one for which neither an EA nor an EIS is necessary, 7/ the action may proceed, in many instances, without the necessity of complying with further NEPA requirements. Thus, for many routine activities, agencies have specified that an EIS will not be required.

For federal actions that are neither within categorical exclusions nor within the category of actions designated by the agency as requiring an EIS, an "environmental assessment" is necessary. 8/ The purpose of an environmental assessment is to provide the basis for determining whether an environmental impact statement is necessary. 9/ The environmental assessment is a concise public document which provides sufficient evidence and analysis to determine whether to prepare an environmental impact statement. 10/ The document must include a discussion of the need for the proposal, the alternatives considered, the environmental impacts of the proposed action and alternatives, and a listing of agencies and persons consulted. 11/ While there are no limits on an environmental

---

7/   40 CFR § 1508.4 defines "categorical exclusion" in pertinent part to mean a category of actions which do not cumulatively have a significant effect on the human environment and which have been found to have no such effect on procedures adopted by a federal agency in implementation of these regulations (§ 1507.3) and, for which, therefore, neither an environmental assessment nor an environmental impact statement is required. 40 CFR § 1508.4. The regulations permit the agency to conduct an environmental assessment even for a categorical exclusion and require that the procedures include a provision for extraordinary circumstances when an excluded subject has a significant environmental effect. Id.

8/   40 CFR § 1501.4(b).

9/   40 CFR § 1501.4(c).

10/   40 CFR § 1508.9(a).

11/   Id.

assessment's length, the CEQ has recommended that the length be no more than 10 to 15 pages. 12/

If the agency finds, based on the environmental assessment, that the project does not significantly affect the environment, the agency must issue a "finding of no significant impact" which briefly explains why an EIS is not necessary. 13/

Assuming that the agency determines that an EIS is necessary, it must publish a notice of intent 14/ and begin the next stage mandated by CEQ regulations—the scoping process. The scoping process is a preliminary step employed to foster participation and focus the agency's EIS. 15/ The agency must determine in the scope of the EIS the range of actions, alternatives and impacts to be considered in an EIS. 16/ The regulations specify that an agency must consider three types of actions: (i) connected actions; 17/ (ii) cumulative actions; and (iii) similar actions. 18/ Likewise, CEQ has broken down the alternatives to be considered in the scoping process into: (i) the no action alternative; (ii) other reasonable courses of

---

12/ See Forty Most Asked Questions Concerning CEQ's National Environmental Policy Act Regulations, 46 FR 18037 (March 23, 1981).

13/ 40 CFR §§ 1501.4(a), 1508.3.

14/ 40 CFR § 1501.7. The "notice of intent" must (i) describe the proposed action and possible alternatives; (ii) describe the proposed scoping process; and (iii) provide the name and address of a person within the agency to contact concerning the EIS. 40 CFR § 1508.22.

15/ 40 CFR § 1501.7.

16/ 40 CFR § 1508.25.

17/ The CEQ has specified that actions are connected if (i) they automatically trigger other actions; (ii) they cannot or will not proceed unless other actions are taken previously or simultaneously; and (iii) they are interdependent parts of a larger action and depend on the larger action for their justification. 40 CFR § 1508.25(a)(1).

18/ 40 CFR § 1508.25(a).

action; and (iii) mitigation measures. 19/ Finally, the regulations specify three separate categories of impacts which must be addressed in the EIS's scope: (i) direct impacts; (ii) indirect impacts; and (iii) cumulative impacts. 20/

The scoping process provides an early opportunity to influence the subject matter of the EIS. Participants wishing to influence the decision may take the opportunity to bring subjects to the agency's attention. Indeed, one might argue that without a proposal that a certain topic be considered within the scope of the EIS, the absence of the topic in the EIS may not be used to overturn the agency decision. 21/ In addition to raising subjects for the EIS, affected parties may request time limits and page limits. Normally the agency is required to set such limits if requested. 22/

Once the scoping process is completed, the agency begins preparation of the EIS. First, a draft EIS is prepared. The draft EIS is prepared to disclose all major points of view on the environmental impacts of the alternatives considered. The draft EIS must "fulfill and satisfy to the fullest extent possible" the requirements of a final EIS. 23/ The agency must solicit comments from various governmental entities and affected parties, 24/ and the draft EIS is subject to a comment period of at least 45 days. 25/

The final environmental impact statement responds to comments on the draft EIS 26/ and meets the criteria set out in Section

---

19/ 40 CFR § 1508.25(b).

20/ 40 CFR § 1508.25(c).

21/ See Vermont Yankee Nuclear Power Corp. v. NRDC, 435 U.S. 519, 551-54 (1977).

22/ 40 CFR § 1501.7(b); 1501.8.

23/ 40 CFR § 1502.9(a).

24/ 40 CFR § 1503.1(a). The provision implements NEPA § 102(2)(C) which requires consultation with and comments from various federal, state and local agencies.

25/ 40 CFR § 1506.10(c).

26/ 40 CFR § 1502.9(b).

102(2)(C) of NEPA. 27/ In general, the final EIS must address the (i) environmental impact of an action; (ii) any unavoidable adverse environmental impacts of the action; (iii) alternatives to the proposed action; (iv) the relationship between short-term uses and long-term productivity; and (v) any irreversible and unretrievable commitments of resources involved in the proposed action. 28/

The regulations prescribe a format for EISs 29/ and some general mechanics of the document. 30/ More substantively, the regulations provide guidance as to the alternatives considered, the affected environment and environmental consequences.

The regulations require that the alternatives in an EIS be presented in a comparative form, "sharply defining the issues and providing a clear basis for choice among options." 31/ The agency

---

27/ NEPA § 102(2)(C), 42 U.S.C. § 4332(2)(C), provides, in pertinent part, that:
all agencies of the federal government shall
(C) Include in every recommendation or report on proposals for legislation and other major Federal actions significantly affecting the quality of the human environment, a detailed statement by the responsible official on—
(i) The environmental impact of the proposed action; (ii) Any adverse environmental effects which cannot be avoided should the proposal be implemented; (iii) Alternatives to the proposed action; (iv) The relationship between local short-term uses of man's environment and the maintenance and enhancement of long-term productivity; and (v) Any irreversible and irretrievable commitments of resources which would be involved in the proposed action should it be implemented.

28/ NEPA § 102(2)(C), 42 U.S.C. § 4332(2)(C).

29/ 40 CFR § 1502.10; see also 40 CFR § 1502.11 (cover sheet requirements).

30/ 40 CFR § 1502.7 dictates that an EIS should not "normally" exceed 150 pages in length. 40 CFR § 1502.8 requires that the agency employ "plain language" and 40 CFR § 1502.12 mandates inclusion of a summary in the EIS. There is also a requirement that preparers be listed, 40 CFR § 1502.17, and directors concerning the appendix, 40 CFR § 1502.18.

31/ 40 CFR § 1502.14.

must: (i) "rigorously" explore and objectively evaluate all reasonable alternatives; (ii) devote substantial treatment to each alternative considered in detail; (iii) include the "no action" alternative; (iv) include reasonable alternatives outside the agency's jurisdiction; (v) identify, if possible, the agency's preferred alternative; and (vi) include appropriate mitigation measures. 32/

The CEQ has prescribed that any EIS is to "succinctly describe" the environment of affected areas. Data and analyses concerning the affected environment are to be commensurate with the importance of the impact; less important material is to be summarized, consolidated or simply referenced. 33/

Discussion of the environmental consequences of an action within the EIS is to be a consolidation of the consideration of criteria within Section 102(2)(C) of NEPA. 34/ The discussion must include: (i) direct effects; (ii) indirect effects; (iii) possible conflicts with land use plans and controls for the area concerned; (iv) environmental effects; (v) energy requirements and conservation potential of various alternatives and mitigation measures; (vi) resource requirements and conservation potential of alternatives and mitigation measures; (vii) urban quality, historic and cultural resources and the design of the built environment; and (viii) means to mitigate adverse environmental impacts. 35/

Beyond this direction, the environmental effects which an agency must consider are not clearly delineated in the regulations. However, the Supreme Court cast some light on the subject in Metropolitan Edison Co. v. People Against Nuclear Energy 36/ which confronted the argument that damage to psychological health and community well-being are among the environmental effects which

---

32/ 40 CFR § 1502.14.

33/ 40 CFR § 1502.15. See Oregon Natural Resources Council v. Marsh, 628 F.Supp. 1557 (D. Or. 1986) (holding that description of the affected area is sufficient if it provides accurate basis for decisionmakers to evaluate environmental consequences).

34/ 40 CFR § 1502.16.

35/ 40 CFR § 1502.16.

36/ 460 U.S. 766 (1983).

must be considered in an EIS. The court held that the statute was intended to embrace only effects on the "physical environment." While human health and welfare are goals of NEPA, Congress intended to reach those ends by protecting the physical environment. Hence, the court reasoned that the terms "environmental effects" and "environmental impacts" in Section 102(2)(C) should be read to require a reasonably close causal relationship between a change in the physical environment and the effect at issue. Because the psychological health damage at issue was so attenuated from the federal action at issue, the causal relationship was not sufficiently close to bring it within the reach of NEPA.

Recently CEQ modified the provisions governing instances when information on environmental consequences is lacking. Where there is incomplete or unavailable information concerning reasonably foreseeable significant environmental effects of an alternative, an agency is to disclose the lack of information. 37/ If this information is essential to a reasoned choice among alternatives and the overall cost to obtain the information is not exorbitant, the agency must include the information in the EIS. If such information cannot be obtained because the cost of obtaining it would be exorbitant or the means to obtain it are not known, the agency must include in the EIS, in addition to a declaration that the information is lacking, a statement of the relevance of the information to evaluating foreseeable significant adverse impacts and the agency's evaluation of such impacts based upon theoretical approaches or research methods generally accepted in the scientific community. 38/

This 1986 regulation supplants its predecessor, which called for a "worst case analysis" in certain circumstances. 39/ The original regulation spawned a great deal of litigation 40/ and

---

37/ 40 CFR § 1502.22.

38/ 40 CFR § 1502.22. The provision applies to "reasonably foreseeable" impacts, which includes impacts which have a catastrophic effect, even if the probability of occurrence is low, so long as the analysis is supported by credible scientific evidence, is not based on pure conjecture and is within the rule of reason.

39/ 40 CFR § 1502.22 (1985).

40/ E.g., Save our Ecosystems v. Clark, 747 F.2d 1240 (9th Cir. 1984); Sierra Club v. Sigler, 695 F.2d 957, 972 (5th Cir. 1983).

presented agencies with a regulatory mandate which was ambiguous at best. 41/ Whether the new regulation will reduce litigation over instances when information is unavailable remains to be seen.

Once the EIS is finalized an agency is to consider its contents in making its decision on the action at issue. 42/ At the time of its decision the agency is to devise a "record of decision"—a concise statement of its decision discussing its choice among alternatives and the means employed to mitigate or minimize environmental harm. 43/ The regulations provide that, in most circumstances, the decision on the action may not be taken or recorded until the later of either ninety days after notice of the draft EIS is provided or thirty days after notice of the final EIS is provided. 44/

3.0 NEPA'S RELATIONSHIP WITH OTHER FEDERAL LAW

One of the most fundamental NEPA concerns is its relationship with other federal law. More specifically, the question is this: How is NEPA to be construed with other federal laws that govern federal agencies?

Although the Supreme Court has held that a _final_ EIS need not be prepared until an agency makes a recommendation or report on a proposal, 45/ NEPA requires all federal agencies to <u>consider</u>

41/ As a condition to proceed with an agency action, the regulation required a "worst case analysis" and its probability when information relevant to adverse impacts is important to the decision and is not known. The probability of the "worst case" was not addressed. Hence, agencies found it difficult to discern the extent to which they were required to analyze very remote environmental effects. See also 51 FR 15618, 15625 (April 25, 1986) (explaining the 1986 regulation's approach).

42/ See generally, 40 CFR § 1501.1.

43/ 40 CFR § 1505.2.

44/ 40 CFR § 1506.10(b).

45/ Aberdeen & Rockfish RR. Co. v. Students Challenging Regulatory Agency Procedures (SCRAP II), 422 U.S. 289 (1975), reaffirmed in dicta in Kleppe v. Sierra Club, 427 U.S. 390 (1976).

environmental impacts at every important stage in the decisionmaking process. This requirement is not explicitly set forth in
NEPA, but it is implicit in its various provisions. It was clearly
enunciated in the still definitive case, Calvert Cliffs' Coordinating
Committee v. AEC. 46/
     Calvert Cliffs' involved Atomic Energy Commission (AEC)
rules implementing NEPA, which, in part, provided that if no party
to a proceeding raised any environmental issue, environmental issues
would not be considered in the decisionmaking process. In reviewing
this rule, the U.S. Court of Appeals for the District of Columbia
Circuit Court said, "We believe that the Commission's crabbed interpretation of NEPA makes a mockery of the Act," 47/ and proceeded
to wonder out loud what possible purpose there could be in requiring
an EIS to "accompany the proposal through the existing agency
review process" or, indeed, in requiring EISs at all, if agencies could
simply ignore their contents. The court then found that:

> NEPA require[s] the . . . agencies to consider environ-
> mental issues just as they consider other matters within
> their mandate. 48/

Thus, Calvert Cliffs' added NEPA's environmental impact provisions
to the decisionmaking criteria set forth in other federal law.
     If NEPA requires agencies to consider environmental factors
when making decisions, does NEPA then expand the authority of
federal agencies beyond what is granted them under other federal
law? There is no case holding that NEPA gives an agency any direct
authority not otherwise afforded it by other federal law. NEPA,
however, was enacted in order to provide federal agencies with a
new tool for protecting the environment, and the authority to deny
agency approval of actions that would result in unacceptable environmental consequences is implicit in the requirement that agencies
consider the environmental consequences of an action before deciding to proceed with it. Thus, an agency's authority does appear to be

---

46/ 449 F.2d 1109 (D.C. Cir. 1971), cert. denied, 404 U.S. 942
   (1972).

47/ 449 F.2d at 1117.

48/ 449 F.2d at 1112 (emphasis supplied).

expanded under NEPA, for an agency might well decide not to proceed with a project based on environmental concerns that, but for NEPA, might be found to be beyond the agency's power to consider.

A related issue is whether when an agency believes, on the basis of an EIS or otherwise, that on balance it should grant its approval if certain conditions are satisfied, but the agency does not have the regular, i.e., non-NEPA based, statutory authority to impose such conditions. For example, the United States Environmental Protection Agency (EPA) once conditioned a grant to Sussex County, Delaware for the construction of a sewage-treatment facility on the County's agreement to halt all rezoning plans (thus effectively blocking major planned construction) until a comprehensive land-use plan was completed. Did NEPA grant EPA the authority to lawfully withhold its approval until this condition was satisfied? The issue was never litigated. How far an agency can go in expanding its authority under the aegis of NEPA, then, remains an open question of considerable importance. 49/

Conflicts between NEPA and provisions of other statutes is also a fundamental concern. Posed directly, the question is: does NEPA override another federal law when the two are in irreconcilable conflict? Sections 102(1), 103, 104 and 105 of NEPA all bear on this question. Section 102 "authorizes and directs that, to the fullest extent possible: (1) the policies, regulations, and public laws of the United States shall be interpreted and administered in accordance with the policies set forth in this Act." Section 103 required all federal agencies to recommend to the president by 1 July 1971, the changes necessary to bring their authority and policies into conformity with NEPA. Section 104 provides that nothing in Sections 102 or 103 changes the specific statutory obligations of any federal agency to comply with other laws protecting the environment, to coordinate or consult with other federal or state agencies, or to act in accordance with the recommendations or certifications of any other

_____

49/ Similarly, EPA maintains that is has the authority under NEPA to impose non-water quality related conditions in NPDES discharge permits under the Clean Water Act, based upon the findings of the EIS, or even to deny a permit on that basis. The agency has consistently asserted this authority in administering its permitting regulations under the Clean Water Act. See 49 FR 37998, 38016-38018 (September 26, 1984).

federal or state agency. Section 105 simply states that the policies and goals set forth in NEPA are "supplementary" to the existing authorizations of federal agencies. These are the statutory provisions upon which the Supreme Court has twice rested decisions finding that NEPA does not override another federal law when the two conflict.

At issue in United States v. Students Challenging Regulatory Agency Procedures (SCRAP I) 50/ was a District Court decision concerning the Interstate Commerce Commission's (ICC) authorization, without first preparing an EIS, of a railroad surcharge. The District Court held that NEPA empowered it to issue an injunction against the Commission's action, notwithstanding another federal law vesting sole and exclusive power from the judiciary. Reversing that decision, the Supreme Court held that NEPA was not intended to supplant other statutes. 51/

50/ 412 U.S. 669 (1973).

51/ The court held that, The statutory language, in fact, indicates that NEPA was not intended to repeal by implication any other statute. Thus, Section 105 specifies that "the policies and goals set forth in NEPA are supplementary to those set forth in existing authorizations of federal agencies," and . . . Section 104 instructs that the Act "shall not in any way affect the specific statutory obligations of any Federal agency . . ." Rather than providing for any wholesale overruling of prior law, Section 103 of NEPA requires all federal agencies to review their "present statutory authority, administrative regulations, and current policies and procedures for the purpose of determining whether there are any deficiencies or inconsistencies therein which prohibit full compliance with the purposes and provisions of NEPA and shall propose to the President . . . such measures as may be necessary to bring their authority and policies into conformity with the intent, purposes, and procedures set forth in NEPA . . . It would be anamolous if Congress had provided at one and the same time that Federal agencies, which have the primary responsibility for the implementation of NEPA, must comply with the present law and ask for any necessary new legislation, but that courts may simply ignore what we described in the previous Arrow case as "a clear congressional purpose to oust judicial power. . . ." 412 U.S. at 694-695 (emphasis supplied and footnote omitted).

In Flint Ridge Development Co. v. Scenic Rivers Association, et al., 52/ the Supreme Court reiterated the holding, but this time relied entirely on Section 102. Flint Ridge addressed the claim of environmental organizations that an EIS was required for approval of a land development project on which an antifraud disclosure document had been filed with the Department of Housing and Urban Development pursuant to the Interstate Land Sales Full Disclosure Act. That act provides that disclosure documents automatically become effective thirty days after filing (thus allowing sales in interstate commerce), unless suspended because of inadequate disclosure. The document at issue was not found to be an inadequate disclosure, nor was it disputed that an EIS could not be prepared within the thirty day period.

The Supreme Court, relying upon the principle announced in SCRAP I, and the language in Section 102, stating that "to the fullest extent possible" (emphasis supplied) all federal agencies shall comply with NEPA's requirements, and concluded:

> Section 102 recognizes . . . that where a clear and unavoidable conflict in statutory authority exists, NEPA must give way. 53/

Thus, it is clear that NEPA will not prevail when it is in irreconcilable conflict with another federal law.

4.0 PROPOSED ACTIONS REQUIRING AN EIS

Section 102(2)(C) requires that an EIS shall be "included in every recommendation or report on proposals for legislation and other major federal actions significantly affecting the quality of the human environment."

Because NEPA makes no pretense of applying its requirements to other than federal agencies, perhaps the best first step toward deciding whether an EIS is required is to determine whether "federal" action is involved. Federal action obviously includes what

---

52/ 426 U.S. 776 (1976).

53/ 426 U.S. at 788.

is undertaken directly by the federal agencies, including operation of programs, construction of facilities, and the provision of funding to others. 54/ Federal action also clearly includes a federal agency's decision on whether to grant its required permission for activities of others, such as private businesses or state or local governments. The CEQ regulations have amplified the judicial interpretation of this element. As a general matter the regulation notes that "major Federal action" encompasses "actions which may be major and which are potentially subject to Federal control and responsibility." 55/

In addition to federal involvement, there must also be a "proposal" for action before preparation of an EIS will be required. 56/ The Sierra Club contended that Interior Secretary Kleppe was required to prepare an EIS on coal development in the Northern Great Plains region of the country. The Supreme Court carefully reviewed Interior's past and contemplated actions. It found that there was no proposal for regional action concerning coal development. All Interior proposals were for actions that were either local or national in scope, even though such actions affected the Northern Great Plains region. Thus, because there was no proposal for regional action, the court held no EIS was required on coal development in the Northern Great Plains region.

The Supreme Court has also held that federal agencies are not required by Section 102(2)(C) to prepare an EIS to accompany appropriations requests as such requests do not constitute "proposals" for legislation or for major federal action. 57/ In so ruling,

---

54/ General Revenue sharing has been held not to require an EIS because it is not sufficiently federal in nature. Carolina Action v. Simon, 389 F. Supp. 1244 (M.D.N.C. 1975), aff'd, 522 F.2d 295 (4th Cir. 1975)). This holding is specifically supported by the CEQ regulations. 40 CFR § 1508.18(a). On the other hand, block grants for more specific projects have been held to require an EIS. See, e.g., Ely v. Velde, 451 F.2d 1130 (4th Cir. 1971).

55/ 40 CFR § 1508.18. The regulation specifically includes: projects financed, assisted, conducted, regulated or approved by federal agencies; new or revised agency rules, regulations, plans, policies or procedures; and legislative proposals. 40 CFR § 1508.18(a).

56/ 427 U.S. 390 (1976).

57/ Andrus v. Sierra Club, 442 U.S. 347 (1979).

the court noted that the language of Section 102(2)(C) is best interpreted as applying to those recommendations or reports that
actually propose programmatic actions, rather than to those that
merely suggest how such actions may be funded.

There are a multitude of cases on the question of whether a
given federal action is "major" and/or "significantly affects" the
quality of the human environment within the meaning of NEPA.
Almost all of these cases, as well as the CEQ regulations, however,
avoid the futile effort of trying to define the amorphous words
"major" and "significantly." 58/ The few cases where definition is
attempted shed no more light on the issue than does the dictionary.
The usual long analysis of those NEPA cases interpreting the meaning of "major" and "significantly affects" is therefore omitted here.
Such an analysis yields no valid criterion for deciding whether any
other federal action is "major" or "significantly affects" the environment.

Practically speaking, the initial decision of whether to
prepare an EIS for any given proposed project lies within the sound
discretion of the various federal agencies. 59/ Accordingly, in the

---

58/ The regulations do provide some limited guidance as to what is
"significant." The term is said to require consideration of both
context and intensity. "Context" means the subjects that are
affected such as society as a whole, the region, interests or the
locality. It includes both short-term and long-term effects.
40 CFR § 1508.27(a). "Intensity" refers to the severity of the
impact. 40 CFR § 1508.27(b).

59/ There has been a split in the circuits of the United States courts
of appeals as to the appropriate standard to employ in reviewing
an agency's "threshold decision" not to prepare an EIS for a
given project. Some circuits have adopted an "arbitrary and
capricious" standard, others have employed a "reasonableness"
standard. See Aertsen v. Landrieu, 488 F.Supp. 314 (D. Mass.
1980) for a discussion of this difference of opinion. Although
the level of judicial scrutiny differs in some measure as a result
of choosing one standard rather than the other, it is generally
true that reviewing courts will simply look for an administrative
record that evidences a rational basis for the agency's
determination on the issue of whether or not to prepare an EIS
on a particular project.

last few years, increasing attention has been given to "findings of no significant impact." 60/

4.1 Findings of No Significant Impact

The CEQ regulations define a "finding of no significant impact" (FONSI) as "a document prepared by a federal agency briefly presenting the reasons why an action, not otherwise excluded 61/ ... will not have a significant effect on the human environment and for which an environmental impact statement therefore will not be prepared." 62/ The regulations further provide that a FONSI must include an environmental assessment or a summary of one. 63/ Although a federal agency need not itself prepare that environmental assessment, the agency is responsible for its content, for if the environmental assessment prepared in connection with the issuance of a FONSI does not provide sufficient evidence to support the agency's finding of no significant impact, that finding will be overturned.

Thus, a FONSI can avoid the lengthy EIS process if properly substantiated. Early NEPA cases confronted many agency determinations that particular actions exerted no significant impact and these determinations were consistently overturned by reviewing courts. This has changed in recent years as agencies have become

---

60/ The CEQ regulations prescribe the use of the term "finding of no significant impact" for such documents. 40 CFR § 1508.13. Before the promulgation of the regulations, these documents were most frequently called "negative declarations."

61/ There are a few exemptions from the EIS requirement. Most notable are the statutory exemptions for United States Environmental Protection Agency actions under most provisions of the Clean Water Act and under all Clean Air Act provisions. 33 U.S.C. § 1371(c)(1); 15 U.S.C. § 793(c)(1). In addition, special exemptions are occasionally granted by Congress for some federal agency projects and for a few private projects that involve some federal agency action. See, e.g., 15 U.S.C. § 793(d). See also, 40 CFR § 1508.4.

62/ 40 CFR § 1508.13.

63/ Id.

more familiar with what is legally required for a FONSI and with the substantiation necessary to support one.

4.2 EIS Requirements for Special Types of Federal Action

Some particular types of federal agency actions merit special mention in connection with the EIS requirement. One is the preparation of an EIS in connection with legislation. In view of the unique nature of legislative recommendations and reports, CEQ's regulations provide for certain special features for EISs that accompany legislative proposals. 64/ First, the statement may be transmitted to the Congress up to thirty days after submission of the proposal in order to allow time for the preparation of an accurate and complete EIS. Second, a legislative EIS is to be prepared in the same manner as an ordinary draft EIS. Draft and final statements are required only in certain limited circumstances. Finally, comments on a legislative EIS are to be collected by the lead agency and forwarded to the Congress, together with the agency's responses to the comments.

A second type of federal agency action that merits special mention in connection with EIS requirements is the agency "program." Although NEPA does not specifically require the preparation of a "programmatic" EIS, the courts have required such EISs in certain circumstances. Although the courts have had considerable difficulty in deciding issues relating to the proper scope of a programmatic EIS, one simple way to state the EIS requirements for a program involving future developments is to say that a programmatic EIS must be prepared if institution of the program will foreclose decisions on whether to approve individual projects that would in themselves require EISs.

Scientists' Institute for Public Information v. Atomic Energy Commission, 65/ is a leading case dealing with EIS requirements for agency programs relating to future developments. In that case, the Commission had concluded that it did not need to prepare a programmatic EIS before deciding to proceed with its liquid metal fast breeder reactor demonstration program because the environmental impact of that program would be evaluated in EISs on each

---

64/ 40 CFR § 1506.08.

65/ 481 F.2d 1079 (D.C. Cir. 1973).

demonstration plant. The court, looking to environmental effects that today's decisions on development of technology may have years hence, held that a programmatic EIS was indeed required.

The applicability of the EIS requirement to ongoing federal agency programs is demonstrated by Minnesota Public Interest Research Group v. Butz, 66/ which held that the cumulative environmental impact of Forest Service decisions on the management of timber in a certain area required a programmatic EIS on what amounted to an ongoing but apparently ad hoc management plan. The applicability of the EIS requirement to ongoing federal agency programs appears to have significant potential for those—both environmentalists and private interests—who seek to change what are to them unacceptable, yet entrenched, federal agency policies and practices.

4.3 Procedure and Time of Required Issuance

As noted above, Section 102(2)(C) requires that an EIS be "included in every recommendation or report on proposals for major federal action significantly affecting the environment." That section also requires an agency, prior to preparing its EIS, to consult with and obtain the comments of any other federal agency that has either jurisdiction by law or special expertise with respect to any environmental impact involved. In addition, copies of the EIS, federal agency comments on it, and the views of appropriate state and local agencies must be made available to the president, CEQ, and the public and must accompany the proposal through the existing agency review process.

The concept of preparing and circulating for comment a draft EIS is embodied in the CEQ regulations where EIS preparation procedures are set out: the draft is to be prepared "early enough so that it can serve . . . as an important contribution to the decision-making process" 67/ and circulated for comment for a period not less than forty-five days. 68/ The regulations also provide that, as a general rule, no agency action should occur earlier than ninety days after the draft EIS or thirty days after the final EIS is made

---

66/   498 F.2d 1314 (8th Cir. 1974).

67/   40 CFR § 1502.5.

68/   40 CFR § 1506.10(c).

available to CEQ and the public. 69/ For informal rulemaking, the draft EIS should normally accompany the proposed rules. 70/

The regulations state that a "proposal" exists at the stage when an agency "has a goal and is actively preparing to make a decision on one or more means of accomplishing that goal and the effects can be meaningfully evaluated. 71/ The CEQ regulation goes on to note that the EIS "should" be timed so that the final EIS may be included in any recommendation or report on the proposal. 72/

In SCRAP, II, 73/ the Supreme Court rejected the holding of several courts of appeals that a final EIS must be prepared prior to agency hearings on an applicant's request for federal action or at other times before the agency actually takes a position on a proposal. The Supreme Court made it clear that "the time at which the agency must prepare the final EIS is the time at which it makes a 'recommendation or report' on a proposal." Since then, the CEQ regulations have prescribed the timing for final EISs in most circumstances.

4.4 Delegation

It is strongly implied, but not explicitly stated, in Section 102(2)(C), that the federal agency or the "responsible federal official" proposing to take action is charged with preparing the requisite EIS. Early in NEPA's history, several courts of appeals decisions addressed the question of whether, and, to what extent, a federal agency can lawfully delegate responsibility for preparing an EIS. The issue divided the courts into three camps: (1) those disallowing

---

69/ 40 CFR § 1506.10(b).

70/ 40 CFR § 1502.5(d).

71/ 40 CFR § 1508.23.

72/ Id.

73/ Aberdeen & Rockfish RR. Co. v. Students Challenging Regulatory Agency Procedures (SCRAP II), 422 U.S. 289 (1975), reaffirmed in dicta in Kleppe v. Sierra Club, 427 U.S. 390 (1976).

any delegation of responsibility; 74/ (2) those allowing some delegation, but requiring the responsible federal official to significantly
and actively participate in the preparation of the EIS 75/ and (3)
those permitting extensive delegation of responsibility, followed
only by review and adoption by the agency. 76/ In August of 1975,
Congress enacted P.L. No. 94-83, adding to Section 102(2) a new
subsection that settled the delegation question with respect to state
officials and agencies, but left open issues involving delegation to
private consultants.

The new subsection, which is designated as Section 102(2)(D),
provides that an EIS "for any major federal action funded under a
program of grants to States shall not be deemed to be legally insufficient solely by reason of having been prepared by a state agency or
official," if (1) the state agency or official has state-wide jurisdiction and is responsible for the action, and (2) the responsible federal
official (a) furnishes guidance and participates in the preparation of
the EIS, (b) independently evaluates it prior to its approval and adoption, and (c) provides early notice to, and solicits the view of, any
other state or any federal land management entity on any action or
alternatives thereto which may affect its responsibilities. The
responsible federal official must also prepare a written assessment
of the impacts on other agencies' responsibilities for incorporation
into the EIS if there is any disagreement. Section 102(2)(D) goes on
to state it does not relieve the federal official of responsibility for
the scope, objectivity and content of an EIS or any other responsibilities under NEPA. The provisions of Section 102(2)(D) have been of
primary importance in situations involving federal grants to states
for highway construction. 77/

74/ See, e.g., Green County Planning Board v. Federal Power Commission, 455 F.2d 412 (2d Cir. 1972), cert. denied, 409 U.S. 849
(1972).

75/ See, e.g., Life of the Land v. Brinegar, 485 F.2d 460 (9th Cir.
1973), cert. denied, 416 U.S. 961 (1974).

76/ See, e.g., Citizens Environmental Council v. Volpe, 484 F.2d 870
(10th Cir. 1973), cert. denied, 461 U.S. 936 (1974).

77/ Congress enacted a special total delegation of responsibility
provision for preparing an EIS to applicants under the Community Development Block Grant Program established by the
Housing and Community Development Act of 1974. 42 U.S.C.
§ 5304(h).

Thus, Congress rejected the per se no delegation rule of Green County in the case of projects involving grants to states and adopted the views expressed by those courts taking the middle course, allowing delegation, but requiring significant, active participation by the responsible federal agency. The law with regard to delegation to private consultants, however, remains unsettled.

4.4.1 The Lead Agency System

Projects requiring "major actions" by more than one federal agency are not uncommon. The concept of a "lead agency" to prepare or to supervise the preparation of an EIS for such an action was developed in order to satisfy the requirements of NEPA in the most efficient manner possible. CEQ's regulations incorporate that concept and require that a "lead agency" be designated to supervise the preparation of an EIS in such circumstances. 78/

Involved agencies are to determine which shall be the lead agency on the basis of five enumerated factors (listed in order of descending importance):

(i)   magnitude of agency's involvement;

(ii)   project approval/disapproval authority;

(iii)   expertise concerning the action's environmental effects;

(iv)   duration of agency's involvement; and

(v)   sequence of agency's involvement. 79/

CEQ will designate the lead agency if there is no consensual selection. 80/

4.5 Contents of an EIS

The broad outline of an EIS is set forth in Section 102(2)(C). The EIS must be a "detailed" statement which is issued only after consultation with other appropriate government agencies and which addresses the environmental impact of the proposed action, unavoidable adverse environmental effects, alternatives, the relationship

---

78/ 40 CFR § 1501.5(a).

79/ 40 CFR § 1501.5(c).

80/ 40 CFR § 1501.5(e) and (f).

between local short-term uses of the environment and the maintenance and enhancement of long-term productivity and irreversible
and irretrievable commitments of resources. Obviously, what a
particular EIS must include depends on the proposal and the facts
surrounding it.

The federal courts have supplemented the statutory requirements on a case-by-case basis. Although each of the cases concerns
a particular EIS and surrounding facts, an individualized analysis
with a composite overview reveals these useful guidelines: (1) the
EIS must be a self-contained document written in language that is
understandable to the layman yet allows for meaningful consideration by decisionmakers and scientists; 81/ and (2) it must also be
responsive to opposing opinions, and of sufficient depth to permit a
reasoned choice.

A fatally defective EIS is usually characterized by one or
more of the following: sweeping conclusions unsupported by the
facts; vagueness as to important issues; internal contradiction; disregard for local land use planning requirements; cursory treatment
of secondary and cumulative environmental impacts; a failure to
include sufficient information on the environmental impact of real-
istic and plausible alternatives, and to make an unbiased comparison
of them with the proposal. Because the consideration of alternatives is accorded the role of "linchpin" of the EIS, it merits some
further mention.

The requirement to consider alternatives embodies the simple
principle that a rational decision requires a knowledge of the available choices and their ramifications. The alternative of no action
must always be discussed. NEPA does not, however, require that the
consideration of alternatives be a "crystal ball" inquiry. 82/ Detailed
discussion and consideration of alternatives that are remote or speculative are not required. Yet, an alternative may not be given short
shrift because it is outside the jurisdiction of the agency or because
it is contrary to existing agency policy. Simply put, the agency's
consideration of alternatives must be reasonable such that a

81/ See 40 CFR § 1502.8 (requiring "plain language").

82/ Natural Resources Defense Council, Inc. v. Morton, 458 F.2d
827, 837 (D.C. Cir. 1972).

reviewing court may conclude that a proposing agency has taken a "hard look" at the decision's environmental consequences. 83/

5.0 "INTERNATIONAL" ENVIRONMENTAL STATEMENTS

There is nothing in Section 102(2)(C) to indicate that actions having international ramifications are to be treated any differently than others subject to the EIS requirement. Indeed, there is precedent for applying the EIS requirement to international programs. 84/ Nevertheless, federal agencies with international responsibilities expressed concern that compliance with EIS requirements could interfere with foreign policy objectives. As a consequence, these agencies and CEQ developed a program designed to accommodate these concerns while meeting the objectives of NEPA. In January of 1979, President Carter approved this program and issued Executive Order No. 12114. 85/

Although Executive Order No. 12114 is not formally based on NEPA, its objective is to further the purposes of the act. It is designed to insure that federal decisionmakers are informed of pertinent environmental considerations concerning actions having effects outside the geographical boundaries of the United States, and that such considerations are taken into account when decisions

---

83/ See, Baltimore Gas & Electric Corp. v. NRDC, 462 U.S. 87,97 (1983); Vermont Yankee Nuclear Power Corp. v. NRDC, 435 U.S. 519 (1978); California v. Block, 690 F.2d 753,761 (9th Cir. 1985).

84/ See, e.g., Sierra Club v. Coleman, 405 F. Supp. 53 (D.D.C. 1975), rev'd and remanded on other grounds, 578 Fed. 384 (D.C. Cir. 1978), in which an EIS was assumed to be required for preliminary construction activities by the Federal Highway Administration in connection with a highway through Panama and Columbia. Cf. Natural Resources Defense Council v. Nuclear Regulatory Commission, 647 Fed. 1345 (D.C. Cir. 1981), in which the court declined to require an EIS for export of a nuclear reactor to the Philippines, holding that NEPA does not impose an EIS obligation with respect to impacts felt solely outside the United States.

85/ 44 FR 1957 (9 January 1979).

are made. The order prescribes the circumstances under which its requirements are applicable and also specifies a number of procedures that must be followed. Affected agencies are further required to develop their own implementing procedures.

Because it is not feasible, from a foreign policy viewpoint, to perform environmental reviews in connection with every action that has environmental impacts outside the United States, specific types of actions are exempted from the requirements of the Order. Examples are intelligence activities, arms transfers and disaster and emergency relief action. Finally, the order specifically does not create any right of judicial review.

In the years since its issuance, the order has had little effect. Its lack of impact has been primarily due to three factors: (1) excepted actions far outnumber the actions to which the order's prescriptions are applicable; (2) even those agency actions to which the order does apply are not judicially reviewable; and (3) the Reagan administration has demonstrated little interest in enforcing its provisions.

6.0 APPLICANT'S ENVIRONMENTAL REPORTS

In situations where the federal action involved is federal agency approval of a non-federal party's proposal, the agency is virtually certain to require an environmental report. The required contents of such a report prepared by an applicant for a permit or other authorization will vary, but are generally spelled out by the federal agency.

In practice, the agency's environmental assessment on which a FONSI may be based is often a rehash of the applicant's environmental report. And, as a practical matter, an EIS itself is often only as good as the applicant's environmental report. Thus, it is apparent that this report is critical to the EIS process and is a document on which the applicant should spend much care and effort.

Despite this, frequent difficulties arise from flawed environmental reports. A variety of problems stem from the frequent failure of such a report to reflect a thorough knowledge and appreciation of the law of NEPA. These problems are avoidable to a great extent. In particular, two potentially serious problems can readily be avoided.

The first problem arises from a failure to write carefully, or to think all the way through the practical or legal ramifications of an issue or position. One should understand at the outset that an applicant's environmental report must state the relevant information in an honest and straightforward manner. 86/ Too often, though, a careful examination of an applicant's environmental report reveals language that is an overstatement, understatement or mistatement of the facts and conclusions. This is damaging to the applicant, for reviewing courts look to the information that was before the agency when its decisions were made and will not themselves undertake to build a more accurate factual record supporting the agency action. Thus, the agency's decision is apt to stand or fall on the accuracy of the applicant's environmental report.

The second problem that can arise in connection with applicants' environmental reports involves the ability of those who conduct the studies and analyses and prepare parts of the report to also serve as convincing expert witnesses if an agency hearing or court action arises at some point. No attempt will be made here to tell an applicant how to select an environmental consultant. Yet it can be a crucial flaw in some cases to discover too late that you have a barely qualified or an inexperienced expert witness or one who is unconvincing or offensive in oral presentations under pressure. Thus, it may be prudent for an applicant to make a careful assessment of the qualifications and the demeanor of the environmental consultant's personnel, particularly those who will be doing the actual work and thus would be the strongly preferred expert witnesses if the need arose.

7.0 THE SEVEN OTHER "ACTION-FORCING" PROVISIONS

In addition to NEPA's EIS requirements, there are seven other "action-forcing" provisions in Section 102(2). They require federal agencies to: (A) utilize an interdisciplinary approach to planning and decisionmaking; (B) insure appropriate consideration of unquantified environmental values; (E) study and develop alternatives to proposals involving unresolved conflicts over use of resources; (F) recognize the worldwide and long-range character of environmental problems; (G) make usable environmental information generally available; (H) initiate ecological information for resource-oriented projects;

86/ There are very few instances of an applicant or an environmental consultant intentionally attempting to deceive.

and (I) assist the CEQ. These sections are discussed briefly below with a view to neither ignoring nor overstating their individual and cumulative potential for important practical significance in the years ahead.

The seven "other" provisions of Section 102(2) are often thought of as relatively unimportant appendages to the EIS requirement. There is, however, a body of case law indicating that courts view at least some of these provisions as imposing on federal agencies duties that are both independent of and wider in scope than NEPA's EIS requirement. This view suggests that increased attention to these provisions could cause a significant change in the nature and extent of scientific data and information that must be compiled by the agencies in order to comply with NEPA. For, as the boundaries of environmental science continue to expand, national concern over mitigation measures and post-operational monitoring programs is likely to increase concomitantly. Thus, the extra-EIS provisions of Section 102(2) may come to play an ever more important role in the law of NEPA, serving as the legal basis for requiring agencies to secure more and better scientific data on environmental impacts both before and after federal action is taken, whether or not an EIS is required.

Section 102(2)(A) authorizes and directs all agencies to "utilize a systematic, inter-disciplinary approach" in planning and decisionmaking through an integrated use of natural and social sciences and environmental design arts. This section has been held to apply to all federal decisions that may have an impact on the environment, even those that do not themselves require the preparation of an EIS. 87/ Hence, its provisions might also be used in conjunction with the EIS requirement to produce greater court scrutiny of federal agency decisions. The result could well be judicial opinions compelling a significantly more systematic and integrated disciplinary approach to planning and decisionmaking, an approach that employs "state-of-the-art" scientific techniques.

Section 102(2)(B) directs federal agencies to "identify and develop methods and procedures . . . which will insure that presently unquantified environmental amenities and values may be given appropriate consideration in decisionmaking along with economic

---

87/ McDowell v. Schlesinger, 404 F. Supp. 212 (D.C. Mo. 1975).

and technical considerations." What Section 102(2)(B) does and does not do is described very well in the Tennessee-Tombigbee decision:

> [Section 102(2)(B)] cannot be fairly read to command an agency to develop or define any general or specific quantification process . . . [I]t requires no more than that an agency search out, develop and follow procedures reasonably calculated to bring environmental factors to peer status with dollars and technology in their decisionmaking. 88/

Section 102(2)(B) clearly adds to the list of factors that must be considered in the agency decisionmaking process, and thus also provides an additional basis upon which to review agency action.

Section 102(2)(E) 89/ requires all federal agencies to "study, develop, and describe appropriate alternatives to recommended courses of action in any proposal which involves unresolved conflicts concerning alternative uses of available resources." 90/ This section, like Section 102(2)(A), has been held to impose duties on federal agencies that are independent of NEPA's EIS requirements. For example, in Trinity Episcopal School Corp. v. Romney, 91/ the Court of Appeals for the Second Circuit reversed and remanded to HUD an agency decision to proceed with a low income housing project in New York City because HUD had not fully considered alternative

---

88/ Environmental Defense Fund, Inc. v. Corps of Engineers, 429 F.2d 1123, 1133 (5th Cir. 1974); see also, Hanly v. Kliendienst, 471 F.2d 823 (2nd Cir. 1972), cert. denied, 412 U.S. 908 (1973).

89/ This provision was originally Section 102(2)(D). It was redesignated when NEPA was amended by PL 94-83 (1975).

90/ The last part of Section 102(2)(E) appears to limit its application to only those proposals which involve unresolved conflicts concerning alternative uses of available resources. It is difficult, however, to conjure up good examples of choices involving environmental impact that are clearly outside the apparent limitation.

91/ 523 F. 2d 88 (2d Cir. 1975), rev'd on other grounds following remand sub nom. Strycher's Bay Neighborhood Council v. Karlen, 444 U.S. 223 (1980).

sites for the project. The court came to this conclusion despite the fact that HUD's decision not to prepare an EIS for the project went unchallenged.

Section 102(2)(F) requires all federal agencies to "recognize the worldwide and long-range character of environmental problems" and to lend such support as is consistent with our foreign policy to international efforts to protect the world environment. This section has received almost no attention from the federal courts. It could in the future, however, provide a basis for claims that agencies must develop and consider more scientific data and information in order to assess "long-range" effects of federal actions. It may also be used to buttress efforts to develop more comprehensive policies on international environmental protection issues.

Section 102(2)(G) requires all federal agencies to "make available to States, counties, municipalities, institutions, and individuals, advice and information useful in restoring, maintaining and enhancing the quality of the environment." This section has been of extremely limited practical utility with respect to particular projects. It does not require by its own terms disclosure of information different from that obtainable under the provisions of the Freedom of Information Act, nor does it add much, if anything, to the Administrative Procedure Act requirement that an agency be fair with public participants and disclose the basis for its decisions.

Another "action-forcing" provision that has received only limited attention to date, but which has great potential significance, is Section 102(2)(H). This section provides that all federal agencies shall "initiate and utilize ecological information in the planning and development of resource-oriented projects." The usual agency practice, evidenced in many EISs, is to make decisions simply on the best available information at the time. The requirement to "initiate" ecological information, then, could be used to require agencies themselves to generate additional information on particular projects before reaching a final decision to proceed.

Section 102(2)(I) simply requires federal agencies to assist the Council on Environmental Quality. At most, this section slightly strengthens the hand of CEQ (which has relatively little funding or staff) when it wants the cooperation of other federal agencies in undertaking a major examination of an environmental problem area.

8.0 STANDING TO SUE FOR ALLEGED VIOLATIONS OF NEPA

Standing is an issue that has received a great deal of attention from the United States Supreme Court since 1970. In general, the Court's opinions on the issue are in conflict and a lengthy analysis of them yields little of predictive value. When environmental interests are at stake, however, the Court has consistently left the door to the courthouse wide open. A brief examination of the two leading Supreme Court decisions on standing in environmental cases reveals the limits to which the Court's liberal stand on this issue goes.

Sierra Club v. Morton 92/ involved a challenge to agency approval of construction of the Mineral King Resort in the Sequoia National Forest. The Sierra Club treated the action as a test case, seeking to establish the principle that a membership organization with a "special interest" in the environment has standing to challenge action that would adversely affect the environment. Accordingly, the Sierra Club intentionally failed to allege that it or any of its members actually used the Mineral King Valley for recreational purposes. Although the Court held that asthetic or environmental harm could constitute "injury in fact" sufficient to confer standing, it denied standing in this case because the Club had not pleaded facts establishing any such injury. The mere fact that the Club had a "special interest" in protecting the environment was not sufficient to allow the Club to challenge the agency action concerned.

The other leading Supreme Court decision on standing in the environmental area is United States v. Students Challenging Regulatory Agency Procedures (SCRAP I). 93/ SCRAP I is generally considered to be among the most liberal standing cases. There an unincorporated association of law students sued the Interstate Commerce Commission for failing to prepare an EIS before allowing railroads to collect a surcharge on freight. They claimed to be "injured in fact" by the Commission's order because they used national parks and forests, and the order would raise the price of recycled materials thereby discouraging the use of such materials, leading in turn to increased mining operations, which would consequently harm national recreational enclaves. The government claimed that the alleged chain of causation was too attenuated to confer standing on the students. The Court, however, responded in a

---

92/ 405 U.S. 727 (1972).

93/ 412 U.S. 669 (1973).

footnote that a "trifle" of injury in fact is enough. 94/ Although subsequent cases 95/ cast some doubt on whether SCRAP I will be followed in the future, no case has directly reversed that decision, and it remains a leading precedent in the environmental area. Thus, when violations of NEPA are alleged, anyone who can claim at least a "trifle" of "injury in fact" has standing to sue.

94/ Id., at 689, n. 14.

95/ See, e.g., Simon v. Eastern Kentucky Welfare Rights Organization, 426 U.S. 26 (1976).

Chapter 11

FEDERAL REGULATION OF PESTICIDES

Marshall Lee Miller
Reid & Priest
Washington, D.C.

1.0 BACKGROUND TO THE FEDERAL REGULATION OF PESTICIDES

The benefits of pesticides, herbicides, rodenticides, and other economic poisons are well known. They have done much to spare us from the ravages of disease, crop infestations, noxious animals, and choking weeds. Over the past two decades, however, beginning with Rachel Carson's Silent Spring, 1/ there has been a growing awareness of the hazards, as well as the benefits of these chemicals, which may be harmful to man and the balance of nature. The ability to balance these often conflicting effects is hampered by our lack of understanding of adverse side effects, a problem which will become even more acute during the next few years as EPA investigations shift from the major pesticides, on which an appreciable amount of research has been conducted, to those for which data is relatively sparse.

1.1 Early Efforts at Pesticide Regulations

Although chemical pesticides have been subject to some degree of federal control since the Insecticide Act of 1910, 2/ the relatively insignificant usage of pesticides before World War II made regulation a matter of low priority. This act was primarily

---

1/ Rachel Carson, Silent Spring (New York, 1962).

2/ 36 Stat. 331 (1910).

concerned with protecting consumers from ineffective products or deceptive labeling, and contained neither a federal registration requirement nor any significant safety standards.

The war enormously stimulated the development and use of pesticides. The resulting benefits to health and farm production made pesticides a necessity and transformed the agricultural chemical industry into an influential sector of the economy. In 1947 Congress responded to the situation by enacting the more comprehensive Federal Insecticide, Fungicide, and Rodenticide Act (FIFRA), 3/ requiring that pesticides distributed in interstate commerce be registered with the United States Department of Agriculture (USDA) and containing a rudimentary labeling provision. The act, like its predecessor, was more concerned with product efficacy than with safety, but the statute did declare pesticides "misbranded" if they were necessarily harmful to man, animals, or vegetation (except weeds) even when properly used. 4/

Three major defects in the new law soon became evident. First, the registration process was largely an empty formality since the Secretary of Agriculture could not refuse registration even to a chemical he deemed highly dangerous. He could register "under protest", but this had no legal effect on the registrant's ability to manufacture or distribute the product. Second, there was no regulatory control over the use of a pesticide contrary to its label, as long as the label itself complied with the statutory requirements. Third, the secretary's only remedy against a hazardous product was a legal action for misbranding or adulteration, and—this was crucial—the difficult burden of proof was on him.

The statute nevertheless remained unchanged for fifteen years. Pesticides were not then a matter of public concern and the USDA was under little pressure to tighten regulatory control. Only a handful of registrations under protest were made during that period, and virtually all these actions involved minor companies with ineffective products. The one notable case in this area involving a

---

3/ 61 Stat. 190 (1947). The present act is still known by this name, although there have been major changes, especially in 1972, in the law since then. For convenience, we will refer to the pre-1972 version as the "Old FIFRA."

4/ Old FIFRA (pre-1972) § 2(z)(2)(d). See H. Rep. 313 (80th Cong., 1st Sess.). 1947 U.S. Code Cong. Serv. 1200, 1201.

fraudulently ineffective product was lost by the USDA at the district court level and mooted by the court of appeals. 5/

In 1964 the USDA persuaded Congress to remedy two of these three defects: the registration system was revised to permit the secretary to refuse to register a new product or to cancel an existing registration, and the burden of proof for safety and effectiveness was placed on the registrant. 6/ This considerably strengthened the act but made little difference in practice. The Pesticide Registration Division, a section of USDA's Agricultural Research Service, was understaffed—in 1966 the only toxicologist on the staff was the division's director—and the division was buried deep in a bureaucracy primarily concerned with promoting agriculture and facilitating the registration of pesticides. The cancellation procedure was seldom if ever used, 7/ and there was still no legal sanction against a consumer's applying the chemical for a delisted use.

The growth of the environmental movement in the late 1960s, with its concern about the widespread use of agricultural chemicals, overwhelmed the meager resources of the Pesticide Division. Environmental groups filed a barrage of law suits demanding the cancellation or suspension of a host of major pesticides such as DDT, Aldrin-Dieldrin, and the herbicide 2,4,5-T. This hectic and bewildering situation demanded a new approach to pesticide regulations.

1.2 Creation of the Environmental Protection Agency

On 2 December 1970, President Nixon signed Reorganization Order No. 3 8/ creating the Environmental Protection Agency (EPA), and assigned to it the functions and many of the personnel previously under Interior, Agriculture, and other government departments. EPA inherited from USDA not only the Pesticides Division but also the environmental law suits against the Secretary of Agriculture. Thus,

---

5/ Victrylite Candle Co. v. Brannan, 201 F.2d 206 (D.C. Cir. 1952).

6/ Act of 12 May 1964, PL 88-30S, 78 Stat. 190. There were other, less significant, amendments in 1959 (73 Stat. 286) and 1961 (75 Stat. 18, 42).

7/ Instead, a Pesticide Registration notice would be sent ordering the removal of one or more listed uses from the registration.

8/ Reorganization Order No. 3 of 1970, §2(a)(1), 1970 U.S. Code Cong. Ad. News 2996, 2998, 91st Cong. 2nd Sess.

within the first two or three months the new agency was compelled to make a number of tough regulatory decisions. The EPA's outlook was considerably influenced by judicial decisions in several of the cases it had inherited from USDA or, concerning pesticide residues, from the Food and Drug Administration (FDA) of the Department of Health, Education, and Welfare (HEW), now the Department of Health and Human Services (HHS). These court decisions consistently held that the responsible federal agencies had not sufficiently examined the health and environmental problems associated with pesticide use. These helped to shape—one might even say force—EPA's pesticide policy during its formative period. 9/

EPA's first policy determination, issued by Administrator William Ruckelshaus in early 1971 in response to a court order, was the "Statement of the Reasons Underlying the Decision on Cancellation and Suspension of DDT 2,4,5-T, and Aldrin-Dieldrin," usually called the 18th of March Statement. This order declared that pesticides would no longer be given only perfunctory review at registration nor be virtually immune from examination thereafter, and reemphasized that the statutory burden of proving a product safe rested with the chemical industry. This meant that EPA and the agricultural chemical industry would henceforth need additional resources for more intensive scientific review.

2.0 PESTICIDE STATUTE

2.1 Key Provisions of the Federal Insecticide, Fungicide and Rodenticide Act

The Federal Insecticide, Fungicide, and Rodenticide Act (FIFRA), 10/ as amended by the Federal Environmental Pesticide Control Act (FEPCA) of October 1972 11/ and the FIFRA amendments of 1975, 12/ 1978, 13/ and 1980, 14/ is a complex statute.

9/ These cases will be discussed in a later section, (9.1).

10/ 7 U.S.C. § 135, et seq.

11/ PL 92-516, 86 Stat. 973, 21 October 1972.

12/ PL 94-140, 28 November 1975.

13/ PL 95-396, 92 Stat. 819, 30 September 1978.

14/ PL 96-539, 94 Stat. 3194, 17 December 1980.

Terms may have a meaning different from, or even directly contrary to, normal English usage. For example, the term "suspension" really means an immediate ban on a pesticide, while the harsher-sounding term "cancellation" indicates only the initiation of administrative proceedings which can drag on for years. There are five key features of the FIFRA; the other points will be discussed more fully in a subsequent section.

The amendments to FIFRA reflect congressional, industry, and environmentalist concern about federal control of pesticide distribution, sale, and use. The 1972 amendments amounted to a virtual rewriting of the law. EPA was given expanded authority over field use of pesticides, and several categories of registration were created which give EPA more flexibility in fashioning appropriate control over pesticides. The 1975 amendments are significant not for what they actually changed but because of the motivations that prompted them. These amendments were viewed by many as, at best, unnecessary and, at worst, a further encumbrance upon an already complicated administrative procedure. EPA was required to consult with the Department of Agriculture and Agricultural Committees of Congress before issuing proposed or final standards regarding pesticides. EPA also got the authority to require that farmers take exams before being certified as applicators.

The 1978 amendments reflected the near-collapse of EPA's pesticide registration program. EPA was given the authority to conditionally register a pesticide pending study of the product's safety and was authorized to perform generic reviews without requiring compensation for use of a company's data. The 1980 amendments provided for a two-house veto over EPA rules or regulations and required the administrator to obtain Scientific Advisory Review (SAR) of suspension actions after they were initiated.

2.2 Registration Procedures

All new pesticide products used in the United States, with minor exceptions, must first be registered with EPA. This involves the submittal of the complete formula, a proposed label, and "full description of the tests made and the results thereof upon which the claims are based." 15/ The administrator must approve the registration if the following conditions are met:

15/ 1 FIFRA § 3(c)(1), 7 U.S.C. § 136(c)(1).

(A)   its composition is such as to warrant the proposed claim for it;

(B)   its labeling and other materials required to be submitted comply with the requirements of this act;

(C)   it will perform its intended function without unreasonable adverse effects on the environment; and

(D)   when used in accordance with widespread and commonly recognized practice it will not generally cause unreasonable adverse effects on the environment. 16/

The operative phrase in the above criteria is "unreasonable adverse effects on the environment", which was added to the act in 1972. This phrase is defined elsewhere in FIFRA as meaning "any unreasonable risk to man or the environment, taking into account the economic, social, and environmental costs and benefits of the use of the pesticide." 17/

This controversial expression, which appears also in the cancellation-suspension section of the act, 18/ disturbed some environmentalists who feared that the word "unreasonable" plus the consideration of social and economic factors would undermine the effectiveness of the cancellation procedure, but experience to date has not indicated a problem.

The registration is not valid for all uses of a particular chemical. Each registration specifies the crops and insects on which it may be applied, and each use must be supported by research data on safety and efficacy. Registrations are for a five-year period, after which they automatically expire unless an interested party petitions for renewal and, if requested by EPA, provides additional data

---

16/   FIFRA § 3(c)(5), 7 U.S.C. § 136a(c)(5).

17/   FIFRA § 2(bb), 7 U.S.C. § 136(bb). The 1975 amendments, as will be discussed, added the specific requirement that decisions also include consideration of their impact on various aspects of the agricultural economy.

18/   FIFRA § 6, 7 U.S.C. § 136d.

indicating the safety of the product. 19/ For the past several years, pre-EPA registrations have been coming up for renewal under much stricter standards than when originally issued. The agricultural chemical companies have justifiably complained that the increased burden of registration is discouraging the development of new pesticides, but there seems no responsible alternative.

2.3 Federal Control over Pesticide Use

Until 1972 the government had no control over the actual use of a pesticide once it had left a manufacturer or distributor properly labeled. Thus, for example, a chemical which would be perfectly safe for use on a dry field might be environmentally hazardous if applied in a marshy area, and a chemical acceptable for use on one crop might leave dangerous residues on another. EPA's only recourse (other than occasional subtle hints to the producer) was to cancel the entire registration—obviously too unwieldy a weapon to constitute a normal means of enforcement. A second problem was that a potential chemical might be too dangerous for general use but could be used safely by trained personnel. There was, however, no legal mechanism for limiting its use only to qualified individuals.

Because of these problems, both environmentalists and the industry agreed that EPA should be given more flexibility than merely the choice between cancelling or approving a pesticide. Congress therefore provided for the classification of pesticides into general and restricted categories, 20/ with the latter group available only to Certified Applicators. There are several categories of applicators, including private applicators and commercial applicators who use or supervise the application of pesticides on property other than their own. A pesticide label permitting use only "under the direct supervision of a Certified Applicator" means that the chemical is to be applied under the instructions and control of a Certified Applicator who, however, curiously is not required to be physically present when and where the pesticide is applied.

The additional flexibility of the certification program was a principal reason the industry eventually supported the 1972 amendments to FIFRA, but some environmentalists were concerned that

---

19/ FIFRA § 6(a), 7 U.S.C. § 136d(a).

20/ FIFRA § 3(d), 7 U.S.C. § 136a(d).

the program might become a farce, especially when administered by certain states. Certification standards are prescribed by EPA, as are requirements for periodic reporting to EPA, but any state desiring to establish its own certification program may do so if the administrator determines that it satisfies the guidelines and statutory criteria. 21/

The efficacy of the entire certification program, however, has become questionable as a result of the 1975 amendments to FIFRA. The amendments considerably loosened the procedures for certification by forbidding EPA to demand any examinations of an applicant's knowledge. 22/   These amendments will be discussed more fully in a separate section. There is a possibility that some states may license anyone who applies, but EPA requirements for periodic reporting and inspection provide some degree of control, and there should be no objection to every farmer becoming a Certified Applicator if he were willing to undergo training.

Finally, since 1972 it has been unlawful either "to make available for use, or to use, any registered pesticide classified for restricted use for some or all purposes other than in accordance with" the registration and applicable regulations. 23/ Stiff penalties for violations of these restrictions include fines up to $25,000 and imprisonment for up to a year. 24/

2.4 Cancellation

While the registration process may be the foundation of the FIFRA, cancellation represents the cutting edge of the law and attracts the most public attention. Cancellation is used to initiate review of a substance suspected of being a "substantial question of safety" to man or the environment. 25/ During the pendency of the proceedings the product may be freely manufactured and shipped in

---

21/ FIFRA § 4, 7 U.S.C. § 136b.

22/ PL 94-140 § 5, amending FIFRA § 4(a)(1).

23/ FIFRA § 12(a)(2)(F), 7 U.S.C. § 136(a)(2)(F).

24/ FIFRA § 14, 7 U.S.C. § 136 1.

25/ EDF v. Ruckelshaus, 439 F.2d 584, 591-92, 2 ERC 1114, 1119 (D.C. Cir. 1971).

commerce. A cancellation order, although final if not challenged within thirty days, usually leads to a public hearing or scientific review committee, or both, and can be quite protracted—a matter of years rather than months. A recommended decision from the agency hearing examiner (now called the administrative law judge) goes to the administrator or his delegated representative, the chief agency judicial officer, for a final determination on the cancellation. If sustained, this would ban the product from shipment or use in the United States. 26/

Even under the old FIFRA 27/ it became clear that there were several quite different types of cancellation. First, there was a cancellation when a substance was, in EPA's opinion, a highly probable threat to man or the environment but for which there was not yet sufficient evidence to warrant immediate suspension. Second, there could be a cancellation when scientific tests indicated some cause for concern and a public hearing or scientific advisory committee was desired to explore the issue more thoroughly. And third, there could be a cancellation issued in response to a citizens' suit when a fact-finding hearing was desired to enable both critics and defenders of the pesticide to present their arguments. These distinctions, although not found in the statute, were nevertheless quite important. State authorities, for example, would often recommend that farmers cease using a cancelled product which they thought had been declared unsafe, although EPA may have considered the action in category two or three above. Conversely, there were occasions when EPA wanted to communicate its great concern over the continued use of a product without resorting to suspension.

This problem is not resolved completely by the amended FIFRA, but two levels of action are distinguished:

> The administrator may issue a notice of his intent either (1) to cancel its registration or to change its classification together with the reasons (including the factual basis) for his action, or (2) to hold a hearing to determine

---

26/ The scientific review committee and other features of this process will be discussed later in more detail.

27/ The cancellation-suspension section of the old act was § 4(c); it is § 6 of the post-1972 FIFRA.

whether or not its registration should be cancelled or its classification changed. 28/

This revision of the law may not have solved EPA's communications problem with local officials, but it does provide a statutory basis for a distinction which EPA sometimes needed to make.

2.5 Suspension

A suspension order, despite its misleading name, is an immediate ban on the production and distribution of a pesticide. It is mandated when a product constitutes an "imminent hazard" to man or the environment, 29/ and may be invoked at any stage of the cancellation proceeding or even before a cancellation procedure has been initiated. According to the 18th of March Statement, "an imminent hazard may be declared at any point in the chain of events which may ultimately result in harm to the public." 30/ There are two types of suspension orders: an ordinary suspension order and an emergency suspension order.

2.5.1 Ordinary Suspension

The purpose of an ordinary suspension is to prevent an imminent hazard during the time required for cancellation or change in classification proceedings. An ordinary suspension proceeding is initiated when the administrator issues notice to the registrant that he is suspending use of the pesticide and includes the requisite findings as to imminent hazard. The registrant may request an expedited hearing within five days of receipt of the administrator's notice. If no hearing is requested, the suspension order can take effect immediately thereafter and the order is not reviewable by a court. 31/

28/ FIFRA § 6(b), 7 U.S.C. § 136d(b). Note that the administrator himself may request a hearing, a power which he did not have under the old FIFRA, although in fact he assumed this authority in his August 1971 cancellation order on 2,4,5-T.

29/ FIFRA § 6(c), 7 U.S.C. § 136d(c).

30/ See 18 March 1971 Statement, p. 6. A suspension order must be accompanied by a cancellation order if one is not then outstanding. FIFRA § 6(b), 7 U.S.C. § 136d(b).

31/ FIFRA § 6(c), 7 U.S.C. § 136d(c).

Suspension procedurally "resembles. . .the judicial proceedings on a contested motion for a preliminary injuction," 32/ hence the tentative connotation of the term, and remains in effect until the cancellation hearing is completed and a final decision is issued by the administrator. 33/ This does not actually accord with reality but has been the consistent theme of judicial decisions since the agency's inception. According to this view, the function of a suspension order is not to reach a definitive decision on the registration of a pesticide but to grant temporary, interim relief. 34/ The Circuit Court of Appeals for the District of Columbia has repeatedly stated this view: "The function of the suspension decision is to make a preliminary assessment of evidence and probabilities, not an ultimate resolution of difficult issues," 35/ and "the suspension order thus operates to afford interim relief during the course of the lengthy administrative proceedings." 36/

The court of appeals has emphasized that "imminent hazard" does not refer only to the danger of immediate disaster: "We must caution against any approach to the term 'imminent hazard' used in the statute, that restricts it to a concept of crises." 37/ In another case, the court declared that the secretary of agriculture:

> has concluded that the most important element of an "imminent hazard to the public" is a serious threat to public health, that a hazard may be "imminent" even if its impact will not be apparent for many years, and that the "public" protected by the suspension provision includes fish and wildlife. These interpretations all seem consistent with the statutory language and purpose. 38/

32/ EDF v. EPA 465 F. 2d 538, 4 ERC 1523, 1530 (D.C. Cir. 1972).

33/ Nor-Am v. Hardin, 435 F. 2d 1151, 2 ERC 1016 (7th Cir. 1970), cert. denied 402 U.S. 935 (1971).

34/ See, In re Shell Chemical, Opinion of the Administrator, pp. 8-11, 6 ERC 2047 at 2050 (1974).

35/ EDF v. EPA, supra, 465 F. 2d at 537, 4 ERC at 1529.

36/ EDF v. Ruckelshaus, supra, 439 F. 2d at 589, 2 ERC at 1115.

37/ EDF v. EPA, supra, 465 F. 2d at 540, 4 ERC at 1531.

38/ EDF v. Ruckelshaus, supra, 439 F.2d at 597, 2 ERC at 1121-22.

2.5.2 Emergency Suspension
     The emergency suspension is the strongest action EPA can take under FIFRA and immediately halts all uses, sales, and distribution. 39/ An emergency suspension differs from an ordinary suspension in that the registrant is not given notice or the opportunity for an expedited hearing prior to the suspension order taking effect. The registrant is, however, entitled to an expedited hearing to determine the propriety of the emergency suspension. The administrator can only use this procedure when he determines that an emergency exists which does not allow him to hold a hearing before suspending use of a pesticide. 40/ This action has only been taken four times: once with 2,4,5-T, twice with ethylene dibromide (EDB), and most recently with Dinoseb.

2.5.3 2,4,5-T
     EPA first used the emergency suspension procedure in 1979 when it suspended the sale and use of 2,4,5-T and Silvex for specified uses. EPA issued the suspension orders based on its judgment that exposure to the pesticides created an immediate and unreasonable risk to human health. EPA's action was reviewed by a Michigan district court in Dow Chemical Co. v. Blum, 41/ where the plaintiffs petitioned for judicial review of EPA's decision and a stay of the emergency suspension orders. In upholding EPA's order, the court analogized the emergency suspension order to a temporary restraining order and defined the term emergency as a "substantial likelihood that serious harm will be experienced during the three or four months required in any realistic projection of the administrative suspension process." 42/
     The court held that this standard required the administrator to examine five factors: (1) the seriousness of the threatened harm; (2) the immediacy of the threatened harm; (3) the probability that

---

39/ Its counterpart in the Toxic Substances Control Act, TSCA, is Section 7, but that provision has remained virtually unused over the past decade.

40/ § 6(c)(3), 7 U.S.C. § 136d(c)(3).

41/ 469 F. Supp. 892, 13 ERC 1129 (E.D. Mich 1979).

42/ Ibid. at 902, 13 ERC at 1135.

the threatened harm would result; (4) the benefits to the public of the continued use of the pesticides in question during the suspension process; and (5) the nature and extent of the information before the administrator at the time he makes his decision. The court also held that an emergency suspension order may be overturned only if it was arbitrary, capricious, or an abuse of discretion or if it was not "issued in accordance with the procedures established by law." 43/

2.5.4 Ethylene Dibromide (EDB)

EDB, a fumigant used on soil, citrus fruit, stored grain, and milling equipment, has been used as a pesticide since 1948. It has also been used since the late 1920s in gasoline to prevent lead deposits in car engines (this has accounted for 90% of its usage), although this use is declining as leaded gasoline is phased out.

Despite a 1975 study by the National Cancer Institute which determined EDB to cause cancer and birth defects in test animals, EPA did not take action on the pesticide until nearly a decade later in September 1983 when it issued an emergency suspension on all soil treatments. 44/ At the same time, EPA issued an 11-month phase-out of post-harvest fruit and vegetable fumigation uses. 45/ However, EPA refused to ban all uses of the chemical. Instead, it issued a "cancellation order" to cover fumigation of stored grain, felled logs and spot fumigation of grain and flour milling machinery.

After several states took action themselves by banning EDB altogether or setting stringent tolerance levels, and after determining the EDB's cancer-causing potential presented a "long-term, chronic, unacceptable health risk," EPA took further action by issuing another emergency suspension on the use of EDB as a fumigant for stored grain and grain milling machinery.

Cancellation of all major uses of EDB took effect 1 September 1984.

43/ Ibid. The court stated that it arrived at its decision to uphold EPA's order "with great reluctance" and would not have ordered the emergency suspension on the basis of the information before EPA, but was not empowered to substitute its judgment for that of EPA's. 469 F. Supp. at 907, 13 ERC at 1140.

44/ 48 FR 46228, 7 October 1983.

45/ 48 FR 46234, 7 October 1983.

2.5.5 Dinoseb

On 7 October 1986 EPA issued an emergency suspension on Dinoseb based on recent findings that exposure of pregnant women to the pesticide poses "serious risk" of birth defects. Dinoseb is used mainly on soybeans, cotton, potatoes, peanuts, alfalfa, snap beans, peas, grapes, and almonds.

2.6 Balancing Test in FIFRA

The balancing of risks versus benefits lies at the heart of the FIFRA, and its importance warrants a separate discussion. There are some who feel that certain types of pesticides, particularly carcinogens, should be forbidden per se as done under the Delaney Amendment to the Food, Drug, and Cosmetics Act. 46/ FIFRA does not require this inflexibility, although the courts have cautioned that the law "places a heavy burden on any administrative officer to explain the basis for his decision to permit the continued use of a chemical known to produce cancer in experimental animals." 47/ EPA Administrator Russell Train in 1974 noted this in his decision regarding Aldrin-Dieldrin:

> Since Aldrin-Dieldrin has been found to be carcinogenic in mice and probably carcinogenic in rats, and to present a high risk of cancer to man, it is arguable that any use of Aldrin-Dieldrin, however significant or beneficial in social or economic terms, cannot be justified, even for the limited period of time until the completion of the cancellation proceedings.
> As indicated in Part I of this opinion, however, it is appropriate that the possible benefits of Aldrin-Dieldrin, or the absence of such benefits, be considered in this proceeding. Nevertheless, it is apparent that any benefits attributable to Aldrin-Dieldrin must be of high order to affect the findings on carcinogenicity. 48/

46/ FDCA § 409(c)(3)(A), 21 U.S.C. § 348(c)(3)(A). The relationship between the FIFRA and the FDCA will be discussed later in more detail.

47/ EDF v. Ruckelshaus, supra, 439 F. 2d at 596, 2 ERC at 1121.

48/ In re Shell Chemical, supra., p. 32, 6 ERC at 2057.

The balancing that is applied during the registration process and, more formally, during the cancellation proceedings is determining whether there are "unreasonable adverse effects on the environment," taking into consideration the "economic, social, and environmental costs and benefits of the use of any pesticide." 49/

In a suspension proceeding, however, the FIFRA does not require a balancing of environmental risks and benefits. It has nevertheless been EPA's policy since its inception to conduct such an analysis, although in practice the benefits would obviously need to be considerable to balance a finding of "imminent hazard." One administrator noted that "the Agency traditionally has considered benefits as well as risks . . . and, in [his] opinion, should continue to do so." 50/

3.0 TRADE SECRETS

The issue in FIFRA that has generated more controversy than any other over the past decade has involved the treatment of trade secrets. 51/ The judicial protection of commercial trade secrets has gradually eroded during the past few years. Many so-called trade secrets were in fact widely known throughout the industry and did not merit confidential status. 52/ Section 10 of FIFRA, added in the

---

49/ FIFRA §§ 2(bb), 3(c)(5), and 6(b), 7 U.S.C. §§ 136(bb), 136a(c)(5), and 136d.

50/ In re Shell Chemical, supra, p. 11, 6 ERC at 2050-51, upheld unanimously by the D.C. Court of Appeals in EDF v. EPA, 510 F. 2d 1292, 7 ERC 1689 (4 April 1975). This practice was also judicially approved in an unrelated case with the same name, EDF v. EPA, supra, 465 F. 2d at 540, 4 ERC at 1530.

51/ FIFRA § 10, 7 U.S.C. § 136h. Trade secrets are also becoming a source of contention in the implementation of the Toxic Substances Control Act.

52/ This is true not merely in the pesticide area but also, for example, in the Clean Air Act under Section 211 pertaining to gasoline additives, where an EPA review a few years ago concluded that most of the hundreds of so-called trade secrets relating to additives in gasoline were in fact either common knowledge in the industry or were easily discoverable by back-engineering.

1972 amendments, provides that trade secrets should not be released but, if the administrator proposes to release them, he should provide notice to the company to enable it to seek a declaratory judgment in the appropriate district court. 53/

It is, of course, desirable that university scientists and others outside industry and government should be able to conduct tests on the effects of various pesticides. In one case debated by the agency for several years, a professor needed to know the chemical composition of a particular pesticide to conduct certain medical experiments. Should EPA or a court furnish this information to a bonafide researcher, with or without appropriate safeguards to preserve confidentiality? EPA resolved that question in the experimenter's favor after an investigation revealed that the chemical composition in fact was not a trade secret within the industry, but the underlying question has yet to be resolved. 54/

Section 10 provides that "when necessary to carry out the provisions of this act, information relating to formulas of products acquired by authorization of this act may be revealed to any federal agency consulted and may be revealed at a public hearing or in findings of fact issued by the Administrator." 55/ Consequently, if the public interest requires, whatever that means, a registrant must assume that the formula for his product can be made available, although in practice this may not occur very often.

Because of the controversy surrounding the disclosure of trade secrets, Congress amended FIFRA in 1975 and 1978. The 1975 amendments 56/ cleaned up an ambiguity created by the 1972 amendments by specifying that the new use restrictions applied only

---

53/ FIFRA § 10 (c), 7 U.S.C. § 136h(c).

54/ The reverse situation, where a chemical company sought an administrative subpoena of the testing files of two university researchers on pesticides, was raised in Dow Chemical Co. v. Allen, 672 F.2d. 1262, 17 ERC 1013 (7th Circ. 1982). The request was rejected as unduly burdensome and not particularly probative, since the EPA had not relied on their data in studies still uncompleted.

55/ FIFRA § 10(b), 7 U.S.C. § 136h(b). Note that state agencies are not mentioned.

56/ PL 94-140, 89 Stat. 75 (1975).

to data submitted on or after 1 January 1970. The definition of trade secrets was left to the administrator.

EPA took the position that the 1972 and 1975 amendments restricted use and disclosure of only a narrow range of data, such as formulas and manufacturing processes, but not hazard and efficacy data. However, the industry challenged this view with some initial success. 57/ In 1978, Congress again amended Section 10 to limit trade secrets protection to formulas and manufacturing processes, thus reflecting EPA's position. This was a significant change and has spawned a host of litigation in recent years. 58/

In Union Carbide Agricultural Products Company v. Costle, 59/ the Second Circuit overturned an injunction that Union Carbide obtained to prevent EPA from disclosing confidential research data under Section 3 of FIFRA. The appeals court held that the lower court applied the wrong legal test in evaluating the plaintiff's request; and that the moving party must show "likelihood of success" on the merits, which Union Carbide did not do. 60/

Union Carbide asserted that disclosure of the data effected a taking of its property, but the Second Circuit expressed doubts that such a taking occurred, noting that a distinction must be made between EPA's use of the data and disclosure to the public. Even if there was a taking, the court stated that Union Carbide must establish that it was without an adequate remedy under the Tucker Act. 61/

57/ Mobay Chemical Corp. v. Costle, 447 F.Supp 811, 12 ERC 1228 (W.D. Mo. 1978), appeal dismissed 439 U.S. 320, reh. denied 440 U.S. 940 (1979); Chevron Chemical Co. v. Costle, 443 F.Supp 1024 (N.D. Cal. 1978).

58/ PL 95-396, 92 Stat. 812.

59/ 632 F.2d 1014, 15 ERC 1113 (2nd Cir. 1980) cert. denied 450 U.S. 996.

60/ Ibid. at 1018, 15 ERC at 1115. The 1978 amendments to FIFRA passed during the pendency of the suit so the plaintiff amended his complaint to attack the new provisions on constitutional grounds.

61/ 28 U.S.C. § 1491. The Tucker Act provides compensation for private property taken for public purposes, thus satisfying the Fifth Amendment requirement that the federal government compensate owners when it takes their property.

In Chevron Chemical Co. v. Costle, 62/ a Delaware district court held that FIFRA authorized EPA's consideration of pre-1970 data for subsequent registrations. It also held that Congress found the use of the data would be a taking for a public, rather than private, purpose. Since FIFRA did not preclude a Tucker Act remedy, the court found that retroactive application of the 1978 amendments did not violate the plaintiff's due process rights.

On appeal, the Third Circuit upheld the district court's decision and clarified the nature of the plaintiff's property rights in its data. 63/ The appeals court found that Congress rejected the idea that there was a common law property right of exclusive use for materials in the government's files prior to 1 January 1970; according to the court, the 1978 amendments, which did not extend the compensation provision to pre-1970 data, was implicit rejection of the exclusive use doctrine for that data. The Third Circuit also held that Chevron's property right on the pre-1970 data was based on 18 U.S.C. Section 1905 which does not confer a private right of action; it only creates a standard by which to judge the legality of an agency's disclosures. That standard is the right of non-disclosure, not of non-use. 64/

A number of other courts reached the same outcome, that there was no unconstitutional "taking" of property, although their reasoning varied considerable in interpreting these murky statutory provisions. 65/ However, a district court judge declared in Monsanto v. Acting Administration that even though federal law establishes no property rights in the submitted data, state law does, and disclosure of this protected interest constitutes a tort, under §757 of the Restatement of Torts. In was inadequate, the court continued, to claim that the company would be compensated for its loss through either arbitration or the Tucker Act: the former was unconstitutional, as a denial of due process under the Fifth Amendment, while the latter was not applicable to this situation.

62/ 499 F.Supp. 732, injunction denied, 499 F.Supp. 745, affirmed 641 F.2d 104 (3rd Cir. 1981), cert. denied 452 U.S. 961.

63/ 641 F.2d 104, 16 ERC 2004 (3rd. Cir. 1981), cert. denied 452 U.S. 961.

64/ Id., at 114, 16 ERC at 2013.

65/ Mobay Chemical Corp. v. Gorsuch, F.2d, 17 ERC 1737 (3rd Circ. 1982).

With these different interpretations, a ruling by the Supreme Court was necessary. In <u>Ruckelshaus v. Monsanto</u>, 66/ the justices held almost unanimously (7-1/2 to 1/2) that while a company did have a property right to the data under state law, the key question was whether it had a reasonable expectation that it would not be disclosed or used by other companies, albeit with adequate compensation. This expectation, the Court found, could only be for the period between the 1972 FIFRA amendments and the 1978 amendments, when the interim change in §10 of the act promised strict confidentiality.

For this period, compensation is available through the Tucker Act, and probably through the statutory arbitration process too, although the Court indicated that matter was sufficiently ripe for judicial review in this case.   .

The one dissent, only on one small part of the opinion, contended that another statute, the trade secret confidentiality section in 18 U.S.C. §1905, provided expectation of confidentiality for the pre-1972 period, but the remainder of the Court found this unpersuasive. 67/

4.0 1972 AMENDMENTS TO FIFRA

The amendments to FIFRA in 1972 which are known as the Federal Environmental Pesticides Control Act (FEPCA) 68/ and amounted to a virtual rewriting of the law. They were considered necessary to (1) strengthen the enforcement provisions of FIFRA, (2) shift the legal emphasis from labeling and efficacy to health and environment, (3) provide for greater flexibility in controlling dangerous chemicals, (4) extend the scope of federal law to cover intrastate registrations and the specific uses of a given pesticide, and (5) streamline the administrative appeals process. Three of the principal changes made by the new law—EPA's expanded authority over field use, the creation of several categories of registration, and trade

---

66/ 104 S. Ct. 2862, 21 ERC 1062 (1984).

67/ More on this pervasive issue can be found in paragraph 4.2 and elsewhere in this chapter.

68/ PL 92-516, 86 Stat. 973, 21 October 1972.

secrets—have already been discussed. The following discussion will consider other important features of the 1972 amendments to FIFRA.

4.1 Indemnities

Section 15 provides financial compensation to registrants and applicators owning quantities of pesticides who are unable to use them because of cancellation or suspension. This section, although not often invoked, was the most controversial in the entire act. The amendment's industry supporters threatened to block passage of the entire 1972 legislation if this section were not attached. Public interest groups complained that it would force taxpayers to indemnify manufacturers for inadequate testing and would encourage the production of unsafe chemicals.

As a partial compromise, a clause was added to bar indemnification to any person who "had knowledge of facts which, in themselves, would have shown that such pesticide did not meet the requirements" for registration and continued thereafter to produce such pesticide without giving notice of such facts to the administrator. 69/ Even under the most expedited agency procedures, that saving clause may disqualify registrants and manufacturers in virtually all cancellation and suspension actions.

The real purpose of the indemnity provision, according to agriculture chemical lobbyists, was not to compensate manufacturers or even retailers and farmers, but to deter EPA from cancellation and suspension actions. A wide-spread belief in the farming community was that EPA would be reluctant to act if it were forced to buy up large quantities of a banned chemical, using funds from EPA's general budget to indemnify pesticide companies and users. This is, of course, somewhat naive. Federal agencies do not, and should not, make decisions involving human safety and the environment because of such factors; but to the degree that it provides an incentive to EPA to consider its own budget, rather than the public welfare, it is poor policy.

There is one situation in which the section may influence EPA action. Following a suspension or final cancellation order, the agency has traditionally not attempted to recall or stop the use of those amounts already in distribution. This tradition, which arose

---

69/ FIFRA § 15(a), 7 U.S.C. § 136m(a).

before the passage of the 1972 amendments, stemmed from the hazards of bulk disposal 70/ and the training time needed before alternative pesticides could be used, but it may now have become standard agency practice. 71/ It is uncertain how much Section 15 unconsciously encourages this practice of condoning the continued use of a chemical which it has declared an imminent hazard.

4.2 "Featherbedding" or "Me-Too" Registrants

The second most contested provision in the 1972 FEPCA, after the question of indemnities, was the issue of "featherbedding" on registration. The original version in the House stated that "data submitted in support of an application shall not, without permission of the applicant, be considered by the Administrator in the support of any other application for registration." 72/ Supporters of the provision, basically the larger manufacturers, claimed that it prevented one company from "free-loading" on the expensive scientific data produced by another company; environmentalists dubbed this the "mice extermination amendment" for requiring subsequent registrants to needlessly duplicate the laboratory experiments of the first registrant.

The groups finally found an acceptable compromise allowing subsequent registrants to reimburse the initial registrant for reliance on its data, adding to the above language the words: "unless such other applicant shall first offer to pay reasonable compensation for producing the test data to be relied upon." 73/ The section provides that disputes over the amount of compensation should be decided by the administrator, but the 1975 amendments deleted the unfortunate clause which ensured that the original registrant should have nothing to lose by appealing to a district court since "in no event shall the amount of payment determined by the court be less

---

70/ Recall and disposal will be discussed later.

71/ See In re Shell Chemical, supra, p. 2, 6 ERC at 2061. Note, however that in this case the cutoff date was the issuance of the Notice of Intent to Suspend, not the date of the final suspension several months later.

72/ FIFRA § 3(c)(1)(D), 7 U.S.C. § 136a(c)(1)(D).

73/ Ibid.

than that determined by the Administrator." 74/ The 1978 amendments removed the unwelcome task from the administrator entirely
by providing for mediation by the Federal Mediation & Conciliation
Service. 75/ The 1975 amendments also pushed back the effective
date of the compensation provision from October 1972, the date of
the enactment of the FEPCA amendments, to 1 January 1970. 76/
     The data compensation provision has created many problems
in the registration process. Pesticide manufacturers brought several
lawsuits to determine the breadth of this provision, the proper use of
the data, and the amount of compensation that a manufacturer is
entitled for use of its data.
     In Amchem Products, Inc. v. GAF Corp., 77/ the primary
issue before the U.S. Court of Appeals for the Fifth Circuit was the
effective date of the 1972 amendments. The plaintiff, a manufacturer of a plant growth regulator, challenged the subsequent registration of the substance by another manufacturer on the grounds
that the plaintiff had not been compensated for use of its data on
which the registration was based.
     In district court, EPA and the second manufacturer success-
fully argued that the effective date of the compensation provision
was controlled by Section 4(c)(1) of FEPCA 78/ which required EPA
to promulgate regulations governing registrations within two years.
Since EPA did not promulgate regulations covering compensation
until after the second manufacturer filed its application, the second
manufacturer argued that the compensation provision did not
apply. 79/

74/ Ibid. This portion was deleted by PL 94-140 § 12.

75/ PL 95-396 § 2(2), 92 Stat. 819.

76/ PL 94-140, §12, amending FIFRA §3(c)(1)(D). The 1972 amend-
     ments had not actually specified an effective date but most
     authorities assumed it was the date of enactment.

77/ 594 F.2d 470 (5th Cir. 1979), reh. denied, 602 F.2d 724 (5th Cir.
     1979).

78/ FEPCA § 4(a), 86 Stat. 998, 999.

79/ Amchem Products, Inc. v. GAF Corp., 391 F.Supp 124, 7 ERC
     1877 (N.D. Ga. 1975). The "taking" issue also arises under cases
     interpreting the 1978 amendments.

The Fifth Circuit reversed the district court's interpretation, holding that Section 4(c)(1) neither deferred the effective date of the FEPCA amendments nor gave EPA any discretion to activate provisions of the act by delaying promulgation of implementing regulations. 80/ The Fifth Circuit also rejected the defendant's argument that the compensation provision applied only to data submitted for the first time by the plaintiff after the FEPCA amendments became law. The court held that construing the provision to apply to data already in EPA's possession would satisfy Congressional intent to "[put] an end to free rides" by subsequent applications. 81/

In Mobay Chemical v. EPA, 82/ Mobay sued EPA claiming that EPA's use of its registration data prior to 1970 which was not compensatable under FIFRA was a "taking" for private use and invalid under the Fifth Amendment. Mobay did not base its claim on FIFRA, but rather the Due Process Clause of the Constitution, claiming that it was deprived of its right to exclusive use of its property. The District Court for the Western District of Missouri upheld the 1972 amendment on the grounds that Section 3 of FIFRA was enacted under the Commerce Clause and that Congress' concern with preventing costly duplicative testing was reasonably related to a legitimate purpose. The court also noted that EPA's use of the data did not create a deprivation of property which rose to the level of a taking.

On appeal, the United States Supreme Court dismissed the case on procedural grounds. The Court held that since FIFRA did not address EPA's use of pre-1970 data, the plaintiff's challenge was to "agency practice, not the statute." 83/ Since the three judge district court panel had been improperly convened, the court held that it did not have jurisdiction to hear the appeal.

80/ 594 F. 2d at 475.

81/ Ibid., at 482. In 1975, this provision was again amended to provide that only "data submitted on or after Jan. 1970" was covered by the section.

82/ 447 F. Supp. 811, 12 ERC 1572 (W. D. Mo. 1975).

83/ 439 U.S. 320, 12 ERC 1581 (per curiam) (1979).

In the case In re Ciba-Geigy Corp. v. Farmland Industries, Inc., 84/ EPA set out criteria to be applied in determining what constitutes reasonable compensation under Section 3(c). Plaintiff Ciba-Geigy claimed that it was entitled to $8.11 million in compensation from Farmland Industries for the latter's use of test data to register three pesticides. The defendant argued that it should pay only a proportional share of the actual cost of producing the data based on its share of the market for the products, approximately $49,000. The plaintiff contended that reasonable compensation should be based on the standards used in licensing technical knowledge: an amount equal to the cost of reproducing the data plus a royalty on gross sales for three years.

The administrative law judge hearing the case ruled that a cost-royalty formula was closer to Congress's intent to avoid unnecessary testing costs. He concluded that the reasonable compensation provision was not intended to provide reward for research and development as the plaintiff's formula would do. The fairest compensatory formula, according to the judge, was using the data producer's cost adjusted for inflation and the defendant's market share two or three years after initial registration. Although no reward for research and development was created, this compensation formula does create an incentive to research because the benefits gained from decreased costs of subsequent registrants outweighs the disadvantages of decreasing the original data producer's projects.

In 1984, the United States Supreme Court ruled in Ruckelshaus v. Monsanto Co. 85/ that pesticide health and safety data was property under Missouri Law Status and thus was protected under the Fifth Amendment of the Constitution. However, the Court overruled a lower court in finding that data submitted prior to 1972 and after 1978 was not a "taking" since the registrant had no expectation of confidentiality. For the period between the 1972 and 1978 amendments, the Court decided there was sufficient ambiguity to warrant a claim. The remedy was not to find FIFRA

84/ Initial Decision, FIFRA Comp. Dockets Nos. 33, 34 and 41 (19 August 1980).

85/ Ruckelshaus v. Monsanto Co., 104 S.Ct. 2862 (1984).

unconstitutional, however, as the lower court had done, but under the Tucker Act, 28 U.S.C. Section 1491.

4.3 Essentiality in Registration

Another registration change obtained by the pesticide industry was a prohibition against EPA refusing to register a substance because it served no useful or necessary purpose. This was not a dispute as to whether, under both the old and new FIFRA, a registration application must demonstrate that a product would "perform its intended function." 86/ The agricultural chemical companies, however, were apprehensive that EPA might refuse to register a new product because an old one satisfactorily performed its intended function. These fears were largely groundless. EPA's best interest lay in as much duplication of pesticides as reasonably possible, since the existence of a similar but safer chemical facilitates the removal of a hazardous pesticide from the market. There was therefore little objection to this non-essential amendment on "essentiality."

4.4 Intrastate Registrations

One important difference between the old and new laws is that under the old FIFRA, 87/ federal authority did not extend to intrastate use and shipment of pesticides with state registrations. This meant that federal authority could be avoided simply by having manufacturing plants in the principal agricultural states. The new FIFRA 88/ broadens the registration requirement to include any person in any state who sells or distributes pesticides.

The states do retain some authority under Section 24 "to regulate the sale or use of any pesticide or device in the state, but only if and to the extent the regulation does not permit any sale or use prohibited by this Act." 89/ States, furthermore, cannot have labeling and packaging requirements different from those required by the act—a measure which was popular among some chemical

---

86/ FIFRA § 3(c)(5)(D), 7 U.S.C. § 136a(c)(5)(D).

87/ Old FIFRA § 4(a).

88/ FIFRA § 3(a), 7 U.S.C. § 136a(a).

89/ FIFRA § 24(a), 7 U.S.C. § 136v(a).

manufacturers who feared that each state might have different labeling requirements. It also seems to exclude a feature common to several of the other environmental laws whereby states may impose stricter requirements than federal on pesticide use within their jurisdiction.

Finally, the section gives a state the authority, subject to certification by EPA, to register pesticides for limited local use in treating sudden and limited pest infestations, without the time and administrative burden required by a full EPA certification. 90/

The fears of pesticide manufacturers that the states would impose more stringent labeling requirements were justified in spite of the 1972 amendments. California imposed additional data requirements under its restricted-use registration. In National Agricultural Chemicals Association v. Rominger, 91/ a California district court declined to issue a preliminary injunction against the state's regulations on the grounds that there was no congressional mandate to occupy the field when Section 24 was enacted, thus there was no federal preemption of restricted-use registrations. 92/

4.5 Scientific Advisory Committees

An important issue for EPA in the 1972 legislation was a revision of the role of scientific advisory committees in the cancellation-suspension process. 93/ According to the old FIFRA, a registrant challenging a cancellation order could request either a public hearing or a scientific advisory committee; and in practice, cases involving several registrants usually resulted in both. EPA was also strongly dissatisfied with the vague and often contradictory reports of the advisory committees.

90/ FIFRA § 24(c), 7 U.S.C. § 136m(a).

91/ 500 F. Supp 465, 15 ERC 1039 (E.D. Cal. 1980).

92/ The court also dismissed challenges to two other provisions of the California laws for lack of ripeness. These challenges were claims that the statute improperly allowed the state to set residue tolerances different from EPA tolerances and that certain labeling requirements for insecticides were improperly imposed.

93/ See FIFRA § 6(d), 7 U.S.C. § 136d(d).

In the 1972 amendments to FIFRA, the advisory committee was transformed into an adjunct of the hearing process, resolving those scientific questions which the administrative law judge or the parties determined were essential to the final decision by the administrator. This enables the advisory committee to consider questions of scientific fact while the public hearing is in process, rather than in a separate proceeding with long delays and divisions of responsibility. By meeting outside of the public hearing, the scientists can also avoid being subject to cross examination and other legal burdens they consider unappealing.

The advisory process, however, was again made more formalistic by the 1975 amendments. The use of a scientific advisory committee is now mandated both for cancellation actions (where they are usually requested anyway) and for any general pesticide regulations; and the composition and selection process for the committee is set forth in considerable detail. 94/

In 1980, Section 25(d) was amended to allow the chairman of a Scientific Advisory Committee to create temporary subpanels on specific projects. 95/ Section 25(d) was also amended to require the administrator to submit any decision to suspend the registration of a pesticide to a scientific advisory panel (SAP) for its comment. 96/ The amendment does not alter the administrator's authority to issue a suspension notice prior to SAP review, it only requires him to obtain SAP review after the suspension is initiated. The 1980 amendments also require the administrator to issue written procedures for independent peer review of the design, protocol and conduct of major studies conducted under FIFRA. The latter two amendments are outgrowths of the General Accounting Office (GAO) study of EPA's controversial decision to suspend 2,4,5-T on an emergency basis. GAO reviewed EPA's decision and concluded that EPA did not have clearly defined peer review procedures. The amendments were enacted to require EPA to proceed on the basis of validated scientific information and to avoid another 2,4,5-T controversy. 97/

94/ PL 94-140, § 7, amending FIFRA § 25. A more detailed analysis of the 1975 changes appears in 5.0.

95/ PL 96-539, 94 Stat. 3195.

96/ Id.

97/ No. 96-1020, 96th Cong., 2d Sess. (1980) p. 4.

4.6 Standing for Registration, Appeals and Subpoenas

The old FIFRA assumed that only registrants would be interested in the continuation of a product's registration or the setting of public hearings and scientific advisory committees. It was increasingly evident, however, that this unintended exclusion of both users and environmentalists needed revision.

A registrant, when faced with cancellation, might prefer not to contest those minor categories of use which it regarded as financially insignificant, but a user might regard them as essential for the protection of his crops. The law was therefore amended by FEPCA to allow not only registrants but any "other interested person with the concurrence of the registrant" to request continuation of the registration. 98/ While this amendment remedies the problem of legal standing, it does not provide the resources and data which a user would need to support his renewal application. 99/

Another problem of standing relates to the right of environmental and consumer groups to utilize the administrative procedures under cancellation-suspension. The old FIFRA did not clearly provide for such groups to request a public hearing or scientific advisory hearing, even though they could obtain judicial review in the court of appeals as a "person who would be adversely affected by such order." 100/ The new act does not specifically give citizens' groups the right to request a public hearing, but the administrator himself is now empowered to call a hearing which he might do at the request of such a group. Furthermore, as already discussed, all

---

98/ FIFRA § 6(a)(1), 7 U.S.C. § 136d(a)(1). See also McGill v. GPA, 593 F. 2d 631, 13 ERC 1156 (5th Cir. 1979).

99/ A good example is the Aldrin-Dieldrin suspension proceeding, in which the registrant was almost solely interested in the use for crops, while the USDA had to join the proceeding to insure that other registrations were properly represented. This USDA action under the new FIFRA, however, was necessary not because the users now lacked legal standing, but presumably because they lacked adequate resources. In re Shell Chemical, supra, 6 ERC 2047.

100/ Old FIFRA § 4(d). The standing environmental groups to contest governmental actions in general is quite complex. See, for example, Sierra Club v. Morton, 405 U.S. 345, 3 ERC 2039 (1972).

interested parties may request consent of the administrative law judge to refer scientific questions to a special committee of the National Academy of Sciences for determination, a right which did not exist before.

The administrative law judge plays a key role in these proceedings, for his approval is necessary for advisory committee referrals and for the power of subpoena, which is given not to the parties but to him. 101/ It was Congress' intent to allow the judge just sufficient discretion to eliminate frivolous or irrelevant issues, hence the statutory language that "upon a showing of relevance and reasonable scope of evidence sought by any party to a public hearing, the hearing examiner shall issue a subpoena to compel testimony or production of documents from any person." 102/ Some commentators, however, have expressed concern that a judge may have excessive latitude to deny reasonable requests. 103/

The issue of standing came up in Environmental Defense Fund v. Costle 104/ when the D.C. Circuit upheld EPA's denial of standing for an environmental group which requested a Section 6(d) cancellation hearing for the continued use of chlorobenzilate in four states. The Environmental Defense Fund (EDF) requested the hearing after the Administrator issued a Notice of Intent to Cancel the registration of chlorobenzilate for all uses other than citrus spraying in four states. The administrator denied the hearing holding that FIFRA was not structured for the purpose of entertaining objections by persons having no real interest in stopping the cancellation from going into effect, but who object to the agency's refusal to propose actions. 105/

101/ See the EPA Rules of Practice 40 CFR § 164.21, 38 FR 19378 (1973) and U.S. v. Allen, 494 F. Supp. 107 (W.D. Wisc. 1980).

102/ FIFRA § 6(d), 7 U.S.C. § 136d(d).

103/ See, for example, William A. Butler, "Federal Pesticide Law," in Erica L. Dolgin and Thomas G. P. Guilbert, Federal Environmental Law (St. Paul, Minn.: West Publishing Co., 1974), p. 1256.

104/ 631 F.2d 922, 15 ERC 1217 (D.C. Cir. 1980), cert. denied 449 U.S. 1112.

105/ Final Decision, FIFRA Docket No. 411 (20 August 1979) at 12-22.

The D.C. Circuit upheld the administrator's decision that EDF was not an "adversely affected" party under Section 6(d), stating that a 6(d) hearing may be used only to stop a cancellation proceeding, not initiate one. The proper procedure for EDF in seeking review of EPA's decision to retain the registration for citrus users was to challenge the notice provisions permitting the limited use in district court under Section 16(a) of FIFRA. 106/

4.7 Judicial Appeals

Under the old FIFRA, 107/ appeals from decisions of the administrator went to the United States court of appeals. According to Section 16 of the amended FIFRA, however, appeals under some circumstances may go to a federal district court: agency "refusals to cancel or suspend registrations, or to change classifications not following a hearing, and other final agency actions not committed to agency discretion by law are judicially reviewable in the district courts." 108/ District courts are also given the authority to "enforce and to prevent and restrain violations of, this act." 109/ Other appeals go to the court of appeals.

This change provoked considerable controversy in EPA during the legislative process. The rationale for change was that courts of appeals are not designed to develop a record if none existed from the proceeding below. It thus seemed logical that in those instances where a record was developed, after public hearing or otherwise, the appeal should be to the court of appeals, whereas in cases where there was no record for the court to review the matter should go to a district court for findings of fact.

Unfortunately, this creates a certain ambiguity which a party might utilize to prolong the judicial review process. In one case that predated the amended FIFRA, an aggrieved registrant appealed to a district court judge whose record for eccentricity was almost

---

106/ 631 F. 2d at 935, 15 ERC at 1229. This case is also noteworthy for its treatment of judicial review under Section 16(b): See discussion of Judicial Review in 4.2.

107/ Old FIFRA § 4(d).

108/ FIFRA § 16(a), 7 U.S.C. § 136n(a).

109/ FIFRA § 16(c), 7 U.S.C. § 136n(c).

legendary. Although he had no jurisdiction whatsoever over the matter, the judge held up the case for almost two years before an order of the court of appeals could be obtained to overturn an injunction which he had issued against the agency. 110/ The legal process could have taken even longer if the statutory exclusion of the district court from jurisdiction had been less explicit.

Section 16 has been the focus of two courts of appeals decisions which reached contrary holdings on the issue of whether the federal courts or the courts of appeals have jurisdiction to review the denial of a request for a FIFRA Section 6(d) hearing on a notice of cancellation. In Environmental Defense Fund v. Costle, 111/ the D.C. Circuit Court held that if an administrative record exists in support of a denial of a hearing request, jurisdiction lies exclusively with the courts of appeals. In AMVAC Chemical Corp. v. EPA, 112/ a divided Ninth Circuit rejected the D.C. Circuit's analysis and held that a denial of a hearing was a procedural action and not an "order" following a "public hearing" within the meaning of Section 16(b). Hence, the Court held that judicial review of hearing request denials lies in the district courts.

The Ninth Circuit attempted to distinguish the Environmental Defense Fund case because the petitioners in that case were able to present their arguments to a Scientific Advisory Panel, whereas the petitioner in AMVAC did not have such an opportunity. 113/ This distinction is rather unpersuasive because the record on which the D.C. Circuit relied included only the proceedings and pleadings on the procedural question of judicial review. Consequently, these two cases present conflicting interpretations of Section 16(b) which may cause procedural nightmares for future review of EPA actions.

110/ Pax Co. v. U.S., 454 F. 2d 93, 3 ERC 1591 (10th Cir. 1972).

111/ 631 F. 2d 922, 15 ERC 1217 (D.C. Cir. 1980) cert. denied 449 U.S. 1112. This case is also important for its treatment of standing, discussed in the previous subsection.

112/ 653 F. 2d 1260, 15 ERC 1467 (9th Cir. 1980) as amended 5 February 1981, reh. denied, 10 April 1981.

113/ Ibid., at 1265.

4.8 Exports and Imports

The old FIFRA 114/ provided that imports should be subject to the same requirements of testing and registration as American products. Section 17 of the new FIFRA kept this provision 115/ and, at the urging of the chemical industry, also retained the controversial provision excluding U.S. exports from the act, other than for certain record keeping requirements. 116/

There were two reasons for this. First, the agricultural chemical producers, seeing the market for some of their products such as chlorinated hydrocarbons drying up in this country, wished to continue exporting the products abroad. They argued that foreign producers would not be stopped from manufacturing these chemicals and they wished to continue to compete, as well as to keep in operation profitable product lines.

A secondary but more compelling reason was that cancellation decisions made in the United States are based upon a risk-benefit analysis that might have little relevance to conditions abroad. For example, DDT is neither needed nor, because of insect resistance, very useful for the control of malaria in the United States. However, the situation in, say, Ceylon, may be quite different (although resistance is becoming an increasing problem there as well) and should be considered separately.

One problem with this approach is that persistent pesticides may be distributed by oceans and the atmosphere in a world-wide circulation pattern that does not stop at national boundaries. A second problem is that there is no requirement that foreign purchasers relying on EPA registration as proof of a product's safety be notified of cancellation-suspension proceedings. Only after a final agency decision—which may take years—is the State Department legally required to inform foreign governments. 117/ The 1978

114/ Old FIFRA § 10.

115/ FIFRA § 17(c), 7 U.S.C. § 136o(c). The old FIFRA provisions on exports is § 3(a)(5)(b).

116/ See FIFRA § 8, 7 U.S.C. § 136f.

117/ FIFRA § 17(b), 7 U.S.C. § 136o(b).

amendments did add a requirement that such exports be labeled that they are "not registered for use in the U.S." 118/

In 1980, EPA issued a final policy statement on labeling requirements. 119/ Under the 1978 amendments, pesticides which are manufactured for export must have bilingual labeling which identify the product and protect persons who come into contact with it. If the pesticide is not registered for use in the United States, the exporter must obtain a statement from the foreign purchaser acknowledging its unregistered status. 120/

The policy statement implements these new requirements by requiring exported products to bear labels containing an EPA establishment number, a use classification statement, the identity of the producer, as well as information about whether the pesticide is registered for use in the United States. In the case of highly toxic pesticides, a skull and crossbones must appear and the word "poison" along with a statement of practical treatment written bilingually. 121/

The policy statement also requires that a foreign purchaser of an unregistered pesticide sign a statement showing that he understands that the pesticide is not registered for use in the United States. The exporter must receive the acknowledgement before the product is released for shipment and submit it to EPA within seven days of receipt. EPA then transmits the acknowledgements to the appropriate foreign officials via the State Department. The acknowledgement procedure applies only to the first annual shipment of an unregistered pesticide to a producer; subsequent shipments of the product to the same producer do not need to comply with the acknowledgement process. 122/

On 15 January 1981, President Carter signed Executive Order 12264 establishing procedures for the export of banned or

---

118/ FIFRA § 17(a)(2), 7 U.S.C. § 136o(e)(f). See also 44 FR 4358, 19 January 1979.

119/ 45 FR 50274, 28 July 1980.

120/ PL 95-396, 92 Stat 833; codified at 7 U.S.C. § 136(o).

121/ 45 FR at 50274, 50278, 28 July 1980.

122/ Ibid., at 50276-77.

significantly restricted substances from the United States. 123/ The comprehensive policy was designed to make present statutory controls over exports more consistent and effective. The cornerstone was a provision requiring that foreign importing countries be notified of the importation of a restricted or banned substance. One of the most restrictive provisions and one that reportedly caused the most disagreement between the federal agencies involved in the policy directed the Department of Commerce to develop regulations for licensing exports of hazardous wastes. The order applied to pesticides, chemicals, drugs, and other products which were restricted in some way by federal statute.

The policy was short-lived because President Reagan rescinded it on 17 February 1981, shortly after he took office. 124/ President Reagan sought instead a review of existing U.S. export controls. The recission resulted in no real changes in the notification requirements under Section 17 of FIFRA.

In the 1986 effort to amend FIFRA, there was little sentiment for changing the present rule allowing importation into the U.S. of food containing residues of pesticides banned by the EPA. 125/

4.9 Disposal and Recall

An important question following a cancellation or suspension action is whether to recall those products already in commerce. 126/ "Misbranded" pesticides may be confiscated, and on several occasions EPA has ordered manufacturers to recall a pesticide when the hazard so warranted, but for both practical and administrative reasons cancellation-suspension orders have generally provided that banned pesticides may be used until supplies are exhausted, without

---

123/ 46 FR 4659, 19 January 1981.

124/ 46 FR 12943, 19 February 1981.

125/ For example, the Senate Agriculture Committee in August 1986 voted to allow continued importation. BNA Chemical Reporter, 10:597, 8 August 1986.

126/ FIFRA §§ 19 and 25, 7 U.S.C. §§ 136q and 136w. See also the previous discussion of indemnities.

being subject to recall. 127/ It may seem inconsistent to ban a substance as an imminent hazard and yet allow quantities already on
the market to be sold, but repeated challenges by environmentalist
groups have been unsuccessful. 128/

This policy was thought necessary, for example, in the mercury pesticides case when EPA scientists concluded that the recall
of certain mercuric compounds would result in a concentration more
harmful to the environment than permitting the remaining supplies
to be thinly spread around the country. In the DDT case the administrator decided that his final cancellation order would not go into
effect for six months to ensure the availability of adequate supplies
of alternative pesticides (namely, organophosphates which can be
very hazardous to untrained applicators) and to allow time for training and educational programs to prevent misuse of the new
chemicals.

EPA promulgated regulations for the storage and disposal of
pesticides in May 1974, 129/ and proposed others which were never
implemented. 130/ These detailed the appropriate conditions for
incinerations, soil injection, and other means of disposal, established
procedures for shipment back to the manufacturers or to the federal
government, directed that transportation costs should be borne by
the owner of the pesticide, and provided standards for storage. The
regulations devote considerable attention to the disposal problem of
pesticide containers, which have caused a significant proportion of
accidental poisonings.

127/ Compare the recall authority of the Consumer Product Safety
Commission under Section 15 of its Hazardous Substance Act,
15 U.S.C. §1274, PL 91-113, which makes recall almost mandatory. The Consumer Product Safety Act, Section 15, on the
other hand, provides several options, 15 U.S.C. 2064, PL 92-
573.

128/ See, e.g., EDF v. EPA 510 F. 2d 1292, 7 ERC 1689 (D.C. Cir.
1975).

129/ 39 FR 15236, 1 May 1974, 40 CFR § 165.

130/ 39 FR 36874, 15 October 1974.

4.10 Experimental Use Permits

FIFRA 131/ provides for experimental use permits for registered pesticides. 132/ The purpose of this seemingly innocuous section is to permit a registration applicant to conduct tests and "accumulate information necessary to register a pesticide under Section 3." 133/ This provision, however, has already been used in at least one successful effort to evade a FIFRA cancellation-suspension order. Under strong political pressure from Western sheep interests and their congressional spokesmen, EPA granted a Section 5 permit for the limited use of certain banned predacides and devices including the "coyote getter." 134/

In March 1974 EPA proposed regulations for experimental permits, noting that in the one-year period from October 1972 to October 1973 almost one hundred experimental permits were issued authorizing the use of a total of 1.5 million pounds of pesticides, and this figure did not include substantial experimental use of federal and state agencies. 135/ These regulations, which became final on 30 April 1975, provided for tighter control over experimental use, including that by governmental agencies, 136/ but did not close the loophole entirely.

EPA issued final regulations on 18 July 1979 under which a state may develop its own experimental permits program. 137/ A

131/ FIFRA § 5, U.S.C. § 136c.

132/ The 1975 amendments added a specific provision for agricultural research agencies, public or private.

133/ FIFRA § 5(a), 7 U.S.C. § 136c(a).

134/ EPA's pesticide regulatory decisions have generally been little affected by such outside pressures, but this action was one of the three exceptions to the rule. The others were an emergency permit for DDT use in the Pacific Northwest, and the protracted deliberations on the ant-killer Mirex.

135/ 39 FR 11306, 27 March 1974, 40 CFR § 172.

136/ Ibid. The regulations point out that, except in limited circumstances, the amended FIFRA "does not grant a blanket exemption to federal or state agencies."

137/ 44 FR at 41783, 18 July 1978; 40 CFR § 172.20.

state, by submitting a plan which meets the requirements of EPA's regulations, may receive authorization to issue experimental use permits to potential registrants under 24(c) of FIFRA (restricted use registration), agricultural or educational research agencies, and certified applicators for use of a restricted use pesticide.

Permits cannot be issued by a state for a pesticide containing ingredients subject to an EPA cancellation or suspension order, or a notice of intent to cancel or suspend or which are not found in any EPA registered product. 138/ The regulations also contain strict limitations on the production and use of a pesticide. Periodic reports must be submitted by the permittee to the state detailing the progress of the research or restricted use. In addition, permits cannot be issued for more than three years.

5.0 1975 AMENDMENTS TO FIFRA

Congress' 1975 amendments to the FIFRA are significant not for what they actually changed but because of the motivations that prompted them. The amendments themselves were viewed by many as, at best, unnecessary and, at worst, a further encumbrance upon an already complicated administrative procedure. They did, however, indicate a strong desire on the part of Congress—or at least the respective agriculture committees—to restrict EPA's authority to regulate pesticides. The situation was summarized by an editorial in a Washington, D.C., newspaper captioned, "Trying to Hogtie the EPA." 139/

5.1 Need for FIFRA Renewal

The authorization for FIFRA under the 1972 act was limited to three years. 140/ Congress was therefore provided the opportunity in 1975 to review the strengths and shortcomings of the 1972 legislation, even though some portions of that law were not

---

138/ 44 FR at 41788. States may, however, issue permits for products containing ingredients subject to the Rebuttable Presumption Against Review process (RPAR).

139/ The Washington Star, 8 October 1975.

140/ FIFRA § 27. Actually the term for the act was less than three years since the act finally went into effect in October 1972 and the authorization expired 30 June 1975.

scheduled to go into effect until four years after enactment. 141/ This review, however, also provided a chance for those, both within and without Congress who believed that EPA had been given too much authority, to seek to redress the balance.

Some environmentalists feared that the Agriculture Committee would allow the bill to lapse altogether, which would have created some uncertainty as to whether the entire FIFRA would have been abolished or merely the 1972 amendments. Practically speaking, it probably would not have made any difference, as EPA could not have administered any part of the law without Congressional authorization of funds. This eventually, however, probably would have created a backlash in favor of the environmentalists and led to much more stringent laws than the House Agriculture Committee or the agricultural chemical industry desired.

Authorization was therefore granted for FIFRA, but the extension was only for one year (to 30 September 1976) rather than the two-year period which EPA originally sought. The reason for this limitation, according to the official House report, was "to give it [Congress] an opportunity to continue to exercise effective oversight activities over its [EPA's] operations," particularly in view of the controversies that had been generated in many of its activities. 142/

5.2 Controversy over USDA's Veto of EPA

The most spirited debate in the Committee hearings was over an amendment submitted by Representative Bob Poage (D-Tex.), the former Chairman of the House Agriculture Committee. The Poage-Wampler Amendment would have permitted the Secretary of Agriculture to veto EPA actions cancelling or suspending a registration, changing the classification of a pesticide, or issuing regulations. The proposed amendment provided no criteria or legal requirements which the secretary had to meet for such a veto, nor was it necessary for the secretary to consider the extensive record developed by

---

141/ One such example is EPA's authority under § 27 to require that a pesticide be registered for use only by a certified applicator.

142/ House Report No. 94-497, "Extension and Amendment of the FIFRA, as Amended," 19 September 1975, for H.R. 8841, p. 5.

EPA for the administrator's decision. Moreover, although less than half of EPA pesticides relate to agriculture, 143/ the secretary would have been granted authority to block EPA actions on all of them. The amendment would have also severely compromised the administering of the act by fragmenting the authority over pesticides between the two agencies. 144/ There was some sentiment in Congress for restoring jurisdiction over pesticides to USDA, but the Department's poor prior record discouraged serious consideration of this idea. 145/

5.3 Requirement of Consultation by EPA with USDA

Congress decided instead to require that EPA engage in formal consultation with USDA and with the Agriculture Committees of the House and Senate before issuing proposals or final standards regarding pesticides. This amended Section 6(b) of the FIFRA to provide that EPA should give 60 days' notice to the secretary of agriculture before a notice is made public. The secretary then must respond within 30 days, and these comments, along with the response of the EPA administrator, are published in the Federal Register. According to the House report, "this represents a real change from present procedures . . . it would have much the same effect as the public exposure of an environmental impact statement. . . ." 146/ These consultations, however, are not required in the event of an imminent hazard to human health for which a suspension order under Section 6(c) is warranted. 147/

143/ See the statement of Russell E. Train, Administrator, EPA before the Senate Agriculture Committee, reprinted in the Senate Report No. 94-452, "Extension of the FIFRA," 10 November 1975, to accompany H. R. 8841, p. 18.

144/ This difficult situation also exists between EPA and FAA, although in that instance the roles are reversed. See the chapter on Noise in this book.

145/ See House Report No. 94-497, p. 7.

146/ House Report No. 94-497, p. 6. These time deadlines may be by agreement between the administrator and the secretary, PL 94-140, § 1.

147/ FIFRA, § 6(c), 7 U.S.C. § 136d(c).

This amendment makes sense only if one assumes either that USDA had not been contacted regularly by EPA before making major decisions in the past, or if it is believed (as the above House report seems to indicate) that USDA's objections to EPA actions had not been given sufficient public attention. Neither assumption is really accurate. The amendment does, however, place USDA in the potentially embarrassing situation of having to respond formally within an unreasonably short period to EPA proposals. The Department of Agriculture was previously in the politically desirable position of being able to criticize EPA actions without having to provide detailed explanation or supportable objections. 148/

At the same time that the administrator provides a copy of any proposed regulations to the secretary of agriculture, he is also required to provide copies to the respective House and Senate Agricultural Committees. The practical impact of this requirement is that Congress is provided an opportunity to communicate displeasure to the administrator before a proposal is issued without necessarily having to subject these comments to scrutiny in the public record. 149/

5.4 Scientific Advisory Committees

One of the reforms of the 1972 amendments had been to streamline the Scientific Advisory Committee process so that Committee deliberations could proceed simultaneously with the administrative hearings, thereby saving time and making them a part of the fact-finding and evaluation system rather than a separate procedure. The 1975 amendments require that the administrator submit proposed and final regulations to a specially constituted scientific

---

148/ The requirement for EPA to consult with USDA is the reverse of the situation regarding small watersheds under PL 566, whereby EPA can formally object to USDA's approval of small watersheds, although USDA does not have to accept the objections. House Report No. 94-497, p. 6. A similar authority is found in EPA's right to object to FAA decisions which might affect emissions into the ambient air.

149/ EPA has often required that congressional communications after the issuance of a proposal be placed on the public record; and where this was not done, as in the DDT proceedings, environmental groups successfully sued to ensure that these contacts and written comments were made public.

advisory panel, separate from the regular Scientific Advisory Committees, at the same time that he provides copies to the secretary of agriculture and to the two agricultural committees of Congress. The advisory committee then has 30 days in which to respond. Membership on this committee is prescribed in unusual detail. The administrator can select seven members from a group of twelve nominees, six nominated by the National Science Foundation, and six by the National Institutes of Health. 150/

One might question the value of yet another advisory committee when, as Administrator Train pointed out, "EPA is already awash in scientific advisory panels." 151/ After all, the statute already provides for a separate scientific advisory committee under the auspices of the National Academy of Sciences for each pesticide cancellation action. EPA has also had, since its inception, a Science Advisory Board (formerly called the Hazardous Materials Advisory Committee) and the administrator has recently created a Pesticides Policy Advisory Committee. Furthermore, one might question how effective the new advisory committee will be, given its thirty-day time limit, considering that the present advisory committees at EPA and other agencies have great difficulty in producing creditable reports under schedules permitting four months of review or longer.

5.5 Economic Impact On Agriculture Statement

The 1975 amendments also reflected the increasing trend in government toward requiring impact statements before regulations can be issued. Congress, borrowing from the environmental impact statement process 152/ and the economic impact statement

---

150/ PL 94-140, § 7, amending FIFRA § 25(d), 7 U.S.C. § 136w.

151/ Statement of EPA Administrator Russell Train to the Senate Agricultural Committee, reprinted in Senate Report No. 94-452, p. 18. This concern apparently did not prevent Congress from amending FIFRA in 1980 to allow the chairman of a SAP to create subpanels. See discussion of 1980 amendments, infra.

152/ National Environmental Policy Act, § 102(2)(c), U.S.C. §§ 4321 et seq., (1969); see also 36 FR 7724 (1971) and 38 FR 20549 (1973).

requirements, 153/ mandated in the new amendment that the administrator, when deciding to issue a proposal, "shall include among
those factors to be taken into account the impact of the action
proposed in such notice on production and prices of agricultural
commodities, retail food prices, and otherwise on the agricultural
economy." 154/

The necessity for this new legal provision is questionable
since the balancing of risks and benefits is at the heart of FIFRA.
No one at EPA or anywhere else has contended that the agricultural
benefits of pesticides should not be taken into consideration in this
balancing equation. In fact, although the courts have stated that
EPA legally need not consider benefits in suspension actions involving an imminent hazard to human health and the environment, EPA
from the beginning has always made the agricultural factor an
essential element in its determinations. 155/ The committees themselves were vague about the actual need for this legislation. The
Senate stated, "The Committee concurs in the House position that
EPA has not always given adequate consideration to agriculture in
its decisions. This concern was also expressed by many witnesses
appearing before the Committee." 156/ However, the House position, at least as indicated in their official committee report, suggests less certainty: "The Committee believes that the [present]
statutory test is a sound one and that changes are not needed in the
formula. There was, however, a strong belief among many witnesses
that the impact on the agrcultural economy of decisions in EPA was
not fully developed by EPA and was not given sufficient recognition." 157/

5.6 Self-Certification of Private Applicators

The clearest illustration of Congress' altered view toward
FIFRA is their treatment of the certification program which had
been a major reason for the enactment of the 1972 amendments.

153/ Presidential Executive Order No. 11821, 29 November 1974.

154/ PL 94-104, § 1, amending FIFRA § 6(b), 7 U.S.C. § 136d.

155/ See the discussion of this in paragraph 2.6 of this chapter.

156/ Senate Report No. 94-452, p. 9.

157/ House Report No. 94-497, p. 6.

This law provided that the pesticides which might be too harmful to the applicators or to the environment if indiscriminately used could continue to be applied by farmers and pesticide operators who had received special training in avoiding these problems.

The program had run into resistance from the beginning from farmers who resented the requirement that they be trained to use chemicals on their own property. As stated in the House report, "The Committee does not see the need for a farmer who would be treating his own farm as he has done for many years to have to go to the county seat or elsewhere for a special training program to get certified." 158/ The changed law does not remove the examination requirement from commercial applicators, who apply pesticides to property other than their own. 159/ It does create an exemption, however, which covers not only the farmer who is applying pesticides to his own land but also his employees. And it must be remembered that the hazards are not necessarily limited to the applicator; organophosphates, which are nerve gases, may be highly toxic to the applicators, but many other substances if improperly used may run off to threaten neighboring farms or the environment in general. The amended law does not seem to recognize this latter problem.

The 1975 amendments also removed the authority of the administrator to require, under state plans submitted for his approval, that farmers take exams before being certified. In other words, EPA may require a training program but may not require a final examination to determine if the information has been learned. 160/ In the opinion of the House Agriculture Committee, "The farmer would be more aware of the dangers of restricted use pesticides if each time he makes a purchase he is given a self-certification form to read and sign." 161/

158/ House Report No. 94-497, p. 9.

159/ See the definition of commercial applicator in FIFRA § 2(e).

160/ States may themselves require an examination of certified applicators but, under the amended FIFRA, EPA could not make this a prerequisite for state plan approval. See PL 94-140 § 5, amending FIFRA § 4, 7 U.S.C. 136b. See also Senate Report No. 94-452, pp. 7-8.

161/ House Report No. 94-497, p. 9.

The report continues, "at the time of purchase of a pesticide, the dealer goes through the information on the label with the prospective buyer and satisfies himself that the buyer understands the limited uses prescribed by the label. Once the dealer is satisfied that the buyer understands the label clearly, he provides the buyer with a certification form for signature in which the buyer certifies he understands the restricted use of the pesticide and will conduct himself accordingly. The dealer is checked periodically to assure that he is informed on the use of the various pesticides that he is licensed to sell and is properly instructing buyers." 162/

6.0 1978 AMENDMENTS TO FIFRA

6.1 Conditional Registration

The near-collapse of EPA's pesticide registration process prompted creation of a system of conditional registration or reregistration. This could be applied when certain data on a product's safety had either not yet been supplied to EPA or had not yet been analyzed to ensure, according to FIFRA § 3(a)(5)(D), that "it will perform its intended function without unreasonable adverse effects on the environment."

Three kinds of conditional registrations are authorized by § 6 of the 1978 law which amends FIFRA § 3(c) with a new section, entitled "Registration Under Special Circumstances": pesticides identical or very similar to currently registered products; new uses to existing pesticide registrations; and pesticides containing active ingredients not contained in any currently registered pesticide for which data need be obtained for registration. These conditional registrations must be conducted on a case-by-case basis, with the last type of conditional registration further limited both by duration and by the requirement that the "use of the pesticide is in the public interest." Conditional registration is prohibited if a Notice of Rebuttable Presumption Against Registration (RPAR) has been issued for the pesticide. And the proposed new use involves use on a minor food or feed crop for which there is an effective registered pesticide not subject to a RPAR proceeding.

Cancellation of conditional registrations must be followed by a public hearing, if requested, within seventy-five days of the

---

162/ Ibid., at 9-10.

request, but must be limited to the issue of whether the registrant has fulfilled its conditions for the registration. 163/

EPA published final regulations implementing conditional registration on 11 May 1979. 164/

6.2 Generic Pesticide Review

EPA has long complained that registration, and especially reregistration reviews, should be conducted for entire classes of chemicals rather than being limited to examining each particular registration as it comes up for five-year renewal. This authority has always existed under FIFRA, but a district court decision in 1975 165/ on compensation for data made this so complicated that the plan was dropped pending a legislative solution.

The amendment that finally emerged under this label in Section 4 of the 1978 act, however, is considerably different in scope: "No applicant for registration of a pesticide who proposes to purchase a registered pesticide from another producer in order to formulate such purchased pesticide into an end-use product shall be required to (i) submit or cite data pertaining to the safety of such purchased product; or (ii) offer to pay reasonable compensation . . . for the use of any such data." 166/

In September 1978, EPA listed 40 chemicals contained in 21,000 pesticides to which it intended to apply generic review within the next two years. This included kelthane, azides, warfarin, naphthalene, and boric acid. 167/

6.3 Greater State Authority

Several sections of the 1978 amendments reflect Congress' intent to give the states greater responsibility in regulating pesticides. This includes not only training and cooperative

---

163/ § 12 of 1978 act, amending FIFRA § 6.

164/ 44 FR 27932, 11 May 1979.

165/ Mobay Chemical Corp. v. Train, 394 F. Supp. 1342, 8 ERC 1227 (W.D. Mo. 1975).

166/ 1978 act, amending FIFRA § 3(c)(2).

167/ BNA 2 Chemical Regulation Reporter, 29 September 1978, pp. 1157-1158.

agreements, but also increasing federal delegation over such matters as intra-state registrations and enforcement. 168/ The EPA administrator, however, retains overall supervisory responsibility and ultimate veto authority.

Because some states, such as California, have promulgated stringent guidelines for pesticide regulations, there has been proposed legislation to limit state authority under Section 24 to gather data about a pesticide for state registration. 169/ Pesticide manufacturers have complained for several years that state registration procedures, which may require additional studies and data gathering, are time-consuming and costly. There have been no changes in Section 24 yet; however, Congress may limit the regulatory authority of the states in future legislation.

6.4 Compensation and Confidentiality

The already overlong FIFRA provisions on the procedures for compensating other firms for their scientific test data have been made even more lengthy and complex. One improvement, however, was shifting the arbitrator role from the EPA administrator to the Federal Mediation and Conciliation Service. 170/ As with TSCA, the controversy over trade secrets will continue to be one of the most troublesome in the law. The amendments did clarify EPA's authority to disclose ecological and toxicological data to the public. 171/

6.5 Efficacy

The requirements for test data on a pesticide's efficacy are now made discretionary for EPA. This does not change the present practice very much, because efficacy information has been increasingly less important over the past few years. But the provision is interesting because it marks a complete reversal from the original

---

168/ §§ 21-27 of 1978 act.

169/ See "Hearings Before the House Agricultural Committee, Federal Insecticide, Fungicide, and Rodenticide Act Amendments," H.R. 5203, Serial No. 97-R, (1982).

170/ § 2 of 1978 act, amending FIFRA § 3.

171/ § 15 of 1978 act, amending FIFRA § 10. The trade secrets provision is discussed in 3.0, and 4.2, infra.

purpose of federal pesticide legislation earlier in this century, which was to protect farmers from "snake oil" pesticide claims. 172/

7.0 1980 AMENDMENTS TO FIFRA

FIFRA was amended again in 1980, but the amendments made only minor changes in Section 25 of the act. These changes are briefly described in the following two sections.

7.1 Two-House Congressional Veto Over EPA Regulations

The 1980 amendments amended Section 25(a) to provide a two-house congressional veto over EPA rules or regulations. 173/ Under the amendments, the administrator is required to submit to each house of Congress new FIFRA regulations. If Congress adopts a concurrent resolution disapproving the new regulation within ninety days of its promulgation it will not become effective. However, if neither house disapproves the regulation after sixty days and the appropriate committee of neither house has reported out a disapproving regulation, the regulation becomes effective.

The constitutionality of congressional vetoes of administrative rules is unsettled. The Supreme Court in 1983 held that one-house vetoes are unconstitutional, and since then legislation has had to be revised to conform to the legislative mode: both houses must pass legislature which is then presented to the president for his approval or disapproval. 174/ Two-house vetoes have not been the subject of litigation as of this writing.

7.2 Changes in the Function and Design of the Science Advisory Panel (SAP)

Section 25(d) of FIFRA was amended by the insertion of two provisions. One authorized the chairman of the FIFRA Scientific Advisory Panel (SAP) to create subpanels. 175/ The other provision

---

172/ § 5 of 1978 act, amending FIFRA § 3 (c)(5).

173/ PL 96-539, 94 Stat. 3194, 3195 amending 7 U.S.C. § 136w(4).

174/ Immigration & Naturalization Service v. Chadha, 462 U.S. 919, 103 S. Ct. 2764 (1983), affirming 634 F. 2d 408 (9th Cir. 1980).

175/ PL 96-539, 94 Stat. 3194, amending 7 U.S.C. 136w(a).

required the administrator to submit emergency suspension orders to the SAP for review of the environmental impacts of the suspension. 176/

The 1980 amendments also added Section 25(e) to the act which requires the administrator to issue written procedures for independent peer review of the design and conduct of major studies performed by EPA. 177/ This provision was an outgrowth of the General Accounting Office (GAO) study of EPA's decision to issue an emergency suspension for 2,4,5-T. GAO concluded that EPA did not have clearly defined peer review procedures and that such procedures were necessary to bolster public confidence in EPA's decision. 178/

8.0 1986 PROPOSED AMENDMENTS

Although not passed in the 99th Congress, these amendments are significant since they were one of the most important legislation considered by the 99th Congress and were the first pesticide amendments proposed in 14 years. Similar amendments will most likely be passed in the 100th Congress.

The proposals included completion of health and safety studies within 10 years for the 600 active ingredients in 35,000 pesticides, re-registration fees, uniform federal tolerances, groundwater protection, and data compensation.

9.0 LEGAL CASES

The usual way to understand a legal field is first to read the statute and then to read the cases involved. This is much less helpful in understanding the FIFRA, however, for several reasons. First, the FIFRA, especially the old FIFRA, had a very complicated legal framework in which the practice had for many years necessarily deviated from the apparent scope of the statute. One such instance was the shift from a mere labeling statute, in which harmful substances would be removed as "mislabeled," to one where the health

---

176/ Ibid.

177/ PL 96-539, 94 Stat. 3195 adding § 25(e), 7 U.S.C. § 136w(e).

178/ H.R. No. 96-1020, 96th Cong., 2d Sess. (1980), pp. 4, 8.

and safety issues were in the forefront. Second, the scientific issues involved in determinations of carcinogenicity, teratogenicity, subacute effects, and the sophisticated chains of causation affecting the environment are understandably not simple matters for a court to follow. Third, as a result, the courts have only hesitantly postulated adjudicatory principles, and some of these if taken literally have been too unrealistic for the Agency to follow. Decisions tend either to be declarations of deference to administrative expertise or remands for further elucidation of a point troubling the court.

Fourth, and now perhaps most important, the litigation over FIFRA for the last decade has shifted from being concerned with product safety to concern with data confidentiality and the financial compensation for its use by other companies. That does not necessarily mean that the former is ignored nor that all sides have reached consensus on what constitutes a health risk, but that the environmental safety issue is now contested more at the staff level within EPA's Pesticide Office than at the administrator's level or in the courts. (There is also, admittedly, much less federal regulatory activity, namely cancellations and suspensions, than there once was.)

The pesticide industry has focused instead of allocating the tremendously expensive costs of developing and registering the few products that survive the testing process and can be marketed. Hence, the preoccupation this past decade has been on trade secrets and compensation, which are discussed at length earlier in this chapter.

But for that reason, the judicial doctrines set forth in EPA's first half dozen years remain the basis for pesticide regulation.

9.1 Basic Cases

The early cases, originating in the period before EPA's creation, generally resulted in court determinations that the responsible federal agency had not sufficiently examined the health and environmental problems.

A leading case in this respect is the 1970 court of appeals decision by Judge Bazelon in Environmental Defense Fund v. Hardin, 179/ which not only gave legal standing to environmental groups under the FIFRA but also determined that the secretary of agriculture's failure to take prompt action on a request for sus-

---

179/ 428 F. 2d 1083, 1 ERC 1347 (D.C. Cir. 1970).

pension of the registration of DDT was tantamount to a denial of suspension and therefore was suitable for judicial review. 180/

That same year the Seventh Circuit Court of Appeals held en banc in Nor-Am v. Hardin 181/ that a pesticide registrant could not enjoin a suspension order by the secretary of agriculture, since the administrative remedies, namely the full cancellation proceedings, had not been exhausted: "The emergency suspension becomes final only if unopposed or affirmed in whole or in part, by subsequent decisions based upon a full and formal consideration. 182/ An under-lying reason for the court's action, which reversed a three-judge court of appeals panel in the same circuit, 183/ was the realization that the suspension procedure, which had been designed to deal with imminent hazards to the public, could effectively be short-circuited by injunctions. In the court's view, therefore, a suspension decision is only equivalent of a temporary injunction which shall hold until the full cancellation proceedings are completed. 184/

One of the most important of the earlier cases was EDF v. Ruckelshaus. 185/ The court in another opinion by Judge Bazelon found that the secretary of agriculture failed to take prompt action on a request for the interim suspension of DDT registration but that the secretary's findings of fact, such as the risk of cancer and its toxic effect on certain animals, implicitly constituted a finding of "substantial question concerning the safety of DDT" which the court

---

180/ As there was no administrative record underlying the secretary's inaction, however, the court remanded the issue to the department of agriculture "to provide the court with a record necessary for meaningful appellate review."

181/ 435 F. 2d 1151, 2 ERC 1016 (7th Cir., en banc, 1970).

182/ Ibid., at 1157, 2 ERC at 1019.

183/ 435 F. 2d 1133, 1 ERC 1460 (7th Cir. 1970).

184/ 435 F. 2d at 1160-1161.

185/ EDF v. Ruckelshaus, 439 F.2d 584, 2 ERC 1114 (D.C. Cir. 1971). This was a sequel to the earlier EDF v. Hardin case, supra, but the name of the administrator of EPA was substituted for the secretary of agriculture since the authority of USDA had been transferred to the EPA the month before.

declared warranted a cancellation decision. The suspension issue was remanded once again for further consideration.

The decision is worthy of attention on two additional points. First, Judge Bazelon made the sweeping statement that "the FIFRA requires the secretary to issue notices and thereby initiate the administrative process whenever there is a substantial question about the safety of the registered pesticide . . . The statutory scheme contemplates that these questions will be explored in the full light of a public hearing and not resolved behind the closed doors of the secretary." 186/ Second, the court approved the findings of the secretary that a hazard may be "imminent" even if its effect would not become realized for many years, as is the case with most carcinogens, and that the "public" protected by the suspension provision includes fish and wildlife in the environment as well as narrow threat to human health. 187/

Wellford v. Ruckelshaus, 188/ another case inherited by EPA from USDA, involved a partial remand of the secretary of agriculture's decision concerning suspension and cancellation of certain uses of the herbicide 2,4,5-T for use around the home, in aquatic areas, and on food crops. This case is primarily important for its articulation of certain procedural ground. It agreed with the contention that suspension is only "a matter of interim relief," 189/ and stated that the criteria for suspension during an administrative process involved the secretary's first determining "what harm, if any, is likely to flow from the use of the product during the course of administrative proceedings. He must consider both the magnitude of the anticipated harm and the likelihood that it would occur. On the basis of that factual determination, he must decide whether anticipated harm amounts to an 'imminent hazard to the public.' "190/

186/ Ibid., at 594, 2 ERC at 1119. Because there may be a "substantial question of safety" about most pesticides, administrative necessity has forced EPA to interpret this as requiring cancellation of only the most harmful chemicals.

187/ Ibid., at 597, 2 ERC at 1121-22.

188/ 439 F. 2d 598, 2 ERC 1123 (D.C. Cir. 1971).

189/ Ibid., at 601, 2 ERC at 1124.

190/ Ibid., at 602, 2 ERC at 1125.

9.2 Label Restrictions: Theory and Practice

One of the most interesting pesticide cases, In re Stearns, 191/ raised the question whether a chemical could be banned that was too toxic to be safely used around the home but which nevertheless was labeled properly with cautionary statements and symbols such as the skull and crossbones. "Stearn's Electric Paste," a phosphorous rat and roach killer, was so potent that even a small portion of a tube could kill a child and a larger dose would be fatal to an adult. There was no known antidote. An incomplete survey of state health officials indicated several dozen deaths and many serious accidents, most involving young children. Because of this hazard and the existence of safer substitutes, the USDA cancelled the registration of the paste in May 1969, before the creation of EPA, and a USDA Judicial Officer upheld this action in January 1971 by relying on the provision in the old FIFRA that "the term misbranded shall apply. . .to any economic poison. . .if the labeling accompanying it does not contain directions for use which are necessary and, if complied with, adequate for the protection of the public." 192/

A year and a half later, however, the Seventh Circuit Court of Appeals concluded that the statutory test for misbranding was whether a product was safe when used in conformity with the label directions, not whether abuse or misuse was inevitable. The court was impressed with the conspicuous "poison" markings and contended that "disregard of such a simple warning would constitute gross negligence." 193/ The hazard of young children left the court unmoved: "such tragedies are a common occurrence in today's complex society and must be appraised as discompassionately as possible." 194/ The cancellation order was set aside.

191/ 2 ERC 1364 (Opinion of Judicial Officer, USDA, 1971); Stearns Electric Paste Company v. EPA, 461 F. 2d 293, 4 ERC 1164 (7th Cir. 1972).

192/ Old FIFRA § 2(z)2(c).

193/ Stearns Electric Paste, supra, 461 F.2d at 310, 4 ERC at 1175.

194/ Ibid., at 308, 4 ERC at 1174.

On the same day, that same panel of the Seventh Circuit also decided Continental Chemiste v. Ruckelshaus, 195/ involving a Lindane (benzene hexachloride) vaporizer, which when lighted emitted a cloud lethal to many insect pests. Studies by USDA demonstrated that these devices in the home produced residues of Lindane on food which "posed a threat to human health." 196/ The vaporizers were registered only for use in commercial and industrial establishments, not for home use, but the registrant's advertising and marketing techniques were specifically designed to promote sales to private consumers. The court declined to rule this illegal, deciding the case on another issue to be discussed later.

The issue was confronted more decisively by the Eighth Circuit a year later in another Lindane case, Southern National v. EPA. 197/ The registrants challenged a proposed EPA label reading in part "Not for use or sale to drug stores, supermarkets, or hardware stores or other establishments that sell insecticides to consumers. Not for sale to or use in food handling, processing or serving establishments." 198/ In EPA's opinion, acceptance of such a label would avoid the necessity of cancelling the entire registration. The court questioned whether EPA was within the scope of its powers under the (old) FIFRA in placing the burden on the manufacturer to discourage distribution to homes but nevertheless sustained the Agency action in all respects.

EPA's policy position, under both the old and new FIFRA, is that if there are safer alternatives to a product which arguably constitutes a substantial question of safety, the hazardous product should be removed from the market. This attitude was clearly expressed In re King Paint, 199/ concerning a paint additive that was toxic to humans but rather ineffective as a pesticide. The judicial

---

195/ 461 F. 2d 331, 4 ERC 1181 (7th Cir. 1972).

196/ See 461 F. 2d at 333, 4 ERC at 1182.

197/ 470 F. 2d 194, 4 ERC 1881 (8th Cir. 1972). This case was decided about a month after the enactment of the new FIFRA on 21 October 1972, but that law was not applied here.

198/ Ibid., at 196, 4 ERC at 1882.

199/ 2 ERC 1819, (Opinion of EPA Judicial Officer, 1971).

officer, after reviewing the benefits and alternatives, concluded, the fact "that many hazardous substances find their way into the homes and all too frequently into the hands of children—is no justification for exposing the consumer to another source of accidents." 200/ Since less toxic and more effective alternatives existed, the registration was cancelled and this decision was not appealed. This agency position has implicitly been approved by subsequent judicial decisions, except for Stearns, for it is difficult to argue the benefits of retaining a hazardous chemical when preferable alternatives exist.

9.3 Administrator's Flexibility

The courts have recognized that EPA in many cases is operating on the frontiers of scientific knowledge. One leading decision, EDF V. EPA, 201/ noted that "it is not an agency in the doldrums of the routine or familiar." 202/ The issues are highly technical, the available scientific data may be inadequate, and "the concept of the safety of the products is an evolving one which is constantly being further refined in light of our increasing knowledge." 203/

> Environmental law marks out a domain where knowledge is hard to obtain and appraise, even in the administrative corridors; in the courtrooms, difficulties of understanding are multiplied. But there is a will in the courts to study and understand what the agency puts before us. And there is a will to respect the Agency's choices if it has taken a hard look at its hard problems. We emphasize again the judicial toleration of wide flexibility for response to developing situations. . . . The Court's concern is for elucidation of basis, not for restriction of EPA's latitude. 204/

200/ Ibid., at 1824.

201/ 465 F. 2d 528, 4 ERC 1523 (D.C. Cir. 1972).

202/ Ibid., at 541, 4 ERC at 1531.

203/ Ibid., at 535 n.5, 4 ERC at 1527, quoting with approval EPA's 18th of March Statement.

204/ Ibid., at 541, 4 ERC at 1531-32.

9.3.1 Concerning the Scientific Advisory Committee

In emphasizing the administrator's regulatory flexibility, the courts have rejected the contention that he must "rubber stamp" the findings of the Scientific Advisory Committee or the administrative law judge. This is illustrated by Dow Chemical v. Ruckelshaus 205/ concerning the herbicide 2,4,5-T. In 1970 the USDA suspended some uses of the chemical and cancelled others because of the high risk that it, or a dioxin contaminant known as TCDD, had proved a potent teratogen in laboratory tests. Most of these uses were not challenged, but Dow did contest the cancellation on rice. A Scientific Advisory Committee convoked by EPA concluded that the "confused aggregate of observations indicated registrations should be maintained" but that there remained serious questions needing further extensive research. The administrator reviewed the report in considerable detail and concluded that a "substantial question of safety" existed sufficient to justify an administrative hearing; in the meantime, the cancellation was maintained. 206/ Dow appealed, but the Court of Appeals for the Eighth Circuit held that the administrator was not compelled to follow the recommendations of the advisory committee if he had justifiable basis for doing otherwise. 207/

205/ 477 F. 2d 1317, 5 ERC 1244 (8th Cir. 1973).

206/ The deficiencies in the advisory report, which was poorly reasoned and internally inconsistent, contributed to the agency's skepticism towards this system of information collection and analysis. The advisory process was improved considerably, however, by providing better staff support to the committee and making it an adjunct of the hearing process.

207/ This case is better remembered for its unconscionable delay of the administrative process. Dow appealed first to a district court in Arkansas and obtained an injunction against further EPA action on 2,4,5-T, although the statute explicitly excluded district courts from jurisdiction. The Eighth Circuit reversed, noting that the court below lacked jurisdiction and that in any case Dow was not entitled to an injunction during a period when "the cancellation orders have no effect on Dow's right to ship and market its product until the administration cancellation process has been completed." Ibid., at 1326, 5 ERC at 1250.

9.3.2 Concerning the Administrative Law Judge

The administrator is also not bound by findings of the administrative law judge. This conclusion follows the general principle of administrative law that a hearing examiner's decision should be accorded only the deference it merits. As the Supreme Court said in Universal Camera, "we do not require that the examiner's findings be given more weight than in reason and in light of judicial experience they deserve." 208/ Only if the decision-maker arbitrarily and capriciously ignored the findings of an examiner, or if the credibility of witnesses was crucial to the case—a situation that rarely exists in an administrative hearing—would a different conclusion be indicated. In the "DDT" case, the court noted that demeanor was not particularly important, adding that the "examiner himself had no particular expertise, for he was a coal mine accident specialist" borrowed from the Department of Interior. 209/

9.3.3 National Environmental Policy Act

The EPA is also not bound by the National Environmental Policy Act (NEPA) 210/ to file environmental impact statements on its pesticide decisions, since the procedures under the FIFRA are an adequate substitute. Although the strict language of NEPA states that all agencies of the federal government should file impact statements, this law was enacted before EPA existed, and courts almost unanimously have found that there is little logic in requiring an agency whose sole function is protection of environment to file a statement obliging it to take into consideration environmental factors. 211/ Courts nevertheless hesitated to grant a blanket exemption to EPA, preferring to stress that EPA actions are mandated by a given statute, although this justification has not exempted certain

---

208/ Universal Camera Corp. v. NLRB, 340 U.S. 474 (1951).

209/ EDF v. EPA ("DDT" case), 489 F. 2d 1247, 1253, 6 ERC 1112, 1117 (D.C. Cir. 1973).

210/ 42 U.S.C. § 4331 et seq., 83 Stat. 852.

211/ For example, Essex Chemical Corp. v. Ruckelshaus, 486 F. 2d 427, 5 ERC 1820 (D.C. Cir. 1973), Portland Cement Assn. v. Ruckelshaus, 486 F. 2d at 375, 5 ERC 1593 (D.C. Cir. 1973).

non-environmental agencies; or they have noted that Environmental Protection Agency procedures for articulating its position and providing for public comment were an adequate substitute for the same procedures under NEPA. The court in EDF v. EPA 212/ ("DDT" case) discussed all the factors:

> We conclude that where an agency is engaged primarily in an examination of environmental questions, where substantive and procedural standards ensure full and adequate consideration of environmental issues, then formal compliance with NEPA is not necessary, but functional compliance is sufficient. We are not formulating a broad exemption from NEPA for all environmental agencies or even for all environmentally protective regulatory actions of such agencies. Instead, we delineate a narrow exemption from the literal requirements for those actions which are undertaken pursuant to sufficient safeguards so that the purpose and policies behind NEPA will necessarily be fulfilled. The EPA action here meets this standard, and hence this challenge to the EPA action is rejected.

10.0 PESTICIDE REGULATION UNDER OTHER FEDERAL STATUTES

Pesticides are not regulated solely under the FIFRA. They may also involve regulatory authority under the Food, Drug and Cosmetic Act (FDCA), under the statutes of several other federal agencies, and under other environmental laws administered by EPA.

10.1 Pesticides Under the Food, Drug & Cosmetics Act
One important function of EPA regarding pesticides is not derived from the FIFRA—the setting of tolerances for pesticide residues in food. This authority, originally granted to the Food and Drug Administration under the Food, Drug and Cosmetic Act, 213/ was transferred to EPA by the 1970 Reorganization Plan establishing the agency and, more specifically, by subsequent detailed memos of agreement between EPA and FDA.

212/ EDF v. EPA, 489 F. 2d at 1257, 6 ERC at 1119.

213/ FDCA § 408, 21 U.S.C. § 346a, et seq.

The reorganization plan provided that EPA should set tolerances and "monitor compliance," while the Secretary of HEW would continue to enforce compliance. The amendments to FIFRA in 1972 also invested EPA with authority to prevent misuse of registered pesticides. Under Section 408 of the FDCA, the administrator issues regulations exempting any pesticides for which a tolerance is unnecessary to protect the public health. 214/ Otherwise, he "shall promulgate regulations establishing tolerances with respect to . . . pesticide chemicals which are not generally recognized among experts . . . as safe for use . . . to the extent necessary to protect the public health." 215/

Pesticide residues are present in most meats, fruits, and vegetables whether or not chemicals are applied to them. DDT, for example, is detectable in most foods, even in mothers' milk. Before registration of a pesticide, a residue tolerance must be set for the maximum level at which that chemical can be safely ingested. Tolerances are usually set at two orders of magnitude (one-hundredth) below the level at which the pesticide has demonstrated an effect on experimental animals. 216/ Some particularly hazardous chemicals are set at "zero residue," but this is causing an increasing problem as the detection capability of analytical equipment is improved. 217/

EPA's pesticide jurisdiction is supposed to cover only residues resulting from a chemical's use as a pesticide but not exposure resulting from, say, dust blowing from a factory (this may be covered by EPA's Clean Air Act) or a truck carrying the chemicals. 218/ In two major cases involving HCB (hexachlorobenzene)

214/ FDCA § 408(c), 21 U.S.C. § 346a(c).

215/ FDCA § 408(b)(c), 21 U.S.C. § 346(b) and (c).

216/ This is an oversimplification. The tolerance margin depends on the particular effects of the chemical.

217/ This problem of the so-called "zero level" exists in other health laws as well. The recent Department of Labor standard on vinyl chloride, for example, set a "no detectable level" arbitrarily defined as one part per million (ppm), plus or minus one-half of a ppm.

218/ FDCA § 306, 21 U.S.C. § 336.

contamination of cattle in Louisiana and sheep in the Rocky Mountains, the HCB was blown from open trucks onto pasture land while being transported from one point to another. EPA assumed responsibility for these cases because the tolerance problems regarding health are really the same whether the chemical entered the food as a result of agricultural use or for some other reason, and FDA was only too glad to oblige.

Several pesticide tolerance cases involved DDT. The leading pre-EPA case was Environmental Defense Fund v. HEW. 219/ EDF proposed that the Secretary of HEW establish a "zero tolerance" for DDT residues in raw agricultural commodities, as they could potentially cause cancer in human beings. 220/ The D.C. Circuit pointed out that the Delaney Amendment, 221/ banning all "additives" found to induce cancer when ingested by man or animal, did not apply to pesticide chemicals, although it did indicate strong congressional concern with potential carcinogens.

The question of whether DDT was a food "additive" in fish within the meaning of the FDCA was raised again in U.S. v. Ewing Bros. 222/ The Seventh Circuit explained that prior to the Delaney Amendment the term did not cover substances present in the raw product and unchanged by processing, but after 1958 the definition was expanded so a single tolerance could cover both raw and processed foods. Since DDT was an additive and EPA had not issued a tolerance, DDT was theoretically a food adulterative and contaminated items were liable to seizure. 223/

219/ 428 F. 2d 1083, 1 ERC 1341 (D.C. Cir. 1970).

220/ FDCA § 408, 21 U.S.C. 301.

221/ FDCA § 409(c)(3)(A), 21 U.S.C. § 348(c)(3)(A), of 1958. See also H.R. Rep. No. 1761, 86th Cong., 2d Sess., Appendix 2 (1960) U.S. Code Cong. & Ad. News 2887, 2936.

222/ 502 F. 2d 715, 6 ERC 2073 (7th Cir. 1974).

223/ Under FDCA § 402(a)(2)(C), 21 U.S.C. § 342(a)(2)(C), this affects only a substance that "is not generally recognized among experts. . .as having been adequately shown. . .to be safe under the conditions of its intended use. . . ." See FDCA § 201(s), 21 U.S.C. § 321(s). Without a tolerance, "the presence of the DDT causes fish to be adulterated without any proof that it is actually unfit as food." 6 ERC 2073, 2077.

This could mean, however, that most foods could be seized as adulterated, including the Great Lakes fish at issue in Ewing. Realizing this in 1969, the FDA had established an interim action level of 5 ppm DDT in fish, thereby excluding all but the most contaminated samples. 224/   This procedure was approved by the Seventh Circuit Court of Appeals in U.S. v. Goodman, 225/ which held that the Commissioner of FDA had "specific statutory authority in the Act empowering him to refrain from prosecuting minor violations," 226/ and that this permitted him to set and enforce action levels in lieu of totally prohibiting the distribution of any food containing DDT at any level.

10.2 Clean Air Act of 1970

Pesticides in the air may be regulated under Section 112 of the Clean Air Act pertaining to hazardous air pollutants. A hazardous pollutant is defined as one for which "no ambient air quality standard is applicable and which in the judgment of the administrator may cause, or contribute to, an increase in mortality or an increase in severe irreversible, or incapacitating reversible illness." 227/   EPA publishes a list of hazardous air pollutants from time to time and, once a pollutant is listed, proposed regulations establishing stationary source emission standards must be issued unless the substance is conclusively shown to be safe. This section has so far not been applied to pesticides but could acquire more significance in the future.

224/ Action levels and enforcement, unlike tolerance setting, remain a prerogative of FDA under Section 306 of the FDCA, 21 U.S.C. § 336.

225/ 486 F. 2d 847, 5 ERC 1969 (7th Cir. 1973).

226/ Ibid., at 855, 5 ERC at 1974; FDCA §306, 21 U.S.C. §336, U.S. v. 1500 Cases, 245 F.2d 208, 210-11 (7th Cir. 1956); U.S. v. 484 Bags, 423 F.2d 839, 841 (5th Cir. 1970).

227/ Clean Air Act, § 112(a)(1), 42 U.S.C. § 1857c-7(a)(1) (1970).

10.3 Federal Water Pollution Control Act of 1972

The Water act as amended in 1972 228/ has at least three provisions applicable to pesticides. Under Section 301, pesticide manufacturers and formulators, like all other industrial enterprises, must apply for discharge permits if they release effluents into any body of water. These point sources of pollution must apply the "best practicable control technology" by 1977 and by 1983 must use "the best available control technology." 229/

Hazardous and ubiquitous pesticides may be controlled under Section 307 governing "toxic substances." 230/ Within one year of the listing of a chemical as a "toxic substance," the special discharge standards set for it must be achieved. There was originally some dispute whether pesticides should properly be regulated under this section because, unless they are part of a discharge from an industrial concern, they generally derive from non-point sources such as runoff from fields and therefore could be controlled under a third provision, Section 208, which is largely under the jurisdiction of the states. 231/

EPA's principal function under Section 208 is to identify and oversee problems of agricultural pollution, regulated at the state and local level. By 1977, according to the statute, state authorities were to have formulated control programs for the protection of water quality, pesticides and other agricultural pollutants such as feed-lots. 232/

228/ Federal Water Pollution Control Act Amendments of 1972 (FWPCA), 33 U.S.C. §1251 et seq., 86 Stat. 816 (1972).

229/ FWPCA § 301, 33 U.S.C. § 1311.

230/ FWPCA § 307, 33 U.S.C. § 1317. The criteria for this list is given in 38 FR 18044 (1973).

231/ EPA, however, has not followed this reasoning. The present § 307 list of 299 toxic pollutants contains many of the major pesticides. See NRDC v. Train (D.C. Cir. 1976) 8 ERC 2120.

232/ FWPCA § 208, 33 U.S.C. § 1288.

10.4 Solid Waste Disposal Acts

The EPA had very limited authority under Section 204 of the Solid Waste Disposal Act, as amended by the Resource Recovery Act of 1970, 233/ to conduct research, training, demonstrations and other activities regarding pesticide storage and disposal. 234/ Enactment of the Resource Conservation and Recovery Act (RCRA) in October 1976 gave EPA an important tool for controlling the disposal of pesticides, particularly the waste from pesticide manufacture. 235/ The role of RCRA is described in detail in a separate chapter of this book.

10.5 Occupational Safety and Health Act

The EPA and the Department of Labor share somewhat overlapping authority under FIFRA and the Occupational Safety and Health Act (OSHA) 236/ for the protection of agricultural workers from pesticide hazards. This produced a heated inter-agency conflict during the first half of 1973, although the FIFRA and its legislative history clearly indicated that EPA had primary responsibility for promulgating re-entry and other protective standards in this area, and that OSHA specifically yielded to existing standards by other federal agencies. 237/ The question was finally settled by the White House in EPA's favor after a court had enjoined Labor's own proposed standards. 238/ Both agencies now seem relatively satis-

---

233/ 42 U.S.C. § 3251 et seq., 79 Stat. 997 (1965), 84 Stat. 1227 (1970); RCRA § 204, 42 U.S.C. § 3253.

234/ RCRA § 212, 42 U.S.C. 3241. Under the Solid Waste Disposal Act, guidelines applicable only to federal agencies have been issued regarding pesticide storage and disposal pertaining to Sections 19 and 25 of the FIFRA. 39 FR 15236, 1 May 1974, and proposed regs., 39 FR 36847, 15 October 1974. See also RCRA § 209, 42 U.S.C. § 3254c.

235/ PL 94-580, 42 U.S.C. 6801 (21 October 1976).

236/ 29 U.S.C. § 651, et seq., 84 Stat. 1590.

237/ OSHA § 6, 29 U.S.C. § 655.

238/ Florida Peach Growers Assn. v. Dept. of Labor, 489 F. 2d 120, (5th Cir. 1974).

fied with the arrangement. Some farm worker groups, however, still contend that the protective standards on EPA pesticide labels are weak and seldom enforced, and that only California and a few other states have adequate statutory and enforcement programs. It may be that local standards, with some federal monitoring of their effectiveness, would be the preferable approach, since the safe re-entry period after spraying can vary dramatically depending on humidity and other local conditions.

Because of OSHA's recent lethargy, Congress has pressured EPA to step into the regulatory vacuum by using TSCA and FIFRA. 239/ In 1983, EPA issued its first notice of violation of pesticide worker safety against an Illinois applicator who sprayed farm workers in the field. 240/

10.6 Federal Hazardous Substances Act

The Federal Hazardous Substances Act of 1970 241/ regulates hazardous substances in interstate commerce. However, pesticides subject to the FIFRA and the FDCA have been specifically exempted by regulation 242/ from the definition of the term "hazardous substance." This statute is administered by the Consumer Product Safety Commission (CPSC) which also adminis-ters the Poison Prevention Packaging Control Act of 1970, 243/ designed to protect children from pesticides and other harmful substances. It is not yet clear how EPA and the CPSC will divide their overlapping authority in this area. EPA might welcome the involvement of CPSC in this limited portion of the pesticide area to the extent that its own hands are tied by the Court of Appeals decision in the Stearns Paste case. 244/

239/ See Chapter 4 on "Toxic Substances" for further discussion of this point.

240/ BNA, Chemical Regulation Reporter, 3 June 1983, p.389.

241/ 15 U.S.C. § 1261 et seq., 84 Stat. 1673.

242/ 16 CFR § 1500 3(b)(4)(ii).

243/ 15 U.S.C. § 1471 et seq., 84 Stat. 1670.

244/ U.S. v. Stearns Electric Paste, supra.

10.7 Federal Pesticide Monitoring Programs

The FDA and USDA assist EPA in monitoring pesticide residues in food. The FDA conducts frequent spot checks and an annual Market Basket Survey in which pesticide residues are analyzed in a representative sampling of grocery items. The FDA's Poison Control Center also compiles current statistics on chemical poisoning. The USDA's Animal and Plant Health Inspection Service conducts spot checks on pesticides in meats and poultry based on samples taken at slaughter houses throughout the country.

The Department of Interior samples pesticide residues in fish and performs experiments to determine the effects of pesticides which may be introduced into the aquatic environment. The Geological Survey Division of Interior also conducts periodic nationwide water sampling for pesticides and other contaminants. The National Oceanic Atmospheric Administration (NOAA) under the Department of Commerce monitors aquatic areas for pesticide levels, and the Department of Transportation's Office of Hazardous Substances records accidents involving pesticides in shipment and distribution.

11.0 THE RPAR PROCESS

The most important new area in pesticides involves the contested reregistration process, usually termed the Rebuttable Presumption Against Registration (RPAR).

Many pesticides are coming up for renewal that were originally registered under the USDA or the early days of EPA when the standards for review were less strict.   These will have to be given much closer scrutiny this time. This is mandated by the 1972 amendments to FIFRA, which directed EPA to assess the risks of all pesticides by October 1976. 245/ (This deadline was missed, as was a congressional extension to October 1977.)

Since there are over thirty thousand registrations, EPA realized early that it could not give adequate individual attention to each one, so it sought a procedural shortcut. The obvious solution was to examine in detail only those for which serious adverse data was alleged. Furthermore, since the law placed the burden of proof

---

245/ Section 4(c)(2) of 61 Stat. 163, 7 U.S.C. § 135.

on the proponent of registration, this feature was naturally incorporated in the new process. 246/

From this uncontroversial basis developed a most controversial program. As set forth in Section 162.11 of the pesticide regulations, 247/ "a rebuttable presumption shall arise . . . upon a determination by the Administrator that the pesticide meets or exceeds any of the criteria for risk set forth in subparagraph (3)." These criteria are extraordinarily detailed; for example, under acute toxicity they specify "an acute dermal LD_{50} of 6g/kg, 'or' an inhalation LC_{50} of 0.04mg/liter or less as formulated." 248/ Chronic toxic effects, such as oncogenicity (cancer) and mutagenicity, are also listed.

The regulations call for EPA then to notify the registrant that a rebuttable presumption exists against the pesticide and allow 45 days (extendable to 105 days) for him to submit scientific data rebutting the allegations of risk. The burden of proof is on him to demonstrate that the product, if used correctly, is not likely to result in any significant adverse, acute, or chronic effects. 249/ If the question is not resolved at this point, a public hearing may be held to assess the balance of risks and benefits.

In practice, the agency has established a multi-stage review process, beginning with the placing of a pesticide on a lengthy suspect list and then a pre-RPAR review of all available scientific literature and test data to determine whether any risk criteria are met. Even this preliminary step can have serious economic consequences, and the chemical industry complains:

> The pesticide suffers in the marketplace because people have a tendency to back away when a possible RPAR is mentioned and is put into "limbo" as far as registration

---

246/ Most of the plan was worked out at an EPA conference in Easton, Maryland, in the summer of 1974.

247/ 40 CFR § 162.11; 40 FR 28268, 3 July 1975; as amended by 40 FR 32329 and 42746.

248/ 40 CFR §§ 162.11 (3)(i)(A)(2) and (A)(3).

249/ 40 CFR § 162.11 (a)(4).

is concerned. Even a label amendment is out of the question as long as RPAR is threatened. 250/

The original RPAR candidate list contained forty-five classes of pesticides, of which twenty-four were still undergoing pre-RPAR review at the end of 1977. 251/ An additional 23 new chemicals were added to the pre-RPAR list on December 1977. 252/ Many more suspect pesticides were scheduled for inclusion on subsequent pre-RPAR.

The Reagan administration has initiated a new policy with respect to RPAR's which will supposedly streamline the process. 253/ Registrants requested a preliminary initial review process, so that chemicals only entered the formal RPAR process when clear risk problems were established. They also sought expedited decisionmaking once RPAR was triggered. As a result, EPA proposed to revise its policy to include more opportunity of negotiations between EPA and a registrant. EPA also proposed a preliminary risk assessment before the public evaluation process is initiated. No new chemicals have been placed on the RPAR or pre-RPAR review under the Reagan Administration, and EPA indicated it would eliminate its backlog of chemicals under review by the end of 1982. 254/ The important but poorly functioning RPAR process is now officially disfavored.

250/ "A Trojan Horse Named RPAR," Farm Chemicals, August 1977.

251/ Six others had been voluntarily cancelled by the registrants, 12 had been RPAR'ed, and 2 were returned to the registration process. Letter of EPA Administrator Douglas M. Costle to Sen. Edward M. Kennedy, 4 November 1977, reprinted in BNA, Chemical Regulation Reporter, p. 1277.

252/ BNA, Chemical Regulation Reporter, 23 December 1977, p. 1493.

253/ Ibid. 9 July 1982, pp. 506-510.

254/ Ibid., 16 July 1982, p. 500.

12.0 BIOTECHNOLOGY

In May 1986, EPA authorized the first permits for the release of a genetically engineered pesticide to a professor from the University of California at Berkeley. The genetically altered bacteria strain, known as "ice-minus" or "Frostban," was developed by the university and licensed by Advanced Genetic Sciences Inc. (AGS). It is designed to retard frost formation on plants. Billions of dollars of crops are lost to frost damage each year. The permits allow the bacteria to be applied to potato seeds before planting and sprayed on young plants.

The University of California had received permission from NIH in 1983 to release the frost retarding bacterium, but The Foundation of Economic Trends, headed by Jeremy Rifkin, an active opponent of genetic engineering, filed suit in U.S. District Court. In a major victory for the anti-biotech crusade, Judge John J. Sirica issued an order on 16 May 1984 blocking the testing (on the narrow grounds that NIH has not followed the correct procedures in approving the experiment) and barring the NIH from approving any other field tests. The University of California appealed this decision, and on 27 February 1985, the U.S. Court of Appeals for the District of Columbia upheld the injunction against the experiment, but overturned the ban on all NIH approvals of other field tests. 255/

However, a subsequent federal court decision held that only NIH-funded biotechnology research needs NIH approval (in addition approval from another agency) in order for genetically modified organisms to be released into the environment. Thus, private research, such as with Frostban, need only get approval from a single, relevant agency for experiments.

On 4 September 1986, EPA also gave its approval for AGS to conduct outdoor tests on Frostban, pending agency review of a test site, reinstating two permits which EPA suspended in March 1986. EPA had alleged that the company violated the federal permit process when it injected Frostban into trees on the open roof of its Oakland, California, facility in February 1985.

255/ Foundation on Economic Trends v. Margaret M. Heckler, 756 F.2d 143).

Now that EPA has decided to allow the testing of Frostban, Rifkin is fighting the pesticide once again. The U.S. District Court for the District of Columbia refused on 8 March 1986 to enjoin the first approval given to AGS, stating that the agency's actions met all the procedural requirements of federal environmental laws. 256/ On 9 July 1986, Rifkin again went to the District Court and asked that it enjoin the EPA from issuing experimental use permits for genetically altered pesticides until the agency establishes "minimal financial responsibility statutes." One week earlier the agency turned down Rifkin's petition seeking a rulemaking to establish liability insurance requirements for companies receiving permits to release organisms mutated through recombinant DNA techniques.

The Department of Agriculture (USDA) has also made efforts to regulate genetically engineered pesticides. For example, on 22 April 1986, the USDA reinstated a license for the first live genetically engineered animal vaccine that the agency temporarily suspended amid allegations made by Jeremy Rifkin that the license was improperly approved. On 26 June 1986, the USDA also proposed a rule to control harmful insects by using biotechnology. Biotechnology companies and universities, however, have criticized these rules for being too restrictive.

After much dispute over statutory jurisdiction over biotechnology products, President Reagan signed on 18 June 1986 a Coordinated Framework for Regulation of Biotechnology, which maps out federal agency jurisdiction over biotechnology products. In general, the EPA is to regulate pesticides and new organisms planned for release from the laboratory into the field, the Agriculture Department will handle products that may be plant pests or cause disease in animals and the FDA will deal with human drugs, foods and food additives. Jeremy Rifkin also intends to challenge this policy in the U.S. District Court, arguing against both the scientific and regulatory bases of the framework.

The biotechnology issue is expected to eventually be legislated in Congress.

256/ Foundation on Economic Trends v. Thomas, F. Supp.

Chapter 12

NOISE CONTROL

Marshall Lee Miller
Reid & Priest
Washington, D.C.

1.0 INTRODUCTION

Noise is such an integral part of life that we take for granted
all but the harshest abuse of our eardrums. This seemingly simple
subject is one we all feel we understand. Where we might be awed
by the intricacies of toxic chemicals or the complexity of ambient
air equation models, we all feel confident that we understand noise.
It is, after all, a loud piece of machinery, or a sonic boom, or a
blaring stereo next door. Noise can be a nuisance and for generations the law has treated it as merely that. If the din became too
oppressive, one could seek remedy in a court of law to restrain
another from violating the right to enjoyment of one's property. 1/
But what once might have been considered merely a nuisance
is now seen, with intensive industrialization and the increasing
crowding of modern life, to be one of the most pervasive health
problems of our society. There has also been a growing awareness of
the technical complexity of noise. The scientific debates about the
physical effects of noise have become just as controversial and
replete with jargon as those concerning teratogenic chemicals or
biological oxygen demand. In fact, a prominent acoustical scientist
recently urged his colleagues to use simpler terms so that laymen

---

1/ For a fuller discussion, see the sections on "Torts" and
    "Nuisance" in Chapter 1.

could continue to follow the debate. Because the traditional common law remedies have proved inadequate to deal with these developments, there has been since 1970 an increasing resort to federal regulation.

Under the deregulatory emphasis of the Reagan administration, EPA's noise program has been almost completely dismantled. Enforcement continues, however, under OSHA and, especially, the Federal Aviation Administration.

1.1 The Characteristics of Sound

Sound intensity is measured in decibels. The zero on the decibel scale is based on the lowest sound level that the healthy human ear can detect. Decibels are not linear units like miles or pounds; rather, they are representative points on a sharply rising, logarithmic curve. Each ten units represents an increase of tenfold, twenty units means a hundredfold (10 x 10), thirty units a thousand-fold (10 x 10 x 10), and so on. Thus, one hundred decibels is 10 billion times as intense as one decibel. This system is used because the human ear can detect such a wide range of acoustical energy that otherwise units in the trillions might be required.

For comparison, the rustle of leaves is rated at 10 decibels, a typical office has about 50 decibels of background noise, moderate traffic noise ranges around 70 decibels, pneumatic drills and heavy trucks at 15 meters range between 80 and 90, and a jet takeoff at 60 meters is 120 or greater. Sound levels are measured at their source, unless otherwise specified, because their intensity is inversely proportional to the square of the distance from that source. 2/

A second important element of noise is frequency or pitch, which is the rate of vibrations of the sound wave. 3/ This is measured in cycles per second and expressed in Hertz (Hz). The audible frequency range of sound is often taken to be between 20 Hz and 20,000 Hz. The ability to hear frequencies declines with age

---

2/   Certain EPA standards, such as for aircraft and trucks, provide that noise measurements be taken at a specified distance from the source. This will be discussed later in this chapter.

3/   There is technically a slight difference between these two concepts.

(presbycusis), 4/ and most adults are limited to the range below 12-15,000 Hz. Some music experts, however, believe we can still "sense" sounds beyond those we can hear.

Sound perception is affected by such factors as background noise level, distance, repetitiveness, tone components, duration, number of sources, insulation, and subjective receiver factors including both conscious and subconscious responses. For outdoor sound there are variables such as baffles, terrain, wind direction and velocity, atmospheric pressure and temperature. Interior sound, in addition to most of these variables, also involves the reverberative and reflective characteristics of various building materials and fixtures, the size and shape of a room, and the absorptive characteristics of its furnishings.

There have been a number of scientific efforts to combine factors such as loudness and duration in one numerical scale which will indicate the degree of human annoyance. One useful scale, the Effective Perceived Noise Level (EPNL), is based upon the relative curve of human discomfort to high frequency sounds such as aircraft or truck engine changes in acceleration. This is then adjusted for the duration and presence of discrete tones such as the whine or scream of jet operations. 5/

2.0 BIOLOGICAL EFFECTS OF NOISE

It has long been recognized that painfully loud sound can produce deafness or impaired hearing; the biophysical mechanisms by which this occurs and the conditions under which individuals are susceptible have yet to be fully explained scientifically. We are also

---

4/   Some authorities believe that presbycusis is less a natural concomitant of aging than the result of years of aural abuse. See statement of Jack Westman, Department of Psychiatry, University of Wisconsin Medical School, Madison, Wisconsin, before the Senate Subcommittee on Government Regulations, Small Business Committee, 23 July 1975, p. 2.

5/   Noise measurement is a complex subject on which the above provides only some of the basic terminology. See, for example, the basic EPA noise criteria document: "Public Health and Welfare Criteria for Noise," 27 July 1973, EPA document, No. 550/9-73-002.

now beginning to realize that noise can harm body organs other than the ears, as well as produce psychological effects which many have long suspected.

2.1 Physical Effects

There is a continuing controversy over definitions of deafness. First, there is a need to distinguish between temporary effects following loud noise from which the ear can easily recover (Temporary Threshold Shift, TTS), and those effects which involve permanent loss of some degree of hearing (Noise Induced Permanent Threshold Shift, NIPTS).

Second, there is a question as to what degree of hearing loss should be considered a serious impairment. There is some scientific feeling that the general population should be protected against a permanent impairment (NIPTS) of more than five decibels, which represents a considerable decrease in aural perceptiveness. 6/ There are others, however, who believe that substantial impairment does not take place until hearing loss reaches 25 decibel attenuation. 7/ This does not represent the beginning of hearing impairment or a satisfactory policy goal but rather is the point at which a severe, compensable handicap is defined. A person with such a hearing loss would be able to understand only 50 percent of monosyllabic words spoken in a quiet room and only 90 percent of all sentences. 8/

Third, at what frequency should hearing impairment be measured? After all, the ability to hear the higher frequencies is usually

---

6/   See, for example, testimony of Daniel L. Johnson, Aerospace Medical Research Laboratory, Wright-Patterson AFB, Ohio, in OSHA Noise Hearings, Washington, D.C., 27 June 1975, transcript 765.

7/   Some scientists have even argued that a hearing impairment should not be considered serious until the loss is 50 decibels or more. W. Dixon Ward, Department of Otolaryngology, Chief, Hearing Research Laboratory, University of Minnesota, testifying on behalf of the American Iron and Steel Institute, OSHA Noise Hearings, 1 July 1975, transcript 1047.

8/   Statement of Joseph H. Hafkenschiel, Economist, Communication Workers of America, Testimony at the OSHA Noise Hearings, July 1975.

lost first. For a proper appreciation of musical harmonics, it is thought important to hear the frequencies between 10,000 and 15,000 Hz which is within the upper range of most normal individuals. The current debate, however, centers around a far more modest expectation: whether good hearing between 2,000 and 4,000 Hz is essential for proper understanding of spoken words. In some of the OSHA noise hearings, the director of that agency's standards office testified in favor of measurements only up to 2,000 Hz, describing those as the "speech frequencies," and defining impairment as a 25 decibel loss in that frequency range. 9/ Witnesses from EPA and NIOSH, on the other hand, have repeatedly emphasized the measurement of hearing loss "in the critical frequencies above 2,000 Hz, which are the soonest and most severely affected by exposure to noise." These frequencies, according to an EPA analysis of the proposed OSHA standard, "are as important as those below 1,900 Hz for determining the intelligibility of speech." 10/

These distinctions, while seemingly technical or trivial, can have important policy consequences. It will be a balancing of the risks to workers against the equally speculative cost to industry that will determine where OSHA will set its important noise standard and what standards EPA and other federal agencies will promulgate for other segments of the economy.

2.2 Physiological Effects

The harmful effects of noise are not limited to the auditory system. Scientific studies have shown, for example, that it also alters moods, reduces learning ability, and increases blood pressure. We are all aware that a sharp sudden noise can cause the adrenaline to flow. Modern man is subject not to occasional stresses but to an unrelenting bombardment of noise which keeps his body on alert. This stress is not something that exists only in the mind, a synonym for a "nervous" condition. This assumption has been corrected by Dr. Jean Tache of the University of Montreal who has declared, "Now, to most people, stress is something bearing a psychological connotation. Stress is something in our heads. I would like to say that stress is something that happens in our body. During stress, the

---

9/   Statement of Dan Boyd, then Director of Standards for OSHA, OSHA Noise Hearings, 23 June 1975, transcript p. 13.

10/   EPA review and report, "Proposed OSHA Occupational Noise Exposure Regulation," 39 FR 43802, 18 December 1974.

size of our organs change, they are modified; the adrenal is
enlarged, the lymphatic system increases in size. So stress is not
something merely in our heads, it is something that happens in our
body." 11/

These manifestations can be demonstrated objectively by
scientific measurements. A hormone, CRF, is secreted by the hypo-
thalmus which stimulates the production of ACTH by the pituitary.
This activates the adrenals producing corticoids which in turn mobi-
lize the entire body for a fight-flight situation. Stress, therefore, is
not merely a situation which can be diagnosed only by a psychiatrist;
it can also be determined quite objectively by, for example, measuring the corticoid level in the blood or the urine. 12/

The effect of these stress hormones on the cardiovascular
system is well known. The arteries constrict, raising the blood pressure and placing greater strain on the heart. It is not possible to
determine precisely what percentage of coronaries and strokes, if
any, might be due in part to the effects of noise. These effects,
according to one authority, "are likely to be distributed over a large
number of common individual cardiovascular and other maladies
whose causation is complex and attributable to other factors as well.
Nonetheless, cardiovascular diseases are such a massive problem in
our society that even if noise increases the incidence or severity by
only a small percentage in the exposed population this would be a
very substantial adverse effect. Major cardiovascular diseases
account for well over half the deaths in the United States, currently
somewhat over a million people per year." 13/

Continuous noise, by putting the body under stress, can lead
to irritation and fatigue. This can be the case even if the noise is
not at an uncomfortably high level, provided it is loud and relatively
continuous. Some observers believe that these tensions can lead to
distractions and a generally higher injury rate, although this point

---

11/   Statement of Jean Tache, Institute of Experimental Medicine
      and Surgery, University of Montreal, Canada, before the
      Senate Small Business Committee, op. cit., p. 23.

12/   Ibid., pp. 23-24.

13/   Statement of Nicholas A. Ashford, Center for Policy Alter-
      natives, MIT, Cambridge, Mass., before the Senate Small
      Business Committee, p. 249.

must await further studies for verification. There is more substantial evidence that noise can reduce efficiency and promote absenteeism, either because of its physical symptoms or because it is a distraction factor among workers subjected to excessive noise levels. 14/

Finally, animal tests suggest that noise may cause yet another barely explored medical hazard. Pregnant mice exposed to high noise levels produced offspring whose skeletal systems were incompletely developed and had a greater susceptibility to gastric ulcers and other gastrointestinal diseases. 15/

3.0 OSHA REGULATION OF NOISE

Most of the severe noise problems are encountered in the occupational context. The former head of EPA's Noise Office has acknowledged, "As far as hearing loss or impairment is concerned, there is absolutely no question that the workplace represents the most serious exposure for the largest group." 16/ The leading standards and enforcement responsibility for noise is thus the Occupational Safety and Health Administration (OSHA) in the Department of Labor.

3.1 The Present OSHA Standard
The Labor Department first began regulating noise under statutes of limited applicability, the most noted being the Walsh-Healey Public Contracts Act of 1936, 17/ which affected employees under private supply contracts with the federal government.

14/ This will be discussed in more detail in the section on the Economic Costs and Benefits of Noise Regulation by OSHA.

15/ Statement of Jean Tache, supra, p. 26. Studies in California have suggested that exactly the same effects—spina bifida, cleft palate, and anencephaly—may be produced in humans, see Washington Post, 20 February 1978.

16/ Statement of Alvin F. Meyer, EPA, Senate Small Business Committee, op. cit., p. 119.

17/ 41 U.S.C. §§ 35-45. Similar noise exposure limits were issued under the (McNamara-O'Hara) Service Contract Act of 1965, 41 U.S.C. § 351 et seq.

Under this statute, on 20 September 1968 the Department proposed for comment an 85 decibel (dB(A)) standard for an eight-hour working day. 18/ This level was adopted as the final standard on 17 January 1969, although companies with an effective hearing conservation program were allowed 92 dB(A) until 1 January 1971. The effective date of the regulation was thirty days from the date of publication. 19/

Just before the effective date, however, on 14 February 1969, the initiation date was postponed three months. 20/ No reason for the delay was given, but the Department later acknowledged that it was due to the advent of the Nixon administration on 20 January 1969. 21/ When the standard finally appeared on 20 May 1969, it differed considerably from the original version. In particular, it established a maximum permissible eight-hour level of 90 dB(A). 22/

In December 1970, with the creation of OSHA, this protection was extended to cover all nongovernmental employees in the United States. 23/

This standard is the one still being enforced today by OSHA. This standard provides, in addition to a noise exposure limit of 90 decibels, a doubling rate of five decibels. This means that for an increase of every five decibels in the sound level, the exposure time must be cut in half. For example, exposure at 90 decibels is permitted for eight hours, at 95 for four hours, and at 100 for two hours.

18/ 33 FR 14258 (1968). The A-scale attempts to relate loudness in decibels to the varying sensitivity of the human ear at different frequencies.

19/ 34 FR 788 (1969), revising 41 CFR 50-204.

20/ 34 FR 2207 (1969).

21/ See the preamble to the 20 May 1969 promulgation, infra.

22/ 34 FR 7946 (1969), esp. 7948-49.

23/ OSH Act § 6(a), 29 U.S.C. § 655(a). The effective date of the Act was April 1971. For two years, OSHA could also adopt other "established federal standards" which might be relevant to safety and health but which had not automatically been adopted under OSHA, and "national consensus standards," set forth by private standard-setting associations. This period ended in April 1973.

PERMISSIBLE NOISE EXPOSURE LIMITS 24/

Duration Per Day In Hours	Sound Level 90 dB(A) Standard	Hypothetical 85 dB(A) For Comparison 25/
8	90	85
6	92	87
4	95	90
3	97	92
2	100	95
1 1/2	102	97
1	105	100
1/2	110	102
1/4 or less	115	105

The standard also provides for a maximum sound level for impact or impulsive noise of 140 decibels, 26/ and a limit for continuous noise at 115 decibels for a fifteen minute period. As in other OSHA standards, employers are required first to control noise by engineering changes and administrative controls. Only if these methods prove infeasible should employers resort to the use of personal protective equipment such as earmuffs and earplugs, along with a hearing conservation program. 27/

24/ Table G-16 in 29 CFR 1910.95.

25/ Note that the 85 dB(A) column is hypothetical, prepared by the author, which also assumes a 5 decibel doubling rate. It is not a part of the Table G-16 or the official standard, although it has been suggested as OSHA's eventual noise standard.

26/ One hundred such 140 dB(A) impacts a day would be allowed with a tenfold increase number each decrease of ten decibels, and ten thousand at 120 decibels. This level, while startlingly high, is in accord with recommendations by the American Conference of Government Industrial Hygienists (ACGIH) and the American Industrial Hygiene Association (AIHA). See BNA, Noise Reporter, 9 June 1975, A-14.

27/ OSHA, "Guidelines to the Occupational Noise Standard," 1971. See also, 29 CFR 1910.95.

3.2 Enforcement

OSHA's enforcement of the present noise standard, although criticized as less than strict, 28/ has exceeded that of many other OSHA health standards. Generally, OSHA inspectors do not make separate inspections for noise, as they might do for toxic chemicals or particular safety hazards, but the ubiquitous nature of noise and its ease of detectability lead to the high citation rate. In 1975, for example, OSHA inspectors cited over 2,400 violations of the noise standard and imposed over a hundred thousand dollars in penalties. These figures, although still inadequate, constituted 4.3 percent of all health citations. This compares with a total of only fifty-one OSHA citations (0.09 percent) in the same year for dangerous carcinogenic chemical hazards. 29/ In 1985, OSHA cited 1,755 noise violations and proposed almost $170,000 in penalties. This represents a decline from 2,400 citations a decade earlier, although the size of the penalties has risen with inflation.

OSHA can impose both civil and criminal penalties for violations. For serious offenses, defined as those liable to cause "death or serious physical harm," the maximum fine is one thousand dollars per incident. Repeated or willful offenses may be punished by fines as high as ten thousand dollars per violation. 30/ Most noise violations, however, are treated as "non-serious", for which the average fine on a first offense is less than a hundred dollars.

3.3 OSHA Noise Hearings

OSHA's present standard, adopted from a regulation under a prior statute, is only an interim measure. Congress never intended that the temporary consensus and other federal standards adopted by OSHA in 1970 would remain the standards for the indefinite future.

28/ Testimony of Nicholas Ashford, MIT, Senate Small Business Committee, op. cit., p. 253. He testified then that, "I think it would be fair to say that, from looking at the compliance history in the noise area by OSHA that there has not been a strict enforcement of the standard."

29/ OSHA, unpublished computer readout of 1975 inspections, 19 February 1976. See also OSHA Press Release, 25 February 1976. The carcinogen category is defined for these calculations as those standards in 29 CFR 1910.1003-1016.

30/ OSH Act § 17, 29 U.S.C. § 666.

The procedure established under Section 6(b) of the OSHA statute is that the National Institute of Occupational Safety and Health (NIOSH), a branch of the Department of Health, Education, and Welfare (HEW, now the Department of Health and Human Services), prepares criteria documents outlining all the relevant scientific information about the health effects of a particular substance or condition. This document is then forwarded to OSHA which conducts its own analysis of the criteria document and other relevant scientific information, often with the help of a special scientific advisory committee, and considers the technological and economic feasibility factors which are beyond NIOSH's statutory purview. OSHA then proposes a standard as a basis for discussions at subsequent public hearings. The proposal is subsequently modified, if deemed necessary, and the final standard is issued. 31/

NIOSH sent its noise criteria document to OSHA on 14 August 1972. 32/ A Standards Advisory Committee on Noise was appointed. 33/ Sixteen months after receipt of the criteria document, the Advisory Committee transmitted its comments and recommendations to the OSHA Standards office on 20 December 1973. The Standards office, after another ten months of deliberation and preparation, issued on 18 October 1974 a proposed occupational noise exposure standard. 34/

OSHA proposed retention of the 90 dB(A) noise level, a peak impulse exposure at 140 decibels, a five decibel doubling rate, and provisions for employee monitoring and audiometric testing with specific recordkeeping provisions. The limited changes in the

---

31/ OSHA's standard setting record is not beyond reproach. Although there are thousands of toxic substances for which no standards exist and NIOSH has submitted a dozen or more criteria documents each year for OSHA consideration, OSHA has averaged less than one final standard a year since its creation, and these generally have been the result of court action or emergency procedures.

32/ This is in accordance with OSH Act § 29(a)(3), 29 U.S.C. § 669.

33/ OSH Act § 76, 29 U.S.C. § 656, requires representation from labor unions, management, government and independent experts.

34/ 39 FR 37773, 24 October 1974.

proposal prompted some critics to wonder why OSHA had bothered to initiate the time-consuming rulemaking procedure.

EPA immediately objected to the OSHA proposal. This was not officiousness by EPA but a duty under Section 4(c)(2) of the Noise Control Act of 1972, 35/ which gave EPA the chief coordinating responsibility for noise within the Administration. Under this statute, EPA Administrator Russell Train notified OSHA on 6 December 1974 that EPA "believes that the proposed regulation does not protect the public health and welfare to the extent required and feasible." 36/ EPA argued that an eight-hour work day exposure standard of 85 dB(A) was more consistent with available scientific evidence. In fact, EPA argued that its scientific data "support a level of 75 dB(A) for an ultimate health goal; EPA believes that the reduction to 85 dB(A) is an important step toward this goal." 37/

EPA also contended that the OSHA-proposed doubling rate of five decibels had no scientific justification; the proper rate, based on the total amount of acoustic energy, should have been three decibels. In addition, EPA criticized OSHA's reliance on audiometric monitoring, since individual variations and the crudeness of measurement techniques could allow a threshold shift as great as 35 decibels before a worker was informed of his hearing loss. 38/

The OSHA public hearing on the proposed noise standard began in June 1975 and continued for several weeks. A team of representatives from the EPA noise office, headed by Alvin Myer, testified strongly against the OSHA proposal, but the anticipated bitter clash between the two agencies never occurred. OSHA's position was not as adamant as it had sometimes been described. OSHA had never held, as some had portrayed, that a 90 decibel standard would protect against all adverse health effects. This misconception arose partially from OSHA's deliberate vagueness, but the proposal document itself clearly stated the following:

35/   PL 92-574, 86 Stat. 1236, 42 U.S.C. § 4903(c)(2).

36/   EPA, "Proposed OSHA Occupational Noise Exposure Regulation," 39 FR 43802.

37/   Ibid.

38/   Ibid., p. 43808.

With regard to the risk of hearing loss, OSHA recognizes
that comparatively more workers would be at lower risk
at 85 dB(A) than at 90 dB(A). However, we also recognize the technical feasibility problems and the economic
impact associated with an 85 dB(A) requirement as reflected in the Bolt, Beranek and Newman study and in
the draft environmental impact statement. Therefore,
OSHA proposes to keep the level at 90 dB(A) until
empirical data and information on the health risks,
feasibility, and economic impact indicate the practi-
cality and necessity of an 85 dB(A) requirement. 39/

3.4 Economic and Technical Feasibility

The major controversy between EPA and OSHA was the
medical and technical basis of the proposed 90 dB(A) standard. EPA
pointed out that NIOSH, while favoring a standard of 85, had stated
it "reluctantly concurs" with the 90 decibel proposal. 40/ EPA
pointed out that this concurrence was solely the result of NIOSH
deferring to OSHA's judgment on economic and technical feasibility,
as set forth in Section 20 of the OSHA statute, 41/ and was not an
independent conclusion by NIOSH that attainment of noise levels
below 90 decibels was generally technically infeasible. 42/

Neither EPA, OSHA, nor any outside experts were really sure
just what was attainable and at what cost. OSHA commissioned a
sweeping economic impact study to determine the anticipated cost
of complying with both 90 decibel and 85 decibel standards. This
study by Bolt, Beranek and Newman (BBN) estimated that the cost
for attaining a 90 dB(A) level would be about $13 billion—even
though this had been the federal standard for a number of years—and

---

39/ OSHA, "Proposed Occupational Noise Exposure," 39 FR 3773,
24 October 1974.

40/ See NIOSH Criteria Document, "Occupational Exposure to
Noise," p. II-3.

41/ OSH Act, § 20(a)(3), 29 U.S.C. § 669(a)(3).

42/ EPA, "Proposed OSHA Occupational Noise Exposure Regulation," 39 FR 43802, 18 December 1974.

that the added cost for reaching the 85 decibel level would be $18
billion. 43/

The benefits of a lower noise standard are even more controversial. The BBN study estimated that a reduction from 90 decibels
to 85 decibels would reduce by 770,000 the number of workers who
would have extreme hearing loss at retirement age. 44/ The reduction from 90 to 85 decibels would also provide protection to an additional 8.2 million workers who would otherwise face serious but not
disabling hearing losses over their working life. 45/

The economic costs of this hearing loss cannot, of course, be
estimated precisely, partially because of the difficulty in assigning
dollar values to human losses. Attempts to quantify some of the
data by using workmen's compensation awards (although they are
notoriously low) produced estimates in the billions of dollars. 46/ A
more interesting, if more speculative, estimate involves estimating
the cost of increased absenteeism as a result of annoying noise. The
Frye Report calculated that if absenteeism could be reduced one day
per year for those workers exposed to noise levels over 85 decibels,
a reasonable assumption, this would add $2 billion a year to the
GNP. 47/

There have also been attempts to calculate the social costs of
irritation annoyance from noise. It is generally accepted that workers prefer quiet working surroundings to the strain of enduring noise
levels of 90 decibels or higher. One study took 10 cents an hour as

---

43/ Bolt, Beranek and Newman, Inc., Cambridge, Mass., "Impact of
     Noise at the Workplace," Report No. 2671. See also OSHA
     Noise Hearings, transcript p. 281, et seq.

44/ Bolt, Beranek and Newman Report, p. 37.

45/ See Bolt, Beranek and Newman Report, Tables III and IV.

46/ See statement of Nicholas Ashford, OSHA Noise Hearings, 23
     July 1975, transcript, p. 84.

47/ U.S. Department of Health, Education and Welfare (HEW),
     Public Health Service, Protecting the Health of 80 Million
     Americans, 1965. The Frye estimate has been recomputed for
     1976 figures. See also Ashford statement in OSHA hearings,
     transcript, p. 85; and Ashford statement before Senate Small
     Business Committee, op. cit., p. 252.

the minimum differential that a worker would accept and 50 cents as a maximum. These computations produced an annoyance estimate ranging from $3 to $14 billion a year. Compliance with a 90 dB(A) standard would produce a yearly benefit of (using the high figure) $3 billion, while attaining an 85 decibel level would yield $4.6 billion. 48/

Another authority has estimated that the benefits to workers from reducing noise-related tension to 85 decibels would be between $5.2 and $13 billion and at least another $11 billion for hearing preservation. 49/

3.5 The Hearing Conservation Amendment

OSHA sought to obtain the benefits of stricter control without the political costs by issuing the hearing conservation amendment 50/ to the OSHA noise standard 51/ on 16 January 1981. This amendment establishes a hearing conservation program, including exposure monitoring, audiometric testing, and training, for all employees whose noise exposure exposures equal or exceed an 8-hour time-weighted average (TWA) of 85 decibels (dB). However, it was soon after stayed for reconsideration and amendment. In August 1981 a major portion of the amendment went into effect; the administrative stay was continued on other portions of the admendment and additional comments were solicited on these stayed portions. 52/ OSHA revoked many of these stayed provisions in a final rule on 8 March 1983. 53/

48/ Ashford, OSHA Noise Hearings, transcript, pp. 87-90.

49/ This, he suggested, however, would still total less than the BBN cost estimates. Robert Stewart Smith, The Occupational Safety and Health Act: Its Goals and Achievements (Washington, D.C.: American Enterprise Institute, 1976), p. 51.

50/ 29 CFR § 1910.95.

51/ 46 FR 4078.

52/ 46 FR 42622.

53/ 48 FR 9738.

3.5.1 Components of the Hearing Conservation Program

The standard requires employers to monitor noise exposure levels in a manner that will accurately identify employees who are exposed at or above significant noise exposures. It is performance oriented in that it allows employers to choose the monitoring and notification method that best suits each individual situation. However, employees are entitled to observe monitoring procedures and must be notified of monitoring results.

Baseline and annual audiometric testing are also required. Audiometric testing not only monitors employee hearing acuity over time, but also provides an opportunity for employers to educate employees about their hearing and the need to protect it. Furthermore, it should indicate whether hearing loss is being prevented by the employer's hearing conservation program.

All workers exposed at or above the action level must be provided with hearing protectors and annual training on the effects of noise, the purpose, advantages, disadvantages, and attenuation of various types of hearing protectors, and the purpose and procedures of audiometric testing.

In addition, noise exposure measurement records must be kept for two years. Records of audiometric test results must be maintained for the duration of employment of the affected employee.

3.5.2 Litigation Over the Hearing Conservation Amendment

On 7 November 1984, a three-judge panel of U.S. Court of Appeals for the Fourth Circuit struck down the entire hearing conservation amendment after it determined that it exceeded OSHA's authority to adopt only standards relating to health and safety at the workplace. 54/ They argued that it failed to make any distinction between hearing losses caused by workplace sources and losses caused by non-workplace sources. Thus, the hearing conservation amendment imposed responsibilities on employers based on non-work-related hazards.

> Under the amendment, an employer whose workers are unaffected by workplace noise may be subject to numerous requirements simply because its

---

54/   Forging Industry Association v. Secretary of Labor, 748 F.2d 210, 12 OSHC 1041 (4th Cir. 1984).

workers choose to hunt, listen to loud music or ride motorcycles during their non-working hours. Hearing loss caused by such activities is regrettable but it is not a problem that Congress delegated to OSHA to remedy. The amendment is therefore vacated. . . . 55/

However, OSHA requested the Fourth Circuit to hear the case en banc. Appeals courts are often asked to have a case reheard by all the judges on the bench to review the decision of the usual three-judge panel, but this request is rarely accepted. In this case, the Fourth Circuit not only agreed to hear the case en banc, but also reversed the earlier ruling by upholding the amendment, an even rarer phenomenon. 56/

3.6 The Feasibility and Balancing Debate

There has been a continuing debate over feasibility and balancing in OSHA noise enforcement. The important issues include the following:

(1) Can OSHA legally consider economic factors in setting health or safety standards levels?

(2) If so, is this consideration limited only to extreme circumstances?

(3) Does the Occupational Safety and Health Act provide for a balancing of costs and benefits in setting standards?

(4) Can OSHA mandate engineering controls although they alone would still not attain the standard?

(5) And, can OSHA require engineering controls even if personal protective equipment (such as ear plugs) could effectively, if often only theoretically, reduce noise to a safe level and at a much lower cost?

55/   12 OSHC 1043.

56/   Forging Industry Association v. Secretary of Labor, 773 F.2d 1436, 12 OSHC 1472 (4th Cir. 1985), en banc.

These questions have been extensively litigated before the Occupational Safety and Health Review Commission (OSHRC) and the courts; most of the debate has been over the interpretation of "feasibility" in Section 6(b)(5) of the act.

One must remember that the OSHA legislation was originally seen by Congress in rather absolutist terms: any standard promulgated should be one "which most adequately assumes . . . that no employee will suffer material impairment of health." Only late in the debate was the Department of Labor able to insert the phrase "to the extent feasible" into the text. This was intended to prevent companies having to close because unattainable standards were imposed on them, but it was not spelled out to what extent economic as well as technical feasibility was included. 57/

Since the term "feasibility" was not clearly defined, there has been much confusion over how to interpret what Congress intended, as the earlier cases show. In Industrial Union Department, AFL v. Hodgson, the D.C. Circuit accepted that economic realities affected the meaning of "feasible," but only to the extent that "a standard that is prohibitively expensive is not 'feasible.' " 58/ It was Congress' intent, the court added, that this term would prevent a standard unreasonably "requiring protective devices unavailable under existing technology or by making financial viability generally impossible." The court warned, however, that this doctrine should not be used by companies to avoid needed improvements in their workplaces:

> Standards may be economically feasible even though, from the standpoint of employers, they are financially burdensome and affect profit margins adversely. Nor

---

57/ This account of the behind-the-scenes machinations is based largely on the views of the late Congressman William Steiger (R-Wisc.), a principal author of the act, and of Lawrence Silberman, then Solicitor of Labor. The legislative history is relatively unhelpful on this subject. See, for example, hearings before the Select Subcommittee on Labor, Committee on Education and Labor, "Occupational Safety and Health Act of 1969," two vols., 1969.

58/ 499 F.2d 467, 1 OSHC 1631 (D.C. Cir. 1974).

does the concept of economic feasibility necessarily guarantee the continued existence of individual employers. 59/

A similar view was adopted in 1975 by the Second Circuit in The Society of the Plastics Industry v. OSHA, written by Justice Clark, who cited approvingly the case above. 60/ He held that "feasible" meant not only that which is attainable technologically and economically now, but also that which might reasonably be achievable in the future. In this case, which concerned strict emissions controls on vinyl chloride, he declared that OSHA may impose "standards which require improvements in existing technologies or which require the development of new technology, and . . . is not limited to issuing standards based solely on devices already fully developed." 61/

Neither court undertook any risk-benefit analysis, such as attempting to compare the hundreds of millions of dollars needed to control vinyl chloride with the lives lost to angiosarcoma of the liver. Those who have attempted to develop such equations have generally concluded the task is undoable, at least for most such chronic health effects. 62/

A third federal appeals court, however, took a strongly contrary position in a case specifically involving noise. In Turner Co. v. Secretary of Labor, the Seventh Circuit Court of Appeals decided that the $30,000 cost of abating a noise hazard should be weighed against the health damage to workers, taking into consideration the availability of personal protective equipment to mitigate the risk. 63/

59/ 1 OSHC 1631 at 1639.

60/ 509 F.2d 1301, 2 OSHC 1496 (2d Circ. 1975), cert. den. 421 U.S. 992.

61/ 509 F.2d at 1309, 2 OSHC at 1502 (2d Cir. 1975).

62/ See, for example, the conclusions of the National Academy of Sciences report, "Government Regulation of Chemicals in the Environment," 1975.

63/ 561 F.2d 82, 5 OSHC 1970. (7th Circ. 1977). The Occupational Safety and Health Review Commission (OSHRC) decisions on Turner and the related Continental Can case can be found at 4 OSHC 1554 (1976) and 4 OSHC 1541 (1976), respectively.

This holding is not unreasonable, but it is based on a highly tenuous interpretation of the law. The court, without providing any clear rationale for its view, held that "the word 'feasible' as contained in 29 CFR § 1910.95(6)(1) must be given its ordinary and common sense meaning of 'practicable.' " (This may be so but is of no analytical value.) From this the court concluded:

> Accordingly, the Commission erred when it failed to consider the relative cost of implementing engineering controls . . . versus the effectiveness of an existing personal protective equipment program utilizing fitted earplugs. 64/

This interpretation does not follow from the analysis. In fact, since the Turner Company had both the financial resources and the technical capability to abate the noise problem, compliance with the regulation would appear to be "practicable." The court, however, considered this term to mean that a cost-benefit computation should be made.

More recently, the U.S. Court of Appeals for the Ninth Circuit, in the case of Donovan v. Castle & Cooke Foods and OSHRC, 65/ also held that the Noise Act and the regulations permit consideration of relative costs and benefits to determine what noise controls are feasible.

OSHA gave the plant a citation on the grounds that, although Castle & Cooke required its employees to wear personal protective equipment, its failure to install technologically feasible engineering and administrative controls 66/ constituted a violation of the noise standard, and that the violation could only be abated by the implementation of such controls. OSHA argued that engineering and

---

64/ 5 OSHC 1790 at 1791.

65/ 692 F.2d 641, 10 OSHC 2169 (1982).

66/ Engineering controls are those that reduce the sound intensity at the source of that noise. This is achieved by insulation of the machine, by substituting quieter machines and processes, or by isolating the machine or its operator. Administrative controls attempt to reduce workers' exposure to excess noise through use of variable work schedules, variable assignments, or limiting machine use. Personal protective equipment includes such devices as ear plugs and ear muffs provided by the employer and fitted to individual workers.

administrative controls should be considered economically infeasible only if their implementation would so seriously jeopardize the employer's economic condition as to threaten continued operation.

However, Castle & Cooke's view was that the use of the personal protective equipment, in conjunction with a plant-wide hearing conservation program, adequately protected employees from exposure to excess noise and that the cost of the proposed engineering and administrative controls did not justify the benefit to the employees.

When the matter was presented to an administrative law judge, the judge concluded that the requirement of "feasible engineering controls" was so vague as to be unenforceable, in that it "compels employers to guess at their peril what controls will be subjectively considered economically feasible." (Emphasis in original). As a result, the citation was vacated.

The Occupational Safety and Review Commission (OSHRC) affirmed this order, but on a different basis. It determined that in order to determine if the proposed engineering controls were economically feasible, it is necessary to "realistically consider the hazard presented by excessive noise and determine whether the health benefits to employees from noise reduction justify the cost to the employer." It concluded that, although implementation of engineering controls would provide some protection to Castle & Cooke employees, the benefits to be gained did not justify the cost of the controls.

On appeal, OSHA argued that neither the OSHRC nor the courts are free to interpret "economic feasibility," because its definition is controlled by the Supreme Court's decision in American Textile Manufacturers Institute, Inc. v. Donovan. 67/ The appeals

---

67/ 101 S.Ct. 2478, 9 OSHC 1913 (17 June 1981). In this case, representatives of the cotton dust industry challenged proposed regulations limiting permissible exposure levels to cotton dust. Section 6(b)(5) of the act requires OSHA to "set the standard which most adequately assures, to the extent feasible . . . that no employee will suffer material impairment of health . . . ." The industry held that OSHA had not shown that the proposed standards were economically feasible. However, the Supreme Court upheld the cotton dust regulations, holding that the "plain meaning of the word "feasible" is "capable of being done, executed, or effected," and that a cost-benefit analysis by OSHA is not required because a feasibility analysis is.

court, however, decided that the Supreme Court's interpretation of the term "feasible" made in American Textile was not deemed controlling for the noise standards. It also affirmed that economic "feasibiity" should be determined through a cost-benefit analysis, and that in the case of Castle & Cooke the costs of economic controls did not justify the benefit that would accrue to employees. Thus, the decision to vacate the citation was upheld.

As a result of the Donovan decision, OSHA has decided to drop its review of the noise standard, contending that its aim of protecting workers' hearing can be achieved through the Hearing Conservation Amendment. 68/ New enforcement instructions were issued on 9 November 1983 by OSHA to its field staff which allow employers to rely on the Hearing Conservation Amendment to comply with the OSHA noise standard, rather than on engineering and administrative noise controls, when the protectors can effectively reduce the noise exposure to levels specified in the standard. However, the debate on this will continue, since many argue that Congress intended both the present noise standard and the Hearing Conservation Amendment to be only interim measures and not final.

3.7 The Long-Anticipated OSHA Noise Standard

Issuance of the final revised OSHA noise standard has been promised for so long that predictions are no longer taken seriously. In May 1976, for example, a senior OSHA official declared that the standard should be published sometime that year. In October another OSHA spokesman said it would be issued within three months.

Meanwhile, several labor leaders hinted darkly that sinister political motives were responsible for the delay, 69/ and one union

---

68/ In the regulatory agenda issued 19 April 1984 (49 FR 16068), the agency listed the noise standard review under rulemaking actions that had been completed, noting that the review was "withdrawn."

69/ In 1972, the then-head of OSHA, George Guenther, wrote a memo to the under secretary of labor indicating that the organization would trim its sails during the presidential election campaign. This memo, uncovered a year later, became a favorite topic for union leaders charging the Agency with crass political sellouts. This criticism was specifically leveled at OSHA on noise by Eric Frumin of the Amalgamated Clothing and Textile Workers Union in October 1976.

brought suit unsuccessfully to require publication of the noise standard within thirty days. In January 1977, a different political party
considered friendlier to labor assumed control of OSHA. The head
of OSHA promised in July 1977 that it would be ready by "early
1978." It was not, however, and when she left office four years later
it too had not released the long-awaited, or long-dreaded, noise
standard.

This delay is due partly, of course, to the extraordinary complexity of the subject. But many of the issues for which additional
information is sought are also ones for which it is probably unobtain-
able in the foreseeable future. Thus, it is correct that a standard
could be issued within three months of a decision on several important questions.

A more important reason for the delay, therefore, is the hesi-
tation of OSHA's leadership, both past and present, to promulgate a
standard with such explosive political consequences for themselves
and the agency.

4.0 ENVIRONMENTAL PROTECTION AGENCY AUTHORITY

Although OSHA has the primary responsibility for controlling
most noise sources in the environment, the Environmental Protection Agency (EPA) has been given statutory authority to oversee
federal actions toward noise pollution in general. EPA also has
responsibility for a number of environmental noise pollutant sources,
ranging from snowmobiles to aviation (in concert with the Federal
Aviation Administration), which are of significant national concern.

The Reagan administration came into office in 1981 determined to eliminate the entire EPA noise program, which then numbered about 110 people. On 17 February 1981, the White House's
Office of Management and Budget (OMB) issued a "no appeal" directive to phase out the office; the only choice was the timing, either
six or eighteen months. Two years later, the staff numbered 2
people, and most of the regulatory programs were rescinded. 70/
The administration was not able to eliminate them entirely, however, because certain strong industry groups and their congressional
supporters wanted federal preemption of a multiplicity of inconsistent and stricter standards. The Noise Act itself was left in place.

_____

70/ Charles Elkins, former director of EPA's Noise Office, 28
    January 1983.

4.1 The Noise Act of 1970

The 1970 Congress enacted the Noise Pollution and Abatement Act, a short act of two sections which was attached as Title IV to the Clean Air Act enacted in the same year. 71/ It directed EPA to establish an Office of Noise Abatement and Control. This office was not then granted any regulatory authority but was to thoroughly investigate the effects of noise on the public health and welfare, to identify major noise sources, and to determine seven statutorily-specified effects of noise. These include the following:

- effects at various levels;

- projected growth of noise levels in urban areas through the year 2000;

- the psychological and physiological effect on humans;

- effects of sporadic extreme noise (such as jet noise near airports) as compared with constant noise;

- effect on wildlife and property (including values);

- effect of sonic booms on property (including values); and

- such other matters as may be of interest in the public welfare. 72/

This information was to be used in the preparation of recommendations to Congress within one year for further legislation on the abatement of noise pollution. 73/

71/   PL 91-604, 42 U.S.C. § 1857, et seq.

72/   Clean Air Act of 1970, § 402(a), 42 U.S.C. § 1858(a).

73/   Clean Air Act § 402(b), 42 U.S.C. § 1858(b). EPA, Report to the President and Congress on Noise, 31 December 1971. This was sent to the White House along with 15 detailed technical reports on noise effects, noise measurement, and other problems.

4.2 The Noise Control Act of 1972

The Noise Control Act of 1972 74/ set forth the broad goal of protecting all Americans from "noise that jeopardizes their health or welfare." 75/ The bill provides four broad duties for EPA: to serve as a coordinator within the federal government for noise control efforts, to establish noise standards based on scientific criteria documents, to regulate noise emissions from products in commerce, and to provide general information to the public concerning the noise emission of such products.

A primary feature of the act, and probably a reason for its attracting support from such divergent interests, was that it delineated the bounds between federal and local jurisdiction over noise. The legislation ostensibly placed principal authority for regulating noise with the states and local communities to ensure that the federal government will not become enmeshed in nationwide noise zoning duties. The practical effect of the 1972 Noise Act, however, was precisely the opposite. While the preamble to the Act acknowledges the "primary responsibility for control of noise rests with state and local governments," the major emphasis of the act is indicated by the phrase that follows: "Federal action is essential to deal with major noise sources in commerce, control of which requires national uniformity of treatment." 76/

There is an interesting contrast here, distinguishing ambient noise and noise sources, between the noise and air laws. Ambient noise, the level of noise in the general environment, is essentially a local problem, while the noise-producing products and machinery are generally those which are used and sold nationally. Under the air pollution laws, however, the ambient levels are set nation-wide by the federal government on health bases, but the sources of air pollution (other than mobile sources) are generally regulated through state authorities under Sections 110 and 111 of the Clean Air Act.

The federal supremacy issue may have been swayed by important commercial interests: while they wanted no regulations for new

---

74/ PL 92-842, 42 U.S.C. §§ 4901, et seq.

75/ Noise Act § 2(b), 42 U.S.C. § 4092(b).

76/ Noise Act § 2(a)(3). The language on the primacy of local governments is lifted almost literally from the preamble to the Clean Air Act, Section 101(a)(3), where it has been retained through successive amendments even though the section has increasingly become an anachronism.

products, they preferred uniform federal rules to a hodge-podge of state and local regulations. These, they feared, might constitute a serious burden on interstate commerce.

Despite contrasting interests, on 8 November 1978 the Quiet Communities Act was approved extending the provisions of the Noise Control Act of 1972 and amending some sections of the act to put more of the burden on state and local governments. Section 14 was expanded to focus more attention on state and local governments providing them with the funds to develop and disseminate information, to conduct and finance research, to purchase monitoring equipment, and in other ways to facilitate the development and enforcement of noise control standards. Nevertheless, the Quiet Communities Act provides that no actions, plans or programs should be "inconsistent with existing Federal authority . . . to regulate sources of noise in interstate commerce." 77/

4.3 Noise Sources and Criteria

In a procedure also modeled after the Clean Air Act, 78/ EPA was required to publish within nine months, i.e., July 1973, noise criteria identifying the effects on health and welfare of different forms and levels of noise. There was also a requirement in the act for a second report three months later indicating what levels of ambient noise were adequate "to protect the public health and welfare with an adequate margin of safety." 79/

The next report, due 18 months after the enactment of the act, i.e., April 1974, called for the identification of those specific products or classes of products which are major noise sources. 80/ This report included information on control techniques, economic and technical feasibility data, and alternative noise control methods. 81/ This list was to be revised and supplemented from

---

77/ Quiet Communities Act, PL 95-609, § 2.

78/ See Clean Air Act § 108, 42 U.S.C. 1857c(3).

79/ Noise Act § 5(a)(2). This second report was essentially superfluous.

80/ This requirement was not in fact met until a further thirteen months later.

81/ Noise Act § 5(b).

time to time and published in the Federal Register along with supporting criteria documents. 82/

4.4 Setting of Noise Emission Standards

Following the identification of the principal noise sources
that are "feasible and are requisite to protect the public health and
welfare," 83/ the administrator was directed to take into account in
determining both feasibility and advisability, "the magnitude and
conditions of use of such products (alone or in combination with
other noise sources), the degree of noise reduction achievable
through the application of the best available technology, and the
cost of compliance." 84/

EPA was required to propose noise emission standards within
18 months of enactment for those products or classes of products
identified under Section 5(b) as major noise sources, if EPA found
such standards were feasible and if the products fell in one of the
following categories:

(i) Construction equipment

(ii) Transportation equipment (including recreational vehicles and related equipment)

(iii) Any motor or engine (including any equipment of which an engine or motor is an
integral part)

(iv) Electrical or electronic equipment 85/

Once a standard was proposed for a noise source, final regulations
were to be issued within six months unless the Administrator determined that noise emission standards were not feasible for such

---

82/ Noise Act § 5(c). Regulatory actions taken by EPA under this
and other sections of the Act will be discussed later in this
chapter.

83/ Noise Act § 6(b).

84/ Noise Act § 6(c)(1).

85/ Ibid.

products. 86/ This congressional device to hasten the administrative process by a rigorous burden of proof is found in few other environmental statutes. 87/

In May 1975 EPA identified a number of products for Section 6 standards, including buses, wheel and crawler tractors, motorcycles, solid waste compactor trucks, and truck-mounted refrigerators. 88/

It should be noted that while the standard procedure for developing standards under Section 6 derives from the identification of the product as a major noise source under Section 5, EPA has the authority to impose noise standards on any product, even though it has not been identified as a major noise source and no control techniques have been set forth. 89/ This provision, therefore, provides an alternative to the congressionally-declared categories under Section 6(a). 90/

Several other features of the standards-setting section merit further brief explanations. First, "any such noise emission standards shall be a performance standard." This is consistent with congressional determination in other environmental acts that industry should not be told how to reduce emissions by design standards but rather should be told only what level should be attained to protect public health and welfare and then be allowed to reach it in any fashion desired. This is a reasonable approach, although it ignores those frequent situations in which industry and government agree on what technology is available but disagree on the levels attainable under varying circumstances. 91/

86/ Noise Act § 6(a)(3).

87/ The most notable are Section 112(b)(1)(B) of the Clean Air Act regarding hazardous air pollutants and Section 307(a)(2) of the Water Pollution Act covering toxic effluent standards.

88/ 40 FR 23105, 28 May 1975.

89/ Noise Act § 6(b).

90/ Noise Act § 6(a)(1)(C).

91/ This was the situation, for example, in EPA air standards involving both mercury and asbestos, and with OSHA standards on the coal tar pitch volatiles (CTPV) from coke ovens.

Second, in standards setting EPA is also required to consider the degree of noise reduction possible using best available technology (BAT), considering the cost of compliance. This can be at odds with the requirement for performance standards. What often occurs in practice is that EPA ascertains what is the best available technology, determines from that what level is achievable under normal circumstances, and then sets a performance standard at that level. Thus, standards are often set on the basis of design criteria but are converted into performance standards.

Third, the requirement to take into consideration the magnitude and use of the product, either by itself or in combination with other noise sources, may result in more severe noise reductions in certain cases because of the likelihood that a number of machines or devices will be operating simultaneously.

4.5 Federal, State and Local Jurisdiction Under Section 6

The noise emission standards under Section 6 affect state and local authority over noise only in one sense: local jurisdictions are preempted from imposing their own noise emission standards on new products for which federal standards apply, unless these standards are identical with federal standards. (The term "new product" means, for practical purposes, virtually any product.) 92/ For those products for which EPA has not yet issued standards, local standards, if any, would continue to apply without preemption. regulate use, operation, or movement of products—except aircraft—without regard to preemption." 93/

During the legislative debates prior to enactment of the Noise Bill, the Nixon administration had favored a complete preemption of state authority once a federal emission standard had

---

92/ § 3(5) defines "new product" as "(a) a product the equitable or legal title of which has never been transferred to an ultimate purchaser, or (b) a product which is imported or offered for importation in the United States and which is manufactured after the effective date of regulation under § 6 or § 8 which would have been applicable to such product had it been manufactured in the United States."

93/ House Committee on Interstate and Foreign Commerce, "Legislative History of Noise Control Act of 1972," March 1972 pp. 8-9, interpreting Noise Act § 6(e).

been set (unless the local standard was identical) to prevent imped-
ing the nationwide distribution of products. The House declined to
accept total state preemption: while states were preempted from
regulating products not yet sold to a consumer, they could control
noise from products once they had reached their ultimate user. 94/
In 1978, the Quiet Communities Act amended Section 6 of the original act giving states or political subdivisions thereof the right to
petition the administrator to revise a federal standard on the
grounds that a more stringent standard is necessary to protect public
health and welfare. 95/

Some consideration was given by Congress to a federal ambient noise standard, similar to the ambient procedure under the Clean
Air Act. 96/ This was rejected, however, because such a standard
"would, in effect, put the federal government in the position of
establishing land use zoning requirements on the basis of noise—i.e.,
noise levels to be permitted in residential areas, in business areas, in
manufacturing and residential areas, and within those areas for
different times of the day or night. It is the committee's view that
this function is one more properly that of the States and their political subdivisions. . . ." 97/

4.6 Warranties

After a standard has been issued, Section 6(d)(1) requires the
manufacturer to warrant to the purchaser that the product was
designed and built to conform with the noise standard at the time of
sale. He does not necessarily warrant that the product will conform
to the standard over its useful life, although EPA might so require.
This warranty makes available to the producer the normal defenses
of wear and tear of the product, misuse, and lack of proper maintenance.

94/ E.L. Dolgin and T.G.P. Guilbert, Editors, Federal Environmental Law (St. Paul, Minn.: West Publishing Co., 1974).

95/ PL 95-609, § 5.

96/ Clean Air Act §§ 108-110.

97/ House Commerce Committee, "Legislative History of Noise
Control Act of 1972," supra, p. 9.

However, where a product is inherently defective, any cost obligation incurred by the dealer to correct the defect must be borne by the manufacturer. The transfer of any such cost obligation from the manufacturer to any dealer through a franchise or other agreement is prohibited. In spite of this prohibition, it would appear that where the responsibility for product performance over a period of time might be involved, this might still fall within the normal arrangements a manufacturer may have with his dealer.

4.7 Advertising Restrictions

In an obvious attempt to keep the manufacturers from exploiting the cost aspects of noise control, Section 6(d)(3) requires that if a manufacturer advertises that his product includes valuable or costly noise emission control devices or systems, such claims are subject to verification by the Bureau of Labor Statistics. Access may be afforded to the manufacturer's books, documents, papers and records. To forestall such investigations, manufacturers' advertising will probably focus on performance, compliance with standards, and other benefits, but not refer to cost or value of the noise emission control devices or systems.

4.8 Labeling

In Section 8 the EPA administrator is required by regulation to designate any product (or class thereof) which (1) emits noise capable of adversely affecting the public health and welfare or (2) is sold wholly or in part on the basis of its effectiveness in reducing noise. The prospective user must be informed of the level of noise the product emits or its effectiveness in reducing noise.

The labeling approach is based on the premise that it constitutes a partial alternative to setting often-arbitrary numerical standards or the outright banning of harmful products. It assumes that consumers will prefer less hazardous products to those which are more hazardous, if they are properly informed of the facts. Or if they prefer the more hazardous, because of lower cost or for some other reason, at least they will have had the opportunity to exercise an informed choice.

Although an advance notice of proposed rulemaking was published in December 1974, 98/ a general labeling proposal was not signed until 10 June 1977. It sets forth the criteria for eventual

---

98/   BNA, Noise Reporter, 9 December 1974, A-12.

selection of candidate products for labeling. They should also be coordinated with other federal agencies, such as the Consumer Prod uct Safety Commission, which also have labeling requirements. 99/

The labeling preemption provision is somewhat vague. 100/ The state or political subdivision is not prevented from regulating product labeling or information in any way which does not conflict with EPA regulations. In other words, the state or political subdivision cannot require information of the type required by EPA to be given in a form different from that prescribed by EPA. The director of EPA's Noise Office declared then that local jurisdictions would indeed be encouraged to instigate their own labeling programs, even though this could have been a serious burden to trade. 101/

With the virtual demise of EPA's noise program, however, this proposal and other regulatory initiatives have been suspended.

4.9 Development of Low-Noise-Emission Products

Low-noise-emission products (LNEP) are defined in Section 15 as any products which emit noise in amounts significantly below the levels specified in noise emission standards applicable at the time of procurement. EPA is empowered to set up procedures to determine which products qualify and to certify them for use in the federal government, if the General Services Administration finds the cost of the product less than that of one for which it would be substituted. Any statutory price limitations would be waived. 102/

In May 1977, EPA proposed LNEP standards for heavy and medium trucks and for portable air compressors. 103/ A month

---

99/   The Department of Commerce adopted in May 1977 an experimental volunteer labeling program and invited companies to participate. See 42 FR 26647. The Home Appliance Manufacturers objected to this plan, claiming it would be costly and would add to already overcrowded labels.

100/   Noise Act § 8(c).

101/   See BNA, Noise Reporter, 27 September 1976, A-1.

102/   Final regulations on procurement were issued in 1974. 39 FR 6670.

103/   42 FR 27442, 27 May 1977.

later, the GSA actually completed an LNEP purchase of quieter push power mowers. 104/

4.10 Prohibitions and Penalties

The Noise act makes illegal the manufacture, distribution, or importation of any new product produced after the effective date of a regulation under either Section 6 (noise standards) or Section 8 (noise labeling information). The act also prohibits the removal or rendering inoperative of noise control devices prior to sale of the product to an ultimate purchaser, 105/ or "the use of a product after such device or element of design has been removed or rendered inoperative by any person." 106/

Section 11 of the Act prescribes fines and imprisonment for willful violations of Section 10. In the original act these sanctions were as high as $25,000 and imprisonment for up to one year, or both, for first violations. The penalty for subsequent violations could reach $50,000 and imprisonment for up to two years. 107/ However, the Quiet Communities Act of 1978 reduced these limits to a maximum of "$10,000 per day of such violation." 108/

4.11 Control of Transportation Noise

Congress recognized in the Noise Act that the primary sources of noise, other than machinery, were the vehicles involved in general transportation. Thus, while Congress provided one section (Section 6) covering general machinery and motors, three detailed sections were incorporated into the Act to deal with aircraft noise (Section 7), railroad noise (Section 19), and noise from motor

---

104/   Reported in BNA, Noise Reporter, 25 April 1977, A-6.

105/   "Ultimate purchaser" is defined as "the first person who in good faith purchases a product for purposes other than resale." Noise Act § 3(4).

106/   Noise Act § 10(a).

107/   Noise Act § 11(a). As in many other acts, each day of a violation may constitute a separate offense under this section. See § 11(b).

108/   PL 95-609, § 4, amending Noise Act § 11(a)(2).

carriers (Section 18). EPA is thus given authority in areas where other federal agencies such as the Federal Aviation Administration (FAA) and the Federal Railroad Administration (FRA) normally exercise sole jurisdiction. Moreover, to the extent that these and other federal agencies have not issued standards and regulations protecting their workers from occupational noise, OSHA has authority under its statute to regulate and enforce its own standards. 109/

4.12 Aviation Noise

Congress' primary concern in the transportation area, as reflected in the legislative history, was with aviation noise. 110/ EPA's regulatory involvement has accordingly been much more extensive in this area, as we shall see in a separate section later. 111/ In 1968 Congress had given the FAA, which is responsible for airline safety, the additional responsibility of regulating aircraft and airport noise. 112/ The 1972 Noise Control Act added to this authority but also extended EPA's authority into the area. The administration had recommended that EPA be given veto power over all noise standards and regulations issued by the FAA. Some environmentalists favored giving EPA even fuller power, allowing the EPA administrator to set aviation noise standards directly.

109/ OSHA Act § 4(b)(1). This authority has not been without legal challenge; in the railroad area, for example, the highest courts have several times considered cases unsuccessfully brought to deny OSHA's jurisdiction to inspect railroad property. The FRA has general jurisdiction in the area but has not issued comprehensive occupational standards.

110/ House Committee on Interstate and Foreign Commerce, "Legislative History of Noise Control Act of 1972," March 1972.

111/ The 1971 EPA Noise hearings revealed that public complaints about noise from aircraft surpassed those from any other source. EPA estimated in its 1971 report to the President, supra, that over 7 million Americans were burdened with aircraft noise.

112/ 1968 amendment to the Federal Aviation Act of 1958, § 611, 49 U.S.C. § 1431.

Congress rejected both these positions, because it felt that EPA lacked the requisite technical expertise concerning aircraft and engine design. Instead, the 1972 act provides for joint regulatory authority for FAA and EPA, although the former retains the leading role. 113/

The basic statutory provision is Section 7 of the Noise Control Act of 1972, along with its Section 7(b) which amends Section 611 of the Federal Aviation Act of 1958. Section 7 provided that within nine months after the enactment of the Noise act, EPA should conduct a detailed and comprehensive study of the adequacy of FAA standards and controls on flight operations and on aircraft, and the available means of reducing the cumulative noise exposure around airports. This important study was sent to the respective committees of the House and Senate on 31 July 1973. 114/

Section 7(b) of the act amended Section 611 of the Federal Aviation Act to provide that the administrator of the FAA "shall prescribe and amend such rules and regulations as he may find necessary to provide for the control and abatement of aircraft noise and sonic boom" and shall consult with others to determine what actions are necessary and whether they are "economically reasonable, technologically practicable, and appropriate for the particular type of aircraft, aircraft engine," etc., for application. 115/ The 1972 amendments specified that the FAA must consult with EPA before taking any regulatory actions on noise.

A more significant authority for EPA is the right to propose noise regulations which the FAA must consider and within thirty days publish a notice of proposed rulemaking. Within a further sixty days FAA must hold a public hearing and after a reasonable time and after further consultation with EPA, the FAA must prescribe the regulations in whole or in part or detail its reasons for not doing

---

113/ House Commerce Committee, "Legislative History of Noise Control Act of 1972," supra, p. 9.

114/ EPA, "Report on Aircraft-Airport Noise," July 1973; this was subsequently published as Senate Committee on Public Works, "Report on Aircraft-Airport Noise," series 93-8, 1973.

115/ FAA § 611(b)(1) and § 611(d)(4), 49 U.S.C. § 1431(b)(1) and § 1431(d)(4).

so. 116/ If EPA believes that the action taken by the FAA "does not protect the public health and welfare from aircraft noise or sonic boom," EPA may request the FAA to reconsider its conclusions and report in writing to EPA in detail as to why the original recommendations were not followed. This already lengthy process may then be followed by publication in the Federal Register, additional consultations, the preparation of a supplemental environmental report, and a list of additional factors for consideration. 117/ The final decision remains with FAA subject to court challenge, but the FAA is given every procedural incentive to heed EPA recommendations.

Another requirement under Section 611 is that the FAA not issue any certificates for previously unmarketed aircraft "for which substantial noise abatement can be achieved by prescribing standards and regulations" unless the FAA has in fact issued regulations which apply to that type of aircraft. 118/

4.13 Railroad and Motor Carrier Noise Standards

These almost identical two sections, Section 17 and Section 18 of the Noise act, were apparently considered of marginal importance by Congress. This conclusion is suggested by the legislative history, in which the House report dealt at length with aviation noise but neglected even to mention the two sections as key items in the summary of legislation. 119/ Nevertheless, these two sections have been the object of considerable activity by the EPA Noise Office. Both sections provide that within nine months of the enactment of the statute, EPA should propose noise emission regulations with specific emission standards for railway and motor carriers engaged in interstate commerce. After years of delay, at the request of the

---

116/   FAA § 611(c)(1).

117/   FAA § 611(c)(2), (3), and § 611(d).

118/   FAA § 611(b)(2). The first certification regulations for aircraft noise were issued in December 1969 as Part 36 of the Federal Aircraft Regulations (FAR 36), see 34 FR 453 (1969).

119/   See House Committee on Interstate Foreign Commerce, "Legislative History of Noise Control Act of 1972," March 1972.

railroad companies, the United States Court of Appeals of the District of Columbia ordered publication of final regulations by 22 February 1979. 120/ However, EPA only issued the proposed regulations on 17 April 1979. 121/

Legislative history indicates that in enacting these two sections Congress may have been more interested in preempting state and local authority than in establishing a federal program. Both of these industries would have been greatly hampered if local regulations could impede their ability to operate in interstate commerce. 122/ According to Section 17(c)(1) (and its twin Section 18(c)(1)), "no state or political subdivision thereof may adopt or enforce any standard applicable to noise emissions resulting in the operation of the same equipment of facility or such carrier unless such standard is identical to a standard applicable to noise emissions resulting from such operations prescribed by any regulation under this section." 123/

A state may still prescribe noise controls which are incidental to other legitimate functions of local government, such as traffic control and licensing regulations, as long as these do not conflict with federal regulations. Also, if particular local conditions require special regulations by state or community, these may be promulgated with the approval of the EPA administrator after consultation with the Secretary of Transportation. 124/

4.14 EPA's Coordination Role Within the Federal Government

EPA's primary role under the Noise Act, other than the setting of standards, is to act as the coordinator of all federal activities relating to noise. This means first of all that EPA oversees federal agencies' compliance with Section 4(a) of the act, which

---

120/ Association of American Railroads v. Costle, (D.C. Cir. 1977) 565 F.2d 1310.

121/ 44 FR 22960, proposing amendment of 40 CFR 201.

122/ See Senate Report No. 92-1160, 92nd Cong., 2d Sess. (1972), pp. 8 and 19.

123/ Noise Act §§ 17(c)(1) and 18(c)(1).

124/ Noise Act §§ 17(c)(2) and 18(c)(2).

directs all federal agencies to "carry out the programs within their control in such a manner to further the policy" set forth in Section 2(b) of promoting an environment free from noise hazards to health or welfare. 125/ This procedure and admonition closely resemble that under the National Environmental Policy Act (NEPA) directing all federal agencies to promote that Act's goal of environmental protection. 126/

The EPA administrator is given direct authority to coordinate the activities of all federal agencies relating to noise research and control, and these agencies are directed to provide him with whatever information he requests. 127/ Moreover, if any federal agency issues a noise regulation or standard which the EPA administrator feels "does not protect the public health and welfare to the extent he believes to be required and feasible," he may request that agency to review that action and report to him on the "advisability of revising such standard or regulation to provide such protection." These detailed findings may be published in the Federal Register, along with supporting documents and detailed statements of findings. The final authority remains with the proposing agency, but the availability of public analysis and comment gives EPA considerable leverage with a recalcitrant agency.

EPA's most notable use of this authority has been in its disagreement with OSHA over the proposed new occupational noise emission standard, which EPA felt was too high to sufficiently protect workers' health. 128/ A similar provision in Section 7 of the Act makes the Federal Aviation Administration (FAA) even more subject to EPA challenge on aviation noise regulations.

EPA is also required under Section 4 to publish periodic status reports on the progress and activities of other federal agencies in noise research and control. This gives EPA the additional sanction of subjecting unresponsive agencies to the full glare of public criticism. 129/

125/ Noise Act §§ 4(a) and 2(b).

126/ See NEPA § 101, 42 U.S.C. § 4321 (1969).

127/ Noise Act § 4(c)(1).

128/ Noise Act § 4(c)(2).

129/ Noise Act § 4(c)(3).

5.0 QUIET COMMUNITIES ACT OF 1978

The Quiet Communities Act of 1978 130/ extended the Noise Control Act of 1972 for one year and amended some of the sections in order to provide state and local governments with funds to promote the development of noise control programs on a local level as long as no actions or programs are inconsistent with federal regulations. 131/

Other than placing more responsibility on state and local governments, the principal changes made by the Quiet Communities Act were: (1) the penalty for violations of Section 10 was reduced from a maximum of $25,000 to a maximum of $10,000 per day, for the first violation; 132/ and (2) the states or political subdivisions thereof were afforded the right to petition the administrator to revise federal regulations on the grounds that a more rigid standard should be imposed to protect the health and welfare of the public. 133/

6.0 CURRENT REGULATORY ACTIONS ON NOISE

Regulatory agencies, principally EPA and the Department of Transportation, have taken actions which affect important industries. These include aviation (both aircraft and airports), motor carriers, heavy equipment, and new products.

6.1 Aviation Noise

In 1968 Congress enacted section 611 of the Federal Aviation Act 134/ granting the FAA broad authority to regulate aircraft noise. In response, the FAA promulgated a series of regulations addressing noise controls, in 1969, on future aircraft design; 135/ in

---

130/ PL 95-609, 92 Stat. 3079, 42 U.S.C. 4901 (8 November 1978).

131/ Ibid., § 2, amending Noise Act § 14(c).

132/ Ibid., § 4, amending Noise Act § 11(a).

133/ Ibid., § 5, amending Noise Act § 6(f).

134/ 40 U.S.C. § 1431 (1982).

135/ 34 FR 18,355, (18 November 1969).

1973, on future production of existing aircraft types; 136/ and, in 1976, on aircraft currently in use. 137/ The final regulations set a 1 January 1985 deadline for domestic operators to bring all four-engine aircraft into compliance with the noise controls by (1) replacing non-compliant aircraft with compliant aircraft, (2) refitting the aircraft with newer, quieter engines, or (3) modifying the aircraft by installation of noise-suppressing kits.

Congress further addressed the noise problem in the Aviation Safety and Noise Abatement Act of 1979, 138/ which took effect in 1985. This act provides that the 1 January 1985 compliance date set by the FAA for domestic aircraft would also apply to foreign aircraft operating in the U.S.

In response, the Federal Aviation Administration (FAA) issued guidelines in granting the exemptions 139/ There has been much debate over the FAA's exemption authority. On 29 March 1985, a federal court of appeals vacated FAA's action on three air carriers and ruled that the FAA acted "capriciously" when it failed to provide consistent reasons for granting exemptions from commercial aircraft noise standards while denying exemptions to other airlines. 140/

6.2 Regulatory Activity Concerning Noise in the Aviation Industry

FAA and EPA have attempted to lower the noise levels around airports by reducing the emissions level from aircraft through retrofit, by the introduction of quieter aircraft, and by the introduction of new operating procedures such as takeoff and landing regulations at airports.

Federal Aviation Regulation (FAR) 36 was introduced in 1969 to cover aircraft thought "most likely to raise the aircraft noise levels in airport neighborhoods." This regulation covered most types

---

136/   38 FR 29,569 (26 October 1973).

137/   41 FR 56,046 (23 December 1976).

138/   PL 96-193, 40 CFR 2101, 94 Stat. 50 (18 February 1980).

139/   45 FR 79302, 79304 (28 November 1980).

140/   Airmark Corp. v. FAA, 758 F.2d 685 (CADC 1985).

of aircraft but not those currently in use or for which a certificate had already been issued. 141/

The regulation set noise levels for approach, takeoff, and sideline measurements based on weight, with the larger aircraft allowed higher noise levels. 142/

FAR 36 specifies a measurement system whereby noise levels are monitored one mile from the beginning of the runway on approach, three and one-half miles from the beginning of the runway on takeoff, and approximately 0.3 of a mile to the side of the runway. These measurements can be converted into a special decibel reading designed to approximate the discomfort to which the human observer would be subjected. This Effective Perceived Noise Level (EPNdB) scale includes the noise level, frequency, duration, and the occurrence of strong tones. (In practice, this scale gives a reading 10 to 15 decibels higher than the standard dB(A) measurement used by OSHA.)

In October 1976, EPA proposed that all new aircraft, both subsonic and supersonic, certified after January 1980, would have to be 6 to 18 decibels quieter than present aircraft. The recommended numbers for takeoff, landing, and sideline measurements were derived by simple subtraction from the average of seventeen aircraft sampled. 143/ FAA, however, in June 1978 decided to set different standards for the two types of aircraft. 144/

6.3 Retrofit of Existing Aircraft

The 1969 FAR 36 noise standards were not designed to result in substantial noise reductions in existing aircraft. After years of debate, on 9 February 1976 the FAA proposed lowering the permissible noise levels from all transport aircraft and all single engine

---

141/   34 FR 453. It did not cover supersonic transports, vertical and short takeoff landing aircraft (V/STOL), and non-jet business and pleasure aircraft.

142/   FAR 36, appendix C.

143/   Aviation Week and Space Technology, 11 October 1976, pp. 24-25.

144/   43 FR 28406, 29 June 1978.

turbo jet aircraft. 145/ The proposed rule would lower the permissible noise levels by up to 10 EPNdB on takeoff, 9 EPNdB on sideline, and 4 EPNdB on landing. 146/

This debate regarding retrofit of existing aircraft, through such means as quieter engines and sound absorbing material, has been one of the most controversial issues at both FAA and the EPA Noise Office. The aviation industry has generally favored the phaseout of older aircraft from U.S. fleets. The shaky financial position of American Airlines in recent years has made them increasingly reluctant to spend the funds necessary for improved, quieter aircraft; but this has also served to reduce the phase-out rate of older aircraft to two percent a year. At this rate, even by 1990 half of the aircraft will fail to meet the modest FAR 36 standards.

For this reason, the former FAA Administrator, John L. McLucas, endorsed retrofit of existing aircraft, along with ongoing replacement, as a necessary and cost effective means of reducing aircraft noise. 147/ The price tag on this proposal was about $1 billion for retrofit of U.S. aircraft and $250 million for retrofit of foreign jets. The benefit-cost ratio, McLucas estimated, would still be over two-to-one, and the cost would amount to less than two-tenths of one percent of the total operating cost during the year the maximum number of planes would be retrofitted.

The Secretary of Transportation announced on 18 November 1976 that existing aircraft would be given until the beginning of 1985 to comply with FAA noise regulations under FAR 36. 148/

145/ The original notice of proposed rulemaking, published on 5 November 1975, was more limited in its scope of application.

146/ FAA, Notice 75-378, Docket No. 15131, as amended 9 February 1976; BNA, Noise Regulation Reporter, 16 February 1976, A-5.

147/ John L. McLucas, FAA Administrator, statement before the House Public Works Aviation Subcommittee, 26 February 1976, reported in BNA, Noise Regulation Reporter, 1 March 1976, A-18.

148/ BNA, Environment Reporter, 26 November 1976, p. 1102.

6.4 Airports and Aircraft Operating Procedures

Airport operators in the United States have been among the strongest proponents of aircraft retrofit, because they have borne much public criticism for excessive aviation noise. In 1962, the United States Supreme Court declared in Griggs v. Allegheny County that the airport operator, usually a local government agency, is responsible for securing sufficient land and easements around the airport to ensure the proper functioning of airport facility. Failure to do so, with resultant noise disruption to the neighboring community, makes the operators of the airport—not the federal government—responsible for any damages. 149/

In September 1975, a California superior court ruled that those subjected to high levels of aircraft noise may sue for mental and emotional distress, and that the same plaintiffs may sue repeatedly if the noise continued. 150/ Some authorities have expressed the fear that this could lead to the closing of the long-embattled Los Angeles Airport and perhaps scores of others around the country.

The position of the airport operators has been particularly confused since 1973 when the Supreme Court held 5 to 4 in City of Burbank v. Lockheed Air Terminal that local communities could not use their general "police" powers to control airport noise. 151/ According to the Court, the comprehensive 1972 Noise Act gave authority over aircraft noise to the FAA and EPA, thereby preempting state and local officials.

In October 1980 the United States Supreme Court declined an appeal of a California State Supreme Court decision, thereby upholding its finding that the federal government's preemption of

---

149/ 369 U.S. 84 (1962). In a dissent, Justices Black and Frankfurter argued that "the United States, not the Greater Pittsburgh Airport, has 'taken' the airspace over Griggs' property necessary for flight." Ibid., at 91.

150/ Greater Westchester Homeowners' Association v. City of Los Angeles, 30 September 1974, report in BNA, Noise Reporter, 13 October 1973, A-29.

151/ 411 U.S. 624 (1973). The dissent by Justice Rehnquist is the better legal argument, but the policy issues are much harder to call.

aircraft noise standards nevertheless did not bar suit for nuisance by a property owners' association against a local airport authority. 152/

In February 1974 EPA proposed that airport operators submit noise abatement plans to the FAA. Failure to comply could mean loss of federal financial support and possibly even the airport's operating certificate. 153/ The FAA, however, seriously questioned the desirability of regulating airports, arguing that this was a complex and cumbersome approach to a problem better solved by making quieter aircraft.

In July 1975 the FAA declared its intention of formulating a national airport noise policy and requested comments by 1 January 1976. The agency outlined four possible policy options: to allow airport operators to develop programs for noise abatement without any constraints from the FAA; to develop a federal airport noise abatement plan, in which the airport operator would play no part and for which he would assume no responsibility; to allow operators to develop abatement plans, with subsequent approval by FAA and possibly EPA; and a continuation of the present policy of reducing aircraft noise at its source—the airplane—and leaving to airport operators the right to take whatever additional measures they felt necessary for operating procedures. Of these choices, the FAA seemed to lean heavily toward the fourth option, but hearings were scheduled for public comment in at least twenty cities around the country. 154/

The FAA has nevertheless proposed a partial noise solution using changes in aircraft takeoff and landing procedures. This would be a further development of the FAA's 1972 recommended "get-em-high earlier" takeoff procedure. So on 20 March 1974 FAA issued an advance notice of proposed rulemaking calling for a change in landing procedures that would incorporate the "two segment" landing

---

152/ Los Angeles v. Greater Winchester Homeowners' Association, U.S., 14 ERC 1074 (1980).

153/ 39 FR 6142 (1974).

154/ 40 FR 28844, 9 July 1975. The hearing announcements are reported in BNA, Noise Reporter, August 1975, A-17; additional hearings were announced. Ibid., 10 November 1975, A-19.

method. This plan, which involves a rapid descent from altitude and then a gradual landing approach, rather than the more common steady gradual descent, has already been used by Northwest Airlines and Air California with considerable success. Not only has landing noise been reduced by 16 decibels, 155/ but there has been a real fuel saving of approximately four million gallons a year for Northwest. 156/

Some experts, however, have questioned the safety of this two segment approach. 157/ One official of the Air Transport Association (ATA), commenting on the proliferation of noise abatement flight procedures, urged the FAA to standardize the system. "We have been begging them to do it." 158/

In August 1976, the State of Illinois threatened suit against the FAA to compel action one way or the other on EPA's numerous proposals for airport and aircraft noise abatement. Included in the list were recommendations for minimum altitudes (December 1974), fleet noise level requirements (February 1975), two segment approaches (August 1975), aircraft noise requirements for operating to and from U.S. airports (January 1976), and others. The state attorney explained, "We're trying to get them off their hands." 159/ The FAA declined to prescribe the above EPA proposals. 160/

155/ Captain J.T. Frederickson, Director, Flying Operations, Northwestern Airlines, reported in BNA, Noise Reporter, 23 June 1975, A-29-30.

156/ Aviation Week and Space Technology, 12 April 1976, pp. 30-31; BNA, Noise Reporter, 10 June 1974.

157/ See statement by H.B. Benninghoff, American Airlines, testifying for the Air Transport Association, FAA Hearings, 5 November 1975, reported in BNA, Noise Reporter, 10 November 1975, A-7-9.

158/ Aviation Week and Space Technology, 12 April 1976, p. 31.

159/ Ibid., 2 August 1976, pp. 28-29.

160/ EPA Noise Control Program—Progress to Date, April 1979.

6.5 DOT's Concorde Decision

The most dramatic aviation noise activity was on the Anglo-French Concorde jet. Supersonic transports (SST) were expressly excluded from coverage under FAR 36 on the grounds that special rules would have to be designed to deal with this unusual aircraft. The United States dropped the development of the SST for a variety of economic and environmental reasons, but the Anglo-French Concorde and, purportedly, the Soviet Tu-144s, were ready for commercial service in early 1976. 161/ The British and French applied for landing rights in New York and Washington, D.C., on a transatlantic route to London and Paris.

There was considerable local and congressional opposition to the granting of these rights, especially from representatives from those two metropolitan areas who characterized the SST as "the noisiest aircraft in the air today." 162/ (A secondary concern was the increase in air pollutants from the aircraft.) Ground monitoring of SST noise indicated that levels were even higher than had originally been indicated: 119.5 EPNdB on takeoff, 116 EPNdB on landing and 112 EPNdB on sideline. 163/

The level for the Concorde was 129.3, compared with 118.3 for the Boeing 707. 164/

161/ Mechanical problems with the Tu-144 kept the aircraft grounded during most of the following years.

162/ See BNA, Noise Reporter, 28 April 1975, A-2.

163/ Ibid., 18 August 1974, A-16. The figures in the FAA Draft Environmental Impact Statement were, respectively, 117.8, 114.9. Moreover, Australian measurements in August 1975 indicated that the production version of the Concorde was significantly noisier than the prototype had been. According to this report, the Concorde was four times louder than the B-707 and eight times louder than the B-747. BNA, Noise Reporter, 29 September 1975, A-25. A somewhat different figure was given by EPA Administrator Train to a Congressional subcommittee on 9 December 1975; he estimated that the Concorde would be twice as loud as the B-707 and four times as loud as the B-747 and DC-10. Ibid., 22 December 1975, A-2.

164/ Ibid., 12 May 1975, A-17.

Congressional attempts to ban the SST outright were narrowly defeated in both houses. In the House, an attempted amendment to the aviation appropriations bill was defeated on 10 July 1975 by a vote of 214 to 196. 165/ The Senate, after considerable debate, rejected a similar move sponsored by Senators William Proxmire (D-Wis.) and Birch Bayh (D-Ind.) on 25 July 1975 by a 46 to 44 vote. 166/

Russell Train, then administrator of EPA, joined the opposition to the Concorde. Although he stressed that his conclusions were preliminary pending a final evaluation of the FAA's environmental impact statement, he declared that approval of landing rights would be inadvisable in New York and "increasingly questionable" in Washington. 167/ Although there were other environmental problems raised by the SST, Train pointed out that his conclusions were based on noise alone, as EPA does not have authority under Section 231 of the Clean Air Act to set air emission standards for SSTs already in production. 168/

Transportation Secretary William T. Coleman had promised a decision on the SST controversy by early February 1976. On 13 January, the last day for receipt of formal comments on the issue, EPA sent him a proposed amendment to FAA noise regulations. EPA proposed to change FAR 91.57 to prohibit non-military SST flights into the United States by any aircraft that did not comply with FAR 36 noise standards as of the end of 1974. This would have prevented all flights to the U.S. by all but three or four existing Concordes. 169/

165/   Ibid., 21 July 1975, A-10.

166/   Ibid., 4 August 1975, A-35.

167/   Testimony of EPA Administrator Russell E. Train, Government Activities and Transportation Subcommittee of the House Government Operations Committee, 9 December 1975, Ibid., 22 December 1975, A-2.

168/   Ibid., A-3.

169/   BNA, Noise Reporter, 19 January 1976, A-10. This EPA proposal was published by DOT as a Notice of Proposed Rulemaking on 12 February 1976. 41 FR 6270, 20 February 1976.

On 4 February 1976, however, Secretary Coleman overrode these objections and granted "limited landing rights for a demonstration period not to exceed sixteen months under certain precise limitations and restrictions." 170/ The Secretary's decision nevertheless contained the following proviso:

> The EIS indicates to me that the marginal impact of six additional flights would be small. Given the subjective nature of human response to noise, however, I must conclude that if any flights at all are justified—that is, if there is sufficient affirmative reason for permitting Concorde flights that we are willing to suffer some environmental effect—those flights should be authorized only on a temporary basis, in order to permit a more intelligent and responsible decision to be made at some point in the future, after we have collected information on the subject response to the Concorde during actual operations. 171/

The matter did not end there. Legal challenges to the decision were brought by environmentalist groups, local governments in the affected states, and by congressmen, who had also introduced legislation to ban the SST. 172/ The most serious threat was posed by the New York Port Authority, which controls Kennedy Airport in New York and which sought to deny SST's access to the airport. 173/

A federal district court in May 1977 found the ban unconstitutional, as contrary to the supremacy clause. This decision was overturned the following month by the Second Circuit, which relied upon the Griggs case mentioned earlier. The Port Authority could set non-discriminatory limits on aircraft noise operations but could not arbitrarily exclude the Concorde. 174/ In October 1977, the

---

170/ DOT, "The Secretary's Decision on Concorde Supersonic Transport," 4 February 1976, p.3.

171/ Ibid., p. 50.

172/ BNA, Noise Reporter, 1 March 1976, A-22.

173/ BNA, Noise Reporter, 19 January 1976, A-4.

174/ British Airways Board v. Port Authority, 431 F. Supp. 1216 (1977); reversed 558 F.2d 75 (2d Cir. 1977).

Supreme Court denied a stay, thereby allowing flights to commence at Kennedy Airport until or unless the local regulations were prepared.

Meanwhile, also in October, the FAA proposed regulations for supersonic aircraft that would allow the present 16 Concordes to operate but would require any beginning operation after January 1980 to meet a limit of 108 EPNdB. 175/

6.5 FAA Noise Certification

The FAA carries out its responsibilities by, in part, certifying various classes of aircraft and providing technical requirements for monitoring.

Under the Reagan administration the concept of Regulation by Objective (RBO) prompted a review of existing noise standards and the methodology for measuring it. For example, the Aerospace Industries Association (AIA) petitioned for modification of FAR 36 rules on turbojets, set twelve years earlier. It is interesting to note, however, that the request disavowed any intent to weaken the standard. 176/ Citizen suits against airports are themselves a considerable deterrent to drastic changes upward in noise levels.

7.0 MAJOR SOURCES OF NOISE

EPA is required under the Noise Control Act to identify the major sources of noise as the first step in the preparation of noise control regulations. 177/

On 19 June 1974 EPA issued its report identifying the major sources of noise, their levels, and the estimated number of people subjected. EPA also acknowledged that this list is "partially subjective," as many factors other than mere loudness are involved. 178/

175/ 42 FR 55176, 13 October 1977. See also 43 FR 28406, 29 June 1978.

176/ 47 FR 47854, 28 October 1982; see Illinois v. Coleman (D.C.D.C., 11 March 1981, No. 76-1961.)

177/ Noise Act § 5(b).

178/ EPA, Identification of Products as Major Sources of Noise, 39 FR 22297 (21 June 1974).

The report concluded that urban traffic noise subjects the most people to annoying levels of noise, based on a 24-hour calculation, followed by aviation noise and construction equipment noise. 179/ According to the report, medium and heavy duty trucks, motorcycles, and snowmobiles were the principal transportation noise sources; and power drivers of rock drills were the most annoying sources of construction noise. Of these listed products, however, only two were officially scheduled for regulation under Section 6 as major sources of noise: medium and heavy duty trucks and portable air compressors. The other listed products remained candidates for possible future regulatory action. 180/

On 20 May 1975 EPA published a second list of products identified as major noise sources under Section 5(b). These included motorcycles, buses, wheel and track loaders and wheel and track dozers, truck transport refrigeration units, and truck-mounted solid waste compactors as special auxiliary equipment on trucks. 181/ Subsequent administrative procedure, as usual, includes the publication before rulemaking of information on control techniques, costs, technology, possible labeling requirements, and alternative methods of noise control. EPA also announced a long list of possible candidates for identification as major noise sources in the immediate

---

179/ Ibid. EPA uses two calculations: the first is the equivalent sound level (Leq), which is used to indicate long term hearing hazards and day-night sound calculation based on a 24-hour period with a 10 dB(A) penalty for sounds occurring at night because of their greater annoyance.

180/ EPA has characterized the information gathering and scientific analysis background to regulation in a slightly different fashion. The first step, they consider, was the Title IV Report, Report to the President and Congress on Noise, Doc. No. 92-63, 92nd Congress, 2nd Session, February 1962; the second step was the publication of the "Criteria Document," Public Health and Welfare Criteria for Noise, EPA, 27 July 1973, pursuant to Section 5(a)(1) of the Noise Control Act of 1972; and, third, the publication of the "Levels Document," Information on Levels of Environmental Noise Requisite to Protect Public Health and Welfare with an Adequate Margin of Safety, EPA, March 1974, pursuant to Section 5(a)(2) of the Noise Control Act.

181/ 40 FR 23105, 28 May 1975.

future. These range from almost all forms of surface transportation, plus tires, to many types of household appliances from electric toothbrushes to movie projectors.

EPA declared its intention to study a number of particular candidates for possible future identification as major noise sources, including the following: light trucks, motor boats, chain saws, tires, pneumatic and hydraulic tools, power drivers, lawn care equipment, and other special auxiliary equipment on trucks. 182/ Relatively little subsequently appeared on these items, however, except for power mowers.

In December 1982 EPA issued a notice of intent to delete from the list of major noise sources the following items: power lawn mowers, pavement breakers, rock drills, wheel and crawler tractors, buses, and truck transport refrigeration units. This reflected the Reagan administration's determination to eliminate the program entirely, even if it meant not considering the jackhammer a noisy device. 183/

7.1 Air Compressors

Air compressors were one of the two products first identified by EPA as major noise sources in June 1974. EPA acknowledged at the time that the current technology which relied upon acoustic insulation was not capable of substantially more development but contended that future noise reduction should stress noise source elimination in compressors themselves. 184/

The report noted that insulation had already allowed equipment manufacturers to lower noise levels by a significant 10-20 decibels, depending on whether the units were diesel or gasoline driven.

Because the mean noise levels reported for the "quieted" models ranged around 75 dB(A) (a significant decrease from previous levels of 82 to 92 dB(A)), EPA's first candidate for noise regulation

---

182/   EPA, "Report on the Identification of Products as Major Sources of Noise," 20 May 1975.

183/   47 FR 54108, 1 December 1982; see also 46 FR 41104, 14 August 1981.

184/   EPA, "Preliminary Cost and Technology Information on Reduction of Portable Air Compressor Noise," June 1974.

under this section was thus a common but relatively quiet machine, quiet at least in comparison with certain heavy metal shaping machines producing noise levels far in excess of 100 dB(A). 185/

Four months later, EPA proposed a noise emissions standard for compressors with a rated capacity of over 75 cfm (2.1 m^3) of 76 dB(A) measured at 7 meters distance. 186/ This standard was expected to benefit approximately 11 percent of the total one million persons severely impacted by construction noise. The cost of this standard, according to EPA estimates, would be approximately $20 million. (Annual sales of air compressors are about $115 million.) 187/

Smaller companies complained that the proposed testing requirements would be a real hardship for them. 188/ Another company representative, on the other hand, noted that the small portable air compressors often made by small companies would be relatively easy to conform to the proposed standard but that larger equipment would become even bulkier and heavier and still might not attain the standard. 189/

EPA held a public hearing on the proposed standard in February 1975 and on 31 December 1975 issued the final regulation. The 76 dB(A) standard was to become effective on 1 January 1978 for compressors with a rated capacity between 75 cfm and 250 cfm; and six months later, on 1 July 1978, for compressors with a capacity over 250 cfm (approximately 7 cubic meters a minute). This extension of the period for compliance, EPA claimed, should have little effect on public health but would reduce the cost of compliance from 16 percent to 12 percent and would avoid the otherwise anticipated 5 percent drop in sales volume. EPA also deferred the requirement that manufacturers certify that their product would meet

---

185/ Ibid.

186/ 100 cubic feet per minute (cfm) corresponds to 2.8 m^3/min.

187/ EPA Assistant Administrator Roger Strelow, press conference, 22 October 1974.

188/ George Fabian, Jaeger Co., Columbus, Ohio, BNA, Noise Reporter, 11 November 1974, A-11.

189/ Gardner-Denver Co., Quincy, Illinois, ibid.

noise standards for the useful life of the device, pending testing to determine the extent of degradation over time. 190/

In a major deregulation, however, the Reagan administration in August 1981 included portable air compressors (along with trucks, motorcycles, and garbage trucks) in a proposal to revoke the reporting and recordkeeping requirements 191/ promulgated in 1976. 192/ Simultaneously, EPA declared its intention to suspend enforcement of these regulations during the period of consideration. 193/ At the end of December 1982, the Agency declared these rules final. 194/

7.2 Trucks

The other major noise source identified by EPA in June 1974 was new medium and heavy duty trucks, defined as vehicles having a gross weight rating over five tons when loaded. 195/ On 2 July 1974, an organization of professional truck drivers (PROD) filed suit in the D.C. District Court seeking to compel EPA to propose regulations on trucks. 196/

In October 1974 EPA proposed an 83 dB(A) noise standard for speeds below 35 mph for model year 1977. This standard was to drop to 80 dB(A) for model year 1981 and to 75 dB(A) by 1983. (Measurements were to be made 50 feet from the center line of traffic.) EPA decided not to propose a regulation for speeds over 50 mph, although a draft proposal a few months earlier had recommended a truck standard of 86 dB(A) at that speed. Because of the uncertainties

---

190/ EPA, Final Noise Emission Limits for Portable Air Compressors, 31 December 1975, published in the Federal Register 14 January 1976; codified in 40 CFR Part 204.

191/ 46 FR 41104, 14 August 1981.

192/ 40 CFR 205.50, et seq.

193/ 46 FR 41057, 14 August 1981.

194/ 47 FR 57709, 28 December 1982; 40 CFR 204.

195/ EPA, "Identification of Products as Major Sources of Noise," 19 June 1974, 39 FR 22297 (21 June 1974).

196/ BNA, Noise Reporter, 8 July 1974, A-12.

about tire noise at higher speeds, further action on truck noise must await a resolution of that problem. 197/

EPA's final regulation on truck noise emissions was announced on 13 April 1976. This draft final differed in a number of respects from the proposed regulation issued in October 1974. The final version postponed for approximately one-half year the 83 dB(A) standard, effective on 1 January 1978, and the 80 dB(A) standard (slated for 1 January 1982). The draft dropped consideration of a 75 dB(A) standard, which had been originally scheduled for 1983, on the basis that further study and research would be necessary for this later period. As with the air compressor standards, the draft regulation also omitted the useful-life provisions from the October proposal which sought to ensure that noise levels did not increase significantly over time.

Administrator Train pointed out that the new standard, although seemingly less stringent than that of Florida and Illinois, was actually more restrictive, because it required that virtually every vehicle meet the standard. This standard, he stated, would slightly increase the initial price of trucks but would reduce the operating costs. 198/

In January 1986, EPA decided to postpone the effective date of the noise emission standard from 1986 to 1988. The level itself remained at 80 dB(A). This rule is the third deferral of the new truck rule. The deferrals, according to the agency, have been granted to give the distressed industry time to coordinate engine design changes for improvement in fuel economy in order to meet the agency's nitrogen oxides and particulate emission standards, promulgated on 15 March 1985. 199/

197/ EPA, Press Release, 13 April 1976. See also EPA, "Proposed Noise Standard for Medium and Heavy Duty Trucks," 22 October 1974, 39 FR 38338, 30 October 1974. Tire and pavement noise could be as significant as the truck noise itself over 40 miles per hour. Crossbar tires were found to be noisier than ribbed treads, and recapped tires ranged 10-15 dB(A) higher.

198/ EPA estimates that this regulation would increase truck prices by about three percent, although this varies with the type and size of the engines. The improved fuel economy, however, was estimated at half a billion a year.

199/ 51 FR 850, 8 January 1986.

7.3 Power Mowers

EPA and the Consumer Product Safety Commission (CPSC) both became embroiled in attempts to regulate noise emissions from power mowers. The CPSC draft proposal in July 1975 called for a limit of 92 dB(A) for walk-behind mowers and 95 dB(A) for riding mowers. This was expected to add a not insubstantial cost of $40 to $112, respectively, to an average machine. The CPSC's interest in power mowers included problems other than noise, particularly the safety hazards. And the need for additional tests on these questions led to several postponements of the planned proposal. 200/

On 12 January 1977 EPA identified power mowers as a major noise source under Section 5(b) and circulated a draft proposal with a standard identical to that originally recommended by CPSC. The agency estimated that forty million operators were exposed to noise loud enough to cause hearing damage, and twice that number to annoying noise levels. 201/ The CPSC, faced with the possibility of a jurisdictional dispute with EPA, deleted the noise section from its proposed power mower standard. 202/

The Outdoor Power Equipment Institute challenged EPA's listing of power mowers as major noise sources. District Judge John Sirica dismissed the suit in October 1977 for lack of jurisdiction, pointing out that a Section 5(b) determination was an inseparable part of the Section 6(b) standard-setting process which, under Section 16(a), could only be reviewed by a court of appeals. 203/

The Reagan administration, however, in December 1982 issued a notice that it did not consider lawn mowers as major noise sources under Section 5, thereby effectively ending plans for regulation in the foreseeable future. 204/

200/   See BNA, Noise Reporter, 19 July 1976, A-11.

201/   Leonard Eiserer, ed., Noise Control Report, 17 January 1977, p. 11 and 14 February 1977, p. 265.

202/   Ibid., 18 April 1977, p. 62.

203/   BNA, Noise Reporter, 10 October 1977, A-9.

204/   47 FR 54108, 1 December 1982.

7.4 Garbage Truck Compactors

EPA proposed noise standards on 12 August 1977 for solid waste compactors. This was scheduled to reduce noise by 4 to 8 decibels in 1979, with a standard of 78 dB(A); and the limit would drop to 75 dB(A) on 1 January 1982. The most controversial feature was the requirement that the manufacturers had to certify the equipment would remain in compliance for three years, or 7500 operating hours, after sale to the ultimate purchaser. 205/

The National Solid Waste Management Association claimed EPA lacked the authority to require a three-year assurance period. New York City officials, however, pointed out that they already had stricter standards than the EPA proposal, and these would be pre-empted once the federal standard became final. 206/

In July 1983, EPA issued a final rule rescinding its noise emission standard for truck-mounted solid waste compactors. 207/ The action was taken in consideration of the costs this regulation imposed on the compactor manufacturing industry.

7.5 Wheel and Crawler Tractors

Wheel and crawler tractors had been identified as a Section 5(b) major noise source on 28 May 1975. On 23 June 1977, EPA issued a proposed rulemaking on these construction vehicles. This contained the controversial requirement, as above, for an assurance period of five years. 208/ The Construction Industry Manufacturers Association (CIMA) objected to this feature and challenged the justification for tractors' identification as a major noise source. 209/

In December 1982, the Reagan administration issued a notice of intention to withdraw the proposed regulation. 210/

205/   42 FR 43226, 26 August 1977. This feature had caused the delay in issuance of the proposal, which was originally due in November 1976.

206/   BNA, Noise Reporter, 24 October 1977, A-20.

207/   48 FR 32502, 15 July 1983.

208/   42 FR 35804, 11 July 1977.

209/   A similar legal challenge concerning power mowers is discussed above.

210/   47 FR 54108, 1 December 1982.

7.6 Buses

On 29 August 1977 EPA announced a proposed regulation on noise emissions, both interior and exterior, for buses weighing over ten thousand pounds. The limit of 83 dB(A) would take effect for new vehicles on 1 January 1979, then would be reduced to 80 dB(A) in 1983 and 77 dB(A) in 1985. Interior limits for the same period would be 83 dB(A) for 1983 and 80 dB(A) by 1985. School buses are included under this regulation. 211/

7.7 Snowmobiles

A more sensitive issue is the continuing debate over snowmobiles. These undeniably noisy vehicles have strong political support in the northern states. This has hampered EPA's effort to impose a 78 dB(A) standard at open throttle, measured at 50 feet. At 15 miles per hour, the limit would be 73 dB(A). Snowmobile manufacturers contend that these levels are unnecessarily strict.

On 31 May 1977, EPA's Deputy Administrator Barbara Blum wrote thirty northern governors for advice on whether there should be legal noise regulations on snowmobiles, or merely informational labeling. The latter would have been useful for operators who are subjected to potentially hazardous levels of 90-100 dB(A), but it would not solve the extreme annoyance problem to others. For this reason, such states as New York and Minnesota have stricter standards than the federal proposal. Although the result of this EPA poll revealed little consensus among "snowbelt" governors, 212/ there has subsequently been little activity on this issue.

7.8 Motorcycles

On 28 May 1975, EPA identified motorcycles as a major source of noise in the environment and began preparing noise emission regulations for new motorcycles and new motorcycle replacement exhaust systems distributed in commerce. 213/ On 15 March 1978, EPA proposed regulations which called for "an average 5 decibel reduction in new street motorcycle sound levels by 1985, and a 2

211/ 42 FR 45776, 12 September 1972.

212/ BNA, Noise Reporter, 6 June 1977, A-19; Ibid., 1 August 1977, A-1.

213/ 40 FR 23105, 28 May 1975.

to 9 decibel reduction in sound levels of new offroad motorcycles." 214/ The proposal also included standards for replacement
mufflers, which EPA hoped would reduce motorcycle noise "by
eliminating the availability of ineffective motorcycle replacement
exhaust systems." 215/

EPA also proposed prohibitions against tampering with or
reducing the effectiveness of muffler systems. 216/ An amendment
to prevent tampering with the noise system, proposed in December
1980, was withdrawn in December 1982. 217/

8.0 EPA MOTOR CARRIER REGULATIONS

EPA issued similar noise emission standards for motor carriers in October 1974. These provided that carriers in interstate
commerce should be limited to 90 dB(A) over 35 mph, 86 dB(A) under
that speed, and 88 dB(A) in a stationary high revving mode. (All
these measurements were based on a distance of 50 feet.) This
standard became effective, one year from publication, in October
1975. 218/ These regulations were the first issued by EPA under the
Noise Act of 1972 to reach final status, enforceable as part of the
noise law.

Once these standards had been issued, it was the responsibility under Section 18 of the act for the secretary of transportation to
issue regulations ensuring compliance with these standards. DOT
proposed regulations at the end of February 1975, 219/ and on 20

214/   43 FR 10822, 15 March 1978.

215/   Ibid.

216/   Ibid.

217/   45 FR 86694, 31 December 1980; 47 FR 54110, 1 December
       1982.

218/   EPA, "Final Interstate Motor Carrier Regulations," 39 FR
       38208, 21 October 1974.

219/   DOT, BMCs, "Proposed Regulations on Compliance with EPA
       Motor Carrier Noise Standards," 40 FR 8658, 28 February
       1975.

September 1975 issued final regulations. 220/ In January 1986, EPA reduced the noise limits for motor carriers engaged in interstate commerce by 3 dB. 221/

8.1 EPA Noise Standard For Railroads

EPA proposed noise emission standards for railroads in July 1974. The noise limit for individual locomotives was set at 93 decibels and at 96 decibels for any combination of locomotives. The standard for railroad cars over 45 mph was also set at 93 dB(A), while for speeds below that a standard was proposed at 88 dB(A). (These measurements were to be made 100 feet from the center of the track.) The proposal also recommended that four years after the date of the final standard, the permissible noise level should decrease to 87 dB(A) for a single locomotive and 90 dB(A) for any combination of locomotives under moving conditions. The proposal exempted steam locomotives, most gas turbines and certain electric locomotives; but approximately 27,000 diesel, electric, road, and switcher locomotives were covered. The proposal, furthermore, did not apply to warning devices such as horns or bells or to special purpose equipment such as cranes or mass transit systems. 222/

According to the statute, these proposed regulations by EPA were to be considered and promulgated by DOT within 90 days and would go into effect 270 days after publication. This timetable foundered, however, when the Department of Transportation strongly objected to many features of the EPA proposal. In its official response, DOT contended that the EPA proposal should have included recommendations for active and inert retarders, a limit of 70 dB(A) for mechanical refrigeration cars, and a 75 decibel limit on overall noise emissions during 90 percent of any 24-hour period by October 1978 and 70 decibels by October 1979.

The final rail carrier emission rule did not appear until January 1976, 18 months after the July 1974 proposal. For locomotives

---

220/ DOT, BMCs, "Final Regulations on Compliance with EPA Motor Carrier Noise Standards," 40 FR 42432, 20 September 1975.

221/ 51 FR 850, 8 January 1986.

222/ EPA, "Proposed Noise Emission Standard for Railroad Locomotives and Cars," 39 FR 24580, 3 July 1974.

manufactured after 31 December 1979, the standard was set at 90 decibels for locomotives in motion and 87 decibels for those under stationary conditions. The requirement for mufflers applied only to these newer vehicles. Locomotives and railcars produced prior to that were required to follow the "best maintenance practice," described as 96 dB(A) for moving locomotives and 93 dB(A) for stationary ones. For railcars, this best maintenance practice meant 93 dB(A) over 45 miles per hour and 88 dB(A) under that speed.

Finally, the new regulation added a series of measurement criteria, such as ambient noise conditions and test specifications, in response to criticism that the measurement parameter in OSHA's July 1974 proposal could be distorted by a number of such extraneous factors. 223/

The EPA standards, however, left significant areas of railroad operation unregulated. Perhaps because of desire for federal pre-emption, the Association of American Railroads brought suit to require noise standards for these other areas also. On 23 August 1977 the Court of Appeals for the District of Columbia Circuit agreed, and ordered EPA within a year to propose additional railroad standards. 224/ The additional standards were not even proposed, however, until 17 April 1979. These proposed regulations state specific noise emission standards for facilities and equipment of the nation's interstate rail carriers. 225/

After EPA promulgated several standards, the parties agreed to dismiss on 12 November 1981. The agency had meanwhile proposed other standards, including one for refrigeration cars and one on railroad property line determinations. In December 1982, these were withdrawn. 226/

Also on 23 August 1977 the Federal Railroad Administration (FRA) issued a final noise enforcement rule to implement EPA's

---

223/ EPA, "Final Railroad Noise Emission Standard," 31 December 1975.

224/ Association of American Railroads v. Costle (CADC 1977) Docket No. 76-1353.

225/ 44 FR 22960, 17 April 1979.

226/ 47 FR 54107, 1 December 1982.

existing noise standards on locomotives and railroad cars. 227/ The regulations, which had been proposed in November 1976, provided that locomotives produced after January 1979 should be limited to 90 dB(A) moving and 87 dB(A) stationary. 228/

EPA had proposed rules allowing states to assure certain responsibilities of a local nature. 229/ Only one locality ever requested consideration under these rules, however, and after seven years the agency formally withdrew the proposal. 230/ A similar determination involving motor carriers was made at the same time. 231/

227/ 42 FR 42342, amending 49 CFR Part 210.

228/ BNA, Noise Reporter, 8 November 1976, A-15.

229/ 41 FR 52317, 29 November 1976.

230/ 47 FR 54313, 2 December 1982.

231/ Ibid.

INDEX

PROTECT YOURSELF — & YOUR COMPANY WITH THESE ENVIRONMENTAL REFERENCES

1. Environmental Information Sources

Now you can save time and effort by beginning and ending your search for environmental information sources all in one place! Details hard-to-find federal government information sources; primary state environmental contacts (in one standard format for ease of access); up-to-date information on environmental publications; key trade and membership organizations; and current environmental databases.
Approx. 230 pp.,   #703

2. Environmental Telephone Directory

Environmental compliance is challenge enough without the extra burden of tracking down that often critical contact. Now this up-to-date telephone directory makes that challenge easier! Contains over 25 pages of EPA information; complete addresses and phone numbers for all Senators and Representatives with their Environmental Aides; full information on Senate and House Committees/Subcommittees and Federal Agencies dealing with environmental issues; and detailed information on State Environmental Agencies.
Approx. 375 pp.,   #709

3. RCRA Hazardous Wastes Handbook, 7th Edition

Get clear, concise answers that take you step-by-step through the maze of RCRA/hazardous wastes regulations. This Handbook carefully analyzes the impact of RCRA on your business and suggests (in non-legalese language) how you can cost-effectively and efficiently comply. This 6th Edition contains a comprehensive analysis plus a copy of the statute as amended by the Hazardous and Solid Waste Amendments of 1984.
Approx. 552 pp.,   #705

4. RCRA Inspection Manual

Now you can better understand what compliance is expected of you and how to best comply with the law—*before* the inspector arrives! Covers key topics to help you eliminate deficiencies and satisfy an inspection, thereby avoiding civil and criminal penalties. Developed by EPA to support its inspectors in conducting the complex field inspections fundamental to hazardous waste enforcement.
Approx. 293 pp.,   #533

5. 1986 Hazardous Material Spills Conference Proceedings

Let 208 experts share with you their state-of-the-art methods for hazardous material spills contingency planning, prevention, and control!

In one comprehensive volume, you will find the newest technologies and tested procedures for cleanup, emergency planning, the latest Governmental programs, personnel safety and training, risk analysis, media relations and much more. Contains numerous charts, tables, figures, graphs, and helpful case histories.
Approx. 565 pp.,   #591

6. Environmental Audits, 5th Edition

Use these checklists and sample procedures to identify your problem areas now and avoid costly compliance expenses later! Learn the details on how to begin—and manage—a successful audit program for your facility. Contains all the step-by-step guidance you need for planning, conducting, and managing your own environmental audit.
Approx. 407 pp.,   #582

7. Superfund Manual: Legal and Management Strategies, 2nd

Understand your business' liability under Superfund—and learn from the experts what you can do about it! Authorities from the Washington, D.C., law firm of Crowell & Moring draw upon their extensive experience to present a comprehensive analysis of federal, state, and common law that will provide you with a workable compliance strategy. This manual clearly interprets Superfund law and regulations plus it explains notification and reporting requirements for hazardous spills, contingency planning, the NPL, EPA's response authority, federal and private party cost recovery action, and more.
Approx. 224 pp.,   #704

8. CERCLA Policy Compendium

Get inside information on the specific policies EPA has developed to ensure compliance with the enforcement of CERCLA/Superfund. Contains internal EPA memorandums written by and for government officials to help guide them in determining liable parties and enforcing cleanup of hazardous waste sites.

Learn about cost recovery actions; documenting costs; contribution among responsible parties; liability of corporate shareholders and successor corporations for abandoned sites; enforcement actions for sites on the National Priorities List; and most importantly, EPA's Settlement Policy—plus much more!
Approx. 584 pp.,   #589

9. General Enforcement Policy Compendium

Fully understand your options for environmental compliance by knowing what EPA requires of you. Forty-three internal EPA policy memorandums detail EPA's general policies on environmental enforcement: Visitors Releases and Hold Harmless Agreements as a Condition for Entry to EPA Employees on Industrial Facilities; Criminal Enforcement Priorities; Liability of Corporate Shareholders and Successor Corporations for Abandoned Sites under CERCLA; Policy on Civil Penalties; Case Referrals for Civil Litigation; and Memorandum of Understanding between the Department of Justice and the EPA are just a few of the EPA policies you can't afford not to know.
Approx. 714 pp.,   #595

Guarantee: Your complete satisfaction with any of these books or you may return your order undamaged within 15 days for a full and immediate refund.

Government Institutes, Inc.
966 Hungerford Drive. #24
Rockville, MD (Washington, DC) 20850
(301) 251-9250

MAY 7 1988

FEB 2 1 1989
MAR 8 1989

DISCHARGED
OCT 2 4 1995
APR 1 1 1988

MAR 8 1988
DISCHARGED